MW01201784

Genealogical History of Deacon Stephen Hart and his Descendants, 1632. 1875

Pg 39   DEACON STEPHEN HART

Pg 364   THOMAS HART

Pg. 366   HAWKINS HART (1)

Pg. 371   HAWKINS HART (2)

Pg. 386   LUKE HART

Pg. 419   STEPHEN HART (FATHER OF CHESTER)

SOLDIERS

14 LT. SAMUEL HART (REV. WAR)   5TH SON OF HAWKINS 1
5 LT. HAWKINS HART (REV WAR)   SON OF HAWKINS 2
19 SELAH HART (REV. WAR)   SON OF LUKE

Simeon Hart.

GENEALOGICAL HISTORY

OF

DEACON STEPHEN HART

AND HIS DESCENDANTS,

1632.   1875.

WITH AN INTRODUCTION OF MISCELLANEOUS HARTS AND THEIR PRO-
GENITORS, AS FAR AS KNOWN; TO WHICH IS ADDED A LIST
OF ALL THE CLERGY OF THE NAME FOUND, ALL THE
PHYSICIANS, ALL THE LAWYERS, THE
AUTHORS, AND SOLDIERS.

BY

ALFRED ANDREWS, NEW BRITAIN, CONN.,

MEMBER OF CONNECTICUT AND WISCONSIN HISTORICAL SOCIETIES, AUTHOR OF "HISTORY OF NEW
BRITAIN, CONN.," "ANDREWS' MEMORIAL," AND "PEDIGREE OF THE HARTS."

PUBLISHED BY

AUSTIN HART, Esq., NEW BRITAIN, CONN.

HARTFORD:
THE CASE, LOCKWOOD & BRAINARD CO., PRINTERS.
1875.

CONTENTS.

1136945

ENGRAVINGS.

PREFACE.

———•••———

THIS pedigree of the Hart family was projected some thirty years since by Deacon Simeon Hart, of Farmington, Conn. He was son of Simeon of Burlington, Conn. ; was a graduate of Yale College, and a noted educator—a man every way fitted for the task, having a natural taste for history, and more especially for antiquarian research. His adopted home was also the home of the Harts. Here the progenitor, Dea. Stephen Hart, fixed his residence, raised his family, made his mark in the world, and here he died. Here, also, are found the land records of the Harts for many generations, as well as other town and probate records ; so that Mr. Hart had the material for starting such a work as this at hand, even at his door.

He spent his leisure hours for several years over the work of corresponding, traveling, and searching the various records, both public and private, until he verily thought he had almost accomplished the object intended. I have been told he began to think of putting the work to press, when he was taken suddenly ill, and died April 30th, 1853, when it was supposed all his labor in this direction was lost. After a delay of some time, and a sad feeling of disappointment on the part of Mrs. Hart, the widow, it was proposed that Rev. Wm. S. Porter, of Farmington, (but later of New Haven,) a friend of the deceased, and a man of much experience in writing up family pedigree, should finish the work and put it to press. But he was poor, and could not work without pay. Mrs. Hart, with her family of little ones, could not advance funds, and here again was a dilemma. Prof. John S. Hart, LL. D., of Philadelphia, was applied to, either to finish and publish, or devise ways and means to have it done. But he declined *politely ;* probably he knew that in *all* jobs of this kind money went out, but none came in. Well, as "necessity is the mother of invention," the proposition then was to raise, by subscription among the Harts near by, a sum of money, to be deposited in the Farmington Savings Bank, with which Mr. Porter could be paid for his time and expense. The sum of three hundred dollars was raised and deposited, on condition that it be refunded to the donors should the work or book fail of being published. In the meantime, Mr. Porter had so

2

far perfected the MS. that he concluded it was ready, or about ready, for the printer, when he *too* died, and the money was refunded and the enterprize abandoned, and the papers laid away for the moths to eat and oblivion to brood over.

In passing, perhaps I ought to say there was a donation or subscription from the South, I think one of the Harts in South Carolina, of twenty-five dollars, never refunded ; probably went directly into Mr. Porter's hands. In the meantime I had published my history of New Britain, in 1867, which contained a partial history of some three hundred Harts—parents and children; and a friend of mine (an expert in pedigree) suggested, since I had at hand so much Hart history, I *could*, and perhaps ought, to publish a work exclusively on the Hart family. *Then* I had never examined the MS. of Hart and Porter above, and called on Mrs. Hart for the loan of it. My friend said to me, after an examination, if you will correspond and gather facts and dates and print it, I will collate the families and make an index. This was about four years ago, and we have been busy ever since in perfecting the work and preparing it for the press. We have insisted upon having full names and full dates in all cases, both males and females, believing mere initials or half-dates are too much of a nuisance to be borne or tolerated by Antiquaries. We have worked for nothing and kept ourselves, furnishing stationery and stamps for correspondence—except a donation of twenty dollars from Mrs. Almira Hart Lincoln Phelps, of Baltimore, for which she has our thanks.

I should never have undertaken the task except for the help and encouragement of my friend and associate, Gad Andrews, Esq., of Southington, above alluded to; so the Hart family may consider themselves indebted to *him* for what both of us have done. But some one may say, how is this? we thought Dea. Hart had almost finished the work, and since that Mr. Porter *had* finished it again, how then could there be so much labor left? In reply it might be said, since Dea. Hart began a whole generation have been born, and a generation more numerous than all that went before them, for they have multiplied exceedingly (like the Israelites), and have filled the land—families numbering from six to seventeen children. When I told one man, a Hart, what I was about, he replied, "you are a fool—you can't write them down as fast as they are born." Now although this is not literally and strictly true, yet it is comparatively so. The great labor is not in writing them *down*, but in *finding* the names, dates, and location of parties. Previous to the Revolutionary war almost every family had the births, marriages, and deaths on the public records, as well as in the old family Bible; now a large majority dispense with the Bible record, and less than one-third of the people have any writ-

ten family record at all, and when called upon for a copy of their
family record, don't seem to know what you mean, or what to say in
response, and after a delay of three months, six months, or in some
cases a year, and by a repetition of other letters of enquiry, they are
at length forced to answer as best they can from tradition or recollec-
tion. The Hart family are not more culpable or indifferent than
others; my experience for twenty years' enquiry shows all familes very
much alike in this respect. Some people see no use in such a work as
this—it deals too much with the past. A young man in active business in New York city said to me—"what do I care for the past, who
my grandfather was, or my great grandfather; show me how to make
a dollar and I will listen to you." Others say, this is a book speculation, a swindle; they have found that the Harts have money in the
Bank of England, and they are forestalling them to secure the money.
I have heard that families have withheld the desired information from
such apprehensions. Notwithstanding all the difficulties and disad-
vantages alluded to, it is hoped and expected that the following pages
will afford much information, instruction, and entertainment to the
reader, especially that portion advanced in life, who always look *back*
on the road they have trodden, while the young look *forward*, hoping
for future good. Money-making is the very last thing hoped for or
expected in a work of this kind. Somebody has to advance or donate
a considerable sum of money to help it through the press, and wait
some months or years for the sales to pay even the printer's bills—to
say nothing of the thirty years of labor bestowed and money advanced to accomplish the end desired. No pains or expense has been
spared to make the work perfect and complete. Books of reference
have been used, friends consulted, records exhausted, and every avail-
able means adopted to make the work full and correct. The sketches
of individuals will be found more or less complete and satisfactory,
according to the material furnished by the parties themselves, if living, or if deceased, by their friends, or public records for the generations past. One man at the West demurred to respond to enquiries
because my name was Andrews, and I had to explain and conciliate
by saying my first wife was a Hart, my eldest aunt married a Hart, I
was born in 1797 among the Harts, was raised and lived seventy-seven
years a neighbor to them, wrote a history of some three hundred of
them in 1869, and hence felt an interest in the matter. After thus
defining my position the man was gained, and a good response too.
Hence it appears that a large share of the indifference manifested
arises from misapprehension, or ignorance of the object and purpose
designed by the author.
    The old town of Farmington, so rich in early history, is the mother

of the Hart family, a family very numerous, honorable, and highly distinguished for piety, industry, and patriotism. Rev. Dr. Smalley settled in 1758 in New Britain, then a parish of Farmington, had his congregation largely composed of Stanleys and Harts, and used to say he looked to Harts for grace, and Stanleys for money—probably the saying was more appropriate *then*, than it would be now, a century later. It is thought the Hart family were formerly rather above a medium size, dark complexioned, with dark hair and eyes; this, however, would not be true in all cases. It has been said of the Harts, that they were domestic, had a great love of home, seldom wandered far for a settlement in life; that they were, on the contrary, more inclined to be clanish. This may be true of former generations, perhaps, but would not apply to the present. They now scatter far and wide, from Saybrook in Connecticut, to the Pacific coast, and are found in all intermediate places, states, and some in the British possessions. I have attempted to locate them all, and give the avocation of each male head of a family, but have failed too often for want of information. The patriotism of the family is proved by the great number found in the ranks of the armies of 1775, 1812, and 1861, either as officers or privates. I have found over two hundred and fifty names of Harts as soldiers, and many are doubtless omitted from the list for want of information. The learned professions are well represented, especially clergymen and physicians, but lawyers and authors are not numerous. I have gathered them in groups in the introduction to the history of the family, that the reader may see a kind of summary at a glance.

In the construction of this pedigree I have followed the plan of numbering used in my former published works, which in their use have proved satisfactory. I refer to my History of New Britain, published in 1867, and my Andrews Memorial, published in 1873. The index used in the Andrews and Hart memorials is *un*like any other ever published (it is thought), saving much waste of time to the reader and much perplexity of mind. The peculiarity referred to is *this:* after a person has a number *pre*fixed to his or her name, the father's and grandfather's name follows, or is *an*nexed, so that a person knowing father and grandfather will find his or her history without a mistake or delay; thus the labor of finding one's own name in a list of fifty to one hundred similar names is greatly facilitated. In addition to those already mentioned as helps, I am under obligations to Col. William Seward Gridley, of Jackson, Mich., who is preparing a Gridley pedigree; to Dr. D. Williams Patterson, of Newark Valley, N. Y., who is an expert in pedigree hunting; and last, but not least, to Rev. James

Dickinson, of Middlefield, Conn., for free access to his very extensive and valuable library.

With these preliminary remarks, which seemed to be necessary to define my position, I submit the following pages to the very numerous posterity of a puritan and venerated progenitor. Should the present living generation be led to honor their parents more, and be more inclined to perpetuate their memory, and the generations to come who peruse this volume be induced to imitate the virtues of their pious ancestors, one great object of the writer will be attained.

I must not forget or neglect to say, that the Hart family are indebted to Austin Hart, Esq., a lawyer of New Britain, Conn., for an engraving representing the face of Dea. Simeon Hart, and placed as frontispiece of this work, and who also has generously volunteered to publish the work itself. This he does without a subscription list to back him up, or recourse to any fund, but relies entirely upon the liberality of the family to patronize its sale, so that the expenses may be met promptly for paper, printing, and binding.

I am also under obligations to W. W. H. Davis, author of a pedigree and history of John Hart, the Quaker, who came over with Wm. Penn, and settled near Philadelphia in 1682. From this pamphlet I have made several extracts in constructing my Introduction, calling them miscellaneous Harts.

ALFRED ANDREWS.

New Britain, Conn., Aug. 4th, 1874.

INTRODUCTION.

THE name of Hart seems to be common to several nationalities ;—England has its Harts, Scotland and Ireland. The origin of the name is not made known. Whether it obtained a place from David's beautiful animal that panted for the water brooks, does not fully appear. The variety in spelling is not as great as appears in many other names. The prevailing is simply Hart,—occasionally Hartt, Harte, Heart, and Hearte. *Maj. Jonathan Hart*, of Kensington, Conn., (in some respects the most distinguished man of the race,) always spelt and signed Heart. *Edmund Harte*, (supposed to be a brother of Deacon Stephen Hart, who stands at the head of this *"Hart Memorial"* as progenitor,) has his name in a list of those who took the freeman's oath May 14th, 1634, as spelled above,—Harte ; while his brother, Stephen, is in the same list of Winthrop's New England,—Hart. So that a difference in spelling (as is the case with many other families,) does not determine the race or family to which they belong. The history of Dorchester, Mass., makes Edmund Hart, above, one of the first settlers of that town, and had his house lot 1632, but subsequently removed to Weymouth. Savage makes his children all daughters, and thus his name disappeared. *Honest John Hart*, (as he is called,) born at Hopewell, N. J., and who died there at an advanced age, in 1780, was the son of Edward, a farmer. He passed the early portion of his life on his estate, and being often elected to the colonial assembly, was prominent, especially in legislating for local improvements. In 1774, he was chosen to the General Congress, at Philadelphia, where he was noted for his sound judgment and inflexible determination ; he was re-elected the two following years, and signed the declaration of Independence with peculiar zeal. New Jersey was soon invaded by the British army ; the estate of Mr. Hart was devastated, and special exertions were made to take him prisoner. He fled from his family and wandered through the woods, from cottage to cottage, and from cave to cave, constantly hunted by his enemies, so that he never ventured to sleep twice in the same place. The capture of the Hessians, by Washington, allowed him to return to his estate, on which he passed the remainder of his life. His descendants are somewhat numerous

nd are scattered over the south and west. He had two sons in the
rar of the Revolution,—Edward and Daniel. He has a grandson,
oseph, living on the top of Rich Mountain, in West Virginia, 1874,
rho is over seventy-six years of age, whose farm was a part of the
attle-field in the late war, who, with his family, were loyal to our flag,
nd who had five sons in the Union army. His long letter, of eleven
ages foolscap, is before me, full of the same kind of patriotism that
noved his grandfather, honest John Hart, the signer of the Declara-
ion of American Independence. He represents the view from the
op of Rich Mountain as beautiful beyond all description. H. S. Hart,
f Circleville, Kansas, is a great-grandson of John, the signer of the
)eclaration.

Joel T. Hart, an American sculptor, was born in Clark Co., Ky.,
bout 1810 ; he was of humble parentage, and while a boy, found
mployment in building chimneys, and other kinds of mason work.
Iis education was restricted to a quarter's schooling, but he became
n indefatigable reader of such books as came within his reach, spend-
ng his evenings over them by the light of a wood fire. In 1830, he
ntered a stone cutter's establishment in Lexington. By degrees, he
ras induced to attempt modeling busts in clay, and succeeded in
btaining good likenesses of many influential persons in Lexington,
nd elsewhere in the West. Among others, Gen. Jackson and Cassius
4. Clay sat to him, and the latter gave him his first commission for a
rust in marble. The work, when completed, proved so satisfactory,
hat the artist was commissioned by the Ladies' Clay Association of
Virginia, to execute a marble statue of Henry Clay. He commenced
is model from the life, in 1846, and after three years labor upon it,
hipped it to Italy, to be executed in marble. He reached Florence
n the latter part of 1849, and after waiting a whole year for the arrival
f his model, which had been lost by shipwreck in the Bay of Biscay,
ras obliged to send to Lexington for a duplicate. This, and other
elays, protracted the completion of the work for several years, and
; was not until the 29th of August, 1859, that the statue was shipped
or the United States. In the interim Mr. Hart had executed many
rusts of eminent men, and some ideal works. He is now engaged
pon a colossal statue of Henry Clay, for the city of New Orleans.

Solomon Alexander Hart, an English painter of history, was born in
'lymouth, April, 1806. He commenced his career by painting minia-
ures, but in 1828, turned his attention to historical subjects, and at
nce achieved a reputation by painting some scenes from the Jewish
eremonial, which his Jewish origin enabled him to treat *con amore.*
Ie next painted scenes from Scott and Shakespeare, and the romantic
pisodes of history ; and again, between 1845–50, recurred to Jewish

subjects. He has also shown a strong partiality for subjects illustrating the ceremonials of the Roman Catholic church. He possesses great technical power, and a feeling for the picturesque, and his works are popular. In 1840, he became an academician, and in 1864, succeeded Mr. Leslie as Professor of Painting in the Royal Academy.

William Hart, an American painter, was born in Paisley, Scotland, in 1823. Emigrating with his parents to the United States, in 1831, he settled in Albany, and in a few years was apprenticed to Messrs. Eaton & Gilbert, coach makers, in Troy, by whom he was employed to paint the panels of coaches. He subsequently painted landscapes, portraits, and even window shades. Since 1848, he has been a regular exhibitor at the National Academy of Design, of which, in 1858, he was elected an academician, having for ten years previous been an associate. He has for some years been a resident of New York. *James M.*, brother of William, born in Kilmarnock, Ayrshire, Scotland, in 1828, a landscape painter, also commenced life as a coach maker, and like his brother, was induced, by a natural taste for art, to adopt the profession of landscape painter. In 1851, he went to Dusseldorf, where he spent nearly a year under the instruction of Schrirmer. He returned to Albany, in 1852, and in 1856, he removed to New York. In 1857, he was elected an associate of the Academy of Design, and in 1859, an academician.

Oliver Hart, M. A., an eminent minister of Charleston, S. C., was born in Warminster, Pa., in 1723, baptized in 1740, on profession of faith, and ordained to the Gospel ministry in 1749. The same year he succeeded Mr. Chandler, at Charleston, as pastor of the Baptist Church, where he labored honorably and successfully for thirty years. Many owned him as a spiritual father, among whom was Rev. Dr. Stillman, of Boston. Mr. Hart was a self-educated man. His countenance was open and manly, his voice clear, harmonious, and commanding, the powers of his mind were strong and capacious, enriched by a fund of knowledge, classical, scientific, and theological, and his taste was elegant and refined. He composed much devotional poetry ;—but as a Christian and pastor was most conspicuous. He walked with God ; the doctrines of free and efficacious grace were precious to him ; his desire for usefulness was ardent and incessant. He was a prime mover in forming an Association of the churches ;—he also originated a society for educating young ministers of the Gospel to enlarged usefulness. In 1775, he was chosen by the council of safety, to travel, in conjunction with Rev. Wm. Tennent and Hon. Wm. H. Drayton, in the interior, to conciliate the inhabitants of South Carolina to the measures of Congress. In consequence of his successful efforts in this way, he was obliged to leave Charleston, in 1780, to avoid falling into

:he hands of the British. He settled at Hopewell, N. J., the same year, where he remained until his death, in 1795, at the age of 72. He died in the triumph of faith, exclaiming, "Enough, enough." —Benedict, vol. 2d, p. 323.

Hon. O. B. Hart, governor of Florida, died March 18th, 1874, after a lingering illness.—*Daily Courant*, of Hartford, Conn.

Capt. S. S. Hart died July 19th, 1873. He was for twenty-five years connected with the Norwich & New York line of steamers.—*Daily Courant.*

Cornelius Hart, Huntington, L. I. ; origin not found. His father, it is said, was of Connecticut, and removed to Suffolk Co., L. I.,—was a farmer, and had six children before the Revolutionary War, viz. :— Cornelius, Michael, Joshua, John, and two daughters ;—Joshua was a minister. Cornelius married and had Ebenezer, who married Margaret Howell, and they had eight children, viz. : 1. Charles ; 2. Betsey ; 3. Polly ; 4. Alfred ; 5. Eunice ; 6. Silas S. ; 7. David ; 8. 1. W. Hart. Alfred was born March 9th, 1797,—removed to Rockford, Winnebago Co., Ill., and married, April 26th, 1826, Betsey Atwater, of Connecticut ; they had six children, three of whom died young. Alfred, Jr., their eldest, is now living, and engaged in mercantile business in Rockford.

Samuel Stryker Hart, Janesville, Rock Co., Wis., son of Andrew T. Hart and his wife Harriet Brown Whitlock, was born in New York City, April 23d, 1840 ; he married, April 5th, 1870, Clarissa Souza. He was admitted to the Congregational Church, Janesville, in 1858. He studied for the ministry partly with Rev. Mr. Goodspeed, at Janesville, and partly at the Chicago Theological Seminary. When the war broke out he, with another young man, raised a company of volunteers, —he being chosen 1st Lieutenant, and his friend being elected Captain. He recruited and drilled until the regiment (the 13th Wisconsin Volunteers,) left for the field, in which he continued to the close of the war,—being, in the mean time, promoted to a captaincy. After the war, he received an appointment in the revenue department, in Chicago, and in April, 1870, went to Helena, Montana. On his return, he was taken sick at Fort Buford, on the Missouri river, Aug. 17th, 1872, and died, aged 32 years, 4 months, and 6 days. His wife had his body embalmed and brought home, and buried by his beloved mother, at Oak Hill cemetery, in Janesville. He left no children.

Hart and *Nixon.*—Married, Nov. 16th, 1869, at Germantown, Phila., by the Rt. Rev. Wm. B. Odenheimer, D. D., bishop of the diocese of New Jersey, Charles Henry Hart, Esq., and Armine, youngest daughter of the late John Nixon. The lady is a great-granddaughter of Robert Morris, the financier of the Revolution, and signer of the

3

Declaration of Independence, as also of Col. John Nixon, who first read the declaration to the people from the steps of Independence Hall, July 8th, 1776.

The following are Harts having money in the Bank of England, as heirs. Taken from Gunn's list of heirs at law, 1872, 3. Lond. :—Christopher Hart, Capt. S. Hart, Miss Sarah Hart, (Co. Sussex,) Henry Hart, Frances Sarah Hart, Martha Hart, Letitia Hart, Louisa Hart.

Dr. John Hart, of Reading, Mass., died 1836, aged 84.

Two men by the name of Hart, hailing from Farmington, Conn.,—one of them almost a giant,—helped to build *"Belcher's Wall."*—See Kendall's Travels, vol. 1, p. 120.

Lucretia Hart, daughter of Col. Thos. Hart, of Lexington, Ky., married April, 1799, Hon. Henry Clay, of Kentucky, one of the most distinguished statesmen and orators of this or any country. They had ten children.

Col. Thos. Hart's widow, Susannah, died at Lexington, Ky., 1832, aged 86 years ; she was the mother of Mrs. Henry Clay.

The mother of Hon. Thos. Hart Benton was a Hart.

Joseph C. Hart, U. S. Consul at Santa Cruz, died July 23d, 1855.

Thomas Hart, Haverhill, Mass., represented that town in the State Legislature, in 1693.

Daniel Hart, of Wheelock, Vt., married Emily Shattuck.

Mary Hart married William Shattuck, of Vermont ; she died in 1822, when he married for a second wife Maria, daughter of Aaron Strong Hart.

Jonathan Hart, Salem, Mass., 1710.—See Felt's Hist. of Salem.

Abijah Hart, Salem, Mass., 1752, a teacher of the grammar school.

Benjamin Hart, Salem, Mass., post rider.—See Felt's History.

Francis Bret Harte, a poet and humorist, was born at Albany, N. Y., in 1837 ; he lost his father, a professor in the Albany Female Seminary, when a child. At the age of seventeen he went to California, where he taught school. Subsequently he became a miner, and then a compositor on a newspaper, at Eureka. Returning to San Francisco, he was compositor, and afterwards editor of the *Golden Era.* He held positions successively in the General Surveyor's office, in the U. S. Marshal's office, and the Branch Mint, and was concerned in the management of the *Californian.* He became known to the public through his poems and characteristic pictures of California life, in the *Overland Monthly,* founded and edited by him in July, 1868. He was author of "Luck of Roaring Camp," and other tales, written in 1869.

Sally Hart, daughter of Ebenezer, married Thos. K. Andrews, of Murray, N. Y.

Harriet Hart, her sister, married James Trumbull.

Olive Hart, another sister, married John Briggs.

John Hart, son of Edward, lives in Medina, Dane Co., Wis.

Edward and *Thomas Hart*, brothers of John, were born in Hunting-:on Co., Eng.

Samuel Hart, Appleton, Outagamie Co., Wis., married Feb. 18th, l844, Eliza Jane, eldest daughter of Lucius Redfield. He was a son)f Samuel and Lucinda P. Hart, and is a mechanic. They had issue, riz. : 1, Francelia Beatrice, born Feb. 17th, 1845 ; 2, Sarah Amelia,)orn March 2d, 1847 ; 3, Lucius, born Aug. 25th, 1849 ; 4, Viola,)orn Nov. 25th, 1851, died March 25th, 1852 ; 5, Ellen, born Jan. 31st, l853, died Sept. 1st, 1856 ; 6, John Hill, born Jan. 13th, 1855, died Aug. 24th, 1855.

William Hart, of Harvard, Ill., son of William and his wife Hannah Mathews, was born Aug. 17th, 1796, at Milton, Vt., and married Julia Hurlburt, of Cornwall, Vt. He has a brother, Lyman Hart, living, :873, at East Berkshire, Vt., who married Sarah Anderson.

John Hart, son of Christopher and his wife Mary, born in England, Nov. 16th, 1651, came over with Penn, and settled in Bucks Co., Pa. ; hey had four children, the eldest of whom, Robert, lived in London, Eng., where he married and had children.

William A. Hart, Friendship, N. Y., son of Joseph S. Hart, and grandson of Timothy Hart, and great-grandson of Joseph, are all of Scotch origin. The sons of Joseph were, Timothy, Theophilus, Aaron, Israel, and Amos. Joseph S. Hart, born Aug. 27th, 1796, married Jan. 9th, 1819, Theodosia Stout, born March 20th, 1795 ; they had 1, George, born Nov. 19th, 1819, died May 10th, 1855 ; 2, Eveline, born Aug. 28th, 1821, died April 19th, 1858 ; 3, Catharine, born July 20th, 823, died Sept. 23d, 1825 ; 4, Jesse S., born July 27th, 1825, died Dec. 15th, 1843 ; 5, William A., born March 30th, 1829, married Jan. 16th, 1855, Mary S. Heakok ; 6, Kate E., born Feb. 13th, 1833 ; 7, Aaron, born March 4th, 1835, died Sept. 22d, 1836. Wm. A. Hart, and Mary S., his wife, had 1, Lewis Eugene, born April 3d, 1858 ; 2, Berth, born and died ; 3, Mary Grace, born April 18th, 1865.

William A. Hart, Litchfield, Conn., married July 5th, 1787, Marga-etta Smith. They had 1, Phileta, born April 8th, 1788 ; 2, William,)orn July 3d, 1790 ; 3, Lorenzo, born May 9th, 1792 ; 4, Nancy, born April 9th, 1795 ; 5, Lurana, twins, born April 9th, 1795 ; 6, Marga-etta, born July 22d, 1797.

Andrew Hart, Jefferson, Jefferson Co., N. Y., married Almira Baird, widow of Abijah Baird, and daughter of Erastus Judd and his wife Ruth Hickox ;—she was born Oct. 25th, 1801, at Jefferson.

Ezekiel Bishop Hart, son of Abram Hart of White Plains, N. Y., and his wife Mary (Coleman). He served as midshipman in the U. S. Navy, under Com. Chauncey, and was killed in the battle at Green Bay, in 1812, being shot through the breast; he was buried with military honors.

Monmouth B. Hart, brother of Ezekiel, was high sheriff at Bloomingdale, N. Y.

Thomas Hart, of Long Island, N. Y., married Mary Denwick, of Setanket, L. I. They had seven children, only one of whom is fully reported, viz.: Andrew Thomas, born July 3d, 1808, now living (1873,) at Janesville, Rock Co., Wis.; he married, May 5th, 1831, Harriet Brown Whitlock, daughter of William and Julia Brown Whitlock, of Elizabethtown, N. J.;—she died Dec. 9th, 1868, and was buried at Oak Hill cemetery, Janesville. He was in mercantile business in New York City until 1838; afterwards fourteen years in the Bank of Commerce, New York, whence he removed to Harmony, "Rock Prairie," Wis., and resided there thirteen years; subsequently he returned and located at Janesville. They also had seven children, only one of whom is reported, viz.: Henry Martyn Hart, born in New York City, Jan. 2d, 1838, married, Oct. 12th, 1858, Harriet Parker. He is an Insurance agent, residing (1874) at Janesville. They have two sons and three daughters.

John Hart, son of Christopher and Mary Hart, was born at Witney, Oxfordshire, Eng., Nov. 16th, 1651, and came to this country with William Penn. He was a Quaker preacher of note, and settled near Philadelphia. He owned one thousand acres of land which he purchased of William Penn, before they left England. He was elected a member of the Assembly for the county of Philadelphia, and took his seat March 12th, 1683. He died at his residence in Warminster, September, 1714, in the 63d year of his age. His widow, Susannah, died Feb. 27th, 1725. In his Will he gave his wife £15 silver money, and all his personal property not already disposed of; to his son John, he gave two hundred acres, his homestead at Warminster; and to his son Thomas, he gave two hundred acres. He bequeathed to his son Josiah the two lots in Philadelphia; and to his daughter Mary, he gave £15 in silver money, and other property;—she is supposed to have died single. This second John was a useful man, both in Church and State, but not so distinguished as his father before him. John Hart, Jr., was born at Byberry, near Philadelphia, 1684, and was married to Eleanor Crispin, in 1708; he seceded from the Quakers, and embraced the Baptists' faith, at the time of the great split in the days of Keith, the agitator. Mr. Hart was patriotic, and held a captain's commission in the militia of Bucks Co., in 1756; he was also a deacon in the Southampton Baptist Church. He died in 1763, in the 80th year of his age; his wife died in 1754, in the 68th year of her age. He left three sons, Joseph, Silas, and Oliver, and one daughter, Edith, living at his death. The eldest son, John, born in 1709, went to Virginia, where, in 1743, he was killed by the accidental discharge of a gun in his own hands.

Joseph Hart became a great patriot, and a distinguished officer, in the days of the revolution,—being best known as Col. Hart ; he had the confidence of Gen. Washington through the war, and was very active. He was appointed, in 1784, one of the judges of the Court of Common Pleas and Quarter Sessions of the county, an office which he held till his death, which occurred at Warminster, in 1788, at the age of 72 years ; his remains were interred at Southampton, near those of his wife, Elizabeth, who had died only six days previous, aged 74 years.

John Hart, 2d, son of Col. Joseph Hart, born in 1743, at Warminster, the old homestead, became a man of some note ; he married, in 1767, Rebecca Rees, who died soon after. He espoused warmly the cause of Independence,—was appointed deputy recorder and treasurer of the county of Bucks, and resided at Newtown, where there were many tories. One evening, while seated at the tea table, some fifteen ruffians rushed into his house, surrounded him, and presenting their pistols at his head, demanded his treasure ; after robbing his house, they repaired to his office, broke it open, and took therefrom 735*l*. 17*s*. 9½*d*. in hard money, which belonged to the effective supplies of Bucks county for the year 1781. One of the robbers was subsequently hanged for a greater crime.

Mrs. Barbara D. E. Hart died at Harrisburg, Pa., July 16th, 1874, aged 101 years and 6 months.

AUTHORS BY THE NAME OF HART.

Col. Hart, American Consul to Santa Cruz, 1855; "Marian Coffin," and other works.

Alexander Hart, Tragical His. of Alexto and Angelica, Lond., 1640.

Andrew Hart, an early printer of Scotland; "a trewe Descrip. of the Nobill race of the Stewards, 1601."

Cheeney Hart, M. D., Electricity, Phil. Trans., 1754–5.

Edward H. Hart, The Bulwark stormed, Lond., 1717; 8vo.

Henry Hart or Harte, L. A. Godly news Short Tretys, &c., 1548; 16mo. 2d, A Godlie Exhortation, 1549; 8vo.

I. Hart, Burning Bush not Consumed, Lond., 1616; 8vo.

James Hart, M. D., professional Treatises, 1623–25–33.

John Hart on Orthographie, 1659; 8vo. 2d, Theolog. Conference, 1584; 8vo.

John Hart, Starch factories, &c., Lond., 1795; 8vo.

Rev. Joseph Hart, Minister at Grey Friars Ch.; 1st, Trans. of Hero-
dian's His. of his own times, 1649; 8vo, privately printed. 2d,
Hymns, &c., with Author's Experience, 1759; 12mo.

Capt. L. W. Hart, Character and Costume Affghanistan, Lond., 1843,
with twenty plates on stone.

Levi Hart and V. R. Osborn, the works of P. Virgilius Maro, &c., with
an Interlinear Translation, &c., Baltimore, 1833; 12mo.

Rev. Oliver Hart, 1723—1795, Minister of Charleston, S. C., Native of
Pennsylvania, published several sermons and tracts; "Dancing Ex-
ploded," Sermon on death of Rev. Wm. Tennant.

Rev. Richard Hart, the importance of the Word of God, Bristol, two
sermons, 1767; 8vo.

Rev. Richard Hart, Sermon, 1804.

Rev. Richard Hart, "Vicar of Catton in the Diocese of Norwich." 1st,
Mediella Conciliorum, &c., Norwich, 1833; 8vo. 2d, Materialism
Refuted. 3d, Ecclesiastic Records of England, Ireland, and Scot-
land from 5th century to Reform; 2d ed., 1846.

Sir Wm. Hart, Lord Chief Justice of Scotland, Examination of G.
Sprot, Lond., 1608, relating to the Gowry conspiracy, and is re-
printed.

Wm. Neville Hart, The Goodness of God, a poem, and Pious Med.,
Lond., 1808.

George Harte, Needfulness of peace in France, 1575, Translated from
French.

Walter Harte, born 1700, died 1774; Poems on several occasions, Lond.,
1727–29; 8vo. 2d, Essay on Satire, 1730; 8vo. Essay on Reason,
1735; Fol. 3d, Unity of Reason, Morality, and Religion, a sermon,
1737; 8vo.

Prof. John Seeley Hart, LL. D., Philadelphia, son of Isaac of Washington Co., Va., born 1810, is a prominent educator and author; his
publications are very numerous and on various subjects, moral, religious, literary, and scientific.

Mrs. Emma Hart Willard, Troy, N. Y., born 1787, at Berlin, Conn.,
daughter of Capt. Samuel Hart, became a noted female educator and
a most splendid writer and author; for a list of her published works,
see a sketch of her in the Memorial, No. 99.

Mrs. Almira Hart Lincoln Phelps, a sister of the above, born 1793, at
Berlin, Conn., became almost equally noted and famous as an educator and writer; both attained the highest honors ever bestowed
upon American women as educators and authors; for list of her
works, see No. 100.

Rev. Levi Hart, D. D., Preston, Conn., now Griswold; published sev-

eral sermons of great interest; born 1738, at Southington, Conn.,
son of Dea. Thomas; he died 1808.

Rev. Wm. Hart, Saybrook; several sermons and other works.

Rev: Luther Hart, Plymouth, Conn.; published tracts, wrote for Spectator and other works.

Rev. Burdett Hart, Fair Haven, son of Dea. Norman of New Britain; graduated at Yale College 1842, settled at Fair Haven, Conn., published several sermons, and wrote for New England and other periodicals.

Rev. Levi Wells Hart, contributor to various periodicals and journals; graduated at Yale College 1846, and resides, 1874, at Brooklyn, N. Y., where he is an educator.

Maj. Jonathan Hart, Berlin, Conn.; "Observations on Ancient works of Art," also on "Native Inhabitants of Western Country." Trans. American Soc.

Francis Bret Harte, known as Bret Harte, a poet and humorist; author of "Luck of Roaring Camp," and other tales, 1869; vol. poems 1870, and "Condensed Novels."

CLERGY BY THE NAME OF HART.

James Porter Hart, New Haven; Grad. at Yale College 1840, studied Theol. there, and resides there, and proposes to represent languages by letters.

Rev. Luther Butler Hart, Bristol, Conn., son of Isaac, a Baptist minister; has labored at Norfolk, Ellsworth, and Bridgeport; Grad. at Union College.

Rev. Burdett Hart, Fair Haven, son of Dea. Norman, an eloquent and distinguished pastor and preacher at Fair Haven, Conn., and elsewhere; Grad. at Yale College 1842.

Rev. Levi Wells Hart, Brooklyn, N. Y., son of Chester of New Britain, a preacher and teacher, a graduate of Yale College 1846; resides at Brooklyn, N. Y., engaged mostly as teacher.

Rev. Charles Edward Hart, Newark, N. J., son of Walter Ward Hart of Freehold, N. J.; Grad. at Priceton, N. J., 1858, settled at Murray Hill church, N. Y., 1863.

Rev. Matthew Hart, New Haven, Conn., of St. Patrick's Church.

Rev. Abram Bloomer Hart, son of Nath'l Coleman Hart of Port Chester, N. Y., and his first wife, Susannah (Stewart); is rector of a church in Apalachicola, Florida.

Rev. John Hart, son of Christopher and his wife Mary, born Nov. 16th, 1651, at Witney, Oxfordshire, Eng.; was a distinguished preacher among the Friends, and came with Wm. Penn to Pennsylvania, and settled near Philadelphia.

Rev. V. C. Hart, a missionary in China now, 1874.

Rev. Oliver Hart, M. A., an eminent minister of Charleston, S. C., born 1723, at Warminster, Pa., was a self-made man, ordained 1749 a Gospel minister in the Baptist Church; died 1795, aged 72.

Rev. Asahel Hart, son of Nathaniel of Kensington, born 1742, settled at North Canaan, Conn., died 1775, aged 33.

Rev. Seth Hart, Hempstead, L. I., second son of Matthew of Kensington, born 1763, graduated at Yale College 1784, became rector of St. George's Church at Hempstead, to the order of priest 1792, by Bishop Seabury, died 1841.

Rev. Wm. Henry Hart, Hempstead, L. I., eldest son of Rev. Seth, born 1790, admitted deacon by Bishop Hobart 1814, ordained priest by Bishop Moore 1816; in 1830 was called to the rectorship of St. Andrew's Church at Walden, Orange Co., N. Y.

Rev. John Clark Hart, Hudson, Ohio, son of Dea. Nathan of Cornwall, Conn., born 1804, died 1871, for several years pastor of Presbyterian church at Springfield, N. J., died at Ravenna, Ohio.

Rev. Levi Hart, Preston, Conn., seventh son of Dea. Thomas of Southington, born 1738, graduated at Yale College 1760; the College of New Jersey gave him in 1800 the degree of D. D.; was eminently useful and successful in Preston, that part now called Griswold; he died October, 1808.

Rev. Henry Elmer Hart, Durham, Conn., son of Reuel of Southington, · Conn., born 1834, graduated at Yale College 1860, studied theology at East Windsor Seminary, settled first at East Hampton, Conn.

Rev. Lucas Hart, settled 1812 at Wolcott, Conn., son of Simeon; born 1784, he died 1813, aged 29 years, at Wolcott, but buried at East Haven.

Rev. Edson Hart, Ohio and Kentucky, eldest son of Obed of Avon, Conn., born 1796, graduated at Yale College and became a very successful preacher; he died 1867, near Louisville, Ky.

Wm. Dickinson Hart, a graduate of Oberlin, studied theology two years at New Haven and the same at Andover; been a missionary in Vermont two summers.

Rev. John Hart, East Guilford, Conn., third son of Capt. Thomas of Farmington, born 1682; he was three years in college at Cambridge, when he entered Yale College at Saybrook 1702, and graduated there alone 1703, and was the second graduate of that college; ordained 1707 at East Guilford; he died there 1732, aged 50 years; was called an eminent preacher of his day.

Rev. Wm. Hart, Saybrook, Conn., eldest son of Rev. John, graduated at Yale College 1732, ordained 1736 at Saybrook, born 1713 at Guilford, and died 1784, aged 71 years; published a sermon 1742.

Rev. Ira Hart, Stonington, Conn., eldest son of Jonathan, born 1771, graduated at Yale College 1797; 1798 was ordained pastor of church at Middlebury, Conn., and installed at Stonington 1809.

Rev. Ichabod Andrews Hart, Southport, Wis., graduated at Hamilton College 1826; pastor of a church at Sandusky City, Ohio, resides at Wheaton, Ill.

Rev. Wm. Hart, youngest son of Thomas of New Britain; graduated at Yale College 1792, licensed to preach by Hartford South 1800— never settled in the ministry, preached only occasionally.

Rev. Luther Hart, Plymouth, Conn., son of David, graduated at Yale College 1807, settled at Plymouth 1810, where he labored with great success; died 1834.

LAWYERS BY THE NAME OF HART.

Noah Harrison Hart, Esq., Lapeer, Mich., third son of Oliver Burnham Hart, born 1813 at Cornwall, Conn.; is a professional lawyer at Lapeer, Lapeer Co., 1874.

Wm. Sherman Hart, Esq., Norwich, Conn., eldest son of Rev. Levi of Preston, born 1767, graduated 1786 at Dartmouth, studied law under Judge Reeve, at Litchfield, Conn., located at Norwich, Conn., and followed his profession.

Levi Hart, Esq., youngest son of Rev. Levi of Preston, born there, graduated at Brown University 1802, married Mary Woodbridge Perkins, went to Ohio, but returned.

Alphonzo Hart, Esq., Ravenna, Ohio, born 1830, son of Chauncey of Burlington; is a lawyer and member of the Senate of the State.

Hon. Alphonzo Hart, a lawyer of Ravenna, Ohio, has been member of the State Senate, was Presidential Elector at large for Grant, now, 1874, Lieut. Governor of Ohio.

Ira Hart, Esq., Lordstown, Trumbull Co., Ohio, eldest son of Levi, born   , admitted, 1860, to the bar.

Bliss Hart, Esq., Brookfield, Trumbull Co., Ohio, born 1823, son of Levi, well educated, and chose the law for a profession; died at Waupan, Fon Du Lac Co., 1847, aged 24 years.

Melanckton Collins Hart, Esq., Warren, Ohio, seventh son of Joseph C., is a lawyer in Warren, and County Clerk of Trumbull Co., Ohio.

Alces Evelin Hart, Esq., only son of Maj. Jonathan of Kensington, born 1782, graduated at Yale College 1801, studied law, opened an office at Hartford, but died suddenly 1805.

Erastus Parmelee Hart, Esq., a lawyer at Elmira, N. Y., second son

4

of Dr. Erastus Langdon Hart, of the same town and county, born May 6th, 1822, at Goshen, Conn.

AUSTIN HART, Esq., New Britain, Conn., son of Simeon of Burlington, born 1824, graduated at Yale College 1853, admitted to the bar at Philadelphia, located at New Britain 1864; married Susan A. Deming, of Farmington.

WM. H. H. HART, Esq., De Witt, Iowa, attorney and counsellor at law, an Englishman by birth, and no kin of Dea. Stephen he thinks.

JOSEPH C. HART, Esq., son of Abram of White Plains, attorney and counsellor at law at Williamsburg, and mayor of the city.

ROBERT STEWART HART, Esq., Bedford, N. Y., son of Nathaniel Coleman Hart, Port Chester, N. Y., and his first wife, Susannah Stewart.

WM. BACKUS HART, Esq., Norwich, Conn., son of Wm. S. Hart, Esq., graduate of Yale College 1817, settled in Bristol, Pa.

PHYSICIANS BY THE NAME OF HART.

DR. REUBEN HART, Pompey, N. Y., seventh son of Job Hart, of Kensington, Conn., was born in 1767, and died in Onondaga Co., N. Y.; see No. 79 in Memorial.

DR. CHARLES PORTER HART, Zenia, Ohio, son of Eliphar, of Norwich, Conn., was born in 1829.

DR. CHARLES REMMINGTON HART, Hartford, Conn., eldest son of Salmon N., was born in 1837, and is now (1874,) in full practice in that city.

DR. WILLIAM HENRY HART, Hudson, N. Y., a dentist of some twenty years experience, son of Newton, of Egremont, was born in 1836.

DR. FREDERIC ALBERT HART, Southington, Conn., a graduate of Yale, located in Southington as a physician, and traveled much in Europe.

DR. CHARLES LANGDON HART, Philadelphia, eldest son of deacon Simeon Hart, of Farmington, was assistant surgeon in the late war, and is now (1874,) located in Philadelphia, as a physician.

DR. ALBERT GAYLORD HART, Clarksville, Pa., eldest son of Ambrose, of Brookfield, Ohio, was born in 1821, and was a graduate of Western Reserve College, and also of the Jefferson Medical College of Philadelphia, and practiced medicine in Mercer Co., Pa.

DR. JOHN HART, East Guilford, second son of Rev. John, was born in 1719, and studied medicine with his uncle, Dr. Jonathan Bull, of Hartford; he began practice in Kensington, Conn., and died in 1849.

DR. JOHN HART, Kensington, Conn., fourth son of deacon Ebenezer, was born in 1753, graduated at Yale in 1776, and after his return from the United States army, as surgeon, he practiced in Farmington, chiefly as surgeon.

DR. JOSIAH HART, New Britain, fourth son of deacon Elijah, was born

in 1742, graduated at Yale in 1762, and was a surgeon in the revolutionary army ; he settled and practiced in Wethersfield, and died
in 1812, near Marietta.

)R. JAMES EVERLIN HART, Natchez, Miss., second son of Dr. John, first
located in Bloomfield, Conn., from whence he removed to Natchez,
and died there in 1823, of yellow fever, aged 33 years.

)R. JOHN ADRIAN HART, Natchez, Miss., third son of Dr. John, was a
great botanist, and was in business with his brother James ; he commenced the practice of medicine in the town of Berlin, Conn., and
died in Natchez, of yellow fever, in 1822.

)R. LUTHER W. HART, Marshall, Mich., graduated at Williams College,
and was for thirty years a practicing physician in Durham, N. Y.,
from which place he removed and located in Marshall, Calhoun Co.

)R. ERASTUS LANGDON HART, only son of Elizur, was born in New
Britain, Conn., in 1787, studied medicine with Dr. Everett, of Canton, and died at Elmira, N. Y., where he located, in 1824.

)R. SAMUEL HART, New Britain, Conn., third son of deacon Elijah,
born in 1786, was for many years a practicing physician in New
Britain, and died in 1863, aged 77 years.

)R. HENRY ABIJAH HART, North Haven, Conn., son of Abijah, studied
and took his medical degree at Yale College ; he commenced practice in North Haven, and died in 1828, aged 22 years.

)R. SETH HART, Harmar, O., son of Joel, born in 1804, has been a
physician since the year 1825, in Harmar and Marietta, and is still
vigorous and active.

)R. BENJAMIN FRANKLIN HART, Marietta, O., born in 1823, son of Benjamin, of New Britain, is a practicing physician of large business in
Marietta.

)R. BENJAMIN KIRTLAND HART, fourth son of Joseph, of New Britain,
was born in 1807, educated in Boston, where he obtained his diploma,
and located at Alton, Ill.

)R. IRA FAYETTE HART, Elmira, N. Y., graduated at Hamilton College
in 1849.

)R. SAMUEL WALDO HART, New Britain, Conn., son of Dr. Samuel, has
an extensive medical practice in New Britain, of which city he is
also now (1874,) mayor.

)R. HENRY ABIJAH HART, New Hartford, only son of Dr. Henry Hart,
of North Haven, graduated an M. D. at the Medical College in New
Haven, and practiced in Bristol and Watertown, Conn. ; he has now
(1864,) abandoned the practice of medicine and engaged in the business of farming ; but (1874) resumed practice in Millerton, N. Y.

)R. SAMUEL HART, Marietta, O., son of Dr. Seth, of Harmar, has an
extensive medical practice in that city.

DR. SIMEON DEMING HART, Washington Co., O., born in 1818, son of Benjamin Hart, of Watertown, O., is a physician at Marietta, O., and superintendent of the Childrens' Home.

DR. JOHN HART, son of John, born at Ipswich, Mass., in 1752, was a lawyer, and a noted musician; he joined Prescott's regiment in the commencement of the revolutionary war, and subsequently, to its close, was a surgeon in the second Massachusetts regiment; he died in South Reading, April 27th, 1836, aged 84 years. He settled in Reading in 1782, was five years in the State Senate, and was a venerable patriot and Christian; when chosen to public office, instead of making a *treat*, as was customary, he gave the money to purchase books for schools.

DR. CLEMENT LEWIS HART, Madison, Wis., son of Edward Buel Hart, born in 1836, at Spencerport, N. Y., married, in 1862, Lutheria N. Thornton, and for a second wife married Ella R. Tolford.

DR. JAMES HARVEY HART, son of Abram, of White Plains, N. Y., is now (1874,) a physician in New York City; his mother's maiden name was Mary Coleman.

SOLDIERS BY THE NAME OF HART.

GENERAL SELAH HART, Kensington, an officer of the Revolution, born 1732, at Kensington, a son of Nathaniel Hart. He served the country as a general during the war, but was two years a prisoner in New York. Died in 1806, aged 74.

CAPTAIN FREDERIC W. HART, New Britain, Conn., son of Salmon, born 1822. In the late war as captain nine months.

CAPTAIN NOAH HARRISON HART, Lapeer, Mich., son of O. B. Hart, of Cornwall, Conn.; was four years in the army of the late war; born 1813, at Cornwall, Conn.; is, in 1874, a lawyer at Lapeer.

EDWARD HART, a son of Julius B. Hart. He was a soldier in the late war, and was killed. He was from Bay City, Mich.

WILLIAM S. HART, youngest son of Almon Hart, of Perry, N. Y. He was killed in 1863, in the army of the late war after dispatches. He was thrown off and kicked to death by a mule.

DR. CHARLES R. HART, son of Salmon N., of Hartford. He was a surgeon in the 10th Regiment Connecticut Volunteers, in the late war, and honorably discharged September 2d, 1865. He was first assistant, and then promoted.

ALFRED DWIGHT HART, Hartford, Conn., son of Salmon N., born 1840, a private in the 25th Regiment Connecticut Volunteers, for nine months.

JOHN OLIVER HART, enlisted when the war began, and died of disease, in the hospital at Louisville, Ky., December 8th, 1862, aged 21 years. Son of Rev. J. C. Hart.

DANIEL KELSEY HART, Candor, N. Y., son of Daniel, born 1838. He was in Company A, 109th Regiment. He was killed in 1864, aged 26 years.

CAPTAIN REUBEN HART, Southington, Conn., son of Deacon Thomas Hart, born 1729. He had a commission as ensign in 1777, of the 3d company of Alarm Lists, 15th Regiment, and a captain's commission signed by Jonathan Trumbull, Governor, and countersigned by George Wyllys, Secretary, dated 1778, and this commission is in possession of his family descendants. Died 1803.

JOSEPH HART, Northington, now Avon, son of Joseph, born 1759. Died in 1777, in camp at Stamford, Conn., and his father died at New Haven on his return from the care of him.

JOEL HART, Southington, son of Amos, born 1753, entered the army of the revolution, and died September, 1776, at Hackensack, N. J., aged 23 years. He was never married.

THOMAS HART, Bristol, son of Thomas, of Southington, born 1755; entered the army of the revolution and in service, September, 1777, in his 23d year, and died of starvation in prison.

JASON HART, Southington, third son of Thomas, born 1757; entered the army of the revolution, and died in that service December 27th, 1777, in his 21st year. He has a tomb-stone in Bristol, Conn.

AMBROSE HART, Burlington, second son of Simeon, of Southington; served in the revolutionary war; died, March, 1834, aged 71. He has a tomb-stone in Burlington, Conn.

SELAH HART, Northington, third son of Noah, born 1760. He became insane in the army in consequence of his captain giving him a severe flogging. He died November 8th, 1816, at Northington, Conn., aged 56 years.

FREDERIC HART, eldest son of Stephen Hart, of New Britain. He was a soldier in the late war, and was killed in North Carolina, January 30th, 1863, aged 27. He was born in 1836, at New Britain.

ABEL HART, Bristol, Conn., son of Thomas. He was a soldier of the revolution, and died of starvation as a prisoner of the British. He lived to reach Milford, Conn. His name is on the monument in the old cemetery there. He was born in 1756.

LIEUTENANT SAMUEL HART, Durham, Conn. He was a lieutenant in the army of the revolution, was wounded at the battle of Saratoga, and drew a pension. Born 1735, at Wallingford; died in 1805, at Durham.

LIEUTENANT HAWKINS HART, Southington, son of Hawkins, born

1736–7. He was first lieutenant of 7th company, 5th battalion, under Colonel Douglass, Bunnel, captain. He died about 1800.

MAJOR JONATHAN HEART, Kensington, second son of Deacon Ebenezer,
born 1744; graduated at Yale in 1768; was in public service in the
army from 1775 to his death at St. Clair's defeat.

DR. JOHN HART, Kensington, fourth son of Deacon Ebenezer. He
was surgeon in the army of the revolution; graduated at Yale in
1776; he also entered the naval service of the United States.

DR. JOSIAH HART, New Britain and Wethersfield. He was a surgeon
in the revolution, and died in 1812, near Marietta, O.

MAJOR-GENERAL WILLIAM HART, Saybrook, Conn.; was in the revolutionary army; born 1746; died 1817, aged 72.

EBENEZER HART, Guilford. He was in the revolutionary army, and
was killed by the British in a skirmish at Leete's Island, June 18th,
1781, aged 23.

BENJAMIN HART, Litchfield, Conn., eldest son of Timothy, of Wallingford, born 1752. He was one of those soldiers of the revolution
who wintered at Valley Forge, and was present at the delivery of
Washington's Farewell to the army.

TITUS HART, Colebrook, Conn., third son of Timothy, of Wallingford,
born 1757, entered the revolutionary army when but 16 years old,
and served until its close.

SELAH HART, Winchester, Conn., second son of Luke. He entered
the revolutionary army at 16, and the war closed when he had served
one year.

ORRIS HART, Oswego, N. Y., second son of Jonathan, of Farmington,
born 1791. He served in the war of 1812, under Captain Hubbard,
Colonel Cleaveland's regiment. He died in 1855, at Oswego.

WARREN ROCKWOOD HART, Volney, N. Y., died in the United States
Army during the Mexican war.

BENJAMIN BRUCE HART, was a soldier in the late war, and died of
wounds received at Bull Run.

DEACON ELIJAH HART, New Britain, was a soldier at the taking of Burgoyne.

WILBUR HART, son of Titus, died in the army, June 5th, 1864, aged 28.

WALTER JOHN HART, Fredonia, N. Y., born 1841. He entered the
army, and was killed on the Peninsula.

WILLARD HART, Winsted, Conn.; was killed at Cold Harbor, Va.

LEWIS HART, Durham, Conn. He served nine months as private in
the 1st Regiment Connecticut Volunteers, but was discharged on
account of ill health, and resides at Pennfield, Ohio.

CHARLES HART, Durham. He served four years in the late war as corporal in the 15th Regiment.

THOMAS HART, New Britain, Conn., second son of Philip, born 1838. He enlisted into the late army in Company F, 14th Regiment, where he was promoted, and was killed, December, 1862, aged 24 years.

HENRY WILLIAM HART, New Britain, eldest son of Deacon William. He enlisted into the 2d Connecticut Light Battery Aug. 5th, 1862, was in many hard fought battles, and was honorably discharged August 10th, 1865.

WILLYS HART, Southington, eldest son of Chauncey, born 1789. He entered the army of 1812, and was stationed at Flatbush, where he deserted. For the third time he was tried by a court-martial, found guilty, and shot, but unjustly, for it was found he was subject to fits and insanity.

SHERMAN HART, second son of Chauncey, of Southington, born 1791; enlisted into the army of 1812, and served out his time; married Elizabeth Smith. He died in 1846.

HENRY CLAY HART, youngest son of Oremus, of Brookfield, Trumbull County, Ohio, born 1833. He entered the army of the late war, and died at Andersonville.

ANDREW EDWIN HART, eldest son of Philip, of New Britain, born 1834. He was a soldier in the 20th Regiment Connecticut Volunteers some nine months.

HENRY HART, Farmington. He. was in Company B, 7th Regiment Connecticut Volunteers, and died at Hilton Head.

RICHARD HART, a veteran soldier of Company B, 7th Regiment Connecticut Volunteers. He returned safe, but died May 7th, 1874.

LEWIS HART, a mechanic of Unionville. He served three years in Company A, Connecticut Cavalry.

DAVIS HART, Winsted, Conn., a veteran private of Company A, 10th Regiment Massachusetts Volunteers; died in the 6th Corps Hospital at Fredericksburg, May 20th, 1864.

GEORGE LEMUEL HART, son of Newton, of Egremont. He was three years a member of Company A, 10th Regiment Massachusetts Volunteers, and one year in the 36th Regiment of the same state.

TIMOTHY ARD HART, West Winsted, Conn., son of Newton. He served as corporal in Company E, 2d Regiment Heavy Artillery.

LEMUEL HART, Sparta, only son of Amos. He was in Company H, 68th Regiment Indiana Volunteers, and was discharged for sickness, but recovered, and enlisted in Company K, 91st Regiment.

FREDERIC MOSES HART, Unionville, Conn., son of Ambrose. He was in Company C, 16th Regiment Connecticut Volunteers, and was made a prisoner at Andersonville and Florence, where he endured every indignity connected with starvation.

ALMON J. HART, Berlin, Conn., son of Joel Hart. He was in Company

B, 21st Regiment Connecticut Volunteers nearly three years, and was in seven battles and not hurt.

DAVID WHITING HART, Southington, son of Collingwood, born 1842. He was in Company E, 20th Regiment Connecticut Volunteers, was wounded in battle May 15th, 1864, and died one week after. A sermon was preached at the funeral by Rev. Mr. Griggs, of Bristol, and published in pamphlet form.

WILLIS HART, aged 38. He was in Company E, 2d Vermont Regiment United States Sharpshooters; mustered in November 9th, 1861; discharged November 24th, 1862.

SIMEON HART, Brookfield, Ohio, son of Oliver E., born 1844. He studied law, but went with Sherman to the sea, in the 105th Regiment Ohio Volunteers.

DR. CHARLES LANGDON HART. He was assistant surgeon during the war.

ANDREW WILLYS HART, second son of Adna T., of Avon, born 1854. He was in Company G, 6th Regiment Connecticut Volunteers, and died in the hospital at Beaufort, S. C., of fever, June 20th, 1863, in his 29th year.

ARTHUR A. HART, Ira, N. Y., son of Noadiah, born 1833. He was a soldier in Battery B for three years. .

THOMPSON TRUXTON HART, born 1843, at Ira, Cayuga County, N. Y. He was hospital steward in the late war, and was present at the surrender of Lee.

ALONZO FRANCISCO HART, Bridgewater, Williams County, Ohio, son of Alonzo, of Avon. He enlisted in the 128th Regiment Ohio Volunteers, and thus served in the late war.

JOHN LUTHER HART, Delivan Station, Minn. He enlisted as a private in Company E, 16th Regiment Connecticut Volunteers.

VELORIUS M. HART, Farmington, Ohio, fifth son of Joseph C. He was first lieutenant in Company D, 2d Regiment Ohio Cavalry, and went through the war.

ADELBERT MIRON HART, Farmington, Trumbull County, Ohio, son of Joseph C. He entered the Union Army in the spring of 1862, was taken prisoner at the battle of Chickamauga, conveyed to Danville, thence to Libby, and from there to Andersonville, where he was exchanged—eighteen months in all—and died on the passage from Charleston, S. C., to Annapolis. .

DR. ALBERT GAYLORD HART, Clarksville, Penn. He entered the army in 1861, as surgeon in the 41st Regiment Ohio Volunteers, and served three years in the late war.

CALVIN C. HART, son of Gad. He was first lieutenant in Company A,

41st Regiment Ohio Volunteers, and was killed at the battle of Stone River, December 31st, 1862.

ALBERT JAMES HART, Unionville and New Britain, son of Deacon Chauncey. He was a veteran in the late war, having served four years as drum-major. He lives at New Britain, 1874.

PHILIP ZENAS HART, son of Deacon Chauncey. He was wounded in the late war, and draws a small pension in consequence.

HENRY CRANE HART, son of Richard, was a private in the late war.

SETH HART, Brookfield, Ohio, son of Robert, of Trumbull County, O. He was a soldier in the late war, and went with Sherman to the sea.

CAPTAIN GEORGE OBED HART, run a steamboat on the Mississippi from Louisville to Memphis.

FREDERIC HART, Durham, fourth son of Wm. A., was four years in late war, first as a private in 1st Regiment Connecticut Volunteers, then as lieutenant in 109th Colored Infantry.

HENRY I. HART, Pennfield, Ohio; served two years in late war, first as color-bearer Ohio Volunteer Infantry, than as sergeant-major in Pioneer Corps; he died at Pennfield, 1863.

CHAS. RICHARD HART, Edenburgh, Ohio, only son of Richard M., born 1825, was a soldier in late war, Company F, Ohio Volunteer Infantry, died at Portage Co., 1862.

STEPHEN PIERCE HART, Berlin, Conn., was a volunteer in 17th Maine Regiment, was wounded at battle of Gettysburg, 1863, is, 1874, in Milwaukee, Wis.

NORMAN HART, son of Selah O., was in army of 1812; died 1813, at Sandusky.

DAVID HART, Illinois, son of Dea. Henry, enlisted 1861 into Company I, 47th Regiment Illinois Volunteers, as 2d sergeant, but promoted to 1st lieutenant of colored regiment; honorably discharged 1866.

MILES HART, Wheeler, Porter Co., Ind., son of Lewis; was nearly four years in late war, mostly guarding prisoners at Johnson's Island, Lake Erie.

WALTER JOHN HART, Fredonia, N. Y., soldier in late war, wounded before Richmond, and died Oct. 28th, 1864, four days after the battle.

LEWIS HART, when the late war broke out, enlisted for three months, then re-enlisted for three years in Company F, 14th Regiment, Capt. Blinn of New Britain; died 1864 at hospital.

NORMAN HART, son of Newton of Winchester, served three years in a Wisconsin regiment.

NELSON HART, son of Selah, a Commissary of U. S. Army at Fort Abercrombie.

FRANKLIN DEWEY HART, son of Nelson, Fort Abercrombie, Min., an assistant commissary.

MORTIMER EDGERTON HART, Cleveland, Ohio, served as a private in late war.

F. W. HART, Waterbury, musician 1st Regiment Connecticut Volunteers; honorably discharged July 31st, 1861.

WILLIS A. HART, New Britain, corporal Company G, 1st Regiment Connecticut Volunteers; honorably discharged July 31st, 1861; reenlisted, died June 20th, 1863.

EDWARD A. HART, New Haven, Company C, 2d Regiment; honorably discharged August 7th, 1861.

GEORGE HART, Columbia, Company A, Cavalry, died Sept. 25th, 1864.

JOSEPH HART, 1st Regiment Connecticut Cavalry, killed April 1st, 1865, at Harper's Farms, Va.

NELSON HART, Sprague, Company K, 1st Regiment Connecticut Cavalry, died March 29th, 1864, at Baltimore, Md.

JOHN HART, Hartford, 1st Regiment Connecticut Cavalry; musician, April, 1864, deserted, May, 1864.

ADAM HART, Southington, 1st Regiment Connecticut Cavalry.

HENRY W. HART, Bridgeport, 2d Light Battery; mustered out August 9th, 1865.

JOSEPH HART, Litchfield, 2d Light Battery; mustered out August 9th, 1865, at New Haven.

LEONARD HART, New Hartford, musician 1st Regiment Heavy Artillery; discharged for disability Oct. 30th, 1861.

EDWARD HART, Bay City, Mich., killed in the late war; son of Julius B. Hart.

FREDERIC J. HART, New Haven, Company F, 1st Artillery; re-enlisted veteran March 22d, 1864.

WM. L. HART, New Haven, Company F, 1st Artillery; discharged for disability Nov. 15th, 1862, at Newark, N. J.

WM. K. HART, Torrington, Company C, 2d Connecticut Artillery; died June 22d, 1864, at Philadelphia, Pa.

CHARLES A. HART, Barkhamsted, Company E, 2d Artillery; mustered out July 7th, 1865, at Washington, D. C.

LUTHER W. HART, Winchester, Company E, 2d Artillery; discharged November, 1863, at Fort Worth.

WM. HART, North Canaan, Company K, 2d Connecticut Artillery, mustered in August 12th, 1862, mustered out May, 1865.

NOAH HART, Barkhamsted, Company L, 2d Connecticut Artillery; mustered in Jan. 21st, 1864, mustered out Nov. 15th, 1864, for disability.

JAMES HART, Hamden, Company L, 2d Connecticut Artillery; deserted June 12th, 1864.

CHARLES HART, Norwalk, Company L, 2d Connecticut Artillery; deserted March 12th, 1864.

CHARLES C. HART, Greenwich, 2d Connecticut Artillery, mustered in Dec. 13th, 1864, deserted August 1st, 1865.

ERASTUS W. HART, New Haven, Company C, 5th Regiment Connecticut Volunteers; mustered in July 22d, 1861, honorably discharged July, 1865.

JOHN HART, New Haven, Company D, 5th Regiment Connecticut Volunteers; killed at Cedar Mountain, Va., August 9th, 1862.

ALVIN H. HART, Cornwall, Company I, 5th Regiment Connecticut Volunteers; promoted from sergeant to 2d lieutenant, Nov. 1st, 1864.

HENRY HART, Windham, Company K, 5th Regiment Connecticut Volunteers; mustered in July 22d, 1861, discharged July 21st, 1864.

JAMES HART, Hartford, 5th Regiment Connecticut Volunteers; mustered in Nov. 18th, 1862, deserted Nov. 27th, 1862.

BURTON W. HART, West Hartford, Company E, 7th Regiment Connecticut Volunteers; discharged June 6th, 1865.

SIDNEY HART, Company F, 7th Regiment Connecticut Volunteers; mustered in Sept. 9th, 1861, re-enlisted veteran, mustered out 1865.

JAMES HART, Canton, Company F, 7th Regiment Connecticut Volunteers; deserted 1863.

HENRY HART, Farmington, Company I, 7th Regiment Connecticut Volunteers; mustered in Sept. 13th, 1861, died July 1st, 1863, in South Carolina.

FRANCIS HART, New Britain, Company A, 8th Regiment Connecticut Volunteers; mustered in Sept. 25th, 1861, discharged May 9th, 1862.

SAMUEL B. HART, New Hartford, Company C, 8th Regiment Connecticut Volunteers; mustered in Oct. 1st, 1861, re-enlisted veteran, discharged for disability, May, 1865.

NELSON HART, Canaan, Company I, 8th Regiment Connecticut Volunteers; mustered in Sept. 21st, 1861, re-enlisted veteran, mustered out 1865.

WILBER F. HART, Meriden, Company K, 8th Regiment Connecticut Volunteers; mustered in Dec. 30th, 1863, mustered out Dec. 12th, 1865.

THOMAS HART, Danbury, Company K, 9th Regiment Connecticut Volunteers; mustered in Dec. 2d, 1861, re-enlisted veteran, mustered out August 3d, 1865.

JAMES HART, Greenwich, Company I, 10th Regiment Connecticut Volunteers; mustered in Oct. 16th, 1861, discharged by civil authority Oct. 22d, 1861.

JOHN HART, Suffield, Company C, 11th Regiment Connecticut Volunteers; mustered in March 17th, 1864, deserted Dec. 1st, 1864.

WILLIAM HEART, Portland, Company F, 11th Regiment Connecticut Volunteers; mustered in March 23d, 1864, died Sept. 20th, 1864, at Andersonville, Ga.

ELMER HART, Avon, Company K, 11th Regiment Connecticut Volunteers; mustered in Nov. 14th, 1861, discharged for disability June 24th, 1862.

ALVERDA S. HART, New, Britain, Company A, 13th Regiment Connecticut Volunteers; mustered in Dec. 22d, 1861, discharged for disability August 8th, 1864.

HENRY C. HART, Farmington, Company A, 13th Regiment Connecticut Volunteers; mustered in Feb. 10th, 1862, discharged Jan. 6th, 1865.

FRANCIS J. HART, Meriden, mustered in Dec. 4th, 1863, transferred to Company E, and died Jan. 8th, 1865. .

THOMAS HART, Danbury, Company D, 13th Regiment Connecticut Volunteers; mustered in Dec. 16th, 1864, mustered out August 25th, 1865.

PATRICK HART, New Haven, Company H, 13th Regiment Connecticut Volunteers; mustered in Feb. 1st, 1862, term expired January 6th, 1865.

JOSEPH HART, Killingly, Company A, 14th Regiment Connecticut Volunteers; mustered in July 14th, 1862, discharged Jan. 8th, 1864.

THOMAS HART, Bristol, Company A, 14th Regiment Connecticut Volunteers; mustered in Sept. 18th, 1863, mustered out August 14th, 1865, at Washington, D. C.

THOMAS HART, New Britain, corporal Company A, 14th Regiment Connecticut Volunteers; killed Dec. 13th, 1862, at Fredericksburg, Va.

WM. W. HART, Madison, first lieutenant Company G, 14th Regiment Connecticut Volunteers; promoted to captain, resigned Oct., 1862.

EUGENE HART, Hartford, Company I, 14th Regiment Connecticut Volunteers; mustered in July 9th, 1862, mustered out May 31st, 1865.

MARTIN HART, Colchester, 14th Regiment Connecticut Volunteers; mustered in Feb. 17th, 1864.

CHARLES E. HART, New Haven, corporal Company I, 15th Regiment Connecticut Volunteers; mustered in July 29th, 1862, mustered out June 27th, 1865.

HENRY C. HART, North Haven, Company K, 15th Regiment Connecticut Volunteers; mustered in August 9th, 1862, mustered out June 12th, 1865.

AUSTIN A. HART, Avon, Company B, 16th Regiment Connecticut Volunteers; mustered in July 22d, 1862, discharged for disability July 14th, 1863.

HIRAM W. HART, Farmington, Company C, 16th Regiment Connecticut Volunteers; mustered in August 16th, 1862, discharged for disability Jan. 4th, 1863.

JOHN L. HART, Canton, Company E, 16th Regiment Connecticut Volunteers; mustered in July 23d, 1862, mustered out June 24th, 1865.

CHARLES L. HART, Farmington, corporal Company G, 16th Regiment Connecticut Volunteers; mustered in August 7th, 1862, discharged for disability Jan. 3d, 1863.

ALGEROY HART, Farmington, Company G, 16th Regiment Connecticut Volunteers; mustered in August 11th, 1862, mustered out June 27th, 1865, at Philadelphia.

ELI A. HART, Avon, Company I, 16th Regiment Connecticut Volunteers; mustered in August 8th, 1862, mustered out June 3d, 1865.

LEWIS HART, Brooklyn, Company A, 18th Regiment Connecticut Volunteers; mustered in July 22d, 1862, mustered out June 19th, 1865.

ANDREW E. HART, New Britain, corporal Company K, 20th Regiment Connecticut Volunteers; mustered in August 8th, 1862, discharged for disability March, 1863.

ALMON J. HART, Wethersfield, Company B, 21st Regiment Connecticut Volunteers; mustered in August 18th, 1862, mustered out June 16th, 1865.

JOHN M. HART, Bethel, Company G, 23d Regiment Connecticut Volunteers; mustered in Sept. 2d, 1862, honorably discharged August 31st, 1863.

CHARLES H. HART, Danbury, sergeant Company K, 23d Regiment Connecticut Volunteers; mustered in August 27th, 1862, honorably discharged August 31st, 1863.

ALFRED D. HART, Hartford, Company K, 25th Regiment Connecticut Volunteers; mustered in August 25th, 1862, mustered out August 26th, 1863.

HENRY F. HART, Branford, Company B, 27th Regiment Connecticut Volunteers; mustered in Aug. 19th, 1862, mustered out July 27th, 1863.

EDWIN R. F. HART, graduate of Beloit College; in late war, capacity not known.

JOHN HART, Weathersfield, Vt., aged 21; 1st Regiment, Company E.

SILAS L. HART, aged 22; Company B, 2d Regiment Vermont Volunteers; died of wounds May 5th, 1864.

ALONZO HART, aged 37; Company D, 2d Regiment Vermont Volunteers; mustered in Sept. 3d, 1861, discharged Feb. 10th, 1863.

FRANK HART, aged 18; Company D, 2d Regiment Vermont Volunteers; mustered in Feb. 19th, 1862.

FREDERIC A. HART, aged 18; Company D, 2d Regiment Vermont Volunteers; mustered in Dec. 31st, 1863.

JEFFREY HART, aged 20; 1st Vermont Cavalry; mustered in Sept. 26th, 1861, died in general hospital 1864.

ANDREW J. HART, aged 20; Company I, 1st Vermont Cavalry; discharged Nov., 1862.

WILLIAM A. HART, aged 18; Company K, 8th Regiment Vermont Volunteers; mustered in Jan. 8th, 1862, re-enlisted Feb., 1864.

JOHNSTON B. HART, aged 22; Company E, 10th Regiment Vermont Volunteers; mustered in Sept. 1st, 1862.

HENRY H. HART, aged 21; mustered in Sept. 1st, 1862, sick in general hospital Aug. 31st, 1864.

CHARLES M. HART, aged 18; Company C, 11th Regiment Vermont Volunteers; mustered in Dec. 16th, 1863.

ORANGE M. HART, aged 25; Company B, 14th Regiment Vermont Volunteers; mustered in Oct. 10th, 1862.

LEONARD HART, aged 35; Company C, 15th Regiment Vermont Volunteers; mustered in Sept. 11th, 1862.

JOHN C. HART, aged 17; Company F, 1st Regiment U. S. Sharp Shooters, promoted to corporal.

GEORGE HART, Company K, 16th Regiment Illinois Cavalry, died at Andersonville, June 30th, 1864.

W. HART, Company K, 16th Regiment Illinois Cavalry, died at Andersonville, June 19th, 1864.

W. HART, Company G, 15th Massachusetts Regiment, died at Andersonville, September 6th, 1864.

JOHN HEART, Company G, 28th Massachusetts Regiment, died at Andersonville, July 18th, 1864.

J. R. HART, Company E, 6th Michigan Regiment, died at Andersonville, May 7th, 1864.

D. R. HART, Company D, 109th New York Regiment, died at Andersonville, August 4th, 1864.

J. HART, Company F, 12th Regiment New York Cavalry, died at Andersonville, August 15th, 1864.

J. HART, Company K, 7th New York Artillery, died at Andersonville, October 26th, 1864.

S. HART, Company B, 146th New York Regiment, died at Andersonville, September 9th, 1864.

S. L. HART, 2d Vermont Regiment, died at Andersonville, October 13th, 1864.

ISAAC HART, teamster, died at Andersonville, September 21st, 1864.

Capt. Samuel Stryker Hart, Janesville, 13th Wisconsin Regiment, was in service to the close of the war.

William Lewis Hart, Janesville, Wis., entered the Union army and served one hundred days. **1136945**

Elias Hart, a private, assisted in taking Louisburg, in 1745.

John Hart, a lieutenant in Col. Samuel Morris' regiment, assisted in taking Louisburg, in 1745.

Ralph Hart, Boston, commissioned a lieutenant by Gov. Shirley, in 1742, preparatory to the taking of Louisburg.

Edwin Hart, Riverside, Cal., received a sergeant's warrant in Company I, 6th Regiment Iowa Cavalry.

Sergeant Peter Hart, of New York, nailed the first flag to the mast at Fort Sumpter, after it had been shot away by a shower of bullets by the rebels.

Maj. William Hart, Marietta, Ohio, was on duty as an officer, and kept watch over the boats in the Muskingham river, to prevent their joining Aaron Burr's insurrection.

William Hart was killed in the battle of Corinth, April 6th, 1862.

Isaac L. Hart, Fall River, Mass., was a sergeant in Company C, 1st Massachusetts Regiment, and discharged for disability, March 27th, 1863.

Daniel Hart, Lawrence, Mass., aged 22, was a member of Company H, 4th Massachusetts Regiment.

Samuel P. Hart, South Danvers, Mass., aged 27, was a member of Company C, 5th Massachusetts Regiment.

Henry T. Hart, Woburn, Mass., aged 25, was a member of Company G, 5th Massachusetts Regiment.

Thomas B. Hart, Lynn, Mass., aged 19, was a member of Company I, 8th Massachusetts Regiment.

Abner P. Hart, Melrose, Mass., aged 23, was a member of Company G, 44th Massachusetts Regiment.

George D. Hart, Barnstable, Mass., aged 32, was a member of Company D, 55th Massachusetts Regiment.

Philip W. Hart, Dartmouth, Mass., aged 33, was a member of Company D, 47th Massachusetts Regiment.

Charles W. Hart, Sheffield, Mass., aged 23, was a member of Company K, 49th Massachusetts Regiment.

James Hart, Blackstone, Mass., aged 21, was a member of Company K, 51st Massachusetts Regiment.

Samuel C. Hart, New Bedford, Mass., was a 1st lieutenant in the 22d Massachusetts Regiment, and was promoted to a captaincy August 20th, 1862.

ISAAC C. HART, New Bedford, Mass., was, Dec. 30th, 1862, a 1st lieutenant in the 23d Massachusetts Regiment.

WILLIAM H. HART, Lynn, Mass., was commissioned 2d lieutenant in the 1st Regiment Massachusetts Artillery, Jan. 28th, 1863.

WILLIAM N. HART, aged 45, was a musician in Company G, 1st Massachusetts Regiment, and was promoted to sergeant.

JOHN HART, a member of Company C, 7th Massachusetts Regiment, was killed in battle, May 5th, 1864.

GEORGE L. HART, aged 22, enlisted as a veteran in Company A, of the 10th Massachusetts Regiment.

HENRY HART, aged 21, was a member of Company H, 9th Massachusetts Regiment, and was mustered out June 21st, 1864.

DAVIS HART, aged 29, was a member of Company A, 10th Massachusetts Regiment, and died at Spottsylvania Court House, May 12th, 1864.

MICHAEL HART, aged 30, was a member of Company C, 12th Massachusetts Regiment.

PHILIP W. HART, aged 34, was a member of Company C, 12th Massachusetts Regiment, and mustered out Nov. 25th, 1863.

JOHN HART, aged 26, was a member of Company B, 13th Massachusetts Regiment, and deserted from Rappahannock, Va., Aug. 21st, 1863.

JOHN HART, aged 22, a member of Company E, 15th Massachusetts Regiment, was transferred to the 15th Battalion, July 12th, 1864.

WILLIAM HART, aged 23, a member of Company G, 15th Massachusetts Regiment, deserted Dec. 4th, 1863.

BERNARD HART, aged 20, was a member of Company A, 16th Massachusetts Regiment, and discharged for disability, Oct. 5th, 1863.

JOHN M. HART, aged   , was a member of Company B, 16th Massachusetts Regiment, and discharged for disability, Dec. 15th, 1862.

JOHN HART, aged 24, a member of Company G, 16th Massachusetts Regiment, re-enlisted into the veteran reserve corps, Nov. 6th, 1863.

CHARLES H. HART, aged 22, a member of Company E, 16th Massachusetts Regiment, re-enlisted into the 11th Massachusetts Battalion, July 11th, 1864.

THOMAS HART, aged 19, was a member of Company G, 16th Massachusetts Regiment, and mustered out July 27th, 1864.

JOHN HART, aged 20, was a member of Company B, 17th Massachusetts Regiment.

SAMUEL C. HART, New Bedford, Mass., was commissioned a 1st lieutenant in the 23d Regiment, Oct. 8th, 1861, and received a captain's commission June 25th, 1862.

Isaac C. Hart, New Bedford, Mass., was a 2d lieutenant in the 23d Regiment, and commissioned a 1st lieutenant Dec. 30th, 1862.

Thomas B. Hart, Lynn, Mass., was a member of the 61st Regiment, and commissioned 1st lieutenant Dec. 30th, 1864.

William H. Hart, Lynn, Mass., was commissioned a 2d lieutenant in the 1st Regiment Heavy Artillery, Jan. 28th, 1863,—subsequently promoted to a captaincy.

Samuel C. Hart, New Bedford, Mass., was commissioned lieutenant-colonel of the 4th Regiment Heavy Artillery, Nov. 14th, 1864.

Capt. Samuel L. Hart, Company D, 41st Wisconsin Regiment, was commissioned June 9th, 1864.

Capt. Samuel S. Hart, Company F, 13th Wisconsin Regiment, was commissioned May 11th, 1864.

Lieut. Edward W. Hart, Madison, Conn., enlisted as a private in the 14th Regiment, was promoted to corporal, and in 1863, received a lieutenant's 'commission, in which capacity he distinguished himself at Chancellorsville ; he died in the service.

Charles Hart, from near Danbury, Conn., was a member of the 23d Regiment, and fell at Brashier City.

Ezekiel Bishop Hart, Westchester, N. Y., son of Abram Hart, White Plains, was a midshipman in the United States Navy, under Com. Chauncey, in the war of 1812; he was shot through the breast at Green Bay.

Benjamin Franklin Hart, brother of Ezekiel, was a purser in the United States Navy.

Elisha Hart, son of Elisha, of Farmington, was in the war of 1812, and died in the service.

Nelson Hart, Dover, Min., was for nearly three years a soldier in the late war.

James Hart, 1st New Jersey Cavalry, was, in 1861, a 1st lieutenant, and for bravery, was promoted to captain; he was killed at "Five Forks," April 1st, 1865.

Thompson D. Hart was a 1st lieutenant in the 104th Pennsylvania Regiment, and in 1862, was promoted to lieutenant-colonel; he was at the siege of Charleston.

Thomas Jefferson Hart was quartermaster in the Missouri home guard, then captain in the 43d and 48th Missouri Regiments, and served in Missouri and Tennessee until January, 1865, when, on account of ill health, he resigned.

HART MEMORIAL.

FIRST GENERATION.

DEACON STEPHEN HART,

BRAINTREE, ENG.; CAMBRIDGE, MASS.; HARTFORD AND TUNXIS, CONN.

1. *Cambridge, Hartford, and Farmington.*

DEACON STEPHEN HART, son of   , and his wife,
                    , born about 1605, at Braintree, in Essex County,
Eng. He came from there to Massachusetts Bay about 1632, and
located for a time at (Newtown,) Cambridge, Mass; married
                    . She died   , when second he
married Margaret, the widow of Arthur Smith, and daughter of
                    . She survived Deacon Hart, and was admitted
to the church in Farmington, March 17th, 1690–1. She died in 1693.
Deacon Hart and his first wife were constituent members of the church
in Farmington, organized November, 1652, with Rev. Roger Newton
pastor. Mr. Hart had been deacon of Rev. Thomas Hooker's church,
at Cambridge, Mass., and at Hartford, Conn. He was one of the fifty-
four settlers at Cambridge, Mass., was a proprietor at Hartford in 1639,
and became one of the eighty-four proprietors of Farmington in 1672.
In 1647 he was one of the "*deputyes*" of the General Court of Connecticut, at their May session. In 1653 he was appointed a commissioner, by the General Court, for the town of Farmington, to aid the
constable in impressing men into the army, then being raised.

Stephen Hart is supposed to have come from Braintree, Essex
County, England, with the company that settled Braintree, Mass., and
subsequently removed to Newtown, since called Cambridge, and constituted the church of which Rev. Thomas Hooker was invited from
England to become their pastor. He was in Cambridge in 1632, and
admitted a freeman there, May 14th, 1634. He came to Hartford with
Mr. Hooker's company in 1635, and was one of the original proprie-

tors of that place. His house-lot was on the west side of what is now called Front Street, near where Morgan Street crosses it, and there is a tradition that the town was called from the ford he discovered and used in crossing the Connecticut River at a low stage of the water, and so from Hart's Ford it soon became Hartford, from a natural and easy transition. Tradition further says that as he and others were on a hunting excursion on Talcott Mountain, they discovered the Farmington River Valley, then inhabited by the Tunxis, a powerful tribe of Indians. The meadows were probably then cleared, and waving with grass and Indian corn. Such lands were then much needed and coveted by the settlers, who soon—probably as soon as 1640—made a bargain with the Indians, and settled among them with their cattle. They still continued, however, connected with the settlement at Hartford, attended public worship, and perhaps wintered there, until about 1645, when the town was incorporated by the name of Farmington, from the excellent farms there.* About this time Mr. Roger Newton, a student in theology with Rev. Thomas Hooker, whose daughter he married, began to preach for them, and in 1652 was ordained their pastor. Stephen Hart was one of the *seven pillars* of the church, and was chosen their first deacon. The other pillars were Rev. Roger Newton, pastor, John Cole (Cowles), John Bronson, Robert Porter, Thomas Judd, and Thomas Thompson.

Stephen Hart appears to have taken the lead in the settlement among the Indians in Farmington, and purchased a large tract on the border of the present town of Avon, and known to this day by the name of Hart's Farm.† He was one of the first representatives in 1647, and continued, with one exception, for fifteen sessions, until 1655, and once in 1660. In short, no man in the town was more active, influential, and useful. His house-lot, which was four or five times as large as any other, was on the west side of Main Street, in the village, opposite the meeting-house, and contained fifteen acres, extending from Mill Lane to the stone store south. This large house-lot was granted to Deacon Stephen Hart as an inducement to erect and continue a mill on the premises, to be perpetuated and kept in motion. The mill was erected originally by the Bronsons, to whom, as a consideration, was granted, viz: a tract of eighty acres, on the Pequabuk River, now known as the "Eighty Acre." The south part of this house-lot he gave to his son John, and the north part to his son Thomas. Thomas

---

* The principal leaders in this settlement were John Steele, William Lewis, Stephen Hart, Thomas Judd, John Bronson, John Warner, Nathaniel Kellogg, Thomas Barnes, Richard Seymour, and Thomas Gridley.

† Probably located at or near what is now called Cider Brook, on the east side of the river, and near the bridge, some three miles north of Farmington Village.

gave it to *his* son Josiah, and it descended to the wife of Roger Hooker, his only surviving child, and to her only son, Thomas Hart Hooker, who sold it to Samuel Deming. The Demings and their descendants hold it to this day—1874. These lots and lands, in some respects, are the most desirable and valuable of any in the old town of Farmington. He was a representative to the General Court of Connecticut in 1647, and most of the succeeding years to 1660, from the town of Farmington. His widow, Margaret, gave her property to her sons, John and Arthur Smith, and daughter, Elizabeth Thompson. She had grandchildren—Elizabeth, John, and Ann Thompson.

Deacon Hart's Will was dated March 16th, 1682-3. He mentions the farm he formerly gave his three sons, John, Stephen, and Thomas, viz: one-half to John, one-fourth to Steven, and one-fourth to Thomas.

Item.—I give my grandson, Thomas Porter, and my son-in-law, John Cole, my plow-land and meadow swamp, which was some time Andrew Warner's farm, abuts on my son Steven, their agreement to my beloved wife being fulfilled.

Item.—I give my sons, Steven and Thomas, and my daughters, Sarah Porter and Mary Lee, my Swamp Lot in the Great Swamp,* and all my uplands to be equally divided between them.

Item.—I give my grandchild, Dorothy Porter, £10.

Item.—I give my grandchild, John Lee, £3.

Item.—I give my grandchild, John Hart, my eldest son's son, £3.

Item.—I give my beloved wife, &c.

The Inventory was taken by   Thomas Hart, } Selectmen.
and John Hart, }

Isaac Moore, } Appraisers.   Taken March 31st, 1682-3.
and Benjamin Judd, }
Amount, £340 4s. House and homestead, £70; land at Nod, east of river, £40.

Deacon Hart was a farmer and large land-holder, located in the village of Farmington, and was a man of great influence, and a leading character. He died March, 1682-3, aged 77 years.

HIS CHILDREN, ALL BY HIS FIRST WIFE, SECOND GENERATION.

2.	Sarah, born	, married Nov. 20th, 1644, Thomas Porter.
3.	Mary, born	, married John Lee; second, Jan. 5th, 1672, Jedediah
	Strong.	
4.	John, born	, married Sarah ———.
5.	Steven, born	, wife not known.
6.	Mehitabel, born	, married John Cole.
7.	Thomas, born	1643, married Ruth Hawkins.

* The Great Swamp means Kensington Parish, now part of Berlin.

SECOND GENERATION.

PORTER.

2. *Farmington.*

SARAH HART, of Farmington, supposed to be the eldest child of Deacon Stephen Hart, and born in England, married, Nov. 20th, 1644, Thomas Porter, who lived on the lot adjacent to her father, a part of which has remained in the family, and was, in 1844, occupied by his descendant, Timothy Porter. They joined the church in 1653, and many of their descendants have been deacons, and some of them clergymen, among the latter, Ebenezer Porter, D. D., President of Andover Theological Seminary. Their children were Thomas, Samuel, Dorothy, Sarah, and Johannah. He died in 1697, and was then a deacon in the church.

LEE.

3. *Farmington.*

MARY HART, of Farmington, second daughter of Deacon Stephen Hart, of Braintree, Eng., Cambridge, Mass., Hartford and Farmington, Conn., born   , married   John Lee, who lived on the lot next north of her father's place, viz., where the Phelps Hotel stands. They joined the church in 1660, and are the progenitors of the Lees of New England. He died in 1690, when second, she married, Jan. 5th, 1692, Jedediah Strong, (his third wife.) Their children, 1, John, born June 11th, 1659, married Dec. 27th, 1682, Elizabeth Loomis; 2, Mary, born Aug. 14th, 1664, married Dec. 28th, 1682, Stephen Upson; 3, Stephen, born April 2d, 1667, married Oct. 1st, 1690, Elizabeth Roys, of Wallingford; 4, Thomas, born in 1671, married Sept. 11th, 1707, Mary Camp, of Hartford, and were the parents of Jared Strong, Esq., of Southington; 5, David, born in 1674; 6, Tabitha, born in 1677, married Preserved Strong, of Northampton, son of her mother's second husband.

COLE.

6. *Hartford.*

MEHITABEL HART, of Farmington, third daughter of Deacon Stephen Hart, of Braintree, Eng., Cambridge, Mass., Hartford and Tunxis, Conn., born   , married   John Cole, a grandson of James Cole, of Hartford, from whom Coles street derives its name. He settled in Farmington, on the place formerly owned by Anson Cowles. Both were members of the church. His sons removed to

Kensington, where their descendants still remain;—the late Mrs. Ruth Hart was one of the family. Their son John, born   , married Jan. 5th, 1691, Mehitabel Loomis, of Windsor.

4.   Farmington.

JOHN HART, of Farmington, eldest son of Deacon Stephen Hart, of Braintree, Eng., Cambridge, Mass., Hartford and Farmington, Conn., born   , in England, married   Sarah   . They resided in Farmington, where he was made a freeman by the General Court, at their May session, 1654. Sarah, his wife, joined the church at Farmington, Oct. 19th, 1653; he was admitted to the church April 2d, 1654. He was one of the first settlers of Tunxis, and bought his house lot of the original owners, and among the list of the eighty-four proprietors of 1672, is numbered the "Estate of John Hart." At the October session of the General Court, in 1660, a committee was raised to examine "Thirty Mile Island," with the view of settlement, when John Hart, of Farmington, was elected one of said committee. His sad and untimely death occurred on this wise, viz.: his house, which was located near the center of the village, was fired in the night by Indians, and he and all his family, with the exception of his eldest son, John, who was that night at Nod, or Northington, since called Avon, looking after the stock on a farm they owned there, perished in the flames. What aggravated the public calamity was the burning of the town records, at the same time. The General Court made diligent search among the Tunxis tribe for the incendiaries, but this neither restored life nor records. This fire occurred   , 1666.

BRANCH OF JOHN HART FOLLOWS, THEIR CHILDREN BEING THIRD GENERATION.

8. Sarah, born in Farmington, about 1653, baptized Oct. 23d, 1653, burned to death in 1666.
9. John, born in Farmington, about 1655, baptized April 2d, 1655, saved from the fire, he being that night at Nod.
10. Steven, born in Farmington, July   , 1657, baptized July 19th, 1657, burned to death in 1666.

9.   Farmington.

CAPT. JOHN HART, of Farmington, eldest son of John Hart and Sarah, his wife, (who were burned to death by the burning of their house, in 1666,) born in Farmington, about 1655, and baptized there April 2d, 1655, married   , Mary, daughter of Deacon Isaac Moore, of Farmington, and both were admitted to the church there Nov. 24th, 1686. He was one of the appraisers of his uncle Stephen Hart's estate in 1689. In May, 1695, he was confirmed by the General Court ensign of the Farmington train-band, and in October, 1703, was commissioned lieutenant, and subsequently promoted captain. He was for four successive years (1702–5,) a deputy from Farmington to the General Court, and was appointed in May, 1705, one of the auditors of the colony. When his father's house was burned by the Indians, he was absent from home, and thus providentially saved to be the progenitor of a numerous posterity. The offices and honors thus bestowed upon him indicate that he stood high in the community. Capt. John Hart died in Farmington, Nov. 11th, 1714, aged 60 years; his wife died Sept. 19th, 1738, aged 74 years.

THEIR CHILDREN, BEING THE FOURTH GENERATION.

11. John, born   , 1684, baptized Nov. 27th, 1686, married March 20th, 1706, Esther Gridley.

12. Isaac, born   , baptized Nov. 27th, 1686, married Nov. 24th, 1721, Elizabeth Whaples.

13. Sarah, horn   , baptized Dec. 11th, 1687, married Feb. 15th, 1705, Ebenezer Steele.

14. Matthew, born   , 1690, baptized Dec. 7th, 1690, married Jan. 10th, 1725, Sarah Hooker.

15. Samuel, born   , baptized Sept. 18th, 1692, married Dec. 5th, 1723, Mary Hooker.

16. Nathaniel, born   , baptized April 14th, 1695, married Dec. 3d, 1719, Abigail Hooker.

17. Mary, born   , married   , John Leffingwell, Esq., of Norwich, Conn.

11.   *Farmington and Kensington.*

DEACON JOHN HART, of Farmington and Kensington, son of Capt. John and his wife Mary (Moore), born   , 1684, baptized in Farmington, Nov. 27th, 1686, married March 20th, 1706, Esther, daughter of Samuel Gridley (the Trader, so called); she was born   , 1687, baptized in Farmington, May 15th, 1687, and both were admitted to the church there Jan. 31st, 1711-12; they lived on his father's place. He was chosen deacon of the church in Farmington, Nov. 19th, 1718, and subsequently removed to Kensington, where he was also a deacon. His wife, Esther, who was the mother of his children, died July 10th, 1743, aged 57 years, when he married, second, Jan. 11th, 1743-4, widow Hannah Hull, who also died, Nov. 27th, 1760, aged 76 years. Deacon John Hart was for many years Town Clerk, and was twenty-three times elected to the General Court, between the years 1717 and 1743. The Will of Deacon John Hart, of Kensington, was dated March 2d, 1752, and is found in probate at Hartford, the substance of which is as follows:

Item.—I give to my beloved wife, Hannah, etc.

Item.—I give my son Judah, besides what I have already given him, 16 acres at the south end of *"Dead Swamp."*

Item.—I give my son John all my house homestead, also my lot called the Meeting-house lot, 3½ acres, bounded East on Stephen Hart, North on highway, and West on Meeting-house yard.

Item.—I give my son Solomon all my lands on *"Fort Hill,"* about 100 acres.

Item.—I give my three daughters, viz., Esther, wife of Nathaniel Newell, Mary, wife of Rev. Samuel Newell, and Sarah, wife of Stephen Root, etc.

He appointed his sons Judah and John executors of his Will, which was witnessed by
                                       James Gridley,
                                       Stephen Hart,
                                       and Thomas Cowles.

The Inventory was taken March 23d, 1754,

by { Giles Hooker, Nehemiah Lewis, Solomon Cowles. } Appraisers amount, £1342 15s. 3d.

The distributors of the estate were { Nehemiah Lewis, Solomon Cowles, and James Judd. }

Deacon John Hart died Oct. 7th, 1753, aged 69 years.

THEIR CHILDREN, BEING THE FIFTH GENERATION.

18. Esther, born Sept. 19th, 1707, married June 29th, 1727, Nathaniel Newell.
19. Judah, born Oct. 25th, 1709, married Feb. 20th, 1734-35, Anna Norton.
20. John, born Oct. 11th, 1714, married   Anna Hall.
21. Mary, born March 9th, 1717, married Dec. 6th, 1739, Timothy Root; second, Rev. Samuel Newell.
22. Sarah, born June 19th, 1719, married June 19th, 1740, Stephen Root; second, Capt. Eldad Lewis.
23. Solomon, born Oct. 1st, 1724, married March 3d, 1749-50, Experience Cole.
    Ruth, born Oct. 25th, 1729, died Oct. 13th, 1745, aged 16 years.

12.   *Berlin.*

ISAAC HART, of Farmington and Kensington, second son of Capt. John and his wife Mary (Moore), born   , baptized Nov. 27th, 1686, in Farmington, married Nov. 24th, 1721, Elizabeth Whaples.

They lived on Hart street, next west of Worthington Village, sometimes called lower lane. The house is still standing, 1873, with the upper story projecting over lower. It is related of him that when at work in Farmington meadows, he observed a bear coming into the lot; he seized his pitchfork and mounted his horse hitched under a tree, and pursued the bear and killed it. This anecdote is related by his great grandson, of Candor, N. Y. He was a deacon in Kensington

7

church, and died Jan. 27th, 1770, aged 84 years. Elizabeth, his widow, died Nov. 14th, 1777. He is said to be one of the early settlers of "*Great Swamp Society.*" In 1753, April 27th, he headed a petition to the General Assembly for a division of this society, and the result was a new society, called New Britain in 1754, now, 1874, the town and city of New Britain.

THEIR CHILDREN, BEING THE FIFTH GENERATION.

24.   Ebenezer, born Nov. 27th, 1722, married   , Martha   .
25.   Isaac, born   , 1724, married   , Ann Mather, of New Britain.
     Elizabeth, born July 12th, 1726, died Jan. 24th, 1726-7.
26.   Mercy, born April 4th, 1729, died March 29th, 1786, aged 57 years.
27.   Job, born Jan. 3d, 1731-2, married March 20th, 1755, Eunice Beckley.
28.   John, born   , 1734, married   , Hepzibah   , died March 23d, 1803.
29.   Lois, born   , 1744, married   , Hezekiah Judd, died August 13th, 1825, aged 81 years.

STEELE.

13.   *Farmington.*

SARAH HART, Farmington, eldest daughter of Capt. John and his wife Mary (Moore), born   , 1687, at Farmington, baptized there Sept. 11th, 1687, married Feb. 15th, 1705, Ebenezer Steele, son of Samuel and his wife Mary Boosey, born August 13th, 1661, in Farmington. They resided there and he inherited his father's large estate, and was a prominent man in the "*Litchfield Land Survey.*" In his will he forbade his widow to marry Gersham Lewis, a dissipated physician. She turned David Steele, his nephew, and heir to his property, out of the house. Their children were, 1, Mary, born June 15th, 1706, married Jan. 24th, 1725, Thomas Smith of Farmington; she died Jan. 4th, 1789; 2, Sarah, born May 25th, 1708, probably died young.

14.   *Kensington, Conn.*

MATTHEW HART, Kensington, third son of Capt. John and his wife Mary (Moore), born   , 1690, in Farmington, and baptized there Dec. 7th, 1690, married, Jan. 10th, 1725-6, Sarah Hooker, daughter of John, born Sept. 11th, 1702, at Farmington. He died at Kensington, Oct. 30th, 1736, aged 48 years; a tombstone shows where he was buried in "*Christian Lane Cemetery.*" She married, second, Huit Strong.

THEIR CHILDREN, BEING THE FIFTH GENERATION.

     Ruth, born Jan. 1st, 1726-7, died Jan., 1741, aged 13 years.
30.   Mary, born July 1st, 1728, married, July 26th, 1750, Amos Peck.

Lois, born May 18th, 1730, died Oct. 11th, 1736, in 7th year.
31. Oliver, born July 15th, 1733, married, Dec. 17th, 1766, Mary Scovill.
32. Matthew, born Jan. 23d, 1736-7, posthumous, married, Nov. 15th, 1759, Elizabeth Hopkins.

15.   Berlin, Conn.

LIEUTENANT SAMUEL HART, Kensington, fourth son of Captain John Hart, of Farmington, and his wife, Mary Moore, born 1692; baptized September 18th, 1692, at Farmington; married December 25th, 1723, Mary Hooker, daughter of John Hooker, Esq., and his wife, Abigail Stanley, born June 11th, 1700. He was a farmer, and held the military rank of lieutenant. She was a constituent member of Worthington Church in 1775. They resided on Hart Street, next west of Main Street, Worthington, where he died, September 30th, 1751, in his 60th year. His widow, Mrs. Mary Hart, died November 22d, 1780, in her 81st year. They have tomb-stones erected to their memory in the South Cemetery at Worthington Parish.

THEIR CHILDREN, BEING THE FIFTH GENERATION.

33. Anna, born September 25th, 1724; married Oct. 15th, 1747, Thomas Hollister.
    Asahel, born May 10th, 1726; died October 5th, 1736, in his 10th year.
34. Mary, born April 13th, 1730; married January 17th, 1754, Dr. Joseph Wells, of Wethersfield.
35. Huldah, born November 2d, 1731; married   , Gideon Porter.
36. Samuel, born January 21st, 1738; married October 10th, 1757, Rebecca Norton; second, Lydia Hinsdale.

16.   Kensington, Conn.

NATHANIEL HART, Kensington, youngest son of Captain John Hart, and his wife, Mary Moore, both of Farmington; born 1695; baptized April 14th, 1695, at Farmington. He married December 3d, 1719, Abigail, daughter of John Hooker, Esq., and his wife, Abigail Stanley, born January 14th, 1797-8. He died October 24th, 1758, in his 64th year. His widow, Mrs. Abigail Hart, died 1761, aged 63 years.

THEIR CHILDREN, BEING THE FIFTH GENERATION.

37. Sarah, born November 13th, 1720; married November 5th, 1747, Dr. Jonathan Marsh, of Norwich.
38. Abigail, born July 21st, 1723; married   , Dr. James Hurlbert.
39. Thankful, born July 4th, 1725; married November 5th, 1747, Charles Bronson.
    Nathaniel, born June 15th, 1728; died June 24th, 1728.
40. Hannah, born August 11th, 1729; married March 21st, 1754, Thomas Stanley, of Kensington.
41. Selah, born May 23d, 1732; married March 14th, 1756, Mary Cole; second Ruth Cole.
42. Nathaniel, born March 17th, 1735; married Nov. 23d, 1758, Martha Norton.
43. Noadiah, born July 30th, 1737; married November 20th, 1760, Lucy Hurlburt.
44. Asahel, born about 1742; graduated at Yale in 1764, and became a minister.

NEWELL.

18.   *Kensington, Conn.*

ESTHER HART, Kensington, Conn., eldest daughter of Deacon John
Hart, of Farmington and Kensington, and his first wife, Esther Gridley, born September 19th, 1707, at Farmington; married June 29th,
1727, Nathaniel Newell, son of Samuel, of Farmington, and his wife,
Mary Hart, born February 20th, 1703. They resided at Farmington,
where he became one of the deacons of that church. He died there
August 31st, 1753, aged 50 years. She inherited a portion of her
father's estate in Kensington, by his Will, the inventory of which was
taken March 23d, 1754. She was a member of the church in Farmington, and died there October 3d, 1762, aged 53 years. Their children were—1, Nathaniel, born July 30th, 1728; 2, Abel, born August
15th, 1730, and became pastor of the church in Goshen, Conn.; and
Elisha, born December 6th, 1732, married Abigail Hart, March 13th,
1755.

19.   *New Britain, Conn.*

JUDAH HART, New Britain, eldest son of Deacon John Hart, of
Farmington and Kensington, and his first wife, Esther, daughter of
Samuel Gridley, the trader; born October 25th, 1709, at Farmington;
married February 20th, 1734–5, Anna, daughter of Sergeant John
Norton, of Farmington and Kensington Parish, and his wife, Anna
Thompson, born January 15th, 1718. They located in Hart Quarter,
New Britain, soon after marriage. His house is still standing, (1874,)
opposite the school-house, and is in good condition. He was a man of
more than ordinary intelligence, of much force of character, and often
employed in public affairs. His first wife, Anna, died, when second
he married September 27th, 1759, Sarah, widow of James North, and
daughter of   Seymour, who died August 20th, 1781, aged
61 years. He died September 14th, 1784, aged 75 years. His Will,
dated September 6th, 1784, gives his son Judah all his estate, on condition that he pay all his debts, funeral charges, tombstones, and the
following legacies, viz:

To the heirs of my son Elias, 20*s.*

To the heirs of my daughter Ann, late deceased.

To my daughter Esther, wife of Eliphaz Alvord, Esq.

To the heirs of my son John, deceased, 10*s.*

He appointed his son Judah sole executor, who exhibited the Will and
proved it in probate court at Farmington, December 6th, 1784. It
was witnessed by Isaac Andrews, Thomas Booth, and Lemuel Hotchkiss.

45. Elias, born February 25th, 1735; married October 17th, 1753, Hope Whaples, of Newington.

Judah, born September 5th, 1737; died November 3d, 1745, aged 8 years.

46. Anna, born May 22d, 1739; married

47. Esther, } born April 4th, 1742; married November 29th, 1764, Eliphaz Alvord, Esq., Winchester, Conn.

Lois, } born April 4th, 1742; died at birth.

48. John, born January 20th, 1743-4; married, October, 1764, Anna Deming, of Southington.

Roger, born May 10th, 1745; died young.

Ruth, born January 19th, 1748; died young.

49. Judah, born September 10th, 1750; married April 19th, 1770, Sarah North, daughter of James and his father's second wife.

20.   *Kensington.*

JOHN HART, Kensington, Conn., second son of Deacon John Hart, of Farmington and Kensington, and his wife, Esther Gridley, born October 11th, 1714, at Kensington. His father's Will, dated March 2d, 1752, makes him one of the executors, and also gives him "all my house and homestead, and my lot, called the Meeting House Lot, of 3½ acres, bounded east on Stephen Hart, north on highway, west on meeting-house yard." (*Query.*—Is it not south on highway?) He removed to Canaan in 1740, but returned and located at Cornwall, Conn., in 1763, having sold the homestead he inherited of his father, in 1765, to Solomon and Amos Cowles. The house is still standing— 1874. He married, in 1744, Anna Hall, who died, when second he married, January 30th, 1749-50, Huldah Gould, who also died, January 19th, 1771, when third he married, May 28th, 1772, Martha Foot. He died December 18th, 1773, aged 59 years, 2 months, and 7 days.

50. John, born November 19th, 1751; died January 1st, 1777, aged 26.

51. Annie, born August 28th, 1753; married   , Seth Pierce, of Cornwall, Conn.

52. Rufus, born April 24th, 1755; died June 28th, 1765, aged 10. A pleasant and obedient child.

53. Thomas, born March 3d, 1756. He lived at Whitestown, N. Y., and at Belvidere, Ill.

54. Silas, born May 19th, 1760; married   , not known who or where.

CHILD BY HIS THIRD MARRIAGE.

55. Rufus, born March 15th, 1773; married   , 1795, Esther Coster.

ROOT. NEWELL.

21.   *Farmington, Bristol.*

MARY HART, Farmington, second daughter of Deacon John Hart, of Kensington, and his wife, Esther Gridley, born March 9th, 1717, at Farmington; married December 6th, 1739, Timothy Root, son of Timothy, and his wife, Margaret Seymour, born 1713, at Farmington. He died at Cape Breton, April 24th, 1746, aged 33, when second she married May 4th, 1749, Rev. Samuel Newell, of Bristol, son of Samuel, of Southington, and his wife, Sarah Norton, born March 1st, 1714, at Southington. He was ordained pastor of the Congregational Church in Bristol, August 12th, 1747, and died there February 10th, 1789. She died November 28th, 1797, aged 80 years, 8 months, 19 days. Her children by Root—1, Timothy born October 16th, 1740; 2, Theodore, born July 17th, 1742; 3, Esther, born July 9th, 1744. Her children by Newell—4, Mary, born October 30th, 1750; 5, Samuel, born June 27th, 1752; 6, Lot, born March 15th, 1754; 7, Anna, born August 3d, 1756; 8, Samuel 2d, born April 11th, 1758.

ROOT. LEWIS.

22.   *Farmington, Southington.*

SARAH HART, Farmington, third daughter of Deacon John Hart, of Farmington and Kensington, and his wife, Esther Gridley, born June 19th, 1719, at Farmington; married June 19th, 1740, Stephen Root, son of Timothy, and his wife, Margaret Seymour, born March 18th, 1711. He died September 5th, 1752, aged 41, when she second married April 11th, 1758, Eldad Lewis, who died at Southington, June 23d, 1784, aged 73 years. He was son of Isaac, of Farmington, and his first wife, Abigail Curtiss, of Wethersfield, born February 11th, 1711, at Farmington. She died at Wallingford, January 25th, 1789, aged 69 years, 7 months, 6 days, and a tablet at the south end burial ground in Southington, says "She was the exemplary mother of ten children." Her children by Root—1, Stephen, born October 21st, 1740; died October 20th, 1767. 2, Sarah, born September 30th, 1743; married Captain Ambrose Sloper. 3, James, born February 23d, 1746; married Mercy Woodruff. 4, Ruth, born March 9th, 1748; married Josiah Newell. 5, David, born January 23d, 1751; died January 28th, 1773. And she had five by Lewis.

23. *Southington, Farmington, Tyringham.*

SOLOMON HART, Kensington, third son of Deacon John Hart, of Farmington and Kensington, and his wife, Esther Gridley, born October 1st,

1724, at Kensington; married March 3d, 1749–50, Experience Cole, daughter of William, of Southington, and his wife, Experience Gaylord, born March 16th, 1728, at Wallingford, and was admitted to the church in Southington, September 27th, 1741. He was a deacon of the church, and lived in Congee, Farmington, where Romanta Porter resides. He removed to Tyringham, Mass., in 1761, and to Cornwall, Conn., in 1765, where he died instantly, August 15th, 1805, aged 80 years, 10 months, 14 days. She died, of hydrothorax, in 1803, aged 75 years.

THEIR CHILDREN, BEING THE SIXTH GENERATION.

56. Ruth, born December 31st, 1750; married   , ——— Brownson. .
57. Esther, born March 26th, 1752; married   , ——— Abbott.
58. Titus, born January 24th, 1754; died October 31st, 1831, aged 77. He was deacon of the church in North Cornwall, Conn.
59. Lot, born   , 1756; married   ; died February 21st, 1826, near Hudson, N. Y., aged 70.
60. Phineas, born   , 1758; married   ; died November 7th, 1828, aged 70.
61. Elias, born   , 1759; married   .   , Philomela Burnham; died February 22d, 1834, aged 75.
    Jemima, born
62. Experience, born   . He was a member of the Methodist Church.
63. Solomon, born May 8th, 1766; married   , 1786, Jerusha Beach.
    Child, born   ; died in infancy.

24.   *Kensington, Conn.*

EBENEZER HART, Kensington, eldest son of Isaac Hart, of Farmington and Kensington, and his wife, Elizabeth Whaples, born November 27th, 1722, at Kensington; married   , Martha He died November 17th, 1753, aged 30 years, 11 months, 20 days.

THEIR CHILDREN, BEING THE SIXTH GENERATION.

64. Abel, born February 22d, 1747; married   , 1769, Mary Galpin.
65. Ebenezer, born January 6th, 1750–1; married   , 1776, Lydia Kent.
66. Elizabeth, born September 14th, 1752.
    Daughter, born   ; married   , ——— Munson, and settled on the Mohawk River.

25.   *Berlin.*

ISAAC HART, Kensington, second son of Isaac Hart of Farmington and Kensington, and his wife Elizabeth Whaples, born   , 1724, at Kensington, married   , Ann Mather, daughter of Joseph of New Britain, and his wife Anna (Booth), daughter of Robert, she born Sept. 15th, 1740. They lived at the north end of Hart street, or as commonly called, "Lower Lane," house standing, 1873. He was admitted to the Congregational Church in Worthington, Feb. 9th, 1775, soon after its organization. He died Feb. 1st, 1776, and on the 10th of March, 1789, Samuel Hart and Zachariah Hart, of Berlin, were appointed by the Court of Probate, District of Farmington, distributors of the estate of Isaac Hart, late of Berlin District—John and Anna Hart being the administrators. They set to Levi, the eldest son, a double portion, viz: £130 1s. 6d.

To Isaac,	65	10	0
To Lorinda Hart,	65	10	1
To Lydia Gridley,	65	11	0
To Chloe Hart,	65	0	10

THEIR CHILDREN, BEING THE SIXTH GENERATION.

67. Levi, born   , baptized Aug. 24th, 1765, married   , Martha Hart.

Lorana, born   , baptized Feb. 8th, 1767, died young.

68. Lydia, born   , baptized June 4th, 1769, married   , Sylvester Gridley.

Isaac, born   , baptized Aug. 11th, 1771, died   , 1772.

69. Chloe, born   , 1774, married   .   , Samuel Gridley.

70. Isaac, born posthumous   , baptized March 9th, 1777, lived single in Hart street, Worthington.

27.   *Kensington and Berlin, Conn.*

JOB HART, Kensington, third son of Isaac Hart, of the same place, and his wife Elizabeth (Whaples), born Jan. 3d, 1731-2, at Kensington, married March 20th, 1755, in Newington, by Rev. Joshua Belden, Eunice Beckley; both admitted to the church in Kensington, Dec. 19th, 1756, and from thence to the church in Worthington, at its formation. He removed to Stockbridge, Mass., about 1781, and was received into the church there in 1782, and Eunice his wife in 1792.

THEIR CHILDREN, BEING THE SIXTH GENERATION.

71. Jabish, born   , 1756, baptized Jan. 2d, 1757, married   , Jemima Brace.

72. Candace, born   , baptized Feb. 8th, 1758, married   , Roswell Barnes, Oneida, N. Y.

73. Job, born   , baptized March 11th, 1759, married   , 1784, widow Rachel Ball.

74. Harvey, born   , baptized Dec. 28th, 1760, died of consumption, single, Dec. 3d, 1780, aged 21 years.   .

75. Leverett, born   , baptized June 27th, 1762, died single.

76. Eunice, born   , baptized Oct. 30th, 1763, married   ·   , Abijah Williamson, Victor, N. Y.

77. Joseph, born   , baptized March 17th, 1765, married   , Beulah Warner.

78.	Simeon, born	, baptized July 21st, 1766, married	, Betsey
	Foot.		
79.	Reuben, born	, baptized Jan. 17th, 1768, married	, widow
	Boughton.		
80.	Comfort, born	, baptized Aug. 25th, 1771, married	,
	Churchill, removed to Pompey, N. Y.		
81.	Hepzibah, born	, married	, Solomon Williams, Chenango,
	N. Y.		
	Betsey, born	, baptized June 4th, 1775, and died young.	

28.   *Berlin, Conn.*

JOHN HART, Kensington, fourth son of Isaac Hart, of Farmington and Kensington, and his wife Elizabeth Whaples, born , 1734, at Kensington, married , Hepzibah , who died Sept. 26th, 1771, in her 27th year. He died March 23d, 1809, aged 75 years. They both have gravestones at the South Cemetery in Worthington. They left no children.

JUDD.

29.   *Kensington, Conn.*

LOIS HART, third daughter of Isaac Hart, of Farmington and Kensington, and his wife Elizabeth Whaples, born in 1744, in Kensington, married Hezekiah Judd of the same place, son of Amos and his wife Keziah Judd, born Oct. 12th, 1737, in Kensington, where he died May 28th, 1823, aged 85 years; she died there, his widow, Aug. 13th, 1825, aged 81 years—was his second wife. They have gravestones at Blue Hills cemetery. They had a child born in 1780, died July 16th, 1782; second, Lois, born , died March 13th, 1807, aged 22 years, single.

PECK.

30.   *Kensington, Conn.*

MARY HART, second daughter of Matthew Hart, of Kensington, and his wife Sarah (Hooker), born July 1st, 1728, in Kensington, married, July 26th, 1750, Amos Peck, son of Samuel and his wife Abigail (Colier), born March 3d, 1715, in Kensington. They lived and died there, he dying April 6th, 1802, aged 88 years, and she died June 22d, 1771, in her 48th year. Tombstones at Blue Hills cemetery show where they are buried. They had Matthew, born July 16th, 1751, married Huldah Rice; Amos, born Jan. 25th, 1754, married, Dec. 4th, 1781, Anna Scovill; Ruth, born Nov. 28th, 1756, married Benj. Hopkins; Mary, born March 9th, 1760, married Elisha Hart; Huldah, born Sept. 13th, 1762; Lemuel, born March 28th, 1765; Lucy, born Dec. 2d, 1767, married Ashbel Dickinson, died Dec. 1st, 1853.

31.   *Kensington.*

OLIVER HART, eldest son of Matthew Hart, of. Kensington, and his wife, Sarah (Hooker), born July 15th, 1733, at Kensington, married, Dec. 17th, 1766, Mary Scovill, sister of Ezra Scovill, Esq. Mr. Hart was a large land-holder, had no heirs, and gave his estate to Ashbel Dickinson. He died Nov. 22d, 1812, aged 79 years. His widow, Mrs. Mary Hart, died at the house of Ashbel Dickinson, in Kensington, Jan. 12th, 1836, aged 89 years. Tombstones are erected to their memory in the Blue Hills cemetery. Their child, Elizabeth, born Dec. 19th, 1769, died young.

32.   *Kensington.*

MATTHEW HART, youngest child of Matthew Hart, of Kensington, and his wife, Sarah (Hooker), born (posthumous) Jan. 23d, 1736-7, at Kensington, married, Nov. 15th, 1759, Elizabeth Hopkins; they lived at Kensington, in the house lately owned and occupied by Shelden Moore, Esq., deceased. He was admitted to the church in Kensington Oct. 5th, 1760, and his wife, Elizabeth, Nov. 27th, 1768. They removed to Whitestown, N. Y., or De Ruyter, N. Y., where he died, 1811.

THEIR CHILDREN, BEING THE SIXTH GENERATION.

82. Matthew, born Aug. 12th, 1760, married, Jan. 11th, 1782, Urania Hooker.
83. Seth, born June 24th, 1763, married, Oct. 7th, 1788, Ruth Hall.
84. Sarah, born Sept. 19th, 1766, married, Feb. 7th, 1788, Bela Strong.
85. Elizabeth, born   , 1769, married, Jan.   , 1790, Dr. James Percival.
86. Oliver, born Aug. 10th, 1774, married, Nov. 25th, 1799, Sally Bronson.
     Daughter, born   , lived with her sister, Mrs. Percival; single.

HOLLISTER.

33.   *Kensington and New Britain.*

ANNA HART, Kensington, eldest daughter of Lieut. Samuel and his wife, Mary (Hooker), born Sept. 25th, 1724, in Kensington, married, Oct. 15th, 1747, Thomas Hollister, of Kensington, and subsequently of New Britain; they lived in the house next north of Elijah Hinsdale, on East street. They had one child, born July 23d, 1748.

WELLS.

34.   *Kensington, Conn.*

MARY HART, Kensington, second daughter of Lieut. Samuel Hart, of the same place, and his wife, Mary (Hooker), born April 13th, 1730, in Kensington, and married, Jan. 17th, 1754, Dr. Joseph Wells, of

Wethersfield, Conn., who was a physician of eminence at Kensington. She died there Nov. 30th, 1792, aged 62 years. He also died there, Nov. 14th, 1793, aged 66 years. They had issue, 1, Joseph, born Nov. 12th, 1754, married, Dec. 31st, 1783, Ruth Allen; 2, Mary, born July 16th, 1759; 3, Sylvester, born May 20th, 1762, was a physician in Hartford; 4, Rhoda, born April 17th, 1764; 5, Nancy, baptized Aug. 30th, 1767; 6, James, baptized April 15th, 1770.

PORTER.

35.   *Kensington and New Britain, Conn.*

HULDAH HART, Kensington, third daughter of Lieut. Samuel Hart, of Kensington, (then a parish of Farmington,) and his wife, Mary (Hooker), born Nov. 2d, 1731, in Kensington, married   , Gideon Porter, of Kensington and New Britain; she died, when he married, second, Dec. 24th, 1778, widow Hannah Heth, widow of Avery. Mr. Porter is said to have lived at Northington, Conn., but he also lived and died in New Britain, Conn., at the house of Simeon Lincoln, Mar. 23d, 1805, aged 84 years. They had issue, viz: 1, Gideon, born   , married   , Hannah Brooks; 2, Huldah, born   , married, April 1st, 1773, John Riley, of Northampton, Mass., where he died; she married second, Simeon Lincoln, of New Britain, Conn.; 3, Abel, born,   , baptized Oct. 2d, 1757, at Kensington, married Eliza- beth, daughter of Solomon Dunham, Esq., who died May 10th, 1783, when he married second, Hannah Elliot; 4, Levi Goodwin, born   , baptized Aug. 3d, 1760, at Kensington; 5, James, born   , baptized April 18th, 1771, at Kensington.

36.   *Kensington and Berlin, Conn.*

CAPT. SAMUEL HART, Kensington, youngest son and child of Lieut. Samuel Hart, of same place, and his wife, Mary (Hooker), born Jan. 21st, 1738, in Kensington, married, Oct. 10th, 1757, Rebecca, daughter of Charles Norton, and his wife, Rebecca (Munson), born May 11th, 1739, died July 28th, 1769, in her 31st year, when he married, second, Oct. 4th, 1770, Lydia, daughter of Capt. John Hinsdale, and his wife, Elizabeth (Cole), born Aug. 11th, 1747. He held the military rank of captain, and lived on Hart street, next west of Main street, in Berlin. Soon after the formation of Worthington Church, in 1775, he became a Universalist in his religious views, and his descendants have adopted more or less the same sentiments. He was a great thinker, but could not speak in public without having his ideas written. He was the first Clerk and Treasurer of the Congregational Church at Berlin, in 1775.

He inherited his father's farm, and was designed for a college course, but his mother could not be induced to send him. His first wife, Rebecca, was admitted to the church in 1758. He died Aug. 21st, 1813, aged 75 years. His widow, Mrs. Lydia Hart, died at the house of John Lee (who had married their daughter), Jan. 18th, 1831, aged 84 years.

THEIR CHILDREN, BEING THE SIXTH GENERATION.

87. Rebecca, born Jan. 30th, 1760, married   , Wm. Cook, of Danbury.
88. Samuel, born May 17th, 1761, married, April 8th, 1791, Mary Wilcox.
89. Charlotte, born Oct. 17th, 1762, married, Dec. 2d, 1784, Orrin Lee.
90. Asahel, born May 6th, 1764, married, Sept. 23d, 1790, Abigail Cowles.
91. Anna, born Feb. 16th, 1766, died of consumption, March 25th, 1784, aged 18 years.
92. Jesse, born Jan. 3d, 1768, married, Nov. 28th, 1792, Lucy Beckley.
    James, born March 5th, 1769, died April 12th, 1770-1.

HIS CHILDREN BY THE SECOND MARRIAGE TO LYDIA HINSDALE.

93. Mary, born Sept. 23d, 1771, married   , John Lee.
94. John, born Jan. 23d, 1773, died Sept. 13th, 1816, aged 44 years.
95. James, born Dec. 26th, 1774, died Dec. 25th, 1796, at Staunton, Del., aged 22 years.
96. Theodore, born Aug. 30th, 1776, died Nov. 1st, 1815, at Petersburg, Va., aged 39 years.
97. Lydia, born Sept. 18th, 1778, married   , Elisha Treat.
    Betsey, born Sept. 21st, 1781, died   , aged 11 years.
    Huldah, born July 12th, 1783, died Jan. 31st, 1784.
98. Nancy, born March 8th, 1785, married   , Joshua Simmons.
99. Emma, born Feb. 23d, 1787, married   , 1812, John Willard, M. D.
100. Almira, born July 13th, 1793, married, Oct. 5th, 1817, Simeon Lincoln; second, John Phelps.

MARSH.

37.   *Norwich, Conn.*

SARAH HART, Kensington, Conn., eldest daughter of Nathaniel Hart of the same parish, and his wife, Abigail, daughter of John Hooker, Esq., born in Kensington, Nov. 13th, 1720, married Nov. 5th, 1747, Dr. Jonathan Marsh, of Norwich, Conn.

HURLBURT.

38.   *Kensington, Conn.*

ABIGAIL HART, Kensington, a parish of Berlin, Conn., second daughter of Nathaniel Hart and his wife Abigail, daughter of John Hooker, Esq., born July 21st, 1723, married James Hurlburt, an eminent physician of that time, and resided in Brandy Lane, a locality of the parish. He was at one time a member in good standing of the church there, but was excommunicated for immoral conduct and neglect of ordinances. Their children were, 1, Summit, born Sept. 5th, 1746; 2, Elizabeth, born Jan. 17th, 1748; 3, Alethena, born   , baptized in Kensington, June 27th, 1759. They probably had other children, not found on record.

BRONSON.

39. *Kensington, Conn.*

THANKFUL HART, of Kensington, a parish of Berlin, Conn., daughter of Nathaniel Hart of the same place, and his wife Abigail, daughter of John Hooker, Esq., born in Kensington, July 4th, 1725, married there Nov. 5th, 1747, Charles Brownson, son of Samuel and his wife Abigail (Ventris), born in Kensington, Sept. 24th, 1723. They lived by the mill which is now owned by J. T. Hart & Co. She died May 20th, 1759, aged 34 years, when he married, second, May 30th, 1759, Martha Barritt.

STANLEY.

40. *Kensington, Conn.*

HANNAH HART, of Kensington parish, fourth daughter of Nathaniel Hart of the same place, and his wife Abigail (Hooker), born in Kensington, Aug. 21st, 1729, married there, March 21st, 1754, Thomas, son of John Stanley, born June 20th, 1726. They had 1, Seth, born May 6th, 1755, married first, Nov.   , 1781, Ann Hooker, second, widow Winchell Stanley, and third, the widow of Josiah Smith; 2, Sibil, born Oct. 17th, 1757, baptized Oct. 30th, 1757; 3, Selah, born June 1st, 1762, baptized June 20th, 1762, married April 3d, 1786, Rhoda, daughter of Samuel Goodrich. The mother died, when he married second, Martha   , and had Hannah and Erastus.

41. *Kensington, Conn.*

GENERAL SELAH HART, of Kensington, a parish of Berlin, Conn., second son of Nathaniel Hart of the same place, and his wife Abigail (Hooker), born in Kensington, May 23d, 1732, married March 4th, 1756, Mary, born Feb. 18th, 1731-2, daughter of Stephen Cole and his wife Abigail (Hart). She died, when he married second, Dec. 22d, 1763, Ruth, born in Kensington, Oct. 29th, 1742, daughter of Matthew Cole and his second wife Mary (Newell); he had but one child, and that by his first wife, named Mary, and she died young. He lived where now (1869,) Oliver Moore does, in the east part of the parish. He was a magistrate, and held many positions of honor and usefulness in his day. He united with the church in Kensington in 1763, in which he held the office of deacon; and Ruth, his second wife, united with the church in 1771. He was the moderator of the first town meeting held in Berlin, June 13th, 1785, and represented the town of Farmington in the General Assembly, four times. He served the country in the capacity of general during the war of the Revolution, with the exception of two years he was held a prisoner in New York, and with the aid of Roger Hooker, his brigade major, he became conspicuous,—Hooker doing his writing.

Having found the last Will of General Selah Hart among his old papers in Berlin, I transcribe it for the benefit of the readers of this memorial:

In the name of God, Amen. I, Selah Hart, of Berlin, in the County of Hartford, and State of Connecticut, in America, being, through the goodness of God, in health and of a sound mind and memory, considering the uncertainty of life, knowing it is appointed unto all men once to die, do make and ordain this my last Will and Testament, in manner and form as follows: That is to say, first, and principally, I give and recommend my soul to God, who gave it, hoping, through the merits of Jesus Christ, to obtain the forgiveness of all my sins, and to inherit eternal life; and my body I commit to the earth, out of which it was taken, to be decently buried.

I give to my dear wife, Ruth Hart, for her sole use and disposal, my chaise, the whole of my household furniture, one-half of my other movable property which shall remain after my debts are paid. Also, I give to her, during her natural life, the use and improvement of one-half of my real estate, the use of one-half of my dwelling-house at the south end, and one-half of my wood-house and corn house, and also one-half of my barns, to be divided in the following manner: the old barn shall be divided east and west through the ridge, and the new barn north and south through the ridge, she having the use of the south part of the old barn, and the east part of the new barn.

Also, I give to Lucy Hart, the widow of Cyprian Hart, lately deceased, so long as she continues to be his widow, the use of the other half of my dwelling-house, and the privilege of keeping two cows on my farm summer and winter, and so much room in my barns as will be necessary to accommodate them; also, the privilege of taking from my farm the necessary firewood during that time, viz., while she remains said Hart's widow.

Also, I give to Selah Hart, my sword, and the said Selah Hart and Cyprian Hart, sons of Cyprian Hart, lately deceased, all my real estate and what of my movable estate that is not disposed of as above, they paying to each of their four sisters, as they arrive to lawful age, two hundred dollars from my movable estate, if they be able, if not, it is my will that they sell those lands for that purpose which can best be spared. If either Selah or Cyprian Hart, as above mentioned, should die without natural heirs, of his own body begotten, this property here given him shall descend to his surviving brother; if both of them die without an heir of their own body, then this property here given them shall descend to their surviving sisters above mentioned.

If hereafter it shall be thought expedient that either Selah or Cyprian Hart, above mentioned, should have a public education, it is my Will that provision for that purpose shall be made from my property, and that in such case the property thus appropriated shall be counted so much towards his portion.

Also, I give my brother, Noadiah Hart, one hundred dollars, to be paid within one year after my decease.

I likewise constitute my wife, Ruth Hart, and Elijah Hooker, Esq., sole executors of this my last Will and Testament, in witness whereof I hereunto set my hand and seal this 29th day of March, 1806.

Signed, SELAH HART and Seal.

Signed, sealed, published, and declared by the said Selah Hart to be his last Will and Testament, in presence of Benoni Upson,
Levia Upson,
Levia Upson, 2d.

He died June 10th, 1806, aged 74 years, and was buried in the cemetery a little distance north-west of his dwelling-house. A monument was erected to his memory bearing the following inscription:

GENERAL SELAH HART,
An Officer of the Revolution,
who died
June 10th, 1806, Æ. 74 years.
"Blessed are the dead who die in the Lord."

His widow, Mrs. Ruth Hart, died Jan. 15th, 1844, aged 101 years 2 months and 16 days, being the oldest person that ever died in that town. Her gravestone bears this inscription:

MRS. RUTH HART,
Wife of General Selah Hart,
Born Oct. 29th, 1742,
Died Jan. 15th, 1844,
Æ. 101 years 2 months and 16 days.
Extraordinary in age, she was not less
distinguished by strength of character, correctness
of moral principle, and holiness of life.
She adorned the profession of the Gospel.
during nearly three-quarters of a century.
A friend of God and her species, her memory
will triumph over the wrecks of time.

Early in life he was considered by the *public* as a man of integrity, sagacity, and thoroughness. In the office of constable he was much employed; and in cases where discretion, great bodily strength, and fearlessness of personal danger were requisite, he was the man for the occasion. When the war for Independence came, his person and his property were at the service of his country, and he was in service or in captivity during the greatest part of the time of the war. In 1776, he commanded a regiment, and when Washington evacuated New York, he was cut off and captured by a body of the enemy's forces which had ascended the Hudson River and landed above him. Ignorant and ill-natured people made many remarks on the occasion, but it was never shown but that he understood his duty, and well performed it. He was stationed in order to cover the retreat of the main body, and if he had been less faithful and less brave, he might have abandoned his post and perhaps have escaped captivity as many others did. The cruelties and miseries which prisoners suffered in New York in those days, have been often told and recorded, and this Col. Hart suffered nearly two years, during the most of which time his wife knew not whether he was living or dead, and when he did return, it was to her as if he had risen from the grave. Subsequently he commanded a brigade until the close of the war. He then resumed his avocation of farming, and the condition of his lands, fences, buildings, utensils, crops, and animals, showed that the owner and master was sagacious and thorough.

Probably no farm near his produced so much at so great a profit, in proportion to the acres used, as did his. He thought more of good crops and the profitable use of labor, than of a large number of acres under partial culture. As he was a man of but few words, some supposed him to be lacking in social feeling, but they were in a mistake. He loved society, and but few would more readily discern and feel what should move human sympathy, or more certainly show it in action. He was hospitable to friends and wayfarers, and he considered the unfortunate and the poor, both to relieve their present necessities and devise for their future welfare. He took a very young colored child to bring up, named Jack, who was legally a slave, but Jack's living, clothing, and education were better than the average of the white lads in the vicinity enjoyed, and when the lad became twenty-one years of age, the master said to him: "The law would give me four years more of your service, but I think you have a right to be *free*, and you are at liberty to go away, or stay with me and receive wages." Gen. Hart was singularly thoughtful and active for the public weal. The interests of the town he made his own in some sort, as when he was its Treasurer, in cases of deficiency, his own funds would be forthcoming in order that the business and the credit of the town might not suffer. As a member of the ecclesiastical society, it was said of him after his death, and by those who reviled him while living, "We have lost the main stud of the building." He had an uncompromising regard for wholesome laws and sound morals, and as a magistrate, he was a "terror to evil doers:" as might be expected, almost all manner of evil was spoken against him, yet but few gave stronger evidence of desiring to see all others prosperous and happy in a course of well doing. And there was no want of proof that there was entire confidence in his wisdom and uprightness, and that the interests, the persons, and the property of the friendless and the orphan were considered safe with him. As a religious man, his creed was conformed, as he believed, to the holiness and the simplicity of the Word of God. Men have invented many things as tests of religious character and practice, but with Selah Hart it was sufficient that all others and himself should *fear God and keep his commandments.* At the beginning and at the close of each day, he with all his household appeared before his and their God, to worship Him in prayer, and to learn His will from His Word. And he considered it as a part of his religious duty so to order every other concern as that nothing should interfere with the stated duties which he considered were owing from himself and each member of his household to their God; and so there was no confusion or loss of time: and in this he was greatly assisted by his wife, a woman of uncommon intelligence, stability, and piety. He was many years a member of the church in Kensington, and one of its deacons until his decease. He died June 10th, 1806, Æ. 74 years, leaving an example which, in most things, it is believed it would be useful, safe, and honorable to follow.

42.   *Kensington.*

NATHANIEL HART, of Kensington, a parish of Berlin, Conn., third son of Nathaniel, and his wife, Abigail Hooker, born March 17th, 1735, at Kensington. He married, Nov. 23d, 1758, Martha Norton, daughter of Thomas, of Kensington. She was admitted to the church there, 1760. He died in Kensington, Oct. 13th, 1773, in his 40th year, and his widow, Martha, removed to Hartford soon after his decease.

THEIR CHILDREN, BEING THE SIXTH GENERATION.

101. Gideon, b. Nov. 28th, 1759, m. June 25th, 1786, Cynthia Langdon.
102. Seth, b. Aug. 19th, 1761, m.   , Anna Goodrich.
103. Salman, b. Jan. 9th, 1763, m. Jan. 31st, 1788, Ruth Norton.
104. Nathaniel, b. May 2d, 1765, m.   , Polly Edwards.
105. Selah, b. Jan. 30th, 1767, m. Oct. 30th, 1793, Sarah Waters.

9

106. Cyprian, born   , baptized Feb. 5th, 1769, married Dec. 25th, 1795, Lucy
      Hooker.
      Norman, born   , baptized March 24th, 1771, died Oct. 17, 1792, Æ. 22
      years.
      Abigail, born   , baptized June 6th, 1773, died Feb. 8th, 1786, Æ. 13 years.

43. *Burlington, Harwinton, Southington.*

NOADIAH HART, of Kensington, fourth son of Nathaniel, of same
place, and his wife, Abigail Hooker, was born July 30th, 1737, at
Kensington. He married, Nov. 20th, 1760, Lucy Hurlburt, daughter
of Stephen, and his wife Hannah. She died in Burlington, Mar. 8th,
1785, Æ. 52 years, having been born Nov. 5th, 1733. He became a
deacon of the church in Harwinton in 1804, removed to Southington,
where he died Oct. 23d, 1817, Æ. 80 years. He lived in Southington,
with Velina, who ran the mill, the site of which is covered now with
"Plant Ponds." His house stood near the mill. He held the military
rank of lieutenant. He married, second, Sept. 25th, 1785, Beulah
Clark (Tubbs).

THEIR CHILDREN, BEING THE SEVENTH GENERATION.

107. Velina, born May 5th, 1761, married, Dec. 3d, 1782, Huldah Green.
108. Luthena, born March 7th, 1763, married   ,   Gillett, died Nov.
      7th, 1781, Æ. 18 years.
109. Stephen Hurlburt, born, Sept. 20th, 1765, died Sept. 15th, 1766.
110. Stephen Hurlburt, 2d, born Nov. 1st, 1767, married, Oct. 18th, 1791, Lucinda
      Cook, daughter of Moses, of Wallingford.
111. Cyprian, born May 23d, 1772, married   , Olive Whedon.
112. Percy, born Aug. 11, 1774, died in Southington, July 11th, 1795, Æ. 20 years.
113. Lucy, born June 21st, 1786, died Sept. 19th, 1795, tombstone in Kensington.

44.   *Kensington and Canaan, Conn.*

REV. ASAHEL HART, of Kensington, youngest son and child of
Nathaniel Hart, of same place, and Abigail Hooker, his wife, born
about 1742, at Kensington, was a graduate of Yale College, 1764.
He qualified himself for the ministry, and was settled pastor of the
church in North Canaan, Conn, March 14th, 1770. He died unmarried, June 28th, 1775, Æ. 33 years. He was the first pastor, the
church being organized Dec. 5th, 1769.

45.   *New Britain, Conn.*

ELIAS HART, of Kensington, eldest son of Judah Hart, of Kensington and New Britain, and his wife, Anna, daughter of Sergt. John
Norton, born Feb. 25th, 1735, at Kensington, married Oct. 17th,
1753, at Newington, Hope Whaples, of that place, before Rev. Joshua

Belden, pastor of the church there—daughter of Jacob, it is thought. He died 1756, when she, second, married, Aug. 18th, 1760, Josiah Wright, jun. The inventory of his estate, amounting to £333 11s., was taken, Jan. 14th, 1757, by Judah Wright and Isaac Lee. The administrators were, the widow Hope and John Judd.

THEIR CHILDREN, BEING THE SEVENTH GENERATION.

114. Jacob, born May 2d, 1754, in East Haddam, and went West, 1776.
115. Rose, born Jan. 8th, 1756, and, Feb. 8th, 1758, Nehemiah Gates, of Middletown, was made her guardian.

ALVORD.

47. *Winchester, Conn.*

ESTHER HART, second daughter of Judah Hart of Kensington and New Britain, and his wife Anna (Norton), was born April 4th, 1742, at New Britain—a twin with Lois, married, Nov. 29th, 1764, Eliphaz Alvord, Esq., of Winchester, Conn., 1770. She was remembered in her father's will, dated 1784. He was a son of Capt. Jonathan, and his wife, Elizabeth Sanford, of Milford, born Jan. 13th, 1742, in Chatham. He was town clerk at the organization of Winchester, and served 46 years, justice of peace, and representative many years to the General Assembly,—one of the pillars of the church and society. She died Nov. 18th, 1818, Æ. 76 years. He died April 15th, 1825, Æ. 83 years. They had ten children, three of whom were born before they removed to, and seven born in, Winchester. He was one of the most prominent men of Winchester in his day.

48. *New Britain.*

JOHN HART, of New Britain, Conn., third son of Judah Hart of Kensington and New Britain, and his wife Anna (Norton), born Jan. 20th, 1743-4, in Kensington, was married Oct. 17th, 1764, at Southington, by Rev. Benj. Chapman, to Anna, daughter of Zebulon Deming, of Southington, and his wife Esther (Adkins), born at Southington. He lived near his father in Hart quarter. The house is now in good condition, 1874, and occupied by the Eddy family. He was a farmer and large land-holder, and died Sept. 17th, 1776, Æ. 33 years. His widow married, second, Aug. 28th, 1777, David Hills. She died Oct. 30th, 1804, Æ. 63 years. Mr. Hart was admitted to Dr. Smalley's church in New Britain, June 8th, 1766.

THEIR CHILDREN, BEING THE SEVENTH GENERATION.

116. Roger, born , 1765, married , Sibil Robinson.
     Chauncey, born , 1767, died , 1787.
     William, born , 1769, died young.

John, born   , 1772, baptized July 12th, 1772, died Sept. 10th, 1776, Æ. 4
years, 6 months.
Roswell, born   , 1775, baptized Aug. 13th, 1775, died Sept. 10th, 1776,
Æ. 14 months.

49.   *New Britain.*

JUDAH HART, JR., of New Britain, Conn., fourth son of Judah Hart,
sen., and his wife, Anna Norton, was born Sept. 10th, 1750, at Kensington, married, April 19th, 1770, Sarah, daughter of James North
and Sarah (Seymour) his wife, born Feb. 22d, 1749. She was a
daughter of Mr. Hart's step-mother. He was a farmer, and inherited
his father's homestead opposite the school-house in the South-west
district, in New Britain. He had a frail constitution, and died April
28th, 1795, aged 45 years. The inventory of his estate amounted to
£1,149 4s. 7d. His widow, Mrs. Sarah Hart, died Sept. 15th, 1822,
aged 74 years. The house they owned and occupied is still, 1874,
standing and in good condition, having been made of heavy white oak
timber.

THEIR CHILDREN, BEING THE SEVENTH GENERATION.

117. Sarah, born November 7th, 1770; married July 30th, 1793, Asahel Hart.
      Anna, born May 3d, 1773; died September 17th, 1776, aged 3 years.
118. Salmon, born May 20th, 1775; married May 2d, 1796, Sarah Goodrich.
119. Judah, born December 16th, 1777; married May 1st, 1800, Abigail Belden.
120. Anna 2d, born March 17th, 1780; married September 17th, 1804, Truman
      Woodruff.
121. Roxana, born October 23d, 1784; married November 22d, 1803, Albert Merri-
      man; second, James Beecher.
122. Lydia, born December 14th, 1786; married June 20th, 1805, Samuel Porter, of
      Southington.
123. Eliphaz, born June 28th, 1789; married December 25th, 1812, Eliza Armstrong,
      of Newport, R. I.
      Henry, born   ; baptized February 11th, 1787.
      Amzi, born July 10th, 1792; drowned in a well.

PIERCE.

51.   *Cornwall.*

AMIE HART, eldest daughter of John Hart, of Kensington and Cornwall, and his wife, Anna Hall, born August 28th, 1753, at Kensington;
married   , Captain Seth Pierce, of Cornwall, Conn., a
prominent man, and extensively known. He held the military rank
of captain, was a pillar in the First Congregational Church, and a large
land-holder. Mrs. Pierce united early with the church. Their issue,
viz: John H., who held the rank of colonel, was killed instantly by a
team starting; Seth, holds the rank of major, and his residence is at
Cornwall, Conn.

52. *Kensington and Cornwall.*

Rufus Hart, Kensington, second son of John Hart, of Kensington and Cornwall, and his wife, Anna Hall, born April 24th, 1755, at Kensington. He went to Canaan and Cornwall with his parents, where he was taken with acute pain in one thigh. He lived but fifty-five hours, and died Friday night, June 28th, 1765. He was a pleasant and obedient child of 10 years.—*Family Record.*

53. *Whitestown, N. Y., Belvidere, Ill.*

Thomas Hart, Belvidere, Ill., third son of John Hart, of Kensington and Cornwall, and his second wife, Huldah Gould, born March 3d, 1756; married   , and removed to Whitestown, N. Y., and thence to Belvidere, Boone County, Ill., where he is said to be located with his sons.

55. *Batavia, N. Y., Coventry, O.*

Rufus Hart, youngest son of John Hart, of Kensington, Canaan, and Cornwall, Conn., and his third wife, Martha Foote, born March 15th, 1773; married, 1795, Esther Coster, born 1771, and died in 1833, when he second married   , and resided in Batavia, N. Y., and subsequently at Coventry, Summit County, Ohio. He was there in 1845 with his second wife.

THEIR CHILDREN, BEING THE SEVENTH GENERATION.

124. Clarissa, born   , 1796; married, June, 1817, Charles Sumner, of Coventry.
125. John C., born   , 1798; married February 21st, 1831, Margaret A. Sterling.
George Washington, born   , 1801; died at Batavia, N. Y., in 1817, aged 16.
126. Hiram, born   , 1804; married   , 1830, Sarah Smith.
127. Lucinda, born   , 1807; married January 1st, 1821, Edward W. Sumner.
128. Elizabeth L., born   , 1810; married December 19th, 1827, Henry Richards.
129. Edward W., born   , 1816; married   , 1838, Rachel Latta.

BROWNSON.

56. *Farmington, Tyringham, Cornwall.*

Ruth Hart, eldest daughter of Solomon Hart, of Kensington, and his wife, Experience Cole, born December 31st, 1750, at Farmington, Conn. She went with her parents, from Congee, in Farmington, to

Tyringham, Mass., in 1761, and from thence to Cornwall, Conn., in 1765. She married · Brownson, and died March 14th, 1837, aged 87 years. She was a member of the church.

ABBOTT.

. **57.** *Farmington, Tyringham, Cornwall.*

ESTHER HART, second daughter of Solomon Hart, of Kensington, and his wife, Experience Cole, born March 26th, 1752, in Farmington. She went with her parents, from Congee, in Farmington, to Tyringham, Mass., in 1761, and from thence to Cornwall, Conn., in 1765. She married Abbott, of . She died December 4th, 1807, aged 55 years.

58. *North Cornwall, Conn.*

TITUS HART, North Cornwall, Conn., eldest son of Solomon Hart, of Congee, in Farmington, and his wife, Experience Cole, born January 24th, 1754, in Farmington; married Esther Hand. He was deacon of the church in North Cornwall, where he lived from the age of ten to his death, October 31st, aged 77 years. "Eminently a man of prayer, he was never known to omit his morning and evening devotions in his family, after which he retired for his private or closet duties."

THEIR CHILDREN, BEING THE SEVENTH GENERATION.

130. Nathan, born June 12th, 1776; married February 8th, 1804, Sylvia Clark.
131. John, born , 1779; married Sally Clark; died June 29th, 1801.

59. *Hudson, N. Y.*

LOT HART, Hudson, N. Y., second son of Solomon Hart, of Farmington and Kensington, and his wife, Experience Cole, born 1756, at ; married . He died near Hudson, N. Y., February 21st, 1826, aged 70 years.

THEIR CHILDREN, BEING THE SEVENTH GENERATION.

132. Lucy, born ; married , Salmon Thompson, Burlington, Conn.
133. Elisha, born , and is a cripple.

60. *Cornwall, Conn.*

PHINEAS HART, New York, third son of Solomon Hart, of Congee, in Farmington, Conn., and his wife, Experience Cole, born 1758, ; married . He lived in Cornwall, where his children were born.

THEIR CHILDREN, BEING THE SEVENTH GENERATION.

134. Lot, born
135. Solomon, born
136. Mary, born   ; married   , Mathew Mooney.
137. Experience, born
138. Jane, born   ; married   ,   Eaton,
          Madison County, N. Y.

61.   *Cornwall, Conn.*

ELIAS HART, Cornwall, Conn., fourth son of Solomon Hart, of Congee, in Farmington, Conn., and his wife, Experience Cole, born 1759; married   , Philomela Burnham, daughter of Appleton, and of his wife, Mary Wolcott, and granddaughter of Rev. William Burnham, of Kensington. She was born May 1st, 1764.

THEIR CHILDREN, BEING THE SEVENTH GENERATION.

139. Enos, born   . He was scalded to death in childhood.
140. Elias, born November 4th, 1784; married   , 1807, Hannah Harrison.
141. Oliver Burnham, born   1787; married   , 1807, Amanda Harrison.
142. Laura, born March, 1790; married   , Ebenezer Harrison.
143. Philomela, born June 17th, 1793; married   , Anson Rogers.
144. Julius, born February 29th, 1796; married January 7th, 1819, Rhoda Rogers.
145. Harriet, born March, 1798; married   , Gideon P. Pangborn.
146. Jerusha, born   , 1801; married   , Palmer Brown.
147. Alvin Nelson, born February 11th, 1804; married   , 1829, Charlotte F. Ball.

63.   *Cornwall, Conn., Hartsville, Mass.*

CAPTAIN SOLOMON HART, New Marlboro, Mass., fifth and youngest son of Solomon Hart, of Congee, in Farmington, Conn., and his wife, Experience Cole, born May 8th, 1766, at Cornwall, Conn.; married July 6th, 1786, Jerusha Beach, daughter of Matthew, and his wife, Martha, born May 21st, 1767, in Stratford, Conn. He was living at Hartsville, New Marlboro, Mass., July, 1849, aged 83 years. His avocation was farming, and he held the military rank of captain. He died June 26th, 1861, aged 95 years, 1 month. His wife, Jerusha, died April 1st, 1845, aged 78 years. They have had twelve children, who are all married, and have families. Mr. Hart is said to have been strictly temperate in all things, (used no tobacco,) which accounts for his good health and long life. He had the use of all his senses until the last, could walk a number of miles in a day, and labored until over 90. He was benevolent and kind, very anxious to suppress all evil habits in the rising generation, and was strictly moral, although a non-professor of religion. He lived to see five generations on the stage, founded the village of Hartsville, and set agoing much machinery in that place, which was a wilderness when he located there at 22 years of age. The village properly takes its name from its founder and patron.

THEIR CHILDREN, BEING THE SEVENTH GENERATION.

148. Reuben, born May 30th, 1787; married May 19th, 1812, Eleanor Kingman.
149. Amanda, born December 28th, 1788; married June 29th, 1808, Amos Marlin, of Owego, N. Y.
150. Elizabeth, born November 11th, 1790; married September 25th, 1811, Jabez Brigham, of New Marlboro.
151. Tynes, born January 31st, 1793; married May 24th, 1814, Tryphena Sage, of Sandisfield, Mass.
152. Polly, born September 17th, 1795; married December 31st, 1815, John Hollister, of Perry, Wyoming County, N. Y.
153. Almon, born September 14th, 1797; married November 30th, 1820, Polly Harmon, of Monterey, Mass.
154. Candace, born October 20th, 1799; married April 26th, 1820, Truman Stone, of New Marlboro.
155. Anna, born April 19th, 1802; married April 19th, 1826, John Powell, of New Marlboro.
156. Solomon Randall, born April 2d, 1804; married September 12th, 1845, Fanny Johnson, of Monterey, Mass.
157. Milan, born December 28th, 1805; married May 1st, 1832, Perlina Nettleton, of Cornwall.
158. Alvira, born September 9th, 1809; married September 26th, 1827, Major Algers.
159. Alfred, born February 12th, 1812; married October 19th, 1833, Cynthia L. Nettleton, of Cornwall, Conn.

64.   *Stockbridge, Mass., Candor, N. Y.*

ABEL HART, Kensington, eldest son of Ebenezer Hart, of the same place, and his wife, Martha   , born February 22d, 1747, at Kensington, then a parish of Farmington; married September 13th, 1769, Mary Galpin, daughter of Caleb, born Oct. 21st, 1753, and sister of Deacon Daniel, of Worthington. About 1774 he removed to Stockbridge, Mass., and from thence to Candor, Tioga County, N. Y. He was a blacksmith by trade and occupation. He died in 1802, aged 55 years. She lived until 1845. They had one son and ten daughters.

THEIR CHILDREN, BEING THE SEVENTH GENERATION.

160.	Abel, born	, 1770; married	, 1795, Rachel Sweeden,
	of Stockbridge.		
161.	Mary, born	, 1772; married	, M. Churchill.
162.	Ruth, born	, 1775; married	, J. Seymour.
163.	Abigail, born	, 1777; married	, Johnson.
164.	Martha, born	, 1780; married	, G. Seymour.
165.	Nancy, born	, 1782; married	, D. Howard.
166.	Esther, born	, 1785; married	, J. Smith.
167.	Lucy, born	, 1788; married	, Orange F. Booth.

168. Electa, born	, 1792; married	, Samuel Smith.
169. Clara, } born	married , 1795;	, S. Leach.
170. Harriet, }	married	, C. Gridley.

65. *Mohawk, N. Y.*

EBENEZER HART, Kensington, second son of Ebenezer Hart, of the same place, and his wife, Martha , born January 6th, 1750–1; married, 1776, Lydia Kent. He settled on the Royal Grant, on the Mohawk River, in New York, and died there in 1798, aged 47 years. He and his wife joined the church in 1771.

67. *Kensington, Conn.; Trenton, N. Y.*

LEVI HART, of Berlin, Conn., eldest son of Isaac Hart, of Kensington, and his wife Ann (Mather), daughter of Joseph, of New Britain, was born in Kensington, and baptized there Aug. 24th, 1765, by Rev. Samuel Clark, pastor of that church. He married , Martha, daughter of Zachariah Hart and his wife Sarah (Parsons), born 1772, in Kensington. They removed to Trenton, N. Y.

THEIR CHILDREN, BEING THE SEVENTH GENERATION.

171. Lorana, born
172. Caroline, born
173. Eliza, born
174. Zenas, born
175. Cyrus, born
176. Horace, born

GRIDLEY.

68. *Kensington, Conn., Clinton, N.Y.*

LYDIA HART, second daughter of Isaac Hart, of Hart street in Kensington, now Berlin, Conn., and his wife, Ann (Mather), daughter of Joseph, of New Britain, was born at Kensington, and baptized there June 4th, 1769. He married, 1829, Sylvester Gridley, said to be a son of Abraham and his wife, Theodocia Horsington, and was a brother of Samuel, who married her sister Chloe. He lived for a time at the Scovill place. He had a former wife, Harriet (Root). They removed to Clinton, N. Y., where he died July 29th, 1845.

71. *Kensington, Conn., Victor, N. Y.*

JABISH HART, of Kensington, eldest son of Job Hart, of same place, and his wife Eunice (Beckley), was born, 1756, at Kensington, and baptized there Jan. 2d, 1757. He married, , Jemima Brace. They removed to Victor, Ontario Co., N. Y., about 1785. She was admitted to the church in Stockbridge, Mass., 1782, and died May 23d, 1823. He died Dec. 20th, 1832, aged 76 years.

10

177. Harvey, born April 9th, 1784, married   , Polly Jackson.
      Tryphena, born Dec. 23d, 1785, married   , Boughton, of Bloom-
      field, N. Y.
179. Theodocia, born Dec. 15th, 1787, married   , Cyrus Jackson.
180. John, born Oct. 20th, 1789, married Betsey Clyne.
181. Demas, born Dec. 13th, 1791.
182. Cyrus, born Nov. 25th, 1794, died Dec. 9th, 1821, aged 27 years.
183. George, born July 4th, 1797, died Aug. 6th, 1802.
184. Eunice, born May 10th, 1799, died   , 1836.
185. Frederic, born Aug. 6th, 1802, married, Sept. 8th, 1825, Sylvia Rowley.

72.   ·   Oneida Co., N. Y.

CANDACE HART, eldest daughter of Job Hart, of Kensington, Ct.,
and his wife Eunice (Beckley), born 1758, at Kensington, and baptized
there by Rev. Samuel Clark, pastor of that church, Feb. 8th, 1758.
She married,   , Roswell Barnes, and removed to Oneida Co.,
New York.

73.   Kensington, Ct., Providence, Pa.

JOB HART, of Victor, N. Y., second son of Job Hart, of Kensington, and his wife Eunice (Beckley), was born 1759, at Kensington,
and baptized there March 11th, 1759. He went with his parents to
Stockbridge, Mass. He married, 1784, widow Rachel Ball, whose
maiden name was Tyrrel, and died 1814. In 1819, with his son Ira,
he removed to Providence, Luzerne Co., Penn., and in 1821, to Victor, Ontario Co., N. Y. He was more than fifty years a member of a
Congregational church. While in Berlin, Conn., he enlisted a soldier
when only sixteen, was captured by the Indians and carried to the
British camp, where he suffered much, escaped from Burgoyne's camp
the day before his surrender, and joined his family at Stockbridge.
His wife Rachel was admitted to the church in Stockbridge, 1791.

186. Isaac, born Dec. 6th, 1785, married, Feb. 12th, 1807, Abigail Stone.
187. Ira, born   , 1790, married

WILLIAMSON.

76.   Stockbridge, Mass., Victor, N. Y.

EUNICE HART, second daughter of Job Hart, of Kensington, Conn.,
and his wife Eunice (Beckley), was born, 1763, at Kensington, and
baptized there Oct. 30th, 1763, by Rev. Samuel Clark, pastor of that
church. She went to Stockbridge, Berkshire Co., Mass., with her
parents. She married,   , Abijah Williamson, and they located
at Victor, Ontario Co., N. Y.

77. *Stockbridge, Mass., Pompey, N. Y.*

JOSEPH HART, of Pompey, Onondaga Co., N. Y., fifth son of Job Hart, of Kensington, Conn., and his wife Eunice (Beckley), was born 1764, and baptized at Kensington, March 17th, 1765; went with his parents to Stockbridge, Mass. He married, , Beulah Warner, and removed to Pompey, where he was for many years an elder in a Presbyterian church. He died about 1840.

THEIR CHILDREN, BEING THE SEVENTH GENERATION.

188. Samuel, born
189. William, born   .

78. *Pompey, N. Y.*

SIMEON HART, of Victor, N. Y., sixth son of Job Hart, of Kensington, and his wife Eunice (Beckley), was born in Kensington, 1766, and baptized there July 21st, 1766. He married, , Betsey Foote. They removed to Pompey, Onondaga Co., N. Y., and thence to Victor, N. Y. He died leaving a numerous family. He was admitted to the church at Stockbridge, Mass., 1791, and his wife Betsey, 1799. No history of their children was found after long and diligent search.

79. *Pompey and Canandaigua, N. Y.*

DOCTOR REUBEN HART, of Pompey, Onondaga Co., N. Y., seventh son of Job Hart, of Kensington, and his wife Eunice (Beckley), was born at Kensington, 1767, and baptized there Jan. 17th, 1768; married widow Boughton. He was a physician, and removed to Canandaigua, N. Y. He was a member of the Assembly, and surrogate of the county for several years. He died   .   .

THEIR CHILD, BEING THE SEVENTH GENERATION.

born,   , married   .

80. *Stockbridge, Mass., Pompey, N. Y.*

COMFORT HART, third son of Job Hart, of Kensington, and his wife Eunice (Beckley), was born in Kensington, Conn., and baptized there by Rev. Samuel Clark, Aug. 25th, 1771. Went with his parents to Stockbridge, Berkshire Co., Mass. He married Sibil Churchill. She was admitted to the church in Stockbridge, with her husband, 1800. They removed from Stockbridge to Pompey, Onondaga Co., N. Y., but all efforts in finding the whereabouts of this family of children failed.

WILLIAMS.

81.   *Chenango Co., N. Y.*

HEPZIBAH HART, third daughter of Job Hart, of Kensington, and his wife Eunice (Beckley), was born   . She married,   , Solomon Williams, and they settled in   , Chenango Co., New York.

82.   *Kensington, Conn., Fabius, N. Y.*

DEACON MATTHEW HART, eldest son of Matthew Hart, of Kensington, Conn., and his wife Elizabeth (Hopkins), was born Aug. 12th, 1760, at Kensington, and baptized Oct. 5th, 1760, by Rev. Samuel Clark. He married, Jan. 11th, 1782, at Kensington, Urania Hooker, daughter of Ashbel and his wife Susannah (Langdon), born at Kensington, and baptized there May 11th, 1760. She died, when, second, he married widow Hopkins, whose maiden name was Rogers, of Wallingford. He and wife Urania were living at Fabius, N. Y., Jan., 1803. He lived also at Truxton. He died 1840, aged 80 years.

THEIR CHILDREN, BEING THE SEVENTH GENERATION.

Infant, born	, died July 22d, 1784.	
" born	, died Nov. 14th, 1787 (2).	
" born	, died March 25th, 1788.	
190.	Ruth, born Feb. 9th, 1782, married, Oct. 25th, 1804, Wm. Bly.	
191.	Edmund, born	, married, , Lefee Jones.
192.	Ira, born , 1792, married , Mary Jones.	
193.	Horatio, born	, died of the epidemic.
194.	Sally, born	; living with Ira, (1873) single.
195.	Betsey, born	, married , Barney.
196.	Rachel, born	, died .
197.	George, born , 1800, married , Deborah Benjamin.	

83.   *Hempstead, L. I.*

REV. SETH HART, Hempstead, L. I., second son of Matthew Hart, of Kensington, and his wife, Elizabeth Hopkins, born June 24th, 1763, at Kensington; baptized June 26th, 1763. He graduated at Yale in 1784, and became an Episcopal preacher, and was rector of St. George's Church, Hempstead, L. I. He was admitted to the order of deacons in 1791, and to the order of priests in 1792, by Bishop Seabury. He was rector of St. John's Church, Waterbury, for several years, then of St. Paul's, Wallingford, until November, 1800, when he received a call to the rectorship of St. George's Church, Hempstead, L. I., vacated by the removal to New York of Rev. Mr. Hobart, who subsequently be-

came bishop. In consequence of a severe attack of paralysis he resigned his charge February 16th, 1829, and died March 16th, 1832,
much beloved and lamented by his former parishioners, whose rector
he had been for more than twenty-eight years. His widow was also
attacked by paralysis, and died November 3d, 1841. At Hempstead
he kept a private boarding school, where his nephew—since the celebrated James Gates Percival—attended about 1809. Rev. Mr. Hart
married, October 7th, 1788, Ruth, daughter of Hon. Benjamin Hall,
of Cheshire.

THEIR CHILDREN, BEING THE SEVENTH GENERATION.

198. William Henry, born January 5th, 1790; married   , 1815, Lydia
Hubbard; second, Maria Graham.

199. Ambrose Gustavus, born October 3d, 1792; died October 15th, 1816, aged 24
years.

Hannah Burnham, born July 16th, 1797; died, September, 1798.

Henry William, born October 26th, 1799; died January 9th, 1813.

200. Elizabeth Ann, born May 9th, 1809; married   , William G.
Clowes, Esq.

201. Benjamin Hall, born February 13th, 1811; married, October, 1837, Elizabeth
Nichols.

202. Edmund Hall, born August 7th, 1813; died August 22d, 1838, aged 25.

STRONG.

84. *Kensington, Conn., Oak Hill, N. Y.*

SARAH HART, eldest daughter of Matthew Hart, of Kensington, and
his wife, Elizabeth (Hopkins), born September 19th, 1766, at Kensington; baptized there September 21st, 1766; married there February
7th, 1788, Bela, son of Bela Strong, of Kensington, and his wife,
Eunice, born at Kensington, and baptized there July 29th, 1764. Bela,
Jr., was grandson of Deacon Hart, of Durham and Kensington. He
died in Kensington, August 21st, 1767, aged 72 years. Sarah Hart
and her husband, Bela Strong, Jr., removed to Oak Hill, Green County,
N. Y.

PERCIVAL. PORTER.

85. *Kensington, Berlin.*

ELIZABETH HART, second daughter of Matthew Hart, of Kensington,
Conn., and his wife, Elizabeth (Hopkins), born 1769, at Kensington;
baptized there December 24th, 1769, and married there, January, 1790,
James Percival, Jr., son of James, and his wife, Dorothy Gates, born
April 20th, 1767, at East Haddam, Conn. He was a physician of
prominence, and lived just west of the meeting-house in Kensington,
where he died suddenly in the midst of his usefulness, Thursday, Jan-

uary 22d, 1807, aged 40 years, when second she married April 6th, 1812, Samuel Porter. Their children were—Harriet, born ,
died February 16th, 1807, aged 17 years; Edwin, born about 1793, died at Troy, N. Y.; James Gates, born September 15th, 1795. He graduated at Yale in 1815, having studied for a physician, and began his practice at Charleston, S. C. He also became very popular as a poet. In 1835, in connection with Charles U. Shepard, was appointed to make a geological and mineralogical survey of Connecticut, the report of which was published in 1842. In 1854 he was appointed state geologist of Wisconsin, and at the time of his death, which occurred at Hazel Grove, Wis., May 2d, 1856, aged 61, he held the office of state geologist in Illinois. He was never married. A life of James Gates Percival, by Julius H. Ward, was published by Ticknor & Fields, Boston, 1866, 1 volume, 583 pages. Oswin Hart, born about 1797; baptized at Kensington, October 29th, 1809. He was never married. Died in the hospital at New Haven.

86. *Kensington, Conn., De Ruyter, N. Y.*

OLIVER HART, Kensington, third and youngest son of Matthew Hart, Kensington, and his wife, Elizabeth (Hopkins), born August 10th, 1774, at Kensington; baptized August 14th, 1774, by Rev. Samuel Clark, pastor of that church; married November 25th, 1799, Sally Bronson, of Kensington, daughter of Captain Luke, and Alma Porter, his wife, born September 1st, 1774, at Kensington. He removed to De Ruyter, Madison County, N. Y. He died in 1864 at the house of an adopted daughter, in Allegany County, N. Y., aged 90 years. They have had no children.

COOK.

87. *Danbury, Conn.*

REBECCA HART, eldest daughter of Captain Samuel Hart, of Kensington, and his first wife, Rebecca, daughter of Charles Norton, born January 30th, 1760, at Kensington; married   , William Cook, of Danbury, Conn. She died January 7th, 1823, aged 63 years. They had William, and Betsey, who married Ebenezer White, and left a son, Howard H., who married Emma Hart, daughter of Jesse.

88. *Berlin, Kensington.*

HON. CAPTAIN SAMUEL HART, eldest son of Captain Samuel Hart, of Kensington, and his first wife, Rebecca, daughter of Charles Norton, born May 17th, 1761, at Kensington; married April 8th, 1791, Mary Wilcox, daughter of Stephen, and his wife, Mary Kelsey, born March

1th, 1772. He resided in the west part of Kensington, where his
on Samuel now (1874) resides. He was much employed in public
usiness, a man of stern independence of character, a prominent mem-
er of the democratic party, was a delegate from Berlin to form the
tate constitution, was a member of the legislature in both branches,
nd in his religious belief a Universalist. He was a proud spirited
1an, an earnest and effective speaker in public, and of very ardent
emperament.* He died March 27th, 1835, aged 73 years. His
vidow, Mrs. Mary Hart, died March 27th, 1850, aged 78 years.

THEIR CHILDREN, BEING THE SEVENTH GENERATION.

03. Cyrus Wadsworth, born March 8th, 1794; married March 11th, 1819, Susanna
Erving, of Ohio.
04. Anna, born March 9th, 1796; died December 23d, 1816, aged 20 years.
05. Samuel, born August 9th, 1802; married November 28th, 1825, Lucy Dickinson.

LEE.

89.   *Berlin, Granby.*

CHARLOTTE HART, second daughter of Captain Samuel Hart, of Ken-
ington, and his first wife, Rebecca, daughter of Charles Norton, born
)ctober 17th, 1762, at Kensington. She married December 2d, 1784,
)rrin Lee, of Worthington and Granby. He was a blacksmith by
rade and occupation. She became partially insane. They had chil-
ren, viz: Norman, Nancy, Hart, and George.

90.   *Kensington, Berlin.*

ASAHEL HART, Worthington, second son of Captain Samuel Hart,
f Kensington, and his first wife, Rebecca, daughter of Charles Nor-
on, born May 6th, 1764, at Kensington; married September 23d,
790, Abigail Cowles, daughter of John, and his wife, Abigail Cole,
orn January 10th, 1769. Mr. Hart was a tailor by trade and occu-
ation, and lived on the east side of Worthington Street, just north of
he Galpin store. She was admitted to the Berlin Church before 1795.
Ie died September 9th, 1821, aged 57 years. His widow, Mrs. Abi-
ail Hart, died September 9th, 1845, in her 77th year.

---

* The Will of Hon. Captain Samuel Hart, of Kensington, Conn., bears date, Feb-
nary 27th, 1824, in which he gave his wife one-third of his personal estate as her
wn, and the use of one-third of his real estate during her natural life. He gave his
on, Cyrus W. Hart, $200, besides what I have already given him, and gave his son
amuel all the rest of his estate, and appointed him sole executor of his Will.
igned, sealed, and declared to be his last Will and Testament, before

(Signed,) SAMUEL HART and *Seal.*

John Dunham 2d, ⎫
Lois Dunham, and ⎬ Witnesses.   This Will proved in Probate Court, May 8th,
Clarinda Hurlburt, ⎭   1835, in the District of Berlin.

THEIR CHILDREN, BEING THE SEVENTH GENERATION.

206.   Laura, born May 25th, 1793; married   , Horace Steele.
207.   Freedom, born August 28th, 1796; married   , 1816, Eunice Beckley.
208.   Sally Cowles, born June 22d, 1798; died July 12th, 1815, aged 17 years.
209.   James, born July 1st, 1801; died at Mobile, Ala., November 21st, 1825, aged
         24 years.

92.   *Berlin.*

JESSE HART, Berlin, third son of Captain Samuel Hart, of Kensington, and his first wife, Rebecca, daughter of Charles Norton, born January 3d, 1768, at Kensington; married November 28th, 1792, Lucy Beckley, daughter of Theodore, and his wife, Lucy Risley, born September 19th, 1772. She died March 30th, 1814, aged 41 years, when he second married March 14th, 1822, Mindwell Porter, daughter of Samuel and Mindwell Griswold, of Windsor. His wife was born July 7th, 1784, and united with the church June 5th, 1812. Mr. Hart was a cabinet-maker by trade, and was for several years a hotel keeper in what is now known as Whaples Hotel, on Berlin Street. He became insane, and died March 15th, 1827, in his 60th year.

THEIR CHILDREN, BEING THE SEVENTH GENERATION.

210.   Lucy, born October 23d, 1793; married April 25th, 1819, Edward Norton.
211.   George, born August 15th, 1795; married March 29th, 1818, Caroline Beckley.
212.   Harriet, born September 22d, 1798; married March 3d, 1822; Norris Wilcox.
         Rebecca, born February 7th, 1802; died February 9th, 1807, aged 5 years.
213.   Elizabeth, born December 17th, 1806; married August 17th, 1828, Frederic
         Weston, of Sandy Hill.
214.   Emma, born September 12th, 1809; married September 19th, 1826, Howard
         White, of Danbury, Conn.

HIS CHILDREN BY THE SECOND MARRIAGE.

       Samuel Porter, born May 24th, 1823; died September 30th, 1823, aged 4
         months.
215.   Jane Porter, born December 1st, 1824; married February 7th, 1856, William
         Dodd, of Hartford and Cincinnati.

LEE.

93.   *Kensington.*

MARY HART, eldest daughter of Captain Samuel Hart, of Kensington, and his second wife, Lydia, daughter of Captain John Hinsdale, born September 23d, 1771, at Kensington; married   , John Lee, of Berlin, and located in Blue Hills District, in Kensington. She became partially insane. Their issue were—Lucy, who married Albert Norton; Cyprian, of Marysville, Ohio; John; and Mary, who married Rodney Picket and William Lee, a merchant of Troy.

Emma Willard

TREAT.

97.

LYDIA HART, second daughter of Captain Samuel Hart, of Kensington, and his second wife, Lydia, daughter of Captain John Hinsdale, born September 18th, 1778, at Kensington; married   ,
Elisha Treat, of Middletown. She was a most lovely character. Their children were Emily, Lorenzo, Mary. This last was adopted by her Aunt Emma, (Mrs. Willard,) and died 1831, aged 21, one of the most perfect of human beings.

SIMMONS.

98.
New Philadelphia, Ohio.

NANCY HART, fifth daughter of Captain Samuel Hart of Kensington, and his second wife, Lydia, daughter of Captain John Hinsdale, born March 8th, 1785, at Kensington; married. ·   , Joshua Simmons, of New Philadelphia, Ohio. She was cheerful, lively, and witty, and regarded as the mother of her neighborhood. Her only surviving daughter, Laura, was educated at Troy Seminary, and was first in her class. She subsequently became a teacher at the Patapsco Institute, Maryland, Mrs. Almira Phelps, her aunt, principal.

99.
Berlin, Conn., Troy, N. Y.

EMMA HART, better known as MRS. WILLARD, of Troy, the sixteenth child of her father, Capt. Samuel Hart, of Kensington, and the ninth by his second wife, Lydia (Hinsdale), was born Feb. 23d, 1787, at Berlin, Conn. A brilliant mind and high aspirations were developed in the child. She taught a common school at seventeen; an academy in Berlin at nineteen; at twenty was preceptress at Westfield Academy, Mass.; was released by the trustees to accept a position at the head of the Female Academy, Middlebury, Vt. In 1809, at the age of twenty-two, she married Dr. John Willard, and opened a boarding school.

After five years, she formed the plan and design of extensively improving female education, chiefly by inducing some state government to establish a female seminary for liberal yet feminine education, and committed her plan to writing. She introduced studies into her school before untaught to females. She had five young ladies in her school of seventy from Waterford, N. Y., to which place she was invited, their leading men to present, 1818, her plan to the legislature of New York. They were to do it, if Gov. Clinton approved: he did so, and brought forward the subject in his message.

Mr. and Mrs. Willard spent the winter in Albany, and presented her plan as a memorial to the legislature. It was approved, and the first law ever made by any legislature to improve the female sex by education, was passed, by which all the legally incorporated female academies in the state have since and do now receive a share of the literature fund. The legislature also incorporated a female seminary at Waterford. In the spring of 1819, after two years, she removed to Troy, as no building was provided for the school at Waterford. The corporation of Troy voted $4,000, and made a fortunate purchase of the ground where the eastern part of the seminary now stands. Further sums were raised, and the school thus founded went on from year to year, increasing in numbers and facilities, until some four hundred pupils had access to nearly the science and literature of the colleges. Many of her methods of teaching, and her illustrations, were peculiar to herself, and would be described in detail had we space. These, however, can be found in her published works.

Dr. Willard died in 1825, leaving the entire responsibility of the school in Mrs. Willard's hands. Its popularity increased so that pupils came from all parts of the Union and Canada, and even from the West Indies. She thus deservedly attained the highly distinguished honor of being the first and most successful female educator in America. In 1838, she resigned her charge to her son and his wife, that she might the better publish her unfinished literary works, and enjoy her travels in Europe. Very interesting biographical sketches of her may be found in Everest's "Poets of Connecticut," and "Appleton's Encyclopedia."

Among the productions of her pen, the best known is the beautiful hymn, "Rocked in the Cradle of the Deep," and in educational literature, her "Historical Series." Her published works are numerous, and some of them of high note and merit.

Thus, in brief, the history of the brilliant *girl*, Emma Hart, culminated in the distinguished Mrs. Willard, of Troy Female Seminary. This was her mission and specialty—this was her forte: here she spent her best days, and here she died at a good old age, Friday, April 15th, 1870; aged 83 years, 1 month, 22 days.*

Their child, John Hart Willard, principal of Troy Seminary, had children, Emma W., John H., Sarah H., Mary T., and Harriet P. The beautiful profile engraving of his honorable mother which embellishes the opposite page, is kindly furnished by him. *He has my thanks.*

---

* She was a great student in chemistry and natural philosophy, and it was these sciences which led her to the great discovery "The motive power in the circulation of the blood." She, in 1837, published a work on the subject, and in 1847, another on "Respiration, and its effects."

Almira Lincoln Phelps.

100.

Berlin, Conn., Troy, N. Y., Baltimore, Md.

ALMIRA HART, better known as MRS. LINCOLN and MRS. PHELPS, was the seventeenth child of Capt. Samuel Hart, of Kensington, and the tenth by his second wife, Lydia Hinsdale, was born July 13th, 1793, at Berlin, Conn. In the following sketch, I transcribe from a letter of her sister, Mrs. Willard, to some extent. She says:

Almira was a pupil of mine for the three years I taught in Berlin, after which, at an early age, she taught a common school. She was subsequently with Mrs. Willard at Middlebury, Vt., and, about eighteen, at the Female Academy in Pittsfield, Mass., under the excellent instruction of a maternal cousin, Miss Nancy Hinsdale. Returning to Middlebury, after having taught for a time a select school in Middletown, Conn., she remained a while with Mrs. Willard, and then took charge of a female academy at Sandy Hill, N. Y. Here she developed the extraordinary talents which have marked her subsequent career. After two years, she married, Oct. 5th, 1817, Simeon Lincoln, Jr., of New Britain, Conn., a printer by trade and occupation, and an editor of a literary paper at Hartford, Conn. They had Jane, who was educated at Troy. Emma Willard, married a lawyer of Reading, Penn. Mr. Lincoln died Oct. 4th, 1823, and she engaged at once in teaching a winter school near her home, although having two small children on her hands. In the spring, she entered Mrs. Willard's Seminary as a teacher, having taken up the Latin language evenings (or nights) of the past winter—her progress was remarkable. Mrs. Willard gave her the department of natural science. About four years after this, she wrote her work on Botany, being then vice-principal of Troy Seminary. This was a decided success, and still holds its place as the first on the subject: it has afforded her an emolument, and made the publisher rich. While Mrs. Willard was in Europe, Mrs. Lincoln managed the Troy Seminary as principal with great ability, and procured of the corporation of Troy an important addition to the grounds. In 1831, Mrs. Lincoln became the wife of Hon. John Phelps, of Vermont, a distinguished jurist and eminent statesman. She then went to reside at Guilford, and subsequently at Brattleboro, Vt. Here she pursued her literary studies, and published a work on Natural Philosophy, and an abridgment of the same; a work on Chemistry, and Chemistry for Beginners; a small work on Geology; a small work entitled Botany for Beginners; a work for the Harpers' Family Library, named "Caroline Westerly;" and published a popular octavo entitled, the *Fireside Friend*,—made up in part of her Saturday Lectures to the pupils of Troy. In 1838, Mrs. Phelps, with the approbation of her husband, accepted an invitation to become the head of a female seminary at West Chester, Pa., which seemed *then* to promise great usefulness; but opposition to religious instruction led her to take a more private establishment at Rahway, N. J.; from which, in 1841, she was invited by the Bishop of Maryland, and trustees of the Patapsco Institute, to found a diocesan church school for girls. Here she labored fifteen years, and sustained Episcopal service and worship, and educated as many as one thousand pupils, among whom were about one hundred and fifty beneficiaries, educated for teachers. This was the great and crowning educational work of Mrs. Phelps. She retired from that field in 1856. The death of Mr. Phelps had occurred in 1849. She takes an interest in the great questions of the day, especially in education and the social condition of women, deeply deploring the agitations caused by restless innovators on the established order of society. She resides in Baltimore; has been a communicant of the Episcopal church since 1816, and is now over eighty years of age, in good health and spirits (July, 1874).*

CHILDREN OF ALMIRA AND SIMEON LINCOLN.

Jane Porter, born 1818, at Hartford, Conn., was a woman of rare accomplishments —a pious and noble character. She was honored and lamented in her death, which was caused by a railroad disaster near Burlington, N. J., Aug. 29th, 1855. The spire of St. John's Church, Troy, is dedicated to her memory. Her remains were interred in the family lot at Greenpoint Cemetery, Baltimore.

James Hart, born 1820, at Hartford, Conn., died 1821.

Emma Willard, born 1822, at New Britain, Conn., married Lewis W.   , now a lawyer in Philadelphia. Their children—Chas. Evans, born 1844, a young man of brilliant promise, died as he was about to graduate in medicine; was an assistant surgeon in the late war. Albert Henry, born 1846, was admitted to the bar in Philadelphia, appointed lieutenant of marines, was in the naval service during the war, at the storming of Fort Fisher, and was commended for bravery. Wm. Dennis, born 1848, an attorney at law in Philadelphia; at sixteen, was a volunteer in a Philadelphia regiment, in active service.

DESCENDANTS OF ALMIRA HART AND JOHN PHELPS, ESQ.

Charles Edward, born 1833, in Vermont; was educated at Princeton, and studied law at Cambridge University; a member of Baltimore city council, and

---

* In her 80th year, she published two volumes, calling them "*Fruits of Autumn.*" "*Preserved in the Winter of Life.*" In June, 1874, she presented, by the hand of Rev. John G. Morris, to the "Maryland Academy of Sciences," her *Herbarium*, containing about six hundred specimens of plants, many of them foreign and rare, accompanied with a letter, which was read when the donation was received. A unanimous vote of thanks was passed, and she was cordially elected a member of the institution. She still later showed her interest in science by personally attending the twenty-third anniversary meeting of the "American Association for the Advancement of Science," held at Hartford, Conn., commencing Aug. 12th, 1874, and continued several days.

major of the Maryland Guards; in 1862, was Lieut. Col. of the 7th Maryland regiment of volunteers; was wounded at the battle of Spottsylvania,
was a Brev. Brig. Gen.

101. *Kensington, Conn., Castleton, Vt.*

MAJOR GIDEON HART, Kensington, eldest son of Nathaniel, of same
place, and his wife, Martha (Norton), was born Nov. 23d, 1759, at Kensington, and baptized May 4th, 1760, by Rev. Samuel Clark, pastor;
married, June 25th, 1786, Cynthia, daughter of Jonathan Langdon, of
Kensington, and his wife, Elizabeth (Edwards), born May 14th, 1765,
baptized May 19th, 1765, at Kensington. They were both admitted
to church there July, 1787. He held the military rank of Major.
He lived for a time at Castleton, Vt., but returned to Farmington,
where he died 1834. She died 1824, aged 59 years.

THEIR CHILDREN, BEING THE SEVENTH GENERATION.

216. Laura, born   , 1787, baptized Sept. 16th, 1787, married,   ,
Erastus Washburn.
Azel Langdon, born 1789, baptized Feb. 2d, 1789.
217. Amanda, born 1791, baptized Aug. 14th, 1791, died 1826; unmarried.
218. Polly, born   , 1793, baptized Sept. 31st, 1793, died 1834; unmarried.
219. Cynthia Langdon, born 1796, baptized July 31st, 1796; lives in Madison, N.C.,
single (1874).
220. Norman, born 1798, baptized May 7th, 1798, died Oct. 16th, 1832.
Salmon, born 1802, baptized May 10th, 1802, died in infancy.
221. Abigail, born   , baptized Dec. 3d, 1803, married,   , James
Bragg, Berrien Co., Mich.
222. Olivia, born 1806, died 1826, aged 20 years.

102. *Kensington and Rocky Hill, Conn.*

SETH HART, Kensington, second son of Nathaniel Hart, of same
place, and his wife, Martha (Norton), was born Aug. 19th, 1761, at
Kensington, married,   , Anna Goodrich. He was a tailor by
trade. He lived for a time in Glastonbury, where he was a member of
that church. He removed to Rocky Hill, and carried with him a letter of recommendation to that church, Dec. 2d, 1787, for himself and
wife, where he became, July 24th, 1808, a deacon. In his tailor shop
in the center of the place, he also had a drug and confectionery connected. His wife Anna died June 27th, 1799, in child-bed, when,
second, he married, Nov. 10th, 1799, widow Lydia Bull, widow of Dr.
Bull, and daughter of Williams. She died March 5th, 1812, aged
fifty years, when, third, he married, Aug. 9th, 1812, Lucy Boardman,
daughter of Elnathan. He died in Rocky Hill, Dec. 12th, 1813, aged
53 years.

223. Nancy, born   , married, Aug. 27th, 1805, Chauncey Buckley, of Rocky Hill.

224. Abigail, born   , married, Nov. 25th, 1804, John Buckley, of Rocky Hill.

225. Roxana, born 1791, baptized Nov. 6th, 1791, married, May 11th, 1808, Nathan Jagger, of Rocky Hill.

Norman, born 1794, baptized Aug. 14th, 1794, died in infancy.

226. Seth,   }
227. Selah,   } twins, born 1796, and baptized Oct. 1st, 1796, at Rocky Hill.

Infant, born   baptized June 26th, 1799, in private, being sick; died.

Caroline, born   , 1801, baptized Oct. 4th, 1801, died Feb. 27th, 1812, aged 11 years.

228. Lucius, born June 14th, 1803, baptized July 31st, 1803, at Rocky Hill, Conn.

229. Norman, born   , 1805, baptized Dec. 22d, 1805; went to Acasto, O.

103.   *Kensington, Conn.*

SALMON HART, Kensington, third son of Nathaniel Hart, of same place, and his wife Martha (Norton), was born Jan. 3d, 1763, at Kensington, and baptized June 7th, 1763, by Rev. Samuel Clark. He married Jan. 31st, 1788, Ruth, youngest daughter of Roger Norton and his wife Mary (Pratt), was born Sept. 5th, 1766, at Kensington, and baptized Sept. 7th, 1766. They resided in that part of Kensington called "Blue Hills." She died Feb. 11th, 1793, aged 26 years. He died Dec. 26th, 1796, in his 34th year. They have tombstones in "Blue Hills" Cemetery.

Lambert, born April 21st, 1789, died May 6th, 1789, aged 15 days.

230. William, born 1790, baptized Oct., 1790, died 1810, at Washington, Penn.

104.   *Kensington, Conn., Castleton, Vt.*

NATHANIEL HART, JR., Kensington, fourth son of Nathan'l Hart, Sr., of the same place, and his wife, Martha (Norton), was born May 2d, 1765, at Kensington, and baptized there May 26th, 1765, by Rev. Samuel Clark, pastor. He married,   , Polly Edwards, and they removed to Castleton, Vt. She died, when, second, he married Jane. He was a pious, useful man. He had no children, and died at Castleton, Vt., but at what time is not reported.

105.   *Kensington, Conn., Watertown, O.*

SELAH HART, of Kensington, Conn., and Watertown, O., fifth son of Nathaniel Hart, of Kensington, and his wife Martha (Norton), was born Jan. 30th, 1767, and baptized there Feb. 8th, 1767. He married, Oct. 30th, 1793, Sarah Walter, born March 5th, 1766. They were both members of the church from early life. They removed to Marietta, O., in 1789, and in 1796, to Watertown, O., and in 1821, to Marion, Morgan Co., Ohio, where he was killed by the fall of a limb from a tree, Jan. 6th, 1836, aged 66 years. All the family are farmers. He was a magistrate for some fourteen years,—a man of excellent mind and judgment, and was greatly missed in the place, and mourned over, so great was the loss.

THEIR CHILDREN, BEING THE SEVENTH GENERATION.

231. Norman, born Aug. 29th, 1795, died Aug., 1813, in the army, at Sandusky, Ohio.
232. Walter, born Dec. 1st, 1796, married, May 30th, 1818, Hannah Potts.
233. Selah, born Mar. 29th, 1797, married, Feb. 23d, 1826, Mary Thompson, daughter of Hugh.
234. Seth, born Dec. 6th, 1799, married, Oct. 27th, 1825, Sally Rush, of Morgan Co., Ohio.
235. Sally, born Nov. 20th, 1801, married,   , Geo. L. Caner.
236. William, born Dec. 11th, 1803, died Dec. 22d, 1847.
237. Hiram, born July 1st, 1805, married, Nov. 24th, 1829, Hannah Smith.
     Cynthia, born Sept. 27th, 1807.
238. Mary, born May 15th, 1809, married,   , John Moody.
     Betsey, born March 31st, 1811, died Sept. 18th, 1817.

106. *Kensington, Conn.*

CYPRIAN HART, of Kensington, sixth son of Nathaniel and his wife, Martha (Norton), was born   , at Kensington, and baptized there Feb. 5th, 1769, by Rev. Samuel Clark, then pastor of that church. He was adopted by his uncle, Gen. Selah Hart, with whom he lived, and whose estate he inherited. He married, Dec. 24th, 1795, Lucy, daughter of Elijah Hooker, of Kensington, and his wife, Susannah (Seymour), was born Jan. 13th, 1772, in Kensington. He resided on the old homestead of his uncle, Gen. Selah Hart, where the late Oliver Moore lived, and died there March 1st, 1806, aged 37 years. His widow Lucy was admitted to Kensington church the same month, and had her six children baptized the subsequent November. She died July 8th, 1851, aged 80 years.

THEIR CHILDREN, BEING THE SEVENTH GENERATION.

239. Selah, born Oct. 19th, 1796, died May 24th, 1838, aged 41 years; unmarried.
240. Ruth, born Dec. 19th, 1797, married, March 25th, 1829, Albert Norton,—his third wife.
241. Abigail, born Sept. 12th, 1799, married, March 25th, 1829, Oliver Moore, died Sept. 2d, 1850.
242. Henry Cyprian, born Jan. 30th, 1801; was a physician; died Mar. 28th, 1831, aged 30 years, at Berlin.
243. Lucy Hooker, born Nov. 14th, 1803, married, Nov. 1st, 1826, Selden Peck.
244. Emily, born May 19th, 1805, died April 3d, 1835, aged 30 years; unmarried.

107.   *Southington, Conn.*

VELINA HART, Southington, eldest son of Noadiah Hart, of Kensington, and his wife, Lucy (Hurlburt), daughter of Stephen, was born
May 5th, 1761. He married, at Southington, before Rev. Wm. Robinson, then pastor of that church, Dec. 3d, 1782, Huldah Green. He
was by occupation a miller, and run what was subsequently called
Carter's Mill; he lived in a small house near the mill, both of which
have long since disappeared, and the place is now covered by Plant's
Pond. Huldah, his wife, died of fever July 29th, 1807, aged 53
years, when he, second, married Hannah Clark, who was received to
the church in Southington, by letter from Burlington church, Oct. 2d,
1808. He died of gout in Southington, April 12th, 1812, in his 51st
year, and a tombstone tells where he lies in Plantsville cemetery. His
widow Hannah was dismissed by a letter to Geneva, Ashtabula Co.,
Ohio, Aug. 26th, 1827.

THEIR CHILDREN, BEING THE SEVENTH GENERATION.

245. Huldah, born   , baptized Nov. 26th, 1809, on account of his second
      wife.
      Hannah, born   , baptized Jan. 15th, 1812, died Jan. 19th, 1812.

GILLET.

108.   *Burlington.*

LUTHENA HART, eldest daughter of Noadiah Hart, of Kensington,
Burlington, Harwinton, and Southington, and his first wife Lucy
(Hurlburt), was born March 7th, 1763. She married   Gillet,
and died soon after marriage, viz., Nov. 7th, 1781, aged eighteen
years.

110.   *Litchfield, Harwinton, Winsted.*

STEPHEN HURLBURT HART, Winsted, son of Noadiah Hart, of Kensington, Burlington, Harwinton, and Southington, and his first wife,
Lucy (Hurlburt), was born Nov. 1st, 1767. He married, Oct. 18th,
1791, Lucinda Cook, daughter of Amos, and perhaps cousin of John
Cook, of Plainville, Conn., born at Wallingford, Oct. 29th, 1771.
They resided in Litchfield, Harwinton, and Winsted. He died Sept.
17th, 1833, aged 66 years, at Winsted, Conn. Mrs. Lucinda Cook
Hart died at Waterbury, Aug. 23d, 1857, aged 85 years, 10 months,
24 days, at the house of her daughter Sophia.

THEIR CHILDREN, BEING THE SEVENTH GENERATION.

246. Asahel, born Oct. 30th, 1793; supposed to be lost at sea.
247. Velina, born Oct. 19th, 1795, married,   , Elizabeth Stevens.

48. Lucy Hooker, born Jan. 26th, 1799, married, Oct. 26th, 1817, Leonard R. Griswold.
49. Roswell Cook, born July 20th, 1801, married, March 11th, 1827, Polly Grant.
50. Lucinda, born Feb. 2d, 1804, married July 23d, 1827, Wm. S. Hungerford.
Rhoda, born Oct. 6th, 1806, died Nov. 20th, 1806.
51. Sophia C., born Sept. 4th, 1809; resides in New Haven; married, April 26th, 1852, Geo. H. Bowditch.
52. Richard P., born Aug. 27th, 1811; resides in Alabama, and says he is second cousin of George, and John, and Henry Cook, of Farmington. He died May 1st, 1859, at Waterbury.

111.
New Britain, Conn., Parishville, N. Y.

CYPRIAN HART, of New Britain, son of Noadiah Hart, of Kensington, and Lucy Hurlburt, his wife, was born May 23d, 1772, at Kensington. He married Olive, daughter of James Wheadon and his wife Dinah, of North Branford, Conn., where she was born June 20th, 1765. He was by occupation a miller; went to New Britain to run Dea. Elijah Hart's mill, and lived by the mill, where his children were born. He lived also, subsequently, where now (1873) Silas Wright does, on the "Mountain Lake" road. She was a member of Dr. Smalley's church in New Britian, made so Dec. 6th, 1812. They removed to Parishville, St. Lawrence Co., N. Y., where both died, he July 5th, 1843, aged 71 years, she June 17th, 1846, aged 81 years.

THEIR CHILDREN, BEING THE SEVENTH GENERATION.

253. Truman, born June 11th, 1793, married, July 4th, 1815, Laura Lewis Steele.
254. Noadiah, born April 16th, 1795.
255. Bera, born March 31st, 1797, married, May 6th, 1819, Mary Whaples.
256. James Griffin, born April 19th, 1799.
257. Leander Sidney, born August 10th, 1801, married, August 23d, 1824, Emeline Thompson; second, married, , Electa Humphrey.
Percy, born June 17th, 1805, died April 3d, 1809, aged 4 years.
Ordelia, born Jan. 17th, 1808, died April 4th, 1809. Both buried in one grave.

116. New Britain, Conn.

ROGER HART, New Britain, eldest son of John Hart, of the same place, and his wife Anna (Deming), was born 1765, at New Britain. He married, , Sibil Robinson, daughter of John and his wife Mary (Strickland), born , 1764, at Middletown. She died Jan. 13th, 1817, aged 53 years, when he, second, married Lavinia, widow of Joseph Tryon, of Southington; she died Nov. 22d, 1822, aged 44 years, when he, third, married, Oct. 24th, 1824, Phebe, widow of Sam'l Gladden, and daughter of Nathaniel Pennfield and his wife Lydia

12

(Barnes), baptized Aug. 19th, 1772. Mr. Hart was left at the death of his father a large land holder; he inherited the old homestead where the late Harlowe Eddy lived and died, in Hart quarter. By speculation and bad trades, he lost all, was hard pressed by poverty, obliged to labor hard to support his large family while they grew up to respectability. He was honest, temperate, and industrious, and lived the last of his days in a small house moved from "Strip lane" to where Solomon Hamblin lived and died, on the Mountain road near the Roswell Steele house—it has (1874) disappeared. He died July 30th, 1828, aged 63 years. He sold, in 1780, to David Hills, his house, barn, and ninety acres of land for £330, reserving to his mother her thirds for life.

THEIR CHILDREN, BEING THE EIGHTH GENERATION.

258. Azuba, born July 7th, 1789, married, Dec. 13th, 1807, Allen Goodrich.
259. Betsey, born Sept. 17th, 1791, married, March 12th, 1815, John Pennfield.
260. Polly, born June 5th, 1793, married, Nov. 27, 1828, George Cook, of Farmington.
261. Chauncey, born Oct. 5th, 1795, married, May 3d, 1821, Polly Markum.
262. John, born   , 1796, married,   , Polly Stephens.
263. Anna, born Sept. 6th, 1800, married,   , Curtiss M. Doolittle.
264. Roswell, born Sept. 1st, 1802, married, Feb. 13th, 1826, Eliza Steele.
265. William S., born Oct. 14th, 1805, married, August 30th, 1827, Sarah Barnes; second, married,   , widow Harriet Dagget.

CHILDREN OF THE SECOND WIFE.

266. Levi, born   , married   , and went to Illinois.

117. *New Britain, Conn.*

SARAH HART, New Britain, eldest daughter of Judah Hart, of the same place, and his wife Sarah (North), was born Nov. 7th, 1770, at New Britain, and married, July 30th, 1793, Asahel Hart, son of Jehudi, and was his second wife. For her history, see his number.

118. *New Britain, Conn.*

SALMON HART, New Britain, Conn., eldest son of Judah Hart, of the same locality, and his wife Sarah (North), was born May 20th, 1775, at New Britain, and married, May 2d, 1796, Sarah Goodrich, daughter of Asahel, and Sarah (Woodruff), his wife, born May 2d, 1777. She died Aug. 2d, 1815, aged 38 years, when, second, he married, June, 1817, Rosetta, widow of Elisha Williams, and daughter of Seth North, of Berlin, and his wife Eunice (Woodford), born Sept. 15th, 1778. She died Oct. 6th, 1863, aged 85 years, at the house of her son, Albert Williams, near Black Rock school-house. Mr. Hart sold his farm to his second wife's son, Henry Williams, and spent the last of his life in New Britain village, with his son, Capt. Frederic Hart. He was lame with rheumatism many years, and died Sept. 18th, 1857, aged 82 years.

THEIR CHILDREN, BEING THE EIGHTH GENERATION.

Sarah Woodruff, born May 24th, 1798, died Jan. 27th, 1813, aged 14 years.

267. Orpha, born April 2d, 1800, married, May 2d, 1820, Ira Hart; second, H. Butler.
268. Lavina, born Sept. 1st, 1802, married, Dec. 9th, 1824, Samuel A. Hamblin.
269. Sophia, born Nov. 18th, 1806, married, July 3d, 1826, Ralph G. Dunham.
270. Salmon North, born June 18th, 1811, married, May 3d, 1832, Martha Corning.

CHILDREN OF SECOND WIFE.

271. Silas Williams, born Sept. 12th, 1818, married, Nov. 24th, 1846, Abigail Merwin.
272. Frederic Woodford, born Nov. 19th, 1822, married June 2d, 1857, Jennie M. Bassett.

119. *New Britain and Norwich, Conn.*

JUDAH HART, New Britain, second son of Judah Hart, of the same place, and his wife Sarah (North), was born Dec. 16th, 1777, at New Britain, Conn., and was by trade a jeweler. He married, May 1st, 1800, Abigail, daughter of Bildad Belden, born Sept. 15th, 1777, at Stepney, now Rocky Hill, Conn. They settled at Middletown, Conn., but in 1805 removed to Norwich, Conn, where they were admitted to Rev. Mr. Kings's church. In 1816, they removed to Griswold, Conn., and from there (1822) to Brownhelm, Lorain Co., O. He died July 26th, 1824, aged 47 years, 7 months, 10 days. She died July 29th, 1824, only three days after her husband, and she repeated the promise of the Lord: "Leave thy fatherless children, and I will preserve them." In 1845, after a lapse of twenty-one years, all her children were alive, and with their wives and husbands, were all members of the church, and some quite efficient.

THEIR CHILDREN, BEING THE EIGHTH GENERATION.

273. Mary Riley, born June 29th, 1801, married, August 13th, 1846, Nathan Porter Johnson.
274. Judah Belden, born Nov. 11th, 1802, married, May 3d, 1825, Sarah T. Jones.
275. Henry, born Feb. 17th, 1805, married, March 24th, 1830, Sarah S. Shepard.
276. Edwin, born May 5th, 1807, married, April 29th, 1832, Eliza J. Glass.
277. Abigail, born March 25th, 1809, married, Nov. 6th, 1832, Henry J. Brooks, of Elyria.
278. William, born April 9th, 1811, married, Dec. 9th, 1834, Betsey Kirk.

279. Asahel, born March 25th, 1813, married, Sept. 12th, 1841, Clarissa Smith.
      Elizabeth, born Oct. 11th, 1815, died April 12th, 1817, aged two years, at Gris-
      wold, Conn.
280. Harriet Elizabeth, born Jan. 2d, 1818, married March 16th, 1837, Ralph L.
      Goslee.

WOODRUFF.

120.   *New Britain.*

ANNA HART, New Britain, third daughter of Judah Hart, of the
same place, and his wife Sarah (North), was born March 17th, 1780,
at New Britain; married, Sept. 17th, 1804, Truman, son of Amos
Woodruff and his wife Sarah (Clark), born Nov. 23d, 1773, at New
Britian. He was a farmer and an Albino, and lived on East street in
New Britain. They had no issue. He died Feb. 15th, 1854, aged 79
years; she died Nov. 20th, 1857, in her 78th year.

MERRIMAN.

121.   *Southington, Conn.*

ROXANA HART, Southington, fourth daughter of Judah Hart, of
New Britain, Conn., and his wife Sarah (North), was born Oct. 23d,
1784. She married, Nov. 22d, 1803, Albert Merriman, son of Eber,
of Southington, born Sept. 6th, 1774, at Southington; he died Aug.
2d, 1827, aged 53 years, when, second, she married, Feb. 5th, 1829,
James Beecher, of Southington, who died Sept. 12th, 1858, aged 80
years. She died Nov. 26th, 1859, aged 75 years, at Southington.

123.   *New Britain, Norwich, Conn.*

ELIPHAZ HART, Norwich, Conn., third son of Judah Hart, of New
Britain, and his wife, Sarah (North), daughter of James, born June
28th, 1789, at New Britain, Conn. He learned the trade of jeweler
of his brother Judah. He married, December 25th, 1812, Eliza, daughter of Oliver Armstrong, and his wife, Elizabeth (Hammond), of Newport, R. I., born December 2d, 1793, at Newport. They resided at
Greeneville, in Norwich, and he died there July 20th, 1866, aged 77
years, 22 days. The widow lives now (1874) with her daughter, at
Hart's Falls, Rensselaer County, N. Y., and both are members of the
Congregational Church there.

THEIR CHILDREN, BEING THE EIGHTH GENERATION.

281. Oliver Armstrong, born February 13th, 1814; married November 16th, 1843,
      Mary E. Hull.
282. Alfred, born March 28th, 1816; married   , Mary E. Gardner.
283. Eliza, born March 2d, 1818. She is living single with her mother at Hart's
      Falls, N. Y.

284. Martha Perrin, born May 4th, 1820; married   , Amos N. Palmer, of Norwich.
285. George, born June 19th, 1822; married August 25th, 1850, Sarah Potter; second, Jennie Davis.
286. Henry Harrington, born April 12th, 1824; married July 18th, 1850, Abby Chase.
287. John, born January 2d, 1827; died June 14th, 1830, of accidental poisoning.
288. Charles Porter, born April 17th, 1829; married November 29th, 1848, Eleanor Beecher.
289. Samuel, born September 8th, 1831; married September 8th, 1854, Olive Bassett; second
290. Harriet, born September 17th, 1833; married   , William Bussey, of
290. Margaretta, born December 20th, 1835; married December 4th, 1859, Thomas Hudson, a wool manufacturer.
    Joseph, born July 21st, 1838; died July 26th, 1839.

125.   *Springfield, Ohio.*

JOHN C. HART, Springfield, Ohio, eldest son of Rufus Hart, of Coventry, Summit County, Ohio, and his wife, Esther (Coster), born   , 1798; married February 21st, 1831, Margaret A. Sterling, born 1811. In 1845 he was living at Middlebury, Summit County, Ohio.

THEIR CHILDREN, BEING THE EIGHTH GENERATION.

292.	George W., born	, 1832.	
293.	John S., born	, 1833.	
294.	Charles S., born	, 1835.	
	Esther E., born	, 1838; died	1841.
295.	Hiram, born	, 1840.	
296.	Frances A., born	, 1844.	

126.   *Coventry, Ohio.*

HIRAM HART, Coventry, Summit County, Ohio, third son of Rufus Hart, of the same place, and his wife, Esther (Coster), born   , 1804, at Batavia; married   , 1830, Sarah Smith.

THEIR CHILDREN, BEING THE EIGHTH GENERATION.

297.	Hiram Delos, born	, 1841.
298.	Milton, born	, 1845.

RICHARDS.

128.   *Ohio.*

ELIZABETH L. HART, third daughter of Rufus Hart, of Coventry, Summit County, Ohio, and his wife, Esther (Coster), born   , 1810, at Batavia, N. Y.; married December 19th, 1827, Henry Richards, of   . They had Maria L., born 1831; died 1841, aged 10 years. The mother died in 1832, aged 22 years.

129.   *Coventry, Ohio.*

EDWARD W. HART, Coventry, Summit County, Ohio, youngest child
of Rufus Hart, of the same place, and his wife, Esther (Coster), born
        , 1816, at   ; married   1838,
Rachel Latta, who died   , 1845, aged   .

THEIR CHILDREN, BEING THE EIGHTH GENERATION.

299. Harriet, born   , 1839.
300. George Washington, born   , 1841.
301. Maria Coster, born   , 1843.

130.   *North Cornwall, Conn.*

DEACON NATHAN HART, North Cornwall, Conn., eldest son of Titus
Hart, of the same place, and his wife, Esther (Hand), born June 12th,
1776, at North Cornwall; married February 8th, 1804, Sylvia, daughter of Hezekiah Clark, and his wife, Sylvia (Hill), born April 8th, 1785.
She died December 4th, 1839, of paralysis. He succeeded his father
as deacon. "Their twelve children all became hopefully pious, and
united with the church before they had completed their twentieth year,
the principal cause of which instrumentality the father ascribes to a
pious, judicious, and unremittèd maternal influence." His son, Titus,
writes of him as follows, dated February, 1872:

"Deacon Nathan Hart left behind him a rich and precious legacy of
prayer, both for the church of which he was for many years a deacon,
as well as for his numerous family, all of whom know in some measure
how to prize so glorious a boon from so good a parent."

THEIR CHILDREN, BEING THE EIGHTH GENERATION.

302. John Clark, born December 10th, 1804; married June 11th, 1834, Emily Irene
        Burnham.
303. Titus Leavitt, born April 26th, 1806; married May 1st, 1833, Harriet S. Cor-
        bin, of West Hartford.
304. Abigail Emelia, born October 11th, 1808; married April 12th, 1837, Peter No-
        dine, of Washington.
305. Hezekiah Milton, born August 21st, 1810; married September 10th, 1836,
        Eunice Judson.
306. Solomon, born September 17th, 1812; married July 9th, 1840, Caroline Rey-
        nolds.
307. Esther Maria, born January 21st, 1815; married March 13th, 1844, Shelden
        Whittlesey, New Preston.
308. Sylvia Ann, born October 3d, 1816; married October 4th, 1855, Shelden Whit-
        tlesey.
309. Mary Eliza, born March 31st, 1818; married August 15th, 1852, Anson B.
        Nodine, Virginia.
310. Clarissa, born December 24th, 1819; married September 11th, 1839, Robert C.
        Nodine, Ohio.

311. Nathan, born December 12th, 1821; married September 8th, 1847, Sarah Amelia Whittlesey.

312. Delia, born June 26th, 1823; married June 26th, 1860, Sherwood Seeley.

313. Uri William, born July 19th, 1825; married July 23d, 1854, Mary Jane Belden.

131. North Cornwall.

JOHN HART, second son of Titus Hart, of North Cornwall, Conn., and his wife, Esther (Hand), born   , 1779, at North Cornwall; married   , Sally Clark. He was a member of the church there, and exhibited great maturity of religious experience. He died June 29th, 1801, aged 22 years. He left no children.

EATON.

138. Madison County, N. Y.

JANE HART, youngest daughter of Phineas Hart, of New York, and Cornwall, Conn., and his wife   , born   , married   Eaton, of Madison County, N. Y. He was killed by the falling of a pile of lumber.

140. Cornwall, Conn.

ELIAS HART, Cornwall, Conn., second son of Elias Hart, of the same town, and his wife, Philomela (Burnham), of Appleton, born November 4th, 1784, at Cornwall; married   , 1807, Hannah Harrison, both members of the church in Cornwall, Conn.

THEIR CHILDREN, BEING THE EIGHTH GENERATION.

314. Albert B., born   , 1809.
315. Flora Ann, born   , 1811.
316. Elias Nelson, born   , 1813; married   , 1835, Caroline Hitchcock.
317. Harriet E., born   , 1815.
318. John Elias, born   , 1817; married   , 1840, Mary Winans.
319. Caroline A., born   , 1819; married   , 1845, William Dickinson.
320. Hannah M., born   , 1821; married   , 1840, Elisha Winans.
321. Juliaette, born   , 1823.
322. Edmund H., born   , 1826; married February 12th, 1849, Mary A. Hunt, of South Canaan.
323. Alvan Henry, born   , 1828.
324. Jerusha R., born   , 1830.

141.   *Lapier, Mich.*

OLIVER BURNHAM HART, Lapier, Lapier County, Mich., third son of
Elias Hart, of Cornwall, Conn., and his wife, Philomela Burnham, born
          , 1787, at Cornwall, Conn; married   , 1807,
Amanda Harrison. They both died at Lapier, Mich., August, 1844,
much lamented, and both were buried in the same grave.

THEIR CHILDREN, BEING THE EIGHTH GENERATION.

Orson, born, September, 1808; died, November, 1808.
Oliver Burnham, born, April, 1810; died, February, 1811.
Caroline, born, January, 1812; died, January, 1819.

325. Noah Harrison, born October 30th, 1813; married September 5th, 1842, Emily
  J. Peck. He is a lawyer at Lapier.

326. Julius Burnham, born   , 1815; married   , 1835, Sarah
  Shafer, of Lapier.

327. Joseph Brown, born   , 1818; married October 23d, 1844, Mary
  M. Hopkins; second, March 7th, 1859.

Henry B., born, March, 1820; died   , 1821.

328. Phila Ann, born   , 1823; married   , 1847, John M. Wattles,
  a lawyer.

329. Sarah Maria, born   , 1825; married   , 1853, Andrew C. Maxwell, a lawyer.

330. Abigail Burnham, born   , 1826; married   , 1851, George Smith, a
  physician of Bay City.

331. Barzillai Brown, born   , 1828; married   , 1853, Elizur Munro, a
  grocer of Lapier.

John E., born, December, 1830; died, February, 1831.

144.   *Cornwall, Conn.*

JULIUS HART, Cornwall, Conn., fourth son of Elias Hart, of the
same town, and his wife, Philomela Burnham, born February 29th,
1796, at Cornwall, Conn.; married January 7th, 1819, Rhoda Rogers,
daughter of Deacon Noah, and his wife, Lydia Cornwall, born June
9th, 1798, at North Cornwall. She died June 11th, 1866, aged 68
years, 2 days.

THEIR CHILDREN, BEING THE EIGHTH GENERATION.

332. Julius Rogers, born December 15th, 1819; died January 31st, 1831, aged 12
  years.

333. Noah Rogers, born September 12th, 1821; married November 22d, 1843, Lucretia Minerva Barnum.

Lydia Julia, ⎫   died June 10th, 1827.
     ⎬ born April 29th, 1826;
334. Julius Leavett, ⎭   was living at West Cornwall in 1872.

335. Elizabeth Wilson, born January 22d, 1829; died September 28th, 1835.

336. Elias Burton, born February 21st, 1834; married October 7th, 1857, Hattie A.
  Canfield.

337. George Spencer, born February 11th, 1837; married February 23d, 1871, Anna
  Dudley, of New York.

147.   *Lapier, Mich.*

Hon. Alvin Nelson Hart, Lapier, Lapier County, Mich., youngest child of Elias Hart, of Cornwall, Conn., and his wife, Philomela (Burnham), born February 11th, 1804, at Cornwall, Conn.; married July 8th, 1828, Charlotte Fox Ball, born June 14th, 1813, at Wendall, Franklin County, Mass., daughter of Dr. Benjamin and Charlotte (Evers) Ball. She died August 14th, 1850, aged 37 years, 2 months. They resided for a time after marriage at Utica, N. Y. He removed thence to the then territory of Michigan, and cut his way fourteen miles through a forest, to Lapier, and was the first to settle there in his log cabin in 1831. He was made a magistrate the next year, made sheriff in 1835, and representative the same year, made supervisor in 1842, made state senator in 1844, and first judge of Lafayette County in 1846, 1847, and 1848. In 1860 he removed to Lansing, and was made alderman of the first ward, which he now (1874) holds. He is engaged in merchandise and real estate. Mr. Hart was educated at Amherst College, Amherst, Mass.

THEIR CHILDREN, BEING THE EIGHTH GENERATION.

338. Benjamin Elias, born July 3d, 1830, at Utica, N. Y. He is living single at Lansing in 1874.
339. Danforth Alvin, born May 15th, 1832, at Lapier; died single, April 20th, 1853.
340. Rodney George, born May 28th, 1834, at Lapier; married December 5th, 1854, Mary Castella Hazen.
341. Isabella Eliza, born July 24th, 1836, at Lapier; married October 1st, 1858, Robert Wilson Hamilton.
     Charlotte Evers, born February 25th, 1838; died December 29th, 1843, at Lapier.
     Mary Josephine, born December 25th, 1840; died December 25th, 1843, aged 3 years.
     Charlotte Josephine, born September 4th, 1845; died August 24th, 1846.
342. Arthur Nelson, born August 16th, 1848; married December 18th, 1866, Helen Augusta Britton.

148.   *Lenox, Ohio.*

Reuben Hart, Lenox, Ashtabula County, Ohio, eldest son of Captain Solomon Hart, of Hartsville, Mass., and his wife, Jerusha (Beach,) born May 30th, 1787, at Cornwall, Conn.; married May 19th, 1812, Eleanor Kingsman. They resided in New Marlboro, Mass., and from thence they removed to Lenox, Ashtabula County, Ohio, in 1833. He lived in Jefferson County, Ohio, in 1871, and died June 22d, 1872, aged 85 years. He was a farmer. His widow is still living in Ohio in 1874.

343. John G., born July 23d, 1813; married February 13th, 1838, Henrietta McNutt; second

344. Laura, born November 14, 1814; married, November, 1835, Amander Hall; she died December, 1870.

345. Amanda, born September 19th, 1816; married February 14th, 1837, James McNutt.

346. James Solomon, born May 11th, 1818; married October 21st, 1851, Eunice Linzey.

347. Nancy, born July 26th, 1824; married, September, 1853, George Carpenter, a farmer of Minnesota.

348. Mary, born April 19th, 1833; married, September, 1857, George M. Loomis, a farmer of Northfield.

MARTIN.

149.   *New Marlboro, Mass.*

AMANDA HART, Tioga Center, Tioga County, N. Y., eldest daughter of Captain Solomon Hart, of Hartsville, in New Marlboro, Mass., and his wife, Jerusha (Beach), born December 28th, 1788, at New Marlboro. She married June 29th, 1808, Amos Martin, a merchant, born at New Marlboro, and died May 14th, 1835. She was living a widow in 1872, at Tioga, N. Y.

BRIGHAM.

150.   *New Marlboro, Mass.*

ELIZABETH HART, second daughter of Captain Solomon Hart, of Hartsville, Mass., and his wife, Jerusha (Beach), born November 11th, 1790, at New Marlboro, Mass.; married September 25th, 1811, Jabez H. Brigham, a farmer, who died September 16th, 1828. She died October 31st, 1868, aged 78.

151.   *Royalton, Niagara Co., N. Y.*

TYRUS HART, New Marlboro, Mass., second son of Captain Solomon Hart, of Hartsville, and his wife, Jerusha (Beach), born January 31st, 1793, at New Marlboro; married May 24th, 1814, Tryphena Sage, of Sandisfield. They went to Royalton, Niagara County, N. Y. He died June 30th, 1831, aged 38 years. He was a clothier by trade.

349. Emily, born

350. Dorlosta, born

351. Chauncey, born   ; married   , Sophia Ross.

HOLLISTER.

• 152. *Perry, N. Y.*

POLLY HART, third daughter of Captain Solomon Hart, of Hartsville, Mass., and his wife, Jerusha (Beach), born September 17th, 1795, at New Marlboro; married December 31st, 1815, John H. Hollister. She died August 26th, 1869, aged 74 years. He was living in 1872 at Perry, Wyoming County, N. Y.

153. *Hillsdale, Mich.*

ALMON HART, Perry, Wyoming County, N. Y., third son of Captain Solomon Hart, of Hartsville, Mass., and his wife, Jerusha (Beach), born September 4th, 1797, at New Marlboro, Mass.; married November 30th, 1820, Polly Harmon, of Monteray, Mass., daughter of Isaac, and his wife, Mary (Rawson), born May 24th, 1800, at Tyringham. He was living in 1872 at Hillsdale, Hillsdale County, Mich.

THEIR CHILDREN, BEING THE EIGHTH GENERATION.

2. Alonzo G., born November 27th, 1821; married December 26th, 1844, Celinda Allen.
3. Gilbert Z., born October 24th, 1823; married October 19th, 1847, Eliza Warren.
4. Jerome W., born August 4th, 1825; married August 8th, 1850, Fanny Kane.
5. William M., born March 9th, 1829; died March 10th, 1832.
6. Alvira S., born October 16th, 1832; married December 29th, 1852, Eugene S. White.
7. Louisa M., born May 19th, 1838; married June 14th, 1857, Eugene S. White.
8. William S., born August 24th, 1840. He was a soldier, and died in service June 21st, 1863, aged 23 years.

STONE.

154. *New Marlboro, Mass.*

CANDACE HART, fourth daughter of Captain Solomon Hart, of Hartsville, Mass., and his wife, Jerusha (Beach), born October 20th, 1799, at New Marlboro, Mass.; married April 26th, 1820, Truman Stone, of New Marlboro. She died November 5th, 1842, aged 43 years.

POWELL.

155. *New Marlboro, Mass.*

ANNA HART, fifth daughter of Captain Solomon Hart, of Hartsville, Mass., and his wife, Jerusha (Beach), born April 19th, 1802, at New Marlboro, Mass.; married April 19th, 1826, John Powell, of the same town. She was living in 1872.

156.   *Perry, N. Y.*

SOLOMON RANDALL HART, Perry, Wyoming County, N. Y., fourth son of Captain Solomon Hart, of Hartsville, Mass., and his wife, Jerusha (Beach), born April 2d, 1804, at New Marlboro; married September 12th, 1845, Fanny Johnson, daughter of Augustus, of Tyringham, Mass., born February 20th, 1803. He was living in 1872 at Perry, N. Y., and was a farmer, justice, and postmaster.

THEIR CHILD, BEING THE EIGHTH GENERATION.

359. William M., born June 21st, 1834; married October 6th, 1853, Jennie Macumber, of Perry, N. Y.

157. *Hartsville, Mass., New Haven, Ct.*

MILAN HART, Hartsville, Mass., fifth son of Captain Solomon Hart, of the same place, and his wife, Jerusha (Beach), born December 28th, 1805, at Hartsville; married May 1st, 1832, Perlina Nettleton, of Cornwall, Conn., daughter of Jehiel, and his wife, Amy (Jackson), born September 7th, 1811, at Cornwall, Conn. He was residing, in 1871, at No. 48 Bradley Street, New Haven, and both were members of the Second Methodist Church there. He has been a farmer, but is now in feeble health.

THEIR CHILDREN, BEING THE EIGHTH GENERATION.

360. Jane Antoinette, born February 20th, 1834; married September 28th, 1852, James Hollister.
361. Edson Solomon, born January 10th, 1836; married September 19th, 1855, Frances J. Fargo; second, Maria
362. Rosalinda Exine, born September 14th, 1837; married June 5th, 1855, George Stephens.
363. John Jay, born September 17th, 1839; married March 20th, 1860, Clara A. Crippen.
       Daughter, born January 26th, 1842; died the same day.
364. Emma Dorothy, born February 12th, 1844; died October 16th, 1861, aged 17 years. She was a member of the Methodist Church.
       Milan Lorenzo, born May 14th, 1846; died June 1st, 1846.

159.   *Hartsville, Mass.*

ALFRED HART, Hartsville, Mass., youngest child of Captain Solomon Hart, of the same place, and his wife, Jerusha (Beach), born February 12th, 1812, at New Marlboro, Mass.; married October 19th, 1833, Cynthia L. Nettleton, of Cornwalll, Conn. He died February 19th, 1864, aged 52 years. He was a farmer.

THEIR CHILDREN, BEING THE EIGHTH GENERATION.

Alonzo M., born July 8th, 1837; died August 11th, 1840.

365. Lucius Whiting, born January 24th, 1842; married January 24th, 1860, Frances S. Ladd.

Amy J., born January 22d, 1845; died May 27th, 1848.

366. Guy H., born December 11th, 1847.

160.   *Candor, Tioga County, N. Y.*

ABEL HART, Candor, Tioga County, N. Y., eldest son of Abel Hart, of Kensington, Conn., and his wife, Mary (Galpin), born   , 1770, at   ; married   , 1795, Rachel Sweeden, of Stockbridge, Mass. They removed from Massachusetts to Candor, N. Y., about 1799, and he died there in 1860, aged 90 years. Their first two children were born in Massachusetts, and the others at Candor, N. Y.

THEIR CHILDREN, BEING THE EIGHTH GENERATION.

367.	Samuel, born	, 1796; married	, Lois Gridley.
368.	Daniel, born	, 1798; married	, M. Kelsey.
369.	Mary, born	, 1800; married	, H. Potter.
370.	Betsey, born	, 1802; married	, J. Rosurance.
371.	Selah, born	, 1805; married	, 1827, Julia Potter.
372.	Susan, born	, 1807; married	, J. Long.
	Ira, born	, 1810; died	, 1813, aged 8 years.
	Henry, born	, 1812; died	, 1823, aged 13 years.
373.	Abel, born second,	, 1814; married	, L. Kirkpatrick ;

BOOTH.

167.   *Candor, N. Y.*

LUCY HART, Candor, Tioga County, N. Y., seventh daughter of Abel Hart, of the same place, and his wife, Mary (Galpin), born 1788, at   ; married   , Orange F. Booth, son of Joseph, of New Britain, and his wife, Elizabeth (Francis), born March 5th, 1782, at New Britain. They both united with the church at Candor in 1819. He died in 1860, aged 78 years.

SMITH.

168.   *Owego, N. Y.*

ELECTA HART, Candor, Tioga County, N. Y., eighth daughter of Abel Hart, of the same place, and his wife, Mary (Galpin), born 1792, at   ; married   , Samuel, son of Joel Smith, formerly of New Britain, but later of Owego, N. Y., and his wife, Hannah (Griswold). They lived at Owego, Tioga County, N. Y., and Nanticoke, Broome County, N. Y.

GRIDLEY.

170.   *Candor, N. Y.*

HARRIET HART, youngest daughter of Abel Hart, of Candor, Tioga
County, N. Y., and his wife, Mary (Galpin), born   , 1795,
t   ; married   , Charles Gridley,
nd both became members of the Congregational Church at Candor,
Tioga County, N. Y., she in 1827, he in 1832.

177.   *Victor, N. Y.*

HARVEY HART, Victor, Ontario County, N. Y., eldest son of Jabish
Hart, of Kensington, Conn., and subsequently of Victor, N. Y., and
is wife, Jemima (Brace), born   , 1784, at Stockbridge,
Mass.; married   , Polly Jackson.

THEIR CHILDREN, BEING THE EIGHTH GENERATION.

74. William, born
75. John, born
76. Martha, born
77. Eunice, born
78. Chauncey, born

180.   *Victor, N. Y.*

JOHN HART, Victor, Ontario County, N. Y., second son of Jabish
Hart, of Kensington, Conn., and subsequently of Victor, N. Y., and
is wife, Jemima (Brace), born October 20th, 1789, at Victor; married
, Betsey Clyne.

185.   *Victor, N. Y.*

FREDERICK HART, Victor, Ontario County, N. Y., sixth son of Jabish
Hart, of Kensington, Conn., a parish of Berlin, and subsequently of
Victor, N. Y., and his wife, Jemima (Brace), born August 6th, 1802,
t Victor; married September 8th, 1825, Sylvia Rowley. He was a
armer, and removed to Guilford, Winnebago County, Ill., where his
hildren married, and settled each on a prairie farm. He died there
'ebruary 7th, 1865, aged 62 years, 6 months, 4 days.

THEIR CHILDREN, BEING THE EIGHTH GENERATION.

79. Sophia, born December 9th, 1827; married February 19th, 1850, Nathan
     Brown.
80. Augustus Frederick, born December 29th, 1830; married January 19th, 1853,
     Fannie J. Newton.
81. Malvina Z., born July 25th, 1832.
82. Jabez D., born November 28th, 1834; married December 10th, 1857, Charlotte
     McIntire.
83. Charlotte Eliza, born December 21st, 1837; married May 6th, 1857, George
     W. Collins.

186. *Stockbridge, Mass., Wilkesbarre, Pa.*

ISAAC HART, Washington County, Va., eldest son of Job Hart, of Victor, N. Y., and his wife, Widow Rachel (Ball), whose maiden name was Tyrrell, born December 6th, 1785, at   ; married February 12th, 1807, Abigail Stone, a sister of John S. Stone, D. D. He removed from Stockbridge, Mass., to Providence, Luzerne County, Penn., in 1812, thence to Wilkesbarre and other places in Pennsylvania until 1836, when he settled in Princeton, N. J. He removed to Carbondale, Penn., in 1841, where his wife died May 29th, 1845, aged   . She early made a profession of religion, and was through life eminent for piety. He subsequently lived with his daughter in Virginia, who was admitted to the church in Stockbridge, Mass., in 1812.

THEIR CHILDREN, BEING THE EIGHTH GENERATION.

384. Rachel Stone, born February 23d, 1808; married, November, 1825, Nathan Jackson, M. D.
385. John Seeley, born January 28th, 1810; married April 21st, 1836, Amelia C. Morford.
386. Harriet Newell, born August 2d, 1820; married July 13th, 1841, Rev. Charles Collins.
    Isaac Newton, born June 22d, 1823; died April 29th, 1824.
    Elizabeth Narcissa, born February 2d, 1828; drowned November 2d, 1829.

187. *Victor, N. Y., Providence, Penn.*

IRA HART, Victor, Ontario County, N. Y., second son of Job Hart, of Victor, N. Y., and his wife, Widow Rachel (Ball), whose maiden name was Tyrrell, born   , 1790, at   ; married   . He was admitted to the church in Stockbridge, Mass., in 1817. He went with his father, in 1819, to Providence, Luzerne County, Penn., and from thence, in 1821, to Victor, N. Y.

THEIR CHILDREN, BEING THE EIGHTH GENERATION.

387. Harriet, born
388. Isaac, born

BLY.

190. *Rensselaer County, N. Y.*

RUTH HART, a daughter of Deacon Matthew Hart, of Kensington, Conn., Fabius and Truxton, Cortland County, N. Y., and his wife, Urania (Hooker), born February 9th, 1782, at Kensington. She went with her parents to Fabius, where she married, October 25th, 1804,

William Bly, born March 2d, 1783, in Renssalaer County, N. Y.   He died February 21st, 1837, aged 54 years.   She died October 9th, 1854, aged 72 years.   They had—1, Hiram G., born September 17th, 1805; married January 29th, 1828, Phebe Keeler; he died January 12th, 1866.   2, William Hart, born October 3d, 1807; married Cynthia Keeler, who died March 4th, 1868.   He is a pattern maker, and was living in Syracuse, N. Y., in 1873.   3, Louisa, born December 14th, 1809; married 1833, J. S. Bentley.   4, Norman, born May 3d, 1812. He was teller in a bank at Elmira, and died in 1867.   5, Edwin P., born August 30th, 1819; married January, 1841, Emeline Neal.   He is a cabinet maker in Janesville, Wis., and was in the late war.   6, Benjamin F., born October 15th, 1821; married July 16th, 1845, Harriet Kemp.   He was a stair-builder in Syracuse, N. Y., in 1873.   The father and mother were both members of the Baptist Church.

191.   *De Ruyter, N. Y.*

EDMUND HART, De Ruyter, Madison County, N. Y., son of Deacon Matthew Hart, of Kensington, Conn., and Fabius, N. Y., and his wife, Urania (Hooker), born   , 1796; married August 18th, 1822, Relief Jones, a sister of Mary, who married his brother Ira.   He died about 1826, leaving a widow and two sons.

THEIR CHILDREN, BEING THE EIGHTH GENERATION.

389.   Matthew, born August 19th, 1823; married   , Mahala Jones.
390.   Charles, born, January, 1825; married   , 1848, Anna Clark.

192.   *Groton, Tompkins County, N. Y.*

IRA HART, Groton, Tompkins County, N. Y., son of Deacon Matthew Hart, of Kensington, Conn., and Fabius, N. Y., and his wife, Urania (Hooker), born October 22d, 1792, at Kensington.   He removed with his parents to the state of New York, and married, August 18th, 1822, Mary Jones.   They were residing at Groton, as above, in 1873, having lived together over fifty years, and both are members of the Congregational Church there.

THEIR CHILDREN, BEING THE EIGHTH GENERATION.

391.   Urania, born June 1st, 1824; married November 13th, 1845, Henri Bradley.
392.   William H., born August 18th, 1825; he was never married; died October 13th, 1853.   He was a farmer.
393.   Mary E., born July 20th, 1827; married January 24th, 1748, Volney Hopkins, of Groton.
394.   Ruth S., born April 23d, 1829, at Truxton.   She was never married.
395.   Oremus Ira, born April 3d, 1830; married   , Mary Hatch.
396.   James B., born October 21st, 1833.   He lives with his parents at Locke, Cayuga County, N. Y.

BONNEY.

195. *Fabius, N. Y.*

BETSEY HART, a daughter of Deacon Matthew Hart, of Kensington, Conn., and Fabius and Truxton, N. Y., and his wife, Urania (Hooker), born   , at   ; married   Bonney. This proved to be an unhappy marriage, and she returned to her father's and died.

197. *Moravia, Angelica, N. Y.*

GEORGE HART, youngest son of Deacon Matthew Hart, of Kensington, Conn., and his wife, Urania (Hooker), born November 23d, 1800, at Berlin, Conn.; married September 7th, 1825, Deborah Benjamin, born April 25th, 1803, at De Ruyter, Madison County, N. Y. She died December 6th, 1871, at Moravia, N. Y. They have had five sons, and he is living with one of them, at Angelica, in 1874. He is a harness maker by trade and occupation.

THEIR CHILDREN, BEING THE EIGHTH GENERATION.

97. Seth Percival, born June 22d, 1826, at Tully, N. Y.; married November 15th, 1853, Susan A. Engle.

98. Martin Van Buren, born September 21st, 1828, at De Ruyter; married July 31st, 1838, Anna E. Ogle.

99. Elias De Puy, born April 12th, 1832, at Venice, Cayuga County, N. Y. He is a light-house keeper at Dunkirk.

00. Edmund Benjamin, born February 24th, 1834, at Venice, N. Y. He is a harness maker at Wellsborough, Tioga County, Penn.

01. Charles Henry, born December 16th, 1836, at Venice, N. Y. He is a book-keeper at Mobile, Ala.

198. *Hempstead, L. I.*

REV. WILLIAM HENRY HART, Hempstead, L. I., eldest son of Rev. Seth Hart, of the same place, and his wife, Ruth (Hall), born January 7th, 1790, at Hempstead; married 1815, Lydia Hubbard, daughter of John Moore, Esq., of Hempstead, brother of Bishop R. C. Moore, of Virginia. She died in 1831, when second he married in 1833, Maria Graham, daughter of Dr. James G. Graham, of Shawangunk, N. Y. He was a clergyman by profession, having graduated at Columbia College in 1811. He was admitted deacon by Bishop Hobart in 1814, and in 1815 took charge of St. John's Church, Richmond Hill, Va. In 1816 he was ordained priest by Bishop Moore. In 1828 he removed to New York, and became principal of the Protestant Episcopal High School. In 1830 he accepted a call to the rectorship of St. Andrew's Church in Walden, Orange County, N. Y., where he resided in 1845.

14

402. Frances Livingston, born October 24th, 1816; married
          Rev. Clement M. Butler.
      Lydia Moore, born May 25th, 1818; died July 13th, 1819.
403. Julia Ann, born June 5th, 1820; married   , Joseph D. Evans.
404. Maria Weymouth, born November 12th, 1821.
405. Elizabeth Elliot, born September 29th, 1823.
406. Mary Anne Horne, born July 8th, 1825; married   , John W. Murrill.
407. William Henry, born January 25th, 1829.

SECOND WIFE.

408. George Graham, born June 26th, 1835.

CLOWES.

200.   *Hartwood, N. Y.*

ELIZABETH ANN HART, second daughter of Rev. Seth Hart, of Hempstead, L. I., and his wife Ruth (Hall), born May 9th, 1809, at Hempstead; married Wm. J. Clowes, Esq., Hartwood, Sullivan Co., N. Y. She died Dec. 4th, 1840, Æ. 31. They had Lydia Moore and Caroline Morgan.

201.   *Hempstead, L. I.*

BENJAMIN HALL HART, Hempstead, L. I., fourth son of Rev. Seth Hart, of the same place, and his wife Ruth (Hall), born Feb. 13th, 1811, at   . He followed the seas until Oct., 1837, when he married Elizabeth Nichols, daughter of Gideon, of Hempstead; he settled as a farmer in Manchester, Dutchess Co., N. Y.; he now, 1871, resides at Poughkeepsie, N. Y.

409. Mary Amelia, born Sept. 18th, 1838.
410. Edward Hall, born Dec. 26th, 1839.
411. Walter Nichols, born Jan. 24th, 1842.
412. Ambrose Burnham, born Jan. 25th, 1844.

203.   *Foxtown, Ohio.*

CYRUS WADSWORTH HART, Kensington, eldest son of Hon. Capt. Samuel Hart, of the same locality, and his wife Mary (Wilcox), born March 8th, 1794, at Kensington. He studied for the law, but in consequence of too close application became for a time partially insane, but recovered, and wrote books and sold them; he married March 11th, 1819, Susannah Ewing, at New Lisbon, Ohio, and settled at Foxtown, Ohio, where his last seven children were born; the first was born at New Lisbon, and the second at Salem, O. He died July 30th, 1854, Æ. 60 years.

THEIR CHILDREN, BEING THE EIGHTH GENERATION.

113. Theodore, born Dec. 5th, 1819, at New Lisbon.
114. William, born Sept. 5th, 1821, at Salem, O.
115. Harriet, born Aug. 8th, 1823.
116. Margaret Ann, born Dec. 16th, 1825, died   , in Iowa.
117. Mary, born Dec. 16th, 1827, died Aug 16th, 1854, Æ. 27.
118. Susannah, born March 21st, 1830.
119. Cyrus W., ⎱ born Jan. 20th, 1832.
120. Lucy,   ⎰ born Jan. 20th, 1832.
121. James E., born March 2d, 1835.

205.   *Kensington, Conn.*

SAMUEL HART, Kensington, second son of Hon. Capt. Samuel Hart, of the same town, and his wife Mary (Wilcox), born Aug. 9th, 1802, at Kensington, a parish of Berlin, Conn.; married Nov. 28th, 1825, Lucy, daughter of Ashbel Dickinson, and his wife Lucy (Peck), born April 5th, 1805, at Kensington. He inherits and resides on his father's old homestead, west part of Kensington, and is a wealthy farmer.

THEIR CHILDREN, BEING THE EIGHTH GENERATION.

22. Willys, born Nov. 6th, 1826, died Oct. 17th, 1848, Æ. 22 years.
23. Sherman, born Oct. 2d, 1828 ; died Sept. 19th, 1863, in Missouri, a soldier.
24. Lucy, born Dec. 13th, 1830; married, Sept. 23d, 1851, Henry R. Lyman.
     Mary Ann, born April 10th, 1834; died April 11th, 1834.
25. Mary Wilcox, born April 30th, 1835; married, Oct. 15th, 1856, Wm. Upson.
     She died. He, second, married
     Anna Eliza, born Aug. 5th, 1837 ; died March 15th, 1857, Æ. 19.
     Samuel, born Feb. 10th, 1840 ; died Sept. 11th, 1842.
26. Samuel Ashbel, born Jan. 15th, 1844.

207.   *Berlin, Conn.*

FREEDOM HART, Berlin, Conn., eldest son of Asahel Hart, the tailor, of the same town, and his wife, Abigail (Cowles), born Aug. 28th, 796, at Berlin; married,   , 1816, Eunice, daughter of David Beckley and Eunice (Williams), of Stepney, now Rocky Hill, his wife; born, March 18th, 1795. She died Aug. 31st, 1823, Æ. 28 years, in child-bed, when, second, he married, Nov. 8th, 1824, Harriet, daughter of Capt. Samuel Norton and Phebe (Edwards), his wife; born April 27th, 1796. He was by trade and occupation a comb-maker, his shop on Main street, in Berlin, on the east side just north of Galpin's store; he inherited his father's homestead, north of the shop. He died March 3d, 1862, Æ. 65 years. His widow, Harriet, died July 7th, 1863, Æ. 7 years.

427.   Julia Beckley, born June 26th, 1816; educated at Troy.
428.   William Cook, born March 13th, 1818; banker, Troy.
429.   Sarah Ann, born Feb. 5th, 1820; married,   , Harlow W. Heath.
       James, born April 1st, 1822; died Dec. 7th, 1822, (8 m.)
       Infant, born Aug. 21st, 1823; died same day.

NORTON.

210.   *Kensington, Berlin, Conn.*

Lucy Hart, Berlin, Worthington Society, eldest daughter of Jesse
Hart, of the same place, and his first wife Lucy (Beckley), born Oct.
23d, 1793, at Berlin; married, April 25th, 1819, Edward Norton, of
"Blue Hills," a locality of Kensington, and was his second wife—he,
son of Roger and his wife, Hannah (Rice). She died Oct. 21st, 1846,
Æ. 53 years. They had, first, Geo. Hart; second, Caroline Elizabeth;
third, Isaac; fourth, Emma Hart; fifth, Lucy Virginia—all baptized
in Kensington, July 17th, 1836.

211.   *Berlin, Conn.*

George Hart, Berlin, Conn., eldest son of Jesse Hart, of the same
place, and his first wife, Lucy (Beckley), born Aug. 15th, 1795, at
Berlin; married, March 29th, 1818, Caroline, daughter of David Beckley and his wife, Eunice (Williams); born Oct. 10th, 1796, at Beckley
quarter in Berlin. He was by occupation a butcher, and died Nov.
16th, 1825, Æ. 30 years, when, second, she married Sept. 12th, 1827,
Col. Wm. Buckley, of Berlin.

THE ONLY CHILD OF GEORGE AND CAROLINE, BEING THE EIGHTH GENERATION.

430. Harriet, born Oct. 27th, 1829; married, June 11th, 1844, Nathaniel Dickinson.

WILCOX.

212.   *Berlin, New Haven, Conn.*

Harriet Hart, second daughter of Jesse Hart, of Berlin, Conn.,
and his first wife Lucy (Beckley), born Sept. 22d, 1798, at Berlin, married, March 3d, 1822, Norris Wilcox, of the same place. He kept the
hotel there for a time and then removed to New Haven, where he became U. S. Collector of that port. She died June 12th, 1863, Æ. 65
years. He died,   , at New Haven, Æ.   years. They had
four children, the eldest is a midshipman in the U. States Navy.

WESTON.

213.   *Sandy Hill, N. Y.*

ELIZABETH HART, fourth daughter of Jesse Hart, of Berlin, Conn., and his first wife Lucy (Beckley), born Dec. 17th, 1806, at Berlin, she married, Aug. 17th, 1828, Frederick Weston, of Sandy Hill, Washington County, N. Y. They have had four children.

WHITE.

214.   *Danbury, Conn.*

EMMA HART, Worthington Society, in Berlin, Conn., fifth daughter of Jesse Hart, of the same locality, and his first wife, Lucy (Beckley), born Sept. 12th, 1809, at Berlin; she was educated at Troy Seminary, and became an eminent teacher there ; married, Sept. 19th, 1826, Howard H. White, of Danbury; her son Howard is the sole survivor of that branch of the family. Howard H. White, above, was a grandson of Rebecca, who was half sister of Mrs. Emma Willard the great educator.

DODD.

215.   *Hartford, Conn., Cincinnati, O.*

JANE PORTER HART, Worthington Society, in Berlin, Conn., youngest daughter of Jesse Hart, of the same place, and his second wife, Mindwell (Porter), born Dec. 1st, 1824, at Berlin; was a teacher of music and drawing at Troy Seminary,—married Feb. 7th, 1856, Wm. Dodd, of Hartford, Conn., and Cincinnati, Ohio.

WASHBURN.

216.   *Farmington, Conn., Middlebury, Vt.*

LAURA HART, Kensington, Conn., eldest daughter of Gideon Hart, of the same parish, and his wife, Cynthia (Langdon), of Jonathan, born 1787; baptized Sept. 16th, 1787; married,   , Erastus Washburn, of Farmington; born in Middletown. He died about 1817, at Farmington, leaving two sons and two daughters, when she became a matron of a Ladies' School at Middlebury, Vt., when the school failed, she married Wm. Carr, of that place, but health failing she returned to Farmington.

219.   *Madison, N. C.*

CYNTHIA LANGDON HART, Madison, N. C., fourth daughter of Gideon Hart, of Kensington, and his wife Cynthia Langdon, of Jonathan; born , 1796; baptized July 31st, 1796, by Rev. Benoni Upson, pastor

of the church in Kensington. She went South, as a teacher; is very
intelligent, and lives in Madison, N. C. She now signs her name
Olynthia L. Hart. She has literary taste, writes a beautiful letter, has
aspirations far above the common level, has made herself very useful,
is still, at this writing, 1873, living in North Carolina, unmarried.

BRAGG.

221.   *Berrien Co., Mich.*

ABIGAIL HART, Kensington, and Michigan, fifth daughter of Gideon
Hart, of Kensington, and his wife Cynthia, daughter of Jonathan
Langdon, of Kensington, and his wife Elizabeth (Edwards), born
, 1803; baptized Dec. 3d, 1803, at Kensington; married,
James Bragg, of Berrian County, Mich.

BUCKLEY,

223.   *Rocky Hill.*

NANCY HART, Rocky Hill, Conn., eldest daughter of Dea. Seth Hart,
of Kensington and Rocky Hill; and his first wife, Anna Goodrich,
born   , married Aug. 27th, 1805, Chauncey Buckley, of Rocky
Hill, Conn.

BUCKLEY.

224.   *Rocky Hill, Conn.*

ABIGAIL HART, Rocky Hill, Conn., second daughter of Dea. Seth
Hart, of Kensington, Glastonbury, and Rocky Hill, and his first wife,
Anna Goodrich, born   , married Nov. 25th, 1804, John
Buckley, of Rocky Hill, Conn.

JAGGER.

225.   *Rocky Hill, Conn.*

ROXANA HART, of Rocky Hill, Conn., third daughter of Dea. Seth,
of Kensington, Glastonbury, and Rocky Hill, and his first wife, Anna
(Goodrich), born   ; baptized Nov. 6th, 1791; married May
11th, 1808, Nathan Jagger, of Rocky Hill.

228.   *Rocky Hill, Conn., N. Y. City.*

LUCIUS HART, Rocky Hill, and New York, son of Dea. Seth Hart,
of Kensington, Glastonbury, and Rocky Hill, and his second wife who
was the widow Lydia Bull when he married her, Nov. 10th, 1799,

widow of Dr. Bull—her maiden name was Lydia Williams. His father died when he was nine years old, Lucius having been born June 14th, 1803, and baptized July 31st, 1803, at Rocky Hill, by Calvin Chapin, D. D., then pastor of that church. At the father's decease, or soon after, Dea. Oliver Hale was made his guardian, and about the first of June, 1819, he was bound an apprentice to T. D. & S. Boardman, of Hartford, to learn the *"pewterers' trade."* After he became of mature age he was sent to their branch house, in New York, and subsequently he was admitted a partner, and eventually succeeded to the whole business, importing metals, and manufacturing britannia, and other wares, until he became wealthy. He made himself very useful. He united in 1826 with Dr. Spring's church. He married at Dr. Spring's church, and before him, Hannah Robinson, of New Brunswick, N. J., date not made known by the family. He was greatly interested in Sunday Schools, had a great love of music, and was very fond of leading the children in their songs at public gatherings and anniversaries. He was an elder in a Presbyterian church some thirty-five years, and a merchant in the city of New York over forty years, and thus became wealthy. He was noted for piety and beneficence. He died at his residence on 14th street, N. Y., Feb. 11th, 1871, Æ. 67. She died Aug. 2d, 1871.

THEIR CHILDREN, BEING THE EIGHTH GENERATION.

431. Elizabeth Robinson, born   ; married   , Charles Fanning, of New York.
432. Martha A., born   • ; married   , Henry N. Beers of N. York, merchant.
433. Mary Seymour, born   ; married   , Wm. T. Booth, New York, merchant.
434. Sarah, born   ; married   , E. Cornelius Benedict, a banker, New York.
435. Lucius, born   ; married   Emilie A. Rundel, New York.

229.   *Acosto, Ohio.*

Norman Hart, Rocky Hill, Conn., Acosto, Ohio, youngest son of Dea. Seth Hart, of Kensington, Glastonbury, and Rocky Hill, and his second wife Lydia (Williams), who was widow of Dr. Bull, born   , 1805, baptized Dec. 22d, 1805, at Rocky Hill, Conn., by Calvin Chapin, D. D., pastor *then*, of that church. He removed to Acosto, Ohio, where, it is said, he had a family, but I can neither find such a place, or family.

232.   *Watertown, Ohio.*

Walter Hart, Watertown, Ohio, second son of Selah Hart, of Kensington, Conn., Marietta and other places in Ohio, and his wife, Sarah

(Waters), born Dec. 1st, 1796, probably at Watertown, O., married, May 30th, 1818, Hannah Potts. Mr. Hart is reported as being dead. All means have failed to secure the dates of birth of these children or their whereabouts, or history. The sons are said to be merchants and lawyers.

THEIR CHILDREN, BEING THE EIGHTH GENERATION.

436. Seth, b.
437. Selah, b.
438. Robert, b
439. Luther, b.
440. Oliver, b.
441. Edwin, b.
442. George, b.
443. Betsey, b.
444. Mary, b.
445. Cynthia, b.
446. Emeline, b.
447. Lucy, b.

233.   *Marion, Morgan Co., O.*

SELAH HART, Jun., Marion, Morgan Co., O., third son of Selah Hart, sen., of Kensington, Conn., Marietta and Watertown, Ohio, and his wife Sarah (Waters), born Nov. 29th, 1797, in Watertown, Washington Co., Ohio, married Feb. 23d, 1826, Mary (Thompson), daughter of Hugh, born Jan. 24th, 1802, by Geo. Corner, Justice of the Peace. He died Sept. 8th, 1870, aged 73 years, 5 months, 9 days. He was a farmer by occupation.

THEIR CHILDREN, BEING THE EIGHTH GENERATION.

448. Janet, born February 20th, 1828; married, May 31st, 1853, John Kobb.
449. Sarah, born April 25th, 1830, at   , is now, 1874, single.
450. John Thompson, born April 26th, 1832; married, March 21st, 1855, Hannah Randal.
451. Mary, born April 26th, 1834; married, March 21st, 1855, Wm. F. Randal.
452. Selah, born August 15th, 1836; married, June 24th, 1869, Rebecca Murphy.
453. Nathaniel, born February 11th, 1839; single, and a soldier in the late war.
454. Hiram, born June 12th, 1841; single, and a soldier in the late war.
455. Emma, born November 7th, 1845; married, March 21st, 1865, John W. Murphy.

234.   *Marion, Ohio.*

SETH HART, Marion, Morgan Co., Ohio, fourth son of Selah Hart, of Kensington, Conn., Marietta, Marion, Watertown, Ohio, and his wife Sarah (Waters), born Dec. 6th, 1799, at Watertown, Washington Co., Ohio, married Oct. 27th, 1825, Sally Rush, of Morgan Co., O. He died September 3d, 1865, aged 65 years, 10 months, 27 days, at Vernon Co., Wis., his wife, now a widow, still living in Muscatine Co., Iowa.

456. Nancy, born August 21st, 1826; single, 1874, living with her mother.
457. Sally Walter, born September 30th, 1827 ; married, 1854, Geo. Worrell, of Morgan Co.
458. John Rusk, born September 15th, 1832; married, 1853, Mary Ann Fell.
459. Elizabeth Ann, born August 9th, 1834; married, March 1st, 1855, Enoch Atkinson, of O. *
460. Selah, born May 27th, 1836 ; married, 1859, Elizabeth Beard.
461. Mary Rusk, born March 22d, 1838 ; married, 1859, William T. Griffith, of Iowa.
462. Seth, jun., born April 9th, 1840 ; married, May 2d, 1862, Margaret McClurg, of Wisconsin.
463. Temperance D, born April 4th, 1842; married, 1858, Nelson C. Rhodes, of Wisconsin.
464. Lucy, born April 9th, 1844 ; married, October 28th, 1860, James McClurg, of Wisconsin.
465. Emroy, born July 17th, 1850.

CANER.

235. *Watertown, Ohio.*

SALLY HART, Watertown, Washington Co., Ohio, eldest daughter of Selah, of Kensington, Conn., Marietta, Marion, and Watertown, Ohio, and his wife Sarah (Waters), born Nov. 20th, 1801, at Watertown, Washington Co., Ohio ; married , Geo. L. Caner. They had children, George, Marcus, Mary, Emily, Lucy, Eliza, Sarah, Ellen, who died, and Martha.

237. *Marion, Ohio.*

HIRAM HART, Marion, Morgan Co., Ohio, sixth son of Selah Hart, of Kensington, Conn., Marietta, Marion, and Watertown, Ohio, and his wife, Sarah (Waters), born July 1st, 1804, at Watertown, Washington Co., Ohio; married Nov. 24th, 1829, Hannah Smith, born April 1st, 1811, in Belmont Co. She died in Morgan Co., January 21st, 1863, aged 51 years, 9 months, 20 days.

466. Sarah Jane, born Nov. 12th, 1830; married, Oct. 18th, 1849, John Croy.
467. Norman, born Aug. 13th, 1833 ; married, Feb. 21st, 1863, Sarah Wollman.
468. George, born Oct. 28th, 1835 ; married, March 26th, 1865, Mary Ann Posey.
469. Martha, born Jan. 4th, 1839 ; married, Oct. 28th, 1858, Isaac A. Randall.
470. Jesse, born May 13th, 1841 ; married Nov. 14th, 1867, Rebecca Jane Moody.
471. Mary Ann, born Oct. 6th, 1843 ; married, Aug. 14th, 1864, Burgess Work.
472. Lydia, born Oct. 11th, 1845 ; married, Jan. 11th, 1863, John W. Randall.
Rebecca, born June 28th, 1849 ; died May 27th, 1857.

15

MOODY.

238. *Watertown, Ohio.*

MARY HART, Watertown, Washington Co., Ohio; third daughter of Selah Hart, of Kensington, Conn., Marietta, Marion, and Watertown, Ohio, and his wife Sarah (Waters), born May 15th, 1809, at Watertown, Ohio, married   , John Moody; they have no issue reported.

NORTON.

240. *Kensington.*

RUTH HART, Kensington, Conn., a parish of Berlin, eldest daughter of Cyprian Hart, of the same place, and his wife Lucy (Hooker), born Dec. 19th, 1797, at Kensington ; married, March 25th, 1829, Captain Albert Norton as his third wife, he son of Roger Norton, Jr., and his wife, Hannah (Rice), born March 26th, 1789, baptized May 24th, 1789, in Kensington. She was admitted to the Congregational church, Kensington, in 1822. Their children, Isabella, born Oct. 15th, 1831, died Dec. 15th, 1840, Harriet Isabel, born July 5th, 1843, living, in 1874, with her father in Blue Hills, Kensington.

MOORE.

241.

ABIGAIL HART, Kensington, Conn., a parish of Berlin, second daughter of Cyprian Hart, of the same place, and his wife Lucy (Hooker), of Elijah, Esq., born September 12th, 1799, at Kensington, and there married, March 25th, 1829, Oliver Moore, his second wife, the son of Roswell Moore, Esq., of Southington, and his wife Lovina (Phillips). They lived at the old homestead of General Selah Hart, in Kensington, where she died September 2d, 1850, aged 51 years. He died May 2d, 1871, at Kensington.

242. *Kensington, Conn.*

HENRY CYPRIAN HART, of Kensington, son of Cyprian, of the same place, and his wife Lucy (Hooker), daughter of Elijah, Esq., born Jan. 30th, 1801. He graduated at Yale College, 1822, became a physician, and practiced in Berlin, where he died Mar. 28th, 1831, aged 30 years. He was unmarried, and a physician of much promise.

PECK.

243.

LUCY HOOKER HART, Kensington, third daughter of Cyprian Hart, of the same place, and his wife Lucy, daughter of Elijah Hooker, Esq., was born Nov. 14th, 1803, at Kensington, and married there, Nov. 1st, 1826, Selden Peck, of "Blue Hills," son of Lemuel and his wife, Lydia Dickinson, born Jan. 25th, 1794, at Kensington. He was a prosperous farmer, became infirm, and late in life they removed to Meriden, where he died July 31st, 1872, aged 78 years. She also died there Nov. 12th, 1872, aged 69 years. Their children were, Sherman, Hattie G., Henry H., George Selden, and Lucy Ann.

244. *Kensington, Conn.*

EMILY HART, Kensington, youngest child of Cyprian Hart, of the same place, and his wife Lucy, daughter of Elijah Hooker, Esq., was born May 19th, 1805, at Kensington; was baptized there Nov., 1806; and there died April 30th, 1835, aged 30 years. A tombstone at the cemetery south of Berlin railroad station shows where she lies. She joined the church in Kensington, 1828. Died single.

247.

Tuscaloosa, Ala., Selada, Bell Co., Texas.

VELINA HART, Tuscaloosa, Ala., second son of Stephen Hurlburt Hart, of Winsted, Conn., Litchfield, and other localities, and his wife, Lucinda (Cook), daughter of Amos, of Wallingford, and wife Hosford, was born Oct. 19th, 1795, at Wallingford. He married, 1821, Elizabeth Stephens, of N. C., born there Jan. 31st, 1801, and they had nine children. He died Oct. 19th, 1867, aged 72 years, at Tuscaloosa, Ala. He was by trade and occupation a *tinner*. The widow Elizabeth lives (1874) at Selada, Bell Co., Texas.

THEIR CHILDREN, BEING THE EIGHTH GENERATION.

473. William, born   , 1823, in Blunt Co., Ala., died 1844. An engineer. No family.

474. Stephen Hurlburt, born Dec.   , 1825, married Dec. 25th, 1848, Sarah C. McCullough.

475. Lucinda Ann, born April 15th, 1827, married,   , John Parker. Russell, born 1831, died 1837.

476. Richard B., born Aug. 15th, 1829, married, Jan. 3d, 1857, Texanna Purdy.

477. Henry A., born July 4th, 1833, died Jan. 10th, 1874, at Salada, Tex. A tinner.

Infant, born , died nine days old.

478. Cornelia Ann, born Nov. 30th, 1837, married John Nix, who died; married, second, Robert L. Quinn.

479. Henrietta V., born Feb. 14th, 1842, married, Dec. 24th, 1866, James K. Quinn. Live in Texas.

GRISWOLD.

248. *Bristol, Conn.*

LUCY HOOKER HART, eldest daughter of Stephen Hurlburt Hart, of Litchfield, and Winsted, Conn., and his wife, Lucinda (Cook), sister of John, Sr., of Plainville, was born Jan. 26th, 1799. She married, Oct. 26th, 1817, Leonard R. Griswold, of Bristol, Conn., and they had four children; only one, Henry, survives (1874).

249. *New Haven, Conn.*

ROSWELL COOK HART, New Haven, Ct., third son of Stephen Hurlburt Hart, of Litchfield, Harwinton, and Winsted, Conn., and his wife, Lucinda (Cook), was born July 20th, 1801. He married, March 11th, 1827, Polly Grant, of , born . They reside in New Haven, Conn., where he keeps a hotel. They have no children.

HUNGERFORD.

250. *Wolcottville, Conn., St. Louis, Mo.*

LUCINDA HART, of Winsted, second daughter of Stephen Hurlburt Hart, of Litchfield, Harwinton, and Winsted, and his wife, Lucinda (Cook), sister of John, Sr., of Plainville, Conn., was born Feb. 2d, 1804. She married, July 23d, , Wm. S. Hungerford, a merchant of Wolcottville, Conn., and St. Louis, Mo. They have four children, viz.: Adelaide, born March 15th, 1828; Sarah S., born April 25th, 1830; Arthur P., born March 10th, 1834; Jane E., born May 12th, 1838. Sarah Sophia, married, , James Brown, a native of New Jersey.

BOWDITCH.

251. *Waterbury, Conn.*

SOPHIA COOK HART, Waterbury, Conn., fourth daughter of Stephen Hurlburt Hart, of Winsted, and his wife Lucinda, daughter of Amos Cook, of Wallingford, and his wife, Horseford, was born Sept. 4th, 1809, and she married, April 26th, 1852, George Henry Blunt Bowditch, born at Salem, Mass.,—living now (1874) at Waterbury, Conn.

253. *Parishville, N. Y.*

TRUMAN HART, New Britain, eldest son of Cyprian Hart, of the same place, and his wife Olive (Wheadon), was born June 11th, 1793, at New Britain. He married, July 4th, 1815, Laura Lewis Steele, daughter of Josiah Steele, Jr., and his wife, Prudence Kilbourn, born Nov. 25th, 1798, at New Britain. Mr. Hart was a blacksmith by trade, tall and erect, and very active; carried on ax-making in Burlington, Ct., for a time. They removed to Parishville, St. Lawrence Co., N. Y., where she died Dec. 20th, 1865, aged 67 years.

THEIR CHILDREN, BEING THE EIGHTH GENERATION.

480. Walter S., born April 13th, 1816, at   , married, Nov. 4th, 1841, Lucy D. Allen.
481. Ordelia, born Sept. 24th, 1817, at New Britain, Conn.; died Oct. 3d, 1817, at New Britain.
Harriet, born March 25th, 1819, died Oct. 22d, 1828.
482. George L., born Oct. 1st, 1822, married Sept. 16th, 1851, Ann M. Bigelow.
483. William W., born June 29th, 1832, married, Feb. 23d, 1860, Laura M. Hoyt.

255.
New Britain, Conn., Parishville, N. Y.

BERA HART, New Britain, Conn., third son of Cyprian, of Kensington, and New Britain, and his wife, Olive Wheadon, was born March 31st, 1797, at New Britian, and learned his trade of clothier there of Moses D. Seymour. He married, May 6th, 1819, Mary Whaples, daughter of Samuel, and Huldah Langdon, his wife, born May 3d, 1797, at New Britain. He removed with his parents and family to Parishville, St. Lawrence Co., N. Y., where he died Mar. 11th, 1872, aged 75 years.

THEIR CHILDREN, BEING THE EIGHTH GENERATION.

484. George, born March 10th, 1821, married, May 4th, 1859, Caroline Harriman.
485. Henry, born July 29th, 1822, married, Nov. 7th, 1843, Elinda Morgan.
486. Nancy, born May 13th, 1824, married, Nov. 29th, 1842, Lewis Allen.
487. James L., born Jan. 20th, 1826, in Parishville, died there Aug. 26th, 1862, aged 36 years.
488. Lucy, born Nov. 3d, 1828, married, March 19th, 1847, Alden Morgan.
489. Samuel, born June 14th, 1830, married, March 27th, 1851, Helen Harriman.
Bera,) Died Feb. 25th, 1843, in 10th year.
 } twins, born Sept. 19th, 1833, at Parishville.
Mary,) Died May 25th, 1850, in 17th year.

257. *New Britain, Ct., Hubbardston, Vt.*

LEANDER SIDNEY HART, New Britain, fifth son of Cyprian Hart, of New Britain, Conn., and his wife Olive (Wheadon), was born Aug.

10th, 1801, at New Britain. He married, Aug. 23d, 1824, Emeline,
daughter of Moses Thompson and his wife Susan (Steele), born Dec.
12th, 1803, and baptized April 15th, 1804, at New Britain. She died
at Hubbardston, Vt., Nov. 1st, 1840, when, second, he married Electa
Humphrey, of Burlington, Conn., daughter of Solomon, and sister of
Rev. Heman Humphrey. No children reported of this family.

FANNING.

431.   *New York City.*

ELIZABETH ROBINSON HART, of New York, eldest daughter of Lucius
Hart, of the same city, and his wife, Hannah (Robinson), born
       ; married   Charles Fanning, of New York City, of the
firm of Lucius Hart & Co., importers of various choice metals, and
manufacturers of Britannia ware, and other metals.

BEERS.

432.   *New York City.*

MARTHA A. HART, New York, second daughter of Lucius Hart, of
Rocky Hill, Conn., and New York City, and his wife, Hannah (Robin-
son), born   ; married   , Henry N. Beers, of New
York, a merchant.

BOOTH.

433.   *New York City.*

MARY SEYMOUR HART, New York, third daughter of Lucius Hart, of
Rocky Hill, Conn., and subsequently a merchant of New York City,
and his wife, Hannah (Robinson), born   ; married   ,
Wm. T. Booth, a merchant of New York City.

BENEDICT.

434.   *New York City.*

SARAH HART, New York, fourth daughter of Lucius Hart, of Rocky
Hill, Conn., and subsequently a merchant of New York City, and his
wife, Hannah (Robinson), born   ; married   , E.
Cornelius Benedict, a banker of New York City.

435.   *New York City.*

LUCIUS HART, New York City, only son of Lucius Hart, of Rocky
Hill and New York, and his wife, Hannah (Robinson). He was admitted a partner with his father in his extensive business, at No. 8 and

10, Burling Slip, in manufacturing britannia, and other wares, and in importing various metals from Europe.   The firm became wealthy, even before the father's death, and is still, 1873, continued under the name of Lucius Hart & Co.   The partners being Chas. Fanning and Lucius Hart,—this son married Emilie A. Randel, and all the family are living and have families in New York City, but decline giving dates of birth, marriage, or children.

KOBB.

448.   *Missouri.*

JANE HART, eldest daughter of Selah Hart of Marion, Morgan Co., Ohio, and his wife Mary, daughter of Hugh (Thompson), of the same County; born Feb. 20th, 1828, in Morgan Co., O.; married May 31st., 1853, John Kobb, before Justice Wm. M. Fergenson; he was born Sept. 19th, 1829; is a farmer in Missouri. They had Wm. A., born April 19th, 1855; second, Emma J., born Feb. 2d, 1857; third, Lemnos Selah, born Dec. 20th, 1859; fourth, Mary A., born April 9th, 1861; fifth, Hiram E. E., born Sept. 29th, 1863; sixth, Sarah Ellen Kobb, born Nov. 7th, 1866; seventh, Ida Bell Kobb, born Jan. 6th, 1870. Hiram E. E. died Aug 14th, 1871—by wagon running over his chest, Aug. 12th, 1871.

450.   *Morgan Co., O.*

JOHN THOMPSON HART, Marion, and Huffman P. O., Morgan Co., O., eldest son of Selah Hart, of the same town and county, and his wife, Mary (Thompson), born April 26th, 1832, at Marion; married before Justice Joseph Mendenhall, March 21st, 1855, Hannah Randal; born Oct. 25th, 1830; occupation, farming; he has my thanks for help in forwarding a copy of his father's family record.

THEIR CHILDREN, BEING THE NINTH GENERATION.

Nathaniel, born Jan. 1st, 1857.
' Sarah Ellen, born Aug. 28th, 1858.
Hiram, born July 4th, 1865.

KENDALL.

451.   *Residence not reported.*

MARY HART, third daughter of Selah Hart, of Marion, Morgan Co., O., and his wife Mary, daughter of Hugh (Thompson), born April 26th, 1834, at Marion; married, March 21st, 1855, at her father's residence in Morgan Co., before Justice Joseph Mendenhall.   Wm. F. Kendall, born Oct. 24th, 1834. They had, first, Mary Ellen, born Jan. 12th, 1856; second, Chas. H., born Nov. 7th, 1858. Mary Ellen, died July 31st, 1865.

452.   *Marion, O.*

SELAH HART, second son of Selah Hart, of Morgan Co., O., and his wife, Mary (Thompson), born Aug. 15th, 1836, at Marion; married, June 24th, 1869, at Chester Hill, Morgan Co., O., before Justice Watson Harris, Rebecca Murphy, born March 13th, 1841. He is a farmer by occupation.

THEIR CHILDREN, BEING THE NINTH GENERATION.

Mary, born June 2d, 1870.
Sarah E., born Nov. 29th, 1871.
Anna, born Feb. 7th, 1873.

453.   *Marion, Ohio.*

NATHANIEL HART, Morgan County, Ohio, third son of Selah Hart, of the same county and state, and his wife, Mary, daughter of Hugh Thompson, born February 11th, 1839, at Marion. He was mustered into the United States service in the late war, September 2d, 1862, in the Ninety-Seventh Regiment Ohio Volunteers, and was wounded at Atlanta, Geo., but soon recovered, and was again wounded at Franklin Seminary, November 30th, 1864, and died there January 3d, 1865.

454.   *Marion, Ohio.*

HIRAM HART, Morgan County, Ohio, fourth son of Selah Hart, of the same town, county, and state, and his wife, Mary (Thompson), born June 12th, 1841, in Marion. He entered the United States service September 2d, 1862, in the Ninety-Seventh Regiment Ohio Volunteers, and was wounded at Missionary Ridge, November 25th, 1863, and died October 4th, 1864, at his father's residence. He was a farmer by occupation.

MURPHY.

455.

EMMA HART, youngest daughter and child of Selah Hart, of Morgan County, Ohio, and his wife, Mary (Thompson), born November 7th, 1845, at Marion; married March 21st, 1865, at her father's residence, before Rev. Daniel Rickatts, John W. Murphy, who was born March 25th, 1838, and is a farmer. They had—1, Augusta Jane, born March

19th, 1868; 2, James Emmet, born August 2d, 1869; 3, Mary Leona, born May 3d, 1871; 4, Sarah Blanch, born October 20th, 1872; 5, Selah Hart, born May 9th, 1873. Mary Leona died October 1st, 1871.

WORRELL.

457. *Morgan County, Ohio.*

SALLY WALTER HART, second daughter of Seth Hart, of Morgan County, Ohio, and his wife, Sally (Rush), born September 30th, 1827, in Morgan County, Ohio; married , 1854, George Worrell, of the same county. They had—1, Jerome, born April 21st, 1855; 2, Frank V., born April 3d, 1858, in Iowa, and died July 18th, 1858; 3, Emma D., born January 25th, 1867, at Atalissa, Iowa; 4, George S., born September 1st, 1870, at Atalissa, Iowa.

458. *Osage County, Kan.*

JOHN RUSH HART, Osage County, Kan., eldest son of Seth Hart, of Morgan County, Ohio, and his wife, Sally (Rush), born September 15th, 1832, in Morgan County, Ohio; married , 1853, Mary Ann Fell, of the same county and state. They removed to Osage County, Kan., about 1862.

THEIR CHILDREN, BEING THE NINTH GENERATION.

490. Sarah Ann, born, December, 1855, in Ohio.
491. Ella Jane, born , 1857, in Ohio.
492. Seth Sherman, born , 1861, in Ohio.
493. Emma, born , at Osage County, Kansas.

ATKINSON.

459. *Morgan County, Ohio.*

ELIZABETH ANN HART, third daughter of Seth Hart, of Morgan County, Ohio, and his wife, Sally (Rush), born August 9th, 1834, at Morgan County, Ohio; married March 1st, 1855, Enoch Atkinson, of the same county and state. They had—1, Ann W., born January 8th, 1856; 2, Francelia, born March 6th, 1858; 3, Sarah E., born March 14th, 1860; 4, Matilda W., born September 6th, 1862; 5, Lucy H., born March 2d, 1869.

460. *Vernon County, Wis.*

SELAH HART, Vernon County, Wis., second son of Seth Hart, of Morgan County, Ohio, and his wife, Sally (Rush), born May 27th, 1836, in Morgan County; married, 1859, at Vernon County, Wis., Elizabeth

16

Beard, of that place. He died February 9th, 1862, aged 25 years, 8 months, 12 days, leaving no children.

GRIFFITH.

461.   *Atalissa, Iowa.*

MARY RUSH HART, fourth daughter of Seth Hart, of Morgan County, Ohio, and his wife, Sally (Rush), born March 22d, 1838, in Morgan County, Ohio; married in the fall of 1859, at Atalissa, Iowa, William T. Griffith, of that place. She died May 28th, 1866, aged 28 years, 2 months, 6 days. They had—1, Bell, born 1860, died 1861; 2, Sarah W., born 1862; 3, Mary E., born 1866, and died in 1866, at Atalissa, Iowa.

462.   *Vernon County, Wis.*

SETH HART, Jr., Vernon County, Wis., third son of Seth Hart, Sr., of Morgan County, Ohio, and his wife, Sally (Rush), born April 9th, 1840, in Morgan County, Ohio. He went to Vernon County, Wis., where he married May 2d, 1862, Margaret McClurg.

THEIR CHILDREN, BEING THE NINTH GENERATION.

494. Eleanor, born, February, 1863, at Vernon County, Wis.
495. John M., born, March, 1866, at Vernon County, Wis.
    Mary B., born, June, 1865, and died the same year.
496. Elizabeth, born   , 1868, at Vernon County, Wis.
497. Kitty, born   , 1870, at Vernon County, Wis.

RHODES.

463.   *Vernon County, Wis.*

TEMPERANCE D. HART, fifth daughter of Seth Hart, of Morgan County, Ohio, and his wife, Sally (Rush), born April 4th, 1842, in Morgan; married, 1858, Nelson T. Rhodes, of Vernon County, Wis. She died November 30th, 1864. They had—1, Mary A., born June 28th, 1860, and was killed in a storm, June 28th, 1865, while attending school; 2, Frank M. Rhodes, born June 6th, 1861, at Vernon, Wis.

McCLURG.

464.   *Vernon County, Wis.*

LUCY HART, sixth daughter of Seth Hart, of Morgan County, Ohio, and his wife, Sally (Rush), born April 9th, 1844, at Morgan County, Ohio; married October 28th, 1860, James McClurg, of Vernon County, Wis. He died May 19th, 1865, a soldier in the late war, and was buried on David's Island, N. Y. He left issue—1, Myra, 2, Mary, twins, born May 3d, 1862; 3, Sarah Laretta McClurg, born January 6th, 1864, when the mother married September 30th, 1870, Joseph Barkhurst. They had—1, John C., born January 24th, 1871; 2, Alice C., born April 4th, 1872.

CROY.

466. *Elliott's X Roads, Ohio.*

SARAH JANE HART, eldest daughter of Hiram Hart, of Washington County, Ohio, and his wife, Hannah (Smith), born November 12th, 1830, at Washington County, Ohio; married October 18th, 1849, John Croy, born September 11th, 1828, at Coshocton County, Ohio. He is a farmer, and resides at Elliott's X Roads, Morgan County, Ohio. They had—1, Richard M., born July 18th, 1850; 2, Hiram H., born April 21st, 1858. Richard M. married August 20th, 1873, Sarah E. J. Steffy, born August 11th, 1855. They reside at Elliott's X Roads, Morgan County, Ohio.

467. *Pennsville, Morgan County, O.*

NORMAN HART, Pennsville, Morgan County, Ohio, eldest son of Hiram Hart, of Washington County, Ohio, and his wife, Hannah (Smith), born August 13th, 1833, in Morgan County, Ohio; married February 21st, 1863, Sarah Woolman, of the same county and state, born January 9th, 1842, in Morgan County. He is a farmer, and his post-office address is at Pennsville. The Harts are greatly indebted to him for gathering and forwarding statistics of the descendants of Selah Hart, Sr., of Kensington, Conn., and Watertown, Ohio, and grandfather of Norman.

THEIR CHILDREN, BEING THE NINTH GENERATION, BORN IN MORGAN COUNTY.

498. Rebecca Jane, born February 20th, 1864.
499. Annie Mary, born November 26th, 1867.
500. Ada May, born September 25th, 1870.
501. Rose Emma, born March 9th, 1872.

468. *Elliott's X Roads, O.*

GEORGE HART, Elliott's X Roads, Morgan County, Ohio, second son of Hiram Hart of the same county and state, and his wife, Hannah (Smith), born October 28th, 1835, in Morgan County; married March 26th, 1865, Mary Ann Posey, born January 25th, 1841. He is a farmer.

THEIR CHILD, BEING THE NINTH GENERATION.

502. Ella Jane, born January 19th, 1866, in Morgan County.

RANDALL.

469.   *Chester Hill, O.*

MARTHA HART, second daughter of Hiram Hart, of Washington
County, Ohio, and his wife, Hannah (Smith), born January 4th, 1839,
in Morgan County, Ohio; married October 28th, 1858, at Morgan
County, Isaac A. Randall, born May 16th, 1837. He is a farmer, and
lives at Chester Hill, Ohio. They have had—1, Rudolph, born November 11th, 1859; 2, Hannah J., born March 2d, 1863; 3, Hiram,
born June 2d, 1864; 4, Eleanor, born July 4th, 1867; 5, John, born
November 1st, 1870.

470.   *Elliott's X Roads, O.*

JESSE HART, Elliott's X Roads, Morgan County, Ohio, third son of
Hiram Hart, of Washington County, and his wife, Hannah (Smith),
born May 13th, 1841, in Morgan County; married November 14th,
1867, Rebecca Jane Moody, of the same county and state, born April
2d, 1845, in Morgan County. She died February 24th, 1872, in Morgan County, aged 26 years, 10 months, 22 days. He is a farmer.

THEIR CHILDREN, BEING THE NINTH GENERATION.

503. Ida May, born September 28th, 1868, in Morgan County, Ohio.
504. Sarah Jane, born June 24th, 1870, in Morgan County, Ohio.
505. Grant, born January 29th, 1872, in Morgan County, Ohio.

WORK.

471.   *Athens Co., Ohio.*

MARY ANN HART, third daughter of Hiram Hart, of Washington
Co., O., and his wife Hannah (Smith), was born Oct. 6, 1843, in Mor-
gan Co. She married, Aug. 14th, 1864, Burgess Work, of Athens
Co., Ohio, born there June 7th, 1841. They had, 1, Mary F., born
May 13th, 1865, in Athens Co., Ohio; 2, Alice, born Jan. 14th, 1871,
died Oct., 1871, in Athens Co.

RANDALL.

472.   *Morgan Co., Ohio.*

LYDIA HART, fourth daughter of Hiram Hart, of Washington Co.,
Ohio, and his wife Hannah (Smith), was born Oct. 11th, 1845, in Morgan Co. She married, Jan. 11th, 1863, John W. Randall, born Oct.
18th, 1843, in the state of Maryland. Their children were, 1, Annie,
born Nov. 6th, 1871; 2, Mary, born Feb. 20th, 1874, in Morgan Co.,
where they reside.

GOODRICH.

258. *Farmington, Conn.*

AzUBA HART, eldest daughter of Roger Hart, of New Britain, and his first wife Sibil (Robinson), was born July 7th, 1789, at New Britain. She married, Dec. 13th, 1807, Allen Goodrich, of Farmington, son of Elias. She died April 15th, 1817, aged 28 years, at New Britain, Conn.

. PENNFIELD. .

259. *New Britain, Conn.*

BETSEY HART, New Britain, second daughter of Roger Hart, of the same place, and his first wife Sibil (Robinson), born Sept. 17th, 1791, at New Britian. She married, March 12th, 1815, John, son of Nath'l Pennfield, of same place, and his wife Eunice (Kelsey), born Oct. 18th, 1791, at New Britain. He was a cooper and farmer, and lived on the place just west of his father's, built for his brother Silas, who died. He lost one leg by the fall of a tree. He was admitted to the Congregational church, in New Britain, Feb. 2d, 1812, and subsequently, about 1830, joined the Methodist church with his wife. She died of cancer Oct. 21st, 1849, aged 58 years; he died July 15th, 1846, aged 55 years—both remarkably devout Christians. They had, 1, Eliza Ann, born Jan. 16th, 1816; 2, Jane Maria, born Sept. 25th, 1818, married, Aug. 28th, 1842, George Williams; 3, Burnham Hart, born April 2d, 1824, married, May 10th, 1846, Annette Judd; 4, Chester, born, Aug. 21st, 1831, married, Dec. 22d, 1850, Sarah Hamilton, of Hartford.

COOK.

260. *Farmington, Conn.*

POLLY HART, New Britain, Conn., third daughter of Roger Hart, of the same place, and his first wife Sibil (Robinson), of Middletown, was born June 5th, 1793, at New Britain. She married, Nov. 27th, 1828, Geo., son of John Cook, of Farmington, and his wife Lucina (Lewis), born March 13th, 1788, at White Oak in Farmington. He was a *nice* farmer, a man of kind impulses and excellent understanding, and resided at the old and noted tavern stand of his father. He died Sept. 8th, 1864, aged 76 years; she died Jan. 27th, 1866, aged 73 years—was a faithful wife and kind mother. They left one son, George (1874), single, and one daughter, Mary, who married Mr. West, Yonkers.

261. *Hartford, Conn., Philadelphia, Pa.*

CHAUNCEY HART, New Britain, eldest son of Roger Hart, of same place, and his first wife Sibil (Robinson), was born Oct. 5th, 1795, at New Britain, and married, May 3d, 1821, Polly Markum, daughter of Isaac, of New Hartford, and his wife Rachel (Boardman), of West Society, Middletown, born Oct. 1st, 1801. He is a carriage-maker, and lives on Windsor street, Hartford. His wife learned to be a tailoress of Jerusha Mather, of New Britain, Conn., but (1874) lives in Philadelphia, as does also his son, Emery Hart.

THEIR CHILDREN, BEING THE NINTH GENERATION.

Margaret Ann, born May 9th, 1825, died   , at   , aged 17 months.

506. Emery Curtis, born Nov. 11th, 1827, married,   , Louisa Warren, of Glastonbury.

507. Mary, born Aug. 6th, 1830, married, Dec. 1st, 1851, Samuel Dunlop, of Hartford, Conn. Went South.

262.   *New Haven, Conn.*

JOHN HART, New Britain, second son of Roger Hart, of same place, and his first wife Sibil (Robinson), was born   , 1796, at New Britain, and married,   , Polly Stephens, of New Haven. He is a cabinet-maker by trade and occupation.

THEIR CHILDREN, BEING THE NINTH GENERATION.

508. Henry, born

509. Mary Ann, born

264.   *Plymouth, Mich.*

ROSWELL HART, New Britain, third son of Roger Hart of the same place, and his first wife, Sibil (Robinson), was born Sept. 1st, 1802, at New Britain, and married, Feb. 12th, 1826, Eliza Steele, daughter of Ebenezer, and his second wife Hannah (Brewer), born Sept. 27th, 1802, at New Britain. He learned harness-making of Bodwell, of Farmington, and lived in Plymouth, Mich.

265. *Shiawassee, Mich., New Britain, Ct.*

WILLIAM STRICKLAND HART, New Britain, fourth son of Roger Hart, of same place, and his first wife Sibil (Robinson), was born Oct. 14th, 1805, at New Britain. He married, Aug. 30th, 1827, Sarah, daughter of Theodore Barnes and his wife Hannah (Bartlett), who died March 24th, 1858, of cancer; when, second, he married, Sept.

19th, 1859, at Hartford, widow Harriet Daggett, daughter of Rev. Benj. Graves, of Middletown, and widow of Isaiah Daggett, of Andover, Conn. Mr. Hart was a shoe-maker by trade.

THE CHILDREN BY FIRST MARRIAGE, BEING THE NINTH GENERATION.

510. Henry Augustus, born April 15th, 1829, married, Nov. 4th, 1857, Lavinia Warren, of Michigan.
511. George Washington, born Aug. 30th, 1831, married, Nov. 4th, 1855, Philanda Ellsworth, of Michigan.
512. Charles Burnham, born June 16th, 1835, died Jan.   , 1855, at Shiawassee, Mich.
    William F., born May 27th, 1834, died July 2d, 1836, in Michigan.
    Mary Jane, born March 22d, 1840, died Aug. 22d, 1845, at Shiawassee, Mich.
513. Sarah Ann, born June 23d, 1842, at Shiawassee, Mich.
514. Martha Ann, born June 2d, 1843, married, about 1862, Alonzo Johnson, of Michigan.
515. Emily Davis, born Feb. 16th, 1846, married, about 1864, John Riley.
    John A., born Aug. 2d, 1851, died Jan. 12th, 1852.

HART. BUTLER.

267.

ORPHA HART, New Britan, second daughter of Salmon Hart, of same place, and his first wife Sarah (Goodrich), was born April 2d, 1800, at New Britain, and married, May 2d, 1820, Ira, son of Dea. Elijah Hart and his wife Anna (Andrews), born July 22d, 1798. He died Dec. 1st, 1824, aged 26 years, when, second, she married, May 2d, 1835, Horace Butler, son of Moses, of East Hartford, and his wife Elizabeth (Forbes), born Feb. 4th, 1789. She, his second wife, was a chair-maker by trade. He became an extensive manufacturer of plated goods in New Britain in company with his sons. She was admitted to the Congregational church, New Britain, Aug. 5th, 1821, when wife of Ira Hart. Had no children.

HAMBLIN.

268. *Bristol, Conn., Whitestown, N. Y.*

LAVINIA HART, New Britain, third daughter of Salmon Hart, of the same place, and his first wife Sarah (Goodrich), was born Sept. 1st, 1802, at New Britain, and married, Dec. 9th, 1824, Samuel Andrews Hamblin, son of John, of "White Oak," in Farmington, and his wife, Eunice Eddy, widow of Samuel Andrews, born April 11th, 1803. He was a carriage-maker, lived in Bristol, and removed to Whitestown, N. Y. He died May 9th, 1871, at New Woodstock, Madison Co., N. Y. She died at Morrisville, same county, April 9th, 1866, in her 64th year. Had two sons.

DUNHAM.

269. *Hartford, New Britain, Conn.*

SOPHIA HART, New Britain, fourth daughter of Salmon Hart, of the same place, and his first wife Sarah (Goodrich), was born Nov. 18th, 1806, at New Britain, and married, July 3d, 1826, Ralph Ives Dunham, son of Elisha, of Berlin, born Dec. 10th, 1801. He is a harness-maker, learned of Moses Beckley at New Britain; worked for Norman Warner, and went into carriage-making with Salmon N. Hart, his brother-in-law, at Hartford. He went to Natchez, Miss., to sell work and there died Nov. 9th, 1833, aged 33 years. She was admitted to the Congregational church, New Britain, Oct. 7th, 1821; was a sabbath-school scholar (1816), and could repeat one thousand verses of Scripture per week. She died Nov. 6th, 1870, aged 64 years, at New Britain. Their children were, 1, Sarah Elizabeth, born July 8th, 1830, died April 14th, 1836; 2, Helen Sophia, born July 4th, 1833, died Aug. 2d, 1835.

270. *Hartford, Conn.*

SALMON NORTH HART, New Britain and Hartford, only son of his father, Salmon Hart, of New Britain, and his first wife Sarah (Goodrich), was born June 18th, 1811, at New Britain, and married May 3d, 1832, Martha Corning, of Hartford, Conn., born April 19th, 1819, and died June 5th, 1846, when he, second, married Dec. 14th, 1846, Joanna F. Gardner, daughter of Ebenezer, of Norwich, Conn., and his wife Matilda D. (Welch), of Colchester, born Jan. 1st, 1820, at Bozrah, Conn. He is a carriage-maker, learned of Mr. Wing, of Hartford. Now (1874) resides at No. 101 Ann street, Hartford, where he owns a fine brick house, and his carriage factory on Albany turnpike. He and both wives were members of Dr. Bushnell's church.

HIS CHILDREN, BEING THE NINTH GENERATION.

517.   Charles Remington, born July 22d, 1837, married, June 15th, 1869, Ella Gardner.
518.   Alfred Dwight, born Sept. 13th, 1840, married, April 18th, 1866, Sarah Daniels.
        Edward Frederick, born Nov. 15th, 1844, died Sept. 23d, 1869.

HIS CHILDREN BY THE SECOND MARRIAGE.

519.   Edward Gardner, born Oct. 9th, 1852.
        Henry North,   ⎫   died May 24th, 1857.
                          ⎬ born November 29th, 1855;
        Martha Fellowes, ⎭   died August 21st, 1856.
520.   Henry Helmer, born November 20th, 1859.

271. *New Britain, New Haven, Conn.*

SILAS WILLIAMS HART, New Britain, second son of Salmon Hart, of New Britain, and his second wife, who was Rosetta North, widow of Elisha Williams, and daughter of Seth North, of Berlin, born September 12th, 1818, at New Britain, Conn.; married November 24th, 1846, Abigail Merwin, of New Haven, where they reside. He is a carriage trimmer. They have no children except one by adoption.

272. *New Britain, Conn.*

CAPTAIN FREDERICK WOODFORD HART, New Britain, third son of Salmon Hart, of New Britain, and his second wife, Rosetta North (Williams), born November 19th, 1822, at New Britain. He learned the jeweler's trade of Wilcox, of New Haven. He married June 2d, 1857, Jennie, daughter of William Bassett, of New Britain, and his first wife, Polly (Judd), born December 10th, 1832. He was captain of Company G, First Regiment Connecticut Volunteers, in the late war. He is an insurance agent in 1874, and is living on West Main Street, New Britain.

THEIR CHILDREN, BEING THE NINTH GENERATION.

520. Frederick Dwight, born February 27th, 1860, at New Britain.
521. Louis Elmore, born June 27th, 1869, at New Britain.

JOHNSON.

273. *Lagrange, Ohio.*

MARY RILEY HART, eldest child of Judah Hart, of New Britain and Norwich, Conn., and Brownhelm, Lorain County, Ohio, and his wife, Abigail (Belden), born June 29th, 1801, at Middletown, Conn. She went with her parents to Brownhelm, Ohio. She married, August 13th, 1846, at Elyria, Ohio, Nathan Porter Johnson, of Hartford, Washington County, N. Y., born January 30th, 1801. They are living, in 1874, at Lagrange, Lorain County, Ohio, where he has been postmaster for the last thirteen years. He was representative in the Ohio legislature four sessions. They have no children.

274. *Brownhelm, Ohio.*

JUDAH BELDEN HART, Brownhelm, Lorain County, Ohio, eldest son of Judah, and Abigail (Belden), his wife, born November 16th, 1802, at New Britain, Conn.; married May 3d, 1825, Sarah T. Jones, who died September 25th, 1835, when second he married   , 1837, Rebecca Smith. He was a farmer in the county of Richland, Ohio,

17

and both were members of the Methodist Church. He died in Michigan, September 18th, 1864, aged 62 years.

520. Henry William, born, February, 1826; married　　　　　　, Caroline Cottrell.
521. James Brown, born January 28th, 1828; married　　　　　, Kate Cottrell.
522. Edward, } born April 15th, 1830;　　married　　　　, Susan Place.
　　　Edwin, }
523. Harriet Ann, born June 4th, 1834; married November 6th, 1852, Elmer D. Bebee.

Lucinda, born, October, 1839.

Child, born

275.　　　　　　*Brownhelm, Ohio.*

HENRY HART, Brownhelm and Elyria, Lorain County, Ohio, second son of Judah Hart, of New Britain, Norwich, and Middletown, Conn., and his wife, Abigail (Belden), born February 17th, 1805, at Norwich; married March 24th, 1830, Sarah S. Shepherd, born August 22d, 1808. He was a carpenter and joiner by trade, and resided at Brownhelm, Ohio, and at Elyria in 1854. He died December 14th, 1860, aged 55 years. She died May 29th, 1864, aged 56 years.

524. Henrietta, born December 27th, 1830; married November 25th, 1848, Chester Curtice.
525. Eliza, born October 8th, 1832; married August 24th, 1850, William Moulton. Levi Shepard, born June 29th, 1836; died November 9th, 1836.
526. Harriet Sophia, born January 2d, 1838; married January 1st, 1862, T. B. Rogers.

Adalaide, born November 20th, 1840; died October 2d, 1841.

527. Sarah Adalaide, born April 17th, 1844; married December 22d, 1872, William H. Fee, of Colorado.
528. Abigail Belden, born November 1st, 1845; married December 1st, Winton Smith, of Colorado.
529. Emma L., born March 18th, 1851; married December 23d, 1873, Charles S. Hill, of Colorado.

276.　　　　　　*Depere, Wis.*

EDWIN HART, Depere, Brown County, Wis., third son of Judah Hart, of Middletown and Norwich, Conn., and Brownhelm, Ohio, and his wife, Abigail (Belden), born May 5th, 1807, at Norwich, Conn.; married April 29th, 1832, Eliza G. Glass. Both are members of the Methodist Church.

George Edwin, born November 28th, 1833.

Levi, born December 22d, 1835.

530. Mary Abigail, born November 22d, 1837; married , Dr. Colman.

531. Clifford Belden, born, November, 1839.

532. Eliza Jane, born ' , 1841; married , Brown, Esq.

BROOKS.

277. *Elyria, Ohio.*

ABIGAIL HART, Elyria, Ohio, second daughter of Judah Hart, of Middletown and Norwich, Conn., and Brownhelm, Ohio, and his wife, Abigail (Belden), born March 25th, 1809, at Norwich, Conn.; married November 6th, 1832, Henry J. Brooks. They reside in Elyria, Ohio, and both are members of the Presbyterian Church. They have one child living, Herbert E., born September 8th, 1838; married August 30th, 1859, Jennie Maria Putnam, of Dunbarton, Me., before Rev. John Putnam. He is a builder, and lives in Cleveland.

278. *Cleveland, Ohio.*

WILLIAM HART, Cleveland, Ohio, fourth son of Judah Hart, of Middletown and Norwich, Conn., and Brownhelm, Ohio, and his wife, Abigail (Belden), born April 9th, 1811, at Norwich; married December 9th, 1834, Betsey Kirk. He is a cabinet maker by trade, and resides at Cleveland, Ohio, in 1874.

279. *Navarino, Brown County, Wis.*

ASAHEL HART, Navarino, Brown County, Wis., fifth son of Judah Hart, of Middletown and Norwich, Conn., and Brownhelm, Ohio, and his wife, Abigail (Belden), born at Norwich, March 25th, 1813; married September 12th, 1841, Clarissa Smith. He is a joiner by trade.

533. Clarissa Adalaide, born , 1842; died at Green Bay, aged 17 years.

GOSLEE.

280. *South Edmonston, N. Y.*

HARRIET ELIZABETH HART, youngest daughter of Judah Hart, of Middletown and Norwich, Conn., and Brownhelm, Ohio, and his wife, Abigail (Belden), born January 2d, 1818, at Griswold, Conn.; married March 16th, 1837, Ralph L. Goslee. They reside at South Edmonston, Chenango County, N. Y. They had—1, Susannah L., born September

8th, 1838; 2, Judah Hart, born February 13th, 1841; 3, Celia Olivia, born October 30th, 1844; 4, Amos Herbert, born September 6th, 1847, died in 1848; 5, Esther Florilla, born February 10th, 1854.

281. St. Louis, Mo.

OLIVER ARMSTRONG HART, St. Louis, Mo., eldest son of Eliphaz Hart, of Norwich, Conn., and his wife, Eliza (Armstrong), born February 13th, 1814, at Norwich, Conn.; married November 16th, 1843, Mary E. Hull, daughter of Abram, born January 2d, 1822, at New York City, and died at their residence, No. 1418 Lucas Place, St. Louis, Mo., February 13th, 1863, aged 41 years. Mr. Hart was formerly an architect and builder, but later was engaged in the manufacture of iron. He is now president of the St. Louis Gas Company, furnishing both St. Louis and Kansas City. He is worth half a million.

THEIR CHILDREN, BEING THE NINTH GENERATION.

534. Eliza, born October 21st, 1844. She is living single with her father in 1874.
535. Augustus Brewster, born March 15th, 1846; married November 26th, 1872, Charlotte Ballantine.
       Samuel Wendell, born February 29th, 1848; died March 2d, 1848.
536. Mary Olivia, born July 16th, 1849; married January 26th, 1871, Edward H. Semple.
537. Anna Cornelia, born June 29th, 1851; married January 12th, 1871, Charles Bartles Bray, of New Jersey.

282. Norwich, Ct., San Francisco, Cal.

ALFRED HART, California, second son of Eliphaz Hart, of Norwich, Conn., and his wife, Eliza (Armstrong), born March 28th, 1816, at Norwich, Conn. He married January 21st, 1841, Mary C. Gardner, daughter of Charles Gardner, of Bozrah, Conn., born March 2d, 1820. In the spring of 1874 she resided at Denver, Col., and he at San Francisco, Cal. He is an artist in the line of painting.

THEIR CHILDREN, BEING THE NINTH GENERATION.

538. Lillie Mitchel, born January 21st, 1842; married September 3d, 1866, Silas M. Stone.
539. Alfred Lawrence, born June 20th, 1843, at Norwich, Conn.; died August 3d, 1844.
540. Georgianna, born August 26th, 1845; married June 19th, 1871, Edward A. Reser.
541. Charles Nelson, born November 24th, 1849, at Hartford, Conn.; married June 22d, 1872, Lizzie A. Arms.
       Eddie White, born June 20th, 1860, at Hartford, Conn.; died May 13th, 1864, at Hartford.

285. *Norwich, Conn., St. Louis, Mo.*

GEORGE HART, Norwich Conn., third son of Eliphaz Hart, of the same place, and his wife, Eliza (Armstrong), born June 19th, 1822, at Norwich, Conn.; married August 25th, 1850, Sarah Potter, of New London, Conn. She died, when second he married   ,
Jennie Davis, of Milwaukie, Wis. He is a tinner by trade, and lived at St. Louis, Mo., for a time.

THEIR CHILDREN, BEING THE NINTH GENERATION.

542. Olivia, born   ; married
543. Mary, born   ; married
544. Oliver Wilgus, born   ; married

286. *Ware, Mass.*

HENRY HARRINGTON HART, fourth son of Eliphaz Hart, of Norwich, Conn., and his wife, Eliza (Armstrong), born April 12th, 1824, at Norwich, Conn. He married April 12th, 1850, Abby Ann Chase, of Yantic, Conn., daughter of Leonard, and his wife, Lucy Ann (Lewis), born March 24th, 1828, at Franklin, Conn. They reside at Ware, Mass. He was a sign and ornamental painter by trade. Their children did not live long. He deals in real estate in 1874. They had—
1, Sarah Eliza, born July 4th, 1854; died September 1st, 1854. They are both members of the Congregational Church.

288. *Norwich, Conn., Zenia, O.*

DOCTOR CHARLES PORTER HART, sixth son of Eliphaz Hart, of Norwich, Conn., and his wife, Eliza (Armstrong), born April 17th, 1829, at Norwich, Conn.; married November 29th, 1848, Eleanor Beecher, of Zenia, Ohio. He is a practicing physician at   , Ohio.

THEIR CHILD, BEING THE NINTH GENERATION.

545. Caroline, born

289.

Norwich, Meriden, Conn., St. Louis, Mo.

SAMUEL HART, Norwich, Conn., seventh son of Eliphaz Hart, of the same place, and his wife, Eliza (Armstrong), born September 8th, 1831, at Norwich. He lived at Meriden, Conn., in 1861. He married September 8th, 1854, Olive Basset, daughter of Charles, of West Meriden, who died, January, 1861, at Meriden, when second he married April 24th, 1863, Mrs. Sarah Sophia Miller, of Cromwell, Conn., daughter of Timlow Bullard, and his wife, Harriet (Sage) Belden, of Cromwell,

Conn. He is a tinman by trade, and is a stove dealer, and resided for a time at St. Louis, Mo. He is a member of the Baptist Church.

HIS 'CHILDREN BY HIS FIRST MARRIAGE, BEING THE NINTH GENERATION.

546. Adah Field, born October 10th, 1857, at Meriden. She was adopted by her grand-parents.
547. George Bassett, born September 8th, 1859, at St. Louis, Mo. He lives in Meriden.

BUSSEY.

290.　　　　　　　　*Norwich, Conn.*

HARRIET HART, third daughter of Eliphaz Hart, of Norwich, Conn., and his wife, Eliza (Armstrong), of Newport, R. I., born September 17th, 1833, at Norwich; married January 1st, 1856, William Bussey, of Norwich, a cotton manufacturer. She is a member of the Methodist Church.

GRUNBACK.

291.

Hartsville, Renssalaer County, N. Y.

MARGARETTA PERRITT HART, Hartsville, N. Y., fourth daughter of Eliphaz Hart, of Norwich, Conn., and his wife, Eliza (Armstrong), of Newport, R. I., born December 20th, 1835, at Norwich, Conn.; married December 4th, 1859, Thomas Hudson Grunback, of Bray, Eng. He is a woolen manufacturer, and resides at Hartsville, N. Y. She is a member of the Methodist Church there. They had Lottie Eliza, born January 24th, 1864.

302.　　　　*Hudson, Summit County, O.*

REV. JOHN CLARK HART, Hudson, Summit County, Ohio, eldest son of Deacon Nathan Hart, of North Cornwall, Conn., and his wife, Sylvia (Clark), born December 10th, 1804, at West Cornwall, and graduated at Yale College in 1831; married June 11th, 1834, Emily Irene, daughter of Hon. Oliver Burnham, and his wife, Sarah (Rogers). She died, July, 1843, at his father's in West Cornwall, when second he married July 19th, 1844, Mrs. Rebecca K. Moore, daughter of Mr. Christopher Starr, of Norwich, Conn., and his wife, Olive (Perkins). He was pastor of the Presbyterian Church at Springfield, N. J., from 1835 to 1843, and subsequently of the Congregational Church at Hudson, Summit County, Ohio, in 1844, and was dismissed in 1853; he was then at Ravenna in 1854, and dismissed in 1861, when he supplied the churches of Edenburg and Charlestown two years, and Kent, Conn., five years.

He preached in the Western Reserve College three months, and other vacant pulpits as his health would admit. He died, September, 1871, at Ravenna, Ohio, aged 67 years. He was a man well known, whose influence was felt wherever he went.

THEIR CHILDREN, BEING THE NINTH GENERATION.

548. Sarah Clarissa, born May 6th, 1835, at Springfield, N. J. She is at Ravenna, Ohio, in 1874.

Mary Jane, born November 5th, 1836; died August 24th, 1838.

Emily Harriet, born September 12th, 1838; died June 12th, 1851, at Hudson, Ohio, aged 13 years.

John Oliver, born February 1st, 1841; died Dec. 8th, 1862, at Louisville, Ky.

Watson Andrews, born, June, 1843, at Kent, Conn.; died, September, 1843, aged 3 months.

CHILD BY SECOND WIFE.

549. Albert Judson, born July 19th, 1845.

303.   *Cornwall, Conn.*

TITUS LEAVITT HART, West Cornwall, Conn., second son of Deacon Nathan Hart, of the same locality, and his wife, Sylvia (Clark), born April 26th, 1806, at Cornwall; married at West Hartford, May 1st, 1833, Harriet S. Corbin, daughter of Woodbridge, and his wife,

(Wadsworth), born February 1st, 1808, at West Hartford. He was a teacher of music four years in Central New York and in New Jersey. As a farmer he loved his profession, and was successful in the pursuit of his calling. In 1852, at the Union Plowing Match inaugurated by P. T. Barnum, and open to competition in all parts of the United States, when twenty-seven of the best plowmen in nearly all the New England States and New York were engaged, he won the first premium of $50. Again in 1853 he was a competitor with the United States and Canada, when thirty plowmen were engaged in the trial, he was admitted to have done the best plowing, thus becoming the champion of the United States and Canada. He was a competitor at all the plowing matches in Litchfield County for some twenty years, and in every instance won the first premium. He is a justice of the peace in Cornwall. He and his adopted son are members of the North Cornwall Church. His wife died November 23d, 1872, aged 65 years. She was also a member of the same church.

THEIR CHILDREN, BEING THE NINTH GENERATION.

Son, born, February, 1854; died at birth.

550. Horace Corbin, born November 15th, 1839—an adopted son.

NODINE.

304. *Washington, D. C.*

ABIGAIL EMELIA HART, eldest daughter of Deacon Nathan Hart, of Cornwall, Conn., and his wife, Sylvia (Clark), born October 11th, 1808, at Cornwall; married April 12th, 1837, Deacon Peter Nodine, a mechanic and manufacturer. He resides at Washington, D. C., and in 1873 was in the Patent Office. They had—1, Nathan Hart, 2, Sylvia Ann, 3, Emily Burnham.

305. *West Cornwall, Conn.*

HEZEKIAH MILTON HART, Cornwall, Conn., third son of Deacon Nathan Hart, of the same place, and his wife, Sylvia (Clark), born August 21st, 1810, at North Cornwall; married September 10th, 1836, Eunice Judson, of Woodbury. He was a farmer of West Cornwall, where he died, December 27th, 1871, aged 61 years. He was judge of probate for several years, also county surveyor, and a music and school teacher.

THEIR CHILDREN, BEING THE NINTH GENERATION.

551. Sylvia Rosalia, born November 26th, 1837.
552. Mary Jane, born February 20th, 1841.
553. John Milton, born June 5th, 1846. He was a graduate of Yale College, and in 1874 is a student in theology.
554. Albert Judson, born August 5th, 1849. He is a farmer.
555. William Clarence, born May 18th, 1851. He is a farmer.

306. *Des Moines, Iowa.*

SOLOMON HART, Des Moines, Iowa, fourth son of Deacon Nathan Hart, of Cornwall, Conn., and his wife, Sylvia (Clark), born September 17th, 1812, at Cornwall; married at Philadelphia, Penn., July 9th, 1840, Caroline Reynolds, of Philadelphia, where he then resided, and was a manufacturer, but in 1873 was a merchant and manufacturer at Des Moines, Iowa.

THEIR CHILDREN, BEING THE NINTH GENERATION.

556. Mary Caroline, born , 1841.
557. Marie Emily, born , 1843.
558. Charles, born ; died February 9th, 1870.
559. Clara Levitt, born
560. Kate Dorman, born

WHITTLESEY.

307. *New Preston, Conn.*

ESTHER MARIA HART, New Preston, Conn., second daughter of Deacon Nathan Hart, of Cornwall, and his wife, Sylvia (Clark), born January 21st, 1815, at Cornwall; married March 13th, 1844, Shelden Whittlesey, of New Preston, his native place. She died there, December 14th, 1854, in her 40th year. He was son of Martin Whittlesey, and his wife, Lorana (Dayton), born August 28th, 1806, at New-Preston, and first married December 13th, 1837, Eunice Smith, who died May 19th, 1843, when he second married as above, and third married October 4th, 1855, Sylvia Ann Hart, sister of Esther Maria. They had—1, Nathan Hart, 2, Robert C. Mills, 3, Judson.

NODINE.

309. *Clifton Station, Va.*

MARY ELIZA HART, Clifton Station, Va., fourth daughter of Deacon Nathan Hart, of Cornwall, Conn., and his wife, Sylvia (Clark), born March 31st, 1818, at Cornwall; married August 15th, 1852, Deacon Anson Baldwin Nodine. They reside at Clifton Station, Va., in 1874. They had—1, Willie Brown, 2, Seward, 3, Arthur Burnham.

NODINE.

310. *Hudson, Ohio.*

CLARISSA HART, Hudson, Ohio, fifth daughter of Deacon Nathan Hart, of Cornwall, Conn., and his wife, Sylvia (Clark), born December 24th, 1819, at Cornwall, Conn.; married September 11th, 1839, Robert Crawford Nodine, a merchant in 1874, at Hudson, Summit County, Ohio. They had—1, Crawford Hart, who died of wounds received at Cedar Mountain; 2, Mary Hart; 3, Clara Leavitt.

311. *West Cornwall, Conn.*

NATHAN HART, West Cornwall, Conn., fifth son of Deacon Nathan Hart, of Cornwall, and his wife, Sylvia (Clark), born December 12th, 1821, at West Cornwall, Conn.; married September 8th, 1847, Sarah Amelia, daughter of Charles Whittlesey, of New Preston, and his wife, Mary Ann (Camp), born April 16th, 1827. She died January 21st, 1871, aged 44 years, when he second married December 19th, 1871, Frances Marion Whittlesey. He is a successful farmer, represented the town of Cornwall in the state legislature of 1860, is presi-

18

dent and active manager of various agricultural societies in Litchfield County, and in 1874 resides at West Cornwall, Conn.

THEIR CHILDREN, BEING THE NINTH GENERATION.

561. Ellen Clarissa, born August 15th, 1848; married September 14th, 1871, John Cotter Sherwood.
562. Charles Whittlesey, born December 9th, 1850.
563. Gould Whittlesey, born November 22d, 1855.

SEELEY.

312.   *Woodbury, Conn.*

DELIA HART, Woodbury, Conn., youngest daughter of Deacon Nathan Hart, of West Cornwall, Conn., and his wife, Sylvia (Clark), born June 26th, 1823, at West Cornwall; married June 26th, 1860, Walter Sherwood Seeley. She died October 12th, 1871, at Woodbury, Conn. He is a farmer there.

313.   *Hamden, Conn.*

URI WILLIAM HART, New Haven, Conn., youngest son of Deacon Nathan Hart, of West Cornwall, Conn., and his wife, Sylvia (Clark), born July 19th, 1825, at Cornwall; married July 23d, 1854, Mary Jane Belden, of Pottsdam, N. Y. They were both admitted to the Congregational Church, New Haven, March 5th, 1865, by letter from the Presbyterian Church, Kanawha, Wis. He resided at Hamden in 1866, and was organist of the First Congregational Church, New Haven, and in 1872 was playing the largest organ in that city. His wife died August 31st, 1855, at Streetsboro, Ohio, when second he married October 26th, 1859, Ann Foot Cowles, daughter of the late Rev. Orson Cowles, of North Haven, Conn., born September 29th, 1833, at Woodstock, Windham County, Conn.

THEIR CHILDREN, BEING THE NINTH GENERATION.
Mary Belden, born July 26th, 1855; died September 19th, 1855.

SECOND WIFE.

564. Agnes Crawford, born June 25th, 1861, at North Haven.
565. Bertha Cowles, born December 13th, 1863, at North Haven.
566. Clara Foot, born August 22d, 1865, at North Haven.
567. Willie Sherwood, born January 4th, 1869, at Hamden, Conn.

316.   *Bridgeport, Conn.*

ELIAS NELSON HART, Cornwall, Conn., second son of Elias Hart, of the same place, and his wife, Hannah (Harrison), born December 25th, 1813, at Cornwall; married December 1st, 1835, at Cornwall, Caroline

Hitchcock, daughter of   , and his wife, Anna (Garlick), born July 24th, 1814, at New Milford. He resided at Bridgeport, Conn., in 1873.

THEIR CHILDREN, BEING THE NINTH GENERATION.

568. Mary Louisa, born September 20th, 1838; married January 15th, 1859, Philander Z. Owens.
569. Sarah Frances, born December 26th, 1839; married   , Henrie Frisbee.
570. Caroline Elizabeth, born September 7th, 1846; married October 3d, 1865, Richard M. Near.
571. Charlotte Maria, born August 31st, 1848.
       William Henry, born May 18th, 1850; died February 18th, 1851.

318.   *Cornwall, Conn.*

JOHN ELIAS HART, Cornwall, Conn., third son of Elias Hart, of the same town, and his wife, Hannah (Harrison), born   , 1817, at Cornwall; married   , 1840, Mary Winans.

THEIR CHILDREN, BEING THE NINTH GENERATION.

572. Elias, born   , 1842.
       Son, born   , 1845.

DICKINSON.

319.   *Cornwall, Conn.*

CAROLINE A. HART, third daughter of Elias Hart, of Cornwall, Conn., and his wife, Hannah (Harrison), born   , 1819, at Cornwall; married   , 1845, William Dickinson.

325.   *Lapier, Mich.*

CAPTAIN NOAH HARRISON HART, Esq., Lapier, Lapier County, Mich., third son of Oliver Burnham Hart, of Cornwall, Conn., and subsequently of Lapier, Mich., and his wife, Amanda (Harrison), born October 30th, 1813, at Cornwall, Conn. He went with his parents, in 1832, to Wisconsin. He married September 5th, 1842, Emily Julia, daughter of Raymond Peck, of Attica, N. Y., and his wife, Fanny (Woodruff), born September 19th, 1824. He is a professional lawyer in Lapier. He was a member of the Constitutional Convention in 1850, and of the state legislature in 1851. He was captain of Company F, Tenth Regiment, in the late war, and was in service until its close in 1865, serving his constituents and country with great acceptance.

Charles Peck, born July 14th, 1846; died March 12th, 1848, aged 1 year and
8 months.
573. Amanda, born April 29th, 1854, at Lapier.
574. Noah Harrison, born March 18th, 1859, at Lapiér.
575. Clarence Maxwell, born August 30th, 1868, at Lapier.

326.   *Bay City, Mich.*

JULIUS BURNHAM HART, Bay City, Mich., fourth son of Oliver Burnham Hart, of Cornwall, Conn., and Lapier, Mich., and his wife, Amanda
(Harrison), born 1815, at Cornwall, Conn.; married, 1835, Sarah Shafer,
of Lapier. He is a merchant and dock owner at Bay City, Mich. She
died in 1845. He second married in 1850.

Child, born   ; died quite young.
576. Edward, born   . He was a soldier, and was killed in the late
war.
577. Emily, born   ; married   , Mr. Patterson.
578. Augusta, born   ; married, not reported; second

327.   *Lapier, Mich.*

JOSEPH BROWN HART, Lapier, fifth son of Oliver Burnham Hart, of
Cornwall, Conn., and Lapier, Lapier County, Mich., and his wife,
Amanda (Harrison), born 1818, at Cornwall, Conn.; married, 1844,
Mary M. Hopkins, of Flint, Mich. He is a fur dealer in 1874. She
died in 1859, when he married, March 7th, 1859, Anna M. Fitch, of
Lapier. There were four children by the first union, but none by the
last.

579. Sabra A., born September 9th, 1846; died in 1856, at Lapier, Mich., aged 9
years.
580. George Arthur, born September 22d, 1849; married, October, 1867, Ella Hammond.
581. Augustus H., born March 14th, 1851. He is single in 1874.
582. Henry Harrison, born April 12th, 1853.

WATTLES.

328.

PHILA ANN HART, second daughter of Oliver Burnham Hart, of
Cornwall, Conn., and Lapier, Mich., and his wife, Amanda (Harrison),
born 1823, at Cornwall, Conn.; married, 1847, John M. Wattles, a

lawyer. They had—1, Greenleaf C., said to be 26 years of age; 2, Olivia Hart, said to be 24 years of age; 3, John M., who died an infant; and 4, Bertha, said to be 16 years of age.

MAXWELL.

329.   *Bay City.*

SARAH MARIA HART, third daughter of Oliver Burnham Hart, of Cornwall, Conn., and Lapier, Mich., and his wife, Amanda (Harrison), born 1825, at Cornwall, Conn.; married, 1853, Andrew C. Maxwell, a lawyer of Bay City. Of their five children two daughters and one son died young. Robert, aged 19, and Jennie, aged 11, are living in 1874.

SMITH.

330.   *Bay City, Mich.*

ABIGAIL BURNHAM HART, fourth daughter of Oliver Burnham Hart, of Cornwall, Conn., and Lapier, Mich., and his wife, Amanda (Harrison), born 1826, at Cornwall, Conn.; married, 1851, George Smith, of Bay City, Mich. He is a physician there. They had—1, Amanda, who died young; 2, Clary, aged 19; 3, Hattie, aged 16; 4, Frankie, a daughter, aged 13; 5, George, aged 10.

333.   *Cornwall, Conn.*

NOAH ROGERS HART, Cornwall, Conn., second son of Julius Hart, of the same town, and his wife, Rhoda (Rogers), born September 12th, 1821, at Cornwall; married November 22d, 1843, Lucretia Minerva (Barnum), daughter of Micajah, and his wife, Rosetta (Pendleton), born March 14th, 1826, at Cornwall. He is a merchant at West Cornwall, and connected with the manufacture of boots and shoes. He resided there until 1859. He then removed to Goshen and resided there until 1870, when he removed to Patterson, Passaic County, N. J., where he resided in 1872, and was closing up his business. In the year 1849 all his early accumulations were lost by a fire. In 1853 he opened a boarding school for boys, and managed it successfully for four years, when his brother, Elias Burton, took it, and he went to Goshen with his brother Julius, where they conducted a very successful mercantile business until 1870, when they sold out. At Goshen he was superintendent of the Sunday School of the Congregational Church—nine years which were very prosperous.

583. Frederick Augustus, born July 25th, 1849, at Cornwall, Conn.
584. Arthur Burton, born June 26th, 1855, at Cornwall, Conn.
585. Mary Elizabeth, born February 8th, 1859, at Cornwall, Conn.
586. Emma Lucretia, born March 15th, 1865, at Goshen, Conn.

334.   *West Cornwall, Conn.*

JULIUS LEAVITT HART, Cornwall, Conn., third son of Julius Hart, of
the same town, and his wife, Rhoda (Rogers), born August 29th, 1826,
at Cornwall; married, at Malone, Franklin County, N. Y., August 1st,
1863, Mrs. Hattie C. Watson, *alias* Hattie C. Smith, daughter of ——
Smith, and his wife, Betsey (Chamberlain), of Vergennes, Vt. She
was born September 6th, 1844, at Kent, Conn. In 1872 he was residing at Englewood, Bergen County, N. J., and was proprietor of the
Palisade House there.

587. Minnie Luella, born November 28th, 1864, at Goshen.
588. George Edward, born May 11th, 1867, at Goshen.
        Grace Elizabeth, born January 9th, 1872, at Ridgewood, N. Y.; died September
        7th, 1872, at Englewood, N. J.

336.   *West Cornwall, Conn.*

ELIAS BURTON HART, West Cornwall, Conn., fourth son of Julius
Hart, of the same locality, and his wife, Rhada (Rogers), born February 21st, 1834, at Cornwall; married October 7th, 1857, Hattie A.,
daughter of Lee Canfield, of Salisbury, Conn. He was principal of a
boarding school for boys at West Cornwall, from 1856 to 1863, at his
residence. The institution was very successful. It had an attendance
of twenty boarding pupils, mostly from New York City. This school
was first organized in 1853, by Noah Rogers Hart, an elder brother,
who never enjoyed a college education, but by personal effort and kind-
ness of Horace Webster, LL. D., a patron of the school, and principal
of the New York Free Academy, he received the honorable degree of
Bachelor and Master of Arts from the University of Vermont. In
1862 he formed a partnership with his youngest brother, and established business in New York City under the firm of George S. Hart
& Co., commission merchants, and wholesale dealers in butter, cheese,
and lard, at 39 Pearl Street. He was thus successfully engaged for
several years, when owing to infirm health, he retired from business to
the quiet of his farm in West Cornwall. The business is still carried
on under the firm of George S. Hart & Howell, at 35 Pearl Street, and
in 1874 is one of the largest and most successful of any similar one on
this continent.

589.   Lee Canfield, born November 15th, 1862.
590.   Elias Burton, born February 11th, 1865.
591.   Charles Julius, born June 29th, 1867.

337.   *New York.*

GEORGE SPENCER HART, No. 35 Pearl Street, New York, youngest son of Julius Hart, of Cornwall, Conn., and Rhoda (Rogers), his wife, born February 11th, 1837, at Cornwall; married February 23d, 1871, Anna Dudley, daughter of Charles H., of New York City, and Anna Eliza (   ), his wife, born April 12th, 1850.   He has been very successful in business, having one of the most extensive cheese houses on the continent, and doing the business of a millionaire.   "He is smart, and as *good* as he is smart."   He is of the firm of George S. Hart & Howell in 1874.

592.   Anna Dudley, born December 25th, 1871.

340.   *Lapier, Lapier County, Mich.*

RODNEY GEORGE HART, Lapier, Mich., third son of Hon. Alvin Nelson Hart, of the same place, and subsequently of Lansing, Mich., and his wife, Charlotte Fox (Ball), born May 28th, 1834, at Lapier; married December 5th, 1854, Mary Castella, daughter of Dr. John Hazen, of Franklin, N. Y., and his wife, Mary (Chamberlain), born September 19th, 1832.   Mr. Hart is a banker, of the firm of R. G. Hart & Co., real estate brokers, farmers, and importers of stock, viz: cattle, sheep, swine, and horses.

593.   Kate Hazen, born January 21st, 1856, at Lapier, Mich.
594.   Belle Charlotte, born June 14th, 1858, at Lapier, Mich.
     Lille Anna, born September 6th, 1864, at Lapier, Mich; died April 18th, 1865.
595.   Mary Ellen, born August 6th, 1866, at Lapier, Mich.

HAMILTON.

341.   *Red Wing, Min.*

ISABELLA ELIZA HART, eldest daughter of Hon. Alvin Nelson Hart, of Lapier and Lansing, Mich., and his wife, Charlotte Fox (Ball), born July 24th, 1836, at Lapier; married October 1st, 1858, Robert Wilson Hamilton, a member of the bar at Red Wing, Min.   He resides at Lapier, Mich.   They have one son in 1874, viz: Alvin Nelson Hamilton, born October 14th, 1859, at Lapier.

342.   *Lansing, Mich.*

ARTHUR NELSON HART, Lansing, Mich., youngest child of Hon. Alvin
Nelson Hart, of Cornwall, Conn., and Lapier and Lansing, Mich., and
his wife, Charlotte Fox (Ball), born August 16th, 1848, at Lapier;
married December 18th, 1866, at Lansing, Mich., Sarah Augusta,
daughter of Claudius ´Britton, and his wife, Sarah (Beaman). Mr.
Hart is the junior partner of the firm of A. N. Hart & Son, hardware,
and sole proprietor of the dry goods store of Arthur N. Hart, at
Lansing.

THEIR CHILDREN, BEING THE NINTH GENERATION.

596. Maude, born September 8th, 1868, at Lansing.

    Lulu, born August 10th, 1871, at Lansing; died May 21st, 1872.

343.   *Dover Center, Min.*

JOHN G. HART, Dover Center, Olmsted County, Min., eldest son of
Reuben Hart, of Lenox, Ashtabula County, Ohio, and his wife, Eleanor
(Kingsman), born July 23d, 1813, at New Marlboro, Mass.; married
February 13th, 1838, Henrietta McNutt, born April 1st, 1816, who
died August 13th, 1847, when he second married August 22d, 1849,
Phebe March. He is a farmer, located at Dover Center, Olmsted
County, Min., to which place he removed from Jefferson, Ohio, in July,
1858.

THEIR CHILDREN, BEING THE NINTH GENERATION.

597. Nelson, born August 23d, 1839; married May 11th, 1867.

598. Caroline, born December 1st, 1840; married October 12th, 1860, George Ro-
    land.

CHILDREN OF THE SECOND MARRIAGE, NINTH GENERATION.

    Frederick E., born May 2d, 1851; died August 21st, 1851.

599. Laura H., born September 27th, 1853. She is teaching in Minnesota.

600. Alfred R., born July 11th, 1856.

601. James W., born June 22d, 1859.

602. John M., ⎱ born May 9th, 1863;
    Milo,   ⎰   died April 24th, 1864.

603. Albert H., born April 12th, 1866.

HALL

344.   *Jefferson, Ashtabula County, O.*

LAURA HART, eldest daughter of Reuben Hart, of Cornwall, Conn.,
New Marlboro, Mass., and Lenox, Ohio, and his wife, Eleanor (Kingsman), born, November, 1814, at New Marlboro; married, November,
1835, Amander Hall, a farmer, located in Jefferson, Ashtabula County,
Ohio. She died, December, 1870, aged 56 years.

McNUTT.

345. *Jefferson, Ohio.*

AMANDA HART, second daughter of Reuben Hart, of Cornwall, Conn., New Marlboro, Mass., and Lenox, Ashtabula County, Ohio, and his wife, Eleanor (Kingsman), born September 19th, 1816, at New Marlboro; married February 14th, 1837, James McNutt, a machinist. His residence is at Jefferson, Ashtabula County, Ohio.

346. *Geneva, Ohio.*

JAMES SOLOMON HART, Geneva, Ashtabula County, Ohio, second son of Reuben Hart, of Cornwall, Conn., New Marlboro, Mass., and subsequently of Lenox, Ohio, and his wife, Eleanor (Kingsman), born May 11th, 1818, at New Marlboro, Mass.; married October 21st, 1851, Eunice Linzey, and resides at Geneva, Ashtabula County, Ohio. They had but one child, a daughter, which was born about 1845, and died about 1862.

CARPENTER.

347. *Northfield, Rice County, Min.*

NANCY HART, third daughter of Reuben Hart, of Connecticut, Massachusetts, and Ohio, and his wife, Eleanor (Kingsman), born July 26th, 1824, at New Marlboro, Mass. She married, September, 1853, George Carpenter, a farmer, of Northfield, Rice County, Min.

LOOMIS.

348. *Jefferson, Ashtabula County, O.*

MARY HART, youngest daughter of Reuben Hart, of Connecticut, Massachusetts, and Lenox, Ohio, and his wife, Eleanor (Kingsman), born April 19th, 1833, at New Marlboro, Mass.; married, September, 1857, George M. Loomis, a farmer, of Jefferson, Ashtabula County, Ohio. They are living there in 1874, and his wife's mother with them.

351. *Royalton, N. Y.*

CHAUNCEY HART, Royalton, Niagara County, N. Y., only son of Tyrus Hart, of New Marlboro, Mass., and his wife, Tryphena (Sage), born   ; married   , Sophia Ross, of Royalton, N. Y. He died before 1871.

THEIR CHILD, BEING THE NINTH GENERATION.

604. Eugene, born, April, 1846.

19

352. *Hillsdale, Mich.*

ALONZO G. HART, Hillsdale, Hillsdale County, Mich., eldest son of Almon Hart, of Perry, Wyoming County, N. Y., and his wife, Mary (Harmon), born November 27th, 1821, at Perry; married December 26th, 1844, Celinda Allen, daughter of Truman, and his wife, Polly (Rutherford), born September 23d, 1822, at Lester, N. Y. He was an insurance agent in 1872, and resided at Hillsdale, Mich.

THEIR CHILDREN, BEING THE NINTH GENERATION.

605. Elizabeth S., born September 23d, 1845, at Lester, N. Y.
606. Josephine M., born July 19th, 1848, at Lester, N. Y.
607. Celestia M., born October 6th, 1853, at Hinsdale, Cattaraugus County, N. Y.

353. *Hillsdale, Mich.*

GILBERT Z. HART, Hillsdale, Hillsdale County, Mich., second son of Almon Hart, of Perry, Wyoming County, N. Y., and his wife, Mary (Harmon), born October 24th, 1823, at Perry; married October 19th, 1847, Elizabeth Warren, daughter of Ira, and his wife, Anna (Tharpsteen), born October 14th, 182-, at Lester, N. Y. They resided at Hillsdale in 1872. He is a farmer by occupation.

THEIR CHILDREN, BEING THE NINTH GENERATION.

608. Henry H., born September 13th, 1845, at Perry, N. Y.
Frank, born December 29th, 1851; died August 11th, 1855.

354. *Hillsdale, Mich.*

JEROME W. HART, Hillsdale, Mich., third son of Almon Hart, of Perry, N. Y., and his wife, Mary (Harmon), born August 4th, 1825, at Perry, Wyoming County, N. Y.; married August 8th, 1850, Fanny Kane, daughter of John, and his wife, Cynthia (Clark), born February 28th, 1826, at Eagle, Wyoming County, N. Y. In 1872 they resided at Hillsdale, Mich. He is a farmer.

THEIR CHILDREN, BEING THE NINTH GENERATION.

609. Augustie A., born May 9th, 1851, at Portage, N. Y.; married December 29th, 1869.
610. Estella R., born April 16th, 1863, at Hillsdale, Mich.

WHITE.

356. *Lester, N. Y.*

ALVIRA S. HART, eldest daughter of Almon Hart, of Perry, N. Y., and his wife, Polly (Harmon), born October 16th, 1832, at Perry, Wyoming County, N. Y.; married December 29th, 1853, Eugene H.

White, born July 15th, 1827, at Lester, N. Y. She died May 25th, 1856, aged 24 years, when second he married, June 13th, 1857, her sister, Louisa M. Hart. He is son of Joseph White, and his wife, Mary (Burdrow). She had—1, Ella C., born October 5th, 1854, at Lester, N. Y.; died September 21st, 1858. 2, Alvira S., born May 13th, 1856.

WHITE.

357. *Hillsdale, Mich.*

Louisa M. Hart, second daughter of Almon Hart, of Perry, Wyoming County, N. Y., and his wife, Polly (Harmon), of Monteray, Mass., born May 19th, 1838, at Perry, N. Y.; married June 13th, 1857, Eugene H. White. She was his second wife, the first being her sister above, who died. She had—1, Mary E., born December 25th, 1861, at Hillsdale; 2, Ellen, born June 19th, 1865, at Hillsdale, Mich.

358. *Perry, N. Y.*

William S. Hart, youngest son of Almon Hart, of Perry, N. Y., and his wife, Polly (Harmon), of Monteray, Mass., born August 24th, 1840, at Perry, Wyoming County, N. Y. He was a soldier in the Union Army of the late war, Company B, Eighteenth Michigan Regiment. He was killed June 21st, 1863, by being thrown from a mule and kicked to death, while sent after dispatches, aged 25. He had no family.

359. *Royalton, N. Y.*

William M. Hart, only son of Solomon Randall Hart, of Perry, Wyoming County, N. Y., and his wife, Fanny (Johnson), born June 21st, 1834, at Royalton, Niagara County, N. Y.; married October 6th, 1853, Jennie Macumber, daughter of Allen, of Perry.

HOLLISTER.

360.

New Haven, Conn., Hartsville, Mass.

Jane Antoinette Hart, eldest daughter of Milan, of Hartsville, Mass., and New Haven, Conn., and his wife, Paulina (Nettleton), born February 20th, 1834; married September 28th, 1852, James, son of Milo Hollister, and his wife, Lydia (Hyde), born September 28th, 1826, at New Marlboro, Mass. He is a mason by trade. He has been a merchant and teacher, and deacon of the Congregational Church in New Haven, and in 1871 was living in Hartsville, unable to labor.

They had—1, Mark James, born April 3d, 1854, died March 9th, 1860; 2, Emma Jane, born November 5th, 1855; 3, Dwight Hart, born October 20th, 1857, died May 18th, 1859; 4, Grace Lydia, born October 28th, 1859, died February 18th, 1862; 5, Clarence F., born August 2d, 1863, died February 14th, 1865.

361.   *Hartsville, Mass.*

EDSON SOLOMON HART, Hartsville, Berkshire County, Mass., eldest son of Milan Hart, of New Haven, and his wife, Paulina (Nettleton), born January 10th, 1836; married September 19th, 1855, Frances J. Fargo, of Hartsville. He second married April 30th, 1871, Maria Starr, of New Haven. His avocation is farming, and he resides at Hartsville, Mass., where he is a member of the Methodist Church.

THEIR CHILDREN, BEING THE NINTH GENERATION.

611.   Cora Paulina, born April 19th, 1857.
612.   Jennie Estella, born February 20th, 1859.
       Albert Milan, born   , 1864; died at the age of 10 months.

STEPHENS.

362.   *Cobourg, Canada.*

ROSALINDA EXINE HART, second daughter of Milan Hart, of New Haven, Conn., and his wife, Paulina (Nettleton), born September 14th, 1837; married June 5th, 1855, George Joel Stephens, born March 3d, 1834. He was educated at college, but was a cabinet maker in 1871, and kept a wareroom at Cobourg, Ontario County, Canada. She is a member of the Methodist Church. They had—1, Carrie Issabel, born August 19th, 1858; 2, George Milan, born August 17th, 1860; 3, Emma Hattie, born, December, 1865, at Cobourg, Canada.

363.   *New Haven, Conn.*

JOHN JAY HART, New Haven, Conn., second son of Milan Hart, of the same city, and his wife, Paulina (Nettleton), born September 17th, 1839; married March 20th, 1860, Clara A. Crippen, of Egremont, Mass.   In 1872 they resided at New Haven, and he was superintending the laying of their Nickelson pavement.   They had no children in 1871.

365.   *Middletown, Conn.*

LUCIUS WHITING HART, second son of Alfred Hart, of Hartsville, Mass., and his wife, Cynthia Louisa (Nettleton), born January 24th, 1842, at New Marlboro, Mass.; married January 24th, 1860, Frances

S. Ladd, of Great Barrington, born November 9th, 1842. He was conductor on the Middletown Railroad to Berlin. Their children did not live long.

367. *Candor, N. Y.*

SAMUEL HART, Candor, Tioga County, N. Y., eldest son of Abel Hart, of that town, and his wife, Rachel (Sweeden), born   , 1796, at   ; married   , 1819, Lois Gridley. He went from Massachusetts to Candor, N. Y., in 1799, where, it is thought, he is a farmer.

THEIR CHILDREN, BEING THE NINTH GENERATION.

613.	Harman P., born	, 1821 ; married	, B. Thorp.
614.	Sarah Emily, born	, 1823 ; married	, R. Day.
615.	Lois Rachel, born	, 1825 ; married	, G. Curtiss.
616.	Mary Elizabeth, born	, 1828 ; married	, W. Dykeman.
617.	Selah Gridley, born	, 1831 ; married	, E. Varmetten.
618.	Rachel Amelia, born	, 1833 ; married	, H. Gilbert.
619.	Nancy Riley, born	, 1836 ; married	, H. Detrich.
	He was a soldier, and was killed.		
620.	Horace William, born	, 1839. He was in Company A, 151st Regiment New York Volunteers. Died at Virginia in 1863.	
621.	Hannah Louisa, born	, 1841 ; married	, S. House.
622.	Julia Ann, born	, 1844 ; married	, A. Knapp.

368. *Candor, N. Y.*

DANIEL HART, Candor, Tioga County, N. Y., second son of Abel Hart, of the same place, and his wife, Rachel (Sweeden), born   , 1798, in Massachusetts; married   , 1824, Mary Kelsey. He went to Candor with his parents in 1799. He is supposed to be a farmer.

THEIR CHILDREN, BEING THE NINTH GENERATION, BORN AT CANDOR.

623.	Mary Elizabeth, born	, 1827 ; married	, W. Hubbard.
624.	Rachel Maria, born	, 1829 ; married	, W. Hubbard.
	Hannah G., born	, 1831 ; died in 1832.	
625.	Sarah Frances, born	, 1833 ; married	, Dr. Dixon.
626.	Daniel Kelsey, born	, 1838. He was in Company A, 109th Regiment, and was killed in the army in 1864.	
627.	Lucia, born	, 1841 ; married	, A. Booth.
628.	Henry Gilbert, born	, 1848 ; married	, L. Guiles.

371. *Candor, N. Y.*

DEACON SELAH HART, Candor, Tioga County, N. Y., third son of Abel Hart, of the same town and county, and his wife, Rachel (Sweeden), born 1805, at Candor; married, 1827, Julia Potter. He was admitted to the Congregational Church at Candor in 1834, and was chosen their deacon in 1836.

THEIR CHILDREN, BEING THE NINTH GENERATION, BORN AT CANDOR.

629.	Horace E., born	, 1827; married	, Hannah Smith.
630.	Ira Norman, born	, 1831; married	, Mary C. Kelsey.
631.	Rachel Mary, born	, 1834; married	, G. Fisher.
632.	Eliza Jane, born	, 1836; married	, J. McCarty.
,	Selah Philemon, born	, 1841; died	, 1843.

373.   *Candor, N. Y.*

ABEL HART, Jr., Candor, Tioga County, N. Y., youngest son of Abel Hart, Sr., of the same town and county, and his wife, Rachel (Sweeden), born 1814, at Candor; married, 1841, L. Kirkpatrick, who died in 1841, when second he married, 1848, Louisa Hall.

THEIR CHILDREN, BEING THE NINTH GENERATION, ALL BORN AT CANDOR.

633.	Lucy Ann, born	, 1841; married	, Dr. Adams.

SECOND WIFE.

634.	George Henry, born	, 1849.
635.	Addie Augusta, born	, 1852.
636.	Lewis Albert, born	, 1853.
	Frank Marion, born	, 1855; died in 1855.

BROWN.

379.   *Victor, N. Y.*

SOPHIA HART, eldest daughter of Frederick Hart, of Victor, Ontario County, N. Y., and his wife, Sylvia (Rowley), born December 9th, 1827, at Victor, N. Y.; married February 19th, 1850, Nathan Brown, at Victor.

380.   *Rockford, Ill.*

AUGUSTUS FREDERICK HART, Rockford, Ill., eldest son of Frederick Hart, of Victor, Ontario County, N. Y., and Guilford, Winnebago County, Ill., and his wife, Sylvia (Rowley), born December 29th, 1820, at Victor; married January 19th, 1853, Fannie J. Newton, of Canandiagua, N. Y. He is a farmer, and lives, in 1874, at Rockford, Ill. His wife died November 24th, 1857, when he second married November 24th, 1858, Nancy Newton, her sister.

CHILDREN OF THE FIRST MARRIAGE, BEING THE NINTH GENERATION.

637. Sylvia Delia, born December 9th, 1853.
638. Fannie J., born November 15th, 1857.

SECOND WIFE.

639. Maryette Eliza, born July 31st, 1866.

Very Truly Yours

John S. Hart

382. *Victor, N. Y.*

JABEZ D. HART, Victor, Ontario County, N. Y., second son of Frederick Hart, of the same town and county, but subsequently of Guilford, Winnebago County, Ill., and his wife, Sylvia (Rowley), born November 28th, 1834, at Victor; married December 10th, 1857, Charlotte McIntire, of   . He is a farmer, and their residence is at Victor in 1874.

THEIR CHILDREN, BEING THE NINTH GENERATION.

640. Christabell, born November 27th, 1858.
641. Albert, born, June, 1861.
642. Frederic Augustus, born February 8th, 1868.
643. Jennie, born May 23d, 1870.

COLLINS.

383. *Rockford, Ill.*

CHARLOTTE ELIZA HART, youngest child of Frederick Hart, of Victor, N. Y., and subsequently of Guilford, Winnebago County, Ill., and his wife, Sylvia (Rowley), born December 21st, 1837, at Victor; married May 6th, 1857, at Rockford, Ill., George W. Collins.

JACKSON.

384. *Carbondale, Penn.*

RACHEL STONE HART, eldest daughter of Isaac Hart, of Washington County, Va., and his wife, Abigail (Stone), born February 23d, 1838, at Stockbridge, Mass. She went with her parents to Pennsylvania when she was four years old. She married, November, 1825, Nathan Jackson, M. D., of Carbondale, Penn. They had—1, Rachel A., 2, Elizabeth R., 3, Isaac, 4, Harriet Newell, 5, Frances, 6, Olive, 7, Nathan D. The mother was for many years a member of the Presbyterian Church.

385.

Princeton, Trenton, N. J., Philadelphia, Penn.

PROFESSOR JOHN SEELY HART, Philadelphia, eldest son of Isaac Hart, of Washington County, Va., and his wife, Abigail (Stone), born January 28th, 1810, at Stockbridge, Mass., and when he was two years old he went with his father to Pennsylvania. He prepared for college under Dr. Orton, of Wilkesbarre, and graduated at Princeton in 1830, when he took charge of the academy in Natchez, Miss., one year, and in 1831 he entered the Theological Seminary at Princeton, and was appointed tutor in college in 1832, and adjunct professor of ancient languages in 1836.   He was licensed as a probationer for the gospel ministry in 1836, but subsequently returned his license to the presbytery, by whom it was cancelled, he having determined to devote his life to the profession of teaching.   In the fall of 1836 he became the proprietor of the Edge Hill Boarding School, near Princeton, which institution he conducted until December, 1841.   In September, 1842, he was appointed principal of the Central High School of Philadelphia. He was brought into the church at the early age of fourteen, mainly through the influence of his mother and Sabbath School teacher.   He married April 21st, 1836, Amelia C. Norford, of Princeton.   He was for a time principal of the State Normal School of New Jersey, but resigned February 7th, 1871.   Thus Professor Hart, from the peculiar structure of his mind and taste, became one of the greatest educators of the age.   From his constant contact with children and youth he could adapt his labors and writings to their wants and necessities.

THEIR CHILD, BEING THE NINTH GENERATION.

644.   James Morgan, born November 2d, 1839.

LIST OF WORKS BY JOHN SEELY HART, LL. D.

For Sale by J. C. Garrigues & Co., No. 608 Arch Street, Philadelphia.

Female Prose Writers of America, 536 pages 8vo, illustrated, - -	$8.00
Spencer and the Faery Queen, 434 pages 12mo, - - - -	2.00
Class Book of Prose, 384 pages 12mo, - - - - -	1.50
Class Book of Poetry, 384 pages 12mo, - - - - -	1.50
Composition and Rhetoric, 384 pages 12mo, - - - -	1.50
First Lessons in Composition, 144 pages 12mo, - - - -	.90
English Grammar, 199 pages 12mo, - - - - -	.60
English Grammar, Part First, Introductory, 12mo, - - - -	.56
Constitution of the United States, an Exposition for Schools, 101 pages 12mo,	.60
Mistakes of Educated Men, 91 pages 18mo, - - - - -	1.50
In the School Room, Chapters in the Philosophy of Education, 276 pp. 12mo,	1.25
Thoughts on Sabbath Schools, 215 pages 12mo, - - - -	.85
The Sunday School Idea, 416 pages 12mo, - - - -	1.50
Removing Mountains, Life Lessons from the Gospels, 306 pages 12mo, -	1.25
The Golden Censer, Thoughts of the Lord's Prayer, 144 pages 12mo, -	.80
Prayer for the School Room (in press).	
English Literature (in preparation).	
American Literature (in preparation).	

COLLINS.

368.   *Washington County, Va.*

Harriet Newell Hart, Washington County, Va., second daughter of Isaac Hart, of the same locality, and his wife, Abigail (Stone), born August 2d, 1820, at Providence, Penn.; married July 13th, 1841, at

Princeton, N. J., Rev. Charles Collins, of the Methodist Church, and President of Emory and Henry College, Washington County, Va. They had—1, Narcissa, born December 24th, 1842; 2, Mary L., born March 30th, 1845; 3, Charles Standish, born October 17th, 1846.

389. *Canisteo, Steuben County, N. Y.*

MATTHEW HART, Canisteo, Steuben County, N. Y., eldest son of Edmund Hart, of De Ruyter, Madison County, N. Y., and his wife, Lefee (Jones), born August 19th, 1823, at Truxton, Cortland Co., N. Y.; married August 28th, 1845, Mahala Jones, daughter of   , and his wife, Betsey (Tillotson), born August 5th, 1820, .at Corinth, Orange County, Vt. He is a blacksmith by trade, and resides at Canisteo, Steuben County, N. Y.

THEIR CHILDREN, BEING THE NINTH GENERATION.

645. Edmund Matthew, born June 13th, 1846; married September 2d, 1872, Anna Merrill.

646. Elma Elizabeth, born June 23d, 1848; married November 18th, 1869, George B. Sherman.

647. Ellen Amelia, born Dec. 28th, 1849, at De Ruyter, Madison County, N. Y.

648. Emma Louisa, born January 26th, 1852, at Canisteo, N. Y.

649. Mary Filuria, ⎰ born October 18th, 1857, at Canisteo, Steuben County, N. Y.
650. Helen Fidelia, ⎱

651. Mahalia Caroline, born Aug. 27th, 1860, at Canisteo, Steuben County, N. Y.

390. *De Ruyter, N. Y.*

CHARLES HART, second son of Edmund Hart, of De Ruyter, Madison County, N. Y., and his wife, Lefee (Jones), born, January, 1825, at Truxton, Cortland County, N. Y.; married   , 1848, Anna Clark, of   .   He is a blacksmith by trade, and resides at   in 1874.

THEIR CHILD, BEING THE NINTH GENERATION.

652. Sackett, born   , 1851.

BRADLEY.

391. *Groton, N. Y.*

URANIA HART, eldest daughter of Ira Hart, of Groton, Tompkins County, N. Y., and his wife, Mary (Jones), of Topsham, Vt., born at Truxton, Cortland County, N. Y., June 1st, 1824; married at Groton, N. Y., November 13th, 1845, Lemi Bradley, a farmer. He died   , and his widow lives at Groton, April, 1874.

20

HOPKINS.

393.   *Groton, N. Y.*

MARY E. HART, second daughter of Ira Hart, of Groton, N. Y., and his wife, Mary (Jones), of Topsham, Orange County, Vt., born July 20th, 1827, at Truxton; married January 24th, 1848, at Groton, Volney Hopkins, a farmer. They live at Groton, N. Y.

395.   *Groton, N. Y.*

OREMUS IRA HART, Groton, Tompkins County, N. Y., second son of Ira Hart, of Kensington, and Locke, Cayuga County, N. Y., and his wife, Mary (Jones), of Topsham, Orange County, Vt., born April 3d, 1830, at Truxton. He is a farmer. He married

Mary Hatch. They live at Groton, N. Y., in 1874.

THEIR CHILDREN, BEING THE NINTH GENERATION.

397.   *Angelica, N. Y.*

SETH PERCIVAL HART, Angelica, Alleghany County, N. Y., eldest son of George Hart, of Kensington, Conn., and Angelica, N. Y., and his wife, Deborah (Benjamin), born June 22d, 1826, at Tully, Onondaga County, N. Y. He is a harness maker by trade and occupation. He married, November 15th, 1853, Susan A. Engle, born June 22d, 1833, at Angelica, N. Y., where they live in 1874.

THEIR CHILDREN, BEING THE NINTH GENERATION.

John Engle, born September 16th, 1854, at Moravia, N. Y.
Sarah Francis, born July 13th, 1856, at Moravia, N. Y.
Rosa Bell, born February 3d, 1861, at Moravia, N. Y.

398.   *Syracuse, N. Y.*

MARTIN VAN BUREN HART, Syracuse, N. Y., second son of George Hart, of Berlin, Conn., and Angelica, N. Y., and his wife, Deborah (Benjamin), born September 21st, 1828, at De Ruyter, Madison County, N. Y.; married July 31st, 1838, Anna E. Ogle, at Syracuse, N. Y., where she was born, July 31st, 1838. He is a sign and ornamental painter at Syracuse, where they reside in 1874.

THEIR CHILDREN, BEING THE NINTH GENERATION.

Jennie, born June 5th, 1870.
Edmund Henry, born

474. *Tuscaloosa, Ala.*

STEPHEN HURLBURT HART, second son of Velina Hart, of Tuscaloosa, Ala., and his wife, Elizabeth (Stephens), born, December, 1825, at Blunt County, Ala.; married December 23d, 1848, Sarah C. McCullough. He was a tinner by trade. He died August 24th, 1857, in his 33d year. His widow is living at Tuscaloosa, Ala., in 1874.

THEIR CHILDREN, BEING THE NINTH GENERATION.

476. *Tuscaloosa, Ala.*

RICHARD B. HART, third son of Velina Hart, of Tuscaloosa, Ala., and his wife, Elizabeth (Stephens), born August 15th, 1829, at Tuscaloosa; married January 3d, 1857, Texanna Purdy. They live in Salado, Bell County, Texas, and his mother is living with them. He is a tinner by trade.

THEIR CHILDREN, BEING THE NINTH GENERATION.

NIX. QUINN.

478. *Bibb County, Ala.*

CORNELIA ANN HART, second daughter of Velina Hart, of Tuscaloosa, Ala., and his wife, Elizabeth (Stephens), born November 30th, 1837, at Tuscaloosa, Ala.; married   , John H. Nix, a farmer, who died August 25th, 1864, leaving one child, William Nix, when she second married August 24th, 1867, Robert L. Quinn, of Bibb County, Ala. They had two children, one of whom died. The name of the living one is Charley Quinn.

QUINN.

479. *Bibb County, Ala.*

HENRIETTA VELINA HART, youngest daughter of Velina Hart, the tinman, of Tuscaloosa, Ala., and his wife, Elizabeth (Stephens), of North Carolina, born February 14th, 1842, at Tuscaloosa; married December 24th, 1866, James Thomas Quinn, of Bibb County, Ala., born August 11th, 1844. They reside in Burnett, Burnett County, Texas. He keeps a tin-shop, is a merchant, and has a farm. They had a daughter, Minnie.

BUTLER.

402. *Boston, Mass.*

FRANCES LIVINGSTONE HART, eldest daughter of Rev. William Henry Hart, of Hempstead, L. I., and his wife, Lydia Hubbard (Moore), born October 24th, 1816, at   ; married
          , Rev. Clement M. Butler, of Grace Church, Boston, son of the late Rev. David Butler, of Troy, N. Y. They had—1, Frances, 2, Helen Moore.

EVANS.

403. *Richmond, Va.*

JULIA ANN HART, third daughter of Rev. William Henry Hart, of Hempstead, L. I., and his wife, Lydia Hubbard (Moore), born June 5th, 1820, at   ; married   ,
Joseph D. Evans, a merchant, at Richmond, Va. They had—1, William Allison, 2, Lydia Moore, 3, Julia Milicent.

MURRILL.

406. *Lynchburgh, Va.*

MARY ANN HORNE HART, sixth daughter of Rev. William Henry Hart, of Hempstead, L. I., and his wife, Lydia Hubbard (Moore), born July 8th, 1825, at   ; married   ,
John W. Murrill, a tobacco manufacturer, of Lynchburgh, Va. They had—1, Alice.

LYMAN.

424. *Montevalla, Ala.*

LUCY HART, eldest daughter of Samuel Hart, of Kensington, and his wife, Lucy (Dickinson), born December 13th, 1830, at Kensington; married September 23d, 1851, Henry R. Lyman, son of Moses, of Kensington. He was a merchant at Montevalla, Ala., in 1873.

UPSON.

425. *Kensington.*

MARY WILCOX HART, Kensington, third daughter of Samuel Hart, of Kensington, and his wife, Lucy (Dickinson), born April 30th, 1835, at Kensington; married October 15th, 1856, William Upson, of Kensington. She died June 30th, 1871, aged 36 years, 2 months, when second he married, at Wolcott, February 23d, 1874, M. Aurelia Hough, before Rev. Samuel Orcutt.

DICKINSON.

430. *New Britain, Conn.*

HARRIET HART, New Britain, Conn., only daughter of George Hart, of Berlin, and his wife, Lucy (Beckley), born October 27th, 1829, at Berlin; married June 11th, 1844, Nathaniel Dickinson, of New Britain, son of Jabez, and his wife, Julia (Bailey), born January 14th, 1817, at Berlin, Conn. He is a carriage painter, and resides in New Britain. They have one daughter, Emma Hart, born May 21st, 1847, and is a graduate of the New Britain High School. Mr. Dickinson's residence is No. 116 Washington Street, and he and his wife are both members of St. Mark's Episcopal Church.

480. *Parishville, N. Y.*

WALTER STEELE HART, eldest son of Truman Hart, the blacksmith, of New Britain, and his wife, Laura Lewis (Steele), born April 13th, 1816, at New Britain, and went to Parishville, St. Lawrence County, N. Y.; married, at Stockholm, St. Lawrence County, N. Y., November 9th, 1841, Lucy D. Allen. They resided in Parishville, where he died, February 7th, 1869, aged 53.

THEIR CHILD, BEING THE NINTH GENERATION.

653. Harriet Lewis, born Feb. 5th, 1843; married August 1st, 1863, Albert E. Flanders.

482. *Parishville, N. Y.*

GEORGE L. HART, Parishville, St. Lawrence County, N. Y., second son of Truman Hart, of New Britain and Burlington, Conn., and Parishville, N. Y., and his wife, Laura Lewis (Steele), born October 1st, 1822, at Burlington, Conn., and went to Parishville, N. Y., with his parents. He married, September 16th, 1851, at Potsdam, St. Lawrence County, N. Y., Ann M. Bigelow. They lived at Parishville in 1873, where their children were born.

THEIR CHILDREN, BEING THE NINTH GENERATION.

Laura Ann, born August 15th, 1852; died October 17th, 1868, at Parishville, aged 16.
Horace B., born January 5th, 1854.
William Harnden, born March 15th, 1857.

483. *Parishville, N. Y.*

WILLIAM W. HART, Parishville, N. Y., youngest son of Truman Hart, of New Britain and Burlington, Conn., and subsequently of Parishville, St. Lawrence County, N. Y., and his wife, Laura Lewis, daughter of Josiah Steele, born June 29th, 1832, at Burlington, Conn. He went with his parents to Parishville, N. Y., and there married, February 23d, 1860, Laura M. Hoyt. They resided at Parishville in 1873, where their children were born.

THEIR CHILDREN, BEING THE NINTH GENERATION.

Truman D., born July 25th, 1865.
Waldo W., born September 17th, 1868.
Herbert W., born March 5th, 1871; died August 7th, 1872, at Parishville.

484.   *Parishville, N. Y.*

GEORGE HART, eldest son of Bera Hart, of New Britain, Conn., and Parishville, St. Lawrence County, N. Y., and his wife Mary (Whaples), born March 10th, 1821, at Rutland, Rutland County, Vt.; married, at Raymondville, N. Y., May 4th, 1859, Caroline Herriman, daughter of Marcus B., and his wife, Charlotte, born November 10th, 1834, at Burke, Franklin County, N. Y. They settled at Parishville, St. Lawrence County, N. Y., where he died, June 24th, 1867, aged 46 years.

THEIR CHILD, BEING THE NINTH GENERATION.

Ira S., born May 4th, 1860, at Parishville.

485.   *Parishville, N. Y.*

HENRY HART, second son of Bera Hart, of New Britain, Conn., and Parishville, St. Lawrence County, N. Y., and his wife, Mary (Whaples), born July 29th, 1822, at Rutland, Rutland County, Vt., and went to Parishville, N. Y., with his parents, about 1823. He married November 7th, 1843, Elinda Morgan. They lived in Parishville in 1873.

THEIR CHILDREN, BEING THE NINTH GENERATION.

654. Candace Olive, born August 17th, 1845, at Parishville; married, 1865, John
      H. Sinclair.
655. Mary Lewis, born April 23d, 1849; married Jan. 1st, 1870, Clark E. Parker.
      John H., born May 8th, 1852, at Parishville.
      Helen L., born October 23d, 1857, at Parishville.
      Bera William, born May 22d, 1860, at Parishville.

ALLEN.

486.   *Parishville, N. Y.*

NANCY HART, eldest daughter of Bera Hart, of New Britain, Conn., and Parishville, N. Y., and his wife, Mary (Whaples), born May 13th, 1824, at Parishville, N. Y.; married there, November 29th, 1842, Lewis Allen, who died there March 29th, 1851. She died October

23d, 1864, at Morrisburg, in Canada. They had—1, Isaac B., born January 29th, 1844, at Parishville, and died there February 1st, 1864; 2, Ellian L., born September 14th, 1846, at Parishville; 3, George H., born April 16th, 1848, at Parishville.

MORGAN. TUPPER.

488. *Parishville.*

Lucy Hart, second daughter of Bera Hart, of New Britain, Conn., and Parishville, St. Lawrence County, N. Y., and his wife, Mary (Whaples), born November 3d, 1828, at Parishville; married March 19th, 1847, at Parishville, Alden Morgan, who died there, March 21st, 1857, when she second married, June 26th, 1862, at Potsdam, Ezra S. Tupper, born November 29th, 1819, at Parishville. Her children by Morgan were—1, Alfred, born May 1st, 1852; married March 2d, 1872, Martha G. Morgan. Her children by Tupper were—2, Clara A., born July 5th, 1863; 3, Charles H., born September 10th, 1866; 4, George E., born September 30th, 1870, at Hopkinton, N. Y.

489. *Parishville, N. Y.*

Samuel Hart, fourth son of Bera Hart, of New Britain, Conn., and Parishville, St. Lawrence County, N. Y., and his wife, Mary (Whaples), born June 14th, 1830, at Parishville, N. Y.; married there, March 27th, 1851, Helen Herriman, daughter of Marcus B., and his wife, Charlotte, born August 5th, 1831, at Bredport, Vt. He resided at Parishville in 1873, and has furnished much material of his father's and brothers' families for this work. Many thanks.

THEIR CHILDREN, BEING THE NINTH GENERATION.

656. Alice C., born February 7th, 1852, at Parishville.
657. Olive Ordelia, born October 3d, 1861, at Parishville.
658. Lulu Lorena, born April 9th, 1870, at Parishville.

506. *Philadelphia, Penn.*

Emery Curtiss Hart, Hartford, Conn., eldest son of Chauncey Hart, of New Britain and Hartford, and his wife, Polly (Markum), born November 11th, 1827, at Hartford; married ,
Louisa Warren, of Glastonbury, Conn. He is a carriage maker, and lives in Philadelphia in 1874.

DUNLAP.

507.   *Georgia.*

MARY HART, youngest child of Chauncey Hart, the carriage maker, of Hartford, and his wife, Polly (Markum), born August 6th, 1830, at Hartford, Conn.; married December 1st, 1851, Samuel Dunlap, of Hartford. She was killed by lightning, June 15th, 1857, at Albany, Baker County, Georgia, aged 26 years, 9 months, 9 days.

517.   *Hartford, Conn.*

DR. CHARLES REMMINGTON HART, Hartford, Conn., eldest son of Salmon North Hart, of the same city, and his first wife, Martha (Corning), born July 22d, 1837, at Hartford. He was educated a physician and surgeon, and entered the service of his country in the late war as assistant surgeon in the Tenth Regiment Connecticut Volunteers, but was promoted to surgeon, and honorably discharged September 2d, 1865. He married June 15th, 1869, Ella, daughter of Rev. H. V. Gardner, of Oneida, N. Y., and his wife, Mary (Foote), born March 29th, 1847, at Harwinton, Conn. He is in full practice in 1874 as physician and surgeon, in Hartford, Conn.

508.   *Hartford, Conn.*

ALFRED DWIGHT HART, Hartford, Conn., second son of Salmon North Hart, the carriage maker, of Hartford, and his first wife, Martha (Corning), born September 13th, 1840, at Hartford. In early life he was trained to the business of carriage making, and became a partner with his father. He went into the late war as a private in the Twenty-Fifth Regiment Connecticut Volunteers for nine months. He married, April 18th, 1866, Sarah, daughter of Aaron Daniels, of Hartford, and his wife, Maria G. (Ensworth), of Andover, Conn., born April 14th, 1848, at East Hartford. He died at Hartford, of quick consumption, July 31st, 1870, aged 29 years, 10 months, 18 days.

THEIR CHILD, BEING THE TENTH GENERATION.

659.   Alfred Dwight, born January 20th, 1867, at Hartford.

535.   *St. Louis, Mo.*

AUGUSTUS BREWSTER HART, St. Louis, Mo., eldest son of Oliver Armstrong Hart, of Norwich, Conn., and St. Louis, Mo., and his wife, Mary E. (Hull), daughter of Abram, of New York City, born March 15th, 1846, at St. Louis, Mo. In 1873 he was teller of the Mechanics Bank in that city. He married, November 26th, 1872, Clara Ballantine, daughter of William, and his wife, Judith (Mullen), of the same city, born August 2d, 1852, at St. Louis.

THEIR CHILD, BEING THE TENTH GENERATION.

660. Oliver Ballantine, born November 30th, 1873, at St. Louis.

SEMPLE.

536. *St. Louis, Mo.*

MARY OLIVIA HART, second daughter of Oliver Armstrong Hart, of St. Louis, Mo., and his wife, Mary E. (Hull), daughter of Abram, of New York City, born July 16th, 1849, at St. Louis; married January 26th, 1871, Edward Humphrey Semple, born August 22d, 1840, at Louisville, Ky. He is a merchant in large business at St. Louis in 1874. They had—1, Mary Emma, born November 24th, 1871, at St. Louis; 2d, Frederick Humphrey, born December 24th, 1872.

BRAY.

537. *St. Louis, Mo.*

ANNA CORNELIA HART, third daughter of Oliver Armstrong Hart, of Norwich, Conn., and St. Louis, Mo., and his wife, Mary E. (Hall), of New York City, born June 29th, 1851, at St. Louis, Mo.; married January 12th, 1871, at St. Louis, Charles Bartles Bray, of New Jersey, born June 22d, 1842, at Kingwood, Hunterdon County, N. J. He is a merchant in large business at St. Louis, Mo., in 1874. They had—1, Oliver Hart Bray, born April 22d, 1872, at St. Louis.

STONE.

538. *Cleveland, Ohio.*

LILLIE MITCHEL HART, Cleveland, Ohio, eldest daughter of Alfred Hart, of Norwich, Conn., and San Francisco, Cal., and his wife, Mary C. (Gardner), born January 21st, 1842, at Lebanon, Conn.; married September 3d, 1866, at Cleveland, Ohio, Silas M. Stone, Esq., attorney and counselor at law, and is residing, March, 1874, at Cleveland.

RESER.

540. *Denver, Col.*

GEORGIANNA HART, Denver, Col., second daughter of Alfred Hart, of Norwich, Conn., and San Francisco, Cal., and his wife, Mary C. (Gardner), born August 26th, 1845, at Norwich, Conn.; married, at

21

Cleveland, Ohio, June 19th, 1871, Edwin A. Reser, a real estate and collecting agent, of Denver, Col.

541.   *Lawrence, Kan.*

CHARLES NELSON HART, second son of Alfred Hart, of Norwich and Hartford, Conn., and California, and his wife, Mary C. (Gardner), born November 24th, 1849, at Hartford, Conn.; married June 22d, 1872, Lizzie Augusta Arms, of North Adams, Mass., born December 7th, 1854, to Leonard, and his wife, Frances (Eldridge). He is a telegraph operator, on Massachusetts Street, Lawrence, Kan. They had— 1, Leonard Arms, born September 20th, 1873; died October 25th, 1873, at Lawrence, Kan.

548.   *Ravenna, Ohio.*

SARAH CLARISSA HART, eldest daughter of Rev. John Clark Hart, of Cornwall, Conn., Springfield, N. J., Hudson, Ohio, and his first wife, Emily Irene (Burnham), born May 6th, 1835, at Springfield, N. J. She was single in 1872, and resided at Ravenna, Portage County, Ohio, and was a member of the Congregational Church there. She made a profession of religion before she was twenty years of age.

Cornwall, Conn.

JOHN OLIVER HART, eldest son of Rev. John Clark Hart, of Cornwall, Conn., Springfield, N. J., and Hudson, Ohio, and his first wife, Emily Irene (Burnham), born February 1st, 1841, at Springfield, N. J. He entered the Western Reserve College, and was a member of the junior class when the war broke out. He then enlisted into the regular army, and after one year of service he died of disease, in the hospital at Louisville, Ky., December 8th, 1862, aged 21 years. He was a member of the college church, and was single.

549.   *Ravenna, Ohio.*

ALBERT JUDSON HART, youngest and only son of Rev. John Clark Hart, of Cornwall, Conn., Springfield, N. J., and Hudson, Ohio, and his second wife, who was Mrs. Rebecca (Moore), born July 19th, 1845, at Hudson, Summit County, Ohio. In December, 1872, he resided at Ravenna, Portage County, Ohio, and was a member of the Congregational Church there.

553.   *New Haven, Conn.*

JOHN MILTON HART, West Cornwall, Conn., eldest son of Hezekiah Milton Hart, of the same town and state, and his wife, Eunice (Judson), born June 5th, 1845, at West Cornwall, and graduated at Yale College in 1867. He was single, and teaching in New Haven in 1872, and his residence was No. 426 Chapel Street.

SHERWOOD.

561. *West Cornwall, Conn.*

ELLEN CLARISSA HART, West Cornwall, Conn., eldest daughter of Nathan Hart, of the same town and state, and his first wife, Sarah Amelia (Whittlesey), born August 15th, 1848, at West Cornwall; married, September 14th, 1871, John Cotter Sherwood.

OWENS.

568. *West Cornwall, Conn.*

MARY LOUISA HART, eldest daughter of Elias Nelson Hart, of Cornwall, Conn., and his wife, Caroline (Hitchcock), born September 20th, 1838, at Cornwall; married January 15th, 1859, Philander Z. Owens, son of   Owens, and his wife, Olive (Dean), born at Sharon, Conn.

FRISBEE.

569. *Onargo, Ill.*

SARAH FRANCES HART, second daughter of Elias Nelson Hart, of Cornwall, Conn., and his wife, Caroline (Hitchcock), born December 26th, 1839, at Cornwall, Conn.; married   , Henry Frisbee, born at Branford. He was a major in the late war. They removed to Onargo, Iroquois County, Ill., where she died, September 8th, 1871, aged 32 years, leaving three children.

NEAR.

570. *Cornwall, Conn.*

CAROLINE ELIZABETH HART, third daughter of Elias Nelson Hart, of Cornwall, Conn., and his wife, Caroline (Hitchcock), born September 7th, 1846, at Cornwall; married October 3d, 1865, Richard M. Near, of

580. *Lapier, Mich.*

GEORGE ARTHUR HART, Lapier, Mich., eldest son of Joseph Brown Hart, of the same town and county, and his wife, Mary M. (Hopkins), born September 22d, 1849, at Lapier; married, October, 1867, Ella Hammond, daughter of John.

609.   *Hillsdale, Mich.*

AUGUSTIE A. HART, eldest daughter of Jerome W. Hart, of Hillsdale, Hillsdale County, Mich., and his wife, Fanny (Kane), born May
9th, 1851, at Portage, N. Y.; married December 29th, 1869.

613.   *Candor, N. Y.*

HERMAN P. HART,   , Wis., eldest son of Samuel Hart,
of Candor, Tioga County, N. Y., and his wife, Lois (Gridley), born
                , 1821, at Candor; married   ,
B. Throope.

THEIR CHILDREN, BEING THE TENTH GENERATION.

661. Sarah Emily, born   ; married   Stratton.
      Elizabeth, born
      Ida, born
      Helen, born

DAY.

614.   *Candor, N. Y.*

SARAH EMILY HART, eldest daughter of Samuel Hart, of Candor,
Tioga County, N. Y., and his wife, Lois (Gridley), born   ,
1823, at Candor; married   , R. Day.

617.   *Illinois.*

SELAH GRIDLEY HART, second son of Samuel Hart, of Candor, Tioga
County, N. Y., and his wife, Lois (Gridley), born   , 1831,
at Candor, N. Y.; married   , E. Vermitten, of
            . They resided at   , Ill., in 1871.

THEIR CHILDREN, BEING THE TENTH GENERATION.

662. Albert, born
663. Elizabeth, born
664. George, born

HUBBARD.

623.   *Candor, N. Y.*

MARY ELIZABETH HART, eldest daughter of Daniel Hart, of Candor,
Tioga County, N. Y., and his wife, Mary (Kelsey), born   ,
1827, at Candor; married   , W. Hubbard. She
died   , 1862.

DIXON.

625.   *Candor, N. Y.*

SARAH FRANCIS HART, fourth daughter of Daniel Hart, of Candor, Tioga County, N. Y., and his wife, Mary (Kelsey), born   , 1833, at Candor, N. Y.; married   , Dr. Dixon.

626.   *Candor, N. Y.*

DANIEL KELSEY HART, Candor, Tioga County, N. Y., eldest son of Daniel Hart, of the same town and county, and his wife, Mary (Kelsey), born   , 1838, at Candor. He was unmarried. He enlisted in Company A, One Hundred and Ninth Regiment, and was killed in 1864, aged 26 years.

BOOTH.

627.   *Candor, N. Y.*

LUCIA HART, Candor, N. Y., fifth daughter of Daniel Hart, of the same town and county, and his wife, Mary (Kelsey), born   , 1841, at Candor; married   , A. Booth, of

628.   *Candor, N. Y.*

HENRY GILBERT HART, Candor, N. Y., youngest son of Daniel Hart, of the same town and county, and his wife, Mary (Kelsey), born · . , 1848, at Candor, N. Y.; married   , L. Guiles.

629.   *Candor, N. Y.*

HORACE E. HART, Candor, Tioga County, N. Y., eldest son of Deacon Selah Hart, of the same town and county, and his wife, Julia (Potter), born   , 1827, at Candor, N. Y.; married   , Hannah Smith.

THEIR CHILD, BEING THE TENTH GENERATION.

665. George Given, born   , 1866.

630.   *Candor, N. Y.*

IRA NORMAN HART, Candor, Tioga County, N. Y., second son of Deacon Selah Hart, of the same town and county, and his wife, Julia (Potter), born   , 1831, at Candor, N. Y.; married   , Mary E. Kelsey. He was admitted to the Congregational Church at Candor in 1846, and his wife in 1864.

THEIR CHILD, BEING THE TENTH GENERATION.

666. Nettie Frances, born   , 1866.

FISHER.

631. *Candor, N. Y.*

RACHEL MARY HART, eldest daughter of Deacon Selah Hart, of Candor, Tioga County, N. Y., and his wife, Julia (Potter), born   ,
, 1834, at Candor; married   , G. Fisher.

McCARTY.

632. *Candor, N. Y.*

ELIZA JANE HART, second daughter of Deacon Selah Hart, of Candor, Tioga County, N. Y., and his wife, Julia (Potter), born
, 1836, at Candor; married   , J. McCarty.

645. *Canisteo, N. Y.*

EDMUND MATTHEW HART, eldest son of Matthew Hart, of Canisteo, Steuben County, N. Y., and his wife, Mahala (Jones), born June 13th, 1846, at De Ruyter, Madison County, N. Y.; married at Canisteo, September 2d, 1872, Anna Merrill. He is a painter by trade, and was residing at Canisteo, N. Y., 1873.

SHERMAN.

646. *Canisteo, N. Y.*

ELMA ELIZABETH HART, eldest daughter of Matthew Hart, of Truxton, Cortland County, and Canisteo, Steuben County, N. Y., and his wife, Mahala (Jones), born June 23d, 1848, at De Ruyter, Madison County, N. Y. She went with her parents to Canisteo, where she married, November 18th, George B. Sherman, who was a wagon maker by trade.

FLANDERS.

653. *Ogdensburgh, N. Y.*

HARRIET LEWIS HART, only daughter of Walter Steele Hart, of Parishville, N. Y., and his wife, Lucy D. (Allen), born February 5th, 1843, at Parishville, St. Lawrence County, N. Y.; married August 1st, 1863, at Ogdensburgh, in the same county, Albert E. Flanders. They are residing at Parishville in 1874, where their children were born, viz: 1, Frederic W., born August 26th, 1866; 2, Laura Olive, born July 3d, 1869.

SINCLAIRE.

654. *Parishville, N. Y.*

CANDACE OLIVE HART, eldest daughter of Henry Hart, of Parishville, St. Lawrence County, N. Y., and his wife, Elinda (Morgan), born August 11th, 1845, at Parishville; married there, September 1st, 1865, John H. Sinclaire.

PARKER.

655. *Parishville, N. Y.*

MARY LEWIS HART, second daughter of Henry Hart, of Parishville, St. Lawrence County, N. Y., and his wife, Elinda (Morgan), born April 23d, 1849, at Parishville; married January 1st, 1870, Clark E. Parker.

597. *Genoa, Min.*

NELSON HART, Dover Center, Min., eldest son of John G. Hart, of Dover Center, Min., and his first wife, Henriettta (McNutt), born August 23d, 1839, at Jefferson, Ashtabula County, Ohio. He removed with his parents to Minnesota, and married, May 11th, 1867, Julia J., daughter of Henry and Elizabeth Smith, born October 28th, 1840, at Avon, Franklin County, Maine. In 1874 his avocation is farming, in Genoa, Min.

THEIR CHILDREN, BEING THE TENTH GENERATION.

667. Henrietta Elizabeth, born June 4th, 1868, at Dover, Olmsted County, Min.
668. Alfred Nelson, born March 20th, 1870, at Chesterfield, Fillmore County, Min.
669. Margaret Frances, born December 13th, 1872, at New Haven, Olmsted County, Minnesota.

ROLAND.

598. *Waseca, Minn.*

CAROLINE HART, eldest daughter of John G. Hart, of Dover Center, Minn., and his first wife, Henrietta (McNutt), born December 1st, 1840, at Jefferson, Ashtabula County, Ohio. She removed to Minnesota with her parents, and married, October 12th, 1860, George Roland, a blacksmith. They live in Waseca, Minn., in 1874.

BRANCH OF STEPHEN HART,

SECOND SON OF DEACON STEPHEN.

670.

STEPHEN HART, 2d, son of Deacon Stephen, the settler, born at Braintree, Essex County, Eng. He located in Farmington, Conn., and had his house east of the meeting-house, opposite the residence of John Hooker. He was made a freeman in Farmington, May, 1654. He died about 1689, and the inventory of his estate was taken by

Isaac Moore,
Thomas Hart, } Am't, £633 14s.
and John Hart.

His seven children were all living at the time of the appraisal, and their ages were fortunately given by the appraisers, viz: Stephen, 27; Thomas, 23; John, 20; Samuel, 17; Sarah, 14; Ann, 11; and Mary, 7.

THEIR CHILDREN, BEING THE THIRD GENERATION.

671. Stephen, born   , 1662; married December 18th, 1689, Sarah Cowles.
672. Thomas, born   , 1666; married December 18th, 1689, Elizabeth Judd.
673. John, born   , 1669; married April 12th, 1694, Widow Hannah Treat.
674. Samuel, born   , 1672; married   , Anna
675. Sarah, born   , 1675; married December 11th, 1695, Samuel Tuttle.
    Anna, born   , 1678.
    Mary, born   , 1682; unmarried; died

671.   *Farmington, Conn.*

STEPHEN HART, 3d, Nod, or Avon, eldest son of Stephen Hart, 2d, and his wife   , born 1662, at Farmington; married December 28th, 1689, Sarah, daughter of Samuel Cowles, and his wife, Abigail (Stanley). She was born December 25th, 1668, at Tunxis, and was admitted to the church in Farmington, February 2d, 1691–2, which fact shows that they resided in Farmington, and not Avon. His Will was dated September 3d, 1728, and gives his wife, Sarah, one-third, to Timothy and Daniel, his sons, to his three daughters, Sarah, Ann,

---

NOTE.—Stephen, the eldest son, being entitled, by the Will and common usage, to a double portion, for some good reason best known to himself, relinquished to his brothers and sisters, by an instrument in writing, dated November 1st, 1689, all his right to a double portion of the estate, provided they never claimed any right to the land at "Nod," now Avon. See probate record at Hartford.

and Abigail, and makes his wife, Sarah, and son, Timothy, sole executors. The inventory of his estate amounted to £939 4s. 1d., taken September 27th, 1733. He died August 18th, 1733, aged 71 years.

THEIR CHILDREN, BEING THE FOURTH GENERATION.

676. Sarah, born October 16th, 1692; married January 19th, 1720-1, Ephraim Smith, Jr.
677. Anna, born August 18th, 1695; married December 23d, 1714, Deacon Samuel Porter.

Stephen, 4th, born March 7th, 1698; died May 9th, 1725.
678. Abigail, born February 28th, 1702; married June 11th, 1729, Stephen Cole, of Kensington.
679. Timothy, born August 31st, 1705; married October 25th, 1728, Elizabeth Cowles.
680. Daniel, born March 21st, 1707-8; married July 18th, 1734, Abigail Thompson.

672. *Farmington, Conn.*

SERGEANT THOMAS HART, Nod and Farmington, second son of Stephen Hart, 2d, and his wife, , born , 1666, at Tunxis; married December 18th, 1689, Elizabeth, daughter of John Judd, and his wife, Mary (Hawkins). She was born in 1670, at Farmington, and united with the church there, February 2d, 1691-2. He had the west half of his father's house-lot, opposite the Female Seminary, which he gave his son, Stephen, in 1724. He was a large landholder. He held the military rank of sergeant. His Will was dated December 8th, 1727, in which he mentions sons—Stephen, Thomas, Daniel, James, and William—and made his wife, Elizabeth, executrix. The inventory amounted to £707 1s. 1d. He died in Farmington, March 23d, 1727-8, aged 62 years. The widow, Elizabeth Hart, died March 18th, 1743, aged 73 years.

THEIR CHILDREN, BEING THE FOURTH GENERATION.

Thomas, born June 5th, 1692; died young.
681. Stephen, born July 30th, 1693; married December 29th, 1720, Eunice Munson.
682. Thomas, born Nov. 3d, 1695; married March 16th, 1720-1, Anna Stanley.
683. Joseph, born , 1700; married December 6th, 1722, Mary Bird.
684. Samuel, born , married February 5th, 1729-30, Elizabeth Thompson.
685. Elizabeth, born ; married May 27th, 1731, Sylvanus Woodruff.
686. James, born December 14th, 1707; married October 10th, 1734, Thankful North.
687. William, born August 20th, 1710; married February 2d, 1737-8, Elizabeth Woodruff.

Mary, born September 7th, 1714; died September 12th, 1716, aged 2 years.

22

673.   *Farmington, Conn.*

JOHN HART, Farmington, third son of Stephen Hart, 2d, of the same place, and his wife, born 1669, in Farmington; married April 12th, 1694, Widow Hannah Treat, of Wethersfield. He held the military rank of lieutenant. He had the east half of his father's house-lot, opposite John Hooker's. They left no children, and he gave his property to his nephews, Stephen Tuttle and Jonathan Hurlburt, whom he brought up. The latter named his first son Hart Hurlburt. She was admitted to the church in Farmington by letter from the Second Church in Hartford, February 23d, 1707–8.

674.   *Farmington.*

SAMUEL HART, Farmington, fourth son of Stephen Hart, 2d, of the same place, and his wife, born 1672, at Farmington; married
          , Anna   . He was a weaver by trade and avocation. On the 10th of January, 1695–6, the town of Farmington voted Samuel Hart ten acres of land, "he to have it on the north side of that which is now given to his brother, Thomas Hart, against Sider brook, up by the Mountain, provided it do not prejudice," &c. At a meeting held January 4th, 1726–7, "voted, the above-mentioned grant to Samuel Hart, deceased, is now made over to Joseph Hart by a deed of Sale, is layd out to Joseph Hart according to the grant, at a place called Syder Brook, which Grant butts West on a highway leading to Simsbury." He died in 1697, leaving no children. His widow, Anna, married second August 20th, 1710, Samuel Judd, who died in 1719, leaving one daughter, Anna, born October 15th, 1712, who married in 1731, Ebenezer Moody. She second married in 1744, David Porter. She third married in 1758, Ezekiel Lewis, who died in 1760. After remaining a widow forty-six years she died in 1806, aged 94 years.

675.   *New Haven.*

SARAH HART, Farmington, eldest daughter of Stephen Hart, 2d, of the same place, born 1675, at Farmington, Conn.; married December 11th, 1695, Samuel Tuttle, of New Haven, Conn.

SMITH.

676.   *Farmington, Conn.*

SARAH HART, eldest daughter of Stephen Hart, 3d, of Farmington, and his wife, Sarah (Cowles), born October 16th, 1692, and was baptized the same day, at Farmington; married January 19th, 1720–1,

Ephraim, son of Ephraim Smith, of Farmington, and his wife, Rachel (Cole), born December 16th, 1690. She died there May 31st, 1744, aged 52 years, when second he married January 24th, 1744–5, Elizabeth Smith. He had no children by his first wife, but three by his second wife.

PORTER.

677. *Farmington, Conn.*

ANNA HART, second daughter of Stephen Hart, 3d, of Farmington, and his wife, Sarah (Cowles), born August 18th, 1695, at Farmington; married there, December 23d, 1714, Samuel Porter, son of Samuel, of Farmington, born there September 17th, 1691, and became a deacon of that church. She died September 13th, 1758, aged 63 years. He died October 8th, 1768, aged 77 years. They had—1, Elijah, born April 27th, 1721; 2, Anna, born December 20th, 1724; and probably others.

COLE.

678. *Kensington, Conn.*

ABIGAIL HART, third daughter of Stephen Hart, 3d, of Farmington, and his wife, Sarah (Cowles), born February 28th, 1702, at Farmington; married June 11th, 1729, Stephen Cole, of Kensington, son of John, and his wife, Mehitabel (Loomis), of Windsor, born October 3d, 1698. She died October 20th, 1736, aged 34 years, when he second married April 26th, 1745, Lydia Benton, of Hartford. He and Abigail had—1, Sarah, born April 15th, 1730; 2, Mary, born February 18th, 1731–2, married March 4th, 1754, Selah Hart; 3, Abigail, born June 25th, 1735.

679. *Farmington, Conn.*

TIMOTHY HART, Farmington, second son of Stephen Hart, 3d, of the same place, and his wife, Sarah (Cowles), born August 31st, 1705, at Farmington; married October 25th, 1728, Elizabeth, daughter of Isaac Cowles, of Farmington, and his wife, Mary (Andrews), born May 24th, 1705, at Farmington, and died November 29th, 1740, aged 39 years. He held the military rank of sergeant. He was killed by a cart-wheel October 3d, 1748, aged 43 years. He lived on his father's place, was a large land-holder, and left an estate of £3,000. He had a second wife, Mary.

THEIR CHILDREN, BEING THE FIFTH GENERATION.

Stephen, born August 11th, 1729; died November 9th, 1740.
688. Elisha, born April 28th, 1731; married July 14th, 1753, Sarah Cole.
Timothy, born September 1st, 1733; died March 23d, 1760, aged 27 years.
Keziah, born October 25th, 1735; died April 29th, 1739.

689.   Abigail, born August 28th, 1737; married March 13th, 1755, Elisha Newell,
        son of Nathaniel.
        Sarah, born March 25th, 1739.
        Keziah, born May 6th, 1740; died December 23d, 1740.

                            680.   *New Britain, Conn.*

DANIEL HART, Farmington, third son of Stephen Hart, 3d, of the
same place, and his wife, Sarah (Cowles), born March 20th, 1707–8,
at Farmington; married July 18th, 1734, Abigail Thompson, daughter
of Thomas, and his wife, Abigail (Woodruff), born September 3d,
1710. He lives at the extreme north end of Stanley Street, in New
Britain, on the east side, at the foot of Clark Hill. His wife, Abigail,
died December 7th, 1760, aged 60, when second he married May 21st,
1761, Comfort Stephens, widow of Benjamin, and daughter of   ,
Kelsey.

HIS CHILDREN, BEING THE FIFTH GENERATION.

        Eldad, born June 6th, 1735; died May 17th, 1736.
690.   Eldad, 2d, born March 22d, 1736–7; married July 8th, 1761, Achsa Stevens.
        Stephen, born March 5th, 1739–10; died March 25th, 1739–40.
691.   Stephen, born December 8th, 1744; married Oct. 8th, 1767, Rhoda Stedman.

                            681.   *Farmington.*

STEPHEN HART, Farmington, second son of Sergeant Thomas Hart,
of the same place, and his wife, Elizabeth (Judd), daughter of John
Judd, born July 30th, 1693, at Farmington, and was baptized there on
the same day; married December 29th, 1720, Eunice Munson. He
lived on his father's place, opposite the Female Seminary in Farmington village. He died there in 1773, aged 80 years. Eunice, his widow,
died at Nod or Northington, November 29th, 1793, aged 92 years.

THEIR CHILDREN, BEING THE FIFTH GENERATION.

692.   Samuel, born December 2d, 1721; married   , 1745, Lydia Gridley.
693.   Mary, born January 5th, 1724; married May 31st, 1744, Ebenezer Dickinson;
        second, Hotchkiss.
694.   Stephen, born July 21st, 1725; married September 13th, 1750, Abigail Gridley.
695.   David, born June 28th, 1734; married February 9th, 1758, Elizabeth Porter.
696.   Eunice, born   , 1738; married, about 1760, Joseph Woodford, as
        his second wife.
697.   Lois, born   ; married, October 31st, 1765, Bethuel Norton,
        of Burlington.

                            682.   *Southington, Conn.*

DEACON THOMAS HART, Southington, Conn., third son of Sergeant
Thomas Hart, of Farmington, and his wife, Elizabeth (Judd), born
November 3d, 1695; married March 16th, 1720–1, Anna Stanley,

daughter of Thomas, and his wife, Anna, daughter of Rev. Jeremiah Peck. She (Anna) was born May 14th, 1699. Mr. Hart settled in Southington, one and a half miles north-east of the village, at what is known as the Ebenezer Finch place. He was chosen deacon of the church in Southington, March 31st, 1742, to fill a vacancy occasioned by the death of Deacon Thomas Barnes. Mr. Hart died October 21st, 1754, in his 59th year. Mrs. Anna Hart, his widow, died October 24th, 1770, in her 72d year.

THEIR CHILDREN, BEING THE FIFTH GENERATION.

698. Amos, born February 20th, 1722; married July 20th, 1749, Ann Gridley.
699. Anna, born September 25th, 1724; married   , Samuel Deming.
700. Thomas, born   , 1727; married August 21st, 1750, Sarah Thomas.
701. Reuben, born September 5th, 1729; married December 21st, 1759, Rhoda Peck.
702. John, born December 9th, 1731; baptized December 12th, 1731; married April 12th, 1755, Desire Palmer.
    Dinah, born February 12th, 1733-4; baptized February 17th, 1734; died August, 1739, aged 5 years.
703. Simeon, born December 29th, 1735; baptized January 4th, 1736.
704. Levi, born March 30th, 1738; baptized August 2d, 1738.
    Dinah, born October 10th, 1742; baptized October 10th, 1742; died September 10th, 1743.

683. *Northington, Conn.*

JOSEPH HART, (Nod,) Avon, fourth son of Sergeant Thomas, of Farmington, and his wife, Elizabeth (Judd), born   , 1700, at Northington; married December 6th, 1722, Mary, daughter of Joseph Bird, Jr., and his wife, Mary (Steele). He was a shoe-maker by trade. They were both constituent members of the church at Northington in 1751, and he was their first deacon. He was also a magistrate there. His home was near the first meeting-house at Cider Brook, where his grandson, Gideon W., lived, and has been in possession of his descendants to this day. She died January 23d, 1774–5. He died March 10th, 1777, aged 77 years.

THEIR CHILDREN, BEING THE FIFTH GENERATION.

705. Joseph, born October 1st, 1723; married June 29th, 1749, Ann Barnes.
706. Ruth, born Dec. 26th, 1724; married June 16th, 1748, Barnabas Thompson.
707. Noah, born October 28th, 1726; married March 30th, 1753, Sarah Miller.
708. Lydia, born August 8th, 1728; married December 15th, 1748, Noah Gillett.
709. Gideon, born September 11th, 1730; married November 15th, 1759, Elizabeth Hart.
710. Ambrose, born August 25th, 1732; married August 20th, 1755, Martha Tuller.
711. Medad, born July 27th, 1734; married November 18th, 1754, Phebe Miller.
712. Mary, born September 11th, 1736; married November 27th, 1760, Obadiah Owen.
713. Dinah, born Nov. 9th, 1738; married April 27th, 1758, Appleton Woodruff.
    Sarah, born October 3d, 1741; died October 25th, 1741.
714. Lois, born   ; married May 30th, 1771, David Bristol, of Northington.

684.   *Northington, Conn.*

SAMUEL HART, (Nod) Northington, fifth son of Sergeant Thomas Hart, of Farmington, and his wife, Elizabeth (Judd), born about 1702, at Farmington; married February 5th, 1729–30, Elizabeth Thompson, daughter of Thomas, born August 8th, 1706, at Farmington. He and his wife were constituent members of the church at Avon, in 1751. He held the military rank of lieutenant. He died April 19th, 1769. She died in Northington, July 9th, 1793, aged eighty-six years.

THEIR CHILDREN, BEING THE FIFTH GENERATION.

715. Anna, born January 31st, 1730–1; married August 5th, 1755, Edward Little.
716. Elizabeth, born September 25th, 1732; married   , 1752, Joseph Woodford.
717. Sarah, born December 26th, 1734; married October 30th, 1754, Benjamin Lewis.
718. Mercy, born January 10th, 1736–7; married May 10th, 1758, Jedediah Case, of Simsbury.
719. Martha, born July 31st, 1739; married February 4th, 1759, Daniel Owen; second,   .
      Samuel, born December 14th, 1741; died January 15th, 1742.
720. Abigail, born February 20th, 1743; married February 10th, 1763; Josiah Woodruff.
721. Anthony, born January 25th, 1750–1; married   , 1776, Eleanor Rowe.
722. Esther, born   ; married May 16th, 1765, Matthew Warren, of Hatfield.
723. Rosanna, born   , 1753; died single, in Avon, August 12th, 1807, aged 54.

686.   *Northington, Conn.*

JAMES HART, Avon, Conn., sixth son of Sergeant Thomas, of Farmington, and his wife, Elizabeth (Judd), born and baptized December 14th, 1707, at Avon; married October 10th, 1734, Thankful, daughter of Thomas North, and his wife, Hannah (Woodford), born July 1st, 1708, at Avon. She died October 6th, 1772, in her 65th year.

THEIR CHILDREN, BEING THE FIFTH GENERATION.

724. Elnathan, born September 10th, 1735; married   , Ruth Judd.
725. Lucy, born October 5th, 1740; died single at Avon, November 30th, 1820, aged 80 years.
726. Hannah, born September 9th, 1741; married October 3d, 1765, Obadiah Andrews.
727. Sarah, born July 15th, 1743; married October 6th, 1766, Ebenezer Merrills.
728. Eunice, born August 9th, 1746; married October 3d, 1765, Eli North.

687.   *Northington, Conn.*

WILLIAM HART, Avon, seventh son of Sergeant Thomas Hart, of Farmington, and his wife, Elizabeth (Judd), born August 20th, 1710;

baptized September 27th, 1710, at Farmington; married February 2d, 1737–8, Elizabeth Woodruff, daughter of Matthew, and his wife, Elizabeth (Baldwin), born May 10th, 1713, at Farmington. They resided in Northington, now Avon, east of the river, and she was a constituent member of the church there.

THEIR CHILDREN, BEING THE FIFTH GENERATION.

729. Elizabeth, born April 9th, 1739; married November 15th, 1759, Gideon Hart.
Mary, born September 13th, 1741; died the same day.
730. William, born October 11th, 1743; married October 13th, 1768, Abigail Thompson.
John, born July 26th, 1745; died the same day.
Susannah, born November 30th, 1746; died December 13th, 1748, aged 2 years.
Huldah, born and baptized October 10th, 1756; died October 3d, 1757, aged 1 year.

688. *Farmington, Conn.*

ELISHA HART, Farmington, second son of Timothy Hart, of Farmington, and his wife, Elizabeth (Cowles), born April 28th, 1731, at Farmington, Conn.; married July 14th, 1753, Sarah Cole. He died insolvent, February 29th, 1768, in his 37th year. His widow second married Sylvanus Woodruff.

The Will of Elisha Hart, of Farmington, was dated February 24th, 1768, by which he gave his children, viz., Elisha, Martin, Timothy, Reuben, and Elizabeth. His inventory, £310, dated April, 1768.

Solomon Whitman,
Noah Stanley, } Appraisers.
Asahel Wadsworth,

THEIR CHILDREN, BEING THE FIFTH GENERATION.

Sarah, born February 25th, 1754; died
Sarah, 2d, born June 3d, 1755; died
731. Elisha, born   , 1757; married   , Hannah .
732. Martin, born October 3d, 1758; married   , Vina .
733. Timothy, born April 7th, 1761.
734. Reuben, born May 31st, 1763; married August 25th, 1783, Elizabeth Kilbourn.
Elizabeth, born May 31st, 1766.
Sarah, born September 6th, 1768, posthumous.

NEWELL.

689. *Farmington, Conn.*

ABIGAIL HART, Farmington, second daughter of Timothy Hart, of the same town, and his wife, Elizabeth (Cowles), born August 28th, 1737, at Farmington; married March 13th, 1755, Elisha, son of Deacon Nathaniel Newell, of Farmington, and his wife, Esther (Hart), daughter of John, born December 6th, 1732. He was brother of Rev. Asahel Newell, pastor of the church in Goshen, Conn.

690. *New Britain, Conn.*

ELDAD HART, New Britain, second son of Daniel Hart, of Farmington, and his wife, Abigail (Thompson), born March 22d, 1736–7, at New Britain. He married, July 3d, 1761, Achsah Stevens, daughter of Benjamin, and his wife, Comfort (Kelsey), born June 13th, 1743. He lived in Stanley Quarter, a section of New Britain, at the foot of Clark Hill. He died September 22d, 1776, aged 40 years. She second married Allen.

THEIR CHILDREN, BEING THE SIXTH GENERATION.

735. Azubah, born February 12th, 1762; married , Ebenezer Combs.
736. Abigail, born August 2d, 1763; married , Westover Eton.
737. Anna, born April 17th, 1765; married , 1785, Jesse Cowles, of New Hartford.
738. Lemuel Stevens, born March 15th, 1767; married .
He went to Oneida County, N. Y.
739. Ozias, born January 25th, 1769; married .
740. Aroxa, born January 25th, 1771; married , 1800, George Porter, of Farmington.
741. Lenda, born January 25th, 1773; married , 1790, Salmon Clark.
742. Daniel, born March 6th, 1775; married .
743. Eldad, born February 16th, 1777, posthumous; married · , 1796.

691. *New Britain, Conn.*

STEPHEN HART, New Britain, Conn., fourth son of Daniel Hart, of Farmington, and his wife, Abigail (Thompson), daughter of Thomas, born December 8th, 1744, at New Britain; married October 8th, 1767, Rhoda, daughter of Charles Stedman, and his wife, Jemima (Gaines), of Wethersfield. He was a farmer, and had an impediment in his speech. He lived in Stanley Quarter, at the foot of Clark Hill, and inherited his father's estate, which was one of the three farms and families excepted in the incorporation of the society or parish of New Britain. He died November 20th, 1816, aged 71 years. She died March 26th, 1832, aged 81 years. She was received by letter from the Farmington Church, December 7th, 1823, to the church of New Britain.

THEIR CHILDREN, BEING THE SIXTH GENERATION.

744. Ebenezer, born February 8th, 1768; married October 2d, 1791, Lucy Jerome.
745. Mary, born June 25th, 1770; married August 1st, 1793, Chauncey Merrill.
746. Christina, born October 22d, 1773; married February 12th, 1795, Theodore Webster.
747. Stephen, born October 21st, 1775; married June 25th, 1797, Sally White.
748. Nancy, born and baptized January 2d, 1789; married November 27th, 1806, Simeon, son of Simeon Kilby.

NOTE.—Administration granted on his estate, November 5th, 1776, to Achsah, the widow, and to Stephen Hart, Jr. The commissioners on the estate were James Lusk and John Fuller.

692.   *Northington, Conn.*

SAMUEL HART, Farmington, eldest son of Stephen, and his wife, Eunice (Munson), born December 2d, 1721; married, August, 1745, Lydia Gridley, daughter of James, and his wife, Susannah (Smith), born July 1st, 1723. He resided in Northington, where he was a member of the church. She died December 19th, 1797, aged 73 years. He died February 2d, 1801, aged 80 years.

THEIR CHILDREN, BEING THE SIXTH GENERATION.

749. Lydia, born February 23d, 1746; married Feb. 14th, 1771, Thomas Newell.
750. Susannah, born October 24th, 1748; married April 6th, 1773, David Gleason.
751. Munson, born March 2d, 1750-1; married March 28th, 1782, Mary Hart.
752. Esther, born August 11th, 1757; baptized August 21st, 1757.
753. Lent, born   , 1760; baptized October 5th, 1760; married July 18th, 1782, Olive Hickok.
754. James Gridley, born   , 1763; baptized May 21st, 1764; married April 24th, 1783, Loraine Derrin.

DICKINSON.

693.   *Farmington, Conn.*

MARY HART, eldest daughter of Stephen Hart, of Farmington, and his wife, Eunice (Munson), born January 5th, 1724, at Farmington; married May 31st, 1744, Ebenezer Dickinson, of Farmington. He died there September 2d, 1751, when second he married   , Hotchkiss. The Dickinson children were—Mary, born December 4th, 1745; Elisha, born   , died June 15th, 1753, aged three years; Ebenezer, born November 23d, 1751, posthumous.

694.   *Farmington, Conn.*

STEPHEN HART, Farmington, second son of Stephen Hart, of Farmington, and his wife, Eunice (Munson), born July 21st, 1725, at Farmington; married September 13th, 1750, Abigail Gridley, daughter of James, and his wife, Susannah (Smith), born September 27th, 1727, at Farmington. They lived at the north end of Farmington Village, on the place occupied in 1845 by John T. Norton. He died in 1773, aged 48 years. She died of small pox.

THEIR CHILDREN, BEING THE SIXTH GENERATION.

755. Abigail, born March 18th, 1751; married   , Seth North, of Farmington.
756. Huldah, born December 27th, 1752; married   Andrews.
757. Mercy, born February 20th, 1755; married   , Theodore Bidwell.
758. Eunice, born February 22d, 1757; married   Goodrich, of Berlin.
759. Gad, born March 24th, 1759; married   , Lorana Winchell.
23

695.   *Farmington, Conn.*

DAVID HART, Farmington, third son of Stephen Hart, of the same place, and his wife, Eunice (Munson), born June 28th, 1734; married February 9th, 1758, Elizabeth Porter, daughter of Ebenezer, and his wife, Anna (Porter), born March 20th, 1737–8, at Farmington. They resided in Farmington Village, on his father's place, opposite the Female Seminary, where he died in 1776, aged 42 years. She became a member of the church at Farmington in 1776, and died April 17th, 1809, aged 71 years.

THEIR CHILDREN, BEING THE SIXTH GENERATION.

760. Asa, born June 14th, 1759.
761. Josiah, born September 22d, 1761; married   , Abigail Kelsey.
762. Lavinia, born October 13th, 1764; married   , Isaac Bidwell.
       Zenas, born August 30th, 1767; died young.
763. Huldah, born   ; married July 13th, 1809, George Porter, of Farmington.
764. Elizabeth, born   ; married   John Coe, of West Stockbridge.

WOODFORD.

696.   *Farmington, Conn.*

EUNICE HART, fourth daughter of Stephen Hart, of Farmington, and his wife, Eunice (Munson), born 1738, at Farmington; married about 1760, Joseph Woodford, and was his second wife. He was the son of Joseph, and his wife, Sarah (North), born March 12th, 1731–2, at Farmington. She died in 1803, aged 65 years. She had thirteen children.

698.   *Southington, Conn.*

AMOS HART, Southington, eldest son of Deacon Thomas Hart, of the same town, and his wife, Anna (Stanley), born February 20th, 1722; married July 20th, 1749, Ann, daughter of Joseph Gridley, of Southington, and his wife, Hannah (Lewis), born May 22d, 1727. She died March 27th, 1755, aged 28 years, when second he married November 23d, 1758, Mary, daughter of Gideon Dunham, and sister of Cornelius, born 1732, and died April 13th, 1790, aged 58 years, when third he married December 8th, 1791, Lois, widow of David Clark, and daughter of Jonathan Andrews, and his wife, Susannah (Richards). She was born June 30th, 1736, at Southington. Mr. Hart lived two and a half miles north-east of the village of Southington, in Flanders District, so called. His house stood opposite that of the late Timothy Hart, deceased, on the corner lot, back in the meadow, which has been since known as the "Hunn Hitchcock Place." He died there April 10th, 1798, aged 76 years. His widow, Mrs. Lois Hart, died of fever, August 26th, 1811, aged 75 years.

At the probate court of Farmington, June 9th, 1800, the heirs of Amos Hart, of Southington, late deceased, signed a mutual agreement, and thus settled the estate of their father, viz: Lois Hart, Lemuel Hart, Ard Hart, Jairus Munson, Anna Munson, Lemuel Hamblin, Mary Hamblin, Jesse Pardee, Clarissa Pardee, and Jude Hart.

THEIR CHILDREN, BEING THE SIXTH GENERATION.

765. Anna, born January 5th, 1751; died January 8th, 1754, in her third year.
766. Joel, born May 8th, 1753; died September 22d, 1776, in the army at Hackensack, N. Y.
767. Amos, born March 16th, 1755; married   , and removed to New York.

CHILDREN BY MARY, THE SECOND WIFE.

768. Lemuel, born August 24th, 1759; married   , Rosanna Winston.
769. Ard, born May 17th, 1761; married March 10th, 1788, Millicent Roberts.
770. Anna, born April 5th, 1764; married February 11th, 1790, Jairus Munson.
      Aaron, born October 28th, 1762; died October 29th, 1762.
771. Jude,   }   married December 9th, 1790, Patience Sloper.
      Twins, } born February 8th, 1766;
772. Chauncey, }   married May 4th, 1789, Lydia Hoadly Bray.
773. Mary, born March 5th, 1769; married July 31st, 1792, Lemuel Hamblin.
774. Ira, born February 25th, 1771; married August 19th, 1792, Margaret Hazzard.
775. Clarissa, born April 28th, 1773; married June 12th, 1799, Jesse Pardee.

DEMING.

699.   *Southington, Plainville, Conn.*

ANNA HART, Southington, eldest daughter of Deacon Thomas Hart, of the same town, and his wife, Anna (Stanley), born September 25th, 1724, at Southington; married   , Samuel Deming, of Plainville, who was father of John and Chauncey Deming, of Farmington, so well known, and Eliakim Deming, of Southington. She died November 23d, 1796, aged 72 years.

700.   *Southington, Conn.*

THOMAS HART, Southington, second son of Deacon Thomas Hart, of the same town, and his wife, Anna (Stanley), born 1727; married   , Lydia Hotchkiss, daughter of John, and his wife,

---

NOTE.—Amos Hart and Mary, his wife, March 2d, 1790, for twenty shillings, sold to Levi Hart one-tenth part of about one-half acre of undivided land in Southington, situated about twelve rods south of the meeting-house, which formerly belonged to Mr. Gideon Dunham, bounded west on highway, northerly and easterly on highway, south on Captain David Peck.

Marian (Wood), of Cheshire, born February 19th, 1733, in Wallingford, probably in that part now called Cheshire. It appears that he
lived where Eli Dunham now lives, or near there, which place he sold
to Captain John Hungerford, and removed to Bristol, Conn., in 1764,
where he died, March 23d, 1777, in his 50th year, when his widow,
Lydia, second married, September, 1777, Captain Ladwick Hotchkiss,
then of Farmington Plains, now called Plainville. She was his third
wife, and they removed to New Durham, N. Y.

THEIR CHILDREN, BEING THE SIXTH GENERATION.

776. Elijah, born November 16th, 1752; baptized November 19th, 1752.
777. Thomas, born January 4th, 1755; baptized February 16th, 1755.
778. Jason, born May 13th, 1757; baptized June 12th, 1757.
779. Ithural, born November 15th, 1759; baptized December 8th, 1759; married
      , Sibil Jerome.
780. Gilbert, born May 24th, 1762; baptized June 27th, 1762; married
      Sarah Lindsley.
781. Seth, born April 19th, 1765; married   , Mary Wilcox.
782. Calvin, born September 23d, 1767; married March 20th, 1791, Anna Yale.
      Lydia, born 1770; died October 9th, 1776, in her 7th year.
      Nancy, born   , 1774; died October 26th, 1776, in her 3d year.

701.

Southington, Conn.

CAPTAIN REUBEN HART, Southington, third son of Deacon Thomas
Hart, of the same town, and his wife, Anna (Stanley), born September
5th, 1729; baptized September 21st, 1729; married December 21st,
1759, Rhoda, daughter of Moses Peck, of Kensington, and his wife,
Sarah (Kellogg), born June 24th, 1735, at Kensington. She was sister
of Sarah, wife of Timo.hy Clark, Esq., of West Street, Southington.
Mr. Hart lived in Flanders, a locality of the town, on the corner, where
the residence of Francis D. Lewis stood in 1869. It was a large
double house, facing the west, with a leanto in the rear, and was torn
down about 1855, to give place to the present structure. He was appointed by the General Assembly in 1777, ensign to the third company
of the Alarm Lists, Fifteenth Regiment. He had a captain's commission, signed by Jonathan Trumbull, Governor, and countersigned by
George Wyllys, Secretary of State, dated at Hartford, May 23d, 1778,
and is now in possession of his grandson, Levi A. Hart, Esq., of Wilmington, N. C. He was a man of strong intellectual powers, and, for
the limited advantages he enjoyed, had a highly cultivated mind. He
died December 6th, 1788, aged 59 years. His widow, Mrs. Rhoda
Hart, died of consumption, March 24th, 1803, in her 68th year.

783. Samuel, born August 31st, 1761; married February 8th, 1786, Rosanna Clark.
Lucy, born May 8th, 1764; died June 6th, 1764.
784. Sarah, born October 18th, 1766; died single, October 17th, 1843, aged 77 years.
785. Roswell, born August 22d, 1768; married   , Sylvia Barnes.
786. Timothy, born July 15th, 1770; married April 24th, 1794, Eunice Woodruff.
787. Lucy, 2d, born   ; married November 6th, 1794, Francis
Hurlburt, of Kensington.

702. *Southington, Conn.*

JOHN HART, Southington, fourth son of Deacon Thomas Hart, of
the same place, and his wife, Anna (Stanley), born December 9th,
1731, at Southington; baptized there December 12th, 1731, by Rev.
Jeremiah Curtiss, then pastor of that church; married April 10th,
1755, Desire Palmer, daughter of Judah, and his wife, Mary (Farrington),* born September 2d, 1735, in Branford, Conn. He settled in
Flanders District, on the east side, on what has been known as the
Jude Hart Place, where, in 1869,   Lewis lived. This place,
consisting of eighty-two acres of land, more or less, with dwelling-
house and barn, he sold to Jude Hart for $1,340, by deed, dated May
22d, 1799. He then removed to Bristol, Conn. He died very destitute, in Lenox, Vt., whither his ungrateful son had taken him, and
then deserted him.

788. John, born   , 1756; baptized January 3d, 1757.
789. Levi, born   , 1759; married May 3d, 1780, Philatœa Allen.
790. Wells, born   , 1771; married August 4th, 1793, Polly Root, of
Bristol.

703. *Southington, Burlington, Conn.*

SIMEON HART, Southington, sixth son of Deacon Thomas Hart, of
the same place, and his wife, Anna (Stanley), born December 29th,
1735, at Southington; baptized January 4th, 1736, by Rev. Jeremiah
Curtiss; married September 14th, 1756, Sarah Sloper, daughter of
Robert, and his wife, Experience (Johnson), born October 13th, 1737.
Mr. Hart's residence stood some sixty rods north of the almshouse, on
the west side of the road, the house having long since been torn away,
and the ground leveled. About three rods south stood another house,
which was torn away a few years since, part of the chimney and cellar
still remaining. About ten feet north of the last-mentioned house was
the well, now covered with boards, which served for both houses.

---

* Her mother, Mary (Farrington), was from Dedham, Mass., and was granddaughter of Micah Palmer, of Branford, and his wife, Damaris Whitehead.

Across the middle of the well, running west from the highway, was the dividing line between the proprietors. He sold his place, consisting of land, dwelling-house, barn, and fruit trees, to Philip M. Farnsworth, for £100, by deed, dated February 14th, 1774. In the deed it is described as being in the south division, east tier of lots, eleventh lot in number, laid out on the right of Captain John Stanley, and lying west of a three-rod highway, beginning in the highway and running west across the middle of the well about twenty-four rods, thence north to land of John Curtiss, bounded east on highway, south on Ichabod Andrews, west on Jonathan Bronson, and north on John Curtiss. Soon after disposing of his farm Mr. Hart removed to Burlington, where his eighth child died, August 10th, 1774, and was buried at the North Cemetery, Bristol, where his five youngest children have tomb-stones. He was active in forming the church at Burlington, and was one of its first deacons, which office he held until excused on account of feeble health. He was justice of the peace for several years. When Bristol, including Burlington, was made a town in 1785, he was their first representative to the state legislature. He lived an eminently useful life, and died instantly, January 12th, 1800, his wife having died the day previous. They were both buried in the same grave, and the inscription on their tomb-stone in the cemetery west of the meeting-house in Burlington, reads thus:

> "Here lieth the bodies of Deacon Simeon Hart,
> and Sarah, his wife;
> She died January 11th, 1800,
> Aged 62, and he died
> January 12th, 1800, Aged 64.
> They were eminent for Piety,
> Charity, and Christian Morality.

> "Inexorable death, thou sweep'st away
> The kind, compassionate, and just,
> All flesh by thee is turned to clay,
> And moulders into common dust.
> Here ends thy reign, the soul shall rise,
> (If Grace the heart hath well refined,)
> Shall join the chorus of the skies,
> In Hallelujahs to the Eternal Mind."

THEIR CHILDREN, BEING THE SIXTH GENERATION.

Levi, born March 22d, 1758; died April 14th, 1758.

791. Ambrose, born March 28th, 1759; married, Aug., 1782, Mercy Bartholomew.

792. Bliss, born March 10th, 1761; married May 17th, 1783, Sylvia Upson.

793. Simeon, born September 8th, 1763; married October 27th, 1783, Mary Warner.

Anna, born October 2d, 1765; died November 11th, 1776, in her 12th year. She was an only daughter.

794. Marcus, born Dec. 20th, 1767; married January 17th, 1786, Rhoda Wiard.

Lucas, born September 14th, 1770; died October 25th, 1776, in his 7th year.

Martin, born June 2d, 1772; died November 15th, 1776, in his 5th year.

Oliver Sloper, born May 29th, 1774; died August 16th, 1774, in his 1st year.

Oliver Sloper, 2d, born November 1st, 1775; died January 21st, 1777, in his 2d year.

704. *Preston, Conn.*

REV. LEVI HART, Preston, Conn., seventh son of Deacon Thomas Hart, of Southington, and his wife, Anna (Stanley), born March 30th, 1738, at Southington, Conn.; baptized August 2d, 1738, by Rev. J. Curtiss, pastor. He graduated at Yale College in 1760, and studied theology with Dr. Bellamy, of Bethlehem, Conn. He settled in the ministry November 4th, 1762, in that part of Preston, Conn., now called Griswold. He married, 1762, Rebecca, daughter of Rev. Dr. Bellamy, and his wife, Frances (Sherman), born September 11th, 1747, at Cheshire, Conn. She died December 24th, 1788, aged 41 years, when he second married December 4th, 1790, the widow of Nathaniel Baccus, of Norwich. He died October 27th, 1808, aged 70 years.

In the year 1800 the college of New Jersey honored him with the degree of D. D. He was a member of the corporation of Dartmouth College from 1784 to 1788, and of Yale College from 1794 to the year preceding his death. Of the intimate friends of Rev. Mr. Hart next to Dr. Bellamy perhaps, was Dr. Hopkins, of Newport, R. I., whose funeral sermon he preached, December 23d, 1803.

The Connecticut Missionary Society owes much to the sympathy and labors of Mr. Hart in its origin and progress. Indeed he was a missionary himself as early as 1769, and with the consent of his people he made a journey into the district of Maine, to preach to the destitute, and again in 1795 he performed a tour of missionary labor at the north, towards Canada. During the great struggle of the country for independence his sympathy was with our army, and his patriotism led him to visit the camp at Roxbury, and preach twice on the Sabbath to Colonel Parsons' regiment. In 1783 he delivered a discourse to an assembly convened at Fort Griswold, Groton, in commemoration of those gallant men who fell there in defence of their country, Colonel Ledyard at their head. But the chief excellence of Mr. Hart appeared as a gospel minister, and pastor to his flock at Griswold, and the savor of his good name has extended down to this date, being spoken of as one of the greatest and best men of the past generation. His funeral was attended by all the neighboring clergymen, and an excellent sermon was preached by Rev. Joel Benedict, of Plainfield, from the words— "Your fathers, where are they? and the prophets, do they live for ever?"—Zechariah 1: 5. A very large and attentive concourse of people hung upon the lips of the preacher while he described some of the prominent features of the character of the deceased, and evidenced that their hearts affectionately responded to the justice of his delinea- tion. His remains were deposited by the side of a deceased wife, at whose grave he had erected a plain stone, with this inscription:

"And Jacob set up a pillar at Rachel's Grave."

CHILDREN BY HIS FIRST WIFE, REBECCA, BEING THE SIXTH GENERATION.

795.   Rebecca, born   ; married   , Rev. Amos Chase.

796.   William Sherman, born   , 1767; married   , Eunice Baccus.

797.   Alice Cogswell, born August 23d, 1772; married November 27th, 1794, Calvin Goddard.

798.   Levi, born   . He graduated at Brown University in 1802.

705.   *Northington, now Avon.*

JOSEPH HART, Northington, eldest son and child of Joseph, of the same place, and his wife, Mary (Bird), born October 1st, 1723, at North- ington; married June 29th, 1749, Ann Barnes, daughter of Thomas, and his wife, Hannah (Day), of Southington, born August 24th, 1727. She was admitted to the church at Southington, September 20th, 1741, and to the church at Northington by letter from Southington, Decem- ber 20th, 1751. He was also a member of the Avon Church. On his return from attending his son, who died in the camp at Stamford, he died at New Haven, February 16th, 1777, aged 53 years. His wife died February 1st, 1786.

THEIR CHILDREN, BEING THE SIXTH GENERATION.

Dorcas, born May 17th, 1750; died June 2d, 1750, aged 15 days.

Hannah, born February 23d, 1752; died June 25th, 1753, about 16 months old.

799.   Asahel, born May 12th, 1754; married November 5th, 1778, Anna Kilbourn.

800.   Ann, born July 21st, 1756; married   , Lot Thompson.

801.   Joseph, born July 29th, 1759; died in camp at Stamford, February 10th, 1777.

802.   Bethel, born December 1st, 1762; married June 24th, 1784, Huldah Steele.

803.   Azubah, born September 28th, 1765; married   , Eben Thompson.

804.   Ezra, born October 5th, 1768; baptized November 1st, 1768.

THOMPSON.

706.   *Northington, now Avon.*

RUTH HART, eldest daughter of Joseph Hart, of Northington, now Avon, and his wife, Mary (Bird), born December 26, 1724, at North- ington; married there, June 16th, 1748, Barnabas Thompson, son of

Samuel, and his wife, Hannah Lathrop, born November 13th, 1723, at Northington. He died September 18th, 1776, in his 53d year. They had children, viz: a daughter, born May 5th, 1749, and died on the 9th; Ruth, born July 11th, 1750; Barnabas, born August 7th, 1752; Levi, born September 13th, 1755; Asa, born March 23d, 1759.

707.   *Northington, now Avon.*

NOAH HART, Avon, second son of Joseph Hart, of the same place, and his wife, Mary (Bird), born October 28th, 1726; married March 30th, 1753, Sarah Miller, who died October 10th, 1776. He died March 22d, 1777, in his 51st year.

THEIR CHILDREN, BEING THE SIXTH GENERATION.

805. Joel, born September 2d, 1754; married   , 1780, Huldah Woodruff.
806. Seth, born May 23d, 1756; married December 9th, 1779, Anna Miller.
807. Mary, born May 20th, 1758; married March 28th, 1782, Munson Hart.
808. Selah, born July 1st, 1760; married   , Sarah
809. Dan, born July 6th, 1762; married
810. Hannah, born   , 1764; baptized July 1st, 1764; married
     James Alderman.
     Noah, ⎫   died June 11th, 1787, aged 19 years.
            ⎬ born   , 1767;
811. Sarah, ⎭   married   Blakesley.
812. Levi, born August 12th, 1770, and removed to Barkhamsted.

GILLETT.

708.   *Northington, now Avon.*

LYDIA HART, Avon, second daughter of Joseph Hart, of the same town, and his wife, Mary (Bird), born August 8th, 1728, at Northington; married December 15th, 1748, Noah Gillett, and had children—Isaac, born January 29th, 1748-9, died February 4th, 1748; Isaac, born January 3d, 1749-50, died June 25th, 1755; Lydia, born August 2d, 1752; Noah, born March 10th, 1755; Titus, born November 7th, 1756; Obadiah, born May 6th, 1763; Amos, born May 16th, 1765.

709.   .   *Northington, now Avon.*

GIDEON HART, Avon, third son of Joseph Hart, of the same place, and his wife, Mary (Bird), born September 11th, 1730, at Farmington; married November 15th, 1759, Elizabeth, daughter of William Hart, and his wife, Elizabeth (Woodruff), of Avon, born April 9th, 1739. She died January 1st, 1825, aged 85. They were both admitted to the church at Farmington in 1814. He was a prosperous farmer, and they lived near the bridge across Farmington River, at Cider Brook, the

24

house being on the north side of the narrow lane leading to the bridge. He died November 17th, 1807, aged 77. The Bible said to have been Joseph Hart's, printed at London in 1585, was given by his wife, Elizabeth, to her daughter, Rhoda Thompson, and was exchanged for a common, large, family Bible, with the Historical Society at Hartford, where it may be seen—"*when found.*"

THEIR CHILDREN, BEING THE SIXTH GENERATION.

813. Huldah, born September 29th, 1760; married February 18th, 1784, Joel Marshall, of Granville.

814. Elizabeth, born May 11th, 1762; married January 11th, 1788, Isaac Gillett, of Avon.

815. Rhoda, born December 27th, 1764; married July 12th, 1814, Eben Thompson, of Farmington.

816. Abner, born December 3d, 1766; married   , 1801, Alma Thompson.

817. Almira, born September 4th, 1769; married Nov. 24th, 1791, Amos Gillett.

818. Alice, born November 5th, 1771; married March 6th, 1796, Samuel Andrews, of Farmington.

Gideon B., born January 13th, 1774; died March 3d, 1775, aged 1 year.

819. Gideon Baldwin, born February 14th, 1776; married December 29th, 1795, Marilla Woodford.

820. Joseph, born June 30th, 1778; married November 5th, 1806, Eunice Fitts.

Noadiah, born November 2d, 1781; died April 9th, 1786, aged 5 years.

710.   *Northington, now Avon.*

AMBROSE HART, Avon, fourth son of Joseph Hart, of the same place, and his wife, Mary (Bird), born August 25th, 1732, at Avon; married March 20th, 1755, Martha Fuller, of Simsbury. He was admitted to Avon Church, March 7th, 1756. The Will of Ambrose Hart was proved in probate court, at Farmington, July 6th, 1799, and Gad and Martha Hart made administrators of the Will annexed.

Item.—I give my wife, Martha, my Loom and tackling, and use of my House and Barn, and half my lands, and the indoors furniture and wearing apparel I give her forever.

Item.—I give my son, Gad.

Item.—I give my daughter, Sabra Whiting.

Item.—I give my daughter, Diadama Cadwell.

Item.—I give my granddaughter, Huldah Brace.

Item.—And I constitute my son-in-law, Lot Woodruff, my sole Executor.   (Signed,) Ambrose Hart, and seal.

The Inventory, £671 18s., taken by Samuel Bishop,

       August 23d, 1799.   and Timothy Crosby.

He died June 23d, 1799, in his 67th year. She died September 26th, 1806, in her 77th year, so says their tomb-stones in the old cemetery east of the river, near the First Church in Avon, Conn.

THEIR CHILDREN, BEING THE SIXTH GENERATION.

21. Asenath, born April 4th, 1756; died single, October 29th, 1784, aged 28.
  Huldah, born June 25th, 1758; died October 14th, 1758, aged 1 year.
22. Martha, born   , 1759; baptized January 20th, 1759; married March
  9th, 1780, Lot Woodruff.
23. Rosa, born   , 1762; baptized March 20th, 1762; married September
  1st, 1785, Titus Goodwin.
24. Abi, born July 8th, 1764; married September 1st, 1785, Zenas Brace.
25. Sibil, born October 14th, 1766; married October 14th, 1793, Abel Thompson,
  of East Farms.
26. Gad, born   , 1770; baptized March 4th, 1770; married July 21st,
  1791, Eunice M. Woodford.
27. Sabre, born September 11th, 1772; married November 19th, 1793, Elijah M.
  Whiting, of West Hartford.
28. Lodama, born   , 1776; baptized October 13th, 1776; married   ,
  1798, Martin Cadwell.

711.   *Northington, now Avon.*

MEDAD HART, Avon, son of Joseph Hart, of the same place, and his
wife, Mary (Bird), born July 27th, 1734, at Avon; married November
8th, 1756, Phebe Miller. He died March 1st, 1777, aged 43. His
widow died December 12th, 1808, aged 78 years.

THEIR CHILDREN, BEING THE SIXTH GENERATION.

29. Dorcas, born January 14th, 1754-5; baptized June 19th, 1755; admitted to the
  church November 7th, 1784; died single.
30. Susannah, born June 12th, 1756; baptized June 20th, 1756; died April 19th,
  1778, aged 21 years.
  Enos, baptized May 20th, 1759. He wandered from home and was never heard
  from.
31. Hosea, baptized March 1st, 1761; married   , Joanna Tuller.
  Phebe, baptized April 24th, 1763; died January 25th, 1784, aged 20.
  Charity Bird, baptized May 12th, 1765; died in 1765.
32. Ruth, baptized February 14th, 1767; married October 7th, 1784, Timothy Alderman, of Simsbury.
33. Lydia, baptized August 26th, 1770; married   , 1791, Stephen Brace,
  of West Hartford.
  Charity Bird, born   , 1772; died March 11th, 1778, aged 6 years.

OWEN.

712.   *Northington, now Avon.*

MARY HART, Avon, third daughter of Joseph Hart, of the same
place, and his wife, Mary (Bird), born September 11th, 1736, in Farm-
ngton; married in Avon, November 17th, 1760, Obadiah Owen.

WOODRUFF.

713.   *Farmington, Conn.*

DINAH HART, Farmington, Conn., fourth daughter of Joseph Hart, of Avon, and his wife, Mary (Bird), born November 9th, 1738; married April 29th, 1768, Appleton Woodruff, of Farmington. They had children—Dinah, Roeda, Lois, Appleton, Roger Hooker, Timothy, born May 24th, 1776; Mary, born September 24th, 1779.

BRISTOL.

714.   *Avon, Conn.*

LOIS HART, Avon, youngest daughter of Joseph Hart, of the same place, and his wife, Mary (Bird), born at Avon; married May 30th, 1771, David Bristol, of Avon.

724.   *Farmington, Conn.*

ELNATHAN HART, Farmington, eldest son of James Hart, of Avon, and his wife, Thankful (North), born September 10th, 1735, at Farmington; married   , Ruth Judd, daughter of Joseph, and his wife, Ruth (Thompson), of Southington. She died November 27th, 1810, aged 70 years. He died August 26th, 1831, aged 96 years. He was a member of the church at Northington for sixty-nine years, being admitted June 13th, 1762. She was admitted June 9th, 1765.

THEIR CHILDREN, BEING THE SIXTH GENERATION.

834. Linas, born September 30th, 1761; married   , 1787, Mary Ann Wilcox.

Martin, born, May, 1767; died August 4th, 1790, aged 23 years.

835. Obed, born June 14th, 1769; married   , 1793, Elizabeth Edson.

725.   *Northington, now Avon.*

LUCY HART, eldest daughter of James Hart, of Avon, and his wife, Thankful (North), born October 5th, 1740, at Farmington. She was never married. She died at Northington, now Avon, November 30th, 1820, aged 80 years.

ANDREWS.

726.   *Northington, now Avon.*

HANNAH HART, second daughter of James Hart, of Avon, and his wife, Thankful (North), born September 9th, 1741, at Farmington, in Avon; married October 3d, 1765, Obadiah Andrews, son of Joseph,

Jr., and his wife, Elizabeth Beckwith, of Southington, born May 4th, 1741. She was admitted to the church at Farmington in 1795. He was named in his father's Will, dated October 13th, 1749, and had 5s. more than he had already given him. No children found for this family.

MERRILLS.

727. *West Hartford.*

SARAH HART, third daughter of James Hart, of Northington, and his wife, Thankful (North), born July 15th, 1743, at Avon; married October 6th, 1766, Ebenezer Merrills, of West Hartford, Conn.

NORTH.

728. *Northington, now Avon.*

EUNICE HART, fourth daughter of James Hart, of Northington, Conn., and his wife, Thankful (North), born August 9th, 1746; married October 3d, 1765, Eli North, her cousin, son of Timothy, and his wife, Hannah (North), born 1743, at Farmington. Both parents were admitted to the church in 1777. They had—1, Eunice, born 1767, married 1790, Daniel Cowles, no children; 2, Elijah, born 1768; married 1796, Mary Hosford; 3, Irene, married 1801, Samuel Gridley, of Collinsville; 4, Timothy, married 1802, Polly Larkum, and in 1829 Widow Anna Day, and went to Candor, N. Y.; 5, James, born 1781, married Lucina Andrews, daughter of Obadiah, died in 1833, aged 52; 6, Roxy, married 1812, Samuel Teel; 7, Cynthia, married Amzi Garrill, of Candor, N. Y.; 8, Sophronia, married William Monroe.

HART.

729. *Cider Brook, Avon.*

ELIZABETH HART, eldest daughter of William Hart, of Northington, and his wife, Elizabeth (Woodruff), born April 9th, 1739; married November 15th, 1759, Gideon Hart, son of Joseph, and his wife, Mary (Bird), of the same place, born September 11th, 1730. They lived near the bridge over Farmington River from Cider Brook District. For children see Gideon Hart.

730. *Northington, now Avon.*

WILLIAM HART, Avon, Conn., eldest son of William Hart, and his wife, Elizabeth (Woodruff), of the same place, born October 11th, 1743, at Avon, Conn.; married October 13th, 1768, Abigail Thompson. He and his wife were admitted to the church in Northington, March tth, 1770. He died in 1812, aged 69 years, and she died in 1811, aged 65 years.

THEIR CHILDREN, BEING THE SIXTH GENERATION.

336. Belinda, born , 1783; married , Isaac Loomis.
   Son, born , 1771; died June 15th, 1771.
   Laflara, baptized May 24th, 1772; died young.
337. Roxalana, baptized July 9th, 1775; married , Charles
   Woodruff.
   Daughter, born , 1777; died June 9th, 1777.
338. Abigail, baptized April 11th, 1779; married , Aaron North.
339. Timothy Thompson, baptized May 6th, 1781; married ,
   Wright, of Guilford.
340. Orrin, born , 1783; married , Sally Gladden,
   daughter of Jedediah.
   William, born , 1785; married
   Clara, born , 1787; died , 1809, aged 22.
   Thomas, born , 1789; died
341. Laflara, born , 1789; married, June, 1812, Ira Cowles, of Farmington. She died a pious woman.

731. *Farmington, New Britain, Conn.*

ELISHA HART, Farmington and New Britain, eldest son of Elisha Hart, and his wife, Sarah (Cole), of Farmington, born at Farmington in 1757; married , Hannah .
She was admitted to the church in New Britain, February 5th, 1791. They lived in a house that he bought of Ezekiel Wright, near Bass River, on the road from New Britain to Farmington, and near the line. He sold his place to Asahel Hart, and soon after, in 1791, removed to Whitestown, where he died during the war of 1812.

THEIR CHILDREN, BEING THE SIXTH GENERATION.

842. Truman, born ; baptized May 10th, 1791.
   Sarah, born ; baptized May 10th, 1791; died May 15th,
   1791.
   Phebe, born ; baptized May 10th, 1791; died ,
   1791.
843. Hannah, born ; baptized May 10th, 1791.
   Rhoda, born ; baptized May 10th, 1791.
   Elisha, born ; baptized May 10th, 1791; died May 17th,
   1791.

734. *Whitestown, N. Y.*

REUBEN HART, Farmington, fourth son of Elisha Hart, of Farmington, and his wife, Sarah (Cole), born May 31st, 1763; married August 25th, 1783, Elizabeth, daughter of Joshua Kilbourn, of Farmington, and his wife, Mehitabel (Mather), born September 24th, 1765. Not long after marriage they removed to Whitestown, N. Y. She died in 1803. He died May 5th, 1824, aged 61 years.

THEIR CHILDREN, BEING THE SIXTH GENERATION.

844. Dorothy, born   ; married   , Reuben
     Heacock, Chili, N. Y.
845. Alpheas, born   ; married   , 1816, Char-
     lotte Mallens, of Ohio.
846. Pluma, born   ; married   , Edward
     Newell, of Whitestown.
847. Amanda, born   ; married   , Asahel
     Mosier.
848. Ansel, born   ; married   ,
     of Spencerport, N. Y.
849. Sophia, born   ; married   , Stephen
     Nourse.
850. Chauncey, born September 10th, 1797; married October 10th, 1819, Rosella
     Hard.
851. Eliza, born   ; married   , Roderic
     Hunt.

COMBS.

735.   *Herkimer County, N. Y.*

AZUBAH HART, eldest daughter of Eldad Hart, of New Britain, and his wife, Achsah (Stevens), born February 12th, 1762, at New Britain. She married   , Ebenezer Combs, of Litchfield, Herkimer County, N. Y. She was a member of the church.

EATON.

736.   *Perrysburg, N. Y.*

ABIGAIL HART, second daughter of Eldad Hart, of New Britain, Conn., and his wife, Achsah (Stevens), born August 2d, 1763, at New Britain. She married   , Westover Eton, and went to Perrysburg, Cattaraugus County, N. Y.

COWLES.

737.   *Warren, Evans, N. Y.*

ANNA HART, third daughter of Eldad Hart, of New Britain, and his wife, Achsah (Stevens), born April 17th, 1765, at New Britain; married   , 1785, Jesse, son of Phineas Cowles, of Farmington, born September 14th, 1765, at Farmington. He removed to Warren, Saratoga County, N. Y., and from there to Evans, Erie County, N. Y., but finally returned to his daughter in New Hartford, Conn. They had five sons and seven daughters, three of whom died in infancy.

738.   *Oneida County, N. Y.*

LEMUEL STEVENS HART, New Britain, Conn., eldest son of Eldad Hart, of New Britain, and his wife, Achsah (Stevens), born March 15th, 1767, at New Britain; married   . He was a farmer, and removed to Augusta, Oneida County, N. Y., where he died in 1820, aged 53 years.

THEIR CHILDREN, BEING THE SEVENTH GENERATION.

852. Erastus, born
      Edward, born   ; died   , 1812.
853. Stephen, born
854. Chauncey, born •
      Ephraim, born   ; died   , aged 11 years.

PORTER.

740.   *Farmington, Conn.*

AROXA HART, fourth daughter of Eldad Hart, of New Britain, and his wife, Achsah (Stevens), born January 25th, 1771, at New Britain; married 1800, George Porter, of Farmington. He was admitted to the church there, August, 1821. She died, and he second married July 13th, 1809, Huldah Hart, before Rev. Noah Porter.

742.   .   *Augusta, N. Y.*

DANIEL HART, Augusta, Oneida County, N. Y., third son of Eldad Hart, of New Britain, Conn., and his wife, Achsah (Stevens), born March 6th, 1775, at New Britain; married   . He settled at Augusta, Oneida County, N. Y., in 1795, as a farmer, and from thence removed to Ohio about 1810. He was a church member. No wife or children reported after much inquiry.

743.   *Augusta, N. Y.*

ELDAD HART, youngest son of Eldad Hart, of New Britain, Conn., and his wife, Achsah (Stevens), born February 16th, 1777, posthumous, at New Britain. He married   , 1796,   , and settled in Augusta, Oneida County, N. Y. He and his wife, and one daughter, are members of the church there.

THEIR CHILDREN, BEING THE SEVENTH GENERATION.

855. Ira, born February 27th, 1798; married
856. William B., born June 25th, 1800; died September 19th, 1831, at South Caro-
      lina, aged 31 years. He was a member of the church.
857. Philo, born December 10th, 1801; married

58. Lucina, born November 14th, 1803; married
59. Aroxa, born August 14th, 1806; married
60. Ephraim, born November 19th, 1817; married
61. Mary, born August 18th, 1820; married

744. *New Britain, Conn.*

EBENEZER HART, New Britain, eldest son of Stephen Hart, of that place, and his wife, Rhoda (Stedman), born February 8th, 1768, at New Britain; married October 2d, 1791, Lucy, daughter of Andrew Jerome, of Bristol, Conn., and his wife, Chloe (Sage), born February 5th, 1773, at Bristol, and was brought up in the Rev. Samuel Newell's family. He died of yellow fever on his passage home from the West Indies, May 30th, 1798, aged 31 years, when she second married July 27th, 1799, Allen Steele, son of Josiah. She died November 24th, 1820, aged 48 years.

THEIR CHILDREN, BEING THE SEVENTH GENERATION.

Emily, born April 27th, 1792; died April 20th, 1796, aged 4 years.
Albert, born November 18th, 1793; died February 29th, 1795, aged 15 months.
62. Dorothy, born September 16th, 1795; married February 3d, 1814, Colonel Joseph Wright.
Ebenezer, born May 21st, 1798; died by the kick of a horse, July 3d, 1802, aged 4 years.

MERRILLS.

745. *New Britain, Conn.*

MARY HART, eldest daughter of Stephen Hart, Sr., of New Britain, Conn., and his wife, Rhoda (Stedman), born June 25th, 1770, at New Britain; married August 1st, 1793, Chauncey, son of Abraham Merrills, of Wethersfield. They lived on the north side of Dublin Hill, in New Britain. She was admitted to the Congregational Church there, February 2d, 1800, and died March 12th, 1825, aged 55 years. They had—1, Rhoda Hart, married January 22d, 1822, Jerry D. Goodrich; 2, Mary Hart, born December 30th, 1802, married, December, 1819, John Bunce; 3, Judith Brace, baptized June 16th, 1805, married September 21st, 1826, Austin Mosier; 4, William Walter, baptized June 26th, 1808, died Æ. 2 years, 6 months.

WEBSTER.

746. *West Hartford, Conn.*

CHESTINA HART, second daughter of Stephen Hart, Sr., of New Britain, and his wife, Rhoda (Stedman), born October 22d, 1773, at

25

New Britain; married February 12th, 1795, Theodore Webster, son of
Stephen, of West Hartford, born April 15th, 1769. She died April
26th, 1828, aged 55 years. He died August 2d, 1851, aged 83 years.

747.   *New. Britain, Conn.*

STEPHEN HART, Jr., second son of Stephen Hart, Sr., of New Britain, and his wife, Rhoda (Stedman), born October 21st, 1775, at New
Britain; married June 25th, 1797, Sally, daughter of Ezra White, and
his wife, Lucy (Stanliff), of Chatham, born June 14th, 1775. He was
a farmer, and lived at the old home of his father, Stephen, and his
grandfather, Daniel, at the foot of Clark Hill, in Stanley Quarter. He
died December 9th, 1816, aged 41 years. She died at the residence of
her son, Philip, on East Street, New Britain, September 6th, 1859, aged
84 years.

THEIR CHILDREN, BEING THE SEVENTH GENERATION.

863.   Stephen, born Feb. 19th, 1798; married August 24th, 1818, Cynthia Steele.
864.   Edmund, born April 23d, 1799; married June 2d, 1824, Mehitabel Dewey.
865.   George, born March 16th, 1801; married March 2d, 1826, Mary Griswold An-
           drews; second
866.   Emily, born March 15th, 1804; married September 21st, 1823, Erastus Parker,
           of Lenox, Mass.
867.   Philip, born June 25th, 1805; married November 16th, 1831, Mary Judd.
868.   William, born October 12th, 1808; married July 28th, 1830, Rhoda Judd;
           second
        Henry, born   , 1811 ; died of dysentery, September 27th, 1814,
           aged 3 years.
869.   Ebenezer, born July 31st, 1814; married January 6th, 1842, Mary Pease,
           of Warehouse Point.

KILBY.

748.   *Wethersfield, Burlington, Conn.*

NANCY HART, youngest daughter of Stephen Hart, Sr., of New
Britain, and his wife, Rhoda (Stedman), born   ;
baptized January 2d, 1789, at New Britain, Conn.; married November
27th, 1806, Simeon, son of Simeon Kilby, of Wethersfield, Conn.

LITTLE.

715.   *Farmington, Conn.*

ANNA HART, eldest daughter and child of Samuel Hart, of Northington, and his wife, Elizabeth (Thompson), born January 31st, 1730-1,
in Farmington (Avon); married August 5th, 1755, Edward Little, of
Farmington.

THEIR CHILD.

Anna, born January 8th, 1757.

WOODFORD.

716. *Northington, now Avon.*

ELIZABETH HART, Avon, second daughter of Samuel Hart, of the same place, and his wife, Elizabeth (Thompson), born September 25th, 1732, in Farmington; married August 1st, 1751, Joseph Woodford, of Avon, son of Joseph Woodford, Jr., and his wife, Sarah North, born March 12th, 1731-2, at Farmington. She died in 1759, aged 27 years. They had children, viz: Elisha, born November 1st, 1752, died November 8th, 1752; Dinah, born March 1st, 1754.

LEWIS.

717. *Northington, now Avon.*

SARAH HART, Avon, third daughter of Samuel Hart, of Northington, and his wife, Elizabeth (Thompson), born December 26th, 1734, at Farmington; married October 30th, 1754, Benjamin Lewis. Their children were—Samuel Hart, Dorcas, Lucy, Benjamin, and Abisha, born May 15th, 1766. See Farmington Record.

CASE.

718. *Simsbury, Conn.*

MERCY HART, fourth daughter of Samuel Hart, of Avon, Conn., formerly Northington, and his wife, Elizabeth (Thompson), born January 10th, 1736-7, at Northington, then a parish of Farmington; married May 10th, 1758, Jedediah Case, of Simsbury, son of Joseph, and his wife, Hannah (Humphrey), born March 30th, 1733. He died at Simsbury, January 11th, 1818, aged 84 years, 9 months, 11 days. They had—1, Jedediah, born 1759; 2, Elihu, born 1761; 3, Humphrey, born 1762; 4, Phebe T., born 1765; 5, Hezekiah, born 1769; 6, Elizabeth, born 1771; Horatio G., born September 21st, 1777. The mother died, February, 1826, aged 89 years.

OWEN. WHITNEY.

719. *Simsbury, Conn., Montville, O.*

MARTHA HART, fifth daughter of Samuel Hart, of Northington, now Avon, and his wife, Elizabeth (Thompson), born July 31st, 1739, at Northington; married February 4th, 1759, Daniel Owen, who died November 7th, 1759, when she second married, February, 1775, Uriah, son of Nathan Whitney, and his wife, Sarah, of Ridgefield, Conn., November 12th, 1737. Martha was his second wife, and he is said to have had Sarah Platt for his first wife. Uriah and Martha had three children, viz: 1, Samuel Platt Whitney, born at Simsbury, November 8th, 1775, and died at Montville, Ohio, December 14th, 1871. He lived with his wife nearly seventy-two years, when they celebrated their diamond wedding. They had twelve children, fifty-seven grandchildren, and fifty-six great-grandchildren—125 in all. 2, Lucy Whitney, born , 1778, at Simsbury, married Jonathan Battles; 3, Thaddeus Whitney, born at Simsbury, December 18th, 1781, married Polly Pratt, and married second, ——— Messenger.

WOODRUFF.

720.   *Northington, now Avon.*

ABIGAIL HART, Farmington, fifth daughter of Samuel Hart, of Avon, and his wife, Elizabeth (Thompson), born February 20th, 1743; married February 10th, 1763, Josiah Woodruff, of Northington. They had—Shubel, born September 25th, 1763; Uriah, born March 16th, 1766; and probably others.

721.   *Northington, now Avon.*

ANTHONY HART, Avon, second son of Samuel Hart, of that place, and his wife, Elizabeth (Thompson), born January 25th, 1750–1; married August 14th, 1776, Eleanor Rowe, of Simsbury. He died August 21st, 1816, aged 66 years, when she second married in 1817, John Hubbard, of Bloomfield.

THEIR CHILD, BEING THE SIXTH GENERATION.
870. Eleanor Hart, born   ; married   , William
        Hickox.

NEWELL.

749.   *Farmington, Conn.*

LYDIA HART, Farmington, eldest daughter of Samuel Hart, of the same place, and his wife, Lydia (Gridley), born February 23d, 1746, at Farmington; married February 14th, 1771, Thomas Newell, son of James, and his second wife, Dinah (Cole), born November 10th, 1744, at Farmington. They had—Samuel, born January 2d, 1774; Thomas, born March 28th, 1776.

GLEASON.

750.   *Northington, now Avon.*

SUSANNAH HART, Avon, second daughter of Samuel Hart, of Farmington, and his wife, Lydia (Gridley), born October 24th, 1748, at Farmington; married April 6th, 1773, David Gleason, of Northington.

751. *Northington, now Avon.*

MUNSON HART, Northington, eldest son of Samuel Hart, of Farmington, and his wife, Lydia (Gridley), born March 2d, 1750–1, at Avon; married March 28th, 1782, Mary Hart, daughter of Noah Hart, and his wife, Sarah (Miller), born May 20th, 1758, at Farmington. She died January 27th, 1827, aged 70 years, and was then a member of the church at Northington, having been received May 4th, 1788. He died at Avon in 1832, aged 82 years. The death of so many of their children is said to be the result of near blood relation of the parents.

THEIR CHILDREN, BEING THE SIXTH GENERATION.

71. Susanna, born 1783; baptized June 8th, 1788; married, 1813, Noah Steele, of New Hartford.
72. Naomi, born 1786; baptized June 8th, 1788; married, 1809, Reuben Hawley, of Avon.
73. Sally, born   ; married, 1814, Alson Thompson, of Avon.
    Rhoda, born 1788; baptized September 21st, 1788; died September 21st, 1793.
    Isaac, born 1791; baptized September 23d, 1792; died May 14th, 1812, aged 21 years.
    Amon, born 1793; died October 19th, 1793, at 4 months.
74. Lydia, born 1794; baptized June 11th, 1797; married December 4th, 1821, Julius Jones, of Harwinton.
    Esther, baptized August 24th, 1800; died October 27th, 1803, aged 3 years, 3 months.
    Huldah, baptized September 26th, 1802; died June 7th, 1808, aged 5 years.

753. *Candor, N. Y.*

LENT HART, Avon, second son of Samuel Hart, of Farmington, and his wife, Lydia (Gridley), born at Farmington, parish of Avon, in 1760. He married July 18th, 1782, Olive Hickox, of Farmington. They removed and located at Candor, Tioga County, N. Y. She was admitted to the church at Avon, November 3d, 1799. She died November 17th, 1836, aged 76 years. He died April 12th, 1837, aged 77 years.

THEIR CHILDREN, BEING THE SIXTH GENERATION.

75. Manna, born 1782; baptized May 24th, 1801; married, 1804, Thede Woodford.
76. Erastus, born 1784; married, 1806, Anna Thompson.
77. Jeptha, born 1786; married   , 1809, Sally Thompson.
78. Almira, born 1788; married   , 1809, Marcus Day, of Avon.
    Hiram, born 1790; died September 23d, 1796, aged 7 years.
79. Arunah, born 1792; baptized May 24th, 1801; married, 1815, Ursula Clark.
80. Samuel, born 1795; died in Mississippi, November 2d, 1821, aged 27. He was a peddler.
    Catharine Hickox, born 1803; baptized April 24th, 1808; died October 7th, 1814, aged 12 years.
81. Emeline Gridley, born November 22d, 1805; married April 26th, 1826, Amaziah Wadsworth.

754.   *Candor, N. Y.*

JAMES GRIDLEY HART, youngest son and child of Samuel Hart, of
Farmington, and his wife, Lydia (Gridley), born 1763; baptized May
21st, 1764, at Northington, Conn.; married April 24th, 1783, Loraine
Derrin, of Northington, born 1766. Mr. Hart was a farmer by avocation, and died in 1850, aged 87 years. They removed to Candor, Tioga
County, N. Y. She was a sister of Timothy Derrin, of Avon, and
died in 1840, aged 74 years.

THEIR CHILD, BEING THE SIXTH GENERATION.

882. Tereucy, born   , 1783, at Avon, Conn.; married   , 1810,
      Sally Smith.

NORTH.

755.   *Farmington, Conn.*

ABIGAIL HART, of Farmington, eldest daughter of Stephen Hart, of
the same town, and his wife, Abigail (Gridley), born March 18th, 1751,
at Farmington; married   , Seth North, son of
Timothy and Hannah North, of Farmington, born 1752, at Farmington. She is called Abigail Bidwell in the Manuscript Genealogy of
the North family, by Rev. William S. Porter, who says her life was
greatly embittered by the cruel treatment of her husband, who seems
to have been a hardened profligate. She died in 1813, aged 62 years.
He died in 1822, aged 70 years. They had one son, Jay, born
      , 1779; married Catharine Provost. She had seven children.
He died in 1815, aged 36 years.

759.   *Farmington, Conn.*

GAD HART, Farmington, only son of Stephen Hart, of the same
town, and his wife, Abigail (Gridley), born March 24th, 1759, at Farmington; married   , Lorana Winchell, born August
11th, 1759. Mr. Hart was a wheelwright by trade and avocation, and
lived on High Street, in Farmington Village, where his wife died,
March 28th, 1809, aged 49 years, 7 months, 17 days, when second he
married   , 1812, Lucina S. Burr. He died October 4th,
1830, aged 71 years, 4 months, 10 days.

THEIR CHILDREN, BEING THE SEVENTH GENERATION.

883. Stephen W., born June 14th, 1781; married   , Sally Bruce.
884. Caty,   )   married   Buck, father of Daniel, of Hartford.
              } born April 17th, 1783;
      Nancy,)   died February 28th, 1809.
885. Julius, born November 17th, 1787; married   , Harriet Prior
      Bruce, of Hartford.
886. Sidney, born October 18th, 1789; married November 13th, 1811, Clarinda S.
      Clark.
887. Hiram, born September 30th, 1791; married   , 1822, Sarah N.
      Woodford.

760.

Farmington, Conn., Loraine County, N. Y.

ASA HART, Farmington, eldest son of David Hart, of the same town, nd his wife, Elizabeth (Porter), born June 14th, 1759, at Farmington; married   . He inherited his father's lace in Farmington, but removed to Loraine County, N. Y.

THEIR CHILDREN, BEING THE SEVENTH GENERATION.

38. David, born
39. Zenas, born 1789; married, September, 1808, Rachel Lewis. He died in 1839, aged 50 years.
Richard, born
Daughter, born
Samuel, born

761.   *Sheffield, Mass.*

JOSIAH HART, of Sheffield, Mass., second son of David Hart, of 'armington, and his wife, Elizabeth (Porter), born September 22d, 761, at Farmington; married   , Abigail Kelsey, of illingsworth, born October 14th, 1767. She died October 7th, 1824, ged 57. He died February 22d, 1826, at Sheffield, Mass., aged 65 ears. He was an exemplary man.

THEIR CHILDREN, BEING THE SEVENTH GENERATION.

)0. Edward, born November 19th, 1791; married   , Sarah Abbe.
)1. Jerusha, born June 3d, 1793; married   , Eli Barnum, of Freedom, Ohio.
)2. Milo, born September 4th, 1800; married   , Julia Ann Sawyer.

BIDWELL.

762.   *Farmington, Conn.*

LAVINIA HART, of Farmington, eldest daughter of David Hart, of 'armington, and his wife, Elizabeth (Porter), born October 13th, 1764, t Farmington; married   , Isaac Bidwell.

766.   *Southington, Conn.*

JOEL HART, Southington, eldest son of Amos Hart, of the same lace, and his first wife, Ann (Gridley), born May 8th, 1753, at South-gton, and was baptized there July 14th, 1754, by the pastor, Rev. eremiah Curtiss. He entered the army of the revolution, and died ; Hackensack, N. J., September 22d, 1776, aged 23 years. He was ever married.

767.   *Ontario County, N. Y.*

AMOS HART, Southington, second son of Amos Hart, of the same place, and his first wife, Ann (Gridley), born March 16th, 1755, at Southington. He was baptized there on the same day, and the mother died ten days after. He married
and removed to New York State, near Lake Ontario.

THEIR CHILDREN, BEING THE SEVENTH GENERATION.

893. Horace, born
894. Theron. born
895. Josiah, born

768.   *Southington, Burlington, Conn.*

LEMUEL HART, Southington, eldest son of Amos Hart, of the same town, and his second wife, Mary (Dunham), born August 24th, 1759, at Southington; married   , Rosanna Winstone, daughter of Stephen, of Southington, and his wife, Rosanna (Cogswell), born January 2d, 1759, at Southington, Conn. He was in the army of the revolution, and in the last years of his life lost the use of one hand by paralysis. He removed to Burlington, Conn., where his wife died, May 23d, 1788, in her 30th year, when he second married Lydia Hefford, of Southington. He removed from Burlington to Hillsdale, Columbia County, N. Y., and taught school there, but returned to Burlington, where he died, May 2d, 1822, in his 63d year. His widow, Lydia, was received into the church in Bristol, by letter from Egremont, Mass., November 30th, 1845. She died May 5th, 1846, at Bristol, aged 78 years, and was buried in Burlington.

THEIR CHILDREN, BEING THE SEVENTH GENERATION.

896. Mary, born   ; married   , John Miller, of
     Canada.
897. Orra, born   ; married   , John Field, of
     Egremont, Mass.
898. Joel, born January 2d, 1788; married February 2d, 1809, Sally Winchell.

HIS CHILDREN BY HIS SECOND WIFE, LYDIA.

899. Newton, born March 23d, 1793; married December 31st, 1836, Martha Sophronia Winchell.
900. Amos, born July 23d, 1800; married March 17th, 1839, Sally Brian.
901. Ard, born January 23d, 1803; married January 3d, 1831, Amanda Hart, of
     Bristol.
902. Jairus, born August 2d, 1804; married, 1825, Hannah Jones.
903. Urania, born   ; married   Crandall, of Petersburg, N. Y.
904. Belinda, born   , 1806; married   , William Spencer.
     Clarinda, born   ; died young.

769. *Burlington, Conn.*

ARD HART, Burlington, Conn., fourth son of Amos Hart, of South-ngton, and his second wife, Mary (Dunham), born May 17th, 1761, at 3outhington; married March 10th, 1788, Millicent Roberts, born Jan-1ary 6th, 1771. He early removed from Southington to the south-east)art of Burlington. He became a deacon of that church, December 30th, 1814, the duties of which office he faithfully discharged until his leath. His wife, Millicent, died at Burlington, February 15th, 1826, 1ged 55 years, when he second married, 1827, Lucy Goodsell, widow)f Isaac Hotchkiss, and daughter of Samuel Goodsell, and his wife, _ucy (Harsington). He died March 5th, 1851, aged 90 years, being .he oldest person in Burlington.

THEIR CHILDREN, BEING THE SEVENTH GENERATION.

05. Nancy, born February 22d, 1789; married , Joel Dorman.
06. Belinda, born April 24th, 1793; married , John Woodford.
07. Delia, born May 19th, 1795; married December 1st, 1814, Billings Hill; second, Leveret Darrow.
    Daughter, born May 28th, 1798, and died without a name.
08. Millicent, born June 14th, 1799; married , John Hart, of Ambrose.
09. Chauncey, born June 9th, 1802; married , Millessendra Hart.
10. William, born September 2d, 1804; married , Mary Ann Bowman.
11. Sarah, born January 26th, 1807; married George Lyman.
12. Elvira, born October 20th, 1812; married October 27th, 1830, Ira Hadsell, now (1874) of Plainville.

MUNSON.

770. *Windham, Green County, N. Y.*

ANNA HART, second daughter of the name in the family of Amos Iart, of Southington, and his second wife, Mary (Dunham), born April 5th, 1764, at Southington; married February 11th, 1790, Jairus Mun-ion of the same town, and removed to Windham, Green County, V. Y. They had Leveret, Jairus, William, and Lemuel.

771. *Southington, Conn.*

JUDE HART, Southington, sixth son of Amos Hart, of the same town, ind his second wife, Mary (Dunham), born February 8th, 1766, at 3outhington, a twin brother with Chauncey; married December 9th, 1790, Patience Sloper, daughter of Daniel, and his wife, Rachel (Lang-lon), born April 3d, 1770, at Southington, and baptized there by Rev. 3enjamin Chapman, July 1st, 1771, and her twin sister, Silence, at the

26

same time. He bought of his Uncle John Hart, by deed, dated May 28th, 1779, for $1,340, his farm in Flanders District, consisting of thirty-two acres, more or less, with dwelling-house and barn thereon, bounded west on eight-rod highway, north part highway and part Timothy Hart, south on Jude Hart. On this place he built a large house about 1820, on the site of the old one, where he spent the remainder of his life. She died September 27th, 1846, aged 76. He died June 12th, 1847, aged 81 years. In 1873 the place was owned and occupied by Lewis.

THEIR CHILDREN, BEING THE SEVENTH GENERATION.

913. Jude, born March 20th, 1790; married November 6th, 1823, Hannah Pardee.
914. Olive, born September 19th, 1791; baptized September 19th, 1795; married March 8th, 1813, Jason Hitchcock.
      Reuel, born August 31st, 1794; baptized September 19th, 1795; died March 3d, 1801, of small pox, aged 6 years.
      Polly, born July 22d, 1803; died single, June 29th, 1857, aged 54.
915. Reuel, born February 1st, 1808; married March 29th, 1832, Rosanna Barnes.

772.   *Southington, Conn.*

CHAUNCEY HART, Southington, seventh son of Amos Hart, of the same town, and his second wife, Mary (Dunham), born February 8th, 1766, at Southington, a twin brother of Jude; márried May 4th, 1789, Lydia Hoadley Bray, daughter of Colonel Asa, of Southington, and his wife, Lydia (Andrews). They were divorced, when second he married, November 17th, 1803, Lucy Gaylord. She died ten days after her fourth child was born, September 22d, 1812, aged 36. He third married, March 20th, 1814, Jemima Dickinson Cowles, daughter of Captain Ashbel, and his wife, Rhoda (Lee), born February 20th, 1772, at Southington. He lived in Flanders District, on the corner, where Henry Whittlesey lived in 1873. He died of cancer, May 27th, 1845, aged 80 years. His third wife died June 23d, 1845, aged 74 years.

THEIR CHILDREN, BEING THE SEVENTH GENERATION.

916. Willys, born November 6th, 1789. He was shot for desertion in 1813.
917. Sherman, born Dec. 14th, 1791; married March 3d, 1819, Elizabeth Smith.
918. Edward, born March 9th, 1794; married   , Anna Beach; second, Rhoda Grannis.
919. Romanta, born June 12th, 1797; died single, May 23d, 1825, aged 28.
920. Almon, born June 12th, 1798; married, 1828, Mary Gates Stewart.

HIS CHILDREN BY HIS SECOND WIFE, LUCY.

921. Chauncey, born September 15th, 1804. He went west, and married Abigail Wright.
922. Henry, born November 25th, 1807; married May 2d, 1834, Harriet Cowles.
923. Lucy Almira, born September 9th, 1809; married March 27th, 1836, Hiram Peck.
      Phebe, born September 19th, 1812; married May 10th, 1835, Edwin Woodruff.

HAMBLIN.

773. *White Oak, in Farmington, Conn.*

MARY HART, Southington, third daughter of Amos Hart, and his second wife, Mary (Dunham), born March 5th, 1769; married July 31st, 1792, Lemuel Hamblin, of White Oak, Farmington, son of Lieutenant John Hamblin, from Suffield, and his first wife, Abi (Phinney), born June 21st, 1770. He was a farmer, and lived on the mountain, next north of Ichabod Bradley. They had seven sons born to them. He died August 15th, 1829, aged 59 years. She died September 16th, 1830, aged 61 years. They had Willys, Chester, Ava, Amos, Noah, Erastus, and Henry.

PARDEE.

775. *Southington, Conn.*

CLARISSA HART, youngest child of Amos Hart, of Southington, and his second wife, Mary (Dunham), born April 28th, 1773, at Southington; married June 12th, 1799, Jesse Pardee, of Southington. He died in 1801. His widow, Clarissa, died at Southington, August 28th, 1854, aged 81 years.

776. *Bristol, Conn.*

ELIJAH HART, Bristol, eldest son of Thomas Hart, of Southington, and his first wife, Sarah (Thomas), of Cheshire, Conn., born November 16th, 1752; baptized November 19th, 1752, at Southington. He went to Bristol with his parents, and married.

777. *Bristol, Conn.*

THOMAS HART, Bristol, Conn., second son of Thomas Hart, of Southington, and his first wife, Sarah (Thomas), born January 4th, 1755, at Southington; baptized February 16th, 1755, by Rev. Jeremiah Curtiss. He went to Bristol with his parents, entered the army of the revolution, and died in the service, September, 1777, of starvation, in the prison of the British in New York, in his 23d year. A tomb-stone has been erected to his memory in the North Cemetery, Bristol, Conn.

778. *Bristol, Conn.*

JASON HART, Bristol, third son of Thomas Hart, of Southington, and his first wife, Sarah (Thomas), born May 13th, 1757, at Southington; baptized June 12th, 1757, by Rev. Benjamin Chapman, then pastor of the church in Southington. He went with his parents to Bristol, Conn. He entered the army of the revolution, and died in the service,

December 27th, 1777, in his 21st year. A tomb-stone has been erected
to his memory in the North Cemetery, Bristol, Conn.

779.   *Bristol, Conn.*

ITHUREL HART, Bristol, fourth son of Thomas Hart, of Southington,
and his first wife, Sarah (Thomas), born November 15th, 1759, at
Southington; baptized there December 8th, 1759, by Rev. Benjamin
Chapman. He went to Bristol, Conn., with his parents, and married,
1783, Sibil Jerome, of Bristol, daughter of Thomas. She was admitted to the church in Bristol, November, 1796, and he was admitted
February 4th, 1816. She died May 15th, 1837, aged 74. He died
May 6th, 1838, aged 78 years. There are tomb-stones at their graves
in the North Cemetery, Bristol, Conn.

THEIR CHILDREN, BEING THE SEVENTH GENERATION.

925. Lydia, born   , 1783; married August 7th, 1816, Samuel Benham.
      Randall, born   , 1785; died November 26th, 1806, aged 21 years. He
        has a tomb-stone in the North Cemetery, Bristol.
926. Thomas, born   , 1788; died at Hazel Green, Ala., May 14th, 1829,
        aged 41.
      Charles, born   , 1802; died February 6th, 1804, aged 16 months.
927. Augustus, born   ; married September 14th, 1819, Sabra Plum.
      Jesse, born   . He went to Missouri.

786.   *Bristol, Burlington, Conn.*

GILBERT HART, Bristol, Conn., fifth son of Thomas Hart, of Southington, and his second wife, Lydia (Hotchkiss), born May 24th, 1762,
at Southington; baptized there June 27th, 1762, by Rev. Benjamin
Chapman. He went to Bristol with his parents, and married Sarah
Linsley of Bristol. He was admitted to the church in Bristol, January, 1796. He removed to Burlington in 1797. He died in 1847,
aged 84 years.

THEIR CHILDREN, BEING THE SEVENTH GENERATION.

Lydia, born   ', 1804; died January 4th, 1805, aged 5 months.
Clark, born   , 1806.

781.   *Bristol, Conn.*

SETH HART, Bristol, sixth son of Thomas Hart, of Southington, and
his second wife, Lydia (Hotchkiss), of Cheshire, born April 19th, 1765;
married Mary Wilcox, of Saybrook, daughter of Elijah, and his wife,
Mary (Bushnell), born 1765, at Cromwell, Conn. Mr. Hart and wife
were admitted to the church at Bristol, January, 1796. He was a
tailor by trade, but was a farmer by occupation, and he located in the
north part of Bristol, just east of Chipen's Hill. His wife died Janu-

ary 22d, 1839, aged 74, when second he married, 1839, Charlotte, widow of William Orvice, of Harwinton. Her maiden name was Charlotte Smith. Mr. Hart was a large land-holder. He died February 21st, 1852, aged 87 years, and he and his first wife were buried in the North Cemetery at Bristol. Charlotte, his widow, died September 8th, 1857, aged 76, and was buried at East Church, Plymouth.

THEIR CHILDREN, BEING THE SEVENTH GENERATION.

William B., born , 1788; died January 20th, 1796, aged 7 years.
928. Seth, born , 1790; died, May, 1813, of yellow fever, aged 23. He was a clothier.
929. Elonzo, born , 1794; married, November, 1815, Lovina Barnes.
Mary B., born, January, 1796; died December 18th, 1796, aged 11 months.
Elias, born , 1797; died September 11th, 1803, aged 6 years.
William, born , 1799; died September 10th, 1803, aged 4 years.
930. Ard, born , 1803; died May 26th, 1850, aged 47.
Marilla, born , 1809; died Sept. 19th, 1810, of croup, aged 1 year.
931. Jason, born . He lives at Plymouth, Mass.
932. Amanda, born , 1805; married January 3d, 1831, Ard Hart, Egremont, Mass.

782. *Burlington, Conn.*

CALVIN HART, Bristol, Conn., seventh son of Thomas Hart, of South-ington, and his second wife, Lydia (Hotchkiss), born September 23d, 1767, at Southington; married March 20th, 1791, Anna Yale, daughter of Abel, born May 12th, 1767. They were both admitted to the church in Bristol, September 29th, 1799. He was a farmer, and was located in the south limits of Burlington. His wife died December 29th, 1809, aged 42 years and 8 months, when second he married Feb-ruary 21st, 1811, Mercy, daughter of James Root, of Southington, and his wife, Mercy (Woodruff), born November 2d, 1771, at Southington. She died July 12th, 1839, aged 68 years. He died July 3d, 1841, aged 74 years.

THEIR CHILDREN, BEING THE SEVENTH GENERATION.

Sylvester, born December 25th, 1791; died April 25th, 1795, in his 5th year.
933. Billy Stanley, born January 9th, 1794.
933½. Sylvester, born March 16th, 1797; married October 14th, 1819, Bathsheba Hayes. He died September 28th, 1821, aged 25.
934. Calvin, born September 18th, 1798; died February 8th, 1825, at Madison County, Ill., in his 27th year.
935. Joel, born May 6th, 1800; married September 7th, 1820, Sally Bowers, of Rocky Hill.
Child, born March 21st, 1802; died March 22d, 1802.
Child, born July 6th, 1803; died in one hour after birth.
936. Anna Charlotte, born August 8th, 1804; married March 27th, 1835, William Morse.
937. Alice, born November 30th, 1795. She was never married, but kept house for her brother, Billy. She died at New Britain, Conn., December 7th, 1870, aged 75 years.

783.   *Southington, Conn.*

COLONEL SAMUEL HART, Southington, eldest son of Reuben Hart, of the same town, and his wife, Rhoda (Peck), born August 31st, 1761, at Southington; married February 8th, 1786, before Rev. William Robinson, Rosanna, only child of Captain John Clark, of Southington, and his wife, Hannah, born February 28th, 1764, at Southington. Colonel Hart became an influential citizen of the town, was much engaged in public business, represented the town in the legislature, was selectman, held many other offices in the gift of the town, and passed through all the military grades up to colonel. He located on West Street, a section of the town of Southington, and was a large and successful farmer. His place was near where his son, Collingwood, had his residence in 1873. His wife died of liver affection, September 1st, 1801, aged 37, when second he married October 10th, 1802, Patience Andrews, daughter of Benjamin Andrews, of Southington, and his second wife, Mary (Barnes), born December 29th, 1779. He died June 23d, 1838, aged 77 years. His widow, Mrs. Patience Hart, died March 30th, 1865, aged 84 years.

HIS CHILDREN BY HIS FIRST WIFE, BEING THE SEVENTH GENERATION.

938. Hiel, born June 22d, 1787; married May 27th, 1810, Harriet Johnson.
939. Vesta, born May 16th, 1789; married November 26th, 1807, Asaph Whittlesey.
940. Nancy, born July 7th, 1791; married   , David Preston.
941. Samuel, born March 29th, 1793; married   , Lucinda Pardee.
942. Lucy, born August 12th, 1795; married May 5th, 1814, Perry Langdon.
      Daughter, born March 4th, 1798, no name.
      Son, born January 16th, 1799; died in one hour after birth.

HIS CHILDRN BY HIS SECOND WIFE.

943. Rosanna,)   married February 17th, 1825, Amon L. Ames.
                 } born June 23d, 1803;
      Patience,)   died September 8th, 1803, of dysentery.
944. John Nelson, born November 4th, 1804; married September 18th, 1827, Sophia Hitchcock.
945. Collingwood, born January 5th, 1806; married October 10th, 1833, Rebecca G. Dunham.
      Patience, born January 14th, 1809; died January 26th, 1810, in her 2d year.
      Mary Ann, born June 7th, 1812; died August 19th, 1812, aged 2 months and 12 days.
      Mary Ann, 2d, born August 13th, 1813; died young.
946. Mary Ann, 3d, born November 29th, 1815; married January 26th, 1836, Loyal Royce.
947. Benjamin, born February 23d, 1818; baptized June 4th, 1818; married   , Lucy Bull.

784.   *Southington, Conn.*

SARAH HART, Southington, second daughter of Captain Reuben Hart, of the same town, and his wife, Rhoda (Peck), born October 18th,

1766, at Southington. She was never married. In the last years of her life she lived much of the time in the family of her brother, Colonel Samuel Hart, where she died, October 17th, 1843, aged 77 years, and was buried at Oak Hill Cemetery, where she has a head-stone.

785. *Southington, Conn.*

ROSWELL HART, Southington, second son of Captain Reuben Hart, of the same town, and his wife, Rhoda (Peck), born August 22d, 1768, at Southington; married ⠀⠀⠀⠀⠀, Sylvia, daughter of Jonathan Barnes, and his wife, Elizabeth (Woodruff), born August 7th, 1771, at Southington. He inherited the old homestead of his father in Flanders District, where he died of consumption, May 17th, 1828, aged 60. His widow died March 21st, 1857, aged 86 years.

THEIR CHILDREN, BEING THE SEVENTH GENERATION.

948. Reuben, born January 8th, 1794; married Nov. 11th, 1819, Abigail Bradley.
949. Julius, born August 9th, 1799; married May 9th, 1827, Diadama Bradley.
950. Roswell, born March 25th, 1806; married May 1st, 1828, Parmelia Amsden.

786. *Southington, Conn.*

TIMOTHY HART, Southington, third son of Captain Reuben Hart, of the same town, and his wife, Rhoda (Peck), born July 15th, 1770, at Southington; married April 24th, 1794, Eunice Woodruff, daughter of John Woodruff, and his wife, Catharine (Bushnell), born May 11th, 1771; baptized September 10th, 1780, at Southington, by Rev. William Robinson. She died of pleurisy, January 9th, 1803, in her 32d year, when second he married August 27th, 1804, Sally Reed, of Simsbury, Conn., born August 17th, 1782. He was a farmer and an old school teacher, was selectman twenty years, and a representative to the legislature one year. He lived in Flanders District, a locality of Southington, about two and a half miles north-east of the village. He died there March 19th, 1855, aged 84 years, 8 months, 4 days. Sarah, his widow, died January 23d, 1859, in her 77th year. Their daughter, Mrs. Eunice Holt, occupies the same premises with her son, John Hart Holt, in 1874.

THEIR CHILDREN, BEING THE SEVENTH GENERATION.

951. Etheta, born June 4th, 1795; married October 3d, 1815, Lemuel Tryon.
952. Rhoda, born October 12th, 1798; married October 6th, 1818, Asahel P. Smith.
953. George, born May 4th, 1801; baptized March 24th, 1822; married February 10th, 1824, Lewia Page.

HIS CHILDREN BY HIS SECOND WIFE.

954. William, born November 15th, 1805; baptized March 24th, 1822; died single.
955. Asahel Woodruff, ⎫ married August 20th, 1833, Verlinda Vantroy.
⠀⠀⠀⠀⠀⠀⠀⠀⠀⠀⎬ born August 7th, 1809; baptized March 24th, 1822;
956. Levi Austin, ⎭ married ⠀⠀⠀⠀⠀, Harriet Kirkland, of New Haven.

957. Alvin, born March 20th, 1813; baptized March 24th, 1822; married, 1835,
       Sarah Stanley.

958. Eunice, born October 24th, 1817; baptized March 24th, 1822; married June
       22d, 1840, Daniel H. Holt.

HURLBÈRT.

787.   *Kensington, Conn.*

LUCY HART, Kensington, Conn., youngest daughter of Captain Reuben Hart, of Southington, and his wife, Rhoda (Peck), born
           ; married at Kensington, November 6th, 1794, Francis Hurlburt, of that parish. She was second of the name in the family of Captain Reuben Hart.

788.   *Southington, Conn.*

JOHN HART, Southington, eldest son of John Hart, of the same town, and his wife, Desire (Palmer), born at Southington in 1756; baptized January 30th, 1757, by Rev. Benjamin Chapman; married Polly Smith, of Boston. He graduated at Yale College in 1776, and studied law, but entered into trade with his brother, Wells, under the firm of J. & W. Hart, of Windsor, Conn.; but the copartnership was dissolved March 22d, 1795, and the said John settled up the business of the firm. Mr. Hart is said to have been a passionate, irritable man. He is said to have taken his father to Lenox, Mass., and there abandoned him to destitution and want. He was a man of splendid talents and education, which he perverted to uses which illy requited his Maker for his gifts, or his father for his anxious, self-denying care.

THEIR CHILDREN, BEING THE SEVENTH GENERATION.

959. Harriet, born
960. Desire, born
961. Heathcote, born
962. Zemina, born   ; married   Hayes.
            She died in New York in 1870.
963. Sherburne, born

789.   ·   *Southington, Conn.*

LEVI HART, Southington, second son of John Hart, of the same town, and his wife, Desire (Palmer), born at Southington in 1759; married May 3d, 1780, Phelathea, daughter of Daniel Allen, of the same town, and his wife, Huldah (Clark), born May 1st, 1764, at Southington. Mr. Hart engaged in the mercantile business, and held the military rank of captain. He built the house now owned and occupied by William Wilcox, just east of Main Street, on the north side of the east road. "He was 6 feet in height, well proportioned, of a lively countenance, quick thought, good native abilities, had a warm imagination, generous, but passionate." [These remarks are by his brother, John, in the old family Bible.—ED.] He died February 13th, 1793, aged 34 years; and on the 15th of February, while the funeral was being attended, word came that Daniel Allen, Mrs. Hart's father, had been found dead in his store at the place owned by Walter Woodruff in 1873, known as the Hobart place. Mrs. Hart second married October 10th, 1796, Asahel Gridley, of the same town. She died August 8th, 1846, aged 82 years. Mr. Hart's Will was dated February 10th, 1793, in substance as follows: I give my wife £20 in household goods, and one-third of my real estate to improve. I give my three sons, Murray, Levi, and John Albert, £20 each, to be paid at majority, and all my real estate to be divided equally.

Item.—I give my brothers, John and Wells, all the debts due me at my decease, except a note due me from my father, John Hart; and I give these brothers my stock in trade, *i. e.*, all merchandize I have in partnership with Elizur Andrews, and all the goods I have at Turkey Hills, and I give my said brothers my sleigh, sulkey, and harness, on condition they pay all my debts, and to my wife £60 to use in support of my children, &c.

THEIR CHILDREN, BEING THE SEVENTH GENERATION.

Phila, born August 7th, 1781; died April 6th, 1783, after five hours illness, aged 1 year and 8 months.
964. Murray, born April 30th, 1784; married August 10th, 1808, Lucy Newell.
965. Levi, born October 15th, 1786; married November 9th, 1809, Polly Newell.
966. John Albert, born May 31st, 1789; married Nov. 22d, 1812, Rachel Newell.

790. *Southington, Windsor, Conn.*

WELLS HART, Southington, third and youngest son of John Hart, of the same town, and his wife, Desire (Palmer), born   ; married in Bristol, Conn., August 4th, 1793, Polly Root, of Bristol. He was a copartner in the mercantile business, at Windsor, Conn., with his brother, John, about 1795, as the following notice, which appeared in the *Connecticut Courant* at that time, will show:

"NOTICE.—The late partnership of John Hart and Wells Hart, known as the firm of John & Wells Hart, was by mutual agreement dissolved, on the 22d day of March, 1795. The subscriber does not consider himself holden by any contract made since that time, unless personally executed by himself. The concerns of the late partnership will be adjusted by the subscriber."
WINDSOR, Dec. 5th, 1796.   (Signed,) JOHN HART."

791. *Burlington, Conn.*

AMBROSE HART, Burlington, second son of Simeon Hart, of Southington, and his wife, Sarah (Sloper), born March 28th, 1759, at South-

27

ington, and went to Burlington with his parents in 1774; married, August, 1782, Mercy Bartholomew, born July 22d, 1762. Mr. Hart served his country in the war of the revolution. He died November 25th, 1811, aged 53 years. His widow died March 24th, 1834, aged 71. There are tombstones to their memory in the east cemetery at Burlington.

THEIR CHILDREN, BEING THE SEVENTH GENERATION.

967. Martin, born June 10th, 1783; married November 29th, 1804, Sally Rowe.
968. Sally, born October 3d, 1784; married November 1st, 1803, John Roberts.
969. John, born May 27th, 1787; married   , Milly Hart.
970. Orrin, born May 5th, 1789; married   , Eunice Ives; second, Lucina Gaylord.
   Alma, born April 10th, 1791; died single, September 13th, 1825.
971. Ambrose, born October 3d, 1793; married   , Chloe E. Moses, of Burlington.
972. Thomas, born, November, 1795; married   , Amanda Barnes.
973. Adna, born May 17th, 1798; married   , Roxana Yale.
   Gad, born February 10th, 1800; died May 12th, 1813, aged 13.

792.   *Brookfield, Trumbull County, O.*

BLISS HART, Burlington, third son of Simeon Hart, of Southington, and his wife, Sarah (Sloper), born March 10th, 1761, at Southington, and went to Burlington with his parents in 1774; married May 17th, 1783, Sylvia Upson, born August 20th, 1765. He was a magistrate, and removed to Brookfield, Trumbull County, Ohio. He entered the continental army in 1777, at the age of 15 years, was in a number of hard-fought battles, and after much hardship, privation, and suffering, was discharged, May, 1780. He was a man of strong powers of mind, was much respected, and had much influence in the church, town, and society of Burlington, which he represented at six sessions of the General Assembly—1811 to 1813—and was a member of the convention to form the Constitution. He died in Brookfield, March 6th, 1831, aged 70 years, and was buried there. His widow died August 20th, 1854, aged 89 years.

THEIR CHILDREN, BEING THE SEVENTH GENERATION.

   Oliver, born September 27th, 1783; died October 17th, 1792, aged 9 years.
974. Orenus, born July 22d, 1785; married September 21st, 1810, Sabra Lewis.
975. Bliss, born September 27th, 1787; married   , Thankful Bronson.
976. Sylvia, born April 1st, 1790; married October 10th, 1811, Dr. Elijah Flowers.
977. Experience, born July 20th, 1792; married   , 1812, Clark Bronson.
978. Levi, born January 8th, 1795; married   , Obedience Fuller.
979. Amanda, born March 13th, 1797; married January 28th, 1824, Garr C. Reed.
980. Oliver Elsworth, born May 20th, 1799; married, May, 1834, Susanna W. Danforth.
981. Rosalinda, born July 20th, 1801; married   , Franklin Peck.
982. Mellissendia, born December 17th, 1803; married   , Chauncey Hart.
   Robert Sloper, born May 23d, 1806; died May 20th, 1809, aged 3 years.

793. *Burlington, Conn.*

SIMEON HART, Jr., Burlington, fourth son of Simeon Hart, Sr., and his wife, Sarah (Sloper), born September 8th, 1763, at Southington, and went to Burlington with his parents in 1774; married October 27th, 1783, Mary Warner, of Middletown. She died February 15th, 1821, when second he married January 30th, 1822, Mrs. Pamelia Wetmore (Pettebone), who was born September 5th, 1782. He improved his early advantages for an education, was an intelligent member of the Congregational Church, was a magistrate thirty or more years, until excused at his own request, and was town clerk eleven years in succession. Having served God and his generation faithfully, he fell asleep in Jesus, December 19th, 1835, aged 72 years. She died January 15th, 1864, aged 82 years. ·

THEIR CHILDREN, BEING THE SEVENTH GENERATION.

983. Lucas, } married November 27th, 1811, Harriet Morris, of East Haven.
born June 5th, 1784;
984. Anna, } married , Daniel Woodruff.
Chester, born January 2d, 1789; died January 26th, 1789, aged 24 days.
Narcissa, born April 26th, 1790; died April 27th, 1790.
985. Jehiel Chester, born February 3d, 1792; married September 2d, 1817, Anna Lowrey, of Southington.
Simeon, born February 5th, 1794; died February 6th, 1794.
986. Simeon, born November 17th, 1795; married December 9th, 1824, Abigail Andrews, daughter of Asa.
987. Polly, born April 18th, 1798; married November 17th, 1818, Joseph Dutton, of Farmington.
988. Fanny, born December 29th, 1800; married , William Hill, who removed to St. Charles.

HIS CHILDREN BY HIS SECOND WIFE.

989. Lucas Wetmore, born December 26th, 1822, at Burlington. He was lost at sea.
990. Austin, born April 17th, 1824; married October 9th, 1867, Susan A. Deming, of Farmington.

794. *Burlington, Conn., Lisle, N. Y.*

MARCUS HART, Burlington, fifth son of Simeon Hart, Sr., of Southington, and his wife, Sarah (Sloper), born December 20th, 1767, at Southington, and went with his parents to Burlington, Conn., in 1774; married January 17th, 1786, Rhoda Wiard, daughter of Seth, of Burlington, and his wife, Dorcas, born March 27th, 1771. She died February 12th, 1804, aged 33 years. He removed to Lisle, Broome County, N. Y., where he died, July 3d, 1832, aged 65.

THEIR CHILDREN, BEING THE SEVENTH GENERATION.

991. Laura, born December 22d, 1788; married , Ezekiel Case.
992. Rhoda, born July 5th, 1791; married , Darius F. Butler.
993. Alice, born September 6th, 1793; married Covel.
Marcus E., born October 13th, 1796; died September 20th, 1827.

CHASE.

795.   *Litchfield, Conn., Pennsylvania.*

REBECCA HART, Preston, Conn., eldest daughter and child of Rev. Levi Hart, of that place, and his wife, Rebecca (Bellamy); married   , Rev. Amos Chase, of Litchfield, South Farms. She died February 25th, 1791, leaving no children. After her death he married Anna, sister of Judge James Lanman, Norwich, and removed to Western Pennsylvania.

796.   *Norwich, Conn.*

WILLIAM SHERMAN HART, Norwich, Conn., eldest son of Rev. Levi Hart, of Preston, and his wife, Rebecca (Bellamy), born 1767, in Preston; married Eunice Backus, of Norwich, Conn. He graduated at Dartmouth College in 1786. He was a lawyer. He studied his profession at Litchfield, under Judge Reeve, and became a practicing attorney at Norwich, Conn.

THEIR CHILD, BEING THE SEVENTH GENERATION.

994.   William Backus, born   ; married

GODDARD.

797.   *Norwich, Conn.*

ALICE COGSWELL HART, Norwich, Conn., second daughter of Rev. Levi Hart, of Preston, Conn., and his wife, Rebecca (Bellamy), born August 23d, 1772, at Preston; married November 27th, 1794, Calvin Goddard, of Norwich, Conn. She died May 3d, 1832, aged 60 years, in the lively faith of a Christian. Her distinguished husband thus speaks of her: "My connection with this family," (Rev. Dr. Hart's,) adds Judge Goddard, "has furnished me with a great proportion of my happiness during a long life; and as well from a knowledge of her Christian life, as from the circumstances of her triumphant death, I can not doubt she was removed to a mansion 'not made with hands, eternal in the heavens.' Our severe loss has been her gain. My children, under God, owe much of what they are to their dear mother, and I trust the influence of her character is not yet lost upon my grandchildren."

Judge Goddard died May 2d, 1842. He graduated at Dartmouth College in 1786, in the class with his brother-in-law, William Sherman Hart. He was one of the most distinguished civilians in Connecticut, being judge of the Superior Court, assistant, &c. His attention was called, among the first, to the moral bearing of lotteries, and, after thorough investigation, brought all his influence to bear against the system, until it was abolished in this state. He then turned his attention to the moral bearings of other great questions of the day, and lent his influence, with that of such men as Judges Sherman, Daggett, Day, and Williams, in favor of moral reformation. He thus prepared the way for an investigation of the bearings of the great moral truths of the Bible on personal character, which resulted in the union with the church of so many of the distinguished civilians of the state of Connecticut, twenty-five or thirty years since. Judge Goddard had six children, "*all*," he said in 1840, "the blessed comforts of my old age," viz:

1, Charles Backus, who graduated at Yale College in 1814, and is a lawyer in Zanesville, Ohio.

2, Alice Hart, married Asa Child, Esq.

3, George Calvin, who graduated at Yale College in 1820, and is a lawyer in New York.

4, Julia Tracy, who remained with her father—"*the comfort of my old age.*"

5, James Burrall, who lived with his father.

6, Levi Hart, born on the day of Dr. Hart's death. He graduated at Yale College in 1828, and was admitted to the bar. He married Mary Woodbridge Perkins, and went to Ohio, but returned, and settled on a farm in Salem, which his wife inherited.

798. *Preston, Conn.*

LEVI HART, Preston, Conn., youngest child of Rev. Levi Hart, of the same parish, and his wife, Rebecca (Bellamy), born in Preston, and graduated at Brown University in 1802. He was a man of superior talents and acquirements, and is supposed to have died at the south, where he became a teacher.

799. *New Britain, Conn.*

ASAHEL HART, New Britain, Conn., eldest son of Joseph Hart, of Northington, and his wife, Ann (Barnes), of Southington, born May 12th, 1754, at Northington; baptized May 25th, 1754, by Rev. Ebenezer Booge; married November 5th, 1778, Anna Kilbourn, daughter of Josiah, of New Britain, and his wife, Anna (Neal), born December 24th, 1759. He was a brick mason by trade and avocation. In 1791 he bought of Elisha Hart his new house, which Ezekiel Wright built on the Farmington road, near Bass River, with two acres and ten rods of land, where he lived for some years. He was a stirring, lively man, and naturally impulsive. After some years he moved to the foot of

Osgood Hill, on the same road. His wife died February 22d, 1803, aged 44, when he second married January 11th, 1804, Chloe Booth, daughter of Nathan, Sr. She died February 10th, 1807, aged 44, when third he married July 29th, 1807, Widow Prudence Gridley. Her former husband was drowned in the whirlpool below Farmington bridge. He had swam the river once safely, when a bet was made that he could not do it again, and he was drowned in the attempt. Mr. Hart was admitted to the church in New Britain, January 26th, 1783. He died in North Granby, Conn., at the house of his son, Joseph. His third wife died in Avon, October 2d, 1852, aged 87 years, and was buried in New Britain Cemetery.

THEIR CHILDREN, BEING THE SEVENTH GENERATION.

995. Anna, born   ; baptized May 18th, 1783; married   , Samuel Coslett, of Granby.

996. Beula, born   ; baptized May 18th, 1783. She was never married, and died at Simsbury.

997. Asahel, born   ; baptized October 3d, 1784; married in Ohio, returned, and was drowned in Farmington River.

998. Joseph, born   ; baptized October 28th, 1787; married   , Sophronia Hart; second, Laura Buel.

999. Eunice, born   ; baptized January 3d, 1790; married September 16th, 1818, Chauncey Clark.

1000. Azubah, born   ; baptized September 16th, 1792; married November 9th, 1809, Apheck Woodruff.

1001. Elizabeth Norton, born   ; baptized May 14th, 1795; married Wakeman Stanley.

1002. Adna Thompson, born   , 1796; baptized May 28th, 1797; married Lydia Woodruff.

1003. Hannah Day, born March 20th, 1799; married   , Ozem Woodruff.

1004. Ezra, born   ; baptized May 17th, 1801. He was unmarried, and occasionally insane.

THOMPSON.

800.   *Farmington, Conn.*

ANN HART, Avon, Conn., third daughter of Joseph Hart, of Northington, and his wife, Ann (Barnes), born   ; baptized July 25th, 1756, at Northington; married Lot Thompson, son of Samuel, and his wife, Hannah (North), born May 4th, 1752, at Farmington.

801. .   *Northington, now Avon.*

JOSEPH HART, Jr., Northington, second son of Joseph Hart, Sr., of the same locality, and his wife, Ann (Barnes), of Southington, born July 29th, 1759, at Northington. He entered the army of the revolution, was wounded by the British at King's Bridge, and died in the hospital at Stamford, Conn., February 10th, 1777, in his 18th year.

802.   *New Britain, Conn.*

BETHEL HART, New Britain, third son of Joseph Hart, of Northington, and his wife, Ann (Barnes), of Southington, born November, 1762; baptized November 28th, 1762, at Avon, by Rev. Ebenezer Booge; married June 24th, 1784, Huldah, daughter of Ebenezer Steele, of New Britain, and his wife, Sarah (Sage), born 1767; baptized January 3d, 1768, at Kensington. He was a farmer, but later in life he became a peddler. His house was opposite the residence of Captain Elam Slater, on Horse Plain. He was lame in one hip late in life, which led him to sell tin and pewter ware for a living. He and his wife, Huldah, were both members of Dr. Smalley's church, and likewise his second wife. His first wife died September 28th, 1810, aged 44, when second he married, May 16th, 1811, the Widow Nancy Seeley, of Rocky Hill. Mr. Hart died December 25th, 1824, aged 62, when she married third, Elias Brown, of Farmington, son of Ephraim, of Windsor, Conn. She died June 8th, 1850, aged 85 years.

HIS CHILDREN BY HIS FIRST WIFE, BEING THE SEVENTH GENERATION.

1005. Huldah, born October 18th, 1786; married March 1st, 1804, Silas Pennfield.
1006. Nancy, born January 2d, 1790; married April 26th, 1809, Shelden Upson.
1007. Sarah Sage, born   , 1794; baptized July 27th, 1794; married February 25th, 1816, Henry Root.
1008. Betsey, born September 28th, 1797; married May 11th, 1813, Romanta Woodford, of Avon.
1009. Lavinia, born December 1st, 1798; married December 5th, 1819, Silas Goff, Jr., of West Springfield.
1010. Salome, born August 14th, 1801; married January 30th, 1832, Henry, son of James Judd.
1011. Adna, born January 28th, 1804; married March 20th, 1825, Lydia Pennfield.
       Daniel, born   ; baptized June 3d, 1806; died June 4th, 1806.
1012. Rosanna, born May 3d, 1807; married   , Joseph Yemons; second,
1013. Caroline Upson, born September 16th, 1809; married July 3d, 1828, Dennis Sweet.

THOMPSON.

803.   *Farmington, Conn.*

AZUBA HART, Farmington, youngest daughter of Joseph Hart, of Northington, and his wife, Ann (Barnes), of Southington, born September 28th, 1765, at Northington; married   , Eben Thompson, of Farmington, Conn.

804.   *Northington, now Avon.*

EZRA HART, Northington, youngest child of Joseph Hart, of the same place, and his wife, Ann (Barnes), Southington, born October 5th, 1768, at Northington. In 1798 he removed to Pompey, Onondaga County, N. Y., from which place he removed to   .
He died   , leaving a large family, but there is no report of them.

805.   *Farmington, East Farms.*

JOEL HART, Northington, eldest son of Noah Hart, of Avon, and his wife, Sarah (Miller), born September 2d, 1754, in Avon. He married, March 15th, 1781, Huldah Woodruff, daughter of Abraham, and his wife, Sarah (North). He lived at East Farms, in Farmington, on the place of his wife's father. She died June 6th, 1796. He died February 14th, 1818, aged 64 years. She was admitted to the church at Farmington in 1780.

THEIR CHILDREN, BEING THE SEVENTH GENERATION.

1014. Sarah, born February 13th, 1782. She lives unmarried on her father's place.
1015. Lucina, born February 4th, 1784; married·   , 1815, Richard Gillett.
       Ruby, born February 23d, 1786; died single in 1812, aged 26.
1016. Mark, born   , 1789; married   , Electa Fisk;
       died March 24th, 1814, aged 25.
       Anna, born   , 1792; died single in 1832, aged 40.
       Amon, born   , 1793; died single, December 11th, 1817, at
       Skaneateles, N. Y.

806.

Barkhamsted, Conn., Bethlehem, N. Y.

SETH HART, Bethlehem, N. Y., second son of Noah Hart, of Avon, and his wife, Sarah (Miller), born May 23d, 1756, at Northington; married December 9th, 1779, Anna Miller, of Northington. He removed to Barkhamsted in 1788, and from thence to Bethlehem, N. Y.

THEIR CHILDREN, BEING THE SEVENTH GENERATION.

· Ethel, born   , 1780. She has ten children in New York State.
   Son, born January 8th, 1782; died January 22d, 1782, aged 14 days.
   Orra, born   , 1783.
   Child, born   , 1785.
   Noah, born   , 1788.
1017. Clement, born   , 1789; married   , 1805, Hancy Walker.
       Seth Riley, born
       Orbin, born
       Sarah, born

808. *Northington, now Avon.*

SELAH HART, Northington, third son of Noah Hart, of the same place, and his wife, Sarah (Miller), born July 1st, 1760, at Avon; married   , Sarah   , who died September 21st, 1786. In 1787 he became insane, in consequence of his captain in the army giving him a severe flogging. He died November 8th, 1816, at Northington, aged 56 years.

THEIR CHILD, BEING THE SEVENTH GENERATION.

Pomeroy H., born   , 1786; baptized July 22d, 1787, at Northington. The child was presented by Widow Phebe Hart, the mother being dead, and the father crazy, so says the record. It is said he wandered from home and friends, and died single.

809. *Northington, now Avon.*

DAN HART, Northington, son of Noah Hart, of the same place, and his wife, Sarah (Miller), born July 6th, 1762, at Avon. He was in Schenectady, N. Y., in 1791, and subsequently lived in Farmington, from which place he removed, but was brought back, and died in the almshouse, February 11th, 1831, aged 69 years. He was a blacksmith by trade. He had a son who was burned to death.

ALDERMAN.

810. *Simsbury, Conn.*

HANNAH HART, Simsbury, daughter of Noah Hart, of Avon, and his wife, Sarah (Miller), born 1764, at Northington; baptized there July 1st, 1764; married James Alderman, of Simsbury.

MARSHALL.

813. *Granville, Mass.*

HULDAH HART, Granville, eldest daughter of Gideon Hart, of Avon, and his wife, Elizabeth (Hart), born September 29th, 1760, at Avon; married February 18th, 1784, Joel Marshall, of Granville, Mass. She died March 26th, 1840, aged 79 years.

GILLETT.

814. *Northington, now Avon.*

ELIZABETH HART, Avon, second daughter of Gideon Hart, of the same place, and his wife, Elizabeth (Hart), born May 11th, 1762, at Avon; married January 11th, 1788, Isaac Gillet, of Avon. She died

28

October 28th, 1828, aged 66. He died November 29th, 1825, aged 68 years, 6 months.

THOMPSON.

815.   *Avon, Conn.*

RHODA HART, Avon, third daughter of Gideon Hart, of the same town, and his wife, Elizabeth (Hart), born December 27th, 1764, at Avon; married July 12th, 1814, Eben Thompson, of Avon. They had only one child, named Levia, born June 10th, 1794. Mrs. Thompson died February 1st, 1842, aged 77 years, 3 months, 4 days. Mr. Thompson died September 28th, 1843, aged 88 years, 6 months.

816.   *Cider Brook, Avon.*

ABNER HART, Avon, eldest son of Gideon Hart, of the same place, and his wife, Elizabeth (Hart), born December 3d, 1766, at Avon; married, 1801, Alma, daughter of Levi Thompson, and his wife, Lucy (Woodford), born May 18th, 1780. He lived on the east side of Farmington River, at Cider Brook, near where the old meeting-house stood, and where his son Austin lived in 1873. His avocation was farming. He died November 30th, 1840, aged 74 years. His widow died of old age, March 31st, 1863, aged 83 years. She was admitted to the church at Avon in 1821.

THEIR CHILDREN, BEING THE SEVENTH GENERATION.

1018. Noadiah, born June 9th, 1801; married Sept. 12th, 1826, Clarissa Dickinson. .
1019. Leffert, born December 14th, 1802; married   , 1826, Nancy
      Woodford.
      Truxton, born November 3d, 1804; died August 14th, 1813, aged 9 years. .
1020. Alonzo, born November 17th, 1806; married *-- /837* , Rachell*//lly*.
1021. Carlos, born November 25th, 1808; married, 1833, Lois Rice; died August
      30th, 1840.
1022. 'Homer, born February 24th, 1811; married   , Delia Loveridge.
1023. Thomas Truxton, born August 10th, 1813; died single, at Houston, July 20th,
      1840, aged 27.
1024. Austin Abner, born November 13th, 1823; married November 20th, 1844,
      Catharine Hart.

GILLETT.

817.   *Avon, Conn.*

ALMIRA HART, Avon, fourth daughter of Gideon Hart, of the same place, and his wife, Elizabeth, daughter of William Hart, born September 4th, 1769, in Avon; married November 24th, 1791, Amos Gillet. She died February 8th, 1799, aged 29 years.

ANDREWS.

818. *Farmington, Conn.*

ALICE HART, fifth daughter of Gideon Hart, of the same place, and
is wife, Elizabeth, daughter of William Hart, born November 5th,
771, at Avon; married March 6th, 1796, Samuel, son of Elijah An-
rews, and his wife, Sarah (Thompson), born April 24th, 1768, at
'armington. She was admitted to the Congregational Church in
'armington, August 2d, 1829, and died August 1st, 1830, aged 58
ears, 8 months, 26 days. He died in 1821, aged about 53 years. His
ather's Will was dated July 2d, 1795, and constituted him, with James,
is brother, as executors. His own inventory was taken August 30th,
821; amount, $3,523.35; and distribution was made August 7th,
822, to the widow and the three children, viz: Hiram, born April
3d, 1799; Huldah, born June 22d, 1803; Emily, born September
2th, 1809.

819. *Avon, Conn.*

GIDEON BALDWIN HART, Avon, Conn., third son of Gideon Hart, of
he same place, and his wife, Elizabeth, daughter of William, born
'ebruary 14th, 1776, at Avon; married December 29th, 1795, Marilla
Woodford, daughter of Joseph, Jr., of Avon, born July 8th, 1777, in
Avon. He resided there east of Farmington River, and died there,
august 31st, 1842, aged 66 years. His widow died in Avon, August
2d, 1863, aged 86 years.

THEIR CHILDREN, BEING THE SEVENTH GENERATION.

025. Luther Woodford, born June 16th, 1796; married   , 1819, Almira
Gillett.

Betsey, born December 26th, 1797; died December 7th, 1808, aged 11. She
was buried at the old cemetery in Avon.

026. Marilla Maria, born March 22d, 1800; married   , Jesse
Frisbee.

027. Joseph Chauncey, born June 23d, 1804; married February 18th, 1824, Rosanna Goff.

028. Gideon Wareham, born June 10th, 1811; married   , 1834, Ann
Rice.

John Woodford, born February 10th, 1814; died February 20th, 1835.

820. *Gustavus, Ohio.*

JOSEPH HART, Gustavus, Ohio, fourth son of Gideon Hart, of Avon,
nd his wife, Elizabeth, daughter of William Hart, born June 30th,
778, at Avon; married November 5th, 1806, Eunice, daughter of
Ioses Fitz, and his wife, Dorothy (Belden), born June 30th, 1787, at

West Hartford. He removed from Northington to Gustavus, Trumbull County, Ohio, in 1811. He died September 19th, 1843, aged 65 years.

THEIR CHILDREN, BEING THE SEVENTH GENERATION.

1029. Joseph, born November 5th, 1800, son of the mother previous to marriage.
1030. Eliza Ann, born July 4th, 1807; married   , Erastus Brainard.
1031. Dorothy Belin, born March 27th, 1809; married   , Russel Bailey.
1032. Joseph Nelson, born January 8th, 1811; married May 16th, 1837, Jane E. Gibson.
1033. Charles Gideon, born September 19th, 1813; married   , Sylvia Russel.
1034. Sarah Emeline, born August 20th, 1815; married   , Norton D. Gleason.
1035. Levia Maria, born March 2d, 1817; married   , Sylvester W. Fitz.
1036. Almira Lucinda, born April 3d, 1819; married   , Albert C. Bradley.
1037. Fannie, born April 4th, 1825; married   , Hiram S. Hart.
1038. James Franklin, born April 3d, 1830; married   , Sarilla Artman.

WOODRUFF.

822.   *Farmington, East Farms.*

MARTHA HART, Farmington, third daughter of Ambrose Hart, of Northington, and his wife, Martha (Tuller), of Simsbury, born at Avon, and baptized there January 20th, 1759; married March 9th, 1780, Lot Woodruff, of Farmington, East Farms.

GOODWIN.

823.   *West Hartford, Conn.*

ROSA HART, West Hartford, fourth daughter of Ambrose Hart, of Northington, and his wife, Martha (Tuller), of Simsbury, born at Avon, Conn., and baptized there March 20th, 1762; married September 1st, 1785, Titus Goodwin, of West Hartford.

826.   *Brookfield, Ohio.*

GAD HART, Brookfield, Trumbull County, Ohio, only son of Ambrose Hart, and his wife, Martha (Tuller), of Avon, Conn., born 1770, and baptized there March 4th, 1770; married July 20th, 1791, Eunice Munson Woodford. They united with the Congregational Church in Northington, November 4th, 1798, and afterwards removed to Brookfield, Ohio.

THEIR CHILDREN, BEING THE SEVENTH GENERATION.

1039. Ambrose, born September 28th, 1792; married February 28th, 1816, Polly Bushnell.
1040. Alva, born May 14th, 1794; married , Fanny W. Borden.
1041. Romeo Thompson, born January 2d, 1796; died single in 1865, aged 69 years.
1042. Ezra, born November 24th, 1797; died , aged 19.
1043. Jeduthan, born August 21st, 1799; married , Hannah Webber.
1044. Gad, born February 19th, 1801; married , Lucretia Moses.
1045. Edwin, born September 24th, 1802; married , Betsey Thompson.
1046. Fanny Woodford, born November 30th, 1804; married , Samuel Brown.
1047. Marilla, born August 6th, 1806; married , William Thompson.
1048. Emeline Matilda, born June 8th, 1808; married , David Cadwell.
1049. Joseph, born March 10th, 1810; married , Prudence Rolph.
1050. Asa, born February 5th, 1812; married , Sarah Richards.
1051. Eunice Munson, born May 19th, 1814; died single, aged 39.
1052. Halsey Phelps, born December 15th, 1815; married , Charles F. Follett.

WHITING.

827. *West Hartford, Conn.*

SABRA HART, seventh daughter of Ambrose Hart, of Avon, and his wife, Martha (Tuller), born September 11th, 1772, at Avon, Conn.; married November 19th, 1793, Elijah M. Whiting, of West Hartford. No farther report of the family.

CADWELL.

828. *Farmington, East Farms, Conn.*

LODAMA HART, Farmington, Conn., youngest child of Ambrose Hart, of Northington, and his wife, Martha (Tuller), of Simsbury, born at Northington, and was baptized there October 13th, 1776; married in 1798, to Martin Cadwell, of Farmington, East Farms.

831. *Avon, Conn.*

HOSEA HART, Avon, second son of Medad Hart, of the same place, and his wife, Phebe (Miller), born in 1761, at Avon, then Northington; married Joanna Tuller. She died in 1839, aged 69 years. He died at Avon in 1837, aged 76 years. They were both made members of the church at Avon, May 5th, 1793.

THEIR CHILDREN, BEING THE SEVENTH GENERATION.

1053. Laura Bird, born , 1790; baptized May 5th, 1793; married , 1819, Jeremiah Morse, of Avon.
 Samuel, born , 1792; baptized May 5th, 1793; died October 11th, 1793, aged 15 months.

1054.   Samuel Tuller, born   , 1794; baptized September 20th, 1795; married
                                , 1814, Electa Woodruff.
        Helena, born   ,·1796; baptized September 24th, 1797.   She was
           burned to death, December 4th, 1797, aged 14 months.
1055.   Asaph, born   ; baptized September 15th, 1799; married
                                , 1828, Widow Lucina Richards.
        Heman, born   , 1801; baptized October 3d, 1802.   He went west,
           and was reported as drowned.
1056.   Jeduthan, born   ; baptized September 4th, 1803; married   ,
           Paulina Wilber.
1057.   Helena, born   ; baptized September 8th, 1805; married   ,
           Irenus Wilbur.
1058.   Jane, born   ; baptized June 11th, 1809; married   ,
           Charles Whitlock.

ALDERMAN.

832.   *Simsbury, Conn.*

RUTH HART, Simsbury, fifth daughter of Medad Hart, of Avon, and
his wife, Phebe (Miller), born at Northington, and was baptized there
February 14th, 1767; married October 7th, 1784, Timothy Alderman,
of Simsbury.

BRACE.

833.   *West Hartford, Conn.*

LYDIA HART, West Hartford, sixth daughter of Medad Hart, of
Avon, and his wife, Phebe (Miller), born at Northington, and was bap-
tized there August 26th, 1770; married, in 1791, Stephen Brace, of
West Hartford, Conn.

834.   *Avon, Conn.*

LINAS HART, Northington, Conn., eldest son of Elnathan Hart, of
the same place, and his wife, Ruth (Judd), born September 30th, 1761,
at Avon; married August 23d, 1787, Mary Ann Wilcox, of Avon.
She was admitted to the church there, March 4th, 1794, and died in
1836, aged 71 years.   He died April 10th, 1810, aged 49.   Administration on his estate was granted to Zina Hart.   Theodore Wolcott
and Samuel Norton were made appraisers.   Done at the probate court
of Farmington, June 4th, 1810.   Amount, $2,271.56.

THEIR CHILDREN, BEING THE SEVENTH GENERATION.

1059.   Zina, born December 2d, 1788; married October 20th, 1813, Rhoda Griswold.
1060.   Adna, born March 27th, 1790; married, April, 1815, Lucy Woodruff.
1061.   Julia, born   , 1791; married   , 1812, Austin Gleason.
1062.   Ruth Judd, born May 3d, 1793; married November 25th, 1812, Phineas Penn-
           field.

1063. Martin, born April, 1795; married   , 1818, Dolly Newell, of
      Farmington.
      Amelia, born May 18th, 1797; died October 30th, 1798, aged 16 months and
      19 days.
1064. Dennis, born September, 1798; married   , 1825, Elvira Dutton.
1065. Ava, born October, 1800; married   , 1827, Julia Crampton.
1066. Amelia, baptized January 26th, 1802; died single, June 8th, 1868, aged 66.

835.   *West Avon, Conn.*

OBED HART, Northington, Conn., third son of Elnathan Hart, of
the same place, and his wife, Ruth (Judd), born June 14th, 1769, at
Northington; married July 23d, 1793, Elizabeth Edson, born March
3d, 1773, was admitted to the church in 1797, and died of consumption, November 16th, 1798, aged 26, when second he married, December 16th, 1799, Charlotte Dorman, born October 16th, 1780. He died
April 14th, 1843, aged 74. They lived at West Avon. She died February 27th, 1865, aged 84. They have tombstones about the center of
West Avon Cemetery. The second wife was admitted to the church
in Avon, September 9th, 1821.

THEIR CHILDREN, BEING THE SEVENTH GENERATION.

1067. Sophronia, born April 21st, 1794; married January 9th, 1810, Joseph Hart.
1068. Edson, born April 12th, 1796; married October 15th, 1821, Helen Priestly.
      He is a clergyman.
      Norman, born May 16th, 1798; died November 9th, 1798, aged 5 months and
      27 days.

SECOND WIFE.

1069. George, born November 16th, 1801; married April 3d, 1827, Esther Hawley.
1070. Hiram, born January 25th, 1804; married May 22d, 1827, Mary Robbins.
1071. Norman, 2d, born October 11th, 1805; married   , 1826, Adaline
      Hart.
1072. Truman, born February 28th, 1808; married   1841, Harriet Langdon.
1073. Harvey, born December 29th, 1810; married September 22d, 1833, Harriet
      Woodford.
1074. Melidtha, born April 9th, 1813; married October 8th, 1835, Aretas Skinner,
      of Sherman, N. Y.
1075. Seth, born April 10th, 1816; married   , Matilda Miller.
1076. Emily, born February 28th, 1819; married   , Joshua S. Heath,
      of Collinsville.

839.   *Rochester, N. Y.*

TIMOTHY THOMPSON HART, second son of William Hart, of Farmington, and his wife, Abigail (Thompson), born   , 1781, at
Farmington; married   Wright, of Guilford. He
lived in Rochester, N. Y., and had six or seven children, but there is
no report of them or the family.

840.   *Farmington, New Britain.*

ORRIN HART, Farmington, third son of William Hart, of Avon, and his wife, Abigail (Thompson), born   , 1783, at Farmington; married   , Sally, daughter of Jedediah Gladden, the pensioner, of Saybrook and Farmington, Conn., and his wife, Elizabeth (Page), of Wallingford, Conn. He lived on the mountain, near the Brown place, so called. He was a farmer and laborer, a noted fox and bee hunter, and a man of great vitality and endurance, but was intemperate. He died in the almshouse of New Britain, January 22d, 1864, aged 81 years.

THEIR CHILDREN, BEING THE SEVENTH GENERATION.

1076½. Julia, born   , 1804; married October 12th, 1823, Edwin Sweet, of Farmington.

Thomas, born   , 1806.
Lucinda, born   , 1810.
Sally, born   , 1812.

1077. Clara, born October 12th, 1816; married September 28th, 1846, Samuel H. Hearsey, of Southington.

Orrin, born   , 1817.
John, born   ; died   , aged 23.

1078. Timothy, born October 7th, 1820, at Farmington. He lived with Captain Elam Slater, and was never married.

Lucy, born   ; died

850.   *Akron, Ohio.*

CHAUNCEY HART, Akron, Ohio, third son of Reuben Hart, of Farmington, Conn., and his wife, Elizabeth (Kilbourn), daughter of Joshua, born September 20th, 1797, at   ; married October 10th, 1819, Rosella Hard, of   . He is a farmer, living at Akron, Ohio, in 1874, but is in feeble health.

THEIR CHILDREN, BEING THE SEVENTH GENERATION.

Amanda, born September 18th, 1820; died July 8th, 1838.

1079. Lydia Amelia, born December 23d, 1824; married   , 1845, W. N. Cunningham.

Henry H., born November 25th, 1836; died August 20th, 1838.

1080. Amanda, born October 13th, 1840; married October 17th, 1861, Avery S. Beardsley.

852.   *Michigan.*

ERASTUS HART, Michigan, eldest son of Lemuel Stevens Hart, of New Britain, Conn., and his wife,

---

NOTE.—A child of Orrin Hart died at Farmington, October 9th, 1808, aged 4 months—so Rev. Dr. Porter's Church Record says.

THEIR CHILDREN, BEING THE SEVENTH GENERATION.

1081.	Edward, born	; married
1082.	Emily, born	; married
1083.	Orlando, born	; married
	Henry, born	
	William, born	
	Sarah, born	
	Lucy, born	

855.   *Augusta, N. Y.*

IRA HART, eldest son of Eldad Hart, Jr., of Augusta, Oneida County, N. Y., and his wife   , born February 27th, 1798, at   ; married

THEIR CHILDREN, BEING THE EIGHTH GENERATION.

1084.	Clarissa Cornelia, born	; married
	William B., born	
	Juliette, born	
	Maria Jane, born	
	Abraham P., born	
	Franklin, born	
	Melissa, born	
	Orena, born	
	Polly Ann, born	

WRIGHT.

862.   *New Britain, Conn.*

DOROTHY HART, New Britain, Conn., second daughter of Ebenezer Hart, of the same town, and his wife, Lucy (Jerome), born September 16th, 1795, at New Britain; married February 3d, 1814, Colonel Joseph Wright, son of Deacon Benjamin, and his wife, Elizabeth (Culver), born October 7th, 1779, at Rocky Hill, then called Stepney. He lived on his father's old homestead, on East Street. He was colonel of militia, judge of probate, selectman, representative of the town to the legislature, and an ardent temperance reformer. In 1850 he sold his place, and built on Chestnut Street, in the city, where he died, July 19th, 1855, aged 76 years. She was admitted to the church, October 5th, 1823. She is living a widow in 1874, and is in comfortable health. They had—1, Lucy Hart, born December 11th, 1814; 2, Benjamin Gaylord, born October 26th, 1816, married April 17th, 1839, Prudence Hubbard; 3, Oliver Cromwell, born September 16th, 1819, married October 6th, 1841, Mary H. Jones; 4, Edwin Culver, born December 4th, 1821, married July 27th, 1852, Louisa C. Jessup; 5, Emily Elizabeth, born December 11th, 1828, died August 30th, 1838; 6, Hercelia Ann, born April 21st, 1833, died December 24th, 1854.

29

863.   *New Britain, Conn.*

STEPHEN HART, Jr., New Britain, Conn., eldest son of Stephen Hart, of the same place, and his wife, Sally (White), born February 19th, 1798, at New Britain; married August 24th, 1818, Cynthia Steele, daughter of William, and his wife, Beccarena (Pennfield), born April 8th, 1796. He was a farmer and butcher, and lived some years on the old homestead of his ancestors, when he sold, and bought in the village of New Britain, where Rev. Mr. Nichols owns in 1874. He died September 6th, 1846, aged 49 years. She died April 4th, 1869, aged 73 years.

THEIR CHILDREN, BEING THE EIGHTH GENERATION.

Infant, born   ; died March 29th, 1822.
1085. Fidelia, born June 7th, 1820; married October 22d, 1846, Mansfield Stacy, of Springfield, Penn.
1086. Nancy, born October 26th, 1822; married July 31st, 1839, Dr. William Allen.
1087. Emily Parker, born May 8th, 1823; married April 13th, 1845, John Proffitt, of Hartford.
1088. Maria, born March 11th, 1827; married October 1st, 1848, Allen Stacy, of Springfield, Penn.
1089. Sarah E., born February 11th, 1834; married November 14th, 1857, Asa Sheldon Parsons.
1090. Frederick, born August 20th, 1840. He was a soldier, and was killed in North Carolina, January 30th, 1863.
Harriet, born, March, 1836; died April 18th, 1839, aged 3 years.
Charles, born March 8th, 1838; died February 28th, 1839.

864.   *New Britain, Conn.*

EDMUND HART, New Britain, Conn., second son of Stephen, of New Britain, and his wife, Sally (White), born April 23d, 1799, at New Britain; married June 2d, 1824, Mehitabel Dewey, daughter of Josiah, and his wife, Mehitabel (Kilbourn), born January 28th, 1797, at New Britain. He lived in various localities, and was a brass founder by trade, which he learned of Cyrus Stanley, in Stanley Quarter. He died January 25th, 1853, aged 54 years. She was admitted to the Congregational Church in New Britain, January 4th, 1829, and died May 26th, 1856, aged 59 years.

THEIR CHILDREN, BEING THE EIGHTH GENERATION.

1091. Antoinette, born April 11th, 1825; married May 24th, 1846, Andrew Rapelye.
1092. Adeline, born March 21st, 1827; married November 26th, 1845, Levi W. Wells, of Wethersfield.
1093. Julia Ann, born March 24th, 1832; married April 10th, 1850, Oscar Butler, and was divorced.
1094. Ellen Maria, born June 12th, 1838; married January 12th, 1860, Richard Wallace Cornish.

865. *New Britain, Conn.*

GEORGE HART, New Britain, third son of Stephen Hart, of the same town, and his wife, Sally (White), born March 16th, 1801, at New Britain; married March 2d, 1826, Mary Griswold, daughter of Ebenezer Andrews, and his wife, Mary (Griswold), born October 22d, 1809. She died August 10th, 1831, aged 23 years, when second he married September 11th, 1832, Elizabeth F., daughter of Cyrus Booth, and his wife, Nancy (North), born October 31st, 1811. She died of consumption, April 25th, 1862, aged 50 years. He was a shoe-maker by trade, but is engaged in teaming and staging, in which he has been successful. His residence is west of Central Park, in the city. He married third on the 6th of May, 1863, Elizabeth, widow of William Perry, of South Windsor, and daughter of Job Elsworth, of East Windsor, and his wife, Laura (Osborn), born September 21st, 1823.

THEIR CHILDREN, BEING THE EIGHTH GENERATION.

  Charles, born   , 1827; died February 27th, 1837, aged 10 years.

1095. William Henry, born July 25th, 1834; married September 19th, 1855, Martha Peck, daughter of Elnathan.

PARKER.

866. *Lenox, Mass.*

EMILY HART, .New Britain, only daughter of Stephen Hart, of the same town, and his wife, Sally (White), born March 15th, 1804, at New Britain. She married September 21st, 1822, Erastus Parker, of Lenox, Mass., son of Richard, of East Haddam, and his wife, Elizabeth (Ellis), born January 5th, 1800, at Bristol, Conn. He was a tanner and currier by trade and avocation, and died November 17th, 1865. They had—1, Sarah Ann, born November 9th, 1825, married March 25th, 1856, J. F. Bassett; 2, Julia Amelia, born December 24th, 1827, died August 13th, 1829; 3, Emily, born May 7th, 1830, died January, 1832; 4, Elizabeth Mary, born November 24th, 1832; 5, William, born December 17th, 1838, and was a graduate of Williams College; married June 30th, 1869, Caroline R. Stansbury; 6, Hattie Amelia, born January 18th, 1847.

867. *New Britain, Conn.*

PHILIP HART, New Britain, fourth son of Stephen Hart, of the same place, and his wife, Sally (White), born June 25th, 1805, at New Britain; married November 16th, 1831, Maria Judd, daughter of William and his wife, Polly (Eddy), born October 22d, 1812, at New Britain. He is a shoe-maker by trade, and lived on East Street until 1871, when they sold, and bought on Seymour Street, in the city. She died February 8th, 1873, of consumption, aged 60 years, 3 months, 16 days.

THEIR CHILDREN, BEING THE EIGHTH GENERATION.

1096. Elizabeth, born October 22d, 1832; married October 22d, 1852, William Burritt, of New Britain.

1097. Andrew Edwin, born February 2d, 1834; married July 1st, 1857, Ann Weltha Clark.

1098. Thomas, born October 16th, 1838. He was a soldier, and was killed December 13th, 1862, aged 24.

Charles, born February 16th, 1842; died September 18th, 1848, of dysentery, aged 6 years, 7 months.

868. *New Britain, Conn.*

DEACON WILLIAM HART, New Britain, fifth son of Stephen Hart, of the same place, and his wife, Sally (White), born October 12th, 1808, at New Britain; married July 28th, 1830, Rhoda, daughter of Daniel Judd, and his second wife, Hannah (Bartholomew), born November 4th, 1809, at New Britain. She died September 2d, 1856, aged .47 years, when second he married May 26th, 1857, Laura Jane Gladden, daughter of Reuben, and his wife, Sarah (Hotchkiss), born January 7th, 1809. He owns a good place on Winter Street, in the city. He is a brass founder by trade, and is a deacon in the Baptist Church.

CHILDREN BY HIS FIRST MARRIAGE, BEING THE EIGHTH GENERATION.

1099. Henry William, born February 10th, 1832; married October 14th, 1862, Elizabeth Black.

1100. Francis, born May 25th, 1834; married May 4th, 1867, Hattie Andrews, widow of J. Slater.

1101. Jane, born April 22d, 1836; married May 19th, 1859, Leonard Orters, of Stratford.

1102. Hannah J., born February 1st, 1840; married March 4th, 1868, William E. Beers, a moulder.

William Delos, born September 30th, 1844; died March 15th, 1845.

1103. Helen Grace, born March 31st, 1846; married November 20th, 1868, William S. Judd.

869.
Wellsburg, N. Y., Fair Haven, Conn.

EBENEZER HART, New Britain, sixth son of Stephen Hart, of the same place, and his wife, Sally (White), born July 31st, 1814, at New Britain; married January 6th, 1842, at Warehouse Point, Mary Pease, daughter of Walter, and his wife, Eliza (Filer), born January 5th, 1824, at Enfield, Conn. They resided at Wellsburg, Chemung County, N. Y., in 1871, where he kept a hotel, but subsequently removed to

Fair Haven, Conn., and there he also kept a hotel. He died there, of liver affection, September 12th, 1874, aged 60 years, and was buried at New Britain, his native place.

THEIR CHILDREN, BEING THE EIGHTH GENERATION.

1104. Charles Edwin, born October 14th, 1842; married June 18th, 1867, Jennie Wainwright.
   Lilian Chase, born April 18th, 1853, at New Haven, Conn.

STEELE.

871. *New Hartford, Conn.*

SUSANNA HART, New Hartford, eldest daughter of Munson Hart, of Northington, and his wife, Mary, daughter of Noah Hart, born 1783, at Northington, and was baptized there, June 8th, 1788; married , 1813, Noah Steele, of New Hartford. Nothing more is reported of their history.

HAWLEY.

872. *Avon, Conn.*

NAOMI HART, Northington, Conn., second daughter of Munson Hart, of the same place, and his wife, Mary, daughter of Noah Hart, and his wife, Mary (Bird), born at Northington, Conn., 1786, and was baptized there, June 8th, 1788; married in 1809, Reuben Hawley, of Avon.

THOMPSON.

873. *Avon, Conn.*

SALLY HART, Northington, Conn., third daughter of Munson Hart, of the same place, and his wife, Mary, daughter of Noah Hart, and his wife, Mary (Bird), born at Avon; married in 1814, Alson Thompson, of Avon, Conn.

JONES.

874. *Harwinton, Conn.*

LYDIA HART, Harwinton, fifth daughter of Munson Hart, of the same place, and his wife, Mary, daughter of Noah Hart, and his wife, Mary (Bird), born 1794, at Avon; baptized June 11th, 1797; married December 4th, 1821, Julius Jones, of Harwinton.

875. *Candor, N. Y.*

MANNA HART, Candor, N. Y., eldest son of Lent Hart, of the same place, and his wife, Olive (Hickox), born at Northington, Conn., 1782;

married, 1804, Thede Woodford. They removed to Candor, Tioga County, N. Y., where their children were all born, and where he died July 23d, 1868, aged 86 years. She died in 1870.

THEIR CHILDREN, BEING THE SEVENTH GENERATION.

1105.	Sarah, born	, 1805; married	, 1827, William Hitchcock.
1106.	Lent, born	, 1807; married	, 1834, Fidelia Hugg.
1107.	Julia, born	, 1810; married	, 1837, Philander Thorp, of
	Spencer, N. Y.		
1108.	Edmund, born	, 1815; married	, 1840, Priscilla McDale.
1109.	Marcus, born	, 1822; married	, 1844, Melissa Mead.

876.   *Avon, Conn.*

ERASTUS HART, Burlington, second son of Lent Hart, of Avon, and his wife, Olive (Hickox), born 1784, at Northington, Conn.; married in 1806, Anna Thompson. He was a farmer and butcher. His wife died July 13th, 1829, aged 34 years, when second he married, March 28th, 1832, Avis French, of Avon. He died May 2d, 1834, aged 50 years.

THEIR CHILDREN, BEING THE SEVENTH GENERATION.

1110.   Amanda Angeline, born, September, 1807; married October 11th, 1826, Elisha Whaples.

1111.   Anna Adaline, born February 6th, 1809; married, October, 1826, Norman Hart.

1112.   Minerva Caroline, born March 17th, 1811; married February 2d, 1834, Lee Lay Rogers.

877.   *Avon, Conn.*

JEPTHA HART, Avon, third son of Lent Hart, of the same place, and his wife, Olive (Hickox), born 1785, at Avon, Conn.; married, October, 1810, Sally Thompson, born April 12th, 1791. He was a farmer by avocation. He died at Avon, July 18th, 1850, aged 65 years. His widow died October 28th, 1870, aged 79 years.

THEIR CHILDREN, BEING THE SEVENTH GENERATION.

1113.   Beulah, born, July, 1812; married, January, 1841, Martin Hart.

1114.   Olive Day, born March 12th, 1815; married January 29th, 1840, Horace Woodruff.

1114½.   Egbert, born   . He went to Candor, N. Y.

DAY.

878.   *Avon, Conn.*

ALMIRA HART, Avon, Conn., eldest daughter of Lent Hart, of the same place, and his wife, Olive (Hickox), born 1788, at Avon; married, 1809, Marcus Day, of Avon.

ARAUNAH HART, Avon, fifth son of Lent Hart, of the same town, and his wife, Olive (Hickox), born 1792, at Avon; married in 1815, Ursula, daughter of Nathaniel Clark, of Avon, born 1794, who died in 1824, when second he married in 1825, Betsey Avery, born 1802. He removed to Granville, Bradford County, Penn., and from there to the state of Wisconsin. This family are all members of the Free Will Baptist Church.

THEIR CHILDREN, BEING THE SEVENTH GENERATION.

1115.	Cibelia, born	, 1817; married	, 1842, Harvey P.
	Smith, of Candor, N. Y.		
1116.	Catharine, born	, 1818; married	, 1837, Edgar M.
	Smith, of Candor, N. Y.		
1117.	Fidelia, born	, 1820; married	Borhen,
	of New York City.		
1118.	Samuel Martin, born	, 1821; married	, 1841, Beulah
	Hart.		
1119.	Amos E., born	, 1823; married	, 1843, Harriet G.
	Smith.		

SECOND WIFE.

1120.	Olive U., born	, 1826; married	, T. Woodford,
	of Danby, N. Y.		
	Jeptha Sylvester, born	, 1829. He was living with his father in	
	1846.		
	Parthenia, born	, 1831; died	, 1844.
1121.	Harriet Ann, born	, 1833; married	, C. Gates.
	Charles Benjamin, born	, 1836.	
	Helen Melissa, born	, 1839.	

WADSWORTH. KILBOURN.

EMELINE GRIDLEY HART, Newington, Conn., youngest daughter of Lent Hart, of Avon, and his wife, Olive (Hickox), born November 22d, 1805, at Avon; married April 26th, 1826, Amzi Wadsworth, a farmer of Northington. He died January 3d, 1829, aged 24, when second she married February 22d, 1836, Henry Kilbourn, a farmer of Newington, Conn. In 1872 they lived next south of the church. She had one child by Wadsworth—Catharine Elizabeth. She had four children by Kilbourn—two sons and two daughters. He died April 18th, 1873, at Newington.

TERENCY HART, Candor, Tioga County, N. Y., only son reported of James Gridley Hart, of the same place, and his wife, Loranie (Derrin), born 1783, at Avon, Conn.; married in 1810, Sally, daughter of Joel Smith, of New Britain, and subsequently of Candor, N. Y., born 1791. She died at Candor in 1854, aged 63 years, and was a member of the Presbyterian Church there. He died in 1864, aged 84 years.

THEIR CHILD, BEING THE SEVENTH GENERATION.

1122. Timothy Edbert, born   , 1821; married   , 1844, Olivia M. Johnson.

883.   *Farmington, Conn.*

STEPHEN WINCHELL HART, Farmington, eldest son of Gad Hart, of the same town, and his wife, Lorana (Winchell), born June 14th, 1781, at Farmington; married   , Sally Bruce. He was a carpenter and wheelwright, with his father. He died June 11th, 1827, aged 46 years.

THEIR CHILDREN, BEING THE EIGHTH GENERATION.

1123. Donald, born June 18th, 1804; married   , 1831, Caroline Pitkin.
1124. Gad Henry, born   , 1806; married   , 1829, Eliza E. Cowles.
1125. Albert B., born   , 1813; died at Macon, Ga., June 27th, 1837, aged 24.
1126. Stephen Decatur, born   . He was a blacksmith, and died at Hartford in 1836.
1127. Nancy, born   ; married   , Alvin Smith.

BUCK.

884.   *Farmington, Conn.*

CATY HART, Farmington, eldest daughter of Gad Hart, of Farmington, and his wife, Lorana (Winchell), born April 17th, 1783, at Farmington, a twin with her sister, Nancy; married Buck, father of Daniel. She died March 14th, 1841, aged 58 years.

885.

JULIUS HART, Farmington, second son of Gad Hart, of the same town, and his wife, Lorana (Winchell), born November 17th, 1787, at Farmington; married December 9th, 1813, Harriet Prior Bruce, of Hartford, Conn., born March 28th, 1792. She died May 13th, 1842, aged 50 years. They were both members of the Congregational Church in Farmington.

THEIR CHILDREN, BEING THE EIGHTH GENERATION.

1128. Lewis Bruce, born December 18th, 1814; married November 17th, 1837, Lydia A. Miller.
1129. Henry Wright, born November 20th, 1816; married   , Lucy Holmes.
        Julius Franklin, born January 13th, 1819; died single.

1130. Jane Ruth, born November 3d, 1821; married   , Silas C.
      Lewis.
1131. Harriet Prior, born January 2d, 1826; married May 31st, 1846, Origen Parker.
1132. Minerva, born July 13th, 1828.
1133. Andrew Jackson, born August 17th, 1831, and lives in Whitneyville, Conn.
1134. Frederic Donald, born April 9th, 1834. He is an engineer at Brooklyn, N. Y.

886. *Farmington, Conn.*

SIDNEY HART, Farmington, third son of Gad Hart, of the same town,
and his first wife, Lorana (Winchell), born October 18th, 1789, at
Farmington; married November 13th, 1811, Clarinda S. Clark. He
was a wheelwright by trade and occupation, which he learned of his
father, and was a very active man. He lived and died in the village
of Farmington.

THEIR CHILDREN, BEING THE EIGHTH GENERATION.

1134$\frac{1}{2}$. Lorana C., born December 30th, 1814; married June 18th, 1837, Charles P.
      James.
1134$\frac{3}{4}$. Catharine, born October 18th, 1817; married   , 1836, William
      Henry Grimes.
1134$\frac{7}{8}$. Sidney, born June 3d, 1819; married   , 1840, Lydia W. Griswold.
1134$\frac{7}{10}$. Hiram Winchell, born February 11th, 1825. He was a joiner in Hartford.

887.

HIRAM HART, Farmington, youngest son of Gad Hart, of the same
town, and his wife, Lorana (Winchell), born February 26th, 1791, at
Farmington; married in 1822, Sarah Woodford. He was a carriage
maker and painter, and was a first rate mechanic. He died July 9th,
1822, aged 31 years.

THEIR CHILD, BEING THE EIGHTH GENERATION.

1135 Emily, born   . She was a school teacher in Hartford.

889. *Farmington, Conn.*

ZENAS HART, Farmington, second son of Asa Hart, of the same
town, and his wife,   , born   , 1789,
at Farmington; married, September, 1808, Rachel, daughter of Jabez
Lewis, and his wife, Clarinda, born April 17th, 1790, at Red Stone
Hill, a locality of Farmington. She died at Unionville, April 2d,
1868, aged 78 years. He was a brick mason by trade and occupation,
and lived on the mountain, near Dr. Cowles' distillery, which was at
the foot of the mountain. He died March 24th, 1838, aged 56 years.

30

Child, born   , 1809; died   , 1810.

1136. Chauncey, born August 26th, 1810; married September 17th, 1832, Jane
       Hooper.

1137. Emily, born June 5th, 1815; married October 6th, 1835, Edward I. Welton,
       of Watertown.

1138. Henry, born   , 1816; married   , 1835, Sarah G. Taylor;
       second

1139. Richard, born January 2d, 1818; married   , Catharine
       Gladden; second

1140. Lewis, born May 20th, 1821; married April 10th, 1840, Julia Ann Root, of
       New Britain.

1141. Lucy Ann, born September 29th, 1823; married March 2d, 1845, Simeon
       Stedman.

890.   *Sheffield, Mass.*

EDWARD HART, Sheffield, Mass., eldest son of Josiah Hart, of the
same place, and his wife, Abigail (Kelsey), born November 19th, 1791,
at Sheffield; 'married   , Sarah Abbe, of Unionvale,
Dutchess County, N. Y., who died September 17th, 1842, when second
he married   , Sabrina Cleavland, of New Marlboro,
Mass., who died February 23d, 184–.

1142. Mary, born August 2d, 1819; married   , John D. Pierce.

1143. Julia Ann, born September 9th, 1820; married   , Isaac Gardner.
       Sarah, born March 6th, 1822.

1144. Amelia,)   married   , Joseph Knok.
               } born February 17th, 1824;
1145. Fidelia,)   married   , Stephen Thorn.
       Edward, born December 31st, 1835.
       Emily Jane, born March 19th, 1838; died April 1st, 1838.
       Emily Jane, born June 16th, 1840.

1146. Stephen, born July 29th, 1844.

BARNUM.

891.   *Freedom, Ohio.*

JERUSHA HART, Freedom, Ohio, only daughter of Josiah Hart, of
Farmington, Conn., and Sheffield, Mass., and his wife, Abigail (Kelsey),
born June 3d, 1793, at Sheffield; married   , Eli
Barnum. Their residence is at Freedom, Portage County, Ohio. She
is a member of the church there.

892.

MILO HART, Freedom, Portage County, youngest son of Josiah Hart,
of Farmington and Sheffield, and his wife, Abigail (Kelsey), born Sep-

tember 4th, 1800; married   , Julia Ann Sawyer.
He is a carpenter and joiner by occupation, and is a professor of religion. They have no children reported.

MILLER.

896.   *Stockton, N. Y.*

MARY HART, Canada, eldest daughter of Lemuel Hart, of Southington, Conn., and his wife, Rosanna (Winstone), born   ;
married   , John Miller, of Canada, and went there
to live, and from there to Stockton, Chatauqua County, N. Y., where,
probably, both died. They had children, viz: Rosanna, married Martin
Winchell; she is now dead; (see the Winchell Genealogy;) William
Henry, Sally, Clarissa, and Mary.

FIELD.

897.   *Egremont, Mass.*

ORRA HART, Egremont, Mass., second daughter of Lemuel Hart, of
Southington, Conn., and his first wife, Rosanna (Winstone), born
                 ; married John Field, of Egremont, Berkshire County,
Mass., where they located, and became members of the Methodist
Church. They both died before 1872. They had children, viz: Lo-
retta, who resides at Princeton, Ill., and is a Methodist; Mary, who is
also a Methodist; Milo, Gilbert, Harry, who is a Presbyterian deacon
at Princeton, Ill., and Joel, who lives in Sheffield, Mass.

898.   *Nelson, Ohio.*

JOEL HART, Egremont, Mass., eldest son of Lemuel Hart, of Southington, and his first wife, Rosanna (Winstone), born January 2d, 1788;
married February 2d, 1809, Sally Winchell, daughter of Amos, of
Egremont, and his wife, Anna (Adams), born November 10th, 1779,
at Egremont. They located at Nelson, Portage County, Ohio, where
she died, April 1st, 1845, aged 66 years. He was a stone mason by
trade and occupation, and both were members of the Methodist Episcopal Church. He died at Freeport, Stephenson County, Ill., October
1st, 1870, aged 82 years.

THEIR CHILDREN, BEING THE EIGHTH GENERATION.

1147. Sarah Ann, born April 6th, 1810; married Sept. 28th, 1837, John Burrows.
1148. Julia Berintha, born June 22d, 1812; married February 11th, 1836, William
R. Nicholson.
Infant son, born   , and died.
1149. Newton Henry, born February 25th, 1816; married August 16th, 1853, Moselle S. McCollum.

1150. Solomon Winchell, born May 21st, 1817; married June 8th, 1843, Eleanor Bancroft.

1151. Lorenzo Dewitt, born October 11th, 1828; married October 13th, 1858, Clarissa Stearns.

1152. Mary Jane, born May 21st, 1831; married September 21st, 1853, Jacob P. Earle.

1152½. Charles Alonzo, born January 8th, 1834; married September 22d, 1866, Amanda M. H. Dobler.

899.   *Egremont, Mass., Winsted, Conn.*

NEWTON HART, Egremont, Mass., eldest son of Lemuel Hart, of Southington, and his second wife, Lydia (Heffards), born May 23d, 1793, at Egremont, Mass.; married December 30th, 1828, Martha Sophronia Winchell, daughter of Amos, of Egremont, and his wife, Anna (Adams), born January 10th, 1803, at Egremont. They lived both at Egremont, and Winsted, Conn., where he died, January 24th, 1868, aged 75 years. She was living with her son, George, at Bristol, Conn., in 1871.

THEIR CHILDREN, BEING THE EIGHTH GENERATION.

1153. Lucinda, born   ; married   , Seth Newman, of Egremont.

Lydia Ann, born Feb. 28th, 1830; died August 28th, 1830, aged 6 months.

1154. Sophronia Urania, born June 13th, 1831; died single, June 12th, 1855, aged 24 years.

1155. Davis, born September 24th, 1833; married   , Amanda Stannard, of Winsted.

1156. William Henry, born January 25th, 1836; married   , Mary E. Brown.

1157. George Lemuel, born September 26th, 1838; married February 13th, 1871, Harriet Jackson.

Martin Van Buren, born February 5th, 1841; died May 4th, 1846, aged 5 years, 3 months.

1158. Timothy Ard, born December 27th, 1843; married   , Emma Tuttle, of Winsted.

901.   *Bristol, Conn.*

ARD HART, Bristol, Conn., second son of Lemuel Hart, of Southington, Conn., and his second wife, Lydia (Heffards), born January 23d, 1803, at Hillsdale, Mass.; married January 3d, 1831, Miss Amanda, daughter of Seth Hart, of Bristol, and his wife, Mary (Wilcox), born July 26th, 1805. He was a hatter by trade, but a farmer by occupation. His farm is located in the north part of Bristol, near Burlington line. He died in Bristol, of small pox, May 26th, 1850, aged 47 years, and was buried in the North Cemetery. She died September 16th, 1863, aged 68 years.

1159. Amos Bushnell, born May 10th, 1832; married November 4th, 1860, Almira Gaylord.
1160. Jason Harvillah, born February 20th, 1834; married June 5th, 1859, Julia Sanford.
1161. Burton, born April 16th, 1836; married February 1st, 1863, Emily Curtiss.
1162. Mary Jane, born October 4th, 1837; married October 26th, 1858, Daniel Post, of Hebron.
1163. Emily Amanda, born May 20th, 1839. She was single in 1871, and living in New Britain.

Orrin, born June 11th, 1841; died June 29th, 1841, aged 2 weeks.

Chloe Nancy, born February 23d, 1843; died June 1st, 1850, of small pox, aged 7 years.

1164. Newton Alphonzo, born January 5th, 1846; married September 20th, 1869, Hattie Emily Geer.
1165. Seth Ransom, born May 17th, 1848; married January 3d, 1869, Evelina Johnson.

901½. *Bristol, Conn.*

HENRY HART, Bristol, Conn., an illegitimate son of Amanda Hart, daughter of Seth, born September 8th, 1830, at Bristol. He was a renegade. He stole small pox clothing from a clothes-line, and so the family of Ard Hart (who married his mother) caught it, and Ard and their daughter, Chloe, died of it. He finally ended his career in the state prison at Wethersfield, where he died, March 15th, 1860, aged 29, and was buried in the North Cemetery at Bristol.

902.

Sheffield, Egremont, Mass., Bristol, Conn.

JAIRUS HART, Bristol, Conn., third son of Lemuel Hart, of Southington, and his second wife, Lydia (Heffards), born August 2d, 1804, probably at Hillsdale, N. Y., where his father taught school; married in 1825, Hannah, daughter of John Jones, of Mount Washington, and his wife, Elizabeth (Kline), born about 1809. She died March 30th, 1839, when second he married in 1844, Elizabeth Sheffel, of Sheffield, Mass., who is an invalid, being nearly helpless. They have lived in Sheffield, Egremont, and Mount Washington, and were living in Bristol in 1871.

Lafanny, born about 1826; died   , aged 10 years.
1166. Esther, born October 30th, 1832. She lives at home and cares for her step-mother.
1167. Salmon Gaylord, born January 3d, 1842, at Bristol. He is single, lives at home, is a wood turner, and was working at Polkville in 1871.

900.   *Sparta, Ind.*

Amos Hart, Sparta, Dearborn County, Ind., fourth son of Lemuel Hart, of Southington, Conn., and his second wife, Lydia (Heffards), born July 23d, 1800; married March 17th, 1839, Sally Brian, born 1808. They reside at Sparta, Ind. His wife died October 2d, 1841, aged 33, when second he married February 20th, 1842, Eliza Ann Roof, daughter of Samuel, and his wife, Willempie (Cozzine), born August 9th, 1817. She died October 8th, 1850, aged 33. He was in trade in 1871, being in feeble health.

HIS CHILD BY HIS FIRST WIFE, BEING THE EIGHTH GENERATION.

1168. Nancy Jane, born March 25th, 1840; married December 20th, 1869, Greensburgh Washington.

HIS CHILD BY HIS SECOND WIFE, ELIZA.

1169. Lemuel, born January 10th, 1845.

CRANDAL.

903.   *Petersburg, N. Y.*

Urania Hart, Burlington, Conn., eldest daughter of Lemuel Hart, of Southington, and his second wife, Lydia (Heffards), born   ; married   , ——— Crandall, of Petersburg, Rensselaer County, N. Y. They had no children, and both were dead in 1871. She was a Seventh Day Baptist.

SPENCER.

904.   *Freeport, Ill.*

Belinda Hart, Burlington, Conn., second daughter of Lemuel Hart, of Southington, and his second wife, Lydia (Heffards), born 1806; married William Spencer, of Burlington. They removed to Freeport, Stephenson County, Ill., and both died there. They left no children. They were both members of the Baptist Church.

DORMAN.

905.   *Charlestown, Ohio.*

Nancy Hart, Charlestown, Portage County, Ohio, eldest daughter of Ard Hart, of Burlington, Conn., and his wife, Millicent (Roberts), born February 22d, 1789, at Burlington; married Joel Dorman. They located at Charlestown, Portage County, Ohio. She died at Hampden, Ohio, June 11th, 1855, aged 66 years. They had children, viz: Delia, Jennet, Rollin, Millicent, Harriet Elvira, Edward, and Julius Hart.

WOODFORD.

906. *West Avon, Conn.*

BELINDA HART, West Avon, second daughter of Ard Hart, of Burlington, and his wife, Millicent (Roberts), born April 24th, 1793; married   , John Woodford, from whom she parted. They lived in West Avon. She died in 1865, aged 72 years. They had children, viz: Corydon, Orson, Annette, Antoinette, and John.

HILL. DARROW.

907. *Plymouth, Conn.*

DELIA HART, Plymouth, third daughter of Ard Hart, of Burlington, and his wife, Millicent (Roberts), born May 19th, 1795; married December 1st, 1814, Billings Hill, a joiner of Burlington, and died, October, 1828, when she second married Leveret Darrow, February 10th, 1839. They resided at Plymouth, Conn. Her children by Hill were —Celia, Harriet, Lewis, Minerva, Edward, and Hart Billings. The mother was a widow, living in Springfield, Mass., but in March, 1874, in Plainville, Conn.

HART.

908. *Burlington, Conn.*

MILLICENT HART, Burlington, Conn., fifth daughter of Ard Hart, of Burlington, and his wife, Millicent (Roberts), born June 14th, 1799; married John Hart, son of Ambrose, of Burlington, and was his second wife. He died May 4th, 1855, aged 68 years. She was a widow, living in Burlington, Conn., in 1871.

909. *Vienna, Ohio.*

CHAUNCEY HART, Burlington, Conn., eldest son of Ard Hart, of Burlington, and his wife, Millicent (Roberts), born June 9th, 1802, in Burlington; married there December 17th, 1823, Millessendra Hart, daughter of Bliss Hart, of the same town, and his wife, Sylvia (Upson), born December 17th, 1803, at Burlington, Conn. They removed to Vienna, Trumbull County, Ohio, in 1825. He died September 18th, 1844, at Brookfield, Ohio, when second she married Samuel Baldwin, and in 1872 they resided at Ravenna, Portage County, Ohio, but in the winter of 1873–4 he died, leaving her again a widow at Ravenna.

THEIR CHILDREN, BEING THE EIGHTH GENERATION.

1170. Helen M., born August 17th, 1824; married December 24th, 1841, Henry H. Long.
1171. William Elsworth, born April 9th, 1826; married in 1852, Rachel Wheelock.

1172.   Alphonzo, born July 4th, 1830. He is a lawyer, a member of the state sen-
        ate, and in 1874 is lieutenant-governor of Ohio.
1173.   Orlando, born July 29th, 1832. He is a tin-man in Blissfield, Mich.
1174.   Edgar L., born April 13th, 1835. He is a merchant in Cleveland, Ohio.

910.   *Palmyra, N. Y., Cleveland, O.*

WILLIAM HART, Palmyra, second son of Ard Hart, of Burlington,
and his wife, Millicent (Roberts), born September 2d, 1804, at Burlington; married April 4th, 1832, Mary Ann Bowman, of Charlestown,
N. H., who died November 10th, 1855, when second he married April
4th, 1860, Mrs. Mary Porter, widow of John, of Farmington. He is
a farmer by occupation, and in 1871 lived at Vineland, N. J., but in
1873 he was a widower, living at Cleveland, Ohio.

THEIR CHILDREN, BEING THE EIGHTH GENERATION.

1175.   William Roberts, born January 15th, 1833; married   , Harriet
        Newell Wilcox.
1176.   Mary H., born October 6th, 1835; married December 22d, 1852, Colonel Wil-
        liam Wisner Hayt, of New York.
1177.   George A., born January 15th, 1841. He is single in 1874, and his residence
        in Philadelphia.
1178.   Edwin R., born March 25th, 1844. He is single in 1874, and his residence
        Western Illinois.
        Emma B., born March 13th, 1848; died at Philadelphia, March 12th, 1871,
        aged 23 years.

LYMAN.

911.   *Newton Falls, Ohio.*

SARAH HART, sixth daughter of Ard Hart, of Southington and Burlington, and his wife, Millicent (Roberts), born January 26th, 1807, at
Burlington; married in 1831, George Lyman. They removed to Ohio,
and she died at Newton Falls, Trumbull County, Ohio, January 8th,
1858, aged 51, when second he married in 1867, Emily Hanscom.
They now reside at Cleveland, Ohio. He is a son of David Lyman, of
New Hartford, and his wife, Rhoda P. (Belden).

HADSELL.

912.   *Burlington, Plainville, Conn.*

ELVIRA HART, Plainville, Conn., seventh and youngest daughter of
Ard Hart, of Southington, and subsequently of Burlington, and his
first wife, Millicent (Roberts), born October 20th, 1812, at Burlington;
married October 27th, 1830, at Burlington, before Rev. Mr. Scranton,
Ira, son of Ira Hadsell, and his wife, Orpha (Sweet), born August

27th, 1802, at Burlington, Conn. He is a wealthy farmer of Plainville, Conn., in 1874. She died June 1st, 1873, aged 62 years, and was buried at the Hill Cemetery. They had but one son, George Ira, born April 6th, 1844, at Farmington; married May 16th, 1865, Martha Clarissa, daughter of Rev. Erastus Clapp, of East Hampton, Mass. They have one daughter and one son in 1874.

<h3 style="text-align:center">913. Scott, N. Y.</h3>

JUDE HART, Jr., Southington, eldest son of Jude Hart, Sr., and his wife, Patience (Sloper), born March 20th, 1799, at Southington; married November 6th, 1823, Hannah Pardee, born February 28th, 1800. They were admitted to the Congregational Church in Southington, December 6th, 1829. They removed to Scott, Cortland County, N. Y., but were residing at Sempronius, Cayuga County, N. Y., in 1871.

THEIR CHILDREN, BEING THE EIGHTH GENERATION.

1179. Albert, born November 1st, 1824; baptized February 5th, 1830. He is a farmer.
1180 Julia Ann, born July 22d, 1833; married, November, 1860, Sherman Williams.
1181. Caroline Augusta, born January 11th, 1837; married July 28th, 1860, Benjamin Williams.
1182. Amos Augustus, born July 17th, 1839; married July 2d, 1866, Mary Wilcox.

<h2 style="text-align:center">HITCHCOCK.</h2>

<h3 style="text-align:center">914. Southington, Conn.</h3>

OLIVE HART, Southington, eldest daughter of Jude Hart, of the same town, and his wife, Patience (Sloper), born September 19th, 1791; baptized September 19th, 1795; married March 8th, 1813, Jason, son of Jason Hitchcock, and his wife, Patience (Langdon), born March 8th, 1794. He died August 23d, 1859, at Southington, aged 69. She died October 5th, 1869, aged 78 years. They had issue, viz: Patience, born May 21st, 1817; Lucy, born July 5th, 1823, died   , aged 3 years; Lucy, 2d, born December 27th, 1825.

<h3 style="text-align:center">915. Southington, Conn.</h3>

REUEL HART, Southington, youngest child of Jude Hart, of the same town, and his wife, Patience (Sloper), born February 1st, 1808; married March 29th, 1832, Rosanna Barnes, daughter of Bebee Barnes, and his wife, Rosanna (Beecher). They reside one mile north-west of the village of Southington, on the road to West Street.

31

1183. Helmer, born June 1st, 1834; married October 5th, 1864, Josephine G. Perry.
1184. Ellen, born August 25th, 1838.
1185. John, born February 23d, 1841.

916. *Southington, Conn.*

WILLYS HART, Southington, eldest son of Chauncey Hart, of the same town, and his first wife, Lydia Hoadley (Bray), born November 6th, 1789, at Southington. He was never married. He entered the army of 1812, and was stationed at Flatbush, N. Y., from whence he deserted for the third time, and came to Southington, where he was arrested by an officer from the army, taken back to Flatbush, tried by court-martial, found guilty, and shot, but unjustly, as he was subject to fits and insanity.

917. *Southington, Conn.*

SHERMAN HART, Southington, second son of Chauncey Hart, of the same town, and his first wife, Lydia Hoadley (Bray), born December 14th, 1791, at Southington, Conn. He enlisted into the army of the war of 1812, and after serving his time he returned, and married March 3d, 1819, Elizabeth Smith, of Southington, daughter of Gideon, and his wife, Lois (Barnes). He removed to Berlin, Worthington Parish, where he died in 1846, aged 54. She was admitted to Worthington Church, October 4th, 1835. She died in 1852, aged 56 years.

1186. Elizabeth, born   , 1820; married   .   , Benjamin
          Goodale, of Rocky Hill.
      Child, born   , 1822; died June 10th, 1823, aged 7 months.
      James, born   , 1824, and lived in Meriden.
      Lois, born   , 1828.
      Frederic, born
      George, born
      John, born
      Harriet, born   , 1836.

918. *Southington, Conn.*

EDWARD HART, Southington, third son of Chauncey Hart, of the same town, and his first wife, Lydia Hoadley (Bray), born March 2d, 1794, at Southington. He was a shoe-maker by trade and occupation, and lived at the north end of Flanders Street, under or at the foot of the mountain. He married Anna, daughter of Daniel Beach, who died at Southington of consumption, June 9th, 1832, aged 42 years, when second he married May 15th, 1835, Rhoda, daughter of Asa Granniss,

and his wife, Keziah (Lewis), born January 25th, 1805, at Wolcott.
He died March 8th, 1869, aged 75 years.

THEIR CHILDREN, BEING THE EIGHTH GENERATION.

1187. Maria, born   , 1821; married September 9th, 1844, Henry P. Pond.

     Jane, born   , 1822; died   , 1825, aged 3 years.

1187½. Samuel Beach, born , 1824; baptized April 5th, 1839; died single in 1869.

1188. Jane Lucretia, born   , 1828; married   , David Fullerton.

1189. Delia Ann, born July 30th, 1836; married November 30th, 1854, Samuel
     Dyer.

1190. Celia L., born August 24th, 1840; married November 15th, 1857, Samuel H.
     Peck.

1191. Almira Eliza, born, January, 1842; married   , Marcus Covell.

1192. Phebe Amelia, born August 18th, 1843; married October 27th, 1869, Francis
     Wright, of New Britain.

1193. Edward Winfield, born August 26th, 1849. He is a farmer and is single.

920.   Geneva, Wis.

ALMON HART, Geneva, Wis., fifth son of Chauncey Hart, of Southington, Conn., and his first wife, Lydia Hoadley (Bray), born June
12th, 1798, at Southington. He was given to David Hart in infancy,
and in the year 1807 was taken to Middletown, Rutland County, Vt.,
where he married in 1828, Mary Gates Stewart, daughter of Samuel,
and his wife, Rebecca (Leach), born September 28th, 1810, at Middletown, Vt. He removed to the west, and has been moving west ever
since, so he writes, and was residing at Geneva, Wis., in 1873, where
he is a farmer. Besides the children below, several died in infancy
without names.

THEIR CHILDREN, BEING THE EIGHTH GENERATION.

1194. Laura Flora, born November 14th, 1829; married   , John
     K. Stamford.

1195. Asa Bray, born March 23d, 1832; married   , Ceda Owen.

1196. David Almon, born August 29th, 1840; married July 3d, 1862, Mary Jane
     Potter.

1197. Mary Jane, born October 18th,   ; married, October, 1860, Hoyt G. Hale.
     Lydia Rebecca, born May 14th, 1845, at Spring Prairie, Wis.

1198. Edward Beriah, born November 14th, 1850.

921.   Southington, Conn.

CHAUNCEY HART, Jr., Southington, eldest son of Chauncey Hart, Sr.,
of the same town, and his second wife, Lucy (Gaylord), born September 15th, 1804, at Southington. He went to Oxford, Chenango County,
N. Y., and married October 1st, 1829, Abigail Wright, born March
20th, 1806, at Southington. She went to Oxford at the age of six
years, and taught school there until her marriage. She died March

20th, 1857, aged 51, when second he married April 13th, 1859, Sally Scott, a member of the Methodist Church, who died December 22d, 1867, aged 52. He third married October 6th, 1868, Mabel Nickerson, born in Guilford, N. Y. She was a member of the Universalist Church. She died November 22d, 1869, aged 56 years, when he fourth married December 30th, 1870, Betsey Hurlburt, born 1810, in Connecticut. He had six children, all by his first wife, and all born in Oxford, four of whom died infants. He was a canvasser for books in 1872.

CHILDREN BY HIS FIRST WIFE, BEING THE EIGHTH GENERATION.

Marcus H., born February 9th, 1832; died March 24th, 1862, aged 30.

1199. Eunice A., born March 4th, 1840; married January 7th, 1869, Egbert G. Willett.

922.   *Southington, Conn.*

HENRY HART, Southington, second son of Chauncey Hart of the same town, and his second wife, Lucy (Gaylord), born November 25th, 1807, at Southington; married May 2d, 1834, Harriet, daughter of George Washington Cowles, and his wife, Amy (Adkins). She was admitted to the church in Southington, February 3d, 1838, and was dismissed, and recommended to the church at Windham, N. Y., October 17th, 1842, to which place they removed, and from thence they removed to East Tennessee, where, on the breaking out of the war, he was confined in jail by the rebels, at Knoxville, for expressing Union sentiments, where he died from starvation. His home was in Bledsoe County.

THEIR CHILD, BEING THE EIGHTH GENERATION.

1200. Henry Washington, born   ; baptized October 15th, 1837.

WOODRUFF.

924.   *Southington, Conn.*

PHEBE HART, Southington, second daughter of Chauncey Hart, of the same town, and his second wife, Lucy (Gaylord), born September 12th, 1812, at Southington; married May 10th, 1835, Edwin, son of Ashbel Woodruff, and his wife, Sibil (Ingraham), born February 28th, 1810, at Southington. He is a farmer, and lives at the south end of Flanders Street, on the east side of the road, where she died October 30th, 1871, of scrofula, after an illness of about three months, aged 59 years. They had no children.

926.   *Bristol, Conn.*

THOMAS HART, Bristol, Conn., second son of Ithurel Hart, of the same place, and his wife, Sibel (Jerome), born 1788, at Bristol; married

. He went south, and died at Hazel Green, Ala., May 14th, 1829, aged 41 years. They had an infant child that died without a name.

927. *Bristol, Conn.*

AUGUSTUS HART, Bristol, Conn., fourth son of Ithurel Hart, of the same town, and his wife, Sibel (Jerome), born at Bristol, and married there September 14th, 1819, Sabra Plum. They had one child, born 1820, and died there February 10th, 1821, aged 10 months. They removed to Missouri.

929. *Bristol, Conn.*

ELONZO HART, Bristol, Conn., third son of Seth Hart, of the same town, and his wife, Mary (Wilcox), born September 4th, 1793, at Bristol; married October 5th, 1815, Lovina, daughter of Josiah Barnes, and his wife, Olive (Cornwall), of Burlington, born March 23d, 1794. He is a farmer, and was living and vigorous in 1871. He has naturally a very active and retentive mind. In 1869 he lost his house by fire, and in 1871 he lived in his horse-shed, about half a mile west of Polk-ville, so called. His wife was divorced from him at the March Court, 1865, when, with the alimony the court gave her, she bought a nice little place on West Main Street, Bristol, at the railroad crossing, on the north side of the town, where she lived in 1871.

THEIR CHILDREN, BEING THE EIGHTH GENERATION.

1200½. Mary Marilla, born January 5th, 1817. She is single, and is a member of the Methodist Church.
1201. Paulina Sophrone, born March 21st, 1819; married Jesse Rose, of Wolcott-ville.
Emeline, born August 3d, 1821; died single, April 4th, 1842, aged 21.
1202. Roxana, born September 14th, 1825; married June 28th, 1846, George L. Atwood; second
1203. Thomas Franklin, born   ; married November 22d, 1855, Sarah E. Weldon.
1204. Lydia Minerva, born   , 1832; married September 22d, 1852, Frederick Hart, of Unionville.
1205. Caroline, born   ; married   , Horatio Gates. They have two sons and one daughter.

933. *Bristol, Conn.*

BILLY STANLEY HART, Bristol, second son of Calvin Hart, of the same town, and his first wife, Anna (Yale), born January 9th, 1794. He was never married. His sister, Alice, kept house for him. He died May 30th, 1863, aged 69 years, and a tombstone has been erected to his memory in the North Cemetery, Bristol.

933½.　　　　　　*Burlington, Conn.*

SYLVESTER HART, Burlington, Conn., third son of Calvin Hart, of
Bristol, and his first wife, Anna (Yale), born March 17th, 1797; mar-
ried October 14th, 1819, Bathsheba Hayes, of Granby, born June 6th,
1790. He was a hatter by trade, which he learned of Abijah Catlin,
Harwinton, and worked as a journeyman in Danbury. He located in
Durham and carried on the business. He returned to Bristol, and died,
September 28th, 1821, aged 25 years. She died January 21st, 1871,
at Granby, Conn., and was buried there.

THEIR CHILD, BEING THE EIGHTH GENERATION.

1206. Sylvester Calvin, born July 7th, 1820; married January 19th, 1842, Penina
B. Norton.

934.

CALVIN HART, Jr., Burlington, fourth son of Calvin Hart, Sr., of
Bristol, and his first wife, Anna (Yale), born September 18th, 1798, at
Burlington; married 　　　　　　　　　　.　They
removed to Madison County, Ill., where he died, February 8th, 1825,
in his 27th year.

THEIR CHILD.

1207. Calvin Sylvester, born 　　　　　　　　, in Wisconsin.

935.　　　　　　*Rocky Hill, Conn.*

JOEL HART, Bristol, fifth son of Calvin Hart, of the same town, and
his wife, Anna (Yale), born May 6th, 1800; married September 7th,
1820, Sally Bowers, daughter of Benajah, of Rocky Hill. She died
July 24th, 1837, aged 39 years, when second he married July 1st, 1838,
Mrs. Mary Green. He lived in various localities—Burlington, New
Britain, Kensington, and Bristol. He died January 8th, 1846, aged
46. Grave-stones in the North Cemetery, Bristol, tell where they lie.

THEIR CHILDREN, BEING THE EIGHTH GENERATION.

1208. Nancy A., born July 17th, 1821; married December 14th, 1845, George Hitchcock.
　　　Sabrina, born 　　　　　　, 1825; died November 27th, 1847, at New Britain,
　　　aged 22.
1209. Lucy, born 　　　　　　　　; married 　　　　　　, Elmer Yale, of
　　　Bristol.
1210. Calvin, born May 12th, 1828, and lives in Bristol.
1211. Cyprian H., born March 10th, 1831; married April 4th, 1853, Eliza Pardew.
1212. Almon G., born May 4th, 1834. He is a farmer, and lives in Berlin, Conn.

MORSE.

936. *New Britain, Conn.*

ANNA CHARLOTTE HART, New Britain, daughter of Calvin Hart, of Bristol, and his first wife, Anna (Yale), born August 8th, 1804, at Burlington; married March 27th, 1835, William, son of Benoni Morse, of Bristol, and his wife, Sarah (Adkins), born March 29th, 1793. He is a wagon maker by trade and occupation, and his residence is on the corner of Washington and Myrtle Streets, New Britain. She was admitted to the Congregational Church, June 4th, 1843. She died May 12th, 1874, aged 70. He died June 13th, 1874, aged 81 years, 3 months. They had children, viz: 1, Anna Rebecca, born 1835, died in 1837; 2, Lucy, 3, Anna Charlotte, 4, Justina Rebecca, and 5, Henrietta Alice, born December 2d, 1842, at New Britain.

938. *Southington, Conn.*

HIEL HART, eldest son of Colonel Samuel Hart, of Southington, and his first wife, Rosanna (Clark), born June 22d, 1787, at Southington; married May 27th, 1810, Harriet Johnson. They had no children. He died January 21st, 1811, aged 23 years, and a tombstone has been erected to his memory at the North Cemetery in Southington.

939. *Talmage, Ohio.*

VESTA HART, Southington, Conn., eldest daughter of Colonel Samuel Hart, of the same town, and his first wife, Rosanna (Clark), born May 16th, 1789, at Southington; married November 26th, 1807, Asaph, son of John Whittlesey, of Washington, Conn., and his wife, Mary (Beale). She died December 20th, 1835, aged 46 years, at Talmage, Summit County, Ohio, to which place they had removed. They had several children. He was a brother of Chester Whittlesey, of Southington.

941. *Southington, Conn.*

SAMUEL HART, Southington, second son of Colonel Samuel Hart, of the same town, and his first wife, Rosanna (Clark), born March 29th, 1793; married   , Lucinda Pardee. She was admitted to the Congregational Church in Southington, March 26th, 1815. They removed to Talmage, Summit County, Ohio, in 1824, where he died, February 21st, 1826, aged 33 years.

THEIR CHILDREN, BEING THE EIGHTH GENERATION.

1213. Henry H., born   , 1815; baptized October 16th, 1815. He resided at Middlebury, Ohio.
Samuel, born

LANGDON.

942.   *Southington, Conn.*

LUCY HART, Southington, third daughter of Colonel Samuel Hart, of the same town, and his first wife, Rosanna (Clark), born August 12th, 1795, at Southington; married May 5th, 1814, Perry Langdon, son of Giles, and his wife, Sarah (Carter), of the same town, born March 12th, 1786. He built near his father, on the road leading from Queen to West Street, the same owned and occupied by Ard Woodruff. She died May 4th, 1850, aged 55 years, when he second married Widow Lucy (Hitchcock) Morse. He died, November, 1871, aged 85 years. They had children, viz: Augustus Perry, John Clark, Frederic, Samuel Hart, Richard, and Lucy Ann.

AMES.

943.   *Southington, Conn.*

ROSANNA HART, Southington, eldest daughter of Colonel Samuel Hart, of the same town, and his second wife, Patience (Andrews), born June 23d, 1803, at Southington; married February 17th, 1825, Amon Langdon Ames, of the same town, son of Daniel, and his wife, Mercy (Langdon), of New Britain and Southington, born August 16th, 1798.

944.   *Southington, Conn.*

JOHN NELSON HART, eldest son of Colonel Samuel Hart, of Southington, and his second wife, Patience (Andrews), born November 4th, 1804, at Southington; married September 18th, 1827, Sophia Hart Hichcock, daughter of Franklin Hitchcock, and his wife, Sophia (Hart). He lived on West Street, in Southington, and taught school in the East Street District one winter. He died of fever, October 26th, 1828, aged 24 years. They had one child, born June 5th, 1828, and died June 8th, 1828, aged 3 days.

945.   *Southington, Conn.*

COLLINGWOOD HART, Southington, second son of Colonel Samuel Hart, of the same town, and his second wife, Patience (Andrews), born January 5th, 1806, at Southington; married October 10th, 1838, Rebecca Irene Dunham, daughter of Harvey Dunham, and his wife, Elizabeth (Tryon), of Southington. He built near his father's old homestead on West Street, where he resided in 1873. He formerly manufactured daguerreotype cases, but is now a farmer, and has a fine location of 136 acres. He is an intelligent man, with good principles, and habits of industry and economy.

THEIR CHILDREN, BEING THE EIGHTH GENERATION.

1214. Charles Collingwood, born July 27th, 1834; baptized June 5th, 1835; married. Cornelia Rebecca, born August 12th, 1836; died September 27th, 1839, aged 3 years.
1215. Samuel Nelson, born September 19th, 1840; baptized July 30th, 1841; married December 24th, 1869, Mary G. Gridley.
1216. David Whiting, born July 25th, 1842; baptized August 4th, 1843.

ROYCE.

946. *Southington, Conn.*

MARY ANN HART, Southington, youngest daughter of Colonel Samuel Hart, of the same town, and his second wife, Patience (Andrews), born November 29th, 1815, at Southington; married January 26th, 1836, Loyal Royce, son of Nathaniel, of Southington, and his wife, Elizabeth (Tuttle), of Cheshire, born March 22d, 1809, at Southington. They had children, viz: Elizabeth Ann, Samuel Nelson, Benjamin Franklin, Aaron Nathaniel, and Irene Rosanna. The family resided at Oxford, Chenango County, N. Y., in 1873.

947. *Southington, Harwinton, Conn.*

BENJAMIN HART, Southington, third son of Colonel Samuel Hart, of the same town, and his second wife, Patience (Andrews), born February 23d, 1818; baptized June 14th, 1818, by Rev. William Robinson, pastor; married in 1843, Lucy Ann, daughter of John Bull, of Harwinton, Conn., and his wife, Dorothy (Austin). He built his house on West Street, where he lived for a time, but became a clerk in Potter's store. His wife was admitted to the Congregational Church in Southington, by letter from Harwinton, May 4th, 1851. They have lived in various localities, and in 1873 was living on her father's farm in Harwinton. They have no children.

948. *Southington, Conn.*

REUBEN HART, Southington, eldest son of Roswell Hart, of the same town, and his wife, Sylvia (Barnes), born January 8th, 1794, at Southington; married November 11th, 1819, Abigail Bradley, daughter of Hemingway Bradley, and his wife, Phebe (Peck), born at Southington, a twin sister with Rachel, who married Adam Smith. Mr. Hart lived on the old homestead of his father and grandfather in Flanders District, on the corner, where the dwelling of Francis D. Lewis stood in 1868. The house was torn away about 1855 to give place to the present structure. He was in poor health for a number of years, and died almost instantly, caused by the rupture of a blood-vessel, on the morning of the 8th of June, 1850, aged 56 years. His widow died March 26th, 1870, aged 72 years.

THEIR CHILDREN, BEING THE EIGHTH GENERATION.

1217. Sylvia D., born April 20th, 1821; married August 13th, 1845, Francis D. Lewis.

Jane A., born January 10th, 1828; died October 3d, 1831, aged 3 years, 9 months.

949.   *Southington, Conn.*

JULIUS HART, Southington, second son of Roswell Hart, of the same town, and his wife, Sylvia (Barnes), born August 9th, 1799, at Southington; married May 9th, 1827, Diadama Bradley, daughter of Ichabod Bradley, of Southington, and his wife, Abigail (Moore). They lived in Flanders District, on the west side, next north of his father's old homestead. He was a farmer by occupation. He died April 16th, 1873, aged 74 years. His funeral was on Saturday, the 19th, at 11 o'clock A. M., in the Methodist Church.

THEIR CHILDREN, BEING THE EIGHTH GENERATION.

1218. Charles A., born April 19th, 1829; married
1219. Abigail B., born April 5th, 1833; married   , Julius Lewis.
1220. Horace, born November 27th, 1835.
1221. Emily Jennette, born, February, 1838. .

950.   *Southington, Conn.*

ROSWELL HART, Jr., Southington, third and youngest son of Roswell Hart, Sr., of the same town, and his wife, Sylvia (Barnes), born March 25th, 1806, at Southington; married May 1st, 1828, Pamelia, daughter of Daniel Amsden, of Southington, and his wife, Lois (Smith). He was a farmer, and lived at the extreme north end of Flanders, a locality of Southington, Conn. He was a member of the Methodist Church, and subsequently of the Second Advent Church. He died of lung fever, January 16th, 1869, aged 63.

THEIR CHILDREN, BEING THE EIGHTH GENERATION.

Daniel Amsden, born March 1st, 1829; died July 7th, 1831, aged 2 years, 4 months.
1222. Reuben Roswell, born November 9th, 1831; married   , Julia A. Clark.
1223. Sarah Jane,   }   died single, January 21st, 1869, aged 35.
                            }   born August 24th, 1833;
1224. Huldah Elizabeth,   }   married December 30th, 1857, George W. Wood.
1225. Daniel Mortimer, born January 6th, 1838; married May 28th, 1860, Jane Clark.

1226. Wilbur Augustus, born April 11th, 1839; married November 10th, 1863, Mary
       Jane Bishop.
1227. John Bunyan, born September 30th, 1844; married November 26th, 1868,
   .   Sarah Francis Buel.
1228. Mary Parmelia, born November 7th, 1846. She lives at home.
       Sylvia Barnes, born October 1st, 1849; died October 10th, 1849, aged 9 days.
       Julia Lois, born December 21st, 1850. She is single, and lives at home.

TRYON.

951.   *Manlius, N. Y.*

ETHETA HART, Southington, eldest daughter of Timothy Hart, of
Southington, and his first wife, Eunice (Woodruff), born June 4th,
1795, at Southington; married October 3d, 1815, Lemuel Tryon, of
Deerfield, Mass. She died July 4th, 1829, at Manlius, N. Y., aged 34.
He left one son.

SMITH.

952.   *Southington, Conn.*

RHODA HART, Southington, second daughter of Timothy Hart, of
the same town, and his first wife, Eunice (Woodruff), born October
12th, 1798, at Southington; married October 6th, 1818, Asahel P.
Smith, of Southington, son of Harvey, and his wife, Elizabeth (Potter). They lived one mile north-east of the village, near his father's,
where she died, August 22d, 1859, aged 61. After her decease he
lived with his son, Charles, in the village, where he died   .
They had three sons and one daughter.

953.

Southington, Guilford, Branford, Conn.

GEORGE HART, Southington, eldest son of Timothy Hart, of the same
town, and his first wife, Eunice (Woodruff), born May 4th, 1801; married at Southington, February 10th, 1824, Lewia Page. She was sister
of Davis Ray's wife, in whose family she was living at the time of her
marriage. Ray at that time lived in the Ebenezer Woodruff house,
just north of the North Cemetery, on the west side of the turnpike.
Mrs. Hart was admitted to the Congregational Church in Southington,
June 2d, 1822. They subsequently removed to Guilford, Conn. He
died at Branford, May 3d, 1865, aged 64. She died, April, 1857.

THEIR CHILDREN, BEING THE EIGHTH GENERATION.

1229. Eliza Etheta, born   .   , 1825; baptized August 4th, 1825; married
                              , Chauncey Hull.
1230. Julia Catharine, born   , 1829; baptized June 5th, 1829; married
                              Hall.

1231. Ellen Verlinda, born   , 1833; baptized October 3d, 1834.
1232. Timothy Henry, born   , 1841.

954.   *Southington, Conn.*

WILLIAM HART, Southington, eldest son of Timothy Hart, of the same town, and his second wife, Sally (Reed), of Simsbury, born November 15th, 1805; baptized March 24th, 1822, by Rev. William Robinson, pastor, he being the second of six children of the same family baptized at the same time. He taught school for several winters. He was never married. He died at the house of his father, in Flanders District, of consumption, November 7th, 1842, aged 37 years.

955.   *Southington, Conn., Missouri.*

ASAHEL WOODRUFF HART, Southington, second son of Timothy Hart, of the same town, and his second wife, Sally (Reed), of Simsbury, born August 7th, 1809, a twin brother with Levi A. He married August 20th, 1833, in Stokes County, N. C., Verlinda Vantoy, of that place, born September 4th, 1812, in Stokes County. In 1851 he removed from there to Henry County, Mo. He was a mechanic. He died November 3d, 1865, aged 56 years, 2 months, 26 days. His widow died April 22d, 1867, aged 54 years, 7 months, 18 days.

THEIR CHILDREN, BEING THE EIGHTH GENERATION.

1233. Melissa Ann, born June 12th, 1834; married September 2d, 1851, Richard R. Walker.
1234. Adarose Alpha, born April 26th, 1836; married March 28th, 1854, Abraham Dudney.
     Etheta Arminta, born February 7th, 1838; died November 1st, 1855, aged 17 years, 8 months, 24 days.
1235. Alonzo Sebaski, born December 17th, 1840.
1236. Sarah Beaufort, born March 14th, 1842; married October 20th, 1867, James H. Platt.
     Levi Austin, born May 6th, 1844; died May 19th, 1845, aged 1 year, 18 days.
1237. Alvin Clinton, born June 4th, 1846; married December 30th, 1869, Lucretia Jane Smith.
1238. Mary Elizabeth, born May 20th, 1849; married February 27th, 1870, James W. Hunt.
1239. Timothy Filmore, born July 19th, 1852. He was a farmer in 1871.
     Sebastian Cabot, born April 15th, 1855.

956.   *Wilmington, N. C.*

LEVI AUSTIN HART, Wilmington, N. C., twin son (with Asahel) of Timothy Hart, of Southington, and his second wife, Sally (Reed), of Simsbury, born August 7th, 1809, at Southington; married Harriet Kirtland, of New Haven. He is a tinman, and set up his business in

S. A. Hart

Wilmington, where he still resides in 1874. Mr. Hart is an active and successful business man, owning a foundry and machine-shop, said to be the largest private enterprise of the kind in the state of North Carolina. The firm is known as Hart & Bailey. He also has a vine-yard, from which a superior kind of wine is made, called the Scupper-nong Champagne. It contains fifty acres, and has 1,000 vines. He is thoroughly practical, and prefers zeal and worth to mere outside dis-play. He is a good father and a respected citizen, and has held posi-tions of honor and trust; one of those of whom we say—"his word is as good as his bond." The family is Presbyterian. Mr. Hart was opposed to secession, and was a Unionist in the late war, but was not an extremist. He lost heavily by the war, but has since felt it his duty to practice moderation and forbearance. He has furnished an engrav-ing, by Sartain, to embellish this work, for which he has my thanks. It is on the opposite page. His wife died of consumption, January 16th, 1853, aged 32, when second he married in 1854, Sarah M. Peck, daughter of Treat Fenn Peck, of New Haven, Conn., and Wilmington, N. C., born October 9th, 1824, at Milford, Conn. She is a member of the First Presbyterian Church, of Wilmington, N. C.

CHILDREN BY HIS FIRST WIFE, BEING THE EIGHTH GENERATION.

1240. Harriet Gilbert, born March 17th, 1842; married January 9th, 1867, Mason Gordon, Esq.
1241. Mary Anna, born November 29th, 1844; married January 22d, 1868, Henry A. Burr, of New York.
1242. Ellen, born June 6th, 1852; died May 22d, 1868, at Wilmington, aged 16 years.

CHILDREN BY HIS SECOND WIFE.

1243. Arietta, born September 22d, 1856, at Wilmington, N. C.
Sarah Loise, born August 4th, 1858, at Wilmington, N. C.
Frederic Levi, born May 22d, 1860; died   , at Wilmington, N. C., aged 8 months.
Leila Austin, born March 10th, 1864, at Wilmington, N. C.

957. *Southington, Conn.*

ALVIN HART, Southington, fourth son of Timothy Hart, of the same town, and his second wife, Sally (Reed), of Simsbury, born March 21st, 1813, at Southington; married October 5th, 1835, Sarah, daughter of Roderick Stanley, of Plainville, and his wife, Sally (Root). He was a shoe-maker by trade, and lived on his father's old place, in Flanders District, in Southington, where he died, March 9th, 1847, aged 33 years, when she second married January 1st, 1850, Timothy St. John Smith, of New Haven, formerly of Kent, Conn., who died in New York, Oc-tober 10th, 1865. His widow resides at Plainville, Conn., in 1874.

1244. Levi Austin, born November 3d, 1837; married   , at Peru,
S. A., a Spanish woman.
1245. Jane Carter, born June 23d, 1842; married February 7th, 1865, Eugene P.
Marks. They are at Ansonia in 1874.

958. *Southington, Conn.*

EUNICE HART, Southington, youngest daughter of Timothy Hart, of the same town, and his second wife, Sarah (Reed), of Simsbury, born October 24th, 1817, at Southington; married June 22d, 1840, Daniel Hemingway Holt, of Harwinton, Conn., son of Daniel, and his wife, Nabby (Bull), born June 17th, 1819, in Harwinton. They lived on the old place of her father's, on Flanders Street, where he died, October 5th, 1865, aged 46. She lives there still in 1874. She has been in feeble health, but has now recovered. They had children, viz: Daniel Hemingway, John Hart, William Edgar, and Henry Clay.

964. *Southington, Conn.*

MURRAY HART, Southington, eldest son of Levi Hart, of the same town, and his wife, Philathea (Allen), born 1784, at Southington; married August 10th, 1808, Lucy Newell, daughter of Charles, and his wife,   (Hazzard), born January 9th, 1785, at Southington. He died at Washington County, Ga., September 23d, 1812, aged 28 years.

1246. Philathea, born July 22d, 1808; married October 9th, 1836, W. R. Blossom.
1247. Lucy, born   , 1810; married   , 1826, Daniel S. Morley, of Ohio.

965. *Southington, Conn.*

LEVI HART, Southington, second son of Levi Hart, of the same town, and his wife, Philathea (Allen), born 1786, at Southington. He married November 9th, 1809, Polly Newell, daughter of Isaac, and his wife, Mary Warren), born November 21st, 1788, at Southington. She was admitted to the Congregational Church there, August 28th, 1808. He resided in the village opposite the churches, where he kept a tavern, and was extensively engaged in trade. Since his death his store has been used for a saloon. He was a tinman by trade, and carried on that business at the south for a time. He died December 3d, 1828, aged 42 years. His widow died at the same place, October 14th, 1868, aged 80 years.

1248. Eluzia A., born August 17th, 1810; baptized January 20th, 1811; married September 2d, 1830, Henry Carter.

1249. Levi, born November 16th, 1815; baptized April 7th, 1816. He is single, and living on the old homestead.

1250. Mary Ann, born May 21st, 1813; baptized August 25th, 1816; married April 26th, 1838, Henry E. Butler.

1251. Angeline, born December 23d, 1822; married October 18th, 1847, John North.

966. *Southington, Conn.*

JOHN ALBERT HART, Southington, youngest son of Levi Hart, of the same town, and his wife, Philathea (Allen), born 1789, at Southington; baptized July 18th, 1790, by Rev. William Robinson; married November 22d, 1812, Rachel Newell, daughter of Deacon Pomeroy, and his wife, Elizabeth (Carter). They lived in the northern part of Southington, on Queen Street, near the school-house, where he died, October 20th, 1823, aged 34 years. His widow died January 6th, 1824, aged 33 years.

1252. Frederick Albert, born January 8th, 1818; married June 21st, 1842, Lucretia S. Lee.

967. *Burlington, Conn.*

MARTIN HART, Burlington, Conn., eldest son of Ambrose Hart, of the same town, and his wife, Mercy (Bartholomew), born June 10th, 1783, at Burlington; married November 29th, 1804, Sally Rowe. He was a farmer. He died March 22d, 1860, aged 77 years, 7 months, 12 days. She died very suddenly while at her work, in Bristol, February 15th, 1853, aged 71 years, and was buried at the North Cemetery in that town.

1253. Julia P., born   ; married   , Lauren Byington.

1254. Edward Ambrose, born   ; died at Bristol, July 4th, 1853, aged 40 years.

1255. Sally Maria, born   ; died at Bristol, September 23d, 1855, aged 34.

969. *Burlington, Conn.*

JOHN HART, Burlington, second son of Ambrose Hart, of the same town, and his wife, Mercy (Bartholomew), born May 27th, 1787, at Burlington; married in 1814, Ursula Beckwith, who died   ;

when second he married Millicent Hart, daughter of Ard Hart, and his wife, Millicent (Roberts), born June 14th, 1799, at Burlington. He died May 4th, 1855, aged 68 years. She was living a widow, at Burlington, in 1871.

THEIR CHILDREN, BEING THE EIGHTH GENERATION.

1256. Ursula Millicent, born March 28th, 1828; married January 17th, 1855, Joel J. Butler.

1257. Augustine, born December 16th, 1829; married   , Martha C. Bird.

1258. Albert John, born November 17th, 1835; married   , Jane M. Chidsey.

970.   *Waterloo, N. Y.*

ORRIN HART, third son of Ambrose Hart, of Burlington, and his wife, Mercy (Bartholomew), born May 5th, 1789, at Bristol; married there, November, 1813, Eunice Ives, of Bristol, born March 11th, 1780. She died June 12th, 1843, at Waterloo, N. Y., when second he married in 1844, Lucina Gaylord. He was a cabinet maker by trade, and was a deacon of the church. He removed from Bristol, Conn., to Waterloo, N. Y., in 1838. He died at Canandaigua, N. Y., at the house of his son-in-law, J. B. Francis, November 14th, 1870, aged 81 years, 6 months, 10 days.

THEIR CHILDREN, BEING THE EIGHTH GENERATION.

1259. Cornelia M., born September 5th, 1814; married April 20th, 1834, George H. Langdon.

1260. George H., born February 20th, 1816; married   , Sarah Edwards.

1261. Henry Cowles, } born August 19th, 1818; married August 20th, 1838, Lucinda Disbrow.

1262. Harriet Ives, } born August 19th, 1818; married April 22d, 1838, J. B. Francis.

1263. Enos Ives, born September 14th, 1823; married June 7th, 1849, Helen E. Belden.

971.   *Burlington, Unionville, Conn.*

AMBROSE HART, Jr., Burlington, fourth son of Ambrose Hart, Sr., of the same town, and his wife, Mercy (Bartholomew), born October 4th, 1793, at Burlington; married Chloe E. Moses, born February 19th, 1794. He died at Unionville, Conn., April 1st, 1846, aged 52, and was buried in the East Cemetery at Burlington.

THEIR CHILDREN, BEING THE EIGHTH GENERATION.

1264. Betsey S., born   , 1816; married   , Andrew Payne.

1265. Samuel Moses, born   , 1819; married   , Sarah A. Colvin.

1266. Frederic Moses, born December 26th, 1826; married September 22d, 1852, Minerva L. Hart; second,   Hamblin.

972. *Medina, Ohio.*

THOMAS HART, Burlington, fifth son of Ambrose Hart, of the same town, and his wife, Mercy (Bartholomew), born, November, 1795, at Burlington; married Amanda Barnes, and removed to Medina County, Ohio.

THEIR CHILDREN, BEING THE EIGHTH GENERATION.

Sarah, born   ; died
Sarah, born
Daughter, born

973. *Bristol, Conn.*

ADNA HART, Bristol, sixth son of Ambrose Hart, of Burlington, Conn., and his wife, Mercy (Bartholomew), born at Burlington in 1797; married February 23d, 1821, Roxana Yale. He died November 21st, 1846, aged 49 years. His widow died September 15th, 1850, aged 50 years. Tombstones have been erected to their memory at the North Cemetery, Bristol.

THEIR CHILDREN, BEING THE EIGHTH GENERATION.

1267. William, born May 15th, 1822; married November 29th, 1849, Emeline Electa Thayer.
John, born   , 1826; died April 28th, 1828, aged 2 years.
1268. John Gad, born February 1st, 1828; married November 12th, 1848, Abigail Benham.
Caroline, born
1269. Thomas, born May 7th, 1832; married November 29th, 1855, Mary Elizabeth Dix.

974. *Brookfield, Ohio.*

ORENUS HART, Brookfield, Trumbull County, Ohio, second son of Bliss Hart, of Burlington, Conn., and his wife, Sylvia (Upson), born July 22d, 1785, in Burlington, Conn.; married September 21st, 1810, Sabra Lewis, of Hartford. They removed to Ohio, September, 1822, where they lived together nearly sixty years. He died at Brookfield, February 24th, 1871, aged 86 years. He was a man of fine intellect, and was a teacher and scholar. His widow was living in 1871 with Robert S., her only surviving son.

THEIR CHILDREN, BEING THE EIGHTH GENERATION.

1270. Charles, born June 29th, 1812; married March 10th, 1841, Rachel Applegate.
1271. Robert Sloper, born June 29th, 1814; married March 16th, 1838, Mary Ann Christy.
1272. Blucher Bliss, born December 19th, 1816; died at Brookfield, January 6th, 1844.
1273. Elizabeth Adaline, born March 10th, 1821; married January 1st, 1840, James Christy.
1274. Henry Clay, born May 1st, 1833. He was a soldier, and died at Andersonville.
33

975.   *Hubbard, Ohio.*

BLISS HART, Hubbard, Ohio, third son of Bliss Hart, of Burlington, Conn., and his wife, Sylvia (Upson), born September 27th, 1787, at Burlington; married   , Thankful Bronson. He died in Williams County, Ohio. She died   .

THEIR CHILDREN, BEING THE EIGHTH GENERATION.

1275. Algernon, born
       Lucas, born
       Son, born
1276. Milisendra, born   ; married   Battleman.
       Daughter, born

FLOWER.

976.   *Brookfield, Ohio.*

SYLVIA HART, Brookfield, Ohio, eldest daughter of Bliss Hart, of Burlington, Conn., and his wife, Sylvia (Upson), born April 1st, 1790, at Burlington, where she married Dr. Elijah Flower, of Connecticut. He died at Brookfield, when second she married ——— Lombra. He died, when third she married ——— Spencer. She died at Brookfield in 1856, aged 65, at the house of her son-in-law, and was buried by the side of her first husband, Dr. Flower. Their children were— Maria Flower, married Edward King; Amanda Flower, married Dr. Theodatus Garlick; Lucy, married Pierce Wallyhard; Sylvia, married and died without issue; Orlando Flower, killed by the kick of a horse, aged 13 years; Lavinia, married Allison Chew, of Brookfield, Ohio.

BRONSON.

977.   *Brookfield, Ohio.*

EXPERIENCE HART, Brookfield, Ohio, second daughter of Bliss Hart, of Burlington, Conn., and his wife, Sylvia (Upson), born July 20th, 1792, at Burlington; married in 1812, Clark Bronson, of Wolcott, Conn., where she died, January 13th, 1864, aged 71 years.

978.   *Brookfield, Ohio.*

LEVI HART, Brookfield, Ohio, fourth son of Bliss Hart, of Burlington, Conn., and Brookfield, Ohio, and his wife, Sylvia (Upson), born January 10th, 1795, at Burlington, Conn.; married there to Obedience Fuller, daughter of Jesse, and his wife, Obedience, of Bristol. He died at Brookfield, December 17th, 1848.

THEIR CHILDREN, BEING THE EIGHTH GENERATION.

1277. Ira, born   ; married   , 1854, Matilda Pierce.
1278. Rosalinda, born   , 1820; died   , 1867, at Newcastle, Penn.

1279. Bliss, born   , 1823; died   , 1847, at Waupun, Wis.,
      aged 24 years.
1280. Sarah, born   , 1824; died   , 1851, at Waupun, Wis.,
      aged 27.
1281. Frances Maria, born February 18th, 1826; married April 30th, 1848, Lucius
      Andrew Baldwin, M. D.
1282. Caroline, born   , 1827; married   , V. R.
      Sullivan.
1283. Phebe, born   , 1829; married   , 1849, William
      Christy.
      Orrin, born   ; died in infancy.
1284. Lucy, born   , 1833; married   , 1858, Abraham
      Applegate.
1285. Mary,   �️   married   , 1855, Elliot Walker.
                     ⎬ born   , 1835;
1286. Robert Lucius, ⎠   married   , 1861, Eva Hough.
      Cornelia, born .   ; died in infancy.
1287. Thomas Corwin, born   , 1840; married   , Melissa Baldwin.

REED.

979.   *Brookfield, Ohio.*

AMANDA HART, Warren, Trumbull County, Ohio, third daughter of
Bliss Hart, of Burlington, Conn., and Brookfield, Ohio, and his wife,
Sylvia (Upson), born March 13th, 1797, at Burlington, Conn. She
went to Brookfield, Ohio, with her parents, and there married, January
28th, 1824, Garry C. Reed, Esq., of Warren, Trumbull County, Ohio,
where she died, October 5th, 1865. They had children, viz: Cynthia,
married S. S. Briggs, M. D., who was a surgeon in the Union Army,
and died; Achsah, married Dr. Hurst; Alvin Hart, married Marion
Ballard; and Philo Elsworth, who was a lawyer, entered the Union
Army as captain, was acting as colonel, when he was shot and instantly
killed at the head of his regiment, while storming a fort. He married
November 22d, 1855, Minerva Drake, who survived him at Warren,
Ohio, in 1871.

980.   *Brookfield, Ohio.*

OLIVER ELSWORTH HART, Brookfield, Ohio, fifth son of Bliss Hart, of
Burlington, Conn., and Brookfield, Ohio, and his wife, Sylvia (Upson),
born May 20th, 1799, at Burlington; married, May, 1834, Susanna
White Danforth, daughter of Samuel, of Palmyra, N. Y. He died
at Brookfield, April 7th, 1846, aged 47.

THEIR CHILDREN, BEING THE EIGHTH GENERATION.

1288. Harriet Eliza, born May 24th, 1835.
1289. Emeline Peck, born, November, 1837; married January 1st, 1856, Oscar F.
      Hurlburt.
      Ellsworth, born   ; died   , aged 3 years.

1290.　Maria, born April 7th, 1841; married July 3d, 1870, Martin Jefferson Barb.

1291.　Simeon, born July 10th, 1844.　He is a real estate broker, and resides, in 1874, at Youngstown, Ohio, unmarried.

PECK.

981.　　　　　　　　　　　　　*Brookfield, Ohio.*

ROSALINDA HART, Brookfield, Ohio, fourth daughter of Bliss Hart, of Burlington, Conn., and Brookfield, Ohio, and his wife, Sylvia (Upson), born July 20th, 1801, at Burlington; married, when about 22 years old, Franklin Peck, of Connecticut.　He was a farmer at Brookfield, Ohio.　They subsequently lived in West Greenville, Mercer County, Penn., where she died, February, 1873, aged 72 years.　They had children, viz: Franklin G., who served during the late war in the Second Ohio Volunteer Cavalry; Byron M., was in the Union Army, in the Second Ohio Cavalry, and married Sarah Brown; Sylvia Ann, married Alexander Adams; Lucy R., married John Christy; Venitia A., married Hugh Montgomery.　They also had five others, who died young.

HART.

982.　　　　　　　　　　　　　*Vienna, Ohio.*

MELLISSENDIA HART, Vienna, Ohio, fifth daughter of Bliss Hart, of Burlington, Conn., and Brookfield, Ohio, and his wife, Sylvia (Upson), born December 17th, 1803; married December 17th, 1823, Chauncey, son of Ard Hart, and his wife, Millicent (Roberts), born June 9th, 1802, at Burlington.　They removed to Vienna, Trumbull County, Ohio, in 1825.　He died September 18th, 1844, at Brookfield, Ohio, when second she married Samuel Baldwin, and they were living at Ravenna, Portage County, Ohio, in 1872, but he died in the winter of 1873–4, leaving her again a widow at Ravenna, Ohio.

983.　　　　　　　　　　　　　*Farmington, Conn.*

REV. LUCAS HART, East Haven, Conn., eldest son of Simeon Hart, of Burlington, and his wife, Mary (Warner), of Middletown, born June 5th, 1784, at Burlington; married November 27th, 1811, Harriet Morris, of East Haven, daughter of Amos, and his wife, Betsey Woodward, born April 6th, 1786.　He was ordained and settled a preacher of the gospel in Wolcott, December 4th, 1811, where he died of dysentery, October 16th, 1813, aged 29 years.　His eldest son died there also of the same disease, October 11th, 1813, aged 1 year, and both were taken to East Haven for interment.　His widow lived to see their second son,

Edward Lucas, educated and established as an educator. She died February 23d, 1839, aged 53.

THEIR CHILDREN, BEING THE EIGHTH GENERATION.

Edward, born September 17th, 1812; died October 11th, 1813, aged 1 year.

1292. Edward Lucas, born December 31st, 1813, posthumous; married April 26th, 1837, N. C. Hooker.

985. *Plainville, Conn.*

JEHIEL CHESTER HART, Plainville, third son of Simeon Hart, of Burlington, Conn., and his first wife, Mary (Warner), born February 3d, 1792; married September 2d, 1817, Anna, daughter of Daniel Lowrey, of Southington, and his wife, Anna (Munson), born December 5th, 1795, on Red Stone Hill, a locality of Plainville, on the west. He was a successful school teacher and book-keeper for many years, and a man of integrity and intelligence. He has collected much history of Burlington and Plainville, and is now in his 83d year. She died February 23d, 1866, aged 70 years.

THEIR CHILDREN, BEING THE EIGHTH GENERATION.

1293. Walter, born August 28th, 1818; married June 4th, 1845, Caroline Wilcox.

1294. Charlotte, born January 4th, 1820; married October 14th, 1845, Charles Wilcox.

1295. Daniel Lowrey, born February 11th, 1825; married January 12th, 1847, Mary Ann Edwards.

1296. Fanny, born April 15th, 1828; married November 15th, 1848, Charles Butler, of Wethersfield.

James, born December 27th, 1832, at Burlington; died single, July 6th, 1855, aged 22 years.

Simeon, born July 21st, 1837; died September 21st, 1839, aged 2 years.

Simeon Edward, born June 2d, 1840; died June 19th, 1844, aged 4 years.

986. *Burlington, Farmington, Conn.*

DEACON SIMEON HART, Farmington, fifth son of Simeon Hart, of Burlington, and his first wife, Mary (Warner), born November 17th, 1795, at Burlington, Conn. He graduated at Yale College, September 10th, 1823, and located at Farmington, Conn., as a teacher of the Academic School. His residence is just south of the Congregational Church, on the same side of the street. He married December 9th, 1824, Abigail Maria, only daughter of Asa Andrews, of Farmington, and his first wife, Hannah (Burnett), of Berlin, born November 14th, 1798, at Farmington. She died August 23d, 1838, aged 39 years, 9 months, 7 days, when second he married November 6th, 1839, Abby Eliza, daughter of Reuben Langdon, of Hartford, and his wife, Patience (Gilbert), of Hebron, born May 20th, 1807, at New London.

Early in life Mr. Hart was interested in the instruction of children and youth, and taught school while fitting himself for college. When he graduated he had in view the gospel ministry, but Providence seemed to direct him to become an educator. After some years of hard and successful labor in the public academy of Farmington, having many applications from abroad to take pupils, he gave up his public school, and enlarged his operations by establishing a private boarding school for boys, and associating himself with his nephew and former pupil, Mr. Edward Lucas Hart, in the enterprise. This boarding school soon became popular and successful. Mr. Hart became a member of the Congregational Church at Farmington in 1825, his first wife in 1818, and his second wife in 1841. He was chosen deacon there in 1827, was a representative of Farmington to the General Assembly several times, was a magistrate, and a superintendent of the Sunday School, and thus made himself actively useful in every good work. He was town clerk after the decease of Horace Cowles, Esq. He originated the savings bank of the town, and was its first secretary. He originated this Memorial, and diligently labored on it to the end of his life, which occurred April 30th, 1853, aged 57 years.

HIS CHILDREN BY HIS FIRST WIFE, BEING THE EIGHTH GENERATION.

1297. Adaline Fanny, born September 29th, 1825; married, September, 1853, Rufus C. Crampton.

Harriet Morris, born July 2d, 1827; died September 18th, 1829, aged 2 years.

HIS CHILDREN BY HIS SECOND WIFE.

1298. Mary Elizabeth, born October 30th, 1840. She excels as a school teacher.
1299. Charles Langdon, born April 8th, 1843; married August 10th, 1865, Sarah Franks.
1300. Ann Gilbert, born March 10th, 1845.
1301. Simeon, born August 5th, 1847.
1302. John Hooker, born May 6th, 1851. He has a great taste for farming, and training steers.

DUTTON.

987. *Farmington, Conn.*

POLLY HART, Burlington, Conn., third daughter of Simeon Hart, of the same town, and his first wife, Mary (Warner), born April 18th, 1798, at Burlington; married November 17th, 1818, Joseph, son of Joseph Dutton, of Farmington. He is a farmer, and lives at Scot's Swamp, a locality of that old town. They had four sons—one of whom was a soldier, and died in that infamous pen at Andersonville, Ga.— and two daughters.

Austin Hart.

HILL.

988. *St. Charles, Mo.*

FANNY HART, St. Charles, Mo., fourth daughter of Simeon Hart, of Burlington, Conn., and his first wife, Mary (Warner), born December 29th, 1800; married William Hill, who removed to St. Charles, Mo., where she died January 26th, 1825, aged 24 years.

989. *Burlington, Conn.*

LUCAS WETMORE HART, Burlington, eldest son of Simeon Hart, of the same town and county, and his second wife, Pamelia Pettibone (Wetmore), born December 26th, 1822, at Burlington, and was educated at Deacon Simeon Hart's school at Farmington. He became first mate in a Liverpool packet, was four years in the service of the United States, sailed to all parts of the world, and was finally lost in the China Sea, from a pilot boat which he commanded, in the year 1862, aged 40 years. He was highly gifted by nature, and well educated, but was never married.

990. *New Britain, Conn.*

AUSTIN HART, Esq., youngest son of Simeon Hart, of Burlington, and his second wife, Mrs. Pamelia Pettibone (Wetmore), born April 17th, 1824, at Burlington, Conn., and graduated at Yale College in 1853. He was admitted to the bar in Philadelphia, Penn., and practiced a few years in Farmington. He settled at New Britain, Conn., in 1864, has his office on Main Street, and his residence is on the west side of Cedar Street, being in the west part of the city, and directly north of the park. He was married October 9th, 1867, before Rev. L. Perrin, D. D., at her father's residence in Farmington, Susan Augusta, daughter of Samuel Deming, and his wife, Catharine (Lewis), born September 8th, 1830, at Farmington. They have had no children to live, at this writing, in 1874. He has generously furnished an engraving of his half brother, Deacon Simeon Hart, for the frontispiece, and also of himself, on the opposite page, for which he has my thanks.

994. *Bristol, Penn.*

WILLIAM BACKUS HART, Norwich, only son of William Sherman Hart, and his wife, Eunice (Backus), born   ; married   . He graduated at Yale College in 1817. He studied law, and settled in Bristol, Penn., where his wife died, when second he married in New York, where he resides.

997. *Worthington, Ohio.*

ASAHEL HART, Jr., New Britain, eldest son of Asahel Hart, Sr., of New Britain, Conn., and his first wife, Anna (Kilborn), born at New Britain, and baptized there October 3d, 1784. He went to Worthington, Ohio, where he married   ,
but returned to Connecticut, and was drowned in Farmington River, December 5th, 1814, aged 34 years. They had Anna, Martha, and a son, but nothing definite about their birth or history has been found.

998. *Cabotville, Mass.*

JOSEPH HART, New Britain, Conn., second son of Asahel Hart, Sr., of the same town, and his first wife, Anna (Kilborn), born September 18th, 1787, at New Britain, where he was baptized, October 28th, 1787; married at Northington, January 9th, 1810, Sophronia, daughter of Obed Hart, of Avon, and his wife, Elizabeth (Edson), born April 21st, 1794, at Avon. She died July 14th, 1814, aged 20 years, when second he married Lura Buel, daughter of William, of Simsbury, born February 18th, 1796. He removed to Cabotville, Mass. He died September 18th, 1840, aged 53 years.

CHILDREN BY HIS FIRST MARRIAGE, BEING THE EIGHTH GENERATION.

Elizabeth Elvira, born September 23d, 1811; died July 4th, 1814, aged 3 years.
Jonathan, born June 19th, 1814; died July 6th, 1814, aged 1 month.

HIS CHILDREN BY HIS SECOND MARRIAGE.

1303. Lura Ann, born April 20th, 1817; married   , David Bradford; died November 20th, 1866.
Joseph Kilborn, born August 18th, 1818; died January 27th, 1819, aged 1 year, 6 months.
1304. Abia, born October 29th, 1821; married   , G. S. Holcomb.
Sophronia Eunice, born November 14th, 1819; died July 25th, 1825.
1305. William Horatio, born June 7th, 1826. He was single in 1873.
1306. Asahel Edward, born June 17th, 1828; married August 4th, 1858, Samantha A. Dibble.
1307. Lovillia Angeline, born May 7th, 1830; married   , Wayne S. Buel, of Johnsonville, Ohio.
Joseph Buel, born April 1st, 1824; died May 10th, 1832.
1308. David Harrison, born July 14th, 1832. He was living single at Johnsonville, Ohio, in 1873.
1309. Sarah Jane, born November 24th, 1836.

CLARK.

999. *New Britain, Conn.*

EUNICE HART, New Britain, Conn., third daughter of Asahel Hart, Sr., of the same town, and his first wife, Anna (Kilborn), born at New Britain, and baptized there, January 3d, 1790, by Rev. John Smalley, pastor; married September 15th, 1818, before Rev. Newton Skinner, Chauncey, son of Solomon Clark, and his wife, Elizabeth (Smith), born April 15th, 1787, at New Britain. She died without children, October 16th, 1819, aged 30 years, when second he married, December 2d, 1824, Mary J. Smith, daughter of Solomon, and his wife, Lucy (Carter). Mr. Clark was a well-to-do farmer, located near the east line of the town, on East Street, and died December 22d, 1855, aged 70 years. His widow died September 2d, 1872, aged 76 years.

WOODRUFF.

1000.   *Avon, Conn.*

Azubah Hart, New Britain, Conn., fourth daughter of Asahel Hart, Sr., of the same town, and his first wife, Anna (Kilborn), born at New Britain, and baptized there, September 16th, 1792; married November 9th, 1809, Apheck Woodruff, of Avon. He was a farmer, and lived on Lovely Street.

STANLEY. WOODRUFF.

1001.   *New Britain, Conn.*

Elizabeth Norton Hart, fifth daughter of Asahel Hart, Sr., of the town of New Britain, and his first wife, Anna (Kilborn), born at New Britain, and baptized there, May 14th, 1795; married Wakeman Norton Stanley, son of Noah, and his third wife, Naomi (Burritt), born March 9th, 1793. He was a plain farmer, and lived in Stanley Quarter. He and his wife were admitted to the church in New Britain, August 5th, 1821. He died with malignant fever, August 19th, 1823, aged 30, when she second married Azmon Woodruff, of Avon. She became a Baptist, and died at Richland, N. Y., January 3d, 1852, aged 54. She left children, viz: Charlotte Stanley, married George Hale; and Horatio Stanley, married Margaret Brace.

1002.   *Avon, Conn.*

Adna Thompson Hart, Avon, third son of Asahel Hart, Sr., of New Britain, and his first wife, Anna (Kilborn), born 1796, and baptized in New Britain, May 28th, 1797; married January 20th, 1820, Lydia Woodruff, daughter of Moses, and his wife, Anna (Woodford), born July 10th, 1793. He went from Avon to New Britain, where he was a shoe-maker by trade, but afterwards ran Judd's Mill, in Avon, several years, and died there, October 4th, 1839, aged 43, and was buried in West Avon Cemetery. She died at Canton, November 3d, 1860, aged 67, and was buried by the side of her husband, in Avon.

34

1310. Caroline M., born January 28th, 1822; married December 1st, 1845, Meriels Roberts.

1311. Catharine, born June 20th, 1824; married November 20th, 1844, Austin A. Hart.

-      Mary Atwell, born August 20th, 1826; died January 2d, 1827.

1312. Philo Woodruff, born December 20th, 1831; married February 6th, 1855, Susan Billings.

1313. Andrew Willis, born November 25th, 1834; died June 20th, 1863. He was a soldier.

1314. Lura Ann, born August 20th, 1836; married October 8th, 1856, Henry Buck. ley Goodrich.

WOODRUFF.

1003.   *Avon, Conn.*

HANNAH DAY HART, Avon, Conn., sixth daughter of Asahel Hart, Sr., of New Britain, and his first wife, Anna (Kilborn), daughter of Josiah, and his wife, Anna (Neal), born March 20th, 1799; baptized May 19th, 1799; married January 13th, 1818, Ozem Woodruff, son of Eldad, of Avon.

1004.   *Avon, Conn.*

EZRA HART, Avon, youngest son of Asahel Hart, Sr., of New Britain, and his first wife, Anna (Kilborn), born at New Britain, and baptized there, May 17th, 1801. He was unmarried. He was occasionally insane, and was found drowned in Farmington River, Avon, April 13th, 1864, aged 63 years.

PENNFIELD. MATHER.

1005.   *New Britain, Conn.*

HULDAH HART, New Britain, eldest daughter of Bethel Hart, of the same town, and his first wife, Huldah (Steele), born October 18th, 1786, at New Britain; married March 4th, 1804, Silas, son of Nathaniel Pennfield, and his first wife, Eunice (Kelsey), born at New Britain, and baptized there, July 1st, 1792. He was a farmer, and built next west of his father, on Horse Plain, in New Britain. He died November 29th, 1812, aged 28, when second she married January 18th, 1814, Cyprian, son of Cotton Mather, and his wife, Rebecca (Steele), born May 30th, 1792. He was a stone mason, a heavy, robust man, with good intellectual powers, was fond of reading, and slow in his movements and conclusions. He lived in various localities. He was admitted to the Congregational Church, August 5th, 1821. She was admitted, January 6th, 1811. He died October 1st, 1845, aged 54. She died June 23d, 1852, aged 67. She had by Pennfield, Caroline Elvira, William, and Caroline 2d; by Mather she had Silas Hart, Caroline, George W., John Newton, and Henry Franklin.

UPSON.

1006.   *New Britain, Conn.*

NANCY HART, New Britain, second daughter of Bethel Hart, of the same town, and his first wife, Huldah (Steele), born January 2d, 1790, at New Britain; married April 26th, 1809, Sheldon, son of Noah Upson, of Plymouth, and his wife, Rachel (Frisbee), born March 24th, 1785. He was a butcher and stone mason, and lived in Stanley Quarter. He was admitted to the church in New Britain, August 5th, 1821. She was admitted, January 6th, 1805. He died March 4th, 1838, aged 53. She was living at West Meriden in 1873. They had Harriet Eliza, married George Stannard, of Southington; Julia Ann, married Homer Curtiss, of Meriden; Jane Nancy, married November 9th, 1841, William L. Coan, of Guilford, Conn.

ROOT.

1007.   *New Britain, Conn.*

SARAH SAGE HART, third daughter of Bethel Hart, of New Britain, and his first wife, Huldah (Steele), born 1794; married February 25th, 1816, Henry, son of Seth Root, and his wife, Tryphena (Warner), born at Farmington in 1797. She died May 15th, 1837, aged 43 years. They had children, viz: Henry, Mary, William, Frederic H., and Amelia, who married Stephen Hubbard, of Birmingham, Conn. Their eldest, Henry, died, aged 2 years.

WOODFORD.

1008.   *Avon, Kensington, Conn.*

BETSEY HART, fourth daughter of Bethel Hart, of New Britain, Conn., and his first wife, Huldah (Steele), born September 28th, 1797, at New Britain; married May 11th, 1813, Romanta Woodford, of Avon, Conn. He was a farmer. Late in life they removed to Kentucky, where their son, Newton, located, and engaged in the brass business with J. T. Hart & Co. Mrs. Woodford was a member of the church in Avon. She was a wonderful woman to dispatch work. She died January 2d, 1873. He died July 20th, 1873, aged 81 years. They had Eveline, Norman, Maryette, Newton, Isaac, Edwin, Julian, Rollin, Louisa, Henry M., Shelden.

GOFF.

1009.   *West Springfield, Mass.*

LAVINIA HART, fifth daughter of Bethel Hart, of Northington and New Britain, Conn., and his first wife, Huldah (Steele), born December 1st, 1798, at New Britain, Conn.; baptized there February 24th, 1799, by Rev. John Smalley; married December 5th, 1819, Silas, son of Silas Goff, of West Springfield, Mass.

JUDD.

1010.   *New Britain, Conn.*

SALOME HART, New Britain, Conn., sixth daughter of Bethel Hart, of Northington and New Britain, Conn., and his first wife, Huldah (Steele), born August 14th, 1801, at New Britain; married January 30th, 1822, Henry, son of James Judd, of New Britain, Conn., and his wife, Esther (Allen), born January 15th, 1801, at New Britain. They lived at the old homestead of his father, on Stanley Street. He was a farmer by occupation. She was admitted to the Congregational Church, August 5th, 1821, and died of cancer, October 20th, 1865, aged 64 years. He died July 7th, 1873, aged 72 years.

1011.   *New Britain, Conn.*

ADNA HART, New Britain, Conn., eldest son of Bethel Hart, of the same town, and his first wife, Huldah (Steele), born January 28th, 1804, at New Britain; married March 20th, 1825, Lydia, daughter of Nathaniel Pennfield, Jr., and his wife, Polly (Steele), born May 1st, 1806. He is a mechanic, and his residence is on Elm Street, in the city of New Britain, Conn., and both are members of the Congregational Church.

THEIR CHILDREN, BEING THE EIGHTH GENERATION.

1314½. Antoinette, born November 13th, 1825; married June 4th, 1848, George H. Booth, of New Britain.
1315. Henry Franklin, born June 1st, 1829; married   , Eliza, daughter of Jefferson Steele.
1316. Jane Melissa, born February 22d, 1833; married November 28th, 1854, Jona-than Nott, of New Britain.
1317. Charles Watson, born October 13th, 1837.
1318. Oliver Dwight, born June 26th, 1840.
1319. George Adna, born December 21st, 1850; married May 5th, 1874, Florence I. Hunter.

YEMONS. BACHELDER.

1012. *Farmington, New Britain, Conn.*

ROSANNA HART, seventh daughter of Bethel Hart, of New Britain, and his first wife, Huldah (Steele), born May 3d, 1807, at New Britain; married in 1827, Joseph Yemons, of Farmington, who died, when second she married in 1835, Moses Bachelder, who was admitted to the church in New Britain, July 19th, 1846. She united with the church in Farmington, April 1st, 1827, and was admitted, by letter from that church, to the church in New Britain, July 19th, 1846. He was born March 7th, 1809, and died February 6th, 1867, at New Haven. They had issue, viz: Victoria Bachelder, born September 21st, 1839, married Eli W. Bassett; Burgess Bachelder, born 1842.

SWEET.

1013. *New Britain, Conn.*

CAROLINE UPSON HART, eighth and youngest daughter of Bethel Hart, of New Britain, Conn., and his first wife, Huldah (Steele), born September 16th, 1809, at New Britain; married July 3d, 1828, Dennis, son of James Sweet, of Farmington, and his wife, Esther (Bidwell), born July 13th, 1807, at Farmington. He is a shoe-maker by trade and avocation, and holds the office of captain in the militia. Their residence is on Elm Street, in the city of New Britain. She united with the church, February 4th, 1827, and he united, April 4th, 1841, and both were admitted to the South Congregational Church in 1842. They had children, viz: Francis James, Charles Harvey, Helen Augusta Sweet, born January 18th, 1848, married December 7th, 1864, Stephen B. Peck, of Winsted.

GILLET.

1015. *New Britain, Conn.*

LUCINA HART, New Britain, second daughter of Joel Hart, of Farmington, and his wife, Huldah (Woodruff), of Northington, born there February 4th, 1784; married in 1815, Richard Gillet, son of Aaron, of Wintonbury, now Bloomfield. He is a joiner by avocation, and lives on Maple Street, New Britain. She died in 1833, aged 49 years, when second he married Julia Boardman, of Wethersfield. Her child, Ruby, married James Orton, of Rome, N. Y.

1017. *Parma, N. Y.*

CLEMENT HART, Parma, N. Y., fourth son of Seth Hart, of Bethlehem, N. Y., and his wife, Anna (Miller), born about 1789, at Bethle-

hem; married about 1805, Hancy Walker, of   . His
avocation was farming. He died about 1826. She died at Parma in
1832.

THEIR CHILDREN, BEING THE EIGHTH GENERATION.

1320. Prudence, born February 16th, 1808; married   , French,
and had one child.
1321. Erastus, born   , 1809; married about 1830, Ruth Wilcox, and had
eight children.
1322. Edmund, born   , 1810; married about 1833, Mahala Jones, and
had six children.
1323. Eliza, born   , 1812; married   , 1833, Jeremiah Smith.
1324. Edward Buel, born October 11th, 1814; married   , 1835, Amret
Irene Nichols.
1325. Ebenezer, born   , 1816; married   , 1836, Elizabeth
Ware, and had ten children.
1326. Riley, born March 9th, 1819; married April 1st, 1847, Mary T. Erig, of
Germany.
1327. Chauncey, born   , 1820; married   , Hannah
John, born   , 1822; died of consumption in 1854.
William, born   , 1824; died in infancy.
1328. William Clement, born , 1827; married   , 1860, Esther Wilsey.

1018.   *Avon, Conn., Lysander, N. Y.*

COLONEL NOADIAH HART, Avon, Conn., eldest son of Abner Hart, of
the same town, and his wife, Alma (Thompson), born June 9th, 1801,
at Avon, and taught school fifteen winters and two summers. He
married in Avon, before Rev. Bela Kellogg, September 12th, 1826,
Clarissa Dickinson, daughter of William, of the family at Hadley,
Mass., and his wife, Elizabeth (Smith), born March 24th, 1800, at Had-
lyme, East Haddam, Conn. He removed to Ira, Cayuga County,
N. Y., October 16th, 1820, and from thence to Lysander, where he
lived in 1872, and was an elder of a Presbyterian Church there, and
has been for some thirty years. He passed through the different
grades in the militia up to colonel. He was admitted to the church at
Avon in 1821.

THEIR CHILDREN, BEING THE EIGHTH GENERATION.

1329. Abner N., born Oct. 4th, 1827; married March 30th, 1865, Jane L. Bennet.
Simeon D., born August 29th, 1829; died September 3d, 1831, aged 2 years.
1330. Homer S., born March 26th, 1831; married December 18th, 1866, H. Augusta
Kelley.
1331. Arthur A., born December 29th, 1833; married January 1st, 1863, Harriet P.
Parker.
1332. Emma Eunice, born January 4th, 1836; married September 17th, 1863, Aaron
C. Keeler.
1333. Thompson T., born March 22d, 1838; married March 27th, 1867, Susan M.
Townsend.
1334. Henrietta Maria, born April 4th, 1840; married April 23d, 1863, Benjamin R.
Howe.
1334½. William D., born April 16th, 1843.

1019. *Avon, Conn., Gerard, Penn.*

LEFFERT HART, second son of Abner Hart, of the same town, and his wife, Alma (Thompson), born December 14th, 1802, at Avon; married September 12th, 1826, Nancy Woodford. He removed to Gerard, Erie County, Penn., where she died, June 5th, 1847, and left seven children, when second he married July 25th, 1848, Eliza M. Dimpsey, of Gerard. His avocation is farming.

CHILDREN BY THE FIRST MARRIAGE, BEING THE EIGHTH GENERATION.

1335. Nancy A., born September 19th, 1827; married , 1844, James Mills. They live at Greenville, Penn.
Oliver W., born August 9th, 1829; died June 14th, 1862.
1336. Ann Elizabeth, born May 9th, 1831; married , 1851, William S. Dreny, a chair maker, of Gerard, Penn.
John L., born February 12th, 1835; died June 2d, 1836.
1337. John L., born March 30th, 1837. He is a merchant tailor in Union City, Mich.
1338. Lucius D., born September 7th, 1839; married December 31st, 1868, Mary E. Guilford. They live at Gerard, Penn.
1339. Henry Clay, born December 27th, 1843; married December 27th, 1869, Stella Whipple. They live at San Gregorio, Cal., where he is in the dry goods business.

CHILDREN BY THE SECOND MARRIAGE.

1340. Emma S., born June 29th, 1849.
1341. Ella M., born March 1st, 1851.
William W., born June 19th, 1853.
James A., born July 10th, 1855.
Edgar C., born November 8th, 1857.
Charles C., born July 22d, 1861.
Frank Joseph, born September 2d, 1863.

1020. *Avon, Conn.*

ALONZO HART, Avon, fourth son of Abner Hart, of the same place, and his wife, Alma (Thompson), born November 17th, 1806, at Avon, Conn.; married November 14th, 1837, Rachel, daughter of Philip Willard, of Pennsylvania, and his wife, Hannah (Thompson), born June 17th, 1821, at Portage County, Ohio, of Dutch extraction. He resided at Bridgewater, Williams County, Ohio, in 1871, and was postmaster, justice of the peace, town clerk, clerk of the board of education, and a farmer. His five eldest sons were all in the army of the late war.

THEIR CHILDREN, BEING THE EIGHTH GENERATION.

1344. Thompson Webster, born February 12th, 1839. He was in the 42d Regiment Illinois Volunteers of the late war.
1345. Edwin Harrison, born July 14th, 1840. He was in the 42d Regiment Illinois Volunteers.

1346. Homer Clay, born March 12th, 1842. He was in the 9th Michigan Cavalry.
1347. Alonzo Francisco, born August 8th, 1843. He was in the 128th Regiment Ohio Volunteers.
1348. Leffert Scott, born November 2d, 1845. He was in the army.
Aaron Philip, born December 29th, 1847.
Alma Adalaide, born August 30th, 1849.
John Sherwin, born August 6th, 1851.
Oran Ozro, born November 15th, 1853.
Ozro Oran, born July 11th, 1856.
Dayton Fremont, born December 6th, 1857.
Bion L., born October 1st, 1860.
Oliver Woodford, born June 6th, 1862.

1021.

CAPTAIN CARLOS HART, Avon, Conn., fifth son of Abner Hart, of Avon, Conn., and his wife, Alma (Thompson), born November 25th, 1808, at Avon; married, June, 1833, Lois, daughter of Gideon Rice, of Barkhamsted, and his wife, Mary Ann Sanderson, born February 14th, 1814, at Barkhamsted, and died January 15th, 1839, at Ravenna, Ohio. He was a teacher at the south, in Georgia and other states. He died at Wheeling, Va., August 3d, 1840, and was buried there, aged 31 years, 8 months, 8 days.

THEIR CHILDREN, BEING THE EIGHTH GENERATION.

1342. Carlos Austin, born December 22d, 1834, at Ira, N. Y.; married Sarah P. Bird.
1343. Anna Lois, born May 14th, 1838, at Ravenna, Ohio; married September 19th, 1860, Azro Spaulding.

1022. *Gerard, Penn.*

HOMER HART, Gerard, Erie County, Penn., sixth son of Abner Hart, of Avon, Conn., and his wife, Alma (Thompson), born February 24th, 1811, at Avon; married   , Delia Loveridge, of Gerard, Penn.

THEIR CHILD, BEING THE EIGHTH GENERATION.

1349. Levi, born   , 1843.

1024. *Avon, Conn.*

AUSTIN ABNER HART, eighth son of Abner Hart, of the same town, and his wife, Alma (Thompson), born November 13th, 1823, at Avon; married November 20th, 1844, Catharine, daughter of Adna Thompson Hart, of Avon, and his wife, Lydia (Woodruff), born June 29th, 1824. He is a farmer by occupation, and was living at Cider Brook, so called, in 1871.

THEIR CHILD, BEING THE EIGHTH GENERATION.

1350. Lena Lydia, born October 27th, 1845. She was a teacher.

1025.
Avon, Conn.

LUTHER WOODFORD HART, Avon, eldest son of Gideon Baldwin Hart, of the same town, and his wife, Marilla (Woodford), born June 16th, 1796, at Avon; married   , 1819; Almira Gillet, of Avon, daughter of Amos, and his wife, Esther (Bishop), born 1800, at Avon. He removed to Farmington, Trumbull County, Ohio, in 1837. They have seven children, all living in Minnesota in 1871, and are all married. His wife died, September, 1852, aged 51 years. In 1872 he was living with his son, George, in Delavan, Faribault County, Minn., s about 79 years of age, and still quite vigorous.

THEIR CHILDREN, BEING THE EIGHTH GENERATION.

1351. Susan Francis, born December 10th, 1818; married April 15th, 1844, Samuel Miller.

1352. Betsey M., born September 20th, 1823; married October 28th, 1841, Noah Miller.

1353. George, born May 9th, 1826; married, second wife, June 17th, 1860, Susan. C. Weir.

1354. Amos Gillet, born November 7th, 1828; married October 19th, 1851, Sarah Miller.

1355. Esther Almira, born February 20th, 1831; married November 30th, 1865, Charles W. Hough.

Joseph, born   , 1832; died   , 1832.

356. John Luther, born September 23d, 1834; married February 10th, 1866, Mary P. Reynolds.

356½. Ann S., born October 5th, 1842; married April 26th, 1866, Seth W. Bishop.

1027.
Farmington, Ohio.

JOSEPH CHAUNCEY HART, Avon, second son of Gideon Baldwin Hart, of the same town, and his wife, Marilla (Woodford), born June 23d, 1804, at Avon, Conn.; married February 18th, 1824, at East Granville, Mass., Rosanna Goff, born September 11th, 1807, at West Springfield, Mass. He kept a tavern at Wethersfield, but removed to Farmington, Trumbull County, Ohio. He died March 19th, 1867, aged 63 years. His widow was living at West Farmington, Trumbull County, Ohio, in 1873.

THEIR CHILDREN, BEING THE EIGHTH GENERATION.

1357. Hiram Samuel, born October 8th, 1825; married   , Fannie Hart, of Gustavus, Ohio.

1358. Joseph Chauncey, born September 22d, 1828; married May 20th, 1852, Margaret Lane, of East Hartford.

1359. Frances K., born July 3d, 1830; married   , Sylvester Fries, a blacksmith.

360. Sarah J., born August 3d, 1832; married November 19th, 1851, Lewis Taft, a farmer.

35

1361. Ann Jennett, born March 23d, 1834; married March 20th, 1856, Sylvanus Pierce, a farmer.

1362. John O., born Feb. 14th, 1836; married, September, 1860, Amy Caldwell.

1363. Ambrose L., born November 2d, 1837. He was living single in California in 1873.

1364. Clinton O., born September 23d, 1839; married , Elizabeth Belden.

1365. Velorus M., born September 11th, 1841; married , Roxana Clark.

1365½. Adelbert Miron, born September 27th, 1843. He was a soldier in the late war.

1366. Melancthon C., born December 15th, 1846; married November 20th, 1872, Mary Camp. He is a lawyer.

1367. Arlington M., born June 15th, 1849. He is assistant clerk for the county.

1028. *Avon, Conn.*

GIDEON WAREHAM HART, Avon, third son of Gideon Baldwin Hart, of the same town, and his wife, Marilla (Woodford), born at Avon in 1811; married November 27th, 1834, Ann Rice, of Barkhamsted, born there, March 9th, 1815, and died June 24th, 1844, aged 29, when second he married at Avon, December 10th, 1844, Mary Susan, daughter of Thomas V. Parsels, of Patterson, Putnam County, N. Y., and his wife, Mary (Squires), born December 10th, 1818, Poughkeepsie, N. Y. He was a farmer by occupation, and resided at Avon, where he died, August 17th, 1871, aged 60 years.

CHILDREN BY HIS FIRST WIFE, BEING THE EIGHTH GENERATION.

Child, still-born, 1835.
Betsey Ann, born July 17th, 1837; died June 3d, 1842, aged 5 years.
Child, still-born, 1844.

CHILDREN BY HIS SECOND WIFE.

1368. Ellen Maria, born March 26th, 1846; married March 24th, 1870, Chauncey Deming, of Farmington.
Gideon Wareham, born February 16th, 1847; died February 16th, 1847.

1369.. Martha Susan, born August 25th, 1850.

1370. George Gideon, born February 16th, 1854.
Mary Esther, born April 20th, 1858.

1029. *Avon, Conn.*

JOSEPH HART, Avon, eldest son of Joseph Hart, of the same place, and his wife, Cynthia (Woodford), born November 5th, 1800, and married July 26th, 1824, Tryphena Rice, daughter of Gideon, of Barkhamsted, and his wife, Mary Ann (Sanderson), of the same place, born August 10th, 1807, at Barkhamsted. He is a shoe-maker by trade and avocation. In 1872 he was in feeble health, and lived a little south of the church in West Avon, Conn.

1371. Noah Humphrey, born January 14th, 1831; married December 7th, 1851, Emeline Butler, of Burlington.

1372. Lucy Jane, born February 3d, 1833; married June 6th, 1852, Ira A. Porter, of Berlin.

1373. Eli Alderman, born July 29th, 1835; married July 10th, 1855, Mary Smith, of Farmington.

1374. Anna Maria, born April 26th, 1838; married   , Nelson Hall, a soldier.

1375. Julia Tryphena, born June 10th, 1841; married   , Henry Hadsell, of Avon.

Cynthia M., born   ; died

Mary P., born   , 1846; died single, at Avon, March 30th, 1864, aged 18 years.

BRAINARD.

1030.   *Avon, Conn.*

ELIZA ANN HART, Northington, eldest daughter of Joseph Hart, of the same place, and subsequently of Gustavus, Ohio, and his wife, Eunice (Fitz), born July 4th, 1807, at Northington, and from thence she went with her parents to Gustavus in 1811, and there married Erastus Brainard, of that place, where they resided in 1873, and she was a member of the Congregational Church.

BAILEY.

1031.   *Gustavus, Ohio.*

DOROTHY BELINDA HART, second daughter of Joseph Hart, of Northington, Conn., and Gustavus, Ohio, and his wife, Eunice (Fitz), born March 27th, 1809, at Northington, Conn. She went from thence with her parents to Gustavus, Ohio, in 1811, where she married Russell Bailey. They located at Gustavus, where they were still residing in 1873. She is a member of the Congregational Church there. They had two sons in the late war, one of whom was killed, and the other returned in safety.

1032.   *Gustavus, Ohio.*

JOSEPH NELSON HART, Gustavus, Ohio, son of Joseph Hart, and his wife, Eunice (Fitz), born January 8th, 1811, in Avon, (then Northington,) Conn.; married May 16th, 1837, at Kinsman, Ohio, Jane Eliza Gibson, daughter of James, and his wife, Mary (Essington), born May 9th, 1818, in Fayette County, Penn.

1376. Maria Jane, born July 1st, 1838; married March 25th, 1856, Jesse Osborn Cooper.

1377. Harriet Rebecca, born July 9th, 1846; married December 3d, 1869, James Wenham.

Albert Joseph, born March 1st, 1849.

1378. Weltha Ann, born January 7th, 1853; married January 17th, 1872, Richard M. Evans.

1033. *Gustavus, Ohio.*

CHARLES GIDEON HART, third son of Joseph Hart, of Avon, Conn., and Gustavus, Ohio, and his wife, Eunice (Fitz), born September 19th, 1813, at Gustavus, and married there, Sylvia Russell, where they were residing in 1873.

GLEASON.

1034. *North Shenango, Penn.*

SARAH EMELINE HART, third daughter of Joseph Hart, of Avon, Conn., and Gustavus, Ohio, and his wife, Eunice (Fitz), born August 20th, 1815, at Gustavus, and married there, Norton D. Gleason. They settled in North Shenango, Crawford County, Penn., where she died, August 2d, 1872, aged 57 years.

FITZ.

1035. *Gustavus, Ohio.*

LEVIA MARIA HART, fourth daughter of Joseph Hart, of Avon, Conn., and Gustavus, Ohio, and his wife, Eunice (Fitz), born March 2d, 1817, at Gustavus; married Sylvester W. Fitz, of that town, where they located. She was a member of the Congregational Church there in 1873.

BRADLEY.

1036. *Farmington, Ohio.*

ALMIRA LUCINDA HART, fifth daughter of Joseph Hart, of Avon, Conn., and Gustavus, Ohio, and his wife, Eunice (Fitz), born April 3d, 1819, at Gustavus; married Albert C. Bradley. They located at Farmington, Trumbull County, Ohio, and resided there in 1873. She is a member of the Congregational Church there.

HART.

1037. *Gustavus, Ohio.*

FANNIE HART, sixth daughter of Joseph Hart, of Northington, and subsequently, of Gustavus, Trumbull County, Ohio, and his wife,

Eunice (Fitz), born April 4th, 1825, at Gustavus, Ohio; married Hiram S. Hart, of the same town, son of Joseph C. Hart, of Avon, Conn., and his wife, Rosanna (Goff), born October 8th, 1821. He is a blacksmith by trade, and they resided at Gustavus in 1873.

THEIR CHILDREN, BEING THE EIGHTH GENERATION.

Lilian, born   ; married   Thompson.
Anna, born about 1862.
Clinton A., born about 1867.

1038.   *Mentor, Ohio.*

JAMES FRANKLIN HART, Gustavus, Ohio, youngest child of Joseph Hart, of Northington, Conn., and Gustavus, Ohio, and his wife, Eunice (Fitz), born April 3d, 1830, at Gustavus; married Savilla Artman. They located at Mentor, Lake County, Ohio, where they resided in 1873.

1039.   *Brookfield, Ohio.*

AMBROSE HART, Brookfield, Ohio, eldest son of Gad Hart, of the same town, and his wife, Eunice Munson (Woodford), born September 28th, 1792, at Northington, Conn., now Avon; married February 28th, 1816, Polly Bushnell, who died, when second he married February 18th, 1829, Lovisa Bushnell, sister of his first wife, and daughters of General Bushnell, of Hartford, Trumbull County, Ohio, the second wife being mother of all his children. He was a merchant at Brookfield, and was well known through all that region. He died in 1849, aged 57 years. He was a man of wealth and influence in his day.

THEIR CHILDREN, BEING THE EIGHTH GENERATION.

1379. Polly, born December 18th, 1819; married December 7th, 1835, Joel Miner, formerly of Hartland, Conn., now of Ann Arbor, Mich.
1380. Albert Gaylord, born August 17th, 1821; married June 6th, 1844, Mary Crosby Hornell.
1381. Edward Harrison, born November 23d, 1833; married August 29th, 1855, Sarah E. Stiles, of Ohio.

1040.   *Avon, Conn.*

ALVA HART, Avon, second son of Gad Hart, of Northington, Conn., and Brookfield, Ohio, and his wife, Eunice Munson (Woodford), born May 14th, 1794, at Avon; married Fanny W. Borden, who died, when second he married   . He died
, 1872, aged 78 years.

1382. Floretta, born   ; married   , G. W. Benton.
1383. Salman, born   ; married, had two children, and both died
       young.
       Francis, born   ; died young.
1384. Henry, born   ; married, lives at La Crosse, Minn., and has
       children.
       Homer, born

1043. *Avon, Conn.*

JEDUTHAN HART, fifth son of Gad Hart, of Northington, Conn., and Brookfield, Ohio, and his wife, Eunice Munson (Woodford), born August 21st, 1799, at Northington, Conn.; married   , Hannah Webber. He died at   , aged 44 years.

1385. Emeline, born   ; married   , James Bell.
       Elbridge, born   . He is single now, 1872.

1044. *Hartford, Ohio.*

GAD HART, Hartford, Trumbull County, Ohio, sixth son of Gad Hart, of Northington, Conn., and Brookfield, Ohio, and his wife, Eunice Munson (Woodford), born February 19th, 1801, at Northington, Conn. He was baptized there, May 4th, 1801; married Lucretia Moses, of Canton, Conn., born October 21st, 1800. She died at Hartford, Ohio, July 12th, 1837, when second he married Celestia Norton, of Hartford, Conn., born June 6th, 1813, who also died at Hartford, Ohio, January 30th, 1848, when third he married April 14th, 1848, Widow Betsey Thompson, born at Preston, Conn., July 27th, 1808. He died in 1863, aged 62 years. His widow was living at Cleveland, Ohio, in 1873.

1386. Mary Jane, born   ; married   , Samuel F.
       Richards.
1387. Franklin, born   ; married   , Rachel Jane
       Stacey.
1388. Calvin C., born July 5th, 1830; married June 2d, 1853, Sarah Elizabeth
       Thompson.
1389. Warren A., born September 23d, 1834; married   , Alice
       Hilyer.

1390. Lucretia Celestia, born November 25th, 1839; married November 12th, 1868,
       James Cedar, of Kinsman.

1391. Anna Matilda, born July 22d, 1843. She is a teacher at Cleveland, Ohio.
1392. Nancy Eunice, born September 17th, 1845; married October 12th, 1870, Robert D. Herrick.

CHILD BY HIS THIRD WIFE.

1393. Seymour Peck, born June 13th, 1849; married August 10th, 1870, Ida M. Thompson, of Hartford, Ohio.

1045. *Avon, Conn.*

EDWIN HART, Avon, Conn., seventh son of Gad Hart, of Northington, Conn., and Brookfield, Ohio, and his wife, Eunice Munson (Woodford), born September 24th, 1802, at Northington (now Avon), Conn.; baptized there, January 2d, 1803; married Betsey Thompson.

THEIR CHILDREN, BEING THE EIGHTH GENERATION.

Lavinia, born   ; died young.
Sarah, born   ; died young.
Sylvestus, born

BROWN.

1046. *Avon, Conn.*

FANNY WOODFORD HART, eldest daughter of Gad Hart, of Avon, and Brookfield, Ohio, and his wife, Eunice Munson (Woodford), born November 30th, 1804, at Avon, Conn.; married Samuel Brown. She died in 1869, aged 65 years. They had issue, viz: Alfred, born   , married   ; Frank, born   , married   , Helen M. Hart.

THOMPSON.

1047. *Avon, Conn.*

MARILLA HART, Avon, second daughter of Gad Hart, of Northington, Conn., and Brookfield, Ohio, and his wife, Eunice Munson (Woodford), born August 6th, 1806; married   , William Thompson. Their children: Lovisa (married John Resher), Ambrose, Newell, William, Porter, Albert.

CADWELL.

1048. *Avon, Conn.*

EMELINE MATILDA HART, third daughter of Gad Hart, of Northington, Conn., and Brookfield, Ohio, and his wife, Eunice Munson (Woodford), born 1808; married David Cadwell, and died about one year afterwards, leaving no children.

1049.　　　　　　　*Avon, Conn.*

JOSEPH HART, eighth son of Gad Hart, of Northington, Conn., and Brookfield, Ohio, and his wife, Eunice Munson (Woodford), born March 10th, 1810; married Prudence Rolph. He died　　　　　，
leaving no children.

1050.　　　　　　　*Brookfield, Ohio.*

ASA HART, ninth son of Gad Hart, of Northington, Conn., and Brookfield, Trumbull County, Ohio, and his wife, Eunice Munson (Woodford), born February 5th, 1812; married Sarah Richards.

THEIR CHILDREN, BEING THE EIGHTH GENERATION.

John Richards, born
Owen, born

Homer, ⎰
Harriet, ⎱ born .

1052.　　　　　　　*Avon, Conn.*

HALSEY PHELPS HART, tenth son of Gad Hart, of Northington, Conn., and Brookfield, Trumbull County, Ohio, and his wife, Eunice Munson (Woodford), born December 15th, 1815 ; married　　　　，
Charlotte F. Follett. He died young.

THEIR CHILDREN, BEING THE EIGHTH GENERATION.

Lucina, born
Eleanor, born

MORSE.

1053.　　　．　　　*Avon, Conn.*

LAURA BIRD HART, eldest daughter of Hosea Hart, of Avon, Conn., and his wife, Joanna (Tuller), born 1790, at Northington, now Avon; baptized there, May 5th, 1793, by Rev. Ebenezer Booge. She married in 1819, Jeremiah Morse, of Avon.

1054.　　　　　　　*Avon, Conn.*

SAMUEL TULLER HART, second son of Hosea Hart, of Avon, Conn., and his wife, Joanna (Tuller), born at Avon in 1794; married in 1814, Electa Woodruff, who died March 15th, 1817, aged 22 years, when second he married in 1817, Sukey Daley, of West Avon, Conn. He died August 5th, 1856, aged 64. His widow died May 7th, 1863.

CHILD BY THE FIRST WIFE, BEING THE EIGHTH GENERATION.

1394.　Electa, born　　　　　　, 1816; married　　　　　, 1842, John Woodruff,
　　　of Unionville.

CHILDREN BY THE SECOND WIFE.

	Albert, born	, 1818. He was living single at Avon in 1871.	
1395.	Delia, born	, 1819; married	, Henry Jones,
	of Otis, Mass.		
1396.	Elmer, born	, 1821; married September 26th, 1855, Jane G. Pike,	
	of East Windsor.		
	Emily, born	, 1823; married	, John Eldridge.
1397.	Mary Ann, born	, 1824; married	; second,
	Ephraim Short.		
1398.	Elvira, born	, 1825; married May 2d, 1846, Erastus Woodruff;	
	second, Egbert Hart.		
1399.	Nelson, born January 6th, 1826; married June 27th, 1850, Elizabeth Duncan.		
1400.	Leonard, born May 14th, 1829; married April 7th, 1849, Harriet Spencer.		
1401.	Jane, born	, 1833; married	, William Haskell, of
	Blanford.		

1055. *Avon, Conn.*

ASAPH HART, Avon, third son of Hosea Hart, of the same town, and his wife, Joanna (Tuller), born 1799, at Northington, (now Avon), Conn.; married in 1828, Widow Lucina Richards, daughter of Jesse Wilcox. He was admitted to the church at Avon in 1821, and was ex-communicated in 1829. His wife left him, and she died a widow, December 23d, 1867, aged 67 years. They had one child, Mary, born 1834; died in 1837, aged 3 years.

1043. *Avon, Conn.*

JEDUTHAN HART, Cincinnati, Ohio, fifth son of Hosea Hart, of Northington, (now Avon,) and his wife, Joanna (Tuller), born 1803; baptized September 4th, 1803, at Avon; married Paulina Wilbur. He was admitted to the church at Avon in 1821, but was subsequently dismissed.

THEIR CHILDREN, BEING THE EIGHTH GENERATION.

Lowly, born
George, born

WILBUR.

1057. *Avon, Conn.*

HELENA HART, Avon, third daughter of Hosea Hart, of the same town, and his wife, Joanna (Tuller), born 1805; baptized September 8th, 1805, at Avon, Conn.; married Ireneus Wilbur.

WHITLOCK.

1058. *Avon, Conn.*

JANE HART, fourth daughter of Hosea Hart, of Avon, and his wife, Joanna (Tuller), born 1808, at Avon, and baptized there, June 11th, 1809; married Charles Whitlock.

36

1059.   *Avon, Conn.*

ZINA HART, Avon, Conn., eldest son of Linas Hart, of Northington, Conn., and his wife, Mary Ann (Wilcox), born December 2d, 1788, at Northington; married October 20th, 1813, Rhoda Griswold, daughter of Ashbel, of New Britain, and his wife, Elizabeth (Woodruff), of Farmington Farms, born August 1st, 1792.   He was a farmer by occupation, and his home was just west of the flag station of West Avon, opposite Harvey Hart's place.   They were both admitted to the Congregational Church there in 1821.   He died October 1st, 1867, aged 79 years.   She was living in 1871.

THEIR CHILDREN, BEING THE EIGHTH GENERATION.

1402.   Linas Omri, born March 20th, 1815; married October 30th, 1839, Mary Ann Pennfield, of New Britain.

1403.   Paulina Griswold, born September 19th, 1817; married January 7th, 1838, Simeon D. Chappell, of Avon.

Ephraim Woodruff, born November 21st, 1819; died March 30th, 1822, aged 2 years and 4 months.

Daughter, born   , 1821.

Diana, born June 5th, 1823; died September 20th, 1825.

1404.   Ephraim Ava, born February 12th, 1825; married October 2d, 1853, Sarah Elizabeth Spencer.

1405.   Russell Dennis, born March 15th, 1833; drowned in Farmington River, May 21st, 1842, aged 9 years.

1060.   *Farmington, East Farms, Conn.*

ADNA HART, Northington, Conn., second son of Linas Hart, of the same place, and his wife, Mary Ann (Wilcox), born March 27th, 1790, at Northington; married April 26th, 1815, Lucy Woodruff, daughter of Solomon, and his wife, Christiana (Curtiss), of Simsbury, born January 11th, 1789.   He was a tallow chandler on Farmington East Farms, and followed his business with diligence and success.   He died January 4th, 1871, aged 80 years.   He was a man of great moral worth.   His son, Newton, was executor of his Will.   His widow died July 2d, 1872, aged 83 years, 6 months.   They were both worthy members of the Farmington Congregational Church.   Adna Hart left an estate of some $15,000, and, until his decease, there had been no death in the family for over sixty-four years.

THEIR CHILDREN, BEING THE EIGHTH GENERATION.

1406.   Dolly, born November 5th, 1817; married   , 1841, George M. Hale, of Burlington.

1407.   Newton, born January 11th, 1821.   He was a soap and tallow chandler, and was single.

1408.   Clarissa, born May 29th, 1825; married   , 1846, David Stoddard, of Avon.

1409.   Lucy, born March 28th, 1827; married April 26th, 1848, Blinn Francis.

1410.   Mary, born April 25th, 1829; married   , Newton Peck.

PENNFIELD.

1062. *New Britain, Conn.*

RUTH JUDD HART, Northington, second daughter of Linas Hart, of the same place, and his wife, Mary Ann (Wilcox), born May 3d, 1793, at Avon; married November 25th, 1812, Phineas Pennfield, of New Britain, son of Phineas, and his wife, Lucy (Osgood), born October 18th, 1785, at New Britain, where he was a farmer. He and his wife were admitted to the Congregational Church there in 1821. He died August 3d, 1845, aged 60 years. She died December 11th, 1848, aged 55 years. They had—1, Mary Ann, born October 4th, 1813; Harvey, born June 7th, 1815; 3, Martin, born August 23d, 1816; 4, Lydia, born May 29th, 1819; 5, Lemuel, born April 17th, 1821; 6, Dennis, born December 24th, 1823; 7, Fidelia, born September 10th, 1826; 8, Emily, born September 11th, 1829; 9, Horace, born June 11th, 1831; 10, Frances Newell, November 25th, 1833; 11, Harriet A., born August 5th, 1835.

1063. *Jacksonville, Ill.*

MARTIN HART, Northington, third son of Linas Hart, of the same town, and his wife, Mary Ann (Wilcox), born   , 1795, at Northington, Conn.; married December 1st, 1818, Dolly Newell, of Farmington. He removed to Jacksonville, Morgan County, Ill.

THEIR CHILD, BEING THE EIGHTH GENERATION.

1411. Anna A., born   , 1821.

1064. *Sherman, N. Y.*

DENNIS HART, Chautauque, N. Y., fourth son of Linas Hart, of Avon, and his wife, Mary Ann (Wilcox), born September 2d, 1798, at Northington; married February 1st, 1825, Elvira, daughter of Joseph Dutton, of Farmington, born December 22d, 1802, at Farmington, and married there by Rev. Dr. Porter. He was a farmer at Sherman, Chautauqua County, N. Y., where he died, September 8th, 1868, aged 70 years.

THEIR CHILDREN, BEING THE EIGHTH GENERATION.

Infant, born   , 1827; died   , 1827.

1412. Cornelia E., born April 4th, 1829; married November 18th, 1852, William H. Keeler.

1413. Mary E., born September 18th, 1830; married May 4th,   , Enoch Sperry.

1414. Joseph Dutton, born August 1st, 1832; married March 28th, 1859, Mary M. Dutton.

1415. Henry M., born May 27th, 1835; died November 3d, 1862, at Chautauqua, aged 27 years.

1416. Elizabeth J., born January 9th, 1838; married October 1st, 1861, Madison J.
       Morse.
1417. Harriet Ann, born October 7th, 1839.
1418. Rollin W., born February 20th, 1842. He was a soldier, and died October
       19th, 1862, in Fairfax Hospital, Virginia.
1419. Abby M., born November 5th, 1844; married October 22d, 1868, John W.
       Spencer.

1065.   *Chautauqua, N. Y.*

AVA HART, Chautauqua, N. Y., fifth son of Linas Hart, of Northington, Conn., and his wife, Mary Ann (Wilcox), born October 24th,
1800, at Avon; married November 6th, 1827, Julia Crampton, daughter of Stephen, and his wife, Amy, of Farmington, born January 14th,
1804, at Farmington, Conn. He is a farmer, and resided at Chautauqua in 1871, where all his children were born. They were married at
Farmington, Conn., before Rev. Dr. Noah Porter, then pastor of the
Congregational Church there.

THEIR CHILDREN, BEING THE EIGHTH GENERATION.

1420. Edmund Crampton, born July 13th, 1829; married October 16th, 1856, Har-
       riet J. Alford.
1421. Ann Maria, born May 22d, 1834.
1422. William Henry, born January 20th, 1836; married October 11th, 1870, Euge.
       nia M. Sperry.
1423. Julius Brewster, born May 20th, 1839; married October 22d, 1868, Julia A.
       Sperry.

HART.

1067.   *New Britain, Avon, Conn.*

SOPHRONIA HART, New Britain, eldest daughter of Obed Hart, of
Avon, Conn., and his wife, Elizabeth (Edson), born April 21st, 1794,
at Avon; married January 9th, 1810, at Avon, Joseph Hart, son of
Asahel, and his wife, Anna (Kilbourn), born September 18th, 1787, at
New Britain, and baptized there, October 28th, 1787. She died July
14th, 1814, aged 20 years, leaving two children, for whom see Joseph
Hart.

1068.   *Louisville, Ky.*

REV. EDSON HART, Ohio and Kentucky, eldest son of Obed Hart, of
Avon, and his first wife, Elizabeth (Edson), born April 12th, 1796, at
Northington, now Avon, Conn.; married October 15th, 1821, Helen
Priestly, of New Brunswick, N. J., born April 11th, 1796. He was
educated at Yale College, and became a very laborious minister of the
gospel. His wife died at New Albany, Ind., April 4th, 1851, aged 55
years, when second he married Miss Martha A. Day, of Morristown,
N. J. He died at his home near Louisville, Ky., September 19th,

1867, aged 71 years. The following appeared in the *Louisville Journal* of September 26th, 1867:

"On Thursday, the 19th instant, the Rev. Edson Hart died at his residence at Baird's Station, Oldham County, Ky. Mr. Hart was born at Farmington, Conn., on the 12th day of April, 1796. He was educated at Yale College, made a profession of his faith in Christ while quite young, entered the ministry in the Presbyterian Church, and continued in the constant and active labors of that sacred calling until partially laid aside by bronchitis. The scene of his earliest labors in the ministry was among the Indians, in the state of Michigan. From thence he removed to Western Ohio, and after several years labor there, removed to Erie County, Penn., where he preached to the two churches of Springfield and Gerard for a number of years. His next field of labor was at Morganfield, Union County, Ky. Here chiefly through his agency, as we understand, a high school was established, in which he felt a deep interest, using his personal influence and efforts in the north to raise funds for its support. He settled at Morganfield about the year 1838, or 1839, and remained there six or eight years. He afterwards spent some years at New Albany, Ind. His health failing he went to New Orleans, and became an agent of the American Bible Society, where he labored until the war interrupted, and in 1862 he came north, and early in 1865 settled at Baird's Station, a quiet place, where he hoped to spend his days in peace. His earnest prayers and exhortations in our little prayer meetings are remembered with a tender interest. He was a man of earnest piety and strong faith. His last illness was lingering, but there were no bands in his death. Peace, hope, and trust, made his death-bed as calm and glorious as the setting sun."

His half brother, Seth Hart, Esq., of New York City, writing of him to the compiler, says of him: "If ever there was a man who sincerely believed in the doctrines he professed, and who truly loved his Saviour and his teachings, it was the late Rev. Edson Hart. It may be said of him as of Noah—'He walked with God.'"

THEIR CHILDREN, BEING THE EIGHTH GENERATION.

1424. Samuel H., born August 23d, 1832; married, May, 1850, Rachel Ellen Emery.
1425. John Priestly, born August 15th, 1824; married
Randolph S., born September 10th, 1826.
Edson R., born October 13th, 1831.
1426. George Obed, born August 7th, 1834; married March 13th, 1855, Addie H. Slent, of Kentucky.
1427. Joseph B., born August 4th, 1829; married   , Juliet   .
Helen E., born April 23d, 1837.

1071. *Sherman, N. Y.*

NORMAN HART, Sherman, Tompkins County, N. Y., fifth son of Obed Hart, of Northington, Conn., and his second wife, Charlotte (Dorman), born October 11th, 1805, at Northington; married October 11th, 1826, at Avon, Conn., before Rev. H. Bushnell, Anna Adaline Hart, daughter of Erastus, and his wife, Anna (Thompson), born February 6th, 1809. They removed from Avon to Sherman, N. Y., and from thence to Westfield, N. Y., where he resided in 1871. He is a farmer. She died December 21st, 1862, at Sherman, Chautauqua County, N. Y., aged 53 years, when he second married at Westfield, N. Y., by Rev. R. T. Van Cleave, April 15th, 1869, Mrs. Eliza A. Barnes, of Westfield, N. Y.

THEIR CHILDREN, BEING THE EIGHTH GENERATION.

1428. Edson Truman, born December 14th, 1827; married March 12th, 1851, Eliza Ann Bush.

1429. Charlotte Ann, born April 21st, 1831; died single, August 26th, 1859, aged 28 years.

1430. George Elnathan, born April 27th, 1833; married February 2d, 1859, Eliza Ann Webster, of Pennsylvania.

1431. Lucelia Malintha, born April 23d, 1835; married March 14th, 1861, Miron Partridge, of Ashville, N. Y.

1432. Minerva Angeline, born October 7th, 1836; married November 30th, 1864, Joseph L. Webster, of Pennsylvania.

Child, born , 1839; died

1433. Esther Lucia, born May 15th, 1843. She was living at Newington, Conn., in 1871, with Aunt Hunn.

1434. Nancy Adalina, born March 9th, 1846; married January 1st, 1868, Timothy T. Root, of Cambridge, Penn.

Mary Adelaide, born September 18th, 1848. She was living single at home in 1871.

1069. *Sherman, N. Y.*

DEACON GEORGE HART, Sherman, N. Y., third son of Obed Hart, of Northington, Conn., and his second wife, Charlotte (Dorman), born November 16th, 1801, at Northington; married April 3d, 1827, Esther Hawley, daughter of Asa, of Farmington, and his wife, Diadama (Root), born September 3d, 1806, at Farmington. He was a clothier by trade. He removed to Sherman, Chautauqua County, N. Y., and followed farming, but returned and died at Scott's Swamp, in Farmington, Conn., April 3d, 1869, aged 67 years, 4 months, 17 days. She was living at Plainville, Conn., in 1872. They had no children.

1070. *Rockford, N. Y.*

HIRAM HART, Avon, Conn., fourth son of Obed Hart, of that town, and his second wife, Charlotte (Dorman), born January 25th, 1804, at

Northington, now Avon; married May 22d, 1827, Mary Robbins, daughter of Enos and Dorothy (Higgins) Robbins, born May 29th, 1803, at Wethersfield. He removed to Lysander, Onondaga County, N. Y., in 1831, and thence to Rockford, Tioga County, N. Y., in 1836, where she died, May 26th, 1839, aged 36 years, when second he married March 22d, 1840, Verona, daughter of Amzi Norton, and his wife, Huldah (Barstow), born January 15th, 1815, at Guilford, Chenango County, N. Y., and died at Lisle, Broome County, N. Y., September 21st, 1868, aged 43 years, when third he married March 22d, 1860, Mary, widow of John Lacy, of Richford, N. Y., daughter of Philip T. Kellogg, and his wife, Huldah (Dikeman), born February 14th, 1809, at Milton, Saratoga County, N. Y. He was residing at Richford, Tioga County, N. Y., in 1871.

THEIR CHILDREN, BEING THE EIGHTH GENERATION.

1435. Ellen Eliza, born June 5th, 1829; married   , Philander Jennings.
Mary Augusta, born October 12th, 1832; died October 24th, 1843, at Berkshire, N. Y., aged 11 years.

SECOND WIFE.

1436. Frances Adelaide, born December 27th, 1842; married   ,
Irving B. Prentice, of Newark.
Edson Harmon, born October 22d, 1845; died September 22d, 1849, at Richford, N. Y., aged 4 years.
Colden Norton, born November 3d, 1850, at Richford, Tioga County, N. Y.
Edson Amzi, born January 31st, 1853.
Sarah Verona, born May 24th, 1855, at Lisle, N. Y.; died May 2d, 1866, at Richford, N. Y., aged 11 years.

1072. *New Haven, Conn.*

TRUMAN HART, New Haven, Conn., sixth son of Obed Hart, of Northington, and his second wife, Charlotte (Dorman), born February 28th, 1808, at Northington, Conn.; married   , Lucia Bliss, who died, when second he married in 1841, Harriet Langdon, who also died, when third he married   , Sarah Halsey.

THEIR CHILD, BEING THE EIGHTH GENERATION.
born   , 1843; died   , 1843.

1073. *West Avon, Conn.*

HARVEY HART, Avon, seventh son of Obed Hart, of Northington, and his second wife, Charlotte (Dorman), born December 28th, 1810, at Northington, Conn.; married September 22d, 1833, Harriet, daughter of Corral Woodford, and his wife, Mary (Woodford), born June

24th, 1814. He lives on his father's old place in West Avon, and has a good farm, and buildings near, just west of the way station of the railroad.

THEIR CHILD, BEING THE EIGHTH GENERATION.

1437. Truman Woodford, born September 9th, 1834; married May 30th, 1856, Mary Jane Woodford.

SKINNER.

1074.   *Sherman, N. Y.*

MELINTHA HART, Avon, Conn., second daughter of Obed Hart, of Northington, and his second wife, Charlotte (Dorman), born April 9th, 1814, at West Avon; married October 8th, 1835, at Sherman, Chautauqua County, N. Y., by Rev. J. Wilson, Aretas Skinner, born October 22d, 1804, at Norwich, Chenango County, N. Y. They resided at Sherman, Chautauqua County, N. Y., where he is a farmer, and where all their children were born. She was admitted to the Congregational Church at Avon, November 6th, 1831. They had—1, Adaline, born September 12th, 1836, died April 6th, 1863; 2, Emily, born June 8th, 1838, married April 15th, 1861, J. F. Cushing; 3, Otis L., born January 26th, 1841; 4, George H., born March 4th, 1844, married December 23d, 1869, Sylvia Eades; 5, Henrietta, born November 28th, 1847, died February 8th, 1848.

1075.   *New York City.*

SETH HART, New York, eighth son of Obed Hart, of Northington, Conn., and his second wife, Charlotte (Dorman), born April 10th, 1816, at Avon; married   , Matilda Miller, a milliner of New York City. He has lived at Macon, Ga., but in 1871 he lived at No. 109 East Eleventh Street, New York.

THEIR CHILD, BEING THE EIGHTH GENERATION.

1438. Charles, born   , 1842.

SWEET.

1076½.   *Farmington, Conn.*

JULIA HART, eldest daughter of Orrin Hart, of the same town, and his wife, Sally, daughter of Jedediah Gladden, and his wife, Elizabeth (Page), born   , 1804, at Farmington; married October 12th, 1823, Edwin Sweet, of Farmington. They lived on the mountain, above Dr. Cowles' distillery, known as the Sweet place, for many years.

HEARSEY.

1077. *Southington, Conn.*

CLARA HART, Farmington, fourth daughter of Orrin Hart, of the same town, and his wife, Sally (Gladden), daughter of Jedediah, and his wife, Elizabeth (Page), born October 12th, 1816, at Farmington. She married September 28th, 1846, Samuel H. Hearsey, of Southington, where they reside in 1874. He is a mechanic.

STACY.

1085. · *New Britain, Conn.*

FIDELIA HART, eldest child (to live long) of Stephen Hart, Jr., of New Britain, and his wife, Cynthia (Steele), born June 7th, 1820, in New Britain; married October 22d, 1846, Mansfield Stacy, then of New Britain. She died childless, August 6th, 1847, aged 27 years, when second he married Maria Morse, daughter of Orson, and his wife, Maria (Kellogg), of Burlington. They removed to Springfield, Bradford County, Penn., where he died about 1848. He was a mechanic in New Britain, but was afterwards a farmer.

ALLEN.

1086. *Meriden, Conn.*

NANCY HART, third daughter of Stephen Hart, Jr., of New Britain, and his wife, Cynthia (Steele), born October 26th, 1822, at New Britain, Conn.; married July 31st, 1839, Dr. William Allen, son of William, then of New Britain. He practiced some years as a physician in Meriden, Conn., where he died, September 6th, 1851, aged 33 years.

PROFFITT.

1087. *Hartford, Conn.*

EMILY PARKER HART, fourth daughter of Stephen Hart, Jr., and his wife, Cynthia (Steele), born May 8th, 1823, at New Britain; married April 13th, 1845, John G. Proffitt, of Hartford, son of John, and his wife, Harriet (Galpin), born March 4th, 1817, at Durham, Conn. He is a carriage painter, and in 1863 resided in Hartford, near the depot. They had—1, Edward Auritius, born September 21st, 1846, died July 17th, 1848; 2, Edward Everett, born January 17th, 1851, died February 6th, 1854; 3, Frederick, born October 13th, 1853; 4, John Hart, February 11th, 1856, at Hartford.

37

STACY.

1088.   *Springfield, Penn.*

MARIA HART, fourth daughter of Stephen Hart, Jr., the butcher, of New Britain, and his wife, Cynthia (Steele), born March 11th, 1827, at New Britain; married October 1st, 1848, Allen Stacy, of Springfield, Bradford County, Penn., a farmer there, but for a time a mechanic in New Britain, where he married. He died about 1853, in Springfield, Penn. His widow is living there, on the farm, in 1874. •

PARSONS.

1089.   *Bridgeport, Conn.*

SARAH E. HART, fifth daughter of Stephen Hart, Jr., of New Britain, and his wife, Cynthia (Steele), born February 11th, 1834, at New Britain; married November 14th, 1857, Asa Sheldon Parsons, of Bridgeport, Conn.

RAPELYE.

1091.   *New Britain, Conn.*

ANTOINETTE HART, eldest daughter of Edmund Hart, of New Britain, and his wife, Mehitabel (Dewey), born April 11th, 1825, at New Britain; married May 24th, 1846, Andrew Rapelye, a cabinet maker of the same place. He was born at New Britain, August 23d, 1824, and was the son of Andrew Rapelye, Sr., of Newtown, L. I., and his wife, Selina Hart (Churchill). His residence is on Chestnut Street. They had—1, Charles Andrew, born March 21st, 1849; 2, William Hart, born March 9th, 1851; 3, George, born October 2d, 1854; 4, Frederic Dewey, born May 6th, 1858; 5, Addie, born October 20th, 1860, died May 25th, 1861; 6, Nellie Antoinette, born November 28th, 1864.

WELLS.

1092.   *New Britain, Conn.*

ADALINE HART, second daughter of Edmund Hart, of New Britain, and his wife, Mehitabel (Dewey), born March 21st, 1827, at New Britain; married November 26th, 1845, Levi W. Wells, of Wethersfield, son of Rossiter, and his wife, Emily (Butler), born September 13th, 1820, at Wethersfield, Conn. They had Emma Adaline, born October 5th, 1853.

CORNISH.

1094. *Simsbury, Conn.*

ELLEN MARIA HART, third daughter of Edmund Hart, of New Britain, and his wife, Mehitabel (Dewey), born June 12th, 1839, at New Britain, Conn.; married January 12th, 1860, Richard Wallace Cornish, of Simsbury, son of James D., and his wife, Roxy (Humphrey), born September 29th, 1835, at Simsbury, Conn. They have no children.

1095. *New Britain, Conn.*

WILLIAM H. HART, second son of George Hart, of New Britain, and his second wife, Elizabeth F. (Booth), daughter of Cyrus, born July 25th, 1834, at New Britain; married September 19th, 1855, Martha Peck, daughter of Elnathan, and his wife, Mary (Dewey), born May 12th, 1837, at New Britain. He is superintendent of the Stanley Works in New Britain, and one of the stockholders of the firm. He now owns and occupies the Dr. Woodruff place, next to his father, on the west side of Main Street, in the center of the city. He has great capacity and dispatch in business operations. Their children were all born at New Britain, and are all living, November, 1874.

THEIR CHILDREN, BEING THE NINTH GENERATION.

1439. Charles William, born August 8th, 1858; baptized April 29th, 1859.
1440. George Peck, born August 22d, 1860; baptized March 3d, 1861.
1441. Howard Stanley, born July 9th, 1867; baptized May 3d, 1868.
1442. Martha Elizabeth, born May 9th, 1869; baptized November 7th, 1869.
1443. Edward Herbert, born October 12th, 1870; baptized May 28th, 1871.
1444. Maxwell Stansbury, born April 15th, 1873; baptized May 3d, 1874, by Rev. Mr. Griffin, Pastor.
1445. Walter H., born August 4th, 1874.

BURRITT.

1096. *New Britain, Conn.*

ELIZABETH MARIA HART, eldest daughter of Philip Hart, of New Britain, and his wife, Maria (Judd), born October 22d, 1832, at New Britain; married October 27th, 1852, William Burritt, of New Britain, son of William, and his wife, Clarissa (Cole), of Kensington, born July 17th, 1830, at New Britain. They reside with her father, on Seymour Street, New Britain, in 1874. They had—1, Ella Elizabeth, born January 16th, 1854; 2, Thomas, born January 20th, 1864. Both children were born at New Britain. The father is a mechanic, and was second lieutenant of Company G., Sixth Regiment Connecticut Volunteers. The mother was admitted to the Center Church, June 6th, 1858.

1097. *New Britain, Conn.*

ANDREW EDWIN HART, eldest son of Philip Hart, of New Britain, and his wife, Maria (Judd), born February 2d, 1834, at New Britain; married July 1st, 1857, Ann Weltha Clark, daughter of Melville, of New Britain, and his wife, Welthy Ann (Pilgrim), of Hartford, born January 11th, 1837, at New Britain. He was a soldier in the Twentieth Regiment Connecticut Volunteers, about nine months, and is now a mechanic, and lives on Glen Street, New Britain, in 1874.

1098. *New Britain, Conn.*

THOMAS HART, New Britain, second son of Philip Hart, of the same place, and his wife, Maria (Judd), born October 16th, 1838, at New Britain. He enlisted in Company F, Fourteenth Regiment Connecticut Volunteers, and was promoted to corporal. He was mustered into service July 22d, 1862, was killed at Fredericksburg, Va., December 13th, 1862, aged 24 years, and was brought home and buried in New Britain.

1099. *Bridgeport, New Britain, Conn.*

HENRY WILLIAM HART, New Britain, Conn., eldest son of Deacon William Hart, of New Britain, and his first wife, Rhoda (Judd), born February 10th, 1832, at New Britain, and is a machinist; married October 14th, 1862, Elizabeth Black, of Bridgeport, Conn., daughter of Alexander, and his wife, Mary, born March 4th, 1838, at Bridgeport, Conn. He enlisted in the Light Battery, in the last war, August 5th, 1862, and was discharged August 10th, 1865. He was in the three days battle at Gettysburg, and many other engagements.

THEIR CHILD, BEING THE NINTH GENERATION.
1446. William Henry, born June 14th, 1867, at Bridgeport.

1100. *New Britain, Conn.*

FRANCIS HART, New Britain, second son of Deacon William Hart, of the Baptist Church of New Britain, and his first wife, Rhoda (Judd), born May 25th, 1834, at New Britain; married May 4th, 1867, Widow Harriet Sophia Slater, daughter of Myron Andrews, of New Britain, and his wife, Lois (Barnes), of Burlington, born April 23d, 1841. She first married March 21st, 1861, Joseph Benjamin Slater, son of Captain Elam, born May 25th, 1840, and died December 10th, 1865, aged 24 years, when she second married Francis Hart as above. Mr. Hart is a mechanic, and is a large, stout built man.

ORTERS.

1101. *Stratford, Conn.*

JANE HART, eldest daughter of Deacon William Hart, of New Britain, and his first wife, Rhoda (Judd), born April 22d, 1836, at New Britain; married May 19th, 1859, Leonard Orters, of Stratford, Conn., a Swede by birth, having been born at Linkaping, Sweden, April 30th, 1828. They have three sons and one daughter.

BEERS.

1102. *Chatham, New Britain, Conn.*

HANNAH JUDD HART, second daughter of Deacon William Hart, of New Britain, and his first wife, Rhoda (Judd), born February 1st, 1840, at New Britain; married March 4th, 1868, William Edward Beers, of Chatham, Conn., born February 8th, 1840, at Chatham. He is an iron moulder by trade, but is a keeper of a livery stable, on Church Street, in 1874.. They have one son, William Edward, born April 5th, 1872, at New Britain.

JUDD.

1103. *New Britain, Conn.*

HELEN GRACE HART, youngest child of Deacon William Hart, of New Britain, and his first wife, Rhoda (Judd), born March 31st, 1846; married November 20th, 1867, William Samuel Judd, son of Philip S., and his wife, Betsey (Howd), born July 7th, 1844. He is a packer and shipper at Corbin's factory in 1874. They have one daughter, Laura J., born September 2d, 1870.

1104. *New Britain, Conn.*

CHARLES EDWIN HART, New Britain, eldest child of Ebenezer Hart, of the same place, and his wife, Mary (Pease), of Warehouse Point, born October 14th, 1842; married June 18th, 1867, Jennie Wainwright, daughter of John, of Manchester, N. J., and his wife, Jane (Skidmore), born June 13th, 1844, at Manchester, N. J. They were living in Hart's Block, New Britain, in 1871. He is a mechanic, and is a contractor at the Stanley Works, New Britain.

THEIR CHILDREN, BEING THE NINTH GENERATION.

Nellie Irene, born June 17th, 1868; died May 28th, 1869, at New Britain.
1447. Lilian Wainwright, born June 3d, 1870, at New Britain.
1448. Havur Emile, born December 7th, 1872, at New Britain.

HITCHCOCK.

1105. *Avon, Conn.*

SARAH HART, eldest daughter of Manna Hart, of Avon, Conn., and Candor, Tioga County, N. Y., and his wife, Thede (Woodford), born at Northington in 1805; married in 1827, William Hitchcock. He was a millwright by trade. They were both members of the church. She died in 1838, aged 33 years.

1106. *Candor, N. Y.*

LENT HART, Candor, N. Y., eldest son of Manna Hart, of Avon, Conn., and his wife, Thede (Woodford), born 1807; married in 1834, Fidelia Hugg. His avocation is farming. They are both members of the Presbyterian Church.

THEIR CHILD, BEING THE EIGHTH GENERATION.

1449. Celestia Louisa, born   , 1835; married   Searles.

THORP.

1107. *Spencer, Tioga County, N. Y.*

JULIA HART, Spencer, N. Y., second daughter of Manna Hart, of Northington, Conn., and his wife, Thede (Woodford), born at Northington, Conn., in 1810; married in 1837, Philander Thorp, of Spencer, Tioga County, N. Y. She is a member of the Presbyterian Church there.

1108. *Hartland, Mich.*

EDMUND HART, Hartland, Livingston County, Mich., second son of Manna Hart, of Northington, Conn., and his wife, Thede (Woodford), born 1815; married in 1840, Priscilla McDale. He is a millwright by trade, and his residence is at Hartland, Livingston County, Mich.

THEIR CHILDREN, BEING THE EIGHTH GENERATION.

1450. Edwin, born   , 1843.
1451. John, born   , 1844.

1109. *Candor, Tioga County, N. Y.*

MARCUS HART, Candor, Tioga County, N. Y., youngest son and child of Manna Hart, of Northington, Conn., and his wife, Thede (Woodford), born 1822; married in 1844, Melissa Mead. His avocation is farming, and his residence is at Candor, Tioga County, N. Y.

THEIR CHILDREN, BEING THE EIGHTH GENERATION.

1452. George, born   , 1846.
       Luther, born   , 1848; died   , 1857, aged 9 years.
1453. Alphonzo, born   , 1858.

WHAPLES.

1 1 1 O. *Newington, Conn.*

AMANDA ANGELINE, eldest daughter of Erastus Hart, of Burlington, Conn., and his wife, Amna (Thompson), born, September, 1807, at Avon; married there, October 11th, 1826, Elisha Whaples, of Newington, Conn. She died November 7th, 1850, aged 43. He died April 5th, 1854, aged 53 years. They have grave-stones to their memory in Newington Cemetery.· Their children were two sons and one daughter.

· HART.

1 1 1 1. *Sherman, N. Y.*

ANNA ADALINE HART, second daughter of Erastus Hart, of Burlington, Conn., and his wife, Amna (Thompson), born February 6th, 1809; married October 11th, 1826, at Avon, before Rev. Mr. Bushnell, Norman, (No. 1071,) a son of Obed Hart, and his second wife, Charlotte (Derrin), born October 11th, 1805. He is a farmer by occupation. They removed from Avon, Conn., to Sherman, N. Y., and from thence to Westfield, N. Y., where he resided in 1871. She died December 21st, 1862, at Sherman, Chautauqua County, N. Y., aged 53 years, when second he married, at Westfield, N. Y., by Rev. R. T. Van Cleave, April 15th, 1869, Mrs. Eliza A. Barnes, of Westfield.

THEIR CHILDREN, BEING THE EIGHTH GENERATION. (SEE OBED.)

1454. Edson Truman, born December 14th, 1827; married March 12th, 1851, Eliza Ann Bush.

Charlotte Ann, born April 21st, 1831; died single, August 26th, 1859, aged 28 years.

1455. George Elnathan, born April 27th, 1833; married February 2d, 1859, Eliza Ann Webster.

1456. Lucelia Malintha, born April 23d, 1835; married March 14th, 1861, Miron Partrige.

1457. Minerva Angeline, born April 23d, 1836; married November 30th, 1864, Joseph L. Webster.

Child, born   , 1839; died

1458. Esther Lucia, born May 15th, 1843. She lives in Newington with Aunt Hunn.

1459. Nancy Adaline, born March 9th, 1846; married January 1st, 1868, Timothy T. Root.

Mary Adalaide, born September 18th, 1848. She is living single at home in 1874.

ROGERS. HUNN.

1 1 1 2. *Vernon, Newington, Conn.*

MINERVA CAROLINE HART, Avon, Conn., youngest daughter of Erastus Hart, of Burlington, Conn., and his wife, Amna (Thompson), born

March 17th, 1811; married February 2d, 1834, Lee Lay Rogers, of Somerville, in Vernon, Conn. He died November 30th, 1836, when second she married December 2d, 1840, Albert Smith Hunn, the cattle dealer, of Newington, Conn., located just north of the railroad depot, where he has a fine farm. She has no children by either husband.

HART.

1113.   *Avon, Conn.*

BEULAH HART, eldest daughter of Jeptha Hart, of Avon, Conn., and his wife, Sally (Thompson), born, July, 1812; married, January, 1841, Samuel Martin Hart, son of Araunah Hart, of Avon, Conn., and his first wife, Ursula (Clark), born 1821. He was brought up by his uncle, Jeptha, whose daughter he married, but they were divorced.

THEIR CHILDREN, BEING THE EIGHTH GENERATION.

1460. Mary Edner, born February 23d, 1841, in Wisconsin; married November 18th, 1869, Charles C. Wolcott, of Fair Haven.
        Fanny, born   , 1848.

WOODRUFF.

1114.   *West Avon, Conn.*

OLIVE DAY HART, Avon, second daughter of Jeptha Hart, of that place, and his wife, Sally (Thompson), born March 12th, 1815, at Avon; married January 29th, 1840, Horace Woodruff, son of Titus, and his wife, Lua, born October 25th, 1807, at Avon. He is a farmer, and they lived on Lovely Street, West Avon, in 1872. She united with the church at West Avon in 1838. They had Thomas D., Almira H., Alathea B., and Marcus W.

1114½.   *Avon, Conn., Candor, N. Y.*

EGBERT HART, Bristol, Conn., only son of Jeptha Hart, of Avon, and his wife, Sally (Thompson), born   , at West Avon. He married the widow of Erastus Woodruff, Jr., and daughter of Samuel T. Hart, of Avon, and his second wife, Susan Daley, born at Avon in 1825. She died at her residence on Lovely Street, in West Avon, February 27th, 1873, aged 48 years.

SMITH.

1115.   *Candor, N. Y.*

CIBELIA HART, Candor, N. Y., eldest daughter of Araunah Hart, of Avon, Conn., and his wife, Ursula (Clark), born 1817; married, 1842,

Harvey P. Smith. Their residence was Candor, Tioga County, N. Y., where he died a hopeful Christian, in 1844.

SMITH.

1116. *Candor, N. Y.*

CATHARINE HART, Candor, N. Y., second daughter of Auranah Hart, of Avon, Conn., and Granville, Bradford County, Penn., and his wife, Ursula (Clark), born 1818; married in 1837, Edgar M. Smith, an architect, of Candor, Tioga County, N. Y. They are both members of the Presbyterian Church there.

1119. *Dodge County, Wis.*

AMOS E. HART, Candor, N. Y., second son of Araunah Hart, of Avon, Conn., and his first wife, Ursula (Clark), born 1823; married in 1843, Harriet J. Smith, of Candor, N. Y. They subsequently removed to Dodge County, Wis.

1122. *Candor, N. Y.*

TIMOTHY EDBERT HART, Candor, N. Y., only son of Terency Hart, of the same place, and his wife, Loraine (Derrin), born 1821; married in 1844, Olivia M. Johnson. They were both members of the Presbyterian Church there. He died in 1869, aged 48 years. Their children were all born at Candor.

THEIR CHILDREN, BEING THE EIGHTH GENERATION.

461.	Orson Edbert, born	, 1845.	He is a banker.
462.	Emma Olivia, born	, 1847.	
463.	Willard Kendrick, born	, 1850.	
464.	Irvin Stanley, born	, 1852.	
465.	Charles Frederic, born	, 1856.	
466.	Mary Alice, born	, 1861.	
467.	Ella Maria, born	, 1864.	

1123. *Hartford, Conn.*

DONALD HART, Hartford, Conn., eldest son of Stephen Winchell Hart, of Farmington, Conn., and his wife, Sally (Bruce), born June 18th, 1804; married in 1831, Caroline Pitkin. He was a wheelwright by trade, and resided in Hartford, Conn. He died without issue, June 21st, 1851.

1124. *Hartford, Conn.*

GAD HENRY HART, Hartford, Conn., second son of Stephen Winchell Hart, of Farmington, and his wife, Sally (Bruce), born   , 1806; married   , 1829, Eliza E. Cowles. He was a carriage

38

maker by trade, and a member of the Congregational Church. He
died February 28th, 1835, aged 29.

1468. Orson, born
1469. Mary, born

1128. *Hartford, Conn.*

LEWIS BRUCE HART, Hartford, Conn., eldest son of Julius Hart, of
Farmington, and his wife, Harriet P. (Bruce), born December 18th,
1815, at Farmington; married November 17th, 1837, Lydia Ann
Miller, daughter of Joseph, and his wife, Mary (Kelsey), of Rocky
Hill, born October 8th, 1824. He is a carriage smith by trade, which
he learned of George and Henry Francis, of Hartford. He is now
registrar of the town and city of Hartford, where he resides at No.
935 Main Street. They had issue, viz: Ellen Bruce, born January
18th, 1848, died   , aged 1 year and 6 months; Lewis Bruce,
born July 12th, 1853, died   , aged 4 years.

1129. *Springfield, Mass.*

HENRY WRIGHT HART, Springfield, Mass., second son of Julius Hart,
of Farmington, and his wife, Harriet P. (Bruce), born November 20th,
1816; married   , Lucy Holmes. His avocation is
painting, and he resides in Springfield, Mass.

1470. Lewis Bruce, born
1471. Charles, born

PARKER.

1131. *New Haven, Conn.*

HARRIET PRIOR HART, New Haven, Conn., second daughter of Julius
Hart, of Farmington, and his wife, Harriet Prior (Bruce), born January 2d, 1826, at Farmington; married May 31st, 1846, Origen, son of
Peter Parker, and his wife, Lovisa (Griswold), born October 11th,
1824, at Enfield, Conn. His avocation is ornamental painting. They
resided at New Haven in 1871, and have two sons and two daughters.

JAMES.

1134½. *Unionville, Conn.*

LORENA HART, Unionville, Conn., eldest daughter of Sidney Hart,
of Farmington, and his wife, Clarissa (Clark), born December 30th,

1814, at Farmington; married June 18th, 1837, Charles P. James, born March 10th, 1815, at Hartford. He is a cabinet maker, and works at Unionville, where they live, and both are members of the Congregational Church. They have had two sons and three daughters, viz: Josephine, Wellington, Roselle, Louisa, and Charles.

GRIMES.

1134¾. *New Britain, Conn.*

CATHARINE HART, Farmington and New Britain, second daughter of Sidney Hart, Sr., of Farmington, and his wife, Clarissa (Clark), born October 28th, 1817; married March 1st, 1835, William Henry Grimes, son of Oliver, of Granby, and his wife, Olive (Gilbert), born June 10th, 1814, at Simsbury. They were married at Farmington, before Rev. Noah Porter, D. D. They had children, viz: George H., born January 25th, 1838; Belle V., born August 11th, 1844.

1134⅞. *Farmington, Conn.*

SIDNEY HART, Farmington, eldest son of Sidney Hart, Sr., of the same place, and his wife, Clarissa (Clark), born June 3d, 1819, at Farmington; married in 1840, Lydia W. Griswold, daughter of Wait, of Rocky Hill, and his wife, Lydia (Wright), born January 19th, 1822. He learned the trade of wheelwright of his father. They reside on Mountain Street, Farmington, he has his shop near the meeting-house, and he is sexton and undertaker to the same.

THEIR CHILDREN, BEING THE NINTH GENERATION.

472. Frances, born August 19th, 1841; married January 26th, 1870, Horton Hoskins, of Bloomfield.

473. Albert Willys, born November 5th, 1842; married January 20th, 1867, Catharine Lewis.

474. Sarah Jane, born November 7th, 1846; married January 4th, 1870, James Bond, of England.

Alonzo James, born Feb. 14th, 1849; died July 29th, 1852, at Farmington.

Jennie Amelia, born January 5th, 1852.

Alonzo James, 2d, born May 6th, 1855.

Kate Adell, born April 24th, 1857.

1134 7/16. *Farmington, Conn.*

HIRAM WINCHELL HART, Farmington, youngest son of Sidney Hart, Sr., of the same town, and his wife, Clarissa (Clark), born February 11th, 1825, at Farmington; married November 25th, 1847, Frances Fidelia Palmer, daughter of Amos, of West Hartford, and his wife, Electa (Wells), born March 21st, 1828. He is a joiner by trade and occupation, and lives on Mountain Street, Farmington. Their children were all born at Farmington.

THEIR CHILDREN, BEING THE NINTH GENERATION.

1475. Horatio Wells, born December 30th, 1848.

Virginia Cowles, born March 12th, 1851; died March 3d, 1855.

1476. Virginia Frances, born April 21st, 1856.

Hattie Cora, born October 12th, 1857; died Feb. 26th, 1862, aged 4 years.

Thomas Palmer, born December 11th, 1859.

1136. *Unionville, Conn.*

DEACON CHAUNCEY HART, Farmington, eldest son of Zenas Hart, of the same town, and his wife, Rachel (Lewis), born August 26th, 1810, at Farmington; married September 16th, 1832, before Rev. Luman Andrus, the Methodist minister, Sarah Jane Hooper, daughter of Philip, of Newington, and his wife, Phebe (Whaples), born January 13th, 1814, at Newington. He was a drum-major in the militia service. He is an ingenious blacksmith and fork maker, an active member and deacon of the Methodist Church, and a temperance man. He has a desirable residence in Unionville, some eighty rods south of the railroad depot. He has a good water power and shops on the south bank of Farmington River, where he and his sons have several men in their employ, and are doing a prosperous business. He learned his trade of Ira Stanley, Jr., of New Britain, while Stanley lived in Farmington.

THEIR CHILDREN, BEING THE NINTH GENERATION.

George Martyn, born November 5th, 1833; died, February, 1835, aged 2 years.

1477. George Lewis, born December 31st, 1834; married, April, 1857, Mary Ann King.

1478. Sarah Jane, born June 5th, 1836; married   , Matthew Foster.

1479. Nancy Tinckham, born December 3d, 1838; married   , Edwin Piper, of Bristol.

1480. Albert James, born August 3d, 1839; married July 19th, 1865, Ellen Barnard.

1481. Sanford Hill, born February 28th, 1841; married February 28th, 1860, Jane Wright.

1482. Hubert Chauncey, born April 14th, 1843; married August 19th, 1862, Eva Moses.

1483. Philip Zenas, born March 14th, 1845; married October 29th, 1864, Margaret Gelshon.

1484. Emma Elizabeth, born March 21st, 1850; married October 15th, 1870, James Alexander McDonald.

WELTON. EDWARDS.

1137. *Hartford, Conn.*

EMILY HART, Hartford, Conn., eldest daughter of Zenas Hart, of Farmington, and his wife, Rachel (Lewis), born June 5th, 1815, at

Farmington; married October 6th, 1835, Edward I. Welton, of Watertown, who died March 14th, 1864, when second she married April 1st, 1868, Porter Edwards, of West Hartford, Conn. They are living at No. 4½ Chestnut Street, Hartford, Conn. Children, all by first marriage, viz: 1, Lewis I. Welton, born May 14th, 1837; 2, Frederick Hart, born May 8th, 1839; 3, Mary E., born March 15th, 1841; 4, Theodore D., born November 27th, 1842, was in the army, and was killed at Fort Wagner, July 11th, 1863; 5, Josephine M., born October 13th, 1844; 6, Julia A., born December 13th, 1846; 7, Jennie E., born February 8th, 1850; 8, Edward H., born July 8th, 1853.

1138.   *Farmington, Conn.*

HENRY HART, Farmington, second son of Zenas Hart, of the same town, and his wife, Rachel (Lewis), born about 1816, at Farmington; married in 1835, Sarah G. Taylor, of Glastonbury, daughter of Benjamin, and his wife, Electa (Chapman), who died, when second he married in 1838, Lucy, daughter of Hubbard Gladdin, and his wife, Maria (Belden). He was a blacksmith by trade and occupation, was a soldier in Company B, Seventh Regiment Connecticut Volunteers, and died at Hilton Head.

THEIR CHILDREN, BEING THE NINTH GENERATION.

1485. Jane, born   ; married   , William Warner, of Manchester, Conn.

1486. Electa, born March 2d, 1836.

SECOND WIFE.

1487. Algeroy, born October 25th, 1839; married   , Lillian Allen, and was divorced.

1488. Harriet S., born July 25th, 1841; married   , Henry L. Johnson, and lives in Farmington, Minn.

1489. Adaline, born   ; married   , George Daly, and was divorced; second, Henry Moore.

Edwin, born January 24th, 1843.

1139.   *New Britain, Conn.*

RICHARD HART, New Britain, Conn., third son of Zenas Hart, of Farmington, and his wife, Rachel (Lewis), born January 2d, 1818, at Farmington; married Catharine Gladden. They parted, and he second married December 23d, 1849, Mary, daughter of John R. Jones, of New Britain, and his first wife, Emeline (Franklin), born August 9th, 1831, at New Britain. His residence is the westernmost house on West Main Street, two miles west of the city. He was a blacksmith by trade, but has been one of the first rule makers in New Britain.

He was a veteran soldier in the Union Army through the late war. He died of lung fever, May 7th, 1874, aged 56 years, 4 months, and 5 days.

HIS CHILD BY HIS FIRST WIFE, BEING THE NINTH GENERATION.

1490. Henry Crane, born October 3d, 1840; married October 23d, 1860, Eunice E. Gilbert.

HIS CHILDREN BY HIS SECOND WIFE.

1491. Frank, born August 29th, 1851; married August 17th, 1874, Mary Jane Rancier.
1492. Emma, born June 6th, 1853.
1493. Caroline, born September 3d, 1856; married July 18th, 1874, George A. Childs.

Charles, born December 25th, 1858.

1140.   *Unionville, Conn.*

LEWIS HART, Unionville, Conn., fourth son of Zenas Hart, of Farmington, and his wife, Rachel (Lewis), born May 20th, 1821, at Farmington; married April 10th, 1840, Julia Ann Root, daughter of Amzi, of New Britain, and his wife, Sally (Hart), daughter of Bethel Hart, born July 13th, 1819. He is a blacksmith by trade, which he learned of his brother, Chauncey. He was in the late war three years, in Company A, Connecticut Cavalry. He lives at Unionville, Conn., in 1874.

THEIR CHILDREN, BEING THE NINTH GENERATION.

1494. Anna Eliza, born December 2d, 1842, at Farmington; married, February, 1860, Thomas F. Clark.

Mary Jane, born October 20th, 1844, at Farmington; died in 1845.

1495. Julia Ann, born April 12th, 1845; married December 25th, 1865, George G. Barnes.
1496. Walter Lewis, born December 2d, 1848. He is a blacksmith, and was single in 1871.
1497. Bernard Dwight, born March 22d, 1851; married, February, 1871, Martha Burton.

Lewis Howard, born May 13th, 1859, at Plainville.

STEDMAN.

1141.   *Unionville, Conn.*

LUCY ANN HART, youngest daughter and child of Zenas Hart, of Farmington, and his wife, Rachel (Lewis), born September 29th, 1823, at Farmington; married March 2d, 1845, Simeon, son of Charles Stedman, of New Britain, and his wife, Betsey (Kellogg), of Kensington, Conn. He is a mechanic in the saw factory, and lives at Unionville. They had—1, Augusta L., born December 18th, 1845; 2, Mortimer D., born July 22d, 1848; 3, Jennie R., born April 27th, 1850; 4, Marion G., born April 10th, 1852; 5, Katie E., born December 12th, 1854;

6, John D., born October 7th, 1857; 7, Frederic, born December 9th, 1862.

PIERCE.

1142. *Sheffield, Mass.*

MARY HART, Sheffield, Mass., eldest daughter of Edward Hart, of the same town, and his wife, Sarah (Abbe), born August 2d, 1819, at Sheffield; married ·, John D. Pierce, a carpenter and joiner.

KONK.

1144. *Sheffield, Mass.*

AMELIA HART, Sheffield, Mass., fourth daughter of Edward Hart, of the same town, and his wife, Sarah (Abbe), born February 17th, 1824, at Sheffield, a twin with Fidelia; married , Joseph Konk. She is a member of the church at Sheffield.

THORN.

1145. *Lee, Mass.*

FIDELIA HART, Lee, Mass., fifth daughter of Edward Hart, of Sheffield, Mass., and his wife, Sarah (Abbe), born February 17th, 1824, a twin with Amelia; married , Stephen Thorn, a paper manufacturer, of Lee, Mass. She was a member of the church there, and died February 15th, 1843, aged 19 years.

BURROWS.

1147. *Nelson, Portage County, O.*

SARAH ANN HART, Nelson, Ohio, eldest daughter of Joel Hart, of Egremont, Mass., and his wife, Sally (Winchell), born April 6th, 1810, at Egremont, Mass.; married September 28th, 1837, John Burrows. He is a boot and shoe maker, and their residence is at Nelson, Portage County, Ohio. They had issue, viz: Julia Augusta, George Hervey, and Charles Henry, who died April 25th, 1864.

NICHOLSON.

1148. *Nelson, Portage County, O.*

JULIA BERINTHA HART, Nelson, Ohio, second daughter of Joel Hart, of Egremont, Mass., and his wife, Sally (Winchell), born June 22d, 1812, at Egremont; married February 11th, 1836, at New Lebanon, N. Y., William R. Nicholson, born September 22d, 1809. He was a farmer in Nelson, Portage County, Ohio, where he died, January 26th, 1859, aged 46 years. They had William Henry, James Wesley, and Augusta Issabel.

1149.   *Petersburg, Mich.*

NEWTON HENRY HART, Petersburg, Monroe County, Mich., second son of Joel Hart, of Egremont, Mass., and his wife, Sally (Winchell), born February 25th, 1816, at Sheffield, Mass. He married August 16th, 1853, Moselle S. McCollum, who died August 27th, 1856, aged 29, when second he married March 27th, 1861, Naome Oram, who died November 24th, 1864, aged 38, when he third married December 12th, 1865, Widow Elizabeth Thompson, who died December 27th, 1870, aged 49 years. He is a mason and rake manufacturer, and was residing at Petersburg in 1872. He sent us, under date of February 3d, 1873, a list of clergymen, copied from the *New York Observer Year Book.*

CHILD BY THE SECOND WIFE, BEING THE NINTH GENERATION.
1498. Millicent M., born December 20th, 1862.

1150.   *Colebrook, Ohio.*

SOLOMON WINCHELL HART, Colebrook, Ohio, third son of Joel Hart, of Egremont, Mass., and his wife, Sally (Winchell), born May 21st, 1817, at Egremont, Berkshire County, Mass.; married June 8th, 1843, Eleanor Bancroft, of Nelson, Portage County, Ohio, daughter of Rodolphus, and his wife, Betsey (King), born September 30th, 1819, at Nelson. His avocation is farming, and he was residing at Colebrook, Ashtabula County, Ohio.

THEIR CHILD, BEING THE NINTH GENERATION.
1499. Julia Amelia, born February 7th, 1848; married August 16th, 1868, Adelbert E. Beckwith.

1151.   *Freeport, Ill.*

LORENZO DE WITT HART, Freeport, Stephenson County, Ill., fourth son of Joel Hart, of Egremont, Mass., and his wife, Sally (Winchell), born October 11th, 1828, at Egremont, Mass; married October 13th, 1858, Clarissa Stearns, born April 13th, 1830. He resides at Freeport, and his avocation is farming. They are both members of the Church of United Brethren, and have two adopted children.

THEIR CHILDREN, BEING THE NINTH GENERATION.
1500. Gertie Ann, born March 2d, 1866.
1501. William A., born August 5th, 1870.

EARLE.

1152. *Windham, Ohio.*

MARY JANE HART, Windham, Ohio, third daughter of Joel Hart, of Egremont, Mass., and his wife, Sally (Winchell), born May 21st, 1831, at Egremont, Mass.; married September 21st, 1853, Jacob P. Earle, a farmer, of Windham, Portage County, Ohio, and both belong to the Free Will Baptist Church there. They had children, viz: Carlisle B., Flora Issabel, and Orville Alonzo.

1152½. *Freeport, Ill.*

CHARLES ALONZO HART, Freeport, Ill., youngest child of Joel Hart, of Egremont, Mass., and his wife, Sally (Winchell), born January 8th, 1834, at Egremont, Mass.; married September 22d, 1866, Amanda M. H. Dobler, whose mother was Catharine S. Kemp, born June 23d, 1840, at Hamilton County, Ohio. He is a farmer at Freeport, Stephenson County, Ill., and both are members of the Church of United Brethren. They have one child by adoption, and one of their own.

THEIR CHILDREN, BEING THE NINTH GENERATION.

1502. Lotta E., born February 7th, 1868—adopted.
1503. · Clara Catharine, born November 28th, 1872—their own.

1155. *Winsted, Conn.*

DAVIS HART, eldest son of Newton Hart, Egremont, Mass., and his wife, Martha Sophrone (Winchell), born September 24th, 1834, at Egremont, Mass.; married Amanda Coles Stannard, daughter of Gershom, and his wife, Lucina (Granger), born June 20th, 1841, at Barkhamsted, Conn. He was a veteran private in Company A, Tenth Regiment Massachusetts Volunteers, was wounded at Spottsylvania Court House, May 12th, 1864, died on the 20th, at the Sixth Corps Hospital, Fredericksburg, Va., and was buried there, aged 30 years. At home his avocation was farming. He had no children. His widow was living at Winsted, Conn., in 1871.

1156. *Hudson, N. Y.*

WILLIAM HENRY HART, Hudson, N. Y., second son of Newton Hart, of Egremont, Mass., and his wife, Martha Sophrone (Winchell), born January 25th, 1836, at Egremont; married at Millerton, N. Y., September 14th, 1864, Mary E. Brown, daughter of Milton, of Millerton, and his wife, Salina (Wheeler), born July 14th, 1845, at Millerton, N. Y., and died there, March 30th, 1868, aged 22 years, 8 months, 15 days, when second he married June 8th, 1870, Mariette W. Cheeney,

39

daughter of Richard, and his wife, Catharine (Hosford), of Hudson, N. Y., born there February 4th, 1844. He has been a resident of Hudson since 1866, where he still resides. He is a dentist, and has been in practice for fifteen years. Previous to 1873 he had a large practice, and more of this world's goods than is common to the Hart family, having been fortunate in speculations.

CHILD BY HIS FIRST WIFE, BEING THE NINTH GENERATION.

1504.   Clarina Brown, born February 8th, 1868.

CHILD BY HIS SECOND WIFE.

1505.   Richard Cheeney, born August 29th, 1871.

1157.   *Egremont, Mass.*

GEORGE LEMUEL HART, Egremont, Mass., third son of Newton Hart, of the same town, and his wife, Martha Sophrone (Winchell), born September 26th, 1838, at Egremont, Mass., and married February 13th, 1871, Harriet Jackson, of Colebrook, Conn. He was three years a member of Company A, Tenth Regiment Massachusetts Volunteers, and about one year in the Thirty-Sixth Regiment, of the same state.

1158.   *West Winsted, Conn.*

TIMOTHY ARD HART, West Winsted, youngest son and child of Newton Hart, of Egremont, Berkshire County, Mass., and his wife, Martha Sophrone (Winchell), born December 27th, 1843, at Egremont; married   , Emma Tuttle, of Winsted. He lives on the old homestead of his father, in Winsted, and his avocation is farming. He served in the late war as corporal in Company E, Second Regiment Connecticut Heavy Artillery.

THEIR CHILD, BEING THE NINTH GENERATION.

1506.   Reuben Elmer, born December 15th, 1869, at West Winsted, Conn.

1159.   *Plymouth, Conn.*

AMOS BUSHNELL HART, Plymouth, Conn., eldest son of Ard Hart, of Bristol, Conn., and his wife, Amanda (Hart), born May 10th, 1832; married November 4th, 1860, Almira, daughter of Sextus Gaylord, and his wife, Lorenda (Preston), born   . His avocation is farming, and he lives at East Church, in Plymouth, Conn.

THEIR CHILDREN, BEING THE NINTH GENERATION.

1507.   Elbert, born June 14th, 1861, at Plymouth.
1508.   Eunice Elizabeth, born August 4th, 1865, at Plymouth.
1509.   Frederic Burdett, born May 31st, 1867, at Bristol.

1160. *Bristol, Conn.*

JASON HARVILLAH HART, Bristol, Conn., second son of Ard Hart, of the same town, and his wife, Amanda Hart, born February 20th, 1834, at Bristol, Conn.; married June 5th, 1859, Julia, daughter of William Sanford, of Plymouth, and his wife, Mary (Todd), born June 20th, 1842. He is a moulder by trade. He has a fine farm east of Chipens Hill, near the old homestead of Seth Hart.

THEIR CHILDREN, BEING THE NINTH GENERATION.

Sidney Harvillah, born September 22d, 1860, at Terryville.
Elmer Elsworth, born March 29th, 1863, at Terryville.
Eddy Leroy, born January 14th, 1865, at Terryville.
Cora Maria, born December 25th, 1869, at Bristol.

1161. *Bristol, Conn.*

BURTON HART, Bristol, Conn., third son of Ard Hart, of the same town, and his wife, Amanda (Hart), born April 16th, 1836, at Bristol; married February 1st, 1863, Emily, daughter of Harlow Curtiss, of Harwinton, Conn., born   . She died in childbed, June 5th, 1864, when second he married April 29th, 1868, Lizzie, daughter of Kirtland Cowles, of Wethersfield, and his wife, Mary (Deming), born January 20th, 1845, at Wethersfield. He kept a grocery at Bristol in 1871.

CHILD BY HIS FIRST WIFE, BEING THE NINTH GENERATION.

1510.   Emily, born May 30th, 1864, at Plymouth.

CHILDREN BY HIS SECOND WIFE.

1511.   Horace Burton, born August 1st, 1869, at Waterbury.
1512.   Alice Cowles, born August 2d, 1871, at Bristol.

POST.

1162. *Bristol, Conn.*

MARY JANE HART, Bristol, eldest daughter of Ard Hart, of the same place, and his wife, Amanda (Hart), daughter of Seth, born October 4th, 1837, at Bristol; married October 26th, 1856, Daniel Post, of Hebron, Conn., born May 29th, 1832. He is a clock maker, and has a fine residence on the north side of Bristol. They have two sons and one daughter.

1164. *New Britain, Conn.*

NEWTON ALPHONZO HART, New Britain, Conn., fifth son of Ard Hart, of Bristol, and his wife, Amanda, daughter of Seth Hart, born January 5th, at Bristol; married September 20th, 1869, Hattie Emily, daughter of Edmund T. Geer, of South Windsor, Conn., and his wife, Henrietta (Hall), of the same place, born August 22d, 1849. In 1871 he was a moulder at the Union Works.

1165.   *Bristol, Conn.*

SETH RANSOM HART, Bristol, youngest son and child of Ard Hart, of the same town, and his wife, Amanda, daughter of Seth Hart, born May 17th, 1848, at Bristol, Conn.; married January 3d, 1869, Elvina, daughter of Horace Johnson, of Plainville, Conn., and his wife, Susan (Adams), born   .   He is a clock maker at Bristol, Conn. They have no children.

WASHINGTON.

1168.   *Decatur, Ind.*

NANCY JANE HART, Sparta, Ind., eldest and only daughter of Amos Hart, of the same place, and his first wife, Sally (Bryan), born March 25th, 1840, in Decatur County, Ind.; married December 20th, 1869, Greensburg Washington, an Englishman. They had one child, Sallie, born September 3d, 1871. There are probably more.

1169.   *Sparta, Ind.*

LEMUEL HART, Sparta, only son of Amos Hart, of the same place, and his second wife, Eliza Ann (Roof), born January 10th, 1845, in Decatur County, Ind. He was in the Union Army for three years, in Company H., Sixty-Eighth Regiment Indiana Volunteers. He was taken sick and discharged, and shortly after enlisted in the six months service, in Company K, Ninety-First Regiment Indiana Volunteers. He lost his health in the service, and has not regained it, and he now follows peddling. He has no family.

LONG.

1170.   *Hubbard, Ohio.*

HELEN MARIA HART, Brookfield, Ohio, eldest daughter of Chauncey Hart, of Burlington, Conn., and Vienna, Ohio, and his wife, Millissendra (Hart), born August 17th, 1824, at Burlington, Conn. She lived at Brookfield, Ohio, with her parents until her marriage, December 24th, 1841, to Henry H. Long, of Hubbard, Trumbull County, Ohio, where they were residing in 1873. They had issue, viz: William, Psyche, Baring, and Mary, who died, May, 1872.

Alphonso Hart

1171. *Newton Falls, Ohio.*

WILLIAM ELSWORTH HART, Cleveland, Ohio, eldest son of Chauncey Hart, of Burlington, Conn., and his wife, Milisendra (Hart), born April 9th, 1826, at Brookfield, Trumbull County, Ohio; married October 19th, 1852, Rachel Wheelock, of Freedom, Portage County, Ohio. They lived at Newton Falls, Trumbull County, Ohio, where their children were born, but they subsequently removed to Cleveland, Ohio, where he was in 1873, in the wholesale grocery trade, and is a very successful business man.

THEIR CHILDREN, BEING THE NINTH GENERATION.

1513. Frank, born September 9th, 1853.
1514. Cora, born December 2d, 1857.

1172. *Ravenna, Ohio.*

HON. ALPHONZO HART, Ravenna, Ohio, second son of Chauncey Hart, of Burlington, Conn., and Brookfield, Ohio, and his wife, Milisendra (Hart), daughter of Bliss, born July 4th, 1830, at Vienna, Ohio, and was residing at Ravenna, Portage County, Ohio, in 1873. He is a young lawyer of much promise, and rapidly rising in the political world. He has been a member of the House of Representatives, is now in the State Senate, and is highly esteemed in that section of the state. He married November 22d, 1856, Phebe Peck, daughter of Joshua Willes Peck, and his wife, Julia E. (Guger), born June 27th, 1832. He lives in Ravenna, where his children were born, and where his wife died, September 22d, 1868, aged 36. He was a republican presidential elector at large for the state of Ohio in 1872, and is lieutenant-governor in 1874.

THEIR CHILDREN, BEING THE NINTH GENERATION.

1515. Edgar Willes, born February 24th, 1859.
1516. Lilla Virginia, born December 21st, 1863.

1173. *Blissfield, Lenawee Co., Mich.*

ORLANDO HART, Blissfield, Lenawee County, Mich., third son of Chauncey Hart, of Burlington, Conn., and Vienna, Trumbull County, Ohio, and his wife, Milisendra, daughter of Bliss Hart, born July 29th, 1832, at Brookfield, Ohio; married February 25th, 1859, Rhoda E. Cook, of Birmingham, Erie County, Ohio. They lived at Blissfield, Lenawee County, Mich., in 1873, where he was engaged in the retail drug business.

THEIR CHILDREN, BEING THE NINTH GENERATION.

1517. Nellie Louise, born February 26th, 1860.
1518. Maria Emma, born   , 1863.

1174.　　　　　*Cleveland, Ohio.*

EDGAR L. HART, Cleveland, Ohio, youngest son of Chauncey Hart, of Burlington, Conn., and Vienna, Ohio, and his wife, Milisendra, daughter of Bliss Hart, born April 13th, 1835, at Brookfield, Trumbull County, Ohio. He is a member of a prominent wholesale trade of millinery and notions. He was never married. His post-office address is Cleveland, Ohio, care of Morgan, Root & Co.

1175.　　　　　*Philadelphia, Penn.*

WILLIAM ROBERTS HART, eldest son of William Hart, of Cleveland, Ohio, and Vineland, N. J., and his first wife, Mary Ann (Bowman), of Charlestown, N. H., born January 15th, 1833, at Charlestown, N. H.; married　　　　　　, Harriet Newell Wilcox, daughter of William, and his wife, Welthy Ann, born January 12th, 1834. He is in the mercantile business at No. 208 South Fourth Street, Philadelphia, Penn.

THEIR CHILDREN, BEING THE NINTH GENERATION.

```
       Infant, born              ; died
       Infant, born              ; died
1519.  Walter Morris, born November 23d, 1872.
```

HAYT.

1176.　　　　　*Patterson, N. J.*

MARY HARRINGTON HART, eldest daughter of William Hart, of Cleveland, Ohio, and Vineland, N. J., and his first wife, Mary Ann (Bowman), born October 6th, 1835, at Charlestown, N. H.; married December 22d, 1852, Colonel William Wisner Hayt, of Patterson, N. J. He was born June 8th, 1825; and was colonel of the One Hundred and Eighty-Ninth Regiment New York Volunteers, in the late war. He died at City Point, Va., November 8th, 1864. They had—1, Frank A., born at Corning, February 23d, 1854; 2, Lucy E., born April 26th, 1855, at Corning.

WILLIAMS.

1180.　　　　　*Auburn, N. Y.*

JULIA ANN HART, Scott, Cortland County, N. Y., eldest daughter of Jude Hart, of Southington, and his wife, Hannah (Pardee), born July 22d, 1833; married, November, 1860, Sherman Williams. He is a farmer by occupation, was residing at Auburn, N. Y., in 1871, and he has two or three children.

WILLIAMS.

1181. *Scott, N. Y.*

CAROLINE AUGUSTA HART, Scott, Cortland County, N. Y., second daughter of Jude Hart, of Southington, and his wife, Hannah (Parlee), born January 11th, 1837; married July 28th, 1860, Benjamin Williams, whose avocation is farming. They were residing at Scott, N. Y., in 1871. They have children, viz: Delia, Eleanor, Leona, Sarah, Edith May, born, June, 1871.

1182. *Southington, Conn.*

AMOS AUGUSTUS HART, youngest son of Jude Hart, of Southington, Conn., and his wife, Hannah (Pardee), born July 17th, 1839; married July 2d, 1866, Mary Wilcox. He is a farmer by occupation.

THEIR CHILDREN, BEING THE NINTH GENERATION.

520. John, born, May, 1868.
521. Isaac, born, February, 1870.

1183. *Southington, Durham, Conn.*

REV. HENRY ELMER HART, Southington, Conn., eldest son of Reuel Hart, of Southington, Conn., and his wife, Rosanna (Barnes), born June 1st, 1834, at Southington. He graduated at Yale College in 1860, studied theology at East Windsor, Conn., was a stated preacher at Bridgewater, Conn., from 1863 to 1866, and was ordained, and installed pastor of the Union Church, East Hampton, Conn., September 9th, 1866. He married October 5th, 1864, Josephine G., daughter of William Perry, of South Windham, and his wife, Elizabeth P. (Elsworth), of East Windsor, born May 18th, 1844, at East Windsor. He s located at Durham, Conn., in 1874, as pastor of the Congregational Church.

THEIR CHILDREN, BEING THE NINTH GENERATION.

522. Ada Louisa, born October 5th, 1866, at East Hampton.
523. William Elmer, born April 8th, 1869, at East Hampton.

POND.

1187. *Lakeville, Minn.*

MARIA ELIZA HART, Southington, eldest daughter of Edward Hart, of the same town, and his first wife, Anna (Beach), born 1821, at Southington; married September 9th, 1844, Harvey R. Pond, of Bristol. He is a farmer, and they are living at Dakota County, Minn. They have had two daughters.

1187½.   *Southington, Conn.*

SAMUEL BEACH HART, eldest son of Edward Hart, the shoe-maker of
Southington, and his first wife, Anna (Beach), born 1824, at Southington; baptized there, April 5th, 1839, by Rev. Elisha C. Jones, and died
there, April 14th, 1870, aged 46. He was never married.

FULLERTON. MOODY.

1188.   *Lakeville, Minn.*

JANE LUCRETIA HART, Southington, third daughter of Edward Hart,
the shoe-maker of Southington, and his first wife, Anna (Beach), born
at Southington in 1828; married David Fullerton, of Mo. He died at
Minnesota, when second she married George Moody, of Lakeville, Dakota County, Minn. She has two daughters and one son by her first
husband, but no children by her second husband.

DYER.

1189.   *Hartford, Conn.*

DELIA ANN HART, Southington, fourth daughter of Edward Hart, of
the same town, and his second wife, Rhoda (Grannis), born July 30th,
1836, at Southington, and was married there, by Rev. E. C. Jones,
pastor, to Samuel Dyer, of Jackson, Me., November 30th, 1854. He
is a mechanic, and was living at Hartford in 1871. They have two
sons and two daughters. She was admitted to the Congregational
Church in Southington, September 3d, 1854. He was admitted by
letter from the church in Vernon, November 5th, 1854.

PECK.

1190.   *Kensington, Conn.*

CELIA LORENA HART, Southington, fifth daughter of Edward Hart,
of the same town, and his second wife, Rhoda (Grannis), born August
24th, 1840, at Southington; married November 15th, 1857, at Southington, before Rev. E. C. Jones, to Samuel H. Peck, of Kensington.
His avocation is farming. She died May 15th, 1862, aged 21 years,
and left two daughters—Celia L. and Rhoda J.

COVILL.

1191.   *St. Anthony, Minn.*

ALMIRA ELIZA HART, Southington, sixth daughter of Edward Hart,
the shoe-maker of Southington, and his second wife, Rhoda (Grannis),

born, January, 1842, at Southington, and married Marcus Covell, of St. Anthony, Hennepin County, Minn., where he is a mechanic. They have five sons.

WRIGHT.

1192. *New Britain, Conn.*

PHEBE AMELIA HART, New Britain, seventh daughter of Edward Hart, the shoe-maker of Southington, and his second wife, Rhoda Grannis), born August 18th, 1843, at Southington; admitted to the church there, May 7th, 1865; married October 27th, 1869, Francis Wright, son of William, and his wife, Lucy (Slater), all of New Britain, born September 5th, 1843. He is a farmer, and lives on West Main Street. They have one son, Francis William, born April 19th, 1871, and one daughter, born July 18th, 1874, named Carrie; died October 2d, 1874.

STANFORD.

1194. *Mercer, Ohio.*

LAURA FLORA HART, Mercer, Ohio, eldest daughter of Almon Hart, of Southington, Conn., and Middletown, Vt., and his wife, Mary Gates Stewart), born November 15th, 1829, at Mercer, Trumbull County, Ohio; married John R. Stanford, who was born at Evansburg, Crawford County, Penn. He died, aged about 40 years. She also died, but when it is not reported.

1195. *Rochester, Minn.*

ASA BRAY HART, Rochester, Olmsted County, Minn., eldest son of Almon Hart, of Southington, Conn., and Middletown, Vt., and his wife, Mary Gates (Stewart), born March 23d, 1832, at Mercer, Trumbull County, Ohio; married at Geneva, Walworth County, Wis., Carda Owen. He resided at Rochester, Minn., in 1872, and his avocation was farming.

1196. *Elgin, Minn.*

DAVID ALMON HART, Wabasha County, Minn., second son of Almon · Hart, of Southington, Conn., and Middletown, Vt., and his wife, Mary Gates (Stewart), born August 22d, 1840, at Evansburg, Crawford County, Penn.; married July 3d, 1862, at Delavan, Wis., Mary Jane Potter, born January 17th, 1843, at Albany, N. Y. Mr. Hart is a blacksmith by trade, and was residing at Elgin, Minn., in 1872.

THEIR CHILDREN, BEING THE NINTH GENERATION.

524. Minnee May, born May 1st, 1866, at Geneva, Wis.
525. David Almon, born March 30th, 1868, at Elgin, Minn.
526. Ernest Dewitt, born August 18th, 1869, at Elgin, Minn.

40

HALE.

1197. *Elgin, Minn.*

MARY JANE HART, Elgin, Minn., second daughter of Almon Hart, of Southington, Conn., and Middletown, Vt., and his wife, Mary Gates (Stewart), born at Sand Lake, Penn., October 18th, about 1843; married at Geneva, Wis., October, 1860, Hoyt G. Hale, a wagon maker by trade. They were residing at Elgin, Wabasha County, Minn.

1198. *Rochester, Minn.*

EDWARD BERIAH HART, youngest child of Almon Hart, of Southington, Conn., and Middletown, Vt., and his wife, Mary Gates (Stewart), born November 14th, 1850, at Geneva, Walworth County, Wis. He is a blacksmith by trade, was a resident of Rochester, Olmsted County, Minn., and was single.

WILLET.

1199. *Afton, N. Y.*

EUNICE A. HART, Afton, only daughter (to live) of Chauncey Hart, of Southington, Conn., and Coventry, Chenango County, N. Y., and his first wife, Abigail (Wright), born March 4th, 1840, at Oxford; married January 7th, 1862, Egbert J. Willet, of Afton, Chenango County, N. Y. He is a carpenter by trade, and was living in the village of Afton. She lived in childhood at Southington, Conn., two years, with her aunt, Mrs. Edwin Woodruff, now deceased. They have children, viz: Ida G., Harmon, Ernest, son.

ROSE.

1201. *Bristol, Conn.*

PAULINA SOPHRONE HART, Bristol, Conn., second daughter of Elonzo Hart, of the same town, and his wife, Lovina (Barnes), born March 21st, 1819, at Bristol; married April 15th, 1840, Jesse Bela Rose, son of Bela, and his wife, Mary (Brocket), of North Haven. He is a worker in wool, and is employed in the Bristol Woolen Mill. They live in her mother's house, near the railroad crossing, and have three sons.

ATWOOD. BLAKESLEY.

1202. *Bristol, Conn.*

ROXANA HART, Bristol, Conn., fourth daughter of Elonzo Hart, of the same town, and his wife, Lovina (Barnes), born September 14th,

1825, at Bristol; married June 28th, 1846, George L. Atwood, of Milford, Conn. He died October 29th, 1853, aged 30 years, when second she married October 15th, 1861, Deacon Leonard Blakesley. She had two sons and one daughter by her first husband, but none by the second. They live in the north part of Bristol, east of Chippin's Hill, on the main road to Burlington. She hears with difficulty.

1203. *Bristol, Conn.*

THOMAS FRANKLIN HART, Bristol, only son of Elonzo Hart, of the same town, and his divorced wife, Lovina (Barnes), born September 1st, 1828, at Bristol; married November 22d, 1855, Sarah E. Weldon, of New Britain, daughter of Samuel H., and his first wife, Sally (Bartholomew), born April 2d, 1833. They parted and were divorced, when second he married Susan Thompson, who died, when he third married Nancy Northrup, of Northfield. He is reported as living at Waterbury in 1871, and had two sons and one daughter by his second wife, viz: John, William, Ida. He is generally considered a miserable specimen of a man.

HART.

1204. *Unionville, Conn.*

LYDIA MINERVA HART, Unionville, Conn., fifth daughter of Elonzo Hart, of Bristol, Conn., and his divorced wife, Lovina (Barnes), born at Bristol in 1832; married September 22d, 1852, Frederic Moses Hart, (No. 971,) son of Ambrose, of Burlington, and his wife, Chloe E. (Moses), born December 26th, 1826, and is a stone mason by trade. His wife died May 21st, 1862, at Unionville, aged 30 years, when second he married March 26th, 1865, Sarah Augusta (Smyth) Hamblin, widow of George Hamblin, of Plainville, and daughter of Willard Smyth, of Springfield, Mass., and his wife, Sarah (Russell), of Vermont, born November 19th, 1827. Mr. Hart was a soldier in the late war, having enlisted in Company C, Sixteenth Regiment Connecticut Volunteers, and was in service three years, eight and a half months of the time being in Andersonville and Florence prisons, where every indignity connected with starvation was endured.

CHILDREN BY HIS FIRST WIFE, BEING THE NINTH GENERATION.

Lewis Frederic, born October 11th, 1854; died December 10th, 1858.

1527. Alfred Elonzo, born June 14th, 1856.

Wallace Frederic, born April 4th, 1862; died November 6th, 1862.

CHILDREN BY HIS SECOND WIFE.

1528. Frederic Ambrose, born March 6th, 1868.

1206.   *Bristol, Conn.*

SYLVESTER CALVIN HART, Bristol, only son of Sylvester Hart, of Burlington, and his wife, Bathsheba (Hayes), of Granby, born at Durham, Conn.; married January 19th, 1842, at Burlington, Pennina Bidwell Norton, daughter of David, of Burlington, and his wife, Dolly (Botsford), of Bristol, born September 7th, 1822, at Burlington. His occupation is farming, at Bristol, where he has 125 acres of land, and lives one mile north of the copper mine.

THEIR CHILDREN, BEING THE NINTH GENERATION.

Mary Alicia, born December 20th, 1846, at Bristol. She is an imbecile, caused by fits.

1529. George Washington, born January 24th, 1849. He is a butcher, and lives at home.

1530. Alice Maria, born December 18th, 1854. She attends school.

Dolly Ann, born April 13th, 1843, at Yorkville, Wis.; died August 20th, 1843.

Emily Louisa, born August 16th, 1844, at Bristol; died June 13th, 1845.

HITCHCOCK.

1208.   *Harbor Creek, Penn.*

NANCY A. HART, Harbor Creek, Erie County, Penn., second daughter of Joel Hart, of Bristol, and other places, and his first wife, Sally Bowers, born July 17th, 1821, and resided in New Britain, Conn., where she married, December 14th, 1845, George Hitchcock, of Southington. They lived at Harbor Creek, Erie County, Penn., in 1861, and had issue, viz: Mary, born at New Britain; Jane, born at Berlin; Andrew, and Charles, born at Harbor Creek.

YALE.

1209.   *Bristol, Conn.*

LUCY HART, Bristol, third daughter of Joel Hart, of the same town, and his first wife, Sally (Bowers), of Rocky Hill, born at Bristol; married Elmer Yale, of the same place. He is a farmer, and they live half a mile south of the copper mine. They have had two sons and two daughters.

1210.

CALVIN HART, Bristol, Conn., eldest son of Joel Hart, of the same town, and his first wife, Sally (Bowers), of Rocky Hill, born May 12th, 1828, at Kensington, Conn.; married December 24th, 1850, Ellen Maria Goodale, daughter of Ebenezer, of Rocky Hill, and his wife, ———— (Chappell), born, September, 1828, at Rocky Hill. He is both a farmer and mechanic. His son works his farm in Burlington, and in 1871 he worked in Sessions' factory at Bristol.

THEIR CHILDREN, BEING THE NINTH GENERATION.

1533. Ella F., born March 24th, 1852, at New Britain; married December 24th, 1870, Perlee Buck, of Bristol.

1534. William Goodale, born July 10th, 1855, at New Britain. He is a mechanic. Lewis C., born March 17th, 1859, at Rocky Hill. Delia, born, September, 1862, at Rocky Hill. Elbert Calvin, born August 20th, 1870, at Burlington.

1211. *Rocky Hill, Conn.*

CYPRIAN HENRY HART, Rocky Hill, Conn., second son of Joel Hart, of Bristol, and other places, and his first wife, Sally (Bowers), of Rocky Hill, born March 10th, 1831, at Bristol; married April 4th, 1853, Eliza Pardew, of English parents. He lived for a time in New Britain, and worked in a factory, but in 1871 he resided in West Rocky Hill, where he has a good farm, is connected with the Methodist Church, and has been superintendent of their Sunday School.

THEIR CHILDREN, BEING THE NINTH GENERATION.

George Augustus, born April 15th, 1855, at New Britain; died May 12th, 1855, at New Britain.

Frank Lewis, born February 14th, 1857, at New Britain; died September 6th, 1858, at Rocky Hill.

1531. Charles Cyprian, born April 10th, 1862, at Rocky Hill.

1532. Arthur Pardew, born April 8th, 1864, at Rocky Hill.

1212. *Berlin, Conn.*

ALMON J. HART, Berlin, Conn., youngest son and child of Joel Hart, of Bristol, Conn., and his first wife, Sally (Bowers), of Rocky Hill, born May 4th, 1834; married January 27th, 1866, Adaline Hull, daughter of Samuel, of Middletown, and his wife, Barbara (Kelsey), of Killingsworth, born January 12th, 1831, at Killingsworth. He is a laboring farmer in Berlin, Conn. He was in Company B, Twenty-First Regiment Connecticut Volunteers, nearly three years. He was in seven battles and not hurt. They had no children in 1871.

1214. *Southington, Conn.*

CHARLES COLLINGWOOD HART, Southington, Conn., eldest son of Collingwood Hart, of the same town, and his wife, Rebecca Irene (Dunham), born July 27th, 1834, at Southington; married November 15th, 1858, Sarah Josephine Merriman, daughter of Joseph, of Southington, and his wife, Amanda (Johnson), born   . He is a farmer and mechanic, and lives in the house with his father, on West Street. He is famous for raising raspberries.

THEIR CHILDREN, BEING THE NINTH GENERATION.

1535. Irving Warren, born October 10th, 1859.
1536. Mary Edith, born September 11th, 1861.
1537. Cornelia Irene, born July 8th, 1863.
1538. Alice May, born September 24th, 1867.

1215.   *Southington, Conn.*

SAMUEL NELSON HART, Southington, second son of Collingwood Hart, of the same town, and his wife, Rebecca Irene (Dunham), born September 19th, 1840, at Southington; baptized July 30th, 1841, by Rev. E. C. Jones; married December 24th, 1869, Mary Jane, daughter of Deacon Joseph Gridley, of Southington, and his wife, Martha (Cowles), born June 5th, 1849, in Southington, and baptized there, September 5th, 1851. They lived on the Munn place, Clark's Farms, Southington, in 1871.

THEIR CHILD, BEING THE NINTH GENERATION.
David Whiting, born February 10th, 1871; died August 27th, 1871.

1216.   *Southington, Conn.*

DAVID WHITING HART, Southington, youngest son of Collingwood, of the same town, and his wife, Rebecca Irene (Dunham), born at Southington, July 25th, 1842; baptized August 4th, 1843, by Rev. E. C. Jones. He enlisted into Company E, Twentieth Regiment Connecticut Volunteers, August 22d, 1862, and was mortally wounded at the battle of Resaca, Ga., May 15th, 1864, and died one week after. His captain, Samuel S. Woodruff, thus speaks of him in a letter published in the *Southington Mirror* of July 1st, 1864:

"It was at this juncture (writing of the battle) that my noble young friend and clerk, David W. Hart, fell by my side, mortally wounded. I asked him where he was hit. He replied that he did not know. He had no sense of pain, but was numb all over. I soon found he was pierced by a minie-ball, and told him he must be carried off. He reluctantly consented, and four of his comrades put him on a blanket. The balls were flying thick and fast among us. He cast his last look at the colors, and his last words to us were—'Boys, I hate to leave you; fight on for the flag.' His bearers soon found a stretcher, and next an ambulance, and then they returned to their company. He was a noble and promising young man, a good soldier, and a devoted Christian, a severe loss to me, and to the company, and to the regiment, and to our country; but this is not to be compared to the crushing blow which falls upon his dear and bereaved family. He lived just one week after he was wounded, suffered but little, and talked cheerfully and hopefully. The ball passed through the spine, thus paralyzing all the lower parts of the body."

He died of his wound in the hospital near Resaca, Ga., May 22d, 1864, and a sermon on the occasion of his death was preached in the Congregational Church, Bristol, Conn., July 3d, 1864, by Rev. Leveret Griggs, printed in pamphlet form, 12 pages, by David B. Moseley, Hartford, 1864.

LEWIS.

1217.   *Southington, Conn.*

SYLVIA D. HART, Southington, eldest daughter of Reuben Hart, of the same town, and his wife, Abigail (Bradley), born April 20th, 1821, at Flanders District, Southington; married August 13th, 1845, Francis Deming Lewis, of Southington, son of Timothy, and his wife, Phila (Tisdale). They lived on the old homestead of her father, grandfather, and great-grandfather, where he built himself a new house on the site of the old one, and was residing there in 1872. She died September 4th, 1852, aged 31, when second he married September 23d, 1855, Elizabeth P. Gilbert.

LEWIS.

1219.   *Southington, Conn.*

ABIGAIL B. HART, Southington, eldest daughter of Julius, of the same town, and his wife, Diadama (Bradley), born April 5th, 1833, at Southington; married   , Julius Lewis, of Southington, son of Timothy, and his wife, Phila (Tisdale).

1222.   *Southington, Conn.*

REUBEN ROSWELL HART, Southington, second son of Roswell Hart, of the same town, and his wife, Pamelia (Amsden), born November 9th, 1831, at Southington; married June 9th, 1856, Julia A., daughter of William Clark, of Southington, and his wife, Jennette (Converse), born February 21st, 1836, at Southington. His avocation is farming, and he owns in part and occupies the Barrett farm, in the north part of the town.

THEIR CHILDREN, BEING THE NINTH GENERATION.

1539. George Reuben, born June 26th, 1863, at Southington.
1540. William Clark, born October 8th, 1865, at Southington.

WOOD.

1224.   *Southington, Conn.*

HULDAH ELIZABETH HART, Southington, second daughter of Roswell Hart, of the same town, and his wife, Pamelia (Amsden), born August 24th, 1833, at Southington; married December 30th, 1857, George W. Wood. He entered the army, and was corporal in Company B, Twenty-First Regiment Connecticut Volunteers. He died February 27th, 1863, at Newport News, and was buried at Oak Hill Cemetery, Southington. He has had one daughter, who lives with her mother at the old homestead.

1225.   *Southington, Conn.*

DANIEL MORTIMER HART, Southington, third son of Roswell Hart, of the same town, and his wife, Pamelia (Amsden), born January 6th, 1838, at Southington; married May 28th, 1860, Jane, daughter of William Clark, of Southington, and Jennette (Converse). He was in D. P. Woodruff's meat-market in 1871.

THEIR CHILD, BEING THE NINTH GENERATION.
1541. Mortimer Converse, born May 3d, 1861, at Southington.

1226.   *Southington, Conn.*

WILBUR AUGUSTUS HART, Southington, fourth son of Roswell Hart, of the same town, and his wife, Pamelia (Amsden), born April 11th, 1839, at Southington; married November 10th, 1863, Mary Jane, daughter of Gad Bishop, of Guilford, and his wife, Mary (Gale), born February 24th, 1836, at Guilford. His avocation is farming, and he lives just north of his father's old place, at the north end of Flanders Street.

THEIR CHILDREN, BEING THE NINTH GENERATION.
1542. Roswell Grant, born September 15th, 1864.
1543. Arthur Chapman, born July 30th, 1867.
1544. Sylvia Pamelia, born December 10th, 1869.

1227.   *Southington, Conn.*

JOHN BUNYAN HART, Southington, fifth son of Roswell, of the same town, and his wife, Pamelia (Amsden), born September 30th, 1844, at Southington; married November 26th, 1868, Sarah Frances Buel, daughter of Lorenzo, and his wife, Lucy (Beckwith).

THEIR CHILD, BEING THE NINTH GENERATION.
1545. Anna Lilian, born November 18th, 1870.

HULL.

1229.   *Southington, Conn.*

ELIZA ETHETA HART, Southington and Guilford, eldest daughter of
Ĝeorge Hart, of the same places, and his wife, Lewia (Page), born at
Šouthington, Conn.; baptized August 4th, 1825, at Southington; mar-
ïed Chauncey Hull.

WALKER.

1233.   *Stokes County, N. C.*

MELISSA ANN HART, Stokes County, N. C., eldest daughter of Asa-
ıel Woodruff Hart, of Southington, Conn., Stokes County, N. C., and
Ĵenry County, Mo., and his wife, Verlinda (Vantroy), born June 12th,
.834, at Stokes County, N. C.; married September 2d, 1851, in Stokes
Ĵounty, N. C., Richard R. Walker. She died September 2d, 1855,
ıged 21 years. His avocation is farming.

1237.   *Montrose, Mo.*

ALVIN CLINTON HART, Montrose, Mo., third son of Asahel Woodruff
Ĥart, of Southington, Conn., Stokes County, N. C., and Henry County,
ıMo., and his wife, Verlinda (Vantroy), born June 4th, 1846, in Stokes
Ĵounty, N. C., and went to Henry, Mo., with his parents, about 1851;
narried in Johnson County, Mo., December 30th, 1869, Lucretia Jane
Šmith, born January 31st, 1850, in Johnson County. His avocation is
arming.

THEIR CHILD, BEING THE NINTH GENERATION.

546. Arthur Wallace, born January 20th, 1870, at Montrose, Mo.

GORDON.

1240.   *Charlottesville, Va.*

HARRIET GILBERT HART, Charlottesville, Va., eldest daughter of Levi
ıAustin Hart, of Wilmington, N. C., and his first wife, Harriet (Kirt-
and), born March 17th, 1842; married January 9th, 1867, at Wilming-
on, Mason Gordon, Esq., a lawyer of Charlottesville, Va. Their chil-
lren were—Harriet Hart, born November 21st, 1867, and William
Ϡobertson, born April 17th, 1869.

BURR.

1241.   *Memphis, Tenn.*

MARY ANNA HART, Memphis, Tenn., second daughter of Levi Austin
Ĥart, of Southington, and subsequently of Wilmington, N. C., and

41

his first wife, Harriet (Kirtland), of New Haven, born November 29th, 1844, at Wilmington; married January 22d, 1868, before Rev. H. L. Singleton, Henry A. Burr, son of J. S. Burr, Esq., No. 129 South Ninth Street, Brooklyn, N. Y., but in 1872 resided in Memphis, Tenn. He went into the cotton press and storage business, and in 1874 became a partner in the firm of Hart & Bailey, N. C. They had issue, viz: 1, Austin Hart, born March 13th, 1869; 2, John Thomas, born October 21st, 1870; 3, Mary Elizabeth, born June 22d, 1872; 4, Henry A., born July 3d, 1874.

1244.   *Paita, Peru, S. A.*

LEVI AUSTIN HART, only son of Alvin Hart, of Southington, Conn., and his wife, Sarah (Stanley), of Plainville, born at Southington, Conn., November 3d, 1837. He went to sea on a whaling voyage when young, and brought up at length at Peru, S. A., where he married a Spanish girl, and has five children in 1874. He lives at Paita, Peru, S. A., and has lately written home to his mother at Plainville. He is making ice artificially as a business.

THEIR CHILDREN, BEING THE NINTH GENERATION.

1547.	John, born	, at Paita, S. A.
1548.	Alvin, born	, at Paita, S. A.
1549.	Paul, born	, at Paita, S. A.
	Sarah Jane, born	, at Paita, S. A.
	Levi, born	, at Paita, S. A.

MARKS.

1245.   *Ansonia, Conn.*

JANE CARTER HART, only daughter of Alvin Hart, the shoe-maker, of Southington, and his wife, Sarah, daughter of Roderic Stanley, of Plainville, Conn., born June 23d, 1842, at Southington; married February 7th, Eugene P. Marks, of Simsbury. He was a soldier in the late war, being in Company H, First Connecticut Heavy Artillery. He is living at Ansonia, Conn., in 1874, and works in the clock factory. They have three children, viz: Carlton Stanley, born July 23d, 1867; Sarah Estella, born May 12th, 1869; Lilian Eunice, born November 25th, 1871.

BLOSSOM.

1246.   *Plainville, Conn.*

PHILATHEA HART, Plainville, Conn., eldest daughter of Murray Hart, of Southington, and his wife, Lucy (Newell), born July 20th, 1808, at Southington, Conn.; married October 9th, 1836, William R. Blossom, who lived in Southington for a time, but removed to Plainville, where he kept a hotel and livery stable. He was found drowned near Belle Dock, New Haven, October 15th, 1869, aged 62 years. It is supposed he was robbed, and then thrown into the water. They had one son and three daughters. His widow is living at Plainville in 1874.

CARTER.

1248. *Southington, Conn.*

ELUZIA HART, Southington, eldest daughter of Levi Hart, of the same town, and his wife, Polly (Newell), born August 17th, 1810, at Southington; married September 2d, 1830, Henry Carter, of Southington, son of John, and his wife, Esther (Tinker), of New London. His avocation was farming, and they lived on West Street, where she died, October 2d, 1831, aged 21. He died October 17th, 1831, aged 25 years. They left one child, Eluzia Hart, born June 22d, 1831; married October 20th, 1859, Reeve L. Knight, of Philadelphia.

1249. *Southington, Conn.*

LEVI HART, Southington, Conn., only son of Levi Hart, of the same town, and his wife, Polly (Newell), born November 16th, 1815, at Southington. He was never married. He lived on the old homestead of his father in the village, on the corner of Main and West Streets. He died October 26th, 1871, aged 56 years. It is stated that he engaged his coffin some years before he died, and kept it in readiness; also a suit of clothes for his body, at an expense of $100. He also named the clergyman to attend his funeral, and directed that he be paid a certain sum for his services.

BUTLER.

1250. *Southington, Conn.*

MARY ANN HART, Southington, second daughter of Levi Hart, of the same town, and his wife, Polly (Newell), born May 21st, 1813, at Southington; married April 27th, 1838, Henry Ensign Butler, of West Hartford, son of James, of the same place. His avocation was teaching and farming. He died July 10th, 1839, in his 28th year. She was living in 1871, on the old homestead of her father, at Southington. No children.

NORTH.

1251. *New York City.*

ANGELINE HART, New York City, youngest child of Levi Hart, the inn-keeper of Southington, and his wife, Polly (Newell), born December 23d, 1822, at Southington. She married October 18th, 1847, John, son of Selah North, of Middletown, Conn. He is an engineer and machinist at Nos. 518 and 520 West Twenty-Second Street, New York. They had John E., Levi Hart, Charles Henry, and Walter Selah. This last has spent two or three years in Southington, and is called the Fat Boy. He was their only living child in 1871.

1252. *Southington, Conn.*

DOCTOR FREDERICK ALBERT HART, Southington, only child of John Albert, of the same town, and his wife, Rachel (Newell), born January 8th, 1818, at Southington. He graduated at Yale College in 1833. He married June 21st, 1842, Lucretia S. Lee, daughter of Martin, and his wife, Sally Hart (Clark), of New Britain, baptized August 7th, 1831, in Southington. He is a physician, and lives on the old homestead of his father-in-law, north of the churches, on the west side. He has traveled much in Europe. They have no children in 1874.

BUTLER.

1256. *Meriden, Conn.*

URSULA MILLICENT HART, Meriden, eldest daughter of John Hart, of Burlington, and his second wife, Millicent (Hart), daughter of Ard, born March 28th, at Burlington; married January 17th, 1855, Joel J. Butler, of Meriden, son of Lemuel, of that town, and his wife, Selina (Merriman), born November 12th, 1811, at Meriden. She was his third wife, and died January 21st, 1863, aged 35, leaving no children. Mr. Butler married first August 27th, 1835, Mary A. Norton, who died August 21st, 1837. He married second July 22d, 1840, Sarah A. Hotchkiss, who died September 11th, 1853. By her he had two children, viz: Mary Ann, and Emma S. He has occupied numerous positions of trust and responsibility in matters pertaining to the government and the town of Meriden. He is president of the Meriden Bank, and United States revenue assessor, and a man in whom the people have the most implicit confidence in every respect.

1257. *Council Bluffs, Iowa.*

AUGUSTINE HART, Council Bluffs, Iowa, eldest son of John Hart, of Burlington, Conn., and his second wife, Millicent (Hart,) daughter of Ard, born December 16th, 1829, at Burlington; married
, Martha Caroline Bird, daughter of Deacon Joshua Bird, of Bethlehem, Conn. She died at Danville, Ky., December 8th, 1865,

aged 28, and her remains were taken to Bethlehem for interment. He is a teacher at Council Bluffs, Pottawattamie County, Iowa.

THEIR CHILD, BEING THE NINTH GENERATION.

Carrie, born

1258.   *Burlington, Conn.*

ALBERT JOHN HART, Burlington, Conn., youngest son of John Hart, of the same town, and his second wife, Millicent, daughter of Ard Hart, born November 17th, 1835, at Burlington; married April 28th, 1853, Jane M. Chidsey, of Avon. He lives at Burlington, and his avocation is market gardening.

THEIR CHILDREN, BEING THE NINTH GENERATION,

1550. Mary Jane, born March 31st, 1854. She is a teacher.
1551. Jennie J., born September 10th, 1855. She is a teacher.
1552. Charles A., born April 14th, 1864.

LANGDON. JONES.

1259.

Waterloo, N. Y., Southington, Conn.

CORNELIA M. HART, Bristol, eldest daughter of Orrin Hart, of the same town, and his wife, Eunice (Ives), born September 5th, 1814, at Bristol; married April 20th, 1834, George H. Langdon, of Burlington, son of Asahel, of Southington, and his second wife, Violetta (Hitchcock), born February 28th, 1809, at Southington. He died October 19th, 1837, at Waterloo, N. Y., aged 28 years, leaving two sons, when second she married, October, 1850, Reuben J. Jones, of Southington, son of Nathaniel, and his second wife, Mabel Crampton. She died February 16th, 1869, aged 54 years. Her children by Langdon were Orrin, Asahel, who died in infancy, and George A., who died in the army, February 22d, 1862. Her child by Jones was Dwight.

1260.   *Waterloo, N. Y.*

GEORGE HART, Waterloo, N. Y., eldest son of Orrin Hart, of Bristol, Conn., and his wife, Eunice (Ives), born February 20th, 1816; married Sarah Edwards, of Otis County, N. Y. He died October 26th, 1866, aged 50 years.

THEIR CHILDREN, BEING THE NINTH GENERATION.

1553. Caroline Lodama, born April 4th, 1843; married February 16th, 1864, Richard Ridley.
1554. Harriet Francis, born July 10th, 1847.
      Iola Jane, born, February, 1849; died, October, 1849.
      Ellie Lucinda, born February 14th, 1853.

1261.   *Waterloo, N. Y.*

HENRY COWLES HART, Waterloo, N. Y., second son of Orrin Hart, of Bristol, Conn., and his wife, Eunice (Ives), born August 9th, 1818; married August 20th, 1838, Lucinda Disbrow. They had no children living in October, 1871.

FRANCIS.

1262.   *Canandaigua, N. Y.*

HARRIET IVES HART, second daughter of Orrin Hart, of Bristol, and his wife, Eunice (Ives), born August 19th, 1818, at Bristol, Conn.; married April 22d, 1838, J. B. Francis. They resided at Canandaigua, N. Y., in 1871. His native place is Wethersfield, Conn. They have no children at this writing.

1263.   *Forestville, Conn.*

ENOS IVES HART, Forestville, Conn., youngest son of Orrin Hart, of Bristol, and his first wife, Eunice (Ives), born September 14th, 1822, at Bristol, Conn.; married June 7th, 1849, before Rev. Dr. Porter, at Farmington, Helen E. Belden, daughter of Ai, of Burlington. He was a cabinet maker by trade, which he learned of his father, and went with him to Canandaigua, N. Y., but returned in 1844, and went to California in 1852, when the gold fever raged, where he spent some five years. He finally returned, and located in Forestville, Conn., where he owned a fine place, and worked in the clock factory. He was a man well read and intelligent. He died May 3d, 1871, aged 48 years.

THEIR CHILDREN, BEING THE NINTH GENERATION.

1555. Ida Jane, born March 31st, 1850, at Farmington. She is a graduate of the New Britain High School.
1556. Enos Ives, born August 19th, 1852.

PAYNE.

1264.   *Avon, Conn.*

BETSEY S. HART, eldest daughter of Ambrose Hart, of Burlington, Conn., and his wife, Chloe E. (Moses), of the same town, born September 22d, 1816, at Burlington. She married   , Andrew Payne, a wheelwright, of Avon.

1265.

SAMUEL MOSES HART, eldest son of Ambrose Hart, of Burlington, Conn., and his wife, Chloe E. (Moses), born November 3d, 1819, at Burlington; married   , Sarah A. Colvin, of Avon.

1266.

FREDERIC MOSES HART, son of Ambrose. (See No. 971), his first wife.

1267. *Foxborough, Mass.*

WILLIAM HART, Foxborough, Norfolk County, Mass., eldest son of Adna Hart, of Bristol, Conn., and his wife, Roxana Yale, born May 15th, 1822, at Bristol, Conn.; married at Bellingham, Norfolk County, Mass., November 29th, 1849, Emeline Electa Thayer, daughter of Sylvanus, and his wife, Olive (Whiting), born August 19th, 1825, at Douglas, Worcester County, Mass. His avocation is a traveling merchant, and he was residing at Foxborough, October, 1871.

THEIR CHILD, BEING THE NINTH GENERATION.
1557. William Thomas, born October 8th, 1850, at Foxborough.

1268. *Bristol, New Britain, Conn.*

JOHN GAD HART, Bristol and New Britain, third son of Adna Hart, of Bristol, Conn., and his wife, Roxana (Yale), born February 1st, 1828, at Bristol; married November 12th, 1848, Abigail Benham, of West Hartford, daughter of Elias, and his wife, Sally (Wooding), born November 23d, 1828, at Burlington. His avocation was butchering, and for a time he lived opposite the house of Mrs. Maria Manross, at Forestville, where he followed his business, but subsequently removed to New Britain, two miles west of the city, a place formerly owned by Selah Andrews. Late in the afternoon of February 24th, 1868, while riding in a snow-storm from the city to his home, in a sleigh with Mr. Frederic Frisbee, of Plainville, they were run over at the crossing one mile west of the city, by the 4 o'clock P. M. train from Waterbury to Hartford. Mr. Frisbee was killed instantly, and Mr. Hart breathed only about an hour. He was 39 years of age, and Mr. Frisbee 30. In 1873 the Treat family owned the place where Mr. Hart lived.

THEIR CHILD, BEING THE NINTH GENERATION.
1558. Helen Marion, born May 4th, 1850; married September 9th, 1867, William Henry Carey.

1497. *Unionville, Conn.*

BERNARD DWIGHT HART, Unionville, Conn., second son of Lewis Hart, of the same place, and his wife, Julia Ann, daughter of Amzi Root, of New Britain, born March 22d, 1851, at Farmington; married, February, 1871, Martha Burton, of Harwinton, of English descent.

BECKWITH.

1499. *Colebrook, Ashtabula Co., O.*

JULIA AMELIA HART, Ohio, only daughter of Solomon Winchell Hart, of Egremont, Mass., and his wife, Eleanor (Bancroft), born February 7th, 1848, at Nelson, Portage County, Ohio; married August 16th, 1868, Adelbert E. Beckwith, a farmer, of Colebrook, Ashtabula County, Ohio, where they resided in 1873.

BUCK.

1533. *Bristol, Conn.*

ELLA F. HART, Bristol, Conn., eldest daughter of Calvin Hart, of Bristol, Conn., and his wife, Ellen Maria (Goodale), daughter of Ebenezer, born March 24th, 1852, at New Britain, Conn.; married December 24th, 1870, Perlee Buck, a butcher, of Bristol.

RIDLEY.

1553. *Waterloo, N. Y.*

CAROLINE LODEMA HART, eldest daughter of George Hart, of Waterloo, N. Y., and his wife, Sarah (Edwards), born April 4th, 1843, at Waterloo, N. Y.; married February 16th, 1864, Richard Ridley. They had—1, Caroline Hart, born October 13th, 1866; 2, Levye Francis, born December 11th, 1867; 3, Daniel Kendie, born March 24th, 1868; 4, Richard, born November 14th, 1870.

1269. *Meriden, Conn.*

THOMAS HART, fourth son of Adna Hart, of Bristol, and his wife, Roxana (Yale), born May 7th, 1832, at Bristol, Conn.; married November 29th, 1855, at Wethersfield, before Dr. Tucker, Mary Elizabeth Dix, daughter of Samuel, and his wife, Elizabeth (Kilbourn), born September 23d, 1832, at Wethersfield. His avocation was making cutlery, and he lived in Meriden some twenty years, where he had a house and lands. He died at Meriden, October 30th, 1862, aged 30 years, leaving an estate of some $1,500. The widow sold it, and built on Hawkins Street, in the south part of the city of New Britain, where she and her daughter were residing in 1873.

THEIR CHILD, BEING THE NINTH GENERATION.
1559. Cora Adella, born December 26th, 1859.

1270. *Brookfield, Ohio.*

CHARLES HART, Brookfield, Trumbull County, Ohio, eldest son of Orenus Hart, of the same place, and his wife, Sabra (Lewis), born

June 29th, 1812; married at Hubbard, Ohio, March 10th, 1841, Rachel Applegate, of Hubbard, Ohio. He died August 10th, 1849, at Brookfield, aged 37.

THEIR CHILDREN, BEING THE NINTH GENERATION.

1560. Charles, born July 6th, 1840.

1561. Adaline, } born July 5th, 1844.
1562. Fanny A., }

1271. *Brookfield, Ohio.*

ROBERT SLOPER HART, Brookfield, Trumbull County, Ohio, second son of Orenus, of the same place, and his wife, Sabra (Lewis), born June 29th, 1814, at Burlington, Conn.; married March 29th, 1838, Mary Ann Christy, of Brookfield, Ohio. His avocation is farming, and was residing at Brookfield in 1871. He is the only son that survives his parents, and is quite wealthy. His wife died June 11th, 1871. Their children were all living in 1871.

THEIR CHILDREN, BEING THE NINTH GENERATION.

1563. Orenus, born July 5th, 1839; married Jan. 24th, 1860, Catharine J. Oliver.
1564. Seth, born July 12th, 1842; married September 29th, 1870, Julia Lucretia Forward.
1565. Blucher Dennis, born August 5th, 1843; married February 5th, 1871, Harriet Stramer.
1566. John, born April 20th, 1849. He is a farmer, and was living with his father in 1872.
1567. Florence E., born May 5th, 1851; married December 25th, 1871, Chauncey Forward.
1568. George, born September 12th, 1852.
1569. Emeline, born December 28th, 1853.

CHRISTY.

1273.

ELIZABETH ADALINE HART, Brookfield, Ohio, only daughter of Orenus Hart, of the same place, and his wife, Sabra (Lewis), born March 10th, 1822, at Burlington, Conn. She went to Ohio with her parents, and married at Brookfield, Trumbull County, January 1st, 1840, James Christy, of the same place. She died at Brookfield, March 28th, 1841, aged 20 years.

1274. *Brookfield, Ohio.*

HENRY CLAY HART, Brookfield, Ohio, youngest son and child of Orenus Hart, of the same place, and his wife, Sabra (Lewis), born May 1st, 1833, at Brookfield. He entered the Union Army in Com-

42

pany C, Second Regiment Ohio Cavalry, where he served two years and three months. He was captured June 29th, 1864, at Ream's Station, Va., and was taken to Andersonville, where he died of starvation, February 1st, 1865, aged 32 years.

1277. *Lordstown, Ohio.*

IRA HART, Esq., Lordstown, Trumbull County, Ohio, eldest son of Levi Hart, of Brookfield, Ohio, and his wife, Obedience (Fuller), daughter of Jesse, of Burlington, Conn., and his wife, Obedience, born   , 1817; married   , 1857, Matilda Pierce, daughter of Benjamin, of Lordstown, where he resided in 1871. He was a teacher until 1860, when he was admitted to the bar.

THEIR CHILD, BEING THE NINTH GENERATION.

Ada, born

1279. *Brookfield, Ohio.*

BLISS HART, Brookfield, Trumbull County, Ohio, second son of Levi Hart, of the same place, and his wife, Obedience (Fuller), born   , 1823, at Brookfield. He was well educated, was of a fine mind and good address, and chose the law for a profession. He went west, and died at Waupan, Fond du Lac County, Wis., 1847, aged 24.

BALDWIN.

1281. *Montville, Ohio.*

FRANCES MARIA HART, Montville, Geauga County, Ohio, third daughter of Levi Hart, of Brookfield, Trumbull County, Ohio, and his wife, Obedience (Fuller), born   ·   , 1825, at Brookfield, Ohio; married April 30th, 1848, Lucius Andrews Baldwin, M. D., who was a resident physician of Montville in 1871. Dr. Baldwin is a son of Julius Baldwin, a farmer of Montville, and his wife, Lucy Ann, eldest daughter of Daniel Andrews,* of Burlington, Conn., and his wife, Polly (Hotchkiss). They had—1, Horace N., born February 21st, 1852; 2, Frank H., born June 3d, 1857; 3, Clayton L., born September 1st, 1867.

SULLIVAN.

1282. *Bristolville, Ohio.*

CAROLINE HART, Bristolville, Trumbull County, Ohio, fourth daughter of Levi Hart, of Brookfield, Ohio, and his wife, Obedience (Fuller), of Burlington, Conn.; born   , 1827, at Brookfield; married

---

* See "*Andrews Memorial,*" No. 1129, for Daniel Andrews' family.

G. R. Sullivan, a farmer of Bristolville, Trumbull County, Ohio. They have seven children, viz: Charles, Frank, Flora, Julia, Margaret, Eva, and Carrie.

CHRISTY.

1283. *Brookfield, Ohio.*

PHEBE HART, Brookfield, Trumbull County, Ohio, fifth daughter of Levi Hart, of the same place, and his wife, Obedience (Fuller), born   , 1829, at Brookfield, Ohio; married there   , 1849, William Christy, a farmer of that town, where the family reside. Their children were—Frank, William, and Clarence.

APPLEGATE. RAND.

1284. *Fowler, Ohio.*

LUCY HART, Fowler, Trumbull County, Ohio, sixth daughter of Levi Hart, of Brookfield, Ohio, and his wife, Obedience (Fuller), born   , 1833; married   , 1858, Abraham Applegate, of Hubbard, Ohio. He died, when second she married Sylvester Rand. Their residence is at Fowler, Ohio.

WALKER.

1285. *Fredonia, Penn.*

MARY HART, Delaware, Mercer County, Penn., seventh daughter of Levi Hart, of Brookfield, Trumbull County, Ohio, and his wife, Obedience (Fuller), of Burlington, Conn., born   , 1835, at Brookfield; married in 1855, Elliot Walker, of Delaware, Mercer County, Penn. His avocation is farming, and they reside at Fredonia, Penn. They have had two children, one of whom died; the other, Eva, was born in 1857.

1286. *Brookfield, Ohio.*

ROBERT LUCIUS HART, Brookfield, Ohio, fourth son of Levi Hart, of Brookfield, and his wife, Obedience (Fuller), of Burlington, Conn., born   , 1835, at Brookfield; married at Sharon, Penn., April 11th, 1861, Eva Hough, daughter of Samuel, and his wife, Susan (Beckwith), of Sharon, Penn., born December 6th, 1844. His avocation is harness making and trimming. They reside at Orangeville, Trumbull County, Ohio, in 1874.

THEIR CHILDREN, BEING THE NINTH GENERATION.

1570. John Duella, born August 6th, 1862.
1571. Claude, born April 26th, 1866.
1572. Alphonzo, born September 12th, 1869.
    Cary, born September 11th, 1871; died August 27th, 1872.

1287.   *Montville, Ohio.*

THOMAS CORWIN HART, Montville, Geauga County, Ohio, youngest
son and child of Levi Hart, of Brookfield, Trumbull County, Ohio,
and his wife, Obedience (Fuller), of Burlington, Conn., born
, 1840, at Brookfield, Ohio; married   , Melissa
Baldwin, of Montville. He was liberally educated, of good mind and
address, is a teacher and a fine musician, and had his residence at
Montville in 1871. They have no children.

1288.   *Warren, Ohio.*

HARRIET ELIZA HART, Warren, Trumbull County, Ohio, eldest
daughter of Oliver Elsworth Hart, of Brookfield, Trumbull County,
Ohio, and his wife, Susanna White (Danforth), born May 24th, 1835,
at Brookfield, Ohio. She resides at Warren, Trumbull County, Ohio,
in 1874, and is single. She is a rising poetical writer for the press, is
a teacher, and has manifested much interest in the "*Hart Genealogy.*"
She has my hearty thanks for aid.

HURLBURT.

1289.   *Hubbard, Ohio.*

EMELINE PECK HART, Hubbard, Trumbull County, Ohio, second
daughter of Oliver Elsworth Hart, of Brookfield, Trumbull County,
Ohio, and his wife, Susanna White (Danforth), born, November, 1837,
at Brookfield, Ohio; married January 1st, 1856, Oscar F. Hurlburt, of
Hubbard, Ohio. Their children are—Horace, Ellis, Frank, and a
daughter, deceased in 1871.

BARB.

1290.   *North Bristol, Ohio.*

MARIA HART, Bristol, Trumbull County, Ohio, third daughter of
Oliver Elsworth Hart, of Brookfield, Ohio, and Susanna White (Danforth), born April 7th, 1841, at Brookfield, Ohio; married July 3d,
1870, Martin Jefferson Barb, a well-to-do farmer of North Bristol,
Ohio, and is residing there in 1874. They have one daughter, Frances,
born August 2d, 1872, at North Bristol, Ohio.

1291.   *Youngstown, Ohio.*

SIMEON HART, Brookfield, Trumbull County, Ohio, second son and
youngest child of Oliver Elsworth Hart, of Brookfield, Ohio, and his
wife, Susanna White (Danforth), born July 10th, 1844, at Brookfield.
He commenced studying law, but entered the army in the One Hun-

ired and Fifth Ohio Volunteers, where he remained until the close of
:he war. He was with Sherman in his grand march to the sea. His
1ealth became so impaired during the campaign that since his return
1e has not been able to finish his studies. He is a young man of fine
mind, good morals, and attractive personal appearance, and was living
it Youngstown, Ohio, in October, 1874.

1292. *Farmington, Conn.*

DEACON EDWARD LUCAS HART, Farmington, second son of Rev. Lucas
Hart, of East Haven and Wolcott, Conn., and his wife, Harriet (Mor-
:is), of East Haven, born December 31st, 1813, in Wolcott. He fitted
'or college under the care and direction of his Uncle Simeon, and
graduated at Yale in 1836. He married April 26th, 1837, Nancy
Champion Hooker, daughter of William G., of New Haven. Having
·esolved to make teaching his profession, he opened a classical school
n New Haven, from which he was transferred to the charge of the
icademy in Berlin, until he permanently located in Farmington as asso-
:iate principal with his uncle in the boarding school for boys. He has
i fine residence in Farmington, with a school-house on the premises,
where he still continues a school for boys, especially in the winter
season. Mr. Hart was chosen deacon of the Farmington Church in
1854. She was admitted to the church in Farmington, December,
1847.

THEIR CHILDREN, BEING THE NINTH GENERATION.

Thomas Hooker, born April 10th, 1839; died May 31st, 1839.
Mary Hooker, born January 16th, 1842; died September 5th, 1842.
Edward Chester, born February 11th, 1843; died October 15th, 1843.
.570¼. Anna Hooker, born November 17th, 1848.
.571½. William Edward, born June 24th, 1850.
572¼. Robert Morris, born November 17th, 1851.

1293. *Redstone Hill, Plainville, Conn.*

WALTER HART, Redstone Hill, eldest son of Jehiel Chester Hart, of
:he same locality, and his wife, Anna (Lowrey), born August 23d,
1818, at Burlington; married June 4th, 1845, Caroline Wilcox, of
Harwinton. She died April 3d, 1847, aged 26 years, when second he
married April 19th, 1848, Elizabeth A. Gibson, of Woodbury. He is
i tinner by trade, but he now works at farming.

CHILD BY HIS FIRST WIFE, BEING THE NINTH GENERATION.

1573. Caroline Wilcox, born March 22d, 1847; married October 26th, 1865, Henry
E. Buel, of Litchfield.

1574. James Hubert, born July 2d, 1854.
1575. Lizzie Gibson, born January 8th, 1857.
1576. Edson Walter, born January 31st, 1861.
1577. Marcia Anna, born May 11th, 1866.

WILCOX.

1294.　　　　　　　*Harwinton, Conn.*

CHARLOTTE HART, Harwinton, Conn., eldest daughter of Jehiel Chester Hart, of Redstone Hill, and his wife, Anna (Lowrey), born January 4th, 1820, at Burlington; married October 14th, 1845, Charles Wilcox, of Harwinton. He is an iron founder and farmer. They have one son and one daughter, viz: Simeon Hart, and Maria Elvira.

1295.

DANIEL LOWREY HART, second son of Jehiel Chester, of Redstone Hill, and his wife, Anna (Lowrey), born February 11th, 1825, at Burlington; married January 12th, 1847, Mary Ann Edwards, of Norwich. He died at Grenada, Central America, May 3d, 1856, aged 31 years. She died May 31st, 1855, aged 31 years.

THEIR CHILD, BEING THE NINTH GENERATION.

1578. Ann Eliza, born June 29th, 1847. She lives in Brooklyn, N. Y.

BUTLER.

1296.　　　　　　　*New Britain, Conn.*

FANNY HART, New Britain, Conn., second daughter of Jehiel Chester Hart, of Redstone Hill, and his wife, Anna (Lowrey), born April 15th, 1828, at Burlington; married November 15th, 1848, Charles Butler, of Wethersfield, son of Harry, and his wife, Lettie (Woodhouse), born August 8th, 1823. He was a jeweler by trade, and his residence was on Lafayette Street, in the city of New Britain. He died January 31st, 1869, aged 45. They had one son and three daughters, viz: Ann Elizabeth, William Henry, Mary A. Lettie, and Fanny H.

CRAMPTON.

·1297.　　　　　　　*Jacksonville, Ill.*

ADALINE FANNY HART, Farmington, only daughter (to live long) of Deacon Simeon Hart, of Farmington, and his first wife, Abigail (Andrews), daughter of Asa, of that town, and his first wife, Hannah (Burnett), born September 29th, 1825, in Farmington; married, September, 1853, Rufus Cowles Crampton, son of William, and his wife, Esther, daughter of Deacon Rufus Cowles, of Farmington and Plainville, born February 24th, 1828. In 1873 Mr. Crampton was professor of mathematics and astronomy at Jacksonville, Morgan County, Ill. He was a graduate of Yale in 1851, having entered that institution in 1847. They have one son, named Edward Hart.

1299. *Philadelphia, Penn.*

DR. CHARLES LANGDON HART, Philadelphia, eldest son of Deacon Simeon Hart, of Farmington, and his second wife, Abby (Langdon), born April 8th, 1843, in Farmington; married August 10th, 1865, Sarah Franks, of Washington, D. C., daughter of Theodore, and his wife, Jane (McCormick). He is a practicing physician in Philadelphia, and was an assistant surgeon in the late war. She died at his mother's residence in Farmington, January 12th, 1874, after an illness of one hundred and ninety-five days.

THEIR CHILDREN, BEING THE NINTH GENERATION.

1579. Mary Adeline Lewis, born September 23d, 1866, at Groving, Ill.; died January 24th, 1871, at Philadelphia.
1580. Theodore Stuart, born February 26th, 1869, at Groving, Ill.

GRIGGS.

1303. *Chicopee, Mass.*

LURA ANN HART, Chicopee Falls, Mass., eldest daughter of Joseph Hart, of New Britain, and his second wife, Lura (Buel), born April 20th, 1817, at   ; married   , David Bradford Griggs, of Chicopee Falls, Mass. She died November 20th, 1866, leaving two sons and one daughter.

HOLCOMB.

1304. *Spencer, Iowa.*

ABIA HART, Spencer, Iowa, third daughter of Joseph Hart, of New Britain, Conn., and Cabotville, Mass., and his second wife, Lura (Buel), born October 29th, 1821; married G. S. Holcomb, of Spencer, Clay County, Iowa. They have one son and two daughters.

1305. *Lowell, Mass.*

WILLIAM HORATIO HART, Lowell, Mass., third son of Joseph Hart, of New Britain, Conn., and Cabotville, Mass., and his second wife, Lura (Buel), born June 7th, 1826. He has been in the manufacturing business for some years in Nashua, and also assistant agent at Vale Mills. He is called a musician of more than ordinary ability. He is unmarried.

1306. *Chester, Washington, Mass.*

ASAHEL EDWARD HART, Washington, Mass., fourth son of Joseph Hart, of New Britain, Conn., and Cabotville, Mass., and his second wife, Lura (Buel), born June 17th, 1828; married August 4th, 1858, Samantha A. Dibble, of Washington, Mass. He is an engineer on the Boston and Albany Railroad. His post-office address was Chester, Mass., in 1873.

THEIR CHILDREN, BEING THE NINTH GENERATION.

1581. Edward Everett, born June 17th, 1859, at Washington, Mass.
Carrie Lovilla, born May 5th, 1862; died August 9th, 1863.
1582. Frank Howard, born July 7th, 1866, at Washington, Mass.
1583. David Alton, born September 14th, 1868, at Washington, Mass.

1308. *Johnsonville, Ohio.*

DAVID HARRISON HART, Johnsonville, Ohio, sixth son of Joseph Hart, of New Britain, Conn., and Cabotville, Mass., and his second wife, Lura (Buel), born July 14th, 1832, at Cabotville. He was single in 1873, and lived at Johnsonville, Trumbull County, Ohio. He is a hame maker.

ROBERTS.

1310. *New Britain, Conn.*

CAROLINE M. HART, New Britain, eldest child of Adna Thompson Hart, of the same place, and his wife, Lydia (Woodruff), born January 28th, 1822, at Avon; married December 1st, 1845, Meriels Roberts, son of John, and his wife, Lois (Deming), born August 9th, 1818. She was admitted to the Congregational Church in New Britain, August 1st, 1858. They live on Chestnut Street, New Britain. They have had—1, Emily May, born April 18th, 1855, died October 14th, 1855; 2, Grace May, born September 28th, 1856—all born at New Britain.

1311.

CATHARINE HART, second daughter of Adna Thompson Hart. (See sketch of Austin Abner Hart, her husband, No. 1002.)

1312. *New Britain, Conn.*

PHILO WOODRUFF HART, New Britain, Conn., eldest son of Adna Thompson Hart, of Avon, and his wife, Lydia (Woodruff), born December 20th, 1831, at West Avon; married February 6th, 1855, Susan Billings, of Norwich. She died August 7th, 1857, at New Britain, aged 26 years, when second he married July 26th, 1864, Sarah Avery, daughter of Daniel, of Wethersfield, and his wife, Emeline, born September 15th, 1840, at Wethersfield. He is a jeweler by trade, which he learned of Churchill & Stanley, New Britain, where he worked in 1873, but in 1874 he is engaged in the grocery business on Park Street, and lives on Chestnut Street.

THEIR CHILD, BEING THE NINTH GENERATION.

1583. Estella Mary, born July 8th, 1865, at New Britain.

1313. *New Britain, Conn.*

ANDREW WILLYS HART, New Britain, second son of Adna Thompson Hart, of Avon, and his wife, Lydia (Woodruff), born November 25th, 1834. He was a jeweler by trade, was a soldier in Company G, Sixth Regiment Connecticut Volunteers, and died in Beaufort Hospital, at South Carolina, of fever, June 20th, 1863, in the 29th year of his age.

GOODRICH.

1314. *New Britain, Conn.*

LURA ANN HART, New Britain, Conn., fourth daughter of Adna Thompson Hart, of Avon and New Britain, and his wife, Lydia (Woodruff), born August 20th, 1836, at Avon; married October 8th 1856, Henry Bulkley Goodrich, of New Britain, son of Elisha Goodrich, and his wife, Sally (Bulkley), of Rocky Hill, born November 10th, 1824, at Glastonbury, Conn. He is a tailor by trade, and lived on Chestnut Street, in the city of New Britain, in 1873. He was a soldier in the late war, where he lost an arm, and for several years past has been a collector of town, city, and school taxes. They have had two sons and one daughter, viz: 1, Frederick M., born October 29th, 1857; 2, Willis Hart, born June 20th, 1859, died July 10th, 1869; 3, Mary E., born June 1st, 1867.

BOOTH.

1314½. *New Britain, Conn.*

ANTOINETTE HART, New Britain, eldest daughter of Adna Hart, of the same place, and his wife, Lydia (Pennfield), born November 13th, 1825, at New Britain; married June 4th, 1848, George Hemsted Booth, son of Osmyn, of New Britain, and his wife, Frances (Hemsted), of Hartford, born August 5th, 1823, at New Britain. She was admitted

43

to the Congregational Church in New Britain, April 2d, 1843; dismissed, and received into the Methodist Church, January 30th, 1856. Their residence is on the Berlin road, in the south part of the city. He is a jeweler, and works at the company's factory. They have one daughter, Jennie Augusta, born July 15th, 1855.

1315.   *New Britain, Conn.*

HENRY FRANKLIN HART, New Britain, Conn., eldest son of Adna Hart, of the same place, and his wife, Lydia (Pennfield), daughter of Nathaniel, born June 1st, 1829, at New Britain; married
, Eliza Steele, of Jefferson, and his wife, Betsey (Goff), of Kensington. He was a brass worker, and lived near his father, in the city. He died of consumption, February 13th, 1861, aged 33 years.

THEIR CHILDREN, BEING THE NINTH GENERATION.

1584. William, born   , 1854, at Southington.
1585. Lilly, born   , 1860, at New Britain; died
      aged 5 years.

NOTT.

1316.   *New Britain, Conn.*

JANE MELISSE HART, New Britain, Conn., second daughter of Adna Hart, of the same place, and his wife, Lydia (Pennfield), born February 22d, 1833, at New Britain, and baptized there in 1841; married November 28th, 1854, Jonathan Nott, of Berlin, but in 1873 of New Britain. Their residence is on Prospect Street. They have no children. Mr. Nott has been a miller, and once owned the grist-mill at the south part of the town.

1319.   *New Britain, Conn.*

GEORGE ADNA HART, New Britain, Conn., fourth son of Adna Hart, of the same place, and his wife, Lydia (Pennfield), born December 21st, 1850; baptized October 23d, 1851, at New Britain; married at New Haven, by Rev. Charles H. Buck, of the Methodist Church, May 5th, 1874, Florence Isabella Hunter, of Southington, Conn., daughter of Lowry, and his first wife, Harriet Maria (Jones), of Southington, born December 9th, 1852, at Southington, Conn. He is a mechanic, and lives in the city of New Britain.

1324.   *Oswego County, N. Y.*

EDWARD BUEL HART, Scriba, N. Y., third son of Clement Hart, of Parma, N. Y., and his wife, Hancy (Walker), born October 11th, 1814,

at Scriba; married at Spencerport, N. Y.,   , 1835, Amret
Irene Nichols, born December 7th, 1817, at Ogden, Monroe County,
N. Y. He is a farmer at Hustisford, Douglas County, Wis., where
they live, and are members of the Methodist Episcopal Church.

THEIR CHILDREN, BEING THE NINTH GENERATION.

1586. Clement Lewis, born August 29th, 1836; married May 18th, 1862, Lutheria
      N. Thornton, of Wis.

Olive Hancy, born	, 1839.		
Mary Helen, born	, 1841.		
1587. John Riley, born	, 1843; married		, 1866, Sarah
Shoults.			
Melvina, born	, 1845.		
Edward, born	, 1848; died young.		
Oscar, born	, 1850; died young.		
Amanda M., born	, 1853.		
Emma Irene, born	, 1855.		
Eli E., born	, 1857.		
Elva, born	, 1861; died young.		

1326.   *Lake, Wis.*

RILEY HART, Lake, Milwaukee County, Wis., fifth son of Clement
Hart, of Parma, N. Y., and his wife, Hancy (Walker), born March
9th, 1819, at Scriba, Oswego County, N. Y.; married April 1st, 1847,
Mary T. Erig, of Germany, where she was born, March 5th, 1831.
His occupation is farming.

THEIR CHILDREN, BEING THE NINTH GENERATION.

1588. Edmund G., born January 31st, 1849, at Lake, Milwaukee County, Wis.
1589. Levi A., born May 13th, 1850, at Lake, Milwaukee County, Wis.
1590. Albert J., born May 19th, 1853, at Lake, Milwaukee County, Wis.
1591. Clara L., born October 25th, 1856, at Portland, Dodge County, Wis.
1592. Lorinda S., born May 11th, 1858, at Portland, Dodge County, Wis.
1593. Minnie C., born March 15th, 1863, at Lima, Pepin County, Wis.
1594. William R., born September 8th, 1865, at Lima, Pepin County, Wis.
1595. Dot E., born October 31st, 1870, at Wheaton, Chippewa County, Wis.

1329.   *Spring Valley, Minn.*

ABNER NOADIAH HART, Spring Valley, Fillmore County, Minn.,
eldest child of Noadiah Hart, of Avon, Conn., and Ira, N. Y., and
his wife, Clarissa (Dickinson), born October 4th, 1827, at Ira, Cayuga
County, N. Y.; married March 30th, 1865, at Ridgefield, Conn., by
Rev. S. G. Coe, Jane L. Bennett. He has taught school, but now resides at Spring Valley, Minn. They have had three children, two of
whom are living. Their names are not reported.

1330.   *Spring Valley, Minn.*

HOMER S. HART, Spring Valley, Fillmore County, Minn., third son of Noadiah Hart, of Avon, Conn., and Lysander, N. Y., and his wife, Clarissa (Dickinson), born March 25th, 1831, at Ira, Cayuga County, N. Y.; married December 18th, 1866, at Owatonna, Minn., by Rev. L. S. Griggs, H. Augusta Kelley. His avocation is printing, and he resides at Spring Valley. He has been in Minnesota some fifteen years.

1331.   *Ira, N. Y.*

ARTHUR A. HART, Ira, N. Y., fourth son of Noadiah Hart, of Avon, Conn., Ira and Lysander, N. Y., and his wife, Clarissa (Dickinson), born December 29th, 1833, at Ira, Cayuga County, N. Y.; married January 1st, 1863, at Freetown, Cortland County, N. Y., by Elder Galpin, Harriet P. Parker. He enlisted for three years in Battery B in the late war, but was taken sick and discharged before his time was out.

KEELER.

1332.   *Ridgefield, Conn.*

EMMA EUNICE HART, Ridgefield, Conn., eldest daughter of Noadiah Hart, of Avon, Conn., and Ira and Lysander, N. Y., and his wife, Clarissa (Dickinson), born January 4th, 1836, at Ira, Cayuga County, N. Y.; married September 17th, 1863, by Rev. J. B. Hall, at Ira, N. Y., Aaron C. Keeler, of Ridgefield, Conn.

1333.   *Lysander, N. Y.*

THOMPSON TRUXTON HART, fifth son of Noadiah Hart, of Avon, Conn., and Ira and Lysander, N. Y., and his wife, Clarissa (Dickinson), born March 22d, 1838, at Ira, Cayuga County, N. Y.; married there, March 27th, 1867, by Rev. R. Townsend, Susan M. Townsend. Mr. Hart was a hospital steward in the army, and was present at the surrender of General Lee.

HOWE.

1334.   *Lysander, N. Y.*

HENRIETTA MARIA HART, Lysander, N. Y., second daughter of Noadiah Hart, of Avon, Conn., and Ira and Lysander, N. Y., and his wife, Clarissa (Dickinson), born April 4th, 1840, at Ira, Cayuga County, N. Y.; married there, April 23d, 1863, by Rev. J. B. Hall, to Benjamin R. Howe, of Lysander, Onondaga County, N. Y.

1334½. *Lysander, N. Y.*

WILLIAM DICKINSON HART, youngest son and child of Noadiah Hart, of Avon, Conn., and Ira and Lysander, N. Y., and his wife, Clarissa (Dickinson), born April 16th, 1843, at Ira, Cayuga County. N. Y. He graduated at Oberlin, studied theology two years at New Haven, Conn., and in 1872 was at Andover, Mass., in his last year of study, when, if he lives, he expects to preach the gospel. He has already spent two summers as a missionary in Vermont.

MILLS.

1335. *Greenville, Penn.*

NANCY A. HART, Greenville, Penn., eldest daughter and child of Leffert Hart, of Avon, Conn., and Gerard, Erie County, Penn., and his first wife, Nancy (Woodford), born September 19th, 1827; married , 1844, James Mills. They live at Greenville, Penn.

DRENY.

1336. *Gerard, Penn.*

ANN ELIZABETH HART, Gerard, Penn., second daughter of Leffert Hart, of Avon, Conn., and Gerard, Erie County, Penn., and his first wife, Nancy (Woodford), born May 9th, 1831, at ; married , 1851, William S. Dreny, a chair maker of Gerard, Penn.

1337. *Union City, Mich.*

JOHN L. HART, Mich., third son of Leffert Hart, of Avon, Conn., and Gerard, Erie County, Penn., and his first wife, Nancy (Woodford), born March 30th, 1837, at . He is a merchant tailor at Union City, Mich.

1338. *Gerard, Penn.*

LUCIUS D. HART, Gerard, Penn., fourth son of Leffert Hart, of Avon, Conn., and Gerard, Penn., and his first wife, Nancy (Woodford), born September 7th, 1839, at ; married December 31st, 1868, Mary E. Guilford. He is a merchant tailor, and they live at Gerard, Penn.

1339. *San Gregorio, Cal.*

HENRY CLAY HART, Cal., fifth son of Leffert Hart, of Avon, Conn., and Gerard, Penn., and his first wife, Nancy (Woodford), born December 27th, 1843, at ; married December 27th, 1869, Stella Whipple. They live at San Gregorio, Cal., where he is a dealer in dry goods.

1345.   *Bridgewater, Ohio.*

EDWIN HARRISON HART, Bridgewater, Williams County, Ohio, second son of Alonzo Hart, of Avon, Conn., and Bridgewater, Ohio, and his wife, Rachel (Millyard), born July 14th, 1840, in Erie County, Penn. He enlisted into the Forty-Second Regiment Illinois Volunteers, and died in Farmer City, Mo., January 16th, 1862, aged 21 years.

1347.   *Bridgewater, Ohio.*

ALONZO FRANCISCO HART, Bridgewater, Williams County, Ohio, fourth son of Alonzo Hart, of Avon, Conn., and Bridgewater, Ohio, and his wife, Rachel (Millyard), born August 8th, 1843, in Portage County, Ohio. He enlisted into the One Hundred and Twenty-Eighth Regiment Ohio Volunteers. His usual avocation is farming. He married July 1st, 1865, Maraby Chisholm.

THEIR CHILDREN, BEING THE NINTH GENERATION.

1596. Edwin, born March 3d, 1867, in Williams County, Ohio.
1597. Dora May, born June 11th, 1870.

1350.   *Farmington, Conn.*

LENA LYDIA HART, Avon, only child of Austin Abner Hart, Avon, Conn., and his wife, Catharine (Hart), born October 27th, 1845, at Avon, Conn. She spent one year in dress-making, taught school some seven years, and died while in that vocation, at Danbury, Conn., January 2d, 1871, aged 25 years, 2 months, 5 days, and her remains were interred at Farmington. This was an untimely death of a very interesting young lady.

1342.   *Hartford, Conn.*

CAPTAIN CARLOS AUSTIN HART, Hartford, Conn., only son of Carlos Hart, of Farmington, and his wife, Lois (Rice), born December 22d, 1834, at Ira, N. Y.; married August 2d, 1858, Sarah Pratt Bird, daughter of Colonel Alpheus, of Foxboro, Mass. She died at Hartford, Conn., June 16th, 1874. He is a jeweler by trade, which he learned of Churchill & Stanley, in New Britain, Conn. He was in the late war, and was captain of Company K, Twenty-Third Regiment Mass. Vols., but resides at Hartford in 1874, and works at his trade.

THEIR CHILDREN, BEING THE NINTH GENERATION.

Arthur Carlos, born November 27th, 1859, at Foxboro, Mass.
Anna Sarah, born December 24th, 1861, at Foxboro, Mass.
Laura Mary, born November 4th, 1864, at Foxboro, Mass.
Herbert Azro, born June 15th, 1866, at New Britain, Conn.
Alice Bird, born October 5th, 1868, at Hartford, Conn.

SPAULDING.

1343.　　　*New Britain, Conn.*

ANNA LOIS HART, New Britain, Conn., only daughter of Carlos Hart, of Farmington, Conn., and his wife, Lois (Rice), of Barkhamsted, born May 14th, 1838, at Ravenna, Ohio; married September 19th, 1860, William Azro Spaulding, of Morristown, Vt. He is an inspector of the work at the Rule and Level Factory in the city of New Britain, where they reside in 1874, and are members of the South Congregational Church. They had issue, viz: 1, Carlos Alva, born June 13th, 1861; 2, Bertha Louise, born March 8th, 1867, died December 10th, 1871, at New Britain; 3, Clara Estella, born February 20th, 1870.

MILLER.

1351.　　　*West Farmington, Ohio.*

SUSAN FRANCIS HART, West Farmington, Ohio, eldest daughter of Luther Woodford Hart, of Avon, Conn., and his wife, Almira (Gillet), born December 10th, 1818, at Avon; married April 15th, 1844, by Joseph Wolcott, Esq., Samuel Miller, son of Samuel, born December 8th, 1822, at Avon. He is a blacksmith by trade, which he learned of Amos Gillet, a brother of Mrs. Miller's mother. In 1873 his post-office address was West Farmington, Trumbull County, Ohio. They have four children, viz: Dora A., Minnie E., Frank B., Anne May.

1353.　　　*Delavan, Minn.*

GEORGE HART, Delavan, Faribault County, Minn., eldest son of Luther Woodford Hart, of Avon, and his wife, Almira (Gillett), born May 9th, 1826, at 4 o'clock A. M., in Avon, Conn.; married there November 22d, 1854. His avocation is farming. She died June 25th, 1855. He second married June 17th, 1860, in Minnesota, Susan Caroline Wier, daughter of William, and his wife, Elizabeth (Latimer), born October 3d, 1830, in Robertson County, Tennessee, and was raised there. His children were all by his second wife, and were all born in Faribault County, Minn., where he has a farm of 200 acres. He went to Farmington, Trumbull County, Ohio, in 1837, but returned to Connecticut in 1847, and worked in Collinsville and Hartford until the spring of 1856, when he removed to Minnesota. His second wife is a member of the Baptist Church.

THEIR CHILDREN, BEING THE NINTH GENERATION.

1598. Dan Luther, born April 7th, 1861.
　　　Georgianna, born October 6th, 1862; died October 7th, 1862.
1599. William Wier, born November 14th, 1863.

1600. Amos Adelbert, born September 14th, 1865.
1601. Elizabeth Almira, born February 19th, 1867.
       George Franklin, born February 6th, 1870.
       Mary Vandelia, born November 24th, 1871.

1354.

Farmington, Ohio, Collinsville, Conn.

AMOS GILLET HART, Collinsville, second son of Luther Woodford Hart, and his wife, Almira (Gillet), born November 7th, 1828, at Avon, Conn. He went with his parents to Farmington, Trumbull County, Ohio, in 1837, where he resided until he was twenty-one years of age, when he returned to Collinsville, where he polished tools one year, and then went back to Ohio and engaged in the same business at Columbus; but for the last few years he has been engaged in making wrenches on contract. He married October 19th, 1851, Sarah, daughter of Samuel Miller, of Avon, and his wife, Harriet (Cornish), of Simsbury, born March 15th, 1830.

THEIR CHILDREN, BEING THE NINTH GENERATION.

1602. Rosa Maria, born September 16th, 1852, at Collinsville, Conn.
1603. Charles Amos, born June 16th, 1855, at Farmington, Ohio.
       Hattie Almira, born March 7th, 1864; died November 11th, 1864, aged 8 months.
       Franklin Samuel, born January 7th, 1867, at Collinsville, Conn.
       Mary Lillian, born December 24th, 1869, at Collinsville, Conn.

1356.   *Delavan Station, Minn.*

JOHN LUTHER HART, Delavan Station, Minn., third son of Luther Woodford Hart, of Avon, Conn., and Farmington, Trumbull County, Ohio, and his wife, Almira (Gillet), born September 23d, 1834, at Avon, Conn.; married in Minnesota, February 10th, 1866, Mary Pamelia Reynolds, daughter of Jesse, and his wife, Sarah (Hicks), born in Michigan, February 3d, 1845. His avocation is farming, and has a farm of 240 acres. In 1872 they had four children, all living in Minnesota. He was in the late war as a private in Company E, Sixteenth Regiment Connecticut Volunteers, and served nearly three years.

THEIR CHILDREN, BEING THE NINTH GENERATION.

1604. Frederick, born December 21st, 1866.
1605. Franklin Earle, born June 28th, 1868.
       Charles Amos, born July 4th, 1870.
       Child, born February 28th, 1872.

BISHOP.

1355. *Hartford, Conn.*

ESTHER ALMIRA HART, second daughter of Luther Woodford Hart, of Avon, Conn., and Farmington, Trumbull County, Ohio, and his wife, Almira (Gillet), born February 20th, 1831, at Avon; married March 21st, 1852, at Avon, before Rev. S. Hubbell, Dan F. Bishop, of Avon. He was a farmer by avocation. He died November 16th, 1862, when second she married November 30th, 1865, Charles W. Hough, son of Ephraim. He is a joiner by avocation, and they were residing at Hartford in 1872.

MILLER.

1352. *West Farmington, Ohio.*

BETSEY M. HART, third daughter of Luther Woodford Hart, of Avon, Conn., and Farmington, Trumbull County, Ohio, and his wife, Almira (Gillet), born September 20th, 1823, at Avon; married October 28th, 1841, Noah, son of Samuel Miller, born September 26th, 1819, at Avon, by Rev. J. J. Steadman, of Farmington, Trumbull County, Ohio. Their post-office address in 1873 was West Farmington, Trumbull County, Ohio. Their children are—1, Melvina E., 2, Diana M., 3, Carns A.

BISHOP.

1356½. *Hartford, Conn.*

ANN S. HART, fourth daughter of Luther Woodford Hart, of Avon, Conn., and Farmington, Ohio, and his wife, Almira (Gillet), born October 5th, 1842, at Avon, Conn.; married April 26th, 1866, Seth W. Bishop. He is a manufacturer, and resided at Hartford in 1872. Their children are—Luther B., born September 10th, 1867, at Hartford; Frederick S., born June 16th, 1869, at Hartford.

1357. *Gustavus, Ohio.*

HIRAM SAMUEL HART, Gustavus, Trumbull County, Ohio, eldest son of Joseph Chauncey Hart, of Avon, Conn., and Farmington, Trumbull County, Ohio, and his wife, Rosanna (Goff), born October 8th, 1825; married   , Fannie Hart, daughter of Joseph Hart, of Gustavus, Ohio, and his wife, Eunice (Fittz), born April 4th, 1825, at Gustavus, where they reside. He is a blacksmith by trade and avocation.

THEIR CHILDREN, BEING THE NINTH GENERATION.

1606. Lilian, born   ; married   , Thompson.
Anna, born
Clinton A., born
44

1358. *Farmington, Ohio.*

JOSEPH CHAUNCEY HART, Farmington, Ohio, second son of Joseph
Chauncey Hart, of Avon, Conn., and Farmington, Ohio, and his wife,
Rosanna (Goff), born September 22d, 1828, at Wethersfield, Conn.;
married May 20th, 1852, Margaret Lane, born April 12th, 1829, to
George D. Lane. His avocation is farming and cheese making, and he
was residing at Farmington, Trumbull County, Ohio, in 1873.

THEIR CHILDREN, BEING THE NINTH GENERATION.

1607. Algernon Dwight, born May 20th, 1853, at Collinsville, Conn.
1608. Carrie Jennette, born June 18th, 1858, at Farmington, Ohio.
Enos Burt, born July 28th, 1871, at Farmington, Ohio.

1362. *Cleveland, Ohio.*

JOHN O. HART, Warren, Trumbull County, Ohio, third son of Joseph
Chauncey Hart, of Avon, Conn., and Farmington, Ohio, and his wife,
Rosanna (Goff), born February 14th, 1836, at Farmington, Ohio; married, September, 1860, Amy Caldwell. He is connected with a wholesale grocery establishment at Cleveland, Ohio, and resides at Warren.

THEIR CHILD, BEING THE NINTH GENERATION.

1609. Minnie, born

1364. *Brookfield, Ohio.*

CLINTON O. HART, Farmington, Ohio, fourth son of Joseph Chauncey
Hart, of Avon, Conn., and Farmington, Ohio, and his wife, Rosanna
(Goff), born September 23d, 1839, at Farmington, Ohio; married
, Elizabeth Belden. He was a dry goods merchant at
Brookfield, Ohio, in 1873.

THEIR CHILDREN, BEING THE NINTH GENERATION.

1610. Harry, born
Frank, born

1365. *Farmington, Ohio.*

VELORUS M. HART, Farmington, Ohio, fifth son of Joseph Chauncey
Hart, of Avon, Conn., and Farmington, Ohio, and his wife, Rosanna
(Goff), born September 11th, 1841, at Farmington, Trumbull County,
Ohio. He was first lieutenant in Company D, Second Regiment Ohio
Cavalry. He went into service at the commencement of the late war,
and remained to its close. He married   , Roxana
Clark. His avocation since the war is farming, and he resides at
Farmington, Ohio.

THEIR CHILD, BEING THE NINTH GENERATION.

1611. Rose, born

1365½. *Farmington, Ohio.*

ADELBERT MIRON HART, Farmington, Trumbull County, Ohio, sixth son of Joseph Chauncey Hart, of Avon, Conn., and Farmington, Ohio, and his wife, Rosanna (Goff), born September 27th, 1843, at Farmington, Ohio. He entered the Union Army in the spring of 1862, was taken prisoner at the battle of Chickamauga, Tenn., and taken to Danville Prison, Va., and from thence to Libby and Andersonville—eighteen months in all. He was exchanged, and died on his passage from Charleston, S. C., to Annapolis, Md., and was buried at sea, December 11th, 1864.

FRIES.

1359. *Farmington, Ohio.*

FRANCES K. HART, Farmington, Ohio, eldest daughter of Joseph Chauncey Hart, of Avon, Conn., and Farmington, Ohio, and his wife, Rosanna (Goff), of West Springfield, Mass., born July 3d, 1830, at Farmington, Ohio; married   , Sylvester Fries, a blacksmith of Farmington, Ohio.

TAFT.

1360. *Farmington, Ohio.*

SARAH JANE HART, Farmington, Ohio, second daughter of Joseph Chauncey Hart, of Avon, Conn., and Farmington, Ohio, and his wife, Rosanna (Goff), born July 3d, 1830, at Farmington, Ohio; married November 19th, 1851, Lewis Taft, a farmer, and they resided at Farmington, Ohio, in 1873.

PIERCE.

1361. *Farmington, Ohio.*

ANN JENNETTE HART, Farmington, Ohio, third daughter of Joseph Chauncey Hart, of Avon, Conn., and Farmington, Trumbull County, Ohio, and his wife, Rosanna (Goff), born March 23d, 1834, at Farmington, Ohio; married March 20th, 1856, Sylvanus Pierce, a farmer of Farmington, Ohio.

1366. *Warren, Ohio.*

MELANCTHON COLLINS HART, Esq., Warren, Ohio, seventh son of Joseph Chauncey Hart, of Northington, (now Avon,) Conn., and Farmington, Ohio, and his wife, Rosanna (Goff), of West Springfield, Mass., born at Farmington, Ohio, December 15th, 1846; married November 20th, 1872, Mary Camp. He is a lawyer, was county clerk in 1873, and resides at Warren, Trumbull County, Ohio.

1367.　　　　　　　　　*Warren, Ohio.*

ARLINGTON M. HART, Farmington, Ohio, eighth son of Joseph Chauncey Hart, of Avon, Conn., and Farmington, Ohio, and his wife, Rosanna (Goff), of West Springfield, Mass., born June 15th, 1849, at Farmington, Trumbull County, Ohio. He was an assistant clerk of the county in 1873, and resided at Warren, Ohio.

DEMING.

1368.　　　　　　　　*Farmington, Conn.*

ELLEN MARIA HART, eldest daughter of Gideon Wareham Hart, of Avon, and his second wife, Mary S. (Parsells), born March 26th, 1846, at Avon, Conn., and was educated at Miss Porter's school in Farmington; married March 24th, 1870, Chauncey, youngest son of Samuel Deming, of Farmington, and his wife, Catharine N. (Lewis), born December 16th, 1838, at Farmington. His avocation is farming, and he inherits and resides on the old home of his father, opposite the Congregational Church, Farmington, Conn. They have one child, Samuel Hart, born January 29th, 1872.

1371.　　　　　　　　　*Chicago, Ill.*

NOAH HUMPHREY HART, Chicago, son of Joseph, of Avon, Conn., and his wife, Tryphena (Rice), born January 14th, 1831, at Avon; married December 7th, 1851, Emeline Butler, of Burlington. He is a brass founder by trade and occupation, and resides in Chicago. She died

THEIR CHILDREN, BEING THE NINTH GENERATION.

1612. Oscar, born August 19th, 1852, at Avon, Conn.
Jennette, born　　　　　　　; died　　　　　　, aged 3 months.
1613. Rosline, born　　　　　　, at Burlington, Conn.

PORTER.

1372.　　　　　　　　　*East Berlin, Conn.*

LUCY JANE HART, East Berlin, Conn., eldest daughter of Joseph Hart, of Avon, and his wife, Tryphena (Rice), born February 3d, 1833, at Avon; married June 6th, 1852, Ira A. Porter, son of David, of Unionville. He is an iron founder by trade and occupation, and was living at East Berlin, Conn., in 1872. He was born March 18th, 1828, and his mother's maiden name was Olive Hadsell. Their children are —Mary Elizabeth, born December 25th, 1854, at Southington; Jane Maria, born August 17th, 1856, at Southington; Lucy Emeline, born

May 17th, 1869, at East Berlin; Grace Hart, born July 6th, 1871, at
East Berlin.

1373.   *Plainville, Conn.*

ELI ALDERMAN HART, Plainville, Conn., second son of Joseph Hart,
the shoe-maker of West Avon, and his wife, Tryphena (Rice), born
July 29th, 1835, at Avon; married July 10th, 1855, Mary Smith, of
Farmington. She died January 1st, 1867, aged 27 years, when he
second married April 18th, 1867, Marilla Fidelia Hart, daughter of
Linas Omri Hart, and his wife, Mary Ann (Pennfield), born September
23d, 1848. He is a joiner by trade and occupation. He was a soldier
in the late war, in Company G, Sixteenth Regiment Connecticut Volunteers, and was a prisoner at Andersonville. He was at work in
Hills' hame shop at Plainville, Conn., in 1871, where they resided.

THEIR CHILDREN, BEING THE NINTH GENERATION.

1614. Kate, born February 2d, 1868, at Avon.
1615. Frederick, born April 18th, 1869, at Avon.
1616. Frank, born September 25th, 1870, at Avon.

HOLT. GLAZIER.

1374.   *Unionville, Waterbury, Conn.*

ANN MARIA HART, second-daughter of Joseph Hart, the shoe-maker
of Avon, and his wife, Tryphena (Rice), born April 26th, 1838, at
Avon; married   , Nelson C. Holt, of Unionville,
who was a soldier in the late war, in Company A, Sixteenth Regiment
Connecticut Volunteers. He died at Florence, a prisoner of the rebels,
and left one son and two daughters. She second married Frederic W.
Glazier, of Waterbury, where they were residing in 1872.

HADSELL.

1375.   *Avon, Conn.*

JULIA TRYPHENA HART, third daughter of Joseph Hart, the shoe-
maker of Avon, and his wife, Tryphena (Rice), born June 10th, 1841,
at   ; married   , Henry Hadsell,
of Avon, who was in the mercantile business in 1871. They have one
son and three daughters.

COOPER.

1376.   *Gustavus, Ohio.*

MARIA JANE HART, eldest daughter of Joseph Nelson Hart, of Gustavus, Trumbull County, Ohio, and his wife, Jane Eliza (Gibson), born

July 1st, 1838, and entered Oberlin College, but not for a full course; married in Pennsylvania, March 25th, 1856, to Jesse Osborn Cooper. His avocation is farming. She is a member of the Congregational Church. They were residing at Gustavus, Ohio, in 1872.

WENHAM.

1377. *Plainville, Mich.*

HARRIET REBECCA HART, second daughter of Joseph Nelson Hart, of Gustavus, Trumbull County, Ohio, and his wife, Jane Eliza (Gibson), born July 9th, 1846, and was at Oberlin College, but not for a full course; married December 9th, 1869, James Wenham, who was in the war four years, and was wounded. They were residing at Plainville, Allegan County, Mich., in 1872. She is a member of the Congregational Church.

EVANS.

1378. *Gustavus, Ohio.*

WELTHA ANN HART, third daughter of Joseph Nelson Hart, of Gustavus, Ohio, and his wife, Jane Eliza (Gibson), born January 7th, 1853; married January 17th, 1872, Richard M. Evans. He is a merchant.

MINER. ·

1379. *Hartland, Conn.*

POLLY BUSHNELL HART, eldest daughter of Ambrose Hart, of Brookfield, Trumbull County, Ohio, and his second wife, Lovisa (Bushnell), born December 18th, 1819, in Hartford, Trumbull County, Ohio; married December 7th, 1835, at Brookfield, Ohio, Joel Miner, of Hartland, Conn., born there June 28th, 1807. They had children, viz: Joel Ambrose, a graduate of Chicago University; George Hart, in college at Ann Arbor; Mary Lovisa, born August 3d, 1853, and is a student at Ann Arbor, Mich., where the family reside in 1874.

1380. *Cleveland, Ohio.*

DR. ALBERT GAYLORD HART, Clarksville, Penn., eldest son of Ambrose Hart, of Brookfield, Trumbull County, Ohio, and his second wife, Lovisa (Bushnell), born August 17th, 1821, at Hartford, Trumbull County, Ohio. He married June 6th, 1844, Mary Crosby, daughter of Rev. George Hornell, of Hornellsville, N. Y., and his wife, Sarah E. (Thacher), born April 4th, 1824, at Hornellsville. He was a graduate of Western Reserve College, Hudson, Ohio, in 1840. He studied medicine and graduated from the Jefferson Medical College, Philadelphia. He practiced medicine in Mercer County, Pennsylvania, until 1861, when he entered the army as surgeon in the Forty-First Regiment Ohio Volunteers, where he served three years, and resumed his practice in Cleveland, Ohio, where he has since remained. He and his wife were formerly members of the Free Presbyterian Church. Before the war this church seceded from the old Presbyterian Church, on account of slavery. They and all their children are members of the Congregational Church. He settled at Clarksville, Penn.

THEIR CHILDREN, BEING THE NINTH GENERATION.

1617. Helen Marcia, born September 28th, 1845; married   , 1864, Frank A. Brown.

1618. William Hornell, born June 25th, 1848, at Clarksville, Penn.; died there, February 28th, 1849.

1619. Hastings Hornell, born December 14th, 1851, at Brookfield, Ohio, and is a student at Oberlin in 1874.

1620. Albert Bushnell, born July 1st, 1854, at Clarksville, Penn. He is a book-keeper in 1874.

1621. Mary Jennette, born July 15th, 1858, at Clarksville, Penn.

1381. *Philadelphia, Penn.*

EDWARD HARRISON HART, second son of Ambrose Hart, of Brookfield, Trumbull County, Ohio, and his second wife, Lovisa (Bushnell), born November 23d, 1833, at Brookfield, Trumbull County, Ohio; married August 29th, 1855, Sarah E. Stiles, born July 5th, 1832, in Cleveland, Ohio, who died in 1858, at St. Louis. Mr. Hart is a traveling agent, and resides in Philadelphia in 1874.

THEIR CHILD, BEING THE NINTH GENERATION.

1622. Albert Dwight, born

BELL.

1385. *Brookfield, Ohio.*

EMELINE HART, eldest daughter of Jeduthan Hart, son of Gad, and his wife, Hannah (Webber), born   ; married   , James Bell, and had children, viz: a daughter who died an infant, Ambrose, and Francis.

RICHARDS.

1386. *Hartford, Ohio.*

MARY JANE HART, eldest daughter of Gad Hart, of Hartford, Trumbull County, Ohio, and his first wife, Lucretia (Moses), born   ; married   , Samuel N. Richards, and had

children, viz: Helen Lucretia, Irwin Hart.   She died
aged 28 years.

1387.   *Hartford, Ohio.*

FRANKLIN HART, eldest son of Gad Hart, of Hartford, Trumbull
County, Ohio, and his first wife, Lucretia (Moses), born
         ; married   , Rachel Jane Stacy.

THEIR CHILDREN, BEING THE NINTH GENERATION.

1623. Sarah Jane, born   ; married   , William
          Horton.
1624. Arthur, born

1388.   *Hartford,. Ohio.*

CALVIN C. HART, second son of Gad Hart, of Hartford, Trumbull
County, Ohio, and his first wife, Lucretia (Moses), born July 5th, 1830,
in Hartford, Ohio; married June 2d, 1853, Sarah Elizabeth Thompson.
He was first lieutenant in Company A, Forty-First Regiment Ohio
Volunteers, in the late war, and was killed at the battle of Stone
River, December 31st, 1862. She remains his widow, and lives at
Hartford, Ohio.

THEIR CHILD, BEING THE NINTH GENERATION.

1625. Frederick Calvin Clayton, born September 17th, 1860, at Hartford, Ohio.

1389.   *Hartford, Ohio.*

WARREN A. HART, third son of Gad Hart, of Hartford, Trumbull
County, Ohio, and his first wife, Lucretia (Moses), born September 23d,
1834, at Hartford, Ohio; married   , Alice Hillyer.
His residence is at Powers Corners, Trumbull County, Ohio.

THEIR CHILDREN, BEING THE NINTH GENERATION.

1626. Francis Dexter, born
1627. Calvin, born

CEDAR.

1390.   *Kinsman, Ohio.*

LUCRETIA CELESTIA HART, eldest daughter of Gad Hart, of Hartford, Trumbull County, Ohio, and his second wife, Celestia (Norton),
born November 25th, 1839; married November 12th, 1868, James
Cedar, of Kinsman, Ohio. His avocation is farming. She died May
3d, 1869.

1391.   *Cleveland, Ohio.*

ANNA MATILDA HART, second daughter of Gad Hart, of Hartford, Trumbull County, Ohio, and his second wife, Celestia (Norton), born July 22d, 1843, and graduated in the ladies' department in Oberlin College. She is a teacher in the public school at Cleveland, Ohio, where she was residing in 1873, an inmate of Dr. Albert Hornell Hart's family. Thanks to her for information.

HERRICK.

1392.   *Champaign, Ill.*

NANCY EUNICE HART, third daughter of Gad Hart, of Hartford, Trumbull County, Ohio, and his second wife, Celestia (Norton), born September 17th, 1845; married October 12th, 1870, Robert D. Herrick. They have one child, Jessie C., born January 8th, 1872, in Champaign.

1393.   *Cleveland, Ohio.*

SEYMOUR PECK HART, youngest and only child of Gad Hart, of Hartford, Trumbull County, Ohio, and his third wife, who was Widow Betsey Thompson, born June 13th, 1849; married August 10th, 1870, Ida M. Thompson, of Hartford, Ohio. He is a music dealer, and their home was in Cleveland in 1873.

THEIR CHILD, BEING THE NINTH GENERATION.

1628. Homer Harland, born November 23d, 1871, at Benton Harbor, Mich.

1396.

ELMER HART, Avon, Conn., second son of Samuel Tuller Hart, of the same town, and his second wife, Sukey (Daley), born at Avon in 1821; married by Rev. Henry Colton, September 26th, 1855, Jane G. Pike, of East Windsor, born 1831.

WOODRUFF. HART.

1398.   *Avon, Conn.*

ELVIRA HART, fifth daughter of Samuel Tuller Hart, of Avon, and his second wife, Suky (Daley), born at Avon in 1825; married May 2d, 1846, Erastus Woodruff, who died, when second she married ————, Egbert, son of Jeptha Hart, of Avon, and his wife, Sally (Thompson). Elvira died on Lovely Street, in West Avon, February 27th, 1873, aged 48 years. For Egbert see No. 1114½.

1399.　　　　　　　　*Bristol, Conn.*

NELSON HART, Bristol, Conn., third son of Samul Tuller Hart, of Avon, and his second wife, Susan (Daley), born January 6th, 1826, at Avon, Conn.; married June 27th, 1850, Elizabeth Duncan, born March 28th, 1826, in Scotland. His avocation is wood turning, and they resided on West Main Street, Bristol, in 1871. They had no children at that date.

1400.　　　　　　　　*Bristol, Conn.*

LEONARD HART, Bristol, Conn., youngest son of Samuel Tuller Hart, of Avon, Conn., and his second wife, Susanna (Daley), born May 14th, 1829, at Avon; married April 7th, 1849, Harriet, daughter of Roman Spencer, of Russell, Mass., and his wife, Electa (Hughes). He is a mechanic, and they lived in the same house with his brother, Nelson, in 1871.

THEIR CHILDREN, BEING THE NINTH GENERATION.

1629. Inez Josephine, born April 30th, 1850.
1630. Wallace Leonard, born September 6th, 1852, at Bakersville, Conn.

HASKEL.

1401.　　　　　　　　*Springfield, Mass.*

JANE HART, Springfield, Mass., youngest daughter of Samuel Tuller Hart, of Avon, Conn., and his second wife, Susanna (Daley), born at Avon in 1833; married　　　　　　　, William Haskell, of Blanford, Mass. He is captain of the guard at the United States Armory in Springfield, Mass., and they had one son in 1871.

1402.　　　　　　　　*Avon, Conn.*

LINAS OMRI HART, Avon, eldest son of Zinas Hart, of the same place, and his wife, Rhoda (Griswold), born March 20th, 1815, at Avon; married October 30th, 1839, Mary Ann Pennfield, daughter of Phineas, of New Britain, and his wife, Ruth Judd (Hart), born October 4th, 1813, at New Britain. He was living on the old homestead of his father, near the flag station in West Avon, in 1871. His wife became a member of West Avon Church, May 7th, 1843. She died at Avon, December 6th, 1853, aged 40 years. He second married August 7th, 1855, Frances R. Beckwith, of New London. She died, when third he married　　　　　　　, Lydia S. Booth, of Simsbury, Rev. Lewis Hyde officiating.

THEIR CHILDREN, BEING THE NINTH GENERATION.

1631. Russel Dennis, born January 18th, 1846; baptized June 28th, 1846.
　　　Child, born May 21st, 1847; died May 24th, 1847, aged 3 days.

1632. Marilla Fidelia, born September 23d, 1848; married April 18th, 1867, Eli
   Alderman Hart.
   Lucy Maria, born July 26th, 1849; baptized June 15th, 1851.
1633. Newell Edward, born November 10th, 1850; married September 14th, 1870,
   Jane E. Bingham.

1404. *New Britain, Conn.*

EPHRAIM AVA HART, New Britain, third son of Zina Hart, of Avon,
and his wife, Rhoda (Griswold), born February 12th, 1825, at Avon;
married October 2d, 1853, Sarah Elizabeth, daughter of Silas Spencer,
and his wife, Mary (Root), of New Britain, born January 20th, 1837.
He was a farmer, and lived in New Britain, on the Farmington road
over the mountain, and near the former home of his grandmother,
Rhoda. His fingers were cramped and disfigured by rheumatism.
After a few years he returned to Avon, where he died May 11th, 1868,
aged 43 years, when second she married George Goodnow, of New
Britain.

THEIR CHILD, BEING THE NINTH GENERATION.
1634. Cornelia Elizabeth, born February 7th, 1859, at New Britain.

HALE. .

1406. *New Haven, Conn.*

DOLLY HART, East Farms, Farmington, daughter of Adna Hart, of
Avon and Farmington, and his wife, Lucy (Woodruff), born November
5th, 1817, at Farmington; married   , 1841, George Martin
Hale, of Burlington. He is a jeweler, and resided at New Haven in
1871, and had one daughter.

STODDARD.

1408. *East Farms, Farmington, Conn.*

CLARISSA HART, East Farms, Farmington, second daughter of Adna
Hart, of Avon and Farmington, and his wife, Lucy (Woodruff), born
May 29th, 1825, at Farmington; married in 1846, David Stoddard, a
wheelwright, of Avon and West Hartford. They reside in West
Hartford, and have one son and two daughters.

FRANCIS.

1409. *Newington, Conn.*

LUCY HART, East Farms, Farmington, third daughter of Adna Hart,
of Avon and Farmington, and his wife, Lucy (Woodruff), born March
28th, 1827, at Farmington; married April 26th, 1848, Blinn Francis,

a mover of buildings, of Newington. He lived at West Hartford in 1871, and they have four sons and five daughters.

PECK.

1410.   *Farmington, Conn.*

MARY HART, fourth daughter of Adna Hart, of Avon and Farmington, and his wife, Lucy (Woodruff), born April 25th, 1829, at Farmington; married   , Newton Peck, son of Asahel, of Scott's Swamp, Farmington, a farmer by occupation. They had two sons in 1871.

KEELER.

1412.   *Chautauqua, N. Y.*

CORNELIA E. HART, Chautauqua, N. Y., daughter of Dennis Hart, of Avon, Conn., and Chautauqua, N. Y., and his wife, Elvira (Dutton), of Farmington, born April 6th, 1829, at Chautauqua; married there by Rev. William T. Reynolds, November 18th, 1852, William H. Keeler.

SPERRY.

1413.   *Chautauqua, N. Y.*

MARY E. HART, Chautauqua, N. Y., second daughter of Dennis, of the same place, and his wife, Elvira (Dutton), born September 18th, 1830, at Chautauqua; married there by Rev. William T. Reynolds, May 4th,   , Enoch Sperry.

1414.   *Chautauqua, N. Y.*

JOSEPH DUTTON HART, Chautauqua, N. Y., eldest son of Dennis Hart, of the same place, and his wife, Elvira, daughter of Joseph Dutton, born August 1st, 1832, at Chautauqua; married at Lawrence, McHenry County, Ill., by Rev. Mr. Brown, March 28th, 1859, Mary M. Dutton. His avocation is farming. No children reported.

MORSE.

1416.   *Chautauqua, N. Y.*

ELIZABETH J. HART, Chautauqua, N. Y., third daughter of Dennis Hart, of the same place, and his wife, Elvira (Dutton), born January 9th, 1838, at Chautauqua; married there by Rev. Henry M. Hazeltine, October 10th, 1861, Madison J. Morse.

SPENCER.

1419. *Chautauqua, N. Y.*

ABBIE M. HART, Chautauqua, N. Y., youngest daughter of Dennis Hart, and his wife, Elvira (Dutton), born November 5th, 1844, at Chautauqua; married at Sherman, Chautauqua County, N. Y., October 22d, 1868, John W. Spencer, before Rev. J. F. Severance, pastor.

1420. *Sherman, N. Y.*

EDMUND CRAMPTON HART, Sherman, Chautauqua County, N. Y., eldest son of Ava Hart, of Avon, and his wife, Julia (Crampton), born July 13th, 1829, at Sherman; married October 16th, 1856, at Farmington, Conn., by Rev. Noah Porter, D. D., Harriet J. Alford, of Harwinton, born November 11th, 1831. His avocation is farming.

THEIR CHILDREN, BEING THE NINTH GENERATION.

1635. Ellen Maria, born June 18th, 1858, at Sherman, N. Y.
1636. Charles Edward, born March 29th, 1860; died September 9th, 1860.
1637. Frederic Alfred, born May 15th, 1862, at Sherman, N. Y.
1638. Henry Stephen, born May 16th, 1866, at Sherman, N. Y.

1422. *Sherman, N. Y.*

WILLIAM HENRY HART, second son of Ava Hart, of Avon, Conn., and Chautauqua, N. Y., and his wife, Julia (Crampton), born January 20th, 1836; married October 11th, 1870, at Sherman, N. Y., Eugenia M. Sperry, of that place, where she was born, April 13th, 1850. He is in the mercantile business there.

THEIR CHILD, BEING THE NINTH GENERATION.

1639. Lilian, born December 18th, 1871, at Sherman, N. Y.

1423. *Sherman, N. Y.*

JULIUS BREWSTER HART, Sherman, Chautauqua County, N. Y., third son of Ava Hart, of Avon, Conn., and subsequently of Chautauqua, N. Y., and his wife, Julia (Crampton), born May 20th, 1839; married October 22d, 1868, at Sherman, N. Y., Julia A. Sperry, of that place, where she was born, June 2d, 1847.

THEIR CHILD, BEING THE NINTH GENERATION.

1640. Minnie May, born September 15th, 1872, at Sherman, N. Y.

1424. *New Albany, Ind.*

SAMUEL H. HART, eldest son of Rev. Edson Hart, of Louisville, Ky., and his first wife, Helen (Priestley), born August 23d, 1822, at

; married, May, 1850, Rachel Ellen Emery, at New Albany, Ind. He died, November, 1867, aged 45 years, and left a wife and five children.

1641. Harry E., born July 7th, 1851; married   , Mary Louisa Klein.
1642. Georgiana, born September 28th, 1853.
1643. Fanny, born February 15th, 1856.
1644. Helen, born August 8th, 1858.
.645. William, born October 19th, 1861.

1425.   *Paducah, Ky.*

JOHN PRIESTLY HART, second son of Rev. Edson Hart, of Louisville, Ky., and his first wife, Helen (Priestly), born August 15th, 1824, at   ; married   . He s a merchant at Paducah, McCracken County, Ky. He has received ι college education.

James E. Cable, born January 8th, 1852; died August 2d, 1852.
Helen Priestly, born July 2d, 1853; died April 5th, 1861.
646. Hannah Cable, born April 21st, 1856.
647. Ann Mariah, born October 11th, 1858.
648. John Priestly, born December 15th, 1860.
Robert E. Lee,.born December 24th, 1862; died May 1st, 1864.
George O., born April 21st, 1865; died July 21st, 1865.
Maggie Turner, born October 15th, 1869.

1426.   *Paducah, Ky.*

CAPT. GEORGE OBED HART, Paducah, McCracken County, Ky., fifth on of Rev. Edson Hart, of Louisville, Ky., and his first wife, Helen Priestly), born August 7th, 1834, at Germany, Penn.; married March 3th, 1855, Addie H. Slent, of Lexington, Ky., born December 3d, 834, in New York City. They were residing at Paducah, Ky., in 871. During the late war he was captain of a steam-boat running on he Ohio and Mississippi Rivers, from Louisville to Memphis and New)rleans, as a steamer was able to get through for the southern army.

Charles Edson, born October 23d, 1858, at New Albany, Ind.; died November 18th, 1858.
649. George Bruce, born May 17th, 1860, at New Albany, Ind.
650. Addie Helen, born March 26th, 1867, at New Albany, Ind.
651. Rosie Annie, born June 9th, 1870, at Paducah, Ky.

1427. *Paducah, Ky.*

JOSEPH B. HART, Paducah, Ky., fourth son of Rev. Edson Hart, of Avon, Conn., Indiana, and Kentucky, and his first wife, Helen (Priestly), born August 4th, 1829, at   ; married   , Juliet   , born January 3d, 1834, at   . He is engaged in the mercantile business.

THEIR CHILDREN, BEING THE TENTH GENERATION.

1652. Thomas Julien, born August 23d, 1855.
1653. Sarah Helen, born March 18th, 1859.
1654. Mary Virginia, born March 24th, 1860.
1655. Joseph Edson, born April 23d, 1862.
1656. Ila Moss, born December 15th, 1869.

1454. *Sherman, N. Y.*

EDSON TRUMAN HART, eldest son of Norman Hart, of Sherman, Tompkins County, N. Y., and his first wife, Adaline Anna (Hart), born December 14th, 1827, at Sherman, N. Y. He married March 12th, 1851, at Chautauqua, by Rev. Mr. Chapin, Eliza Ann Bush. His avocation is farming.

1455. *Chautauqua, N. Y.*

GEORGE ELNATHAN HART, Chautauqua, N. Y., second son of Norman Hart, of Sherman, N. Y., and his first wife, Adaline Anna (Hart), born April 27th, 1833, at Sherman, N. Y.; married February 2d, 1859, at Cambridge, Crawford County, Penn., by Rev. Mr. Hampson, Eliza Ann Webster, of Cambridge. His avocation is farming.

PATRIDGE.

1456. *Ashville, N. Y.*

LUCELIA MELINTHA HART, second daughter of Norman Hart, of Sherman, N. Y., and his first wife, Adaline Anna (Hart), born April 23d, 1835, at Sherman, Chautauqua County, N. Y.; married at Sherman, by Rev. Mr. Husted, March 14th, 1861, Myron Patridge, of Ashville, N. Y.

WEBSTER.

1457. *Cambridge, Penn.*

MINERVA ANGELINE HART, third daughter of Norman Hart, of Sherman, N. Y., and his first wife, Adaline Anna (Hart), born October 7th, 1836, at Sherman, Chautauqua County, N. Y.; married November 30th, 1864, at Sherman, by Rev. H. M. Hazeltine, Joseph L. Webster, of Cambridge, Crawford County, Penn.

ROOT.

1459. *Cambridge, Penn.*

NANCY ADALINE HART, Cambridge, Penn., fifth daughter of Norman Hart, of Sherman, N. Y., and his first wife, Adaline Anna (Hart), born March 9th, 1846, at Sherman, Chautauqua County, N. Y.; married there January 1st, 1868, by Rev. A. S. Merrifield, to Timothy T. Root, of Cambridge, Crawford County, Penn., son of Sylvester, and his wife, Mercy (Thomas), born February 25th, 1831, at Cambridge Village, Venango Township, Crawford County, Penn., where they lived in 1871. They had issue, viz: Clarence C., born June 3d, 1869.

1473. *Farmington, Conn.*

ALBERT WILLYS HART, Farmington, eldest son of Sidney Hart, of Farmington, and his wife, Lydia (Griswold), born November 5th, 1842, at Farmington; married January 20th, 1867, Katie Lewis, daughter of Henry, of Farmington, and his wife, Nancy (Woodruff). He is a wheelwright by trade, which he learned of his father, and he worked and lived with him in 1871.

THEIR CHILD, BEING THE TENTH GENERATION.
1657. Mary Jane, born June 8th, 1871, at Farmington.

HOSKINS.

1472. *Bloomfield, Conn.*

FRANCES HART, Bloomfield, Conn., eldest daughter of Sidney Hart, of Farmington, and his wife, Lydia W. (Griswold), born August 19th, 1841, at Farmington; married January 26th, 1870, Horton Hoskins, of Bloomfield, Conn. He is a joiner by trade and occupation. They have one son.

BOND.

1474. *Unionville, Conn.*

SARAH JANE HART, Farmington, second daughter of Sidney Hart, of the same town, and his wife, Lydia W. (Griswold), born November 7th, 1846, at Farmington; married January 4th, 1870, James Bond, a wood turner, of England, and works at Unionville. They live with her father, and in 1871 they had no children.

1477. *New Britain, Conn.*

GEORGE LEWIS HART, New Britain, second son of Deacon Chauncey Hart, of Farmington and Unionville, and his wife, Sarah Jane (Hooper), born December 21st, 1834, at Farmington; married, April, 1857, Mary Ann King, daughter of Orrin, of New Hartford, and his wife, Philena (Root), born March 12th, 1836, at New Hartford. He worked at the cutlery business in New Britain, Conn., in 1871. He lived for a time at Unionville, Conn.

THEIR CHILDREN, BEING THE TENTH GENERATION.

1658. Charles Edward, born March 7th, 1858, at Unionville.
Sarah, born May 5th, 1860; died in 1864, aged 4 years.
1659. John Chauncey, born August 20th, 1862, at Southington.

1480.

ALBERT JAMES HART, Unionville and New Britain, Conn., third son of Deacon Chauncey Hart, of Farmington and Unionville, and his wife, Sarah Jane (Hooper), born August 3d, 1839, at Farmington; married July 19th, 1865, Ellen Barnard, daughter of John, and his wife, Mary (Wright), of Weatogue, Simsbury, born July 19th, 1847. He is a blacksmith by trade, and is a superior workman. He is living in New Britain in 1874, and is a contractor at Humason & Beckley's. He was a veteran in the late war, and served four years. He was a drum-major.

THEIR CHILDREN, BEING THE TENTH GENERATION.

Hubert, born December 22d, 1867, at Unionville; died young.
Albert Wilcox, born January 29th, 1869, at West Haven; died at New Britain, aged 6 months.
Everet Wilcox, born June 10th, 1870, at New Britain, Conn., and died there.
Child, born   ; died young.

1481.   *Unionville, Conn.*

SANFORD HILL HART, Unionville, fourth son of Deacon Chauncey Hart, of Farmington and Unionville, Conn., and his wife, Sarah Jane (Hooper), born February 28th, 1841, at Farmington; married February 28th, 1860, Jane Wright, of Burlington. He is a blacksmith, and worked with his father at Unionville in 1871.

THEIR CHILDREN, BEING THE TENTH GENERATION.

Clinton, born July 16th, 1868, at Unionville.
Hudson, born May 1st, 1871, at Unionville.

1482.

HUBERT CHAUNCEY HART, Unionville, fifth son of Deacon Chauncey Hart, of Unionville, and his wife, Sarah Jane (Hooper), born April 14th, 1843, at Farmington; married August 19th, 1863, Eva Moses,

46

laughter of Orrin, of Burlington. He is a skilled mechanic and an
inventor, has obtained six patents, and resides at Unionville, Conn.

THEIR CHILDREN, BEING THE TENTH GENERATION.

1660. Arthur Hubert, born August 12th, 1863, at Unionville.
1661. Ernest Moses, born October 12th, 1868, at Unionville.

1483.   *Unionville, Conn.*

PHILIP ZENAS HART, Unionville, sixth son of Deacon Chauncey Hart,
of the same place, and his wife, Sarah Jane (Hooper), born March
4th, 1845, at Farmington; married October 29th, 1864, Margaret
Felshon, of Farmington, born in Ireland, November 29th, 1847. He
has been a circus performer, and can lift 1,800 pounds dead weight.
He was wounded in the late war, and draws a small pension. His wife
was divorced from him May 3d, 1869, when he second married
                           , of Plymouth, and Margaret, when
divorced, married Charles Andrews, son of Royal, of Farmington.

THEIR CHILD, BEING THE TENTH GENERATION.

662. Augustus Jones, born July 19th, 1866, at Farmington. He is living with his
mother at New Britain, Conn., in 1874.

McDONALD.

1484.   *New Brunswick, Unionville.*

EMMA ELIZABETH HART, Unionville, Conn., youngest daughter of
Chauncey Hart, of Farmington and Unionville, and his wife, Sarah
Jane (Hooper), born March 21st, 1850, at Unionvile; married October
5th, 1870, James Alexander McDonald, of Woodstock, N. B. He is
a photographer, and lives at Unionville. They have one son, who was
born there. In 1871 they boarded with her father, some eighty rods
south of the Unionville Depot.

1490.   *Farmington, Conn.*

HENRY CRANE HART, Farmington, eldest son of Richard Hart, of
New Britain, and his first wife, Catharine (Gladden), born October 3d,
1840, at Farmington; married October 23d, 1860, Eunice Elizabeth,
daughter of Linas Gilbert, and his second wife, Abigail, who was the
widow of Jason Porter, born July 19th, 1844. He was in the late
war. He is a house painter by occupation, and lived at Farmington in
1873.

THEIR CHILDREN, BEING THE TENTH GENERATION.

362. Ella Maria, born July 29th, 1865, at White Oak, Farmington.
363. Wilbur Henry, born July 18th, 1867, at White Oak, Farmington.
364. Lewis, born September 3d, 1869, in Farmington.

1491.   *New Britain, Conn.*

FRANK HART, New Britain, Conn., eldest son of Richard Hart, of Farmington and New Britain, and his second wife, Mary (Jones), born August 29th, 1851, at New Britain. He is a rule maker by occupation, and works at the factory of the Stanley Rule and Level Company. His residence is on West Main Street, and his lot is bounded on the . line of Plainville, being the last dwelling in the town of New Britain. He married August 17th, 1874, at Patterson, N. J., before Rev. Zelotes Grenell, Mary Jane, daughter of Andrew Rancier, and his wife, Eliza (Perrin), born March 14th, 1849, at Patterson, N. J.

CHILDS.

1493.   *New Britain, Conn.*

CAROLINE HART, New Britain, second daughter of Richard Hart, of the same town and county, and his second wife, Mary (Jones), daughter of John R. Jones, and his first wife, Emeline (Franklin), born September 3d, 1856, at New Britain; married July 18th, 1874, at Farmington, before Rev. Mr. Smith, George Arthur Childs, son of Charles Childs, deceased, and his wife, Frances Irene (Childs), formerly of New Haven, but now of New Britain; born December 12th, 1853, at Derby, Conn. He is a house painter.

CLARK. DUFF.

1494.   *Unionville, Plainville, Conn.*

ANNA ELIZA HART, Unionville, eldest daughter of Lewis Hart, of the same place, and his wife, Julia Ann (Root), of New Britain, born December 2d, 1842, at Farmington; married, February, 1860, Thomas F. Clark, of Plainville. They were divorced in 1863, when second she married, May, 1870, George Duff, of Unionville. She had one daughter by her first husband.

BARNES.

1495.

JULIA ANN HART, Unionville, Conn., third daughter of Lewis Hart, of the same place, and his wife, Julia Ann (Root), of New Britain, born April 12th, 1845, at Farmington; married December 25th, 1865, George G. Barnes, of Unionville, a joiner by avocation. They were residing at Unionville in 1871, and had one daughter.

1497. *Unionville, Conn.*

BERNARD DWIGHT HART, second son of Lewis Hart, of Unionville, Conn., and his wife, Julia Ann (Root), of New Britain, born March 22d, 1851, at Unionville. He married, February, 1871, Martha Burton, of Harwinton. She is of English descent.

BECKWITH.

1499. *Colebrook, Ohio.*

JULIA AMELIA HART, only child of Solomon Winchell Hart, of Colebrook, Ashtabula County, Ohio, and his wife, Eleanor (Bancroft), born February 7th, 1848, at Nelson, Portage County, Ohio; married August 16th, 1868, Adelbert Beckwith, a farmer, of Colebrook, Ohio.

BUCK.

1533. *Bristol, Conn.*

ELLA F. HART, Bristol, Conn., eldest daughter of Calvin Hart, of Burlington, Conn., and his wife, Ellen Maria (Goodale), of Rocky Hill, Conn., born March 24th, 1852, at Burlington, Conn.; married December 24th, 1870, Perlee Buck, a butcher, of Bristol.

RIDLEY.

1553. *Waterloo, N. Y.*

CAROLINE LODEMA HART, eldest daughter of George Hart, of Waterloo, N. Y., and his wife, Sarah (Edwards), born April 4th, 1843, at Waterloo, N. Y., and married February 16th, 1864, Richard Ridley. They had issue, viz: Caroline Hart, Levey Francis, Daniel Kendie, and Richard, born November 14th, 1870.

CARY.

1558. *Lawrence, Kan.*

HELEN MARION HART, only child of John Gad Hart, of Bristol and New Britain, and his wife, Abigail (Benham), born May 4th, 1850, at Burlington, Conn.; married September 9th, 1867, at New Britain, before Rev. Mr. Walker, the Baptist minister, William Henry Carey, a butcher, of Stockbridge, Mass. In 1870 they removed to Lawrence, Kan., where he herds stock for market. They had one son, Henry William, born at New Britain, in June, about 1870; died of fever, July 31st, 1874, aged 4 years.

1563. *Brookfield, Ohio.*

ORENUS HART, eldest son of Robert Sloper Hart, of Brookfield, Ohio, and his wife, Mary Ann (Christy), born July 5th, 1839, at Brookfield; married January 24th, 1860, Catharine J. Oliver, of Hubbard, Trumbull County, Ohio. They were residing at Brookfield in 1871.

THEIR CHILDREN, BEING THE TENTH GENERATION.

1665. Horace Burke, } born January 29th, 1861.
1666. Dora, }
1667. Lulu, born March 21st, 1864.

1564. *Brookfield, Ohio.*

SETH HART, Brookfield, Trumbull County, Ohio, second son of Robert Sloper Hart, of the same town, and his wife, Mary Ann (Christy), born July 12th, 1842, at Brookfield; married September 29th, 1870, Julia Lucretia Forward, of the same place. His avocation is farming. He was a soldier under Sherman in the late war, and went with him through the campaign.

1565. *Atwater, Ohio.*

BLUCHER DENNIS HART, Atwater, Portage County, Ohio, third son of Robert Sloper Hart, of Brookfield, Ohio, and his wife, Mary Ann (Christy), born August 5th, 1843, at Brookfield, Ohio; married February 5th, 1871, Harriet Stramer, of Atwater, where they were residing in 1871. His avocation is farming.

FORWARD.

1567. *Brookfield, Ohio.*

FLORENCE E. HART, eldest daughter of Robert Sloper Hart, of Brookfield, Trumbull County, Ohio, and his wife, Mary Ann (Christy), born May 5th, 1851, at Brookfield; married December 25th, 1871, Chauncey Forward.

BUEL.

1573. *Plainville, Conn.*

CAROLINE WILCOX HART, eldest daughter of Walter Hart, of Redstone Hill, and his first wife, Caroline (Wilcox), born March 22d, 1847, at Plainville; married October 26th, 1865, Henry E. Buel, of Litchfield. He lived in Plainville in 1871, and worked at lamps in Forestville. They have one son and one daughter.

BROWN. WRIGHT.

1617.

HELEN MARCIA HART, eldest daughter of Dr. Albert Gaylord Hart, of Cleveland, Ohio, and his wife, Mary C. (Hornell), born September 28th, 1845, at Clarksville, Mercer County, Penn.; married in 1864, Frank A. Brown, of Cleveland, who died in 1867, when she second married, April, 1872, Rev. Walter E. C. Wright, pastor of Plymouth Church, Philadelphia. Her address is 1410 North Nineteenth Street, Philadelphia.

1619.   *Cleveland, Ohio.*

HASTINGS HORNELL HART, Cleveland, Ohio, second son of Dr. Albert Gaylord Hart, of Clarksville, Penn., and his wife, Mary C. (Hornell), born December 14th, 1851, at Brookfield, Ohio. He entered Oberlin College in the fall of 1871, and was a sophomore in 1873. He is a junior in 1874. He has manifested much interest in the publication of this Memorial by forwarding a history of his immediate ancestors.

1620.   *Cleveland, Ohio.*

ALBERT BUSHNELL HART, third son of Dr. Albert Gaylord Hart, of Clarksville, Penn., and Cleveland, Ohio, and his wife, Mary C. (Hornell), born July 1st, 1854, at Clarksville. He is a graduate of the Cleveland High School, and was a book-keeper in 1873.

JENNINGS. BARROWS.

1435.   *Hazel Green, Iowa.*

ELLEN ELIZA HART, eldest child of Hiram Hart, of Avon, Conn., and his first wife, Mary (Robins), born June 5th, 1829, at Sandisfield, Mass.; married   , Philander Jennings, son of Alfred. She second married   , Levi Barrows. They are living at Hazel Green, Delaware County, Iowa.

PRENTICE.

1436.   *Newark Valley, N. Y.*

FRANCES ADALADE HART, third daughter of Hiram Hart, of Avon, and his second wife, Verona (Norton), daughter of Amzi, born December 27th, 1842, at Richford, Tioga County, N. Y.; married , Irving B. Prentice, of Newark Valley, N. Y.

1437.   *West Avon, Conn.*

TRUMAN WOODFORD HART, West Avon, Conn., only son of Harvey of the same place, and his wife, Harriet (Woodford), born September 9th, 1834, at Avon; married May 30th, 1856, Mary Jane Woodford, daughter of Asahel, of Avon, and his wife, Flora (Humphrey), born March 25th, 1837, at Orwell, Bradford County, Penn. He is a farmer and mechanic, and was living with his father in 1871.

THEIR CHILDREN, BEING THE NINTH GENERATION.

1668. Gertrude Louise, born October 2d, 1862, at Collinsville, Conn.
1669. Hattie Woodford, born February 5th, 1868, at Avon, Conn.

1586.   *Madison, Wis.*

DOCTOR CLEMENT LEWIS HART, Madison, Wis., eldest son of Edward Buel Hart, of Scriba, Oswego County, N. Y., and his wife, Amret Irene (Nichols), born August 29th, 1836; married May 18th, 1862, Lutheria N. Thornton, daughter of Hon. O. W. Thornton, of Dane, Marshall County, Wis. She died of consumption, January 24th, 1869, when he married second, May 18th, 1871, Ella R. Talford, of Madison, Wis., born May 10th, 1850, at Woodstock, New Brunswick. He is a practicing physician at Madison in 1874, and stands high in his profession.

CHILD BY HIS FIRST WIFE, BEING THE TENTH GENERATION.

1670. Edith Lutheria, born May 31st, 1868, at Columbus, Wis.

CHILD BY HIS SECOND WIFE, BEING THE TENTH GENERATION.

1671. Effie Irene, born March 27th, 1872, at Madison, Wis.

1587.   *Maugaska, Minn.*

JOHN RILEY HART, Maugaska, Martin County, Minn., second son of Edward Buel Hart, of Spencerport, N. Y., and his wife, Amret I. (Nichols), born October 15th, 1843, at Franklin, Wis.; married December 3d, 1865, at Hustisford, Dodge County, Wis., Sarah A. Shoults, born August 24th, 1848, at New Portland, Me. They are living at Maugaska, Martin County, Minn., in 1874.

THEIR CHILDREN, BEING THE TENTH GENERATION.

1672. Eliza Day, born October 1st, 1866, at Pepin County, Wis.
1673. Elba Buel, born August 17th, 1867, at Lima, Pepin County, Wis.
1674. Delmont Alton, born March 1st, 1869, at Hustisford, Dodge County, Wis.
1675. Cora Ellen, born April 24th, 1870, at Hustisford, Dodge County, Wis.
1676. Merton Lata, born September 16th, 1872, at Maugaska, Martin County, Minn.
1677. Clement Vernon, born May 7th, 1874, at Maugaska, Martin County, Minn.

BRANCH OF THOMAS HART.

1678.

THOMAS HART, Farmington, third son and youngest child of Deacon tephen Hart, of Cambridge, Mass., and Hartford and Farmington, onn., and his wife,   , born 1644, at ·
; married   , Ruth, daughter of Anthony [awkins,* of Farmington, born October 24th, 1649, at Windsor, onn. Mr. Hart inherited a portion of his father's homestead, oppo- te the meeting-house. He was made a freeman by the General Court, t their May session, 1664. He is on the list of freemen of Farming- ן, October 12th, 1669; confirmed ensign of Farmington train-band y the General Court, May session, 1678, lieutenant in 1693, and was eputy to the General Court the same year, was captain, May, 1695, nd was appointed on a committee "To return the Thanks of the Court ℩ the Rev. Mr. Samuel Hooker for his great *paynes* in preaching the lection Sermon, and that they desire him to grant a copy thereof to e disposed and improved by the General Court for the people's good." [e was also deputy from Farmington in 1690, 1692, 1694, 1695, 1696, 697, 1698, 1699, 1700, 1702, 1704, 1705, and 1706, and was chosen peaker of the General Court in 1700, 1704, 1705, and 1706. At the ʲeneral Court, October session, 1700, "This Court doth allow unto ʲapt. Thos. Hart, Speaker, *thirtie* Shillings in pay for his *conduct* in the ʲeneral Court in May last;" and at their October session, 1704, it was oted that "This Court allows to Capt. Thos. Hart *five* and *thirtee* Shil- ngs in pay as Speaker this session;" and at their October session, 705, it was voted that "This Assembly doth allow to Capt. Thos. [art, Speaker, Thirtee Shillings for his conduct this session;" also at ıeir May session, 1706, it was voted "That this Court grants unto 'hos. Hart, Speaker, Thirtee Shillings." He was appointed commis- ioner for Farmington by the General Court, in 1692, 1693, 1694, 1695, nd 1697. He was appointed justice for Hartford County in 1698, 701, 1702, 1703, 1704, 1705, and 1706. He was member of the

---

* Anthony Hawkins was a distinguished man in Farmington. His wife was the aughter of Governor Wells, of Connecticut. His only son died childless.

Council in 1697. At their October session, 1699, the General Court appointed Captain Thomas Hart and others a committee "to take care of the countries interest in the undivided lands, and to indevour the preventing and detecting all illegall trading with the natives for land, and to implead such persons as have trespassed upon the countries land by intrusion." By a vote at the May session, 1700, he and others were continued on the same committee. In May, 1701, he was appointed a committee for a similar purpose and object. In October, 1702, he was appointed a committee to settle a line between Connecticut and Rhode Island. At the same session he was appointed on a committee "to draw a Bill to prevent disorders in Retailers of strong drinke and excessive drinking, and to prepare a Bill to put in execution the reformation Lawes." At their May session, 1703, the General Court passed the following: "This Assembly doth appoint and empower Capt. Thos. Hart and Mr. Caleb Stanley, to survey or to lay out to James Bird 100 acres of land granted to him in October last according to his grant." Captain Hart and his wife were members of the church in Farmington, March 1st, 1679-80. "He was a man of wealth, activity, and usefulness. He represented the town in the General Court twenty-nine sessions—from 1690 to 1711—of which body he was several times clerk and speaker, and a candidate for the Upper House. He and John Hooker were the two prominent men of the town, and conspicuous in the colony. They were the justices of the peace, filled the more important town offices, and executed important public trusts." His wife died October 9th, 1724, aged 75 years. Captain Hart died August 27th, 1726, in his 83d year, and was buried with military honors.

His Will was dated 1721, in which he gives his beloved wife, Ruth.

To his son, Hawkins.

To his son, Thomas.

To his son, Hezekiah, all his lands at Great Swamp,

To his son, John.

To his son, Josiah.

To his two daughters, Mary Newell and Margaret Strong, £5 each.

To Richard Negro, our Servant, 15 acres.

He makes his sons, Thomas and John, executors. Inventory taken September 7th, 1726. A large estate—about 2,000 acres.

Isaac Cowles,
John Hart, } Appraisers.

THEIR CHILDREN, BEING THE THIRD GENERATION.

1679. Mary, born ; married December 20th, 1683, Samuel Newell.
1680. Margaret, born ; married June 11th, 1689, Asahel Strong.
1681. Hawkins, born , 1677; married September 7th, 1701, Sarah Royce.

47

1682. Thomas, born, March, 1680; baptized April 4th, 1680; married December
          17th, 1702, Mary Thompson.
1683. John, born April 12th, 1682; baptized April 23d, 1682; married March 20th,
          1712, Rebecca Hubbard.
1684. Hezekiah, born   , 1684; baptized November 23d, 1684.
1685. Josiah, born   , 1686; baptized December 6th, 1686.

NEWELL.

1679.   *Farmington, Conn.*

MARY HART, Farmington, eldest child and daughter of Captain
Thomas Hart, of the same town, and his wife, Ruth (Hawkins), born
about 1666; married December 20th, 1683, Samuel Newell, son of
Thomas, of Farmington, and his wife, Rebecca; baptized December
5th, 1660, and was admitted to the church there in 1687. His wife
died April 28th, 1752, aged 86 years. He died February 15th, 1753,
in his 93d year. He held the military rank of ensign. They had
seven children, viz: Samuel, Thomas, John, Mary, Daniel, Nathaniel,
and Sarah.

STRONG.

1680.   *Northampton, Mass.*

MARGARET HART, second daughter of Captain Thomas Hart, of the
same town, and his wife, Ruth (Hawkins), born   ;
married June 11th, 1689, Asahel Strong, Esq., of Northampton, Mass.,
who settled in Farmington, where he was a member of the church,
and died in 1739. She died in 1735. Rev. Cyprian Strong, of Chatham, was their grandson.

1681.   *Wallingford, Conn.*

HAWKINS HART, Wallingford, eldest son of Captain Thomas Hart, of
Farmington, and his wife, Ruth (Hawkins), born at Farmington in
1677; married September 7th, 1701, Sarah Roys, of Wallingford,
daughter of Nathaniel, and his wife, Sarah (Lathrop), born April 3d,
1683, at Wallingford, he being aged 24 years, and she 19, at the time
of marriage (so says the record). He lived for a time in Farmington,
where their first two children were born, on the 4th of October, 1705
(says the record). They removed to Wallingford, where his wife died,
January 31st, 1733, aged 49 years, when second he married January
30th, 1734, Mary Street. He lived on the farm of his first wife's
father. He held the military rank of lieutenant. He died at Wallingford, May 24th, 1735, aged 58 years. His second wife is said to have
been Mary, widow of ——— Street, and daughter of Rev. Joseph
Elliot, of Guilford, and his second wife, Mary, daughter of Hon.

Samuel Willys, of Hartford. She was born in 1687. After the death of Lieutenant Hart she third married Rev. Abraham Pierson, of Killingworth, who died, when fourth she married ——— Hooker, of Farmington. Shew as granddaughter of Rev. John Eliot, the apostle to the Indians, and the author of a translation of the Bible into the Indian language, a copy of which was sold at auction, in New York City in 1869, for the enormous sum of $1,130. Mr. Hart represented Wallingford in the General Court nine sessions between 1714 and 1732.

THEIR CHILDREN, BEING THE FOURTH GENERATION.

1686. Nathaniel, born June 13th, 1702; married December 20th, 1727, Martha Lee.

1687. Ruth, born August 13th, 1704; married March 24th, 1726, William Merriam. Child, born September 16th, 1706; died September 22d, 1706.

1688. Hawkins, born March 1st, 1708; married November 30th, 1730, Susanna Merriam.

1689. Sarah, born May 21st, 1710; married October 25th, 1730, Stephen Ives.

1690. Esther, born August 12th, 1712; married October 26th, 1730, John Webb.

1691. Thomas, born September 29th, 1714; married March 23d, 1743, Hannah Coe.

1692. Elizabeth, born , 1716; married November 13th, 1738, William Jeroms.

1693. Mary, born June 21st, 1719; married July 1st, 1741, Ebenezer Hawley.

1694. Benjamin, born January 28th, 1722; married , 1744, Phebe Rich.

SECOND WIFE.

1695. Samuel, born July 18th, 1735, posthumous; married , Abridget Fowler.

1682. *Kensington, Conn.*

DEACON THOMAS HART, Kensington, Conn., second son of Captain Thomas, of Farmington, and his wife, Ruth (Hawkins), born, April, 1680, at Farmington; married December 17th, 1702, Mary, daughter of John Thompson, of Farmington, and his wife, Mary (Steele). He was admitted to the church in Farmington, February 2d, 1706–7. The church in Kensington was organized December 10th, 1712, and consisted of ten members, among whom were Thomas Hart and wife. He was chosen deacon of that church, January 27th, 1718–19. He resided a short distance south-east of the present railroad depot, as appears by the following: "The inhabitants of Kensington having fallen into a dispute about where to locate their second meeting-house, application was made to the Legislature, who, at their May session, 1732, directed it to be built on Deacon Thos. Hart's home lot." The meeting-house stood on the corner, east of the present Middletown Turnpike, and west and north of the road passing Cyrus Root's present place, near the old Thomas Hart place of the present century, well known to the public. He was the most influential man in Kensington Society, having been a justice of the peace, and represented the town of Farmington six sessions between 1739 and 1747. His wife died, October, 1763, aged 83 years, when he second married January 11th, 1764, Elizabeth Norton, widow of Isaac Norton, of Berlin, and daughter of ——— Galpin, of Stratford, Conn. She too was a member of the church in Kensington. At the time of his second marriage he was 84 and his bride 79. Deacon Thomas Hart, of Kensington, March 14th, 1760, for love to his grandson, Elijah Hart, of New Britain, gave him, by deed and will, all the tools of whatsoever name he used in making reeds for weaving by looms; also all the cane he might have at his decease. Signed by Ebenezer Hart and Elizabeth Hart as witnesses. His second wife died March 28th, 1771, aged 86 years, and was buried by the side of her first husband, at the South Cemetery in Berlin. Deacon Thomas Hart died January 29th, 1773, aged 93 years (wanting three months, says the record).

THEIR CHILDREN, BEING THE FOURTH GENERATION.

1696. Mary, born September 29th, 1703; married July 4th, 1728, John Hooker, Jr.
1697. Ebenezer, born April 13th, 1705; married June 9th, 1741, Widow Elizabeth Lawrence.
       Elijah, born February 1st, 1706-7; baptized February 2d, 1706-7; died young.
1698. Hannah, born February 1st, 1709; married July 11th, 1728, Joseph Porter.
1699. Elijah, born June 18th, 1711; married December 26th, 1734, Abigail Goodrich.
1700. Ruth, born August 14th, 1713; married May 15th, 1740, William Wadsworth.
       Mercy, born January 13th, 1724; died November 8th, 1726, in her third year. The oldest stone in Great Swamp Yard.

1683.   *East Guilford, Conn.*

REV. JOHN HART, East Guilford, Conn., third son of Captain Thomas Hart, of Farmington, and his wife, Ruth (Hawkins), born April 12th, 1682, at Farmington; baptized April 23d, 1682. He entered Yale College in 1702, not long after its organization at Saybrook. Previous to this he had been three years in college at Cambridge. He graduated alone at Yale in 1703, and was the second who had graduated there. He was ordained pastor of the church at East Guilford, Conn., November, 1707. He married March 20th, 1712, Rebecca Hubbard, of Boston, born November 11th, 1692. She died December 7th, 1715, aged 23 years, when he second married August 12th, 1717, Sarah Bull, daughter of Jonathan, of Hartford. She died February 4th, 1719, aged 32 years, when third he married December 6th, 1720, Mary Hooker, of Guilford, daughter of Hon. James, and granddaughter of Rev. Samuel. He died at East Guilford, March 4th, 1732, aged 50 years. He was called an eminent preacher of his day. His third wife was born November 5th, 1693, and died September 6th, 1756, aged 63 years. In his Will Mr. Hart gave his negro woman, Fillis, to his wife, Mary. He served Yale College as its only tutor three years. His predecessor was Daniel Hooker, of Farmington, son of Rev. Samuel. Mr. Hart commenced his labors in East Guilford about 1705, and was mainly instrumental in gathering a church of thirteen mem-bers, over which he was ordained at its formation in November, 1707, and continued pastor until his death. Rev. Mr. Chauncey, of Durham, preached his funeral sermon, and gave him an exalted character. He was greatly beloved by his people, and his memory is yet cherished.

THEIR CHILDREN, BEING THE FOURTH GENERATION.

1701. William, born May 9th, 1713; married June 18th, 1742, Mary Blague.
1702. Rebecca, born August 20th, 1714; married September 25th, 1734, Rev. Thomas Ruggles, Jr.

CHILD BY HIS SECOND WIFE.

1703. John, born January 31st, 1719. He was a physician, and died single.

CHILDREN BY HIS THIRD WIFE.

James, born January 16th, 1722; died March 28th, 1733, aged 11 years.
1704. Thomas, born May 27th, 1723; married November 28th, 1750, Concurrence Bartlett.
Mary, born May 29th, 1724; died August 28th, 1724.
1705. Benjamin, born June 1st, 1725; married November 21st, 1750, Mabel Fowler.
1706. Sarah, born March 1st, 1727; married Henry Hill; second, Dr. Thomas Adams; third, Rev. Amos Fowler.
1707. Samuel, born   , 1730; died single at Madison, September 4th, 1747, aged 17 years.

1684.

Hezekiah Hart, Kensington, fourth son of Captain Thomas Hart, of Farmington, and his wife, Ruth (Hawkins), born 1684; baptized November 29th, 1684, at Farmington; married   ,
Martha, daughter of Benjamin Beckley, and his wife, Rebecca, born October 15th, 1692, in Beckley Quarter, then in Wethersfield. She had a portion of her father's estate by his Will, dated June 28th, 1728. Mrs. Hart died September 7th, 1752, in her 61st year, and Mr. Hart died September 29th, 1752, in his 68th year. They have tombstones to their memory in the South Cemetery at Berlin.

THEIR CHILDREN, BEING THE FOURTH GENERATION.

1708. Rebecca, born August 27th, 1711; married   , Nathaniel Sage, of Middletown.
Hezekiah, born December 11th, 1714; died March 29th, 1730, aged 15 years.
1709. Martha, born August 5th, 1717; married December 16th, 1736, Joseph Deming, of Wethersfield.
1710. Lucy, born September 5th, 1720; married January 28th, 1742, Jacob Deming, Jr., of Wethersfield.
1711. David, born August 11th, 1724; married   , Lucy Peck.

1712. Ruth, born November 1st, 1726; married   , Daniel Beckley.
1713. Zerviah, born December 16th, 1728; married John Allis; second, David Webster.
1714. Hezekiah, born January 7th, 1730; married January 10th, 1757, Abigail Adkins.
1715. Hepzibah, born April 16th, 1732; married January 18th, 1753, Isaac North.
1716. Zachariah, born January 5th, 1733–4; married March 23d, 1758, Abigail Beckley.

1685.   *Farmington, Conn.*

CAPTAIN JOSIAH HART, Farmington, youngest son and child of Captain Thomas, of the same town, and his wife, Ruth (Hawkins), born at Farmington in 1686; baptized there December 6th, 1686; married January 7th, 1713–14, Sarah, daughter of Deacon Thomas Bull, of Farmington, and his wife, Esther (Cowles), born November 5th, 1684. She died July 1st, 1737, aged 53 years, when he second married February 22d, 1738, Lois, daughter of Nathaniel Goodwin, and his wife, Lois (Porter), born September 10th, 1694. She has a tombstone by the side of her husband, in the old cemetery at Farmington, but without date or age. He inherited the old homestead of his father, nearly opposite the meeting-house in Farmington, and on this place he lived and died. He was the wealthiest and one of the most influential men of his day in that town. He was a justice of the peace, and possessed negro servants. He represented the town in the General Court six sessions—from 1731 to 1734. He held the military rank of captain. The General Court, at their October session, 1733, appointed "Capt. Wm. Wadsworth and Capt. Josiah Hart, of Farmington, a committee to provide for the Dieting of the Indian lads at 4 shillings per week for the time they attend the Schoole in said town until the session of the Assembly in May next, and they then make report thereof." He and his first wife were admitted to the church in Farmington after January 21st, 1711–12. He died January 28th, 1758, aged 72 years.

THEIR CHILDREN, BEING THE FOURTH GENERATION.

1717. Thomas, born November 7th, 1714; died   , leaving no posterity.
   Ruth, born May 13th, 1717; died May 20th, 1717.
1718. Mercy, born August 23d, 1719; married January 29th, 1740, Roger Hooker, Esq.
   Josiah, born January 24th, 1721–2; died January 28th, 1722.
1719. Sarah, born April 17th, 1723; married July 11th, 1750, Elijah Cowles.
   Jonathan, born February 7th, 1726; died September 28th, 1736, aged 10 years.

1686.   *Wallingford, Conn.*

NATHANIEL HART, Wallingford, Conn., eldest son of Hawkins Hart, of the same town, and his wife, Sarah (Roys), born June 19th, 1702, at Farmington; married December 21st, 1727, Martha, daughter of Captain Stephen Lee, of Farmington, and his wife, Elizabeth (Roys), born February 17th, 1701–2, at Farmington. He died October 2d, 1750, aged 48 years, and his widow married second Joseph Francis. She died before July, 1760.

THEIR CHILDREN, BEING THE FIFTH GENERATION.

1720. Nathaniel, born September 5th, 1729; married January 23d, 1753, Alice Hall.
1721. Timothy, born May 24th, 1731; married March 6th, 1751, Phebe Fenn.
1722. Martha, born June 21st, 1733; married   , 1752, Joseph Curtiss, of Wallingford.
1723. Hawkins, born, February, 1736; married February 12th, 1761, Abigail Hall.
1724. Ebenezer, born March 26th, 1739. He was a farmer, and probably died single in Wallingford.
1725. Josiah, born February 22d, 1741–2; married January 10th, 1765, Lydia Moss.
1726. Phebe, born April 20th, 1746; married   Preston.
1727. Esther, born   ; married   Curtiss.

1687.   *Wallingford, Conn.*

RUTH HART, Wallingford, Conn., eldest daughter of Hawkins Hart, of the same town, and his wife, Sarah (Roys), born August 13th, 1704; married March 24th, 1726, William Merriam, son of John, of Lynn, Mass., born February 12th, 1697. He died October 5th, 1751, and she second married September 3d, 1762, Deacon Edward Parker, born 1692, and died October 21st, 1776, aged 84.

1688.   *Southington, Conn.*

HAWKINS HART, Southington, second son of Hawkins Hart, of Wallingford, Conn., and his wife, Sarah (Roys), born March 1st, 1708, at Wallingford; married there November 30th, 1730, Susanna Merriam. Soon after marriage they removed to Southington, and located on East Street, at what has since been known as the Ezekiel Sloper place, on the west side of the highway. His wife died February 23d, 1736–7, when he second married April 5th, 1738, Esther, daughter of Thomas Gridley, born March 17th, 1706, at Farmington. He died at Southington, April 17th, 1756, in his 49th year, and his widow married December 14th, 1758, Robert Cook.

THEIR CHILDREN, BEING THE FIFTH GENERATION.

Hawkins, born March 8th, 1732; died April 4th, 1732.
· Sarah, born May 1st, 1733; died December 1st, 1742, aged 9 years.
Susanna, born December 31st, 1734; died December 3d, 1742, aged 8 years.
1728. Hawkins, born January 3d, 1736–7; married March 23d, 1758, Huldah Woodruff.

NOTE.—The estate of Widow Elizabeth (Roys) Lee, the grandmother of these children on the maternal side, was £60, and they had one-third of it by her Will, exhibited in court, July 15th, 1760.

1729. Luke, born January 8th, 1738; married, March, 1764, Deborah Barnes.

1730. Josiah, born June 30th, 1740; married September 11th, 1763, Elizabeth Moss.

Sarah, born November 27th, 1742; died November 25th, 1756, aged 15 years.

1731. David, born July 22d, 1745; married   , Lucy Codner.

Susanna, born January 12th, 1747–8; died October 26th, 1757, aged 9 years.

1732. Benjamin, born January 4th, 1750–1; married February 25th, 1776, Jerusha Rich.

IVES.

1689. *Wallingford, Conn.*

SARAH HART, second daughter of Hawkins, of Wallingford, and his first wife, Sarah (Roys), born May 21st, 1710, at Wallingford; was married there October 25th, 1730, to Stephen Ives, of the same town, son of Nathaniel, and his wife, Mary (Cook), born at Wallingford, March 24th, 1704. He sold his place in Wallingford, consisting of a dwelling-house and twenty-three acres of land, to Moses Lyman, of Durham, Conn., for £230, deed dated February 16th, 1731–2. They had issue, viz: Sarah, Mary, and Lois, born January 9th, 1737.

WEBB.

1690.

ESTHER HART, third daughter of Hawkins Hart, of Wallingford, and his first wife, Sarah (Roys), born October 12th, 1712, in that part of Wallingford now called Meriden; married there by Rev. Theophilus Hall, October 26th, 1730, to John Webb. She died in 1806, aged 34 years.

1691. *Farmington, Bristol, Conn.*

THOMAS HART, Wallingford, third son of Hawkins Hart, of the same place, and his first wife, Sarah (Roys), born September 29th, 1714, in Wallingford; married March 23d, 1742, Hannah Coe, born April 12th, 1712, and died, November, 1783. He settled in Farmington, where his first three children were born. He removed to Bristol about 1747, and second married   , Rachel Barnes. He died July 12th, 1801, aged 87 years. His widow died March 26th, 1810, aged 87 years. The inventory of her estate was taken May 1st, 1810, at Bristol, Conn., by Abel Lewis and Bryan Hooker, appraisers; amount, $68.70. See Probate Records of Farmington.

THEIR CHILDREN, BEING THE FIFTH GENERATION.

1733. Mary, born March 23d, 1743; married June 25th, 1761, Luke Gridley, of Bristol.

1734. Ruth, born October 1st, 1744; married June 2d, 1768, Dan Hills.

1735. Jonathan, born March 22d, 1746; married   , Lucia Clark.
1736. Hannah, born October 10th, 1747; married   , Jacob Byington.
1737. Thomas, born September 10th, 1749; married , 1772, Mary Hungerford.
1738. Esther, born November 16th, 1751; married November 2d, 1769, Zebulon Peck.
1739. Amasa, born June 19th, 1754; married   , Phebe Roberts.
1740. Abel, born September 5th, 1756. He was a soldier of the revolution, and died in prison of starvation.
1741. Barbara, born May 24th, 1758; married   , Zerubabel Jerome.
1742. Benjamin, born March 25th, 1761.
1743. Lydia, born   , 1770; admitted to the church in 1816.

JEROMS.

1692.   *Bristol, Conn.*

ELIZABETH HART, fourth daughter of Hawkins Hart, of Wallingford, and his first wife, Sarah (Roys), born about 1716, in that part of Wallingford now called Meriden; married there by Rev. Theophilus Hall, November 13th, 1738, to William Jeroms, son of Timothy Jeroms, and his wife, Abigail, born August 28th, 1717, in Wallingford. They removed to Bristol, and were the ancestors of those of the name of Jerome in that town. He died there, June, 1794, aged 77 years, and was buried in the north yard.

HAWLEY.

1693.   *Farmington, Conn.*

MARY HART, Farmington, fifth daughter of Hawkins Hart, of Wallingford, and his first wife, Sarah (Roys), born June 21st, 1719, in Wallingford; married July 1st, 1741, Ebenezer Hawley, of Scot's Swamp, in Farmington, son of Joseph, born December 10th, 1713, at Farmington. His wife died, when second he married Mrs. Kesiah Root, widow of Joseph, and daughter of Deacon James Smith, of Southington, October 10th, 1757. He died March 3d, 1769, in his 56th year. Children of the first wife—Sarah, Asa, Benjamin, Ebenezer, Mary, twin with Ebenezer, Esther. Child of the second wife— James, born October 8th, 1758.

1694.   *Wallingford, Conn.*

BENJAMIN HART, Wallingford, fourth son of Hawkins Hart, of the same town, and his first wife, Sarah (Roys), born January 28th, 1722, at Wallingford; married, 1744, Phebe Rich. He died in 1745, aged 23 years, when second she married July 17th, 1747, John Grave, 3d,

48

of Guilford, who died December 13th, 1759, when third she married in 1761, Jonathan Crampton, of East Guilford.

CHILD BY HIS FIRST WIFE, BEING THE FIFTH GENERATION.

Benjamin, born March 27th, 1744–5; died, January, 1768, at North Guilford, aged 23.

1695.   *Durham, Conn.*

· SAMUEL HART, Durham, Conn., fifth son of Hawkins Hart, of Wallingford, and his second wife, Mary (Street), born July 18th, 1735, at Wallingford; married October 9th, 1759, at Durham, Abridget Fowler. He took the oath of fidelity in Durham, August 27th, 1777, and was made a freeman, September 16th, 1777. He was admitted to the church there in half-way covenant, August 8th, 1762, and at the same time had his eldest child baptized. He and his wife were admitted to the church in full communion, August 18th, 1771. He held the military rank of lieutenant in the army of the revolution, and was wounded at the battle of Saratoga, after which he drew a pension. He settled in Durham, on a farm given to his grandfather, Rev. Joseph Elliot, by the legislature, for preaching an election sermon. When asked if he was one that Arnold drove up, with the flat of his sword, to action, he replied, "No! I was so near the enemy that Arnold dare not come." He died January 12th, 1805, aged 71 years. She died November 6th, 1827, aged 93 years.

THEIR CHILDREN, BEING THE FIFTH GENERATION.

Mary, born June 24th, 1762; died   , 1782, aged 20 years.

Samuel, born February 23d, 1764; died   , 1769, aged 5 years.

1744. Ruth, born June 8th, 1766; married   , Charles Dudley, of Guilford.

1745. Daniel, born June 29th, 1768; baptized July 13th, 1768; married   , Hannah Hubbard.

1746. Samuel, born July 12th, 1770; married March 3d, 1803, Patience Hubbard.

1747. John,   ⎫   married July 15th, 1801, Sally Coe.
           ⎬ born September 11th, 1772:
Rebecca, ⎭   baptized October 25th, 1772; died in 1776, aged 4 years.

1748. Lois, born   ; baptized March 12th, 1775; married   , Selah Parker.

HOOKER.

1696.   *Kensington, Conn.*

MARY HART, Kensington, Conn., eldest daughter of Deacon Thomas Hart, of the same place, and his first wife, Mary (Thompson), born September 29th, 1703, at Kensington, Conn.; married July 4th, 1728, John Hooker, Jr., father of Rev. John Hooker, of Northampton,

Mass., whose descendants are among the most distinguished families in Massachusetts. Their issue, viz: John, Seth, Ashbel, and Elijah, born April 12th, 1746; married August 26th, 1767, Susanna Seymour.

1697. *Kensington, Conn.*

EBENEZER HART, Kensington, Conn., eldest son of Deacon Thomas Hart, of the same place, and his first wife, Mary (Thompson), born April 13th, 1705, in Kensington; married June 9th, 1741, Widow Eliz.beth Lawrence. He was chosen deacon of the church in Kensington, December 9th, 1762, and died in 1773, aged 68 years. She died in .914, aged 96 years.

THEIR CHILDREN, BEING THE .FIFTH GENERATION.

749. Ebenezer, born July 29th, 1742; married April 5th, 1770, Lydia Benton.
750. Jonathan, born , 1744; married , 1777, Abigail Riley.
Elizabeth, born May 20th, 1746; died November 4th, 1766. She was a school teacher.
751. Elihu, born March 4th, 1751; married December 31st, 1777, by Dr. Smalley, Mary Peck.
752. John, born March 11th, 1753; married November 9th, 1786, Hannah Williams.
752¼. Thomas, born December 6th, 1754, at Kensington. He was never married.
752½. Hannah, born , 1758; died single, of measles, in 1810, aged 52 years.

PORTER.

1698. *Kensington, Conn.*

HANNAH HART, Kensington, Conn., second daughter of Deacon Thomas Hart, of Kensington, Conn., and his first wife, Mary (Thompson), born February 1st, 1709, at Kensington, Conn.; married July 11th, 1728, Deacon Joseph Porter, of Kensington, Conn., son of Deacon Samuel Porter, of Farmington, Conn. She died , 1795, aged 86 years. They had no children.

1699. *New Britain, Conn.*

DEACON ELIJAH HART, New Britain, Conn., third son of Deacon Thomas Hart, of Kensington, Conn., and his first wife, Mary (Thompson), born June 18th, 1711, at Kensington, Conn.; married December 6th, 1734, Abigail Goodrich, daughter of Allen, and his wife, Elizabeth, born December 14th, 1714. He located in New Britain, and built his house near the site of what is known as the State House, in Hart Quarter. He and his wife were members of the church in Kensington, and became constituent members of the first church in New Britain, which was organized April 19th, 1758, and he was soon after elected deacon. He was a stout, athletic man, and his avocation was farming, yet in carrying a stick of fence timber on his shoulder, he stepped into a hole in the ground, was crushed with the weight, and died in consequence. The following is a copy of the inscription on his grave-stone in New Britain Cemetery: "In memory of the greatly esteemed and much lamented Deacon Elijah Hart, who provided for his own, and served his generation with great diligence and fidelity, even to the last day of his life, was taken suddenly to his inheritance above, on the 3d day of August, 1772, in the 61st year of his age." His widow died in Simsbury, at the residence of her daughter, Mrs. Eno, January 21st, 1809, aged 95.

THEIR CHILDREN, BEING THE FIFTH GENERATION.

1753. Elijah, born September 26th, 1735; married　　　　　　, Sarah Gilbert.

1754. Thomas, born January 12th, 1738; married February 2d, 1758, Mehitabel Bird.

1755. Jehudah, born December 12th, 1739; married July 9th, 1767, Mary Munson.

1756. Josiah, born April 28th, 1742; married　　　　, 1765, Abigail Sluman.

1757. Mary, born October 26th, 1744; married January 7th, 1765, Jonathan Eno.

1758. Benjamin, born October 16th, 1747; married August 19th, 1772, Mary Fuller.

1759. Joseph, born May 17th, 1750; married November 5th, 1772, Huldah Smith.

1760. Elizur, born December 25th, 1752; married January 1st, 1778, Sarah Langdon.

Aaron, born October 1st, 1756; died February 12th, 1761, aged 5 years.

WADSWORTH.

1700.　　　　　　　　*Farmington, Conn.*

RUTH HART, Farmington, third daughter of Deacon Thomas Hart, of Kensington, and his first wife, Mary (Thompson), born August 14th, 1713, at Kensington; married May 15th, 1740, William Wadsworth, Esq., of Farmington, who died August 6th, 1769, in his 60th year, when second she married July 30th, 1778, Solomon Whitman, Esq., of Farmington. She was his third wife, his second wife, Ruth Strong, having died at Farmington, September 18th, 1777.

1701.　　　　　　　　*Saybrook, Conn.*

REV. WILLIAM HART, Saybrook, Conn., eldest son of Rev. John Hart, of East Guilford, and his first wife, Rebecca (Hubbard), born May 9th, 1713, at Guilford; married June 18th, 1742, Mary Blague,* daughter of Deacon Joseph. He graduated at Yale College in 1732, studied for the ministry, and was ordained pastor over the First Church of Saybrook, November 17th, 1736. A sermon of his entitled "A Discourse concerning the Nature of Regeneration, and the way wherein it is

---

* Joseph Blague, father of Mrs. Hart, came from Scotland, and was a deacon of Mr. Hart's church at Saybrook. His wife was Mary Hamlin, of Middletown.

wrought," was published by T. Green, New London, 1742, 57 pages. He died July 11th, 1784, aged 71 years. She died December 11th, 1800, aged 80 years. On his tombstone is inscribed:

> "Wise in Council,
> Mighty in the Scriptures, and
> Instructive in his life and Ministry.
> 'Blessed are the dead who die in the Lord.'"

He acquired, by descent, marriage, and accumulation, a large estate, inherited by his descendants. He was much respected by his brethren in the ministry, and was highly revered by his people, enjoying their confidence and affection through a ministry of nearly forty-eight years. He distinguished himself as a vigorous controversial writer. He had the reputation of being an Arminian. He zealously justified the council that acted in the ordination of Mr. Dana at Wallingford in 1760, and published a narrative of the proceedings—a joint production of himself and Rev. Jonathan Todd—in 1759; Remarks on Dangerous Errors, (Hopkinsianism,) 1770; Remarks on President Edwards' Dissertation on Virtue, 1771; A Treatise on Qualification for the Sacrament, published in 1772. The sermon at his own ordination was preached by Rev. Jared Elliot, of Killingworth, and his funeral sermon by Rev. John Devotion, of the Third Church in Saybrook, and was published. They had nine children, all living at the time of his decease, and all but one were present at the funeral.

THEIR CHILDREN, BEING THE FIFTH GENERATION.

1761. Mary, born July 13th, 1743; married February 26th, 1770, William Bull, of Hartford.

1762. Rebecca, born January 22d, 1745; married   , William Lynde, of Saybrook.

·1763. William, born June 24th, 1746; married   , Esther Buckingham.

1764. Samuel, born June 24th, 1748; married February 22d, 1770, Lucy Bushnell.

1764½. John, born September 24th, 1750; married   , Widow Nancy Bull; died April 28th, 1828.

Sarah, born December 14th, 1752; died single, June 24th, 1788.

1765. Joseph, born January 13th, 1755; married   , Eunice Ellery.

1766. Elisha, born September 3d, 1758; married   , Jennette McCurdy, of Lyme.

1767. Amelia, born January 26th, 1761; married August 29th, 1790, Frederic William Hotchkiss.

RUGGLES.

1702. *Guilford, Conn.*

REBECCA HART, eldest daughter of Rev. John Hart, of East Guilford, and his first wife, Rebecca (Hubbard), born at East Guilford, Conn.,

August 20th, 1714; married September 25th, 1734, Rev. Thomas Ruggles, Jr., of Guilford. She died February 17th, 1760, aged 45.

1703.   *Farmington, Conn.*

DR. JOHN HART, of East Guilford, second son of Rev. John Hart, of the same town, and his second wife, Sarah (Bull), born January 31st, 1719, in East Guilford, Conn. His mother died when he was four days old, and her brother, Dr. Jonathan Bull, of Hartford, was appointed his guardian, with whom he studied medicine. He commenced practice in Kensington, Conn., and died while on a visit to Guilford, his native place, March 21st, 1749, aged 30 years. He was unmarried. In his Will he calls himself John Hart, of Farmington, for Kensington was then a portion of that old town.

1704.   *Guilford, Conn.*

THOMAS HART, Guilford, Conn., fourth son of Rev. John Hart, of that town, and his third wife, Mary (Hooker), born May 27th, 1723, at East Guilford, Conn.; married November 28th, 1750, Concurrence Bartlett, daughter of Ebenezer, of Guilford. Mr. Hart died February 26th, 1813, aged 90 years. She died October 30th, 1813, aged 83 years.

THEIR CHILDREN, BEING THE FIFTH GENERATION.

1768. Mary, born August 17th, 1751; married March 12th, 1777, Nathaniel Dudley.
1769. Deborah, born May 22d, 1753; married July 26th, 1775, Samuel Fairchild, of Middletown.
Rebecca, born December 6th, 1754; died single at Guilford, December 25th, 1827, aged 73 years.
1769½. Ebenezer, born October 3d, 1757. He was a revolutionary soldier, and was killed.
1770. Ruth, born April 23d, 1760; married January 7th, 1784, Hooker Bartlett, Jr.
1771. Thomas, born September 8th, 1762; married October 8th, 1787, Mary Parmelee.
1772. Elizabeth, born July 17th, 1765; married February 15th, 1792, Jonathan Parmelee.
Sarah, born June 8th, 1768; died single, June 29th, 1825.
1773. John, born January 15th, 1773; married   , Betsey, daughter of Luke Field.

1705.   *East Guilford, Conn.*

BENJAMIN HART, East Guilford, fifth son of Rev. John Hart, of the same town, and his third wife, Mary (Hooker), born June 1st, 1725, at East Guilford, Conn.; married November 21st, 1750, Mabel Fowler, daughter of Abraham, Jr., of East Guilford. He died February 28th, 1804, aged 79 years. His widow died September 13th, 1814.

1774. Sarah, born August 6th, 1751; died single, February 2d, 1841, aged 90.
1775. James, born February 27th, 1753; died single at Madison, September 12th, 1836, aged 83.

John, born, March, 1755; died October 1st, 1756, aged 1 year.

1776. John, born October 9th, 1757; died single at East Guilford, April 30th, 1782, aged 24.

Mabel, born October 26th, 1759; died

Mabel, born October 26th, 1760; died single, August 13th, 1822, aged 62 years.

Samuel, born April 29th, 1765; died single, November 2d, 1820, aged 55.

1777. Benjamin, born October 25th, 1772; married March 31st, 1804, Mary Meigs.

HILL. ADAMS. FOWLER.

1706. *Guilford, Conn.*

SARAH HART, Guilford, third daughter of Rev. John Hart, of East Guilford, and his third wife, Mary (Hooker), born March 1st, 1727, at East Guilford; married January 9th, 1750, Henry Hill, of Guilford, who died July 17th, 1751, when second she married Dr. Thomas Adams, of East Haddam, son of Rev. Eliphalet Adams, of New London, who died, September, 1758, when third she married Rev. Amos Fowler, of Guilford. She died June 30th, 1789, aged 67 years.

SAGE.

1708. *Middletown, Conn.*

REBECCA HART, Kensington, eldest child of Hezekiah Hart, of the same place, and his wife, Martha (Beckley), born August 27th, 1711, at Kensington; married   , Nathaniel Sage, of Middletown.

DEMING.

1709. *Wethersfield, Conn.*

MARTHA HART, Kensington, second daughter of Hezekiah Hart, of the same place, and his wife, Martha (Beckley), born August 5th, 1717, at Kensington; married there by Rev. William Burnham, December 16th, 1736, Joseph Deming, of Wethersfield, son of Jacob, and his wife, Dinah (Churchill), born November 24th, 1711, at Wethersfield. He held the military rank of lieutenant. She died November 26th, 1748, in her 33d year, when second he married August 2d, 1750, Elizabeth Wright. He died February 28th, 1774, in his 63d year, and has a tombstone in the cemetery at Beckley Quarter, Berlin, Conn. His widow died October 11th, 1788. The children of Joseph and Martha Deming are—Joseph, David, Gideon, and Asahel; also five children by the second wife.

DEMING.

1710.   *Wethersfield, Conn.*

LUCY HART, Kensington, third daughter of Hezekiah Hart, of Kensington, and his wife, Martha (Beckley), born September 5th, 1720, at Kensington; married January 28th, 1742, Jacob Deming, of Wethersfield, son of Jacob, and his wife, Dinah (Churchill), born at Wethersfield in 1713, and was a brother of Joseph, who married Martha. He died July 29th, 1791, in his 78th year. His widow died March 7th, 1802, in her 82d year, and both have tombstones in Beckley Quarter Cemetery.

1711.   *Berlin, Conn.*

DAVID HART, Worthington, Conn., second son of Hezekiah Hart, of Kensington, and his wife, Martha (Beckley), born August 11th, 1724, at Kensington; married   , Lucy Peck. He died in 1786, aged 62 years, and his estate was· represented insolvent. Samuel Hart and Jedediah Sage were appointed commissioners to adjust the claims, who, by notice dated Berlin, August 28th, 1786, were to meet at the house of Roger Riley, Esq., in said Berlin, for the purpose aforesaid.

THEIR CHILD, BEING THE FIFTH GENERATION.

1777½. David, born   ; married   , Ann Benjamin.

BECKLEY.

1712.   *Wethersfield, Conn.*

RUTH HART, Kensington, fourth daughter of Hezekiah Hart, of Kensington, and his wife, Martha (Beckley), born November 1st, 1726, at Kensington; married   , Daniel, son of Daniel Beckley, of Wethersfield, and his wife, Martha, daughter of Thomas North, of Farmington, born November 29th, 1724, in Wethersfield. He died March 4th, 1760, in his 36th year, and has a tombstone in Beckley Quarter Cemetery. They had issue, viz: Seth, born July 28th, 1753, died February 27th, 1769, aged 16 years; Daniel, born   , baptized June 18th, 1758, in Kensington.

ALLIS. WEBSTER.

1713.   *Kensington, Conn.*

ZERVIAH HART, Kensington, fifth daughter of Hezekiah Hart, of the same place, and his wife, Martha (Beckley), born December 16th, 1728, at Kensington; married John, son of William Allis, born September

11th, 1726, who died May 18th, 1756, aged 30 years, when second she married December 19th, 1761, David Webster, Esq., son of John, and his wife, Esther (Judd), born January 29th, 1721, at Glastonbury. He was a graduate of Yale College in 1741, studied law, and practiced in Farmington and elsewhere. She was his second wife, and died January 17th, 1786, aged 57 years, when he third married November 22d, 1786, Widow Olive Smith. He died May 12th, 1806, aged 85 years. She had one child by Allis, viz: Abel, born 1755; married Widow Thankful Gilbert; died July 3d, 1816. Her children by Webster were—Hepzibah, born November 3d, 1763, married Israel Deming; Lydia, born September 28th, 1765, married Elijah Bevins; John, born April 7th, 1768, married January 28th, 1790, Eunice Deming; Selah, born September 20th, 1770, died November 13th, 1776.

1714. *Kensington, Conn.*

HEZEKIAH HART, Kensington, third son of Hezekiah, of the same place, and his wife, Martha (Beckley), born January 7th, 1730, at Kensington; married January 10th, 1757, Abigail Adkins. They were both admitted to the church in Kensington, August 6th, 1758. They had a negro servant. Mr. Hart died April 14th, 1804, aged 74 years. His widow died November 24th, 1820, aged 92 years, and both have tombstones in the burial ground near Merritt Cowles' dwelling-house in Kensington.

THEIR CHILDREN, BEING THE FIFTH GENERATION.

1778. Hezekiah, born May 25th, 1758; died single, September 24th, 1840, aged 82 years.

1778¼. Lucy, born August 10th, 1760; died single, May 15th, 1791, aged 31 years.

1778½. Abigail, born December 14th, 1761; died single, January 7th, 1785, aged 22 years.

Daniel, born October 10th, 1763; died single in the almshouse.

1778¾. Jabish, } died single, June 18th, 1800, aged 35 years.
born October 3d, 1765;
1779. Hannah, } married August 12th, 1792, Stephen Kelsey.

1780. Ruth, born   , 1767; baptized January 17th, 1768; married , Job Cole.

1781. Rebecca, born   , 1770; baptized April 29th, 1771; married October 20th, 1805, Jedediah Gladden.

Reuben, born   , 1774; baptized June 27th, 1774; died March 23d, 1781, aged 7 years.

NORTH.

1715. *Kensington, Conn.*

HEPZIBAH HART, Kensington, fifth daughter of Hezekiah Hart, of the same place, and his wife, Martha (Beckley), born April 16th, 1732,

49

at Kensington; married January 18th, 1753, Isaac North, son of Isaac, and his wife, Mary (Woodford), born 1729. They lived in Kensington. She died in 1792, aged 61 years. He died in 1804, aged 75 years. They had children, viz: Joseph, Hepzibah, Abel, Selah, Lydia, Salmon, and Isaac, born 1771; married   , 1810, Sally North.

1716.   *Berlin, Conn.*

ZACHARIAH HART, Kensington, fifth son of Hezekiah Hart, of Kensington, and his wife, Martha (Beckley), born January 5th, 1733-4, at Kensington; married March 23d, 1758, Abigail, daughter of Joseph Beckley, and his wife, Mary (Judd), born November 22d, 1737, in Beckley Quarter. She died July 12th, 1765, aged 28 years, when second he married, June, 1766, Sarah Parsons. They lived at the North House, on Hart Street, next west of Berlin Street. He and his first wife were admitted to Kensington Church, September 30th, 1759, and when the church in Berlin was organized in February, 1775, he and his second wife were constituent members there. He died December 26th, 1811, aged 77 years. Mrs. Sarah Hart died January 26th, 1813, in her 80th year.

THEIR CHILDREN, BEING THE FIFTH GENERATION.

1782. Olive, born June 24th, 1759; married   , Solomon Flagg.
Joseph, born October 14th, 1760, died, November, 1760.
Zachariah, born September 1st, 1761; died January 3d, 1762.
1783. Caroline, born October 21st, 1762; married   , Abel Hollister.
Zachariah, 2d, May 26th, 1764; died November 17th, 1764.
1784. Abigail, born May 21st, 1768; married March 27th, 1788, Josiah Norton.
1785. Sarah, born   , 1770; baptized February 11th, 1770; married   , Shubel Patterson.
1786. Martha, born   , 1772; married   , Levi Hart, son of Isaac.
Zenas, born   , 1774; baptized August 3d, 1774; died   , 1775.
1787. Submit, baptized January 21st, 1776; married May 9th,   .

HOOKER.

1718.   *Farmington, Conn.*

MERCY HART, Farmington, second daughter of Captain Josiah Hart, of the same town, and his first wife, Sarah (Bull), born August 23d, 1719, at Farmington; married January 29th, 1740, Roger Hooker, of Farmington. They had children—1, Sarah, born December 16th, 1740, died April 19th, 1741; 2, Sarah, 2d, born September 16th, 1742, married Jonathan Leavett, Esq., of Greenfield; 3, Thomas Hart, born 1745, and died in the army in 1776, aged 31 years. He inherited an immense estate from his grandfather, Captain Josiah Hart, being his only male heir, most of which he expended in extravagance and dissipation, and finally married in 1769, Sarah, daughter of Deacon John Whitman, of West Hartford, and granddaughter of Rev. Samuel Whitman, of Farmington, and settled in West Hartford They left two children—Abigail Pantry, who married Samuel Talcott, and Thomas Hart.

COWLES.

1719. *Farmington, Conn.*

SARAH HART, Farmington, third daughter of Captain Josiah Hart, of the same town, and his first wife, Sarah (Bull), born April 17th, 1723, at Farmington; married July 11th, 1750, Elijah, son of Isaac Cowles, and his third wife, Elizabeth (Smith), born January 12th, 1727. She died July 12th, 1751, in her 29th year, when second he married   , Eunice   . He died June 29th, 1793, in his 66th year. His widow died January 12th, 1810, in her 79th year. His first wife had one child—Jonathan, born July 7th, 1751; died July 23d, 1751. There were seven children by his second wife, viz: Elijah, Jonathan, Sarah Hart, Gad, Seth, Eunice, Gad, 2d.

1720. *Wallingford, Conn.*

CAPTAIN NATHANIEL HART, Wallingford, eldest son of Nathaniel, of Farmington and Wallingford, and his wife, Martha (Lee), born September 5th, 1729, at Wallingford; married January 23d, 1753, Alice, daughter of David Hall, and his wife, Alice (Case), born September 8th, 1731, at Wallingford. She died September 9th, 1775, aged 44 years, when second he married February 15th, 1778, Phebe, widow of ——— Johnson. She died September 23d, 1803. He held the military rank of captain. He removed to Goshen, Conn., and lived there with his sons in his old age. He died about 1810, aged 80 years.

THEIR CHILDREN, BEING THE SIXTH GENERATION.

Nathaniel, born November 8th, 1754; died   , aged 23 years.

1788. David, born November 22d, 1756; married, May, 1781, Hannah Hudson.

Samuel, born September 10th, 1758; died November 5th, 1763, aged 5 years. He was scalded.

1789. Sarah, born February 29th, 1760; married   , Joseph Doolittle, of North Haven.

1790. Lois, born December 22d, 1761; married   , Joel Doolittle, of Wallingford.

1791. Reuben, born July 4th, 1763; married, November, 1784, Ruth Ives, of Wallingford.

1792. Lucy, born September 29th, 1764; married   , Moses Hall. They lived at Ballston, N. Y.

1793. Samuel, 2d, born January 7th, 1766; married
   They lived at Coos and Granby, Vt.
1794. Stephen, born June 3d, 1767; married   Seymour.
   They lived in Turin, Black River. He died in 1857.
1795. Ruth, born September 27th, 1768; married   , Asahel Munson,
   of Branford.
1796. Mary, born August 7th, 1770; married   , Samuel Doolittle.
1797. Phebe, born April 29th, 1772; married   , Jeremiah Hull, of
   Wallingford.
1798. Levi, born November 3d,·1773; married November 15th,·1796, Esther Barnes.
   They live in Turin, Black River.

SECOND WIFE.

Alice Hall, born September 6th, 1780; died January 19th, 1790, aged 10 years.

1721.   *Wallingford, Conn.*

TIMOTHY HART, Wallingford, second son of Nathaniel Hart, of the same town, and his wife, Martha (Lee), born August 24th, 1731, at Wallingford; married March 6th, 1751, Phebe Fenn, of Wallingford, daughter of Theophilus, and his wife, Martha (Doolittle), born February 12th, 1735, in Wallingford.

THEIR CHILDREN, BEING THE SIXTH GENERATION.

1799. Benjamin, born March 25th, 1752; married December 15th, 1775, Hannah
   Curtiss.
1800. Timothy, born April 26th, 1754; died, September, 1812, at Steubenville, Ohio.
1801. Titus, born July 10th, 1756; married December 21st, 1780, Lucy Johnson.
1802. Jonathan, born October 13th, 1758.
   Isaac, born December 4th, 1760; died January 1st, 1775, aged 15 years.
1803. Phebe, born May 3d, 1763; married   Sackett.
1804. Joel, born January 24th, 1766; married   , Phebe Dallas.
1805. Amos, born February 3d, 1768; married   , Lois Anthony.
1806. Amasa, born July 1st, 1770; married   , Abigail Fenn.
1807. Elizabeth, born August 24th, 1772; married   , Benjamin Baldwin.
1808. Jesse, born August 23d, 1774; married   , Esther Derby.
1809. Ebenezer, born   ; married his first, second, and third wife, and
   lived in Batavia, Ohio.

CURTISS.

1722.   *Wallingford, Conn.*

MARTHA HART, Wallingford, eldest daughter of Nathaniel Hart, of Farmington and Wallingford, and his wife, Martha (Lee), born June 21st, 1733, at Wallingford; married in 1752, Joseph Curtiss, of Wallingford.

1723.   *Wallingford, Barkhamsted, Conn.*

HAWKINS HART, Wallingford, third son of Nathaniel Hart, of Farmington and Wallingford, and his wife, Martha (Lee), born, February,

1736, in that part of Wallingford called Meriden; married February 12th, 1761, Abigail Hall, daughter of Peter, and his wife, Rebecca (Bartholomew), born May 15th, 1737. Mr. Hart was a carpenter and joiner by trade and occupation. His wife died May 20th, 1807, aged 70 years. He removed to Barkhamsted in 1789, and died there, May 26th, 1824, aged 88 years.

THEIR CHILDREN, BEING THE SIXTH GENERATION.

1810. Rebecca, born November 23d, 1761; married   , Joel Cook.
1811. Josiah Hall, born June 3d, 1764; married January 14th, 1790, Phebe Hall.
1812. Hannah, born September 20th, 1766; married   , Joel Parker.
1813. Aaron, born February 8th, 1770; married   , Aunis Austin.
1814. Hiel, born July 25th, 1772.
      Abigail, born February 1st, 1775; died February 20th, 1775, aged 20 days.
1815. Abigail, 2d, born June 8th, 1778.
1816. Hawkins, born January 28th, 1781; married   , Lois Slade.
1817. Jerre, born October 11th, 1784; married   Ives.

1725.   Wallingford, Conn.

JOSIAH HART, Wallingford, fifth son of Nathaniel Hart, of Farmington and Wallingford, and his wife, Martha (Lee), born February 22d, 1741–2, at Wallingford; married January 10th, 1765, Lydia Moss. He is called Josiah Hart, Jr., on the Wallingford records. After the revolutionary war he removed to Nova Scotia.

THEIR CHILDREN, BEING THE SIXTH GENERATION.

1818. Rama, born June 26th, 1766.
1819. Joseph, born July 20th, 1767.
1820. Jairus, born February 17th, 1769.
1821. Irad, born January 2d, 1771.
1822. Tyrus, born January 13th, 1773.
1823. Punthia, born June 10th, 1775.
1824. Lydia, born April 19th, 1777.
1825. Lee, born August 23d, 1779.
1826. Ithiel, born December 17th, 1782.

1728.   Southington, Conn.

LIEUTENANT HAWKINS HART, Southington, second son of Hawkins Hart, of the same town, and his wife, Susannah (Merriam), born January 3d, 1736–7, at Southington, and baptized there by Rev. Jeremiah Curtiss, May 1st, 1737; married March 23d, 1758, Huldah, daughter of David Woodruff, and his wife, Mary (Porter), born 1737, and baptized June 26th, 1737, in Southington, by the pastor, Rev. J. Curtiss. They lived on East Street, in the house owned and occupied by his son-in-law, Amos Woodruff. It stood a few feet south of the residence of

Truman Barnes in 1869. His wife died December 31st, 1795, aged 58
years, when he second married   , Ruth Chubs, of
Barkhamsted, Conn., to which place he removed. He bore the military
rank of lieutenant. In 1776 the General Assembly ordered six bat-
talions to be raised, to march immediately to New York and join the
continental army. Hawkins Hart was appointed first lieutenant in the
seventh company, Fifth Battalion, under William M. Douglas, colonel;
Nathaniel Bunnel, captain; Thomas Lyman, second lieutenant; Miles
Hull, ensign. They had but one child, Phebe, who married Amos
Woodruff. In 1784 her father gave her, for love, four acres of his
home lot, reserving to himself the fruit of thirteen apple trees. He
subsequently, in 1788, sold his son-in-law other portions of his farm.
He lived in the town of Berlin January 26th, 1800, as appears from
his deed to Amos Woodruff bearing that date.

THEIR CHILD, BEING THE FIFTH GENERATION.

1827. Phebe, born   ; married   , Amos Woodruff.

1729.   *Southington, Conn.*

LUKE HART, Southington, eldest son of Hawkins Hart, of the same
town, by his second wife, Esther (Gridley), born January 8th, 1738–9,
in Southington; married, March, 1764, Deborah, daughter of Benjamin
Barnes, of Southington, and his wife, Hannah (Abbot), born November
10th, 1734, in Branford, Conn. They were married at Southington,
before Rev. Benjamin Chapman, then pastor. He lived on the old
homestead of his father, at or near what has since been known as the
Ezekiel Sloper place, on the west side of East Street, recently occupied
by Stephen Judd. He removed to Winchester, Conn., in 1786, and
his name is on the tax list there in that year. In 1787 his wife became
owner of a lot on the west side of Spruce Street Road, nearly opposite
Amos Pierce, on which they lived in a log house, and where they
probably died. They deeded their place at Southington in 1786, to
Samuel Newell, for £215, containing twenty-one acres, with house and
barn thereon, and another piece of twenty-one acres in Blue Hills, to
extend to the top of the mountain. This was in Shuttle Meadow
Division.

THEIR CHILDREN, BEING THE SIXTH GENERATION.

       Josiah, born   , 1765; died young.
1827½. Selah, born   , 1766; baptized March 23d, 1766; married
                   , Rachel Hemsted.
1828. Stephen, born   , 1767; married   , Sarah Munson.
1829. Samuel, born   , 1771; died at Winchester in 1826, aged 55 years.
1830. Lydia, born July 13th, 1775; married, January, 1799, Hawley Oakley.

1730.   *Rutland, Vt.*

JOSIAH HART, Southington, second son of Hawkins Hart, of the same town, and his second wife, Esther (Gridley), born June 30th, 1740, at Southington, and baptized there by Rev. Jeremiah Curtiss, pastor; married September 1st, 1761, Elizabeth Moss, of Wallingford. They lived at Farmingburg Parish, in Southington, but sold his place here in 1785, to Rachel Truesdale, of Harwinton, for £40, containing seventeen acres, with a cider-mill thereon, and his buildings standing on lands of Joshua Porter. He removed to Rutland, Vt., and February 13th, 1789, there gave a quitclaim deed of five acres of land in Farmingburg Parish, in Southington, for £2 consideration, to Amos Beecher.

THEIR CHILDREN, BEING THE SIXTH GENERATION.

831. Esther, born December 3d, 1762.
832. Sarah, born August 17th, 1765.

1731.   *Middletown, Vt.*

DAVID HART, Southington, third son of Hawkins Hart, of the same town, and his second wife, Eunice (Gridley), born July 22d, 1745, at Southington, and baptized there, July 28th, 1745; married Lucy Codner. He had an impediment in his speech. He and his wife, Lucy, sold to Jotham Woodruff, March 14th, 1807, for the consideration of $800, their place, consisting of two pieces of land—the first, part of an ancient highway of two and one-half acres, and the second, a piece of nine acres, with a dwelling-house and barn attached; and at the same date they sold to Ruth, wife of William Tisdale, eight acres for $200. The same land was conveyed to said Lucy by James Curtiss. They removed from Southington to Middletown, Rutland County, Vt., in 1807, where, it is said, they both died, after 1828 and before 1835. They had no children.

1732.   *Wallingford, Conn.*

BENJAMIN HART, Southington, youngest son of Hawkins Hart, of the same town, and his second wife, Esther (Gridley), born January 4th, 1750–1, at Southington; baptized January 6th, 1751, by the pastor, Rev. J. Curtiss. He married at Wallingford, February 25th, 1776, Jerusha Rich, where he located. He died at Meriden, October 7th, 1836, aged 85 years. She died August 26th, 1832.

THEIR CHILDREN, BEING THE SIXTH GENERATION.

1833. Esther, born November 8th, 1776; married   Hall;
          second, January 24th, 1822, Marvel Andrews.
1834. Lucy, born December 20th, 1779.

1835. Susannah, born January 15th, 1782.
1836. Webb, born February 21st, 1786; married
1837. Jerusha, born September 11th, 1788.
1838. Samuel Ives, born November 22d, 1792; married September 20th, 1814, Abigail D. Hall.

GRIDLEY.

1733.   *Bristol, Conn.*

MARY HART, Wallingford, eldest daughter of Thomas, of Wallingford, and his wife, Hannah (Coe), born March 23d, 1743, at Wallingford; married June 25th, 1761, Luke Gridley, of Bristol, son of Hezekiah, and his wife, Sarah (Newell), born September 31st, 1734, at Farmington. He died at Bristol of old age, (so the record says,) March 1st, 1810, aged 76. His widow died May 30th, 1817, aged 74 years. (See Bristol record of deaths.) They had Mary, born April 17th, 1762; Elisha, born May 17th, 1765; Chloe, born April 25th, 1769; Rachel, born October 17th, 1771; Lott, born April 2d, 1774.

HILLS.

1734.   *Bristol, Conn.*

RUTH HART, Bristol, second daughter of Thomas Hart, of Wallingford and Bristol, and his wife, Hannah (Coe), born October 1st, 1744, at Wallingford; married at Bristol, (where she went with her parents about 1747,) Dan Hills, born 1734. She was his second wife. He died in Bristol of dropsy, June 9th, 1799, aged 65 years. She died there of consumption, February 8th, 1809, aged 64 years.

1735.   *Paris, N. Y.*

JONATHAN HART, Paris, Herkimer County, N. Y., eldest son of Thomas Hart, of Wallingford, Farmington, and Bristol, Conn., and his wife, Hannah (Coe), born March 22d, 1746, at Farmington, and went with his parents to Bristol, Conn. He married   ,
Mary Coe, who died about 1787, when second he married about 1788, Lucia Clark, of Southington, daughter of David, and his wife, Lois (Andrews), born November 4th, 1760, at Southington. He removed to Paris, N. Y., about 1794. She died there, February 26th, 1803, aged 42 years. He died at the same place, March 2d, 1806, aged 60 years.

THEIR CHILDREN, BEING THE SIXTH GENERATION.

1839. Ira, born September 18th, 1771; married, December, 1798, Maria Sherman.
1840. Jonathan, born April 22d, 1773; married   , Orphia Chapin.
1841. Samuel, born June 3d, 1775; married
1842. Hester, born August 9th, 1777; died December 2d, 1795, in Brotherton, (now Marshall,) Oneida County, N. Y.

343. Polly, born October 3d, 1779; married   , Elisha Hills.
344. Seth, born November 25th, 1781; married   , Louisa Hickox.
345. Josiah, born April 2d, 1784; married   , Sophronia Gridley.
346. Eunice, born June 27th, 1787; married   , Jacob Hemingway.

SECOND WIFE.

347. Alvaro, born November 4th, 1788; married   , 1812, Betsey Burr.
348. Orris, born February 13th, 1791; married, January, 1812, Elizabeth Bigelow.
349. Warren, born August 29th, 1793; married, December, 1814, Harriet Page.
    Lowly, born October 27th, 1795; died at Paris, N. Y., September 11th, 1813, aged 18 years.
350. Lucia, born February 19th, 1798; married   , 1816, Ambrose Lyman.
351. Edwin Clark, born December 14th, 1800; married March 10th, 1823, Aurel Anderson.
352. Ichabod Andrews, born February 16th, 1803; married October 13th, 1830; Emeline F. Frisbee.

BYINGTON.

1736.   Bristol, Conn.

HANNAH HART, Bristol, Conn., third daughter of Thomas Hart, of Vallingford, Farmington, and Bristol, Conn., and his wife, Hannah Coe), born October 10th, 1747, in that part of Farmington now called Bristol; married Jacob Byington, of that town.

1737.   Clinton, N. Y.

THOMAS HART, Clinton, Oneida County, N. Y., second son of Thomas Hart, of Wallingford, Farmington, and Bristol, Conn., and his wife, Hannah (Coe), born September 10th, 1749, at Bristol, Conn.; married in 1772, Mary Hungerford, daughter of Benjamin. She was admitted to the church in 1796. He was a member of the New York Legislature, judge of the county court, &c., a man of wealth, and a supporter of religious institutions as the basis of civil liberty. He and his brothers, Amasa and Jonathan, emigrated from Bristol, Conn., to Paris, Oneida County, N. Y., about 1794. He died at Clinton, N. Y., leaving a large estate.

THEIR CHILDREN, BEING THE SIXTH GENERATION.

353. Jemima, born   ; married   , Ava Woodruff.
354. Hannah, born   ; married   , Ava Woodruff.
355. Ephraim, born   ; married   , 1821, Martha Seymour.
356. Prudence, born   ; married   , Dr. Sewell Hopkins.
357. Eli, born   ; married   , Mary
357½. Roswell, born   ; married   , Eliza Pixley.
358. Truman, born   , at Palmyra, N. Y.; married   ,
    Susan
359. Thomas, born   . He is wealthy, and lives in Rochester
    unmarried.
360. Mary, born   ; married   Allen.

PECK.

1738.　　　　　　　　　　　　　　*Bristol, Conn.*

ESTHER HART, Bristol, Conn.; fourth daughter of Thomas Hart, of Wallingford, Farmington, and Bristol, Conn., and his first wife, Hannah (Coe), born November 16th, 1751, in that part of Farmington now called Bristol, where she married Zebulon, son of Zebulon Peck, of Bristol, and his wife, Mary (Edwards), born April 15th, 1743, in Meriden. He was a brother of Captain David Peck, of Southington. She died at Bristol in 1777, aged 26, when he second married June 11th, 1778, Widow Mary Watson, and third he married Widow Mindwell Chubb. He was a very prominent man in Bristol, having been a justice of the peace many years, was a member of the legislature fourteen sessions, was a delagate to the convention to act upon the adoption of the United States Constitution, and voted yea, and was a deacon of the Congregational Church. He removed to Clinton, N. Y., 1801, and died at Marshall, N. Y., January 23d, 1820, aged 70 years. His children by his first wife were—Esther, Roxana, Isaac, Beulah, Silas, born March 30th, 1776, married Betsey Chubb, died October 31st, 1839.

1739.　　　　　　　　　　　　　　*Paris, N. Y.*

AMASA HART, Paris, N. Y., third son of Thomas Hart, of Wallingford, Farmington, and Bristol, Conn., and his wife, Hannah (Coe), born June 19th, 1754, at Bristol; married　　　　　　, Phebe Roberts. They removed from Bristol, Conn., to Paris, N. Y., about 1794, and from thence to Clinton, Oneida County, N. Y.

THEIR CHILDREN, BEING THE SIXTH GENERATION.

1861. Susannah, born　　　　　　, 1775; married　　　　　　, Samuel Foot, of Clinton, N. Y.

1862. Rhoda, born　　　　, 1777; married　　　　　, Jesse Hale.

1863. Abel, born November 5th, 1778; married　　　, 1798, Lovina Gridley, of Paris, N. Y.

1864. Lovina, born　　　, 1782; married　　　　Pierce, of Otsego, N. Y.

1865. Jesse, born　　　, 1784; married　　　　, Ruth Stebbins, of Clinton, N. Y.

1865½. William, born　　　, 1786; married　　　　Adams, Jefferson County, N. Y.

Amasa, born　　　, 1788.

1866. Phebe, born　　　, 1790; married　　　, 1807, William C. Gridley; second,　　　　　　　Wells.

1740.　　　　　　　　　　　　　　*Bristol, Conn.*

ABEL HART, Bristol, Conn., fourth son of Thomas Hart, of Wallingford, and that part of Farmington called Bristol, and his first wife,

Hannah (Coe), born September 5th, 1756, at Bristol, Conn. He entered the army of the revolution, and died of starvation. He was a prisoner of the British in New York, but was released, and lived to reach Milford, Conn. His name is inscribed on a monument erected in the old cemetery at Milford to perpetuate the memory of revolutionary soldiers.

JEROME.

1741.   *Bristol, Conn.*

BARBARA HART, Bristol, Conn., fifth daughter of Thomas Hart, of Wallingford, and that part of Farmington now called Bristol, and his first wife, Hannah (Coe), born May 24th, 1758, in Bristol, and married _____, Zerubabel Jerome, of Bristol. They had issue, viz: Robert, Stephen, John, Randall, Hannah, and Nancy.

1742.

BENJAMIN HART, Bristol, Conn., fifth son of Thomas Hart, of Wallingford, and that part of Farmington called Bristol, after it was called New Cambridge a few years, and his first wife, Hannah (Coe), born March 25th, 1761, at Bristol; married _____, Mehitabel Jerome, daughter of Thomas, and sister of Sibil, wife of Ithurel Hart, born May 6th, 1765. He died at Bristol April 17th, 1828, in his 68th year. She removed to Pittsford, N. Y., in 1834, but returned, and died at Bristol, December 4th, 1848, aged 84 years, and was buried in the North Yard.

THEIR CHILDREN, BEING THE SIXTH GENERATION.

1867. Ruth, born October 2d, 1784; married November 26th, 1805, Clark Carrington.
1868. James, born September 18th, 1786; married January 1st, 1821, Betsey Johnson.
1869. Orra, born May 28th, 1788; married January 6th, 1807, Moses Moss, Jr.
1870. Mehitabel, born July 6th, 1790; married February 19th, 1810, George Bulkley, of Farmington.
1871. Eber Jerome, born September 12th, 1791; married, March, 1815, Sophia Root.
1872. Fanny, born February 7th, 1793; married March 31st, 1834, Moses Moss, Jr.
1873. Roswell, born February 21st, 1795; married June 27th, 1820, Phebe Johnson.
1874. Romanta, born March 19th, 1800; married _____, lives at the west, and has five children.
1875. Emeline, born January 25th, 1804; married February 13th, 1825, Linas Wilcox.
1876. Thomas Coe, born July 7th, 1806; married _____, Emily Atwater, of Bristol.

DUDLEY.

1744.   *Durham, Conn.*

RUTH HART, Durham, Conn., second daughter of Samuel Hart, of the same town, and his wife, Abridget (Fowler), born June 8th, 1766, and baptized June 15th, 1766, in Durham; married Charles Dudley, of Guilford, and removed to Litchfield, Conn. They had children, viz: Susan, Lois, Samuel, Frederic, and Ruth.

1745.   *Durham, Conn.*

DANIEL HART, Durham, Conn., second son of Samuel Hart, of the same town, and his wife, Abridget (Fowler), born June 29th, 1768; baptized July.13th, 1768, in Durham; married   , Hannah Hubbard, daughter of Abraham, and his wife, Hannah (Hedges), of Guilford. His avocation was farming. He was made a freeman in Durham, September 15th, 1800. He was a very quiet and industrious man. He died January 3d, 1845, aged 76 years. His wife died December 27th, 1845.

THEIR CHILD, BEING THE SIXTH GENERATION.

1877. Ruth, born August 6th, 1800; married December 12th, 1821, Henry Maltby.

1746.   *Durham, Conn.*

SAMUEL HART, Durham Conn., third son of Samuel Hart, of the same town, and his wife, Abridget (Fowler), born July 12th, 1770; baptized July 22d, 1770, in Durham; married March 3d, 1803, Patience Hubbard, daughter of Eber, and his wife, Patience (Chittenden), born, August, 1772. He was made a freeman in Durham, September 21st, 1801. He was a farmer, and lived on the old homestead of his father. Like his brother, Daniel, he was quiet and industrious. He died December 25th, 1857, aged 87 years. His wife was an excellent woman and mother, and during the last part of her life was a great sufferer from broken limbs, which suffering she bore with Christian resignation, agreeing in spirit with her given name. She died March 15th, 1864, aged 91 years and 7 months.

THEIR CHILDREN, BEING THE SIXTH GENERATION.

1878. William A., born April 26th, 1806; married June 23d, 1828, Sally Jones.
1879. Edward, ⎫ married December 25th, 1834, Emma Merriman, of Wallingford.
            ⎬ born January 14th, 1808;
1880. Edmund, ⎭ married December 28th, 1833, Mary Hurlburt.
1881. George, born April 18th, 1810. He was killed by the falling of a tree, December 19th, 1835, aged 25 years.
            Amos, ⎫   died March 8th, 1831, aged 18 years.
            ⎬ born January 1st, 1813;   .
1882. Mary, ⎭   married November 1st, 1835, Seneca Barnes, of Northford.
1883. Samuel, born April 15th, 1815; married October 28th, 1838, Lydia R. Davidson, of Lyme.

1747.   *Durham, Conn.*

CAPTAIN JOHN HART, Durham, Conn., fourth son of Samuel Hart, of the same town, and his wife, Abridget (Fowler), born September 11th,

1772, a twin with Rebecca, and both were baptized October 25th, 1772, in Durham. He married July 15th, 1800, Sally Coe, daughter of Morris, and his wife, Lucy (Rossiter), of Durham. He held the military rank of captain. He was admitted to the church in Durham, November 4th, 1827; his wife was admitted in 1804. He settled on a farm half a mile from his father, and was a selectman for a number of years. He was made a freeman in Durham, September 21st, 1801. He died February 19th, 1847, aged 74 years. She died July 12th, 1861, aged 83 years. She is said to have been a driving, hard-working woman.

THEIR CHILDREN, BEING THE SIXTH GENERATION.

Emeline Rebecca, born September 28th, 1803; died November 13th, 1813, aged 10 years.

Leander, born January 30th, 1809; died June 8th, 1824, aged 15 years.

1884. Harriet, born June 20th, 1811; married October 12th, 1831, Amos Harrison.

1885. Catharine, born January 25th, 1816. She is a seamstress.

PARKER.

1748. *Kensington, Conn.*

Lois Hart, Durham, Conn., fourth daughter and youngest child of Samuel Hart, of the same town, and his wife, Abridget (Fowler), born in Durham, and baptized there March 12th, 1775; married

, Selah Parker, of Kensington, son of Job, and brother of Huldah, who married Seth K. Smith, of Southington. She was admitted to the Congregational Church in Durham, November 6th, 1803. They lived in Kensington, in a house standing just east of the barn of Levi Stoddard, now Hiram Galpin's. The house still remained in 1870. He fell dead while threshing in the barn of Ashbel Dickinson, January 5th, 1818, aged 40 years. Their children were—1, Betsey, baptized September 12th, 1807, married June 11th, 1834, Thomas Camp, of Durham; 2, Mary, baptized, September, 1814, married in 1837, Lewis Jones, of North Madison, Conn. They have since moved to Pennfield, Ohio.

1749.

Kensington, Conn., Charlestown, N. H.

Ebenezer Hart, Kensington, Conn., eldest son and child of Deacon Ebenezer Hart, of the same place, and his wife, Elizabeth (Lawrence), born July 29th, 1742, at Kensington, Conn.; married April 5th, 1770, Lydia Benton, who died, when second he married in 1780, Sally Whitmore, and after her decease he married third in 1792, Mary Hands, who removed to Clarendon, Vt. He removed to Charlestown, N. H., where he died in 1796, aged 54 years. His estate was represented as insolvent. The following notice appeared in the *Connecticut Courant,* October, 1796:

"We, the subscribers, being appointed Commissioners to examine the claims of the creditors of the estate of Ebenezer Hart, late of Charlestown, (in New Hampshire State,) deceased, represented insolvent, do hereby give notice that we will attend to the business of our appointment on the 2d of January, 1797, at the dwelling-house of the deceased in said Charlestown, from 1 o'clock P. M. until 7, after which time those who neglect to exhibit their claims will forever be debarred. No account will be allowed unless properly authenticated.

Charlestown, Oct. 19th, 1796.

George Hubbard,
Ezra Rice,   } Commissioners."
Bill Barnes,

CHILDREN BY HIS FIRST WIFE, BEING THE SIXTH GENERATION.

1885.	Betsey, born February 21st, 1771; married	, 1790; George Atkins.	
	Romeo, born	; baptized February 8th, 1778, at Worthington.	
	Era B., born	; died young.	
1886.	Era Benton, born Gilbert.	, 1779; married September 17th, 1810, Lydia	
1887.	Lydia, born New Britain.	, 1780; married	, 1834, Theron Hart, of
1888.	Hannah, born Hartford.	, 1782; married	, 1810, Caleb Church, of
1889.	Ichabod W., born	, 1784; married	, 1814, Lucy Atkins.
1890.	George W., born	, 1786; married	, Polly Hitchcock.
1890½.	Josiah, born	, 1788; married	, Friendly Rice.

1750.   *Berlin, Conn.*

MAJOR JONATHAN HART, Kensington, Conn., second son of Deacon Ebenezer Hart, of the same place, and his wife, Elizabeth (Lawrence), born at Kensington, Conn., in 1744, and graduated at Yale College in 1768. He went to New Jersey, and taught school for several years. He returned to Kensington, and entered into trade with the minister of the place, with whom he had a serious quarrel, and was thrown into jail, where he remained until the revolution. He joined the army, was in the public service from 1775 to 1791, and was slain by the Indians at St. Clair's defeat, in the autumn of 1791, at which time he held the military rank of major. He married in 1777, Abigail Riley, who, after her husband's decease, married second, Rev. Cyprian Strong, of Chatham, Conn., August 3d, 1797. Major Hart left one child only, who married, and died childless.

At probate court, Farmington, Conn., July 5th, 1792, administration was granted to Abigail Hart on the estate of Jonathan Hart, late of Berlin, deceased, and June 4th, 1794, she was appointed guardian to Everlin Hart, a minor of said town of Berlin, and in said probate district of Farmington. The following biographical sketch is copied from

he *Connecticut Gazette*, published by John M. Niles and J. T. Pease, in
.819, at Hartford, Conn.:

"Major Jonathan Hart was a native of this town, (Berlin.) He was
₁ gallant and distinguished officer, and one of the victims of the un-
ortunate defeat of General St. Clair, November 4th, 1791. His life
and those of his command were literally offered a sacrifice for the
afety of the rest of the army. When all were in confusion and dis-
nay Major Hart was ordered to charge the enemy with the bayonet,
with a view to facilitate a retreat, or rather a flight, to the shattered
emains of the army. This charge was made with gallantry and spirit,
under circumstances which language is too feeble to describe—the des-
olation of the place, the confusion of the scene, and the whoop and
rells of a savage foe flushed with victory and thirsting for blood, the
general consternation which prevailed, and the groans of the dying in
every direction. But the intrepid major and almost every man of his
party were killed in the desperate enterprise, and their bones were left
o bleach upon the borders of the waters of the Wabash, the dreary
abode of wild beasts, and of savage men more wild than they."

While Major Hart was marching up and down the rivers of Ohio,
and perambulating the country as a soldier, he had a good opportunity
to observe the soil, climate, and value of the lands with reference to
the claims of Connecticut for the reserve, and the commissioners who
had the location of those claims in charge wisely availed themselves of
his knowledge. He wrote some thirty letters to his friend, Major William Judd, of Farmington, on the subject, and these letters are still
in good condition, preserved by the posterity of Major Judd, who reside in the city of New Britain in 1875. They are interesting, but too
lengthy for this work. They have been in Ohio and copied.

THEIR CHILD, BEING THE SIXTH GENERATION.

1891. Alces Evelin, born October 10th, 1782; married   , Charlotte
    Overton.

1751.   *Kensington, Conn.*

ELIHU HART, Kensington, Conn., third son of Deacon Ebenezer Hart,
of the same place, and his wife, Elizabeth (Lawrence), born March 4th,
1751, at Kensington; married December 31st, 1777, Mary Peck, before
Dr. John Smalley, of New Britain. He removed to New Durham,
N. Y. He was unfortunate in business, was imprisoned for debt, and
died in jail at Coxsackie. N. Y.

THEIR CHILDREN, BEING THE SIXTH GENERATION.

Amos, born   . He left home and was never heard from.

1892. Jonathan, born   ; married   ,
    at Fayetteville, N. C.

Lavira, born   ; died at Coxsackie, N. Y.

1752.   *Kensington, Conn.*

Doctor John Hart, Kensington, Conn., fourth son of Deacon Ebenezer Hart, of the same place, and his wife, Elizabeth (Lawrence), born March 11th, 1753, at Kensington, Conn. He graduated at Yale College in 1776, and soon after entered the army of the revolution as surgeon. After his return he settled at Farmington, where he practiced chiefly in surgery until about 1798, when his health being impaired, he resolved upon a sea voyage, and entered the naval service of the United States. He married November 9th, 1786, Hannah, daughter of Gideon Williams, of Kensington, Conn., and his first wife, Patience (Graham), born October 15th, 1766, at Kensington, Conn. For some years after his death she was a female physician, and practiced obstetrics. It is said that she would ride any time of night to visit his patients. She second married J. Stoddard Wightman, of Southington, Conn. She died at Blendon, Franklin County, Ohio. Dr. Hart was an ensign at the surrender of Cornwallis. In company with General Lyman and others he attempted to settle on the Mississippi, near Natchez, but was compelled to swim the Father of Waters, and flee through the forests to Florida. He then engaged as surgeon on the armed schooner Retaliation. He died at sea in latitude 39°, and west longitude 73° 33′, October 3d, 1798, aged 45 years.

THEIR CHILDREN, BEING THE SIXTH GENERATION.

Son, born December 8th, 1787; died   , aged 13 days.

1892¼. James Everlin, born November 8th, 1788; died   , 1821.

1893. John Ariadna, born November 17th, 1790; married February 27th, 1815, Joanna Porter.

1893¼. Elizabeth Lawrence, born April 9th, 1793; died November 13th, 1807, aged 14 years.

1894. Gideon Williams, born July 21st, 1795; married Nancy Langdon.

1895. Thomas Joseph, born January 11th, 1798; died in Blendon, Ohio, by eating poisoned pork.

1752¼.   *Kensington, Conn.*

Thomas Hart, Kensington, Conn., fifth son of Deacon Ebenezer Hart, of the same place, and his wife, Elizabeth (Lawrence), born December 6th, 1754, at Kensington, Conn. He was never married. He gave his farm in Kensington to his niece, Lydia Hart, April 27th, 1834, who married Theron, son of Benjamin Hart, of New Britain; Conn. After the Middletown Turnpike was built, by order of the legislature of the state, Thomas Hart lived on the corner opposite the Second Church, near an apple tree in Deacon Thomas Hart's lot. Thomas Hart died at Kensington, September 26th, 1832, aged 77 years, 9 months, 20 days. Deacon Thomas Hart was grandfather of the above.

1752½.

HANNAH HART, Kensington, Conn., second daughter and youngest child of Deacon Ebenezer Hart, of the same parish, and his wife, Elizabeth (Lawrence), born at Kensington in 1758. She died of measles in 1810, having never been married.

1753.   *New Britain, Conn.*

DEACON ELIJAH HART, Jr., New Britain, Conn., eldest son of Deacon Elijah Hart, of Kensington and New Britain, Conn., and his wife, Abigail (Goodrich), born September 26th, 1735, in Kensington. He united with the church there in 1757, came to New Britain with his parents, and became one of the constituent members of Dr. Smalley's church there, April 19th, 1758, when the church was organized. He married Sarah Gilbert, daughter of Ebenezer, and his wife, Mercy (Cowles), born May 11th, 1737. He first located in the south part of Hart Quarter, where Horace Hart lived, and after him Levi O. Smith, but built a large house near the mills, and September 10th, 1793, he deeded the south part to his son, Elijah, third of the name in as many generations. He was a man of strictly puritanical habits, stern virtue, great diligence, and economy. He was a plain farmer, with a large family and large property. He was chosen deacon, June 1st, 1780, which office he held for twenty years. His business was all laid aside at 4 o'clock Saturday afternoon, by himself, workmen, and servants, his face shaved, his long boots brushed, and his cows milked before sunset. His best boots would last him seven years, and his best surtout coat twenty years. He led the singing in church many years, having a grand voice, and good musical taste for that age. He died December 10th, 1800, aged 66 years. His widow died September 22d, 1809, aged 73 years.

THEIR CHILDREN, BEING THE SIXTH GENERATION.

1896. Elijah, born May 7th, 1759; married December 21st, 1780, Anna Andrews.
1897. Aaron, born October 16th, 1761; married March 4th, 1790, Sarah Francis.
1898. Sarah, born February 21st, 1765; married March 3d, 1785, Robert Cornwall.
1899. Ozias, born August 8th, 1768; married   , Sarah Lee.
1900. Selina, born August 30th, 1770; married December 30th, 1790, Solomon Churchill.
1901. Olive, born   , 1775; baptized August 27th, 1775; married August 8th, 1803, Seth Merill.

1754.   *New Britain, Conn.*

THOMAS HART, New Britain, Conn., second son of Deacon Elijah Hart, of the same place, and his wife, Abigail (Goodrich), born Janu-

51

ary 12th, 1738, at Kensington; married February 2d, 1758, Mehitabel, daughter of Jonathan Bird, of Farmington, and his wife, Hannah (Thompson), born July 15th, 1738, at Farmington. He was a farmer and shoe-maker, and lived on ·West Main Street, New Britain, in the same house owned and occupied by Henry K. Smith in 1873. He was a man of great industry and economy, scrupulously honest, and re- markably inoffensive. He first built his house at the east corner of his home lot, but found no water for a well; and just as his house was nearly finished, while the joiners were at dinner, it took fire from the shavings and burned down. He was admitted to the New Britain Church, June 4th, 1762. His wife was admitted January 9th, 1785. She was a sister of Jonathan Bird, M. D., who was also a preacher of the gospel. Mr. Hart died January 7th, 1830, aged 93 years. His wife died March 18th, 1825, aged 87 years.

THEIR CHILDREN, BEING THE SIXTH GENERATION.

1902. Ruth, born November 10th, 1758; married Feb. 17th, 1785, Aaron Roberts.
1903. Abigail, born October 27th, 1761; married February 15th, 1781, Jonathan Seymour.
1904. Abijah, born April 7th, 1764; married September 22d, 1794, Anna Hall.
1905. Ismena, born   , 1768; baptized July 17th, 1768; never married; died February 20th, 1854.
1906. William, born   , 1772; baptized March 16th, 1772; married   , 1798, Hannah Bridge Campe.

1755.   *New Britain, Conn.*

JEHUDAH HART, New Britain, Conn., third son of Deacon Elijah Hart, of Kensington and New Britain, and his wife, Abigail (Good- rich), born December 12th, 1739, in Kensington; married July 9th, 1767, Mary, daughter of Reuben Munson, of Southington, and his wife, Mary, born 1751; baptized April 14th, 1751, at Southington. She died in childbed, October 28th, 1786, aged 36 years, when he second married in 1787, Elizabeth, widow of Phineas Judd, Jr., and daughter of Mark Mazuzen, a Frenchman. Mr. Hart's residence was some twenty rods south of his father's, in Hart Quarter, the same house owned and occupied by Mr. Chauncey Beckwith in 1873. His avocation was farming, and he was an honest and inoffensive man. He was admitted to the New Britain Church, September, 1769. He had such a fondness for home that it is said he never saw the city of Hartford, although living to an old age within twelve miles of it. His second wife died April 26th, 1825, aged 73 years. He died Au- gust 25th, 1825, aged 86 years.

CHILDREN BY THE FIRST WIFE, BEING THE SIXTH GENERATION.

1907. Mary, born August 5th, 1769; married December 24th, 1806, Eliphalet Wads- worth, being his second wife.

1908. Asahel, born May 24th, 1771; married , 1790, Hannah Langdon;
   second, Sarah   .
1909. James, born May 22d, 1773; married, June, 1793, Sylvia Pennfield.
   Sylvia, born August 15th, 1774; died November 19th, 1776.
1910. Sylvia, 2d, born April 15th, 1777. She lived at her father's home, and died
   May 9th, 1864.
1911. Joel, born June 14th, 1779; married September 17th, 1800, Lydia North.
1912. Benjamin, born Nov. 20th, 1781; married July 28th, 1805, Honor Deming.
1913. Abigail, born October 28th, 1786; married January 29th, 1807, Moses D.
   Seymour.

CHILDREN BY THE SECOND MARRIAGE.

1914. Oliver, born December 19th, 1788; married January 3d, 1838, Deborah E.
   Hurlburt.
   Laura, born   ; baptized August 4th, 1791; died   ,
   1793.
1915. Elizur, born October 9th, 1794; married September 11th, 1832, Sophronia
   Jerome, of Bristol.

1756.

Wethersfield, Conn., Marietta, Ohio.

Dr. Josiah Hart, New Britain, Conn., fourth son of Deacon Elijah Hart, of Kensington and New Britain, and his wife, Abigail (Goodrich), born April 28th, 1742, in Kensington. He prepared for college under Rev. Dr. Norris, and graduated at Yale College in 1762. He studied medicine with Dr. Potter, of Wallingford, became a physician, and was a surgeon in the army of the revolution. He married in 1765, Abigail Sluman, of Stonington, Conn., and settled as a physician, at Wethersfield, on Broad Street, where Simeon Hale resided in 1874, which town he represented in the legislature several times. His wife died June 4th, 1777, at Wethersfield, of small pox, when second he married March 25th, 1778, Abigail Harris, of Wethersfield, widow of Thomas Harris, and daughter of Joshua Robbins. He removed to her place on Harris Hill, a little south of the village. He was chosen deacon of the church at Wethersfield, April 17th, 1793. His second wife was a descendant of John Robbins, one of the first settlers of Wethersfield, and a blood relation on the mother's side to the celebrated Miles Standish. She died August 8th, 1796, at Wethersfield, when Dr. Hart removed to Marietta, Ohio, where his two sons had settled early in life. Here he continued his avocation as physician, and married third, Miss Anna Moulton, a maiden lady of Newburyport, Mass. At the formation of the Congregational Church in Marietta he was elected deacon, which office he filled several years. In person Dr. Hart was below the medium size, but well formed, with a mild, pleasing, and intelligent countenance. In his manners he was very gentlemanly and kind, exhibiting a true Christian spirit in his intercourse with his fellow-men. In 1811, having become too aged for practice, he removed to a farm in Lowell, Ohio, on the Muskingum River, some ten miles from Marietta, where he died of spotted fever, August, 1812, aged 70 years. His widow died a few hours after him, and both were buried the same day.

NOTE.—After the death of his first wife Dr. Hart removed to the house of his second wife, on Harris Hill, a place now occupied and owned by the Harris family, where I found an old ledger in the handwriting of Dr. Hart, in which his autograph is on several pages of the book. The oldest date found was 1777, and the latest was 1799. Here are charges of his visits and services as physician, to the people of Wethersfield, Newington, Berlin, Stepney, (now Rocky Hill,) and to other places more remote, embracing a period of some twenty years of active labor. The book is somewhat mutilated, but is still a precious relic of a good and worthy ancestor.

CHILDREN BY HIS FIRST WIFE, BEING THE SIXTH GENERATION.

1916. Abigail, born February 3d, 1766; married   , Thomas Wells, of Wethersfield.

Josiah, born December 10th, 1768; died January 15th, 1769, aged 1 month.

1917. Hannah, born   24th, 1769; married   , Joshua Robbins, of Wethersfield.

1918. Emily, born February 3d, 1771; married, March, 1789, Gideon Wells, of Wethersfield.

1919. Josiah Sluman, born January 10th, 1773; baptized February 7th, 1773, by Dr. Smalley, at New Britain; died young.

1920. William, born March 4th, 1775; married   , Sarah Waters Wolcott, and lived at Marietta, Ohio.

1921. Thomas, born December 14th, 1776; married   , Elizabeth McClelland.

CHILDREN BY HIS SECOND WIFE.

1922. Betsey, born December 22d, 1778; married   , Titus Buck, of Wethersfield, Conn., and Marietta, Ohio.

1923. Clarissa, born   ; married   ; in Ohio, Wing Devoe, of Marietta, Ohio.

1924. Cynthia, born   ; married   , in Ohio, ——— Vance, of Columbus.

ENO.

1757.   Simsbury, Conn.

MARY HART, New Britain, Conn., only daughter of Deacon Elijah Hart, of Kensington and New Britain, and his wife, Abigail (Goodrich), born October 26th, 1744, at New Britain; married January 7th, 1765, Jonathan, son of David Eno, of Windsor, and his wife, Mary (Gillett), born 1739. She owned the covenant at New Britain Church, April 14th, 1765. Their children were—1, Polly, born December 21st, 1764, married Elijah Tuller, of Simsbury; 2, Rhoda, born August 12th, 1766, married Daniel Phelps, of Simsbury; 3, Jonathan, born March

5th, 1769, married Theodosia Case, of Simsbury; 4, Lucretia, born 'ebruary 13th, 1771, married David Humphrey, of Simsbury; 5, Elizbeth, born August 9th, 1773, at New Britain, married December 12th, 793, Alexander Phelps, of Simsbury; 6, Sintha, born May 28th, 1777, married Hezekiah Case, of Simsbury; 7, Salmon, born December 13th, 779, married June 2d, 1805, Polly Richards; 8, Chauncey, born December 19th, 1782, married Amarilla Case, of Simsbury; 9, Abigail, born February 28th, 1785, married October 2d, 1805, John Viets, of imsbury.

1758.   *New Britain, Conn.*

BENJAMIN HART, New Britain, Conn., fifth son of Deacon Elijah Hart, of Kensington and New Britain, and his wife, Abigail (Goodich), born October 10th, 1747, at Kensington; married August 19th, 772, by Rev. Samuel Clark, pastor of Kensington Church, Mary, daughter of Ephraim Fuller, of Berlin, and his wife, Mary (Dunham), born and baptized January 2d, 1757, at Kensington. His house and arm is at the head of the mill-pond, which was formerly owned by Ozias Hart, and in 1873 by Frederic North. He was a tall, bony man, f industrious and regular habits, and a successful farmer. He and his wife were admitted to the New Britain Congregational Church, December 12th, 1773. He died February 21st, 1827, aged 80 years. His widow died October 22d, 1834, aged 79 years.

THEIR CHILDREN, BEING THE SIXTH GENERATION.

925.   Benjamin, born February 7th, 1773; married January 30th, 1800, Hannah Kellogg.

     Mary, born   , 1775; died July 6th, 1790, aged 15 years.

     Esther, born November 8th, 1776; died young.

     Rhoda, born January 10th, 1778; died May 9th, 1786, aged 9 years.

926.   Roxana, born June 21st, 1780; married November 9th, 1797, Leonard Belden, Jr.

927.   Theron, born December 29th, 1782; married   , Abia Warner.

928.   Fanny, born February 17th, 1785; married   , Dr. Chauncey Andrews.

929.   Rhoda, 2d, born February 8th, 1788; married March 28th, 1839, Asa Tuller, of Simsbury.

     Ephraim, born November 4th, 1790; died young.

930.   Polly, born May 2d, 1792; married   , David Walkley, of Haddam.

931.   Cyrus, born July 19th, 1795; married March 31st, 1819, Betsey Clark.

932.   Esther, born March 5th, 1798; married March 16th, 1819, Edwin Gridley, of Southington.

1759.   *Seneca, N. Y.*

DEACON JOSEPH HART, New Britain, Conn., sixth son of Deacon Elijah Hart, of Kensington and New Britain, and his wife, Abigail (Goodrich), born May 17th, 1750, at Kensington; married November 5th, 1772, Huldah, daughter of Jedediah Smith, and his wife, Susannah (Cogswell), born January 4th, 1749. He built in Hart Quarter, New Britain, next north of his father's, the same house since owned and occupied by Edwin Francis and others, which house and farm he sold to Oliver Gridley, and removed to New Durham, N. Y., about 1804, and from thence to Seneca, Ontario County, N. Y., about 1814, where he died   . He was chosen deacon, probably at New Durham, now called Windham Center.

THEIR CHILDREN, BEING THE SIXTH GENERATION.

1933. Joseph, born November 20th, 1773; baptized September 11th, 1785; married Lucy Kirtland.
1934. Luther W., born September 2d, 1778; baptized September 11th, 1785; married April 27th, 1806, Sibil Selden.
1935. Huldah, born   ; baptized September 11th, 1785.
1936. Selah, born   ; baptized September 11th, 1785. Resides in Castleton, N. Y.
       Daughter, born

1760.   *New Britain, Conn.*

ELIZUR HART, New Britain, Conn., seventh son of Deacon Elijah Hart, of Kensington and New Britain, and his wife, Abigail (Goodrich), born December 25th, 1752, at Kensington; married January 1st, 1778, Sarah, daughter of Captain John Langdon, of New Britain, and his wife, Mercy (Eno), born December 9th, 1756. He was a noted school teacher, having taught seventeen seasons. He was called Landlord Hart, from having kept a tavern in Hart Quarter. In 1873 the house was in good condition, and called the State House, wherein was a famous dancing hall. In 1794 Mr. Hart went to the West Indies for his health, and died of yellow fever, at Kingston, Jamaica, in 1794, aged 42 years, when his widow married second, Seth Wadsworth, of Farmington. She died at Farmington, June 14th, 1822, aged 65.

CHILDREN OF ELIZUR AND SARAH, BEING THE SIXTH GENERATION.

1937. Sally, born November 9th, 1778; married Manly Clark; second, Martin Lee.
1938. Polly, born October 5th, 1781; married September 8th, 1800, John Hills, son of David.
1939. Sophia, born September 3d, 1785; married November 30th, 1809, Franklin Hitchcock.
1940. Erastus, born May 8th, 1787; married September 12th, 1810, Mary Parmelee, of Goshen.

BULL.

1761.   '

MARY HART, eldest daughter of Rev. William Hart, of Guilford and Saybrook, Conn., and his wife, Mary (Blague), born July 13th,

743, at Saybrook; married there February 26th, 1770, William Bull,
f Hartford, son of Caleb, Jr., and his wife, Martha (Cadwell), born
Lugust 22d, 1748, at Hartford. She died at Saybrook, October 14th,
791, aged 48 years, when he second married   ,
Jrsula Bull, daughter of Isaac, of Litchfield, who survived him. He
ied at Litchfield, October 13th, 1799, aged 51 years, leaving no chil-
ren, and gave his property, by Will, to his poorest relative, Russel
Iull proving himself entitled to the estate.

LYNDE. JONES.

1762.   *Saybrook, Conn.*

REBECCA HART, Saybrook, second daughter of Rev. William Hart,
f the same town, and his wife, Mary (Blague), born January 22d,
745, at Saybrook; married   , William Lynde, of
Iaybrook. They had—1, Henry. 2, John Hart, who graduated at
Tale College, and was a lawyer; married Elizabeth, daughter of John
Jichol, and had five children; died December 17th, 1817. 3, Joseph,
orn   ·   ; married Elizabeth Jones, and had three
hildren. Mr. Lynde, the husband of Rebecca, died, when second she
narried Timothy Jones, son of Timothy, grandson of Isaac, great-
randson of Deputy-Governor William, and great-great-grandson of
Colonel John, the regicide.

1763.   *Saybrook, Conn.*

MAJOR-GENERAL WILLIAM HART, Saybrook, Conn., eldest son of Rev.
William Hart, of the same town, and his wife, Mary (Blague), born
une 24th, 1746, at Saybrook; married   , Esther
Buckingham, of Haddam, daughter of Joseph, and his wife, Sarah
Tully, born March 8th, 1745. His avocation was a merchant. He
vas in the war of the revolution, became a major-general, and was for
everal years a candidate for governor of the state. In 1795 the
Western Reserve, (so called,) belonging to the state of Connecticut,
vas purchased by subscription, by a company of wealthy citizens of
he state, for $1,200,000. William Hart was one of the company, and
1is subscription was $30,462. In 1785 he was engaged in the mercan-
ile business with his brother, Joseph, in Hartford, and were much en-
raged in the West India trade. His wife died March 15th, 1811, aged
36 years, when second he married January 28th, 1812, Lucy Bucking-
1am, daughter of Samuel, and his wife, Lydia (Watrous), born November 6th, 1775. General Hart died August 29th, 1817, in his 72d
year, when second she married General Matson Smith, of New Ro-
:helle, N. Y. She died at Norwich, Conn., June 26th, 1851, aged 75.

General Hart attained a high rank in society, and an unusual public esteem and consideration. The following is copied from his tombstone in the ancient burial ground on Saybrook Point:

"Sacred to the memory of Major-General William Hart, eldest son of Rev. William Hart, of Saybrook, who was born June 24th, 1746, and died August 29th, 1817, in the 72d year of his age."

In youth active and enterprising, he early entered on mercantile pursuits, and sustained a character of unquestionable integrity and extensive respectability. By his talents he rose to some of the first civil and military honors of this state, and commanded unusual influence at home and abroad. He loved order, was an able counsellor, a professor of religion, a benefactor to the church, a pillar in society, and has left a memory respected by his friends, instructive to his family, and honorable to the place in which he lived.

"One eye on death, and one full fixed on heaven,
Became a mortal and immortal man."

· CHILD BY HIS FIRST WIFE, BEING THE SIXTH GENERATION.

1941.   Richard William, born January 15th, 1768; married October 29th, 1795, Elizabeth Bull.

1764.   Saybrook, Conn.

SAMUEL HART, Saybrook, Conn., second son of Rev. William Hart, of the same town, and his wife, Mary (Blague), born June 24th, 1748, in Saybrook; married February 22d, 1770, Lucy, daughter of Joshua W. Bushnell, of Saybrook. He died November 8th, 1823, aged 75 years. She died October 23d, 1841, aged 87 years.

THEIR CHILDREN, BEING THE SIXTH GENERATION.

Lydia, born July 18th, 1772; died November 6th, 1790, aged 18 years.
1942.   Mary, born July 18th, 1775; married   Sill.
1943.   Samuel, born February 13th, 1778; married April 3d, 1813, Mercy Pratt, of Saybrook.
1944.   Harriet, born October 13th, 1781; married William Willard.
1945.   Maria, born March 13th, 1788; died June 13th, 1810, aged 22 years.
1946.   Nathaniel Lynde, born October 25th, 1791; married February 17th, 1822, Emeline E. Ingraham.

1764½.   Saybrook, Conn.

JOHN HART, Saybrook, Conn., third son of Rev. William Hart, of the same town, and his wife, Mary (Blague), born September 24th, 1750, at Saybrook; married Widow Nancy Bull, who died August 20th, 1825, aged 69 years. He was a merchant at Saybrook. He resided also in Hatfield, Mass., from 1793 to 1797, and he and his wife

united with the church at Amherst in 1802. He died April 28th,
1828, aged 78 years.

1947. John, born March 11th, 1784; married, June, 1811, Nancy Matthews.
1948. Rebecca, born
1949. William, born
1950. Julia Ann, born
1951. Nancy, born   , 1793; died   , 1793.
1952. Richard Morrison, born May 9th, 1795; married, May, 1813, Betsey Ingham,
     and lives in Ohio.
1953. George A., born
1954. Charles Edward, born, January, 1797; married   , Betsey
     , and lives in New York.
1955. Alexander, born

1765.   Hartford, Conn.

Joseph Hart, Saybrook, fourth son of Rev. William Hart, of the
same town, and his wife, Mary (Blague), born January 13th, 1755, at
Saybrook; married   , Eunice Ellery, of Hartford,
Conn., daughter of John, and his wife, Eunice (Hooker). He was engaged in the mercantile business at Hartford, from 1785 to 1800, and
probably later, first in company with his brother, General William
Hart, and subsequently by himself, and was much engaged in the
West India trade. His store was located near the river, and he appears to have been in the wholesale business. He became connected,
by marriage and business, with the most noted families in Hartford,
but for some cause became embarrassed, left the country, and was lost
overboard at sea about 1810.

1956. John Ellery, born June 12th, 1785; married Sarah Woodbridge; died Novem-
     ber 4th, 1821.
     Amelia, born July 16th, 1788; died February 5th, 1809.
1957. Joseph William, born May 11th, 1790; died November 16th, 1821.
     Frederic Austin, born January 21st, 1794; died, May, 1819.
1958. Ferdinand Austin, born September 10th, 1796; married June 12th, 1827, Sarah
     A. Cook.
1959. Edward Bonner, born March 12th, 1798; married in Boston; died, May, 1865.
     Henry F., born May 22d, 1800. There is no account of him, but it is sup-
     posed he was lost at sea.

1766.   Saybrook, Conn.

Elisha Hart, Saybrook, fifth son of Rev. William Hart of the same
town, and his wife, Mary (Blague), born September 3d, 1758, at Saybrook, Conn.; married Jannette McCurdy, of Lyme. She died April

7th, 1815. He died May 28th, 1842, aged 84. Their daughters have been distinguished for beauty and elegant accomplishments, and moved in the highest circles of wealth and honor.

THEIR CHILDREN, BEING THE SIXTH GENERATION.

1960. Sarah McCurdy, born   , 1787; married   , Rev. Samuel F. Jarvis, of Middletown.

1961. Ann McCurdy, born   , 1790; married   , Commodore Isaac Hull, United States Navy.

Mary Ann, born   , 1792; died single, October 30th, 1830, aged 38 years.

1962. Jannette M. McCurdy, born   , 1794.

1963. Elizabeth, born   , 1796; married   , Hon. Heman Allen.

1964. Amelia, born   , 1799; married   , Captain Joseph Hull, United States Navy.

1965. Harriet Augusta, born   , 1804; died   , 1840, aged 36 years.

1767.   *Saybrook, Conn.*

AMELIA HART, youngest daughter and child of Rev. William Hart, of the same town, and his wife, Mary (Blague), born January 26th, 1761, at Saybrook; married August 29th, 1790, Rev. Frederick William Hotchkiss, successor of Rev. William Hart as pastor of the First Church of Saybrook. He graduated at Yale College in 1778, and died March 31st, 1844. She died August 8th, 1845, aged 84 years, 6 months, and 12 days.

1769½.   *Guilford, Conn.*

EBENEZER HART, Guilford, Conn., eldest son of Thomas Hart, of the same town, and his wife, Concurrence (Bartlett), born October 3d, 1757, at Guilford. He was killed by the British in a skirmish at Leete's Island, Guilford, Conn., June 18th, 1781, aged 23 years, 8 months, and 15 days. He was unmarried.

1771.   *Guilford, Conn.*

THOMAS HART, Guilford, second son of Thomas Hart, of the same town, and his wife, Concurrence (Bartlett), born September 8th, 1762; married October 8th, 1787, Mary Parmelee, of Guilford, daughter of William. His avocation was farming, and he was a deacon of the church. He died May 29th, 1829, aged 67 years. She was living, August, 1847.

THEIR CHILDREN, BEING THE SIXTH GENERATION.

1966. William, born May 5th, 1788; married November 29th, 1814, Lydia Griffin.

1967. Ruth, born January 14th, 1790; married March 18th, 1813, George Landon.

1968. George, born February 8th, 1794; married March 27th, 1818, Clarissa Par-
mela.

1969. Polly, born September 13th, 1797; married April 10th, 1817, Richard Fowler.

1970. Eliza, born, March, 1800; married August 31st, 1823, Stephen Trowbridge.

1773. *Guilford, Conn.*

JOHN HART, Guilford, third son and youngest child of Thomas Hart,
of the same town, and his wife, Concurrence (Bartlett), born January
15th, 1773, at Guilford, Conn.; married October 1st, 1803, Betsey
Field, daughter of Luke, of Guilford. He died in 1858, aged 85
years.

THEIR CHILDREN, BEING THE SIXTH GENERATION.

1971. John, born May 15th, 1805. He was a mariner, and died in South America.

1972. Betsey, born January 29th, 1807; married January 4th, 1826, Daniel Loomis,
of Guilford.

1973. Samuel S., born November 7th, 1808; married   , Mary
Coulter.

1974. Julia, born January 5th, 1811; married William Fowle; second, Samuel C.
Davis.

1975. Sarah E., born October 11th, 1814; married November 26th, 1839, Miles Dudley, of Guilford.

1976. Deborah, born April 27th, 1817; married May 5th, 1842, Benjamin Candee,
of New Hampshire.

1977. Thomas, born August 8th, 1819; married   , Elizabeth
Fuller.

1978. Elisha, born November 11th, 1823; married October 14th, 1862, Sarah E.
Beardsley.

1979. Mary, born October 5th, 1826; married   , Oliver Brooks.

1777. *Madison, Conn.*

BENJAMIN HART, East Guilford, fifth son and youngest child of
Benjamin Hart, of the same town, and his wife, Mabel (Fowler), born
October 25th, 1772; married March 31st, 1804, Mary, daughter of
Timothy Meigs, who died October 26th, 1809, aged 35 years, when
second he married May 14th, 1811, Lucy Baldwin, daughter of Timo-
thy, and his wife, Olive (Norton), born July 9th, 1786, at Guilford.
His residence was at Madison, and he became a deacon there. He died
June 4th, 1852, in his 80th year. His widow died December 31st,
1861, aged 75 years, 4 months, and 22 days.

THEIR CHILDREN, BEING THE SIXTH GENERATION.

Mary, born March 31st, 1805; died September 26th, 1805.

Mabel, born January 28th, 1808; died February 25th, 1826, aged 18 years.

Mary, born September 16th, 1809; died March 13th, 1810.

Benjamin, born August 8th, 1812; died May 16th, 1815, in his 3d year.

1980.   Baldwin, born March 12th, 1815; married December 23d, 1841, Charlotte J.
        Wells.

1981.   William Winthrop, born March 19th, 1835; married July 14th, 1859, Rox-
        anna Scranton.

1777½.

DAVID HART, Jr., Worthington, Conn., only son and child of David
Hart, Sr., and his wife, Lucy (Peck), born at Berlin; married
                , Ann Benjamin.   He died in 1783, when second she
married   , Josiah Smith.

THEIR CHILD, BEING THE SIXTH GENERATION.

1982.   Roxanna, born   ; married October 31st, 1799, Bridgman
        Brown.

1778.   *Kensington, Southington, Conn.*

HEZEKIAH HART, Kensington, eldest son of Hezekiah Hart, of the
same place, and his wife, Abigail (Adkins), born May 25th, 1758, at
Kensington, and baptized there August 6th, 1758.   He was *non compos
mentis*, and was never married.   He lived several years in the family
of Roswell Moore, Esq., in the east part of Southington, where he
was boarded out by the selectmen of Berlin, he in the mean time sup-
posing himself on wages.   Esquire Moore kept a herd of cows, which
were milked in great part by females of the family, and as Hart was
extremely fond of women, he claimed the privilege of carrying in the
pails of milk, with which right if any of the masculine gender inter-
fered, he became angry.   It was his invariable custom to attend the
yearly military regimental review, with his market basket in hand, and
lay in a large stock of gingerbread, a part of which he distributed
among his favorites of the female sex in his neighborhood—a card to
each one.   He was a tall, slim man, and was very irritable.   He died
at the house of Widow Polly Merriman, September 24th, 1840, aged
82 years.

1778¼.

LUCY HART, Kensington, eldest daughter of Hezekiah Hart, of the
same place, and his wife, Abigail (Adkins), born August 10th, 1760, at
Kensington; baptized there August 10th, 1760, by Rev. Samuel Clark.
She was never married.   She died there May 15th, 1791, in her 31st
year.   A tombstone in the cemetery near the house of Merrit Cowles,
in Kensington, shows where she was buried.

1778½. *Kensington, Conn.*

ABIGAIL HART, Kensington, second daughter of Hezekiah Hart, of the same place, and his wife, Abigail (Adkins), born December 14th, 1761, at Kensington; baptized there April 25th, 1762, by Rev. Samuel Clark. She was never married. She died January 7th, 1785, aged 23 years, was buried in the cemetery near Merrit Cowles, and a tombstone marks the place.

1778¾. *Kensington, Conn.*

JABISH HART, Kensington, Conn., third son of Hezekiah Hart, of the same place, and his wife, Abigail (Adkins), born October 3d, 1765, at Kensington, where he died unmarried, June 18th, 1800, aged 34, and the inventory of his estate, amounting to £41 14s. 8d., was exhibited at probate court, Farmington, July 15th, 1800, Joseph Peck and Jabez Cowles, appraisers. He was a twin with his sister, Hannah.

KELSEY.

1779. *Berlin, Conn.*

HANNAH HART, Kensington, third daughter of Hezekiah Hart, of Kensington, and his wife, Abigail (Adkins), born October 3d, 1765, a twin with Jabish, her brother; married August 12th, 1792, Stephen Kelsey, son of Enoch, and his wife, Mary (Bidwell), of Glastonbury, born May 28th, 1764. He died February 21st, 1833, aged 69 years. They had four daughters, the first being Abigail, who married Jerry Dickinson, and died March 22d, 1830, aged 32 years.

COLE.

1780. *Kensington, Conn.*

RUTH HART, Kensington, fourth daughter of Hezekiah Hart, of the same place, and his wife, Abigail (Adkins), born at Kensington in 1767; baptized there January 17th, 1768; married   ,
Job Cole, of Kensington. From tombstones in the burial ground near the house of Merrit Cowles, in Kensington, it appears that Job Cole died October 19th, 1825, aged 64 years; his widow died November 13th, 1838, aged 71 years; and Lucy H., their daughter, died August 14th, 1815, aged 22 years.

GLADDEN.

1781. *Kensington, Conn.*

REBECCA HART, Kensington, fifth daughter of Hezekiah Hart, of the same place, and his wife, Abigail (Adkins), born 1770; baptized

April 29th, 1771, at Kensington; married October 20th, 1805, Jedediah Gladden, who died in Kensington, February 6th, 1859, aged 78 years. She died October 6th, 1843, aged 73 years. There are tombstones in the grave-yard near the house of Merrit Cowles, Kensington, a parish of Berlin.

FLAGG.

1782.   *Berlin, Conn.*

OLIVE HART, Kensington, eldest daughter of Zachariah Hart, of the same place, and his wife, Abigail (Beckley), born at Kensington, and baptized there September 30th, 1759; married Solomon Flagg, son of Abijah, and his wife, Sarah (Clark), who was the widow of Joseph Bills. Mr. Flagg was born at Bristol, Conn., in 1758, and he and his wife were members of Berlin Church. They lived on the road leading from Hart Street to the church, in the house in which his father died, and where he himself died, September 9th, 1793, aged 35 years, when second she married Ithamar Morgan, and went to the Black River country. She died October 2d, 1833, aged 73 years. Mr. Flagg's Will was made and proved October 7th, 1793, in which he says he gave his proportion for the support of his mother, and the balance he gave his four children, viz: Joseph, Sarah, Roxy, and Abijah. The house was old and small, and disappeared some fifty years since. Mr. Flagg's father bought the place, containing two acres, of Mrs. Flagg's father.

HOLLISTER.

1783.   *Berlin, Kensington, Conn.*

CAROLINE HART, Kensington, second daughter of Zachariah Hart, of the same place, and his first wife, Abigail (Beckley), born October 21st, 1762, in that part of Middletown which is now in Berlin. She married   , Abel Hollister, of Kensington, who died there May 25th, 1809, aged 48. His widow died October 26th, 1841, aged 79 years. Tombstones in the south burial yard at Worthington show where they were buried. He was a son of Ephraim Hollister, and his wife, Ann Beckley, baptized February 15th, 1761, at Kensington.

NORTON. SMITH. STANLEY. BECKLEY.

1784.   *Berlin, Conn.*

ABIGAIL HART, Worthington, Conn., third daughter of Zachariah Hart, and his first wife, Sarah (Parsons), born May 21st, 1768; married March 27th, 1788, Josiah Norton, who died, when second she married October 19th, 1804, Josiah Smith, who died April 9th, 1821, aged 66 years, when she third married in 1822, Seth Stanley, who died June 22d, 1827, aged 72 years, when she fourth married Elias' Beckley, who died October 4th, 1828, aged 69 years. She died July 4th, 1845, aged 77 years.

PATTERSON.

1785.   *Berlin, Conn.*

SARAH HART, Berlin, Conn., fourth daughter of Zachariah Hart, of the same place, and his second wife, Sarah (Parsons), born 1770; baptized February 11th, 1770, at Kensington; married   , Shubel Patterson, who died in New York City, November 8th, 1828, aged 64 years, and was buried at the Bridge Cemetery, North Worthington. Mrs. Patterson, of Buffalo, N. Y., died December 18th, 1846, aged 77 years, and was buried by the side of her husband at the Bridge Cemetery; also three children, viz: Ira, died February 24th, 1818, aged 22 years; Lois, died October 17th, 1805, aged 2 years; Henry, died March 23d, 1806, aged 6 weeks.

HART.

1786.   *Trenton, N. Y.*

MARTHA HART, Berlin, fifth daughter of Zachariah Hart, of Berlin, and his second wife, Sarah (Parsons), born at Kensington in 1772; married   , Levi Hart, son of Isaac, and his wife, Ann (Mather), of New Britain, baptized August 24th, 1765, at Kensington. They removed to Trenton, N. Y.

THEIR CHILDREN, BEING THE SIXTH GENERATION.

1983. Lorana, born
       Caroline, born
       Eliza, born
       Zenas, born
       Cyrus, born
       Horace, born

1787.   *Berlin, Conn.*

SUBMIT HART, Berlin, fifth son of Zachariah Hart, of the same place, and his second wife, Sarah (Parsons), born at Berlin in 1776, and married there May 9th, 1797, Clarissa Hopkins, daughter of Benjamin, born 1779. He lived at the north end of Hart Street, or Lower Lane, west of Worthington Street. He died May 9th, 1810, aged 34 years, and has a tombstone at the Bridge Cemetery, when second she married   Wright, and these last were parents of Clarissa, wife of Russell Wells. The estate of Mr. Hart was settled by Levi Hart, who married Patty (or Martha) Hart, a sister of Mr. Hart.

CHILDREN OF SUBMIT AND CLARISSA, BEING THE SIXTH GENERATION.

1984. Lois, born   , 1797; married   , 1826, N. Williams;
        second, Sylvester Elton.
1985. Marilla, born   , 1799; married   , Russel Hollister.
1986. Lucy, born   , 1805; married   , Franklin Deming.
1987. Harriet, born   , 1807; married   , Talmage Hale, of
        Black River, N. Y.
1988. Submit, born September 28th, 1810, posthumous; married   ,
        Mary Cone.

1788.   *Goshen, Torrington, Conn.*

DAVID HART, Wallingford, second son of Captain Nathaniel Hart, of the same town, and his wife, Alice (Hall), born November 22d, 1756, at Wallingford; married, May, 1781, Hannah, daughter of John Hudson, of Southampton. He owned and occupied the house now occupied by the heirs of Lyman Hall, and known as the Aaron Yale place. He was a man of worth, and was much respected. In early life he removed to Goshen, Conn., where he resided in 1783, and then to Torrington in 1798. He was a carpenter by trade. His wife was a superior woman, and came from a family on Long Island. She was admitted to the church in Goshen, September 1st, 1816. She died in Goshen, October 14th, 1835, having been helpless many years. He died September 13th, 1845, aged 89 years.

THEIR CHILDREN, BEING THE SEVENTH GENERATION.

1989. Luther, born July 27th, 1783; married, September, 1811, Minerva Potter, of
        Plymouth.
1990. Henry, born February 28th, 1785; married   , Ann Street.
1991. Miles, born December 10th, 1786; married January 1st, 1820, Laura Clark.
1992. Alpha, born September 17th, 1788; married December 15th, 1814, Betsey
        Dutton.
        Polly, born   ; died   , aged 16 months.

1791.   *Goshen, Conn.*

REUBEN HART, Goshen, Conn., fourth son of Captain Nathaniel Hart, of Wallingford, and his first wife, Alice (Hall), born July 4th, 1763, at Wallingford; married, November, 1784, Ruth, daughter of Abel Ives, of Wallingford, born 1761, and died August 24th, 1843, aged 82 years. He died in Goshen, Conn., May 22d, 1836, aged 73 years.

THEIR CHILDREN, BEING THE SEVENTH GENERATION.

        Infant, born   ; died
1993. Lois, born July 17th, 1787; married   , Asa Ward, of
        Cornwall.

1994. Alice, born November 28th, 1790; married , Daniel Beach.

Seeley, born February 28th, 1793; died , aged 2 years.

1995. Amanda, born February 29th, 1796; married May 21st, 1823, Alva Wise, of Warren.

1996. Seeley, 2d, born February 1st, 1798; married October 16th, 1823, Jemima Thirza Chapman.

1997. Betsey, born October 14th, 1801; married , Rufus Carrier.

1998. Reuben, born May 2d, 1803; married July 2d, 1829, Nancy Ann Law.

1999. Elias, born May 2d, 1807; married January 20th, 1830, Julia Ann Page.

HULL.

1797. *Wallingford, Conn.*

PHEBE HART, Wallingford, sixth daughter of Captain Nathaniel Hart, of the same town, and his wife, Alice (Hall), born April 25th, 1772, at Wallingford; married Jeremiah, son of Jeremiah Hull, of Wallingford, and his wife, Mary (Merriman).

1798. *Turin, N. Y.*

HON. LEVI HART, Winchester, Conn., youngest son of Captain Nathaniel Hart, of Wallingford, and his first wife, Alice (Hall), born November 3d, 1773, at Wallingford, and went to Goshen with his father; married in Bristol, Conn., November 15th, 1796, Esther Barnes, of Bristol. At that time he was a resident of Winchester, Conn., so the record says. They removed to Turin, Lewis County, Black River Country, N. Y., where he died, June 30th, 1861, aged 87 years, 7 months, and 27 days. He was judge of the court, and representative to the General Assembly. There were no children reported.

1799. *Litchfield, Conn.*

BENJAMIN HART, Litchfield, Conn., eldest son of Timothy Hart, of Wallingford, and his wife, Phebe (Fenn), born March 5th, 1752, at Wallingford; married there December 15th, 1775, Hannah Curtiss, of Wallingford, born 1754. He removed from Wallingford to Litchfield soon after the war of the revolution. He was one of the non-commissioned officers who wintered at Valley Forge, and was present at the delivery of Washington's farewell address to the army. He took his first deed of land in Litchfield, February 22d, 1786, and two others the same year. His wife died at Litchfield, April 2d, 1833, aged 79 years. He died January 30th, 1831, aged 78 years, 10 months, and 25 days. They were buried on Litchfield Hill.

THEIR CHILDREN, BEING THE SEVENTH GENERATION.

2000. Lois, born October 4th, 1775; married , Heman Bartholomew.

2001. Hannah, born March 8th, 1778; married , Timothy Stone.

53

2002. Benjamin, born October 7th, 1779; died single in 1830, and was buried on Litchfield Hill.

2003. Phebe, ⎫   married   , White Webster.
⎬ born August 28th, 1784;
2004. Lucy, ⎭   married   , Eliakim Curtiss.

2005. Jonathan, born August 11th, 1786. He went to Kingsville, Ashtabula County, Ohio.

2006. Isaac, born April 1st, 1788; married   , 1812, Hannah Butler.

2007. Merab, born   ; married   , Abner Stone.

2008. Ann, born   ; married   , Roswell Knapp, of Ohio.

2009. Lydia, born September 3d, 1794; married   Huntley, of Ohio.

1801.   *Colebrook, Conn.*

TITUS HART, Colebrook, Conn., third son of Timothy Hart, of Wallingford, and his wife, Phebe (Fenn), born July 4th, 1757, at Wallingford. He married there, December 21st, 1780, Lucy Johnson, of Litchfield, Conn., who bore to him eight children, when she died September 22d, 1803, aged 38 years, and second he married January 8th, 1804, Elizabeth, daughter of Elijah Andrews, of Windsor and Winchester, and his wife, Mary (Roberts). He entered the army of the revolution when he was sixteen years old, and remained to its close. After the war and soon after his marriage he removed to Litchfield, and from thence to the south part of Colebrook about 1794, on the same farm on which he died. He was a carpenter and joiner by trade, but followed farming mostly. While he lived his descendants were accustomed to hold family gatherings with him annually on thanksgiving day, sometimes to the number of 200 and over—children, grandchildren, great-grandchildren, and friends. He died July 27th, 1844, aged 87 years and 23 days. His widow died July 31st, 1844—only four days later—aged 67 years.

CHILDREN BY HIS FIRST WIFE, BEING THE SEVENTH GENERATION.

2010. Truman, born November 23d, 1785, at Litchfield; married, April, 1812, Polly Spencer.

2011. Polly Johnson, born July 17th, 1788; married James Gillet, of Hartland.

2012. Elizabeth, born March 28th, 1791, at Litchfield; married April 11th, 1810, Asa Barnard.

2013. Lewis, born September 30th, 1793; married November 1st, 1815, Persis Swift.

2014. Titus, born May 5th, 1795; married July 14th, 1820, Amanda Webster.

2015. Lucy, born January 1st, 1799; married February 22d, 1824, Lester North.

2016. Orpha, born April 11th, 1802; married December 13th, 1831, William Vining, of Simsbury.

     Child, born   , 1803; died   , 1803.

CHILDREN BY HIS SECOND WIFE.

     Phebe, born March 3d, 1805; died March 7th, 1807.

2017. Milo Roberts, born June 30th, 1806; married   , Julia Anna Cowdry.

2018. Phebe Fenn, born February 29th, 1808; married   , Leonard Gillet.

2018½. Timothy Orson, born November 30th, 1809.

2019. Thomas West, born September 11th, 1811; married November 26th, 1838, Grace Morse.

2020. Jerusha, born August 31st, 1813; married ⎯⎯⎯⎯, Nelson Rogers.

2021. Sylvia, born October 10th, 1815; married ⎯⎯⎯⎯, James Hubbard Mills.

2022. Charles William, born January 2d, 1818; married ⎯⎯⎯⎯, Ann Camp.

2023. Jane Minerva, born August 23d, 1820; married Henry Arnold; died July 5th, 1847, aged 27 years.

1804. *Wallingford, Vt.*

JOEL HART, Vermont, sixth son of Timothy Hart, of Wallingford, Conn., and his wife, Phebe (Fenn), born January 24th, 1766, at Wallingford; married ⎯⎯⎯⎯, Phebe Dallas, and removed to Wallingford, Rutland County, Vt.

THEIR CHILDREN, BEING THE SEVENTH GENERATION.

2024. George, born
Philo, born
Joel, born

1805. *Guilford, Conn., Wallingford, Vt.*

AMOS HART, Guilford, Conn., seventh son of Timothy Hart, of Wallingford, and his wife, Phebe (Fenn), born February 3d, 1768, at Wallingford; married ⎯⎯⎯⎯, Lois Anthony. He lived at Guilford, Conn., but removed to Vermont.

THEIR CHILDREN, BEING THE SEVENTH GENERATION.

2025. Alanson, born ⎯⎯⎯⎯, married ⎯⎯⎯⎯, Roxana Dudley.

2026. Damaris, born

1806. - *North Wallingford, Vt.*

AMASA HART, North Wallingford, Vt., eighth son of Timothy Hart, of Wallingford, Conn., and his wife, Phebe (Fenn), born July 1st, 1790, at Wallingford, Conn.; married ⎯⎯⎯⎯, Nabby Fenn. He removed to Vermont.

1808. *Springfield, Ohio.*

JESSE HART, New York, ninth son of Timothy Hart, of Wallingford, and his wife, Phebe (Fenn), born August 25th, 1774, at Wallingford, Conn.; married ⎯⎯⎯⎯, Esther Derby, of Rutland County, Vt. She died there, when second he married ⎯⎯⎯⎯, Freelove Ives. They removed to Ohio in 1812. He died at Springfield, Summit County, Ohio, July 18th, 1864, aged 90 years.

2027.	Worthy, born	; married	, Ransom Baldwin.
2028.	Amy, born	; married	, Reuel Lang.
2029.	Esther, born	; married	, Jonathan Niles.
2030.	Patience, born	; married	, Elijah T. Banning.
	Welcome, born	; died young.	

2031.	Louisa, born	; married	, Homer Root.
2032.	Jesse, born	; married	Richards.
2033.	Phœbe, born	; married	, Otis Merriman.
2034.	George, born	; married	Nelson.
2035.	Elizabeth, born	; married	, John Hickson.
	Amos, born	; died	
2036.	Harriet, born	; married	, William W. Chapman.
2037.	Sarah M., born	; married	, Joseph R. Conrad.
	Benjamin, born	. There is no report of him.	

1809.   *Batavia, N. Y.*

EBENEZER HART, Genesee, N. Y., tenth and youngest son of Timothy Hart, of Wallingford, and his wife, Phebe (Fenn), born
, at Wallingford; married three times. He located in Vermont, but removed to Genesee, N. Y., and in 1852 was living at Batavia, N. Y. All the means used have failed to bring further information of this family.

COOK.

1810.   *Wallingford, Conn.*

REBECCA HART, Wallingford, eldest daughter of Hawkins Hart, of Wallingford, and his wife, Abigail (Hall), born November 23d, 1761, at Wallingford; married January 1st, 1784, Joel, son of Colonel Isaac Cook, and his wife, Martha, daughter of Benjamin Cook, of Wallingford, born October 12th, 1760, at Wallingford. He became captain, entered the army of the revolution with his father in 1776, and served through the war. In 1812 he was a distinguished officer under General Harrison, in many hard battles with the Indians. He was at Flatbush, N. Y. She died February 22d, 1838, aged 77 years. He died at Deer Park, L. I., December 18th, 1851, aged 92 years. They had children, viz: Lucy, Minerva, Leander, Patty, Rebecca, Phebe, Jennette, and Joel Wilcox.

1811.   *Barkhamsted, Conn.*

JOSIAH HALL HART, Wallingford, eldest son of Hawkins Hart, of the same town, and his wife, Abigail (Hall), born June 3d, 1764, at Wallingford; married January 14th, 1790, Phebe Hall, daughter of

Benjamin, and his wife, Phebe, born August 20th, 1763, at Wallingford. He removed to Barkhamsted, February 8th, 1790, and was elected a member of the General Assembly in 1816. She died in Barkhamsted, October 7th, 1844, aged 81 years. He died March 16th, 1850, aged 86 years.

THEIR CHILDREN, BEING THE SEVENTH GENERATION.

2038. Almira, born May 17th, 1792; married , Allen Rixford.
2039. Lovisa, born October 12th, 1793; married , Timothy Tiffany.
2040. Lyman, born March 2d, 1797; married May 11th, 1820, Charlotte Gilbert.
2041. Phebe, born December 15th, 1798; married August 4th, 1819, Amos Beecher.

PARKER.

1812. Ohio.

HANNAH HART, Wallingford, second daughter of Hawkins Hart, of the same place, and his wife, Abigail (Hall), born September 20th, 1766, at Wallingford; married , Joel Parker, and removed to , Ohio, about 1816.

1813. Pomfret, N. Y.

AARON HART, Pomfret, Chautauqua County, N. Y., third son of Hawkins Hart, of Wallingford; and his wife, Abigail (Hall), born February 8th, 1770, at Wallingford; married . , Annis Austin. He was a mason and trader, and removed from Wallingford to Barkhamsted, from there to Bristol, Ontario County, N. Y., and from thence to Fredonia, Chautauqua County, N. Y., where he died June 9th, 1851, aged 81 years. She died February 15th, 1845.

THEIR CHILDREN, BEING THE SEVENTH GENERATION.

2042. William Austin, born January 13th, 1797; married January 22d, 1821, Mary Ann Sumerton.
2043. Sally, born ; married , Norman Hills.
2044. Hila, born ; married , John B. Roberts.
2044½. Ira Wilder, born . . He was married three times, and is a stage agent in Erie, Penn.
2045. Salmon, born September 19th, 1807; married ;
second, Mary Reddington.
2045½. Phebe L., born ; married , Isaac Avery.
2045½. Aaron H., born September 19th, 1810; married August 29th, 1833, Hepsibah Hart.

1816. Barkhamsted, Conn.

HAWKINS HART, Barkhamsted, fourth son of Hawkins Hart, of Wallingford, and his second wife, whose name is unknown, born January 28th, 1781, at Wallingford. He went to Barkhamsted with his

parents in 1789; married December 5th, 1805, Lois Slade, born April
6th, 1785, at Barkhamsted.   He was a carpenter and joiner by trade
and occupation.   He died at Barkhamsted, October 8th, 1836, aged 55
years.

THEIR CHILDREN, BEING THE SEVENTH GENERATION.

2046.   Chester, born July 16th, 1806; married March 13th, 1833, Julia Case.
        Rebecca, born March 6th, 1808; died, April, 1842.
        Betsey, born May 6th, 1810; died February 6th, 1822.
2047.   William H. H., born August 28th, 1812; married October 26th, 1840, Eliza
          Scovil.
        Fanny, born November 10th, 1814; died January 3d, 1816.
        Fanny Amilla, born January 2d, 1816; died, January, 1840, aged 24 years.
2048.   Sarah, born January 24th, 1818; married
        Olive, born September 2d, 1820; died February 5th, 1822.
2049.   Abner S., born July 15th, 1823; married, April, 1848, Julia Rose.
        Lois, born September 14th, 1825; died, December, 1825.
2050.   Hannah Amanda, born July 8th, 1827; married

1817.   *Wayne, Ohio.*

JERRY HART, Wayne, Ashtabula County, Ohio, fifth son of Hawkins
Hart, of Wallingford, and his second wife, whose name is unknown,
born October 11th, 1784, at Wallingford.   He went with his parents
to Barkhamsted in 1789; married   .   , Ives, of
        . He was a carpenter by trade.   He removed
to Wayne, Ashtabula County, Ohio.

THEIR CHILDREN, BEING THE SEVENTH GENERATION.

2051.   David, born
        Josiah, born
        Jassa, born
        Levi, born
        Elon, born

WOODRUFF.

1827.   *Southington, Conn.*

PHEBE HART, Southington, only daughter and child of Hawkins
Hart, of Southington, and his wife, Huldah (Woodruff), born about
1760, at Southington; married   , Amos Woodruff,
of Southington, son of Jonathan, and his wife, Phebe (Wiers), born
at Southington, and baptized there September 17th, 1749.   He was a
cooper by trade, and lived at the old homestead of his father-in-law,
Hawkins Hart, on the west side of East Street.   The house stood its
width south of the present residence of Truman Barnes.   It was a
large two-story house, with two front rooms, and a lean-to in the rear,
after the model of the better class of houses of that date.   His wife

died May 26th, 1816, aged 56 years. His daughter, Diantha, kept house for him, after the death of Mrs. Woodruff, for several years, and the last years of life he spent with his children. The old house was finally drawn away and converted into a cement mill. He died at the house of Gad Andrews, who had married his daughter, Diantha. Their children were—1, Keziah, born April 12th, 1780, married October 28th, 1800, Levi Barnes; 2, Amanda, born June 5th, 1782, married October 25th, 1802, Joel Gridley; 3, Phebe, born June 20th, 1785, died January 5th, 1794, in her 9th year; 4, Diantha, born November 12th, 1803, married May 1st, 1833, Gad Andrews.

1827½. *Winchester, Conn.*

SELAH HART, Winchester, Conn., second son of Luke Hart, of Southington, and his wife, Deborah (Barnes), born 1766; baptized March 23d, 1766, at Southington. He went to Winchester with his parents in 1786. He lived in Winchester until about 1812, when he removed to Canaan, Conn., and on the 16th of January, 1817, Selah Hart, for $30 of David Andrus, of Norfolk, deeded to him two acres of land. He was the tallest man in Winchester, measuring six feet, five and one-half inches. He labored at laying stone wall, and was poor in this world's goods, but rich in faith, love, and charity. He was a father and strong pillar of the Methodist Church, and a devout, kind hearted, and much loved man. He married   , Rachel Hemsted. He entered the army of the revolution at sixteen years of age, and served one year, when the war closed. He was a stone mason by trade. His wife died about 1830. He died February 17th, 1834, aged 72 years.

THEIR CHILDREN, BEING THE SEVENTH GENERATION.

2052. Deborah, born   ; married   , Zenas Alvord.
2053. Diadama, born   , 1793; married   , Luke Hadsell, of Canaan.
2054. Sally, born   ; married   , 1812, David Andrews.
2055. Phœbus, born April 19th, 1798; married   , 1833, Rhoda Dorman, of Canaan.
2056. Newton, born January 11th, 1800; married March 1st, 1824, Ruth Hadsell.

1828. *Winchester, Conn.*

STEPHEN HART, Winchester, Conn., third son of Luke Hart, of Southington, and his wife, Deborah (Barnes), born at Southington in 1767. He went to Winchester with his parents in 1786, and married Sarah Munson, of Middlebury, Conn. He died at Winchester, September 17th, 1833, aged 66 years.

THEIR CHILDREN, BEING THE SEVENTH GENERATION.

2057. Chester, born
2058. Roswell, born
2059. Lovina, born

1829.   . *Winchester, Conn.*

SAMUEL HART, Southington, fourth son of Luke Hart, of the same town, and his wife, Deborah (Barnes), born at Southington in 1771. He went to Winchester with his parents in 1786, and married Mariam Bassett, of Vermont and Winchester. His avocation was farming. He died at Winchester in 1826, aged 55 years.

THEIR CHILDREN, BEING THE SEVENTH GENERATION.

  Sally, born   ; died young.
2060. Willard, born, January, 1798; married May 29th, 1828, Maria Andrews.
2061. Sylvester, born May 22d, 1800; married June 22d, 1822, Charlotte Walter.
2062. Amelia, born   , 1802; married   , Samuel Bandall.
2063. Polly, born   ; married   , Levi Tuttle.
2064. Wells, born February 4th, 1805; married November 1st, 1826, Susan Tryon.
2065. Hawley, born February 10th, 1807; married   , Hannah Tryon.
  Harriet, born about 1809; died single at Winchester; aged about 18 years.
2066. Lucy, born about 1810, in Granville, Mass. She is single.
2067. Sylvia, born about 1811; married   , Edward Albro.
2068. Julia, born about 1812; married   , Jason Lilley, of Vermont, and lived in East Windsor in 1871.
2069. Samuel, born May 25th, 1813; married November 14th, 1833, Laura Benedict.

OAKLEY.

1830.   *Barkhamsted, Canaan, Conn.*

LYDIA HART, Canaan, Conn., youngest child of Luke Hart, of Southington and Winchester, and his wife, Deborah (Barnes), born July 13th, 1775, at Southington; married, January, 1799, Hawley Oakley, and settled in Barkhamsted, where their first four children were born, and from thence, about 1807, they removed to Canaan, Conn., where they lived over forty years. They were members of the Methodist Church. He died   . She died   . They had Alma, Stata, Alva, Luke, William, Sally, Emma, and Lucinda.

HALL. ANDREWS.

1833.   *Wallingford, Meriden, Conn.*

ESTHER HART, Meriden, eldest daughter of Benjamin Hart, of Wallingford, and his wife, Jerusha (Rich), born November 8th, 1776, at Wallingford; married   Hall, of   , who died, when second she married January 24th, 1822, Marvel Andrews, of Meriden, son of Nicholas, and his wife, Lydia (Hull), born October 20th, 1765. She was his fourth wife. She died December 26th, 1854, aged 78 years. He died at Meriden, Conn., December 5th, 1848, aged 83 years, 1 month, and 15 days.

1836. *Meriden, Conn.*

WEBB HART, Meriden, eldest son of Benjamin Hart, of Southington and Wallingford, and his wife, Jerusha (Rich), born February 21st, 1786, at Meriden; married   , Clarissa Peck.

THEIR CHILDREN, BEING THE SEVENTH GENERATION.

2070. Harriet, born about 1807.
2071. Norman, born about 1809; married   ; second   .
2072. Benjamin, born June 26th, 1811; married August 5th, 1835, Jane Brooks.

1838. *Meriden, Conn.*

SAMUEL IVES HART, Meriden, youngest son of Benjamin Hart, of Southington and Wallingford, and his wife, Jerusha (Rich), born November 22d, 1792, at Meriden; married September 20th, 1814, Abigail D. Hall, born August 25th, 1793. They resided in the east part of Meriden, where he died September 10th, 1870, aged 78 years.

THEIR CHILDREN, BEING THE SEVENTH GENERATION.

2073. Daniel Hall, born June 19th, 1815; married May 14th, 1840, Harriet G. Miller.
Edmund, born August 12th, 1817; died February 16th, 1818.
2074. Jerusha,   married May 5th, 1844, Horace Pratt, of Meriden.
born August 22d, 1822;
2075. Elizabeth,   married October 24th, 1852, Edward B. Miller, of Meriden.

1839. *Stonington, Conn.*

REV. IRA HART, Stonington, Conn., eldest son of Jonathan Hart, of Paris, Herkimer County, N. Y., and his wife, Mary (Coe), born September 18th, 1771, at Farmington, Bristol Society, Conn. He united with the church of Yale College in 1795, where he graduated in 1797, studied theology with President Dwight, and in November, 1798, was ordained pastor of the church at Middlebury, Conn. He married, December, 1798, Maria Sherman, daughter of John, and granddaughter of Hon. Roger Sherman, of New Haven, who signed the Declaration of Independence. She died September 21st, 1857, and lacked but nine days of being 83 years old. The following is from her pen:

"'His natural temperament was ardent,' in the language of his friend, the writer of his obituary. By an amount of personal exertion which few have ever made, and in prospect of pecuniary embarrassment, which would have dismayed a mind less resolved, he carried himself through a collegiate course, and graduated with high reputation. In the personal friendship and respect of the late President Dwight he ever held a distinguished place."

Three seasons of special revival of religion were enjoyed under his

ministry in Middlebury.   The first occurred in 1799, and resulted in
large additions to the church, an account of which appears in the *Connecticut Evangelical Magazine*, Volume III., 64th and 102d pages, and
lately re-published by President Tyler, of East Windsor, one of his
spiritual children, and who fitted with him for college.   He was dismissed from that people, April, 1809, in the midst of an uncommon
religious inquiry, especially among the youth, for daring to reprove sin
in an aggravated case, the parties being wealthy, and of high standing
in society, to the grief of many of his friends.   During the summer
following he supplied the pulpit in North Stonington, and in the autumn
of the same year he received a unanimous call to be pastor over the
church and society in Stonington Borough.   He was installed on the
6th of December.   For twenty years he continued to discharge the
duties of his office, almost without interruption, until within two weeks
of his death, which occurred October 29th, 1829.   As a preacher he
was earnest and popular.   He was very ready, no exigency finding him
unfurnished with appropriate thoughts and language, many of his best
efforts being extempore.   He was successful, referring only to the last
scene of his labors, the stability, union, and strength of a society that
had previously languished from the want of a regular ministry for
several years alone furnishing ample testimony.   In 1822 sixty were
added to the church, and some were added nearly every year of his
ministry.   As a pastor we have room to mention only one prominent
trait in his character.   He was distinguished for tenderness and sympathy towards the sick and bereaved, and was rendered more so by
the loss of his son in 1819—Charles Theodore, of beloved memory—
a youth whom his classmates in college will long remember as the most
amiable of their number, and as a candidate for the very first collegiate
honors, and concerning whom his marble says truly, " of great promise
and of hopeful piety."   Though this loss deeply wrung the father's
heart with anguish, yet the man of God triumphed over the feelings
of the father, and as he closed the eyes of his son, he said with true
Christian dignity, "the will of the Lord be done."   I will add, like
Leigh Richmond he mourned over this child of his fondest hopes to
the day of his death.   It eminently gratified him to be a "son of con-
solation" to the bereaved, and this trait greatly endeared him to his
people.   The remote occasion of his death was a severe contusion in
his side, received by a fall from his carriage in the middle of September, 1829.   He was confined to the house only two weeks.   Early in
his confinement he said, as if anticipating the result, "Now I want
dying grace, and I have it."   Subsequently, of a Saviour supreme and
divine he said: "Here is firm footing; here is solid rock.   With
Hooker I will say, 'I am going to receive mercy.'"   To his wife he

said, "Here is a precious promise for you—'1 will *never* leave thee, nor forsake thee.' Take it; it is yours; you will need it. I have indeed found abundant need of it, and it has been literally fulfilled in my experience." He died suddenly at last, with but momentary pain. He fell "asleep in Jesus," aged 58 years. Affectionate friends among his people have reared a tablet to his memory. He still lives in their affections, and his remembrance is precious to their hearts.

THEIR CHILDREN, BEING THE SEVENTH GENERATION.

2076. David Sherman, born September 26th, 1799. He lives single in Stonington.
2077. Charles Theodore, born June 14th, 1801; died October 13th, 1819, aged 18 years.
2078. Harriet Eliza, born March 12th, 1803; married December 31st, 1833, Benjamin F. Palmer.
2079. Louisa Maria, born April 11th, 1805. He resides in Stonington.
2080. Henry Austin, born September 26th, 1809; died March 5th, 1837.

1840.   *Kirkland, N. Y.*

JONATHAN HART, Kirkland, Oneida County, N. Y., second son of Jonathan Hart, and his first wife, Mary (Coe), born April 23d, 1772, in Bristol. He married Orphia Chapin, of Granby, Mass., and was a farmer by occupation. He took the name of John when he was a young man. She was born September 25th, 1776, and died January 17th, 1844. He died May 18th, 1852, aged 80 years, and 25 days.

THEIR CHILDREN, BEING THE SEVENTH GENERATION.

2081. Susan Luana, born September 18th, 1797; married March 14th, 1815, Nathan Heaton.
2082. Caroline Maria, born August 31st, 1799; married January 8th, 1821, Truman Loomis. She died July 15th, 1823.
2083. Seth Chapin, born February 25th, 1801; married February 8th, 1831, Nancy Oothout.
2084. Theodore Ephraim, born December 22d, 1802; married January 11th, 1826, Eliza Collins.
2085. Polly Sophronia, born November 25th, 1804; married March 24th, 1832, John M. Roe.
2086. Jonathan Walter, born August 2d, 1806.
2087. Orpha Harriet, born November 20th, 1808; married September 8th, 1833, Rufus Edwards, of Virgil, N. Y.
2088. Hiram George, born September 11th, 1810; married February 25th, 1834, Mariette Terry, of Clinton, N. Y.
2089. Eber Coe, born June 21st, 1813; died May 26th, 1869, at Shreveport, La.
2090. David Wood, born January 24th, 1815; died in 1837, at Lockport, N. Y.

1841.   *Paris, N. Y.*

SAMUEL HART, Black River, N. Y., third son of Jonathan Hart, of Paris, N. Y., and his wife, Mary (Coe), born June 3d, 1775, at Bristol,

Conn. He went with his parents to Paris, Herkimer County, N. Y.; married   . They settled in the Black River Country, N. Y., where he died December 13th, 1800, aged 25 years.

2091. Samuel, born   . He went to Missouri, and is deacon of a
      Baptist Church there.

HILLS.

1843.

POLLY HART, second daughter of Jonathan Hart, of Paris, Herkimer County, N. Y., and his first wife, Mary (Coe), born October 3d, 1779; married   , Elisha Hills, of Marshall, Oneida County, N. Y. She died about 1850. They had Ira Hart, Mary Eliza, who married Rev. Luther Myrick, and seven others, viz: Leander, Esther, Nelson, Seth, Jane, Polly, and Lowly.

1844.   *Clinton, N. Y.*

SETH HART, Clinton, Oneida County, N. Y., fourth son of Jonathan Hart, of Herkimer County, N. Y., and his first wife, Mary (Coe), born November 25th, 1781, at Bristol, Conn.; married   ,
Louisa Hickox, of Clinton, N. Y. He died January 15th, 1806, aged 24 years, 1 month, and 20 days, when second she married
      Thrall, and removed with her son to St. Louis, Mo.

2092. Seth, born about 1806, posthumous; died at Galena, Wis.

1845.   *Cortlandville, N. Y.*

JOSIAH HART, Virgil, Cortland County, N. Y., fifth son of Jonathan Hart, of Paris, Herkimer County, N. Y., and his first wife, Mary (Coe), born April 2d, 1784, at Bristol, Conn. He went with his parents to Paris, and about 1805 he married Sophronia Gridley, daughter of Noadiah, formerly of Southington. Mr. Hart has been a member of the New York Legislature one term, and was justice of the peace several years. In the spring of 1815 he removed to Paris, and from thence to Hartford, Cortland County, N. Y., where he lived until 1853, when he retired from active business, and removed to Cortlandville, where he died, July 19th, 1866, aged 80 years. He possessed a strong mind and vigorous constitution, and liberally supported the Universalist Church at Hartford, N. Y., where his wife died, February 1st, 1851.

THEIR CHILDREN, BEING THE SEVENTH GENERATION.

2093. Alonzo Orville, born February 1st, 1806; married February 19th, 1829, Eveline M. Tobey.

2094. Samuel, born December 14th, 1807; married January 17th, 1832, Sarah S. Potter.

Raymond Brace, born June 1st, 1811; died in 1860.

2094½. Esther Maria, born November 27th, 1813.

Jonathan Seth, born August 14th, 1814; died in 1814.

2095. Sophronia, born November 25th, 1817; married   , J. W. Montgomery, of Dryden.

2096. Josiah, born July 27th, 1819.

2097. Lester Orson, born May 7th, 1821; died in 1858.

Jonathan Fayette, born June 4th, 1823; died in 1825.

HEMINGWAY.

1846.

EUNICE HART, third daughter of Jonathan Hart, of Paris, N. Y., and his first wife, Mary (Coe), born June 27th, 1787. She married   , Jacob Hemingway, of   , and died in 1826. They had issue, viz: Paulina and Mary Ann.

1847.   *Paris, N. Y.*

ALVARO HART, Paris, Herkimer County, N. Y., eldest son of Jonathan Hart, of Farmington and Bristol, Conn., and Paris, N. Y., and his second wife, Lucia (Clark), born November 4th, 1788, at Bristol, Conn.; married Betsey Burr in 1812. He died at Paris, November, 1824, aged 36 years.

THEIR CHILDREN, BEING THE SEVENTH GENERATION.

2098. Jonathan Alvaro, born   ; married

2099. Lowly Eliza, born   ; died   , 1835, at Oswego, N. Y.

Lucia, born

Jane,

Elizabeth, born

1848.   *Oswego, N. Y.*

HON. ORRIS HART, Oswego, Oswego County, N. Y., second son of Jonathan Hart, of Farmington and Bristol, Conn., and subsequently of Paris, N. Y., and his second wife, Lucia (Clark), born February 13th, 1791, at Bristol, Conn., and went with his parents to Paris, N. Y. He married, January, 1818, Elizabeth Bigelow. She died December 19th, 1840. He was a merchant, judge of the Court of Common Pleas, sheriff from 1819 to 1824, and a member of the New York Legislature in 1826 and 1827. He was a man of excellent qualities of head and heart, and commanded the respect and esteem of all who knew him. He served in the war of 1812 in Colonel Cleaveland's regiment, under Captain Hubbard. During his residence in Oswego County he served as county judge under the old constitution, was for many years canal commissioner, and represented the county in the state constitutional convention of 1846. He died at Oswego, November 30th, 1855, aged 64 years.

THEIR CHILDREN, BEING THE SEVENTH GENERATION.

2100. Julia Ann, born March 2d, 1814; married February 24th, 1830, William Bullen.
2101. Jeanette, born June 20th, 1817; married, August, 1837, Joseph O. Glover.
2102. Mary Gertrude, born April 25th, 1819; married, September, 1840, Dr. Frank K. Hamilton.
2103. Ellen, born April 23d, 1821; married, September, 1841, John S. Randall.
2104. Elizabeth, born June 24th, 1823; married Hon. B. C. Cook, of Chicago.

1849.   *Volney, N. Y.*

WARREN HART, Volney, Oswego County, N. Y., third son of Jonathan Hart, of Farmington and Bristol, Conn., and subsequently of Paris, Herkimer County, N. Y., and his second wife, Lucia (Clark), born August 29th, 1793; married, December, 1814, Harriet Page. His avocation was farming. She died, April, 1837, when second he married, August, 1838, Widow Maria Alexander, having seven children. He died at White Pigeon, Mich., April 28th, 1868, aged 75 years.

THEIR CHILDREN, BEING THE SEVENTH GENERATION.

2105. Lucia Louisa, born September 25th, 1815; married   , R. Austin.
2106. Orlando Palmer, born November 21st, 1817; married   , 1840, Goodrich.
2107. Lucius Leander, born August 30th, 1819; married   , 1844, Goodrich.
2108. Edwin Clark, born May 6th, 1821; died January 13th, 1846, aged 25 years. Betsey Amelia, born March 20th, 1824; died March 8th, 1844.
2109. Ephraim Alvaro, born March 3d, 1825; married Marinda Goodrich, and they reside in Wisconsin.
2110. Orris Josiah, born December 11th, 1826; married September 12th, 1855, Laura Betsey Young.
2111. Warren Rockwood, born March 10th, 1828. He died in the Mexican war.
2112. Benjamin Bruce, born April 18th, 1829. He was a soldier, and died of wounds at Bull Run.
2113. Hiram Lorenzo, born July 30th, 1830; married January 15th, 1857, Catharine A. Hubbard.
2114. Harriet Emeline, born January 5th, 1832; married October 23d, 1855, Isaac Jenks, a lawyer; died, April 7th, 1863.

2115. Sophronia Jane, born July 1st, 1833; married January 4th, 1855, Edwin O.
Lyman.

Ichabod, born May 6th, 1835; died September 5th, 1853.

2116. Cornelia Maria, born April 25th, 1837.

CHILDREN BY HIS SECOND WIFE.

2117. Elonzo Alexander, } born September 15th, 1839.
2118. Elphonzo Philander, }

LYMAN.

1850.   *Lycoming County, Penn.*

LUCIA HART, Pennsylvania, second daughter of Jonathan Hart, of
Farmington and Bristol, Conn., and of Paris, N. Y., and his second
wife, Lucia, daughter of David Clark, of Southington, and his wife,
Lois (Andrews), born February 19th, 1798, at Paris, N. Y.; married
there October 1st, 1816, Ambrose Lyman, of Lycoming County, Penn.,
son of Eleazar, and his wife, Clarissa (Hitchcock), of Springfield,
Mass. She died at Jersey Shore, Lycoming County, Penn., January,
1823, aged 26 years. He died about the same time. They left three
children—Edwin Clark, James Williamson, and Lucia Jane.

1851.   *Oswego, N. Y.*

EDWIN CLARK HART, Oswego, N. Y., fourth son of Jonathan Hart,
of Farmington and Bristol, Conn., and Paris, N. Y., and his second
wife, Lucia, daughter of David Clark, of Southington, Conn., and his
wife, Lois (Andrews), born December 14th, 1800, at Paris, Oneida
County, N. Y.; married March 10th, 1823, Aurel Anderson, born September 1st, 1802, at Windsor, Conn. He is a merchant at Oswego,
N. Y., where he resides. His wife died there January 22d, 1870, aged
68 years, when he second married May 17th, 1871, Mrs. Warren N.
Hawks. Her maiden name was Wilber, and she was born August
17th, 1817, in Madison County, N. Y.

THEIR CHILDREN, BEING THE SEVENTH GENERATION.

Marion Violetta, born November 9th, 1824; died November 20th, 1835, at
Oswego, N. Y.

Velona, born July 3d, 1828; died November 16th, 1835, at Oswego, N. Y.

Mary Frances, born November 9th, 1832; died November 7th, 1835, at Oswego, N. Y.

Edwin Augustus, born January 14th, 1835, at Oswego, N. Y.; died there
September 5th, 1853, aged 18 years.

2119. Aurel Augusta, born October 25th, 1837; married August 17th, 1859, John
Dunn, Jr.

Lucia Gertrude, born Sept. 2d, 1839; died June 26th, 1841, at Oswego, N. Y.

2120. Haynes Lord, born March 13th, 1844; married Rosie Jones, and was living in
1872.

1852.   *Wheaton, Ill.*

Rev. Ichabod Andrews Hart, Southport, Wis., youngest son of
Jonathan Hart, of Farmington and Bristol, Conn., and subsequently of
Paris, Herkimer County, N. Y., and his second wife, Lucia, daughter
of David Clark, of Southington, Conn., and his wife, Lois (Andrews),
born February 16th, 1803, at Paris, N. Y.; married October 13th,
1830, Emeline F. Frisbee, of Westmoreland, N. Y., daughter of Benjamin, born August 6th, 1803, and died January 16th, 1836, at Franklin, Delaware County, when he second married November 3d, 1836,
Damask Rose Frisbee, half sister of his former wife, who died January 13th, 1840, at Sandusky, Ohio, when he third married May 4th,
1841, Harriet Eliza Whitcomb, of Templeton, Mass., born April 22d,
1819.   He graduated at Hamilton College in 1826, was pastor of a
Church in Sandusky City, Ohio, removed to Southport in 1845, and
was residing at Wheaton, Du Page County, Ill., in 1872.   Ten days
after his birth his mother died of puerperal fever, hence his name—
Ichabod.

CHILDREN BY HIS SECOND WIFE, BEING THE SEVENTH GENERATION.

Frances Emeline, born July 22d, 1837, at Franklin, N. Y.; died September
12th, 1838.

Henry, born November 19th, 1838, at Sandusky, Ohio; died November 19th,
1838.

2120½. Edwin Rose Frisbee, born December 31st, 1839, at Sandusky, Ohio; married
Maggie Elizabeth Kull.

CHILDREN BY HIS THIRD WIFE.

2121.   Charles Carlton, born December 6th, 1842, at Sandusky, Ohio; married Emma
A. Alden.

2122.   Walter Osgood, born October 13th, 1844, at Medina, Ohio; married Maggie
Furgeson.

2123.   Eliza Floretta, born January 28th, 1847, in Kenosha.

2124.   Ellen Cornelia, born May 2d, 1852, at Greenwood, Ill.

2125.   Sarah Adah, born April 6th, 1855, at Greenwood, Ill.; died February 26th,
1856.

1855.

Hon. Ephraim Hart, Utica, N. Y., eldest son of Thomas Hart, of
Clinton, Oneida County, N. Y., and his wife, Mary (Hungerford), born
            ; married   , 1821, Martha Seymour,
of Hartford, Conn.   He is a merchant, and soon after the opening of
the Erie Canal was elected commissioner, and was twice elected a senator to the New York Legislature.   His store at Paris was in Clinton
Society, and was broken open by a burglar July 22d, 1801, and $1,800
cash taken from a trunk.   The thief was pursued and taken, and the
money recovered.

THEIR CHILDREN, BEING THE SEVENTH GENERATION.

2126. Cornelia, born
2127. Verona, born
2128. Henry R., born
2129. Mary, born   ; married   Porter.
2130. George, born
2131. Caroline, born
2132. James, born
2133. Louisa, born

1857.

Eli Hart, New York, fifth son of Thomas Hart, of Paris, (now Clinton,) N. Y., and his wife, Mary (Hungerford), born   , married   , Mary   . He is an extensive flour merchant in New York City.

THEIR CHILDREN, BEING THE SEVENTH GENERATION.

Nelson, born
Frances, born

1857½.   *Rochester, N. Y.*

Roswell Hart, Rochester, N. Y., second son of Thomas Hart, of Clinton, N. Y., and his wife, Mary (Hungerford), born ; married   , Eliza Pixley.

THEIR CHILDREN, BEING THE SEVENTH GENERATION.

2134. Charlotte, born   ; married   Cummings.
2135. Thomas P., born
2136. Jane, born   Rochester.
2137. George W., born
2138. Mary E., born   ; married   , M. F. Reynolds.
2139. Roswell, born   . He graduated at Yale College in 1843.

1858.   *Palmyra, N. Y.*

Truman Hart, Palmyra, Wayne County, N. Y., third son of Thomas Hart, of Clinton, N. Y., and his wife, Mary (Hungerford), born   ; married   , Susan   . He has been a member of the New York State Senate.

THEIR CHILDREN, BEING THE SEVENTH GENERATION.

2140. Abby, born   ; married
        Strong, of Palmyra.
2141. Ann, born   ; married
        Mumford, of Rochester.
2142. Charles, born
2143. Helen, born
2144. Susan, born

FOOT.

1861.   *Clinton, N. Y.*

SUSANNAH HART, Clinton, N. Y., eldest daughter of Amasa Hart, of Bristol, Conn., and Paris, (now Clinton,) N. Y., and his wife, Phebe (Roberts), of Bristol, born   , 1775, at Bristol, Conn.; married   , Samuel Foot, of Clinton, where they died.

HALE.

1862.   *Adams, N. Y.*

RHODA HART, Adams, Jefferson County, N. Y., second daughter of Amasa Hart, of Bristol, Conn., and Paris, (now Clinton,) N. Y., and his wife, Phebe (Roberts), born   , 1777, at Bristol. In 1794 she went with her parents to Paris, (now Clinton,) and there married   , Jesse Hale, and they lived and died in Adams, Jefferson County, N. Y.

1863.   *Kirkland, N. Y.*

ABEL HART, Kirkland, N. Y., eldest son of Amasa Hart, of Bristol, Conn., and Kirkland, N. Y., and his wife, Phebe (Roberts), of Bristol, born November 5th, 1778, at Bristol, Conn.; married   , 1798, Lovinia Gridley, of Paris, (now Kirkland); born August 20th, 1780, at Kirkland, where she died, June 6th, 1856, aged 76 years. He died April 6th, 1864, aged 86 years.

THEIR CHILDREN, BEING THE SEVENTH GENERATION.

2145.   Enrotas, born October 25th, 1799; married October 28th, 1823, Betsie S. Walker.

2146.   George, born   ; married August 28th, 1826, Sally Bennet.

2147.   Phebe, born   ; married   , Eli Monger, a blacksmith.

2148.   Lucinda, born   ; married   , Eli Monger.

2149.   Louisa, born   ; married   , Lyman Ealy, of Kirkland.

2150.   William O., born   ; married   , Weltha Crocker.

2151.   Caroline, born   ; married   , Charles Everet.

2152.   Jane, born

2153.   Hiram, born

2154.   Emery, born

1865.   *Cincinnati, Ohio.*

JESSE HART, Cincinnati, Ohio, son of Amasa Hart, of Bristol, Conn., and subsequently of Paris, N. Y., and his wife, Phebe (Roberts), of Bristol, born   , 1784, at Bristol, Conn. He went with his

parents to Paris, (now Kirkland,) N. Y., married ,
Ruth Stebbins, of Clinton, and removed to Cincinnati, Ohio. Every
effort to obtain a report of their family has failed.

1865½.   *Adams, N. Y.*

WILLIAM HART, Adams, Jefferson County, N. Y., son of Amasa
Hart, of Bristol, Conn., and subsequently Paris, (or Kirkland,) N. Y.,
and his wife, Phebe (Roberts), of Bristol, Conn., born ,
1786, at Bristol, and went with his parents to Paris, N. Y.; married
. They lived in Adams,
Jefferson County, N. Y., where he owned a farm, made potash, and
had a dry goods store. No report of their children could be obtained.

GRIDLEY.

1866.   *Adams, N. Y.*

PHEBE HART, Bristol, Conn., and Paris, N. Y., youngest child of
Amasa Hart, of Bristol, and his wife, Phebe (Roberts), born
, 1790, at Bristol, and went with her parents to Paris, (now
Clinton,) N. Y., where she married , 1807, William C.
Gridley, a clerk in Clinton, and they removed to Adams, Jefferson
County, where he was also a clerk, and where he died.

CARRINGTON.

1867.   *Huron, Ohio.*

RUTH HART, Bristol, Conn., eldest child of Benjamin Hart, of the
same town, and his wife, Mehitabel (Jerome), born October 2d, 1784,
at Bristol; married there November 26th, 1805, Clark Carrington, of
the same place. They removed to Huron, Erie County, Ohio, and had
six children.

1868.   *Brighton, N. Y.*

JAMES HART, Bristol, eldest son of Benjamin Hart, of the same town,
and his wife, Mehitabel (Jerome), born September 18th, 1786, at Bristol; married January 1st, 1821, Betsey Johnson. They removed to
Brighton, N. Y.

THEIR CHILDREN, BEING THE SEVENTH GENERATION.

Francis, born , 1825; died May 29th, 1830, at Bristol, aged 5
years.
2155. Jerome, born
2156. Francis Grove, born

MORSE.

1869.   *Litchfield, Conn.*

ORRA HART, Bristol, Conn., second daughter of Benjamin Hart, of the same place, and his wife, Mehitabel (Jerome), born May 28th, 1788, at Bristol; married January 6th, 1807, Moses M. Morse, Jr., of Litchfield. She died September 29th, 1834, aged 46 years, when second he married her sister, Fanny.

BULKLEY.

1870.   *Farmington, Conn.*

MEHITABEL HART, Bristol, third daughter of Benjamin Hart, of the same town, and his wife, Mehitabel (Jerome), born July 6th, 1790, at Bristol; married there February 19th, 1810, George Bulkley, of Farmington, by whom she had nine children.

1871.   *Brighton, N. Y.*

EBER JEROME HART, Bristol, second son of Benjamin Hart, of the same town, and his wife, Mehitabel (Jerome), born September 12th, 1791; married, March, 1815, Sophia Root, daughter of Elijah, of Plainville, Conn., and his wife, Ruth (Judd), born March 1st, 1788. They removed from Bristol, Conn., to Brighton, Monroe County, N. Y. They had six children, and two of his sons are married.

1873.   *Brighton, N. Y.*

ROSWELL HART, Bristol, third son of Benjamin Hart, of the same town, and his wife, Mehitabel (Jerome), born February 21st, 1795; married June 27th, 1820, Phebe Johnson, sister of his brother James' wife. They removed to Brighton, N. Y. She died September 24th, 1823, aged 27 years.

1874.   *Brighton, N. Y.*

ROMANTA HART, Brighton, Monroe County, N. Y., fourth son of Benjamin Hart, of Bristol, Conn., and his wife, Mehitabel (Jerome), born March 19th, 1800, at Bristol, Conn.; married
Ruth Cowles. He removed from Bristol, Conn., to Brighton, Monroe County, N. Y. No children reported in this or his brother's family preceding.

WILCOX.

1875. *Brighton, N. Y.*

EMELINE HART, Bristol, Conn., fifth daughter of Benjamin Hart, of the same town, and his wife, Mehitabel (Jerome), born January 25th, 1804, at Bristol; married there February 13th, 1825, Linas Wilcox. They removed to Brighton, Monroe County, N. Y., where she died, May 6th, 1826, aged 22 years, and was buried there.

1876. *Bristol, Conn.*

THOMAS COE HART, Bristol, Conn., youngest son and child of Thomas Hart, of the same town, and his wife, Mehitabel (Jerome), born July 7th, 1806, at Bristol; married   , Emily Atwater, who died at Bristol, September 21st, 1837, aged 29 years, and was buried at the North Yard, so the record says. He died December 8th, 1838, aged 32 years, 5 months, and 1 day. They had two children.

MALLORY.

1877. *Durham, Conn.*

RUTH HART, Durham, Conn., only child of Daniel Hart, of the same town, and his wife, Hannah (Hubbard), born August 6th, 1800, at Durham; married December 12th, 1821, Henry Mallory, of Northford, Conn. They live on the old homestead of her father, in Durham. They had—1, Jane, born March 29th, 1823, died June 23d, 1843, aged 20 years; 2, William, born March 19th, 1825, married Esther Hale, of Wallingford; 3, Henry, born January 8th, 1828, married Sophia Lindsley, of Northford.

1878. *Durham, Conn.*

DEACON WILLIAM A. HART, Durham, Conn., eldest son of Samuel Hart, of the same town, and his wife, Patience (Hubbard), born April 26th, 1806, at Durham; married June 23d, 1828, Sally Jones, of North Madison, Conn., daughter of Joseph, and his wife, Lucy (Austin). He was trained to farming, but being of an intellectual turn of mind he gave his attention to study as much as his limited means would allow, and taught school winters for a good many seasons in succession. He subsequently became a butcher for many years, until he failed in business, and has since worked on a farm. He was made a freeman, April 3d, 1830, and in 1853 a deacon of the South Congregational Church in Durham. He was active in forming the first temperance society in Durham in 1828, when he signed the pledge with some twenty others. He was an anti-slavery man in the first efforts in that direction. He has been a justice of the peace and school visitor. His wife is an energetic, Christian woman.

2157. Elizabeth, born May 17th, 1831; married January 15th, 1855, Charles E. Camp.
2158. Franklin, born April 29th, 1834; married December 25th, 1840, Adaline Jackson.
2159. Mary E., born July 10th, 1836. He was residing at Hartford in 1872.
2160. Lewis, born December 28th, 1838; married March 31st, 1867, Widow Harriet Hart.
2161. Ellen, born March 11th, 1841; married August 29th, 1861, Isaac Hale.
2162. Charles, born April 2d, 1843; married February 8th, 1870, Isabella Burns.
2163. Frederic, born February 26th, 1845; married November 27th, 1867, Fannie J. Frost.
2164. Catharine, born August 17th, 1847. She was a teacher in 1872.
2165. Alice, born April 19th, 1852.

1879. *Pennfield, Ohio.*

EDWARD HART, Durham, Conn., a twin brother of Edmund, second son of Samuel Hart, of the same town, and his wife, Patience (Hubbard), born January 14th, 1808, at Durham; married December 25th, 1834, Emma, daughter of Caleb Merriman, of Wallingford, born October 20th, 1808. He removed to Pennfield, Ohio, October 31st, 1837. His avocation is farming. His wife died August 1st, 1868, when second he married February 8th, 1871, Mrs. Jemima Head, of Saratoga, N. Y., daughter of   Chapman, of Ohio. He and his wives were members of the Baptist Church.

2166. George F., born May 4th, 1836; married February 18th, 1857, Harriet S. Hull.
2167. Henry I., born September 26th, 1838. He was a brave soldier in the late war. Leander, born February 7th, 1846; died May 24th, 1846.

1880. *Wethersfield, Conn.*

EDMUND HART, Durham, Conn., a twin brother of Edward, third son of Samuel Hart, of Durham, and his wife, Patience (Hubbard), born January 14th, 1808, at Durham; married December 28th, 1833, Mary Hurlburt, of Wethersfield, daughter of Elizur, and his wife, Mary (Deming), born July 31st, 1810, at Wethersfield. He settled there, and was a shoe-maker by trade, but is occupied in farming. He was admitted to the Congregational Church in Durham, November 4th, 1827, but is now a member of the Methodist Church. They live on the bank of the Connecticut River. His four sons were all living at home unmarried in 1871.

2168. Allen Hurlburt, born February 20th, 1837. He is a member of the Congregational Church.

2169. George Edmund, born October 25th, 1839.

Robert Newton, born October 27tb, 1841; died January 16th, 1845.

2170. Robert Newton, born September 4th, 1843.

2171. Francis Edgar, born July 1st, 1847.

BARNES.

1882. *Northford, Conn.*

MARY HART, Durham, Conn., only daughter of Samuel Hart, of the same town, and his wife, Patience (Hubbard), born January 1st, 1813, at Durham, Conn.; married November 1st, 1835, Seneca Barnes, of Northford. They had—1, George, born March 15th, 1837; married, January, 1870, Carrie Bailey. He is a farmer, and lives in Northford. He served two years in the Fifteenth Regiment Connecticut Volunteers. 2, Amelia, born July 18th, 1839; married January 27th, 1869. Edward Buel, of Northford, Conn. 3, Theodore, born September 12th, 1841. He is a farmer. 4, Charlotte, born October 25th, 1845. She is a teacher. Mrs. Barnes was a twin with Amos, who died at the age of 18.

1883. *Durham Center, Conn.*

SAMUEL HART, Durham, youngest son and child of Samuel, Sr., of the same town, and his wife, Patience (Hubbard), born April 15th, 1815, at Durham, Conn.; married October 28th, 1838, Lydia R. Davidson, of Lyme, Conn. His avocation is farming, and he lives on the old homestead of his father.

2172. Jane, born March 22d, 1841; married January 1st, 1863, William Hale, of Wallingford.

2173. John, born July 15th, 1844. · He is a mechanic.

2174. Walter, born August 19th, 1848. He is a farmer.

HARRISON.

1884. *Northford, Conn.*

HARRIET HART, Durham, Conn., second daughter of Captain John Hart, of Durham, and his wife, Sally (Coe), born June 20th, 1811, at Durham; married October 12th, 1831, Amos Harrison, of Northford, and removed there to live. Their children, viz: 1, Caroline, born November 10th, 1834, married David Durand, of Milford; 2, Corridon, born April 2d, 1838; married Stella Hull, and second, Emily Hull; 3,

Charlotte, born October 13th, 1842, died July 14th, 1867; 4, Roderick, born September 11th, 1845, married Ella Nettleton, of Durham; 5, Imogene, born March 13th, 1853, died July 2d, 1856, aged 3 years.

1886.   *Kensington, Conn.*

ERA BENTON HART, Kensington, Conn., third son of Ebenezer Hart, of the same place, and his wife, Lydia (Benton), born at Kensington in 1779; married September 17th, 1810, Lydia Gilbert, daughter of John, and his wife, Anna Steele, born September 8th, 1791. He was a miller by occupation. He died June 10th, 1825, aged 46 years, and has a tombstone in the west cemetery at Kensington. His widow died June 17th, 1870, aged 78 years, 9 months, and 9 days.

THEIR CHILDREN, BEING THE SEVENTH GENERATION.

2175. Elizabeth Lawrence, born   , 1810; baptized June 7th, 1818; married , Riley Gladden, of Iowa.
2176. Eliza Benton, born   , 1815; baptized June 7th, 1818; married , Truman Cole, of Kensington.
2177. Jonathan Thomas, born December 2d, 1818; married June 3d, 1842, Maria Woodruff.

HART.

1887.   *Berlin, Conn.*

LYDIA HART, Kensington, second daughter of Ebenezer Hart, of the same place, and his wife, Lydia (Benton), born at Kensington in '1780; married in 1834, Theron Hart, of New Britain, son of Benjamin, and his wife, Mary (Fuller), born December 29th, 1792, at New Britain. She was his second wife, and an adopted daughter of her uncle, Thomas Hart, of Kensington; and, as he was a bachelor, he made her his heir, so that his farm was inherited by her. The house was situated on the corner west of the old church, and south-east of the railroad depot in Berlin. She and her husband lived on this farm many years. They had no children. She died July 18th, 1850, aged 70 years. He has a grave-stone at the Bridge Cemetery in Worthington. Previous to this marriage and after her death he lived on Arch Street, in New Britain, and was a prominent member of the Methodist Church. He died at New Britain, January 16th, 1859, aged 76 years, 2 months, and 17 days.

1889.   *West Claremont, N. H.*

ICHABOD W. HART, West Claremont, Sullivan County, N. H., fourth son of Ebenezer Hart, of Kensington, and his wife, Lydia (Benton), born at Kensington in 1784. He went to Charlestown, N. H., with his parents, and married in 1811, Lucy Atkins. He was living at West Claremont, N. H., June 19th, 1860. His sister, Lydia, who became the wife of Theron Hart, of New Britain, gave him by Will, proved in probate court, July 25th, 1850, the sum of $300, to be paid to him by J. T. Hart, to whom she gave the use of her estate during his life, and then to be divided equally between his living male heirs at his decease.

THEIR CHILDREN, BEING THE SEVENTH GENERATION.

2178. Wetmore, born
2179. Josiah, born
2180. John, born
2181. George, born
2182. Ebenezer, born
2183. Thomas, born

1890.   *Canada.*

GEORGE W. HART, Canada, fifth son of Ebenezer Hart, of Kensington, Conn., and Charlestown, N. H., and his wife, Lydia (Benton), born 1786; married   , Polly Hitchcock, of   . He fled into Canada, where he still resides.

THEIR CHILDREN, BEING THE SEVENTH GENERATION.

2184. Stephen, born
2185. Lewis, born
2186. Lydia, born
2187. Elizabeth, born

1890½.   *Claremont, N. H.*

JOSIAH HART, Claremont, Sullivan County, N. H., sixth son of Ebenezer Hart, of Kensington, Conn,, and Charlestown, N. H., and his wife, Lydia (Benton), born 1788; married Friendly Rice. He removed to Claremont, Sullivan County, N. H., where he was killed by a fall while building a mill.

THEIR CHILD, BEING THE SEVENTH GENERATION.

2188. Josiah, born

1891.   *Hartford, Conn.*

ALCES EVELIN HART, Kensington, only son of Major Jonathan Hart, of the same place, and his wife, Abigail (Riley), born October 10th, 1782. He graduated at Yale College in 1801 with the highest honor. He studied law, and opened an office in Hartford with the most brilliant prospects, but died suddenly in 1805, aged 23 years. He married

56

Charlotte Overton, daughter of Seth, of Chatham, Conn. They had no children.

<h3 style="text-align:center">1892½.   Natchez, Miss.</h3>

DOCTOR JAMES EVERLIN HART, Natchez, Miss., second son of Dr. John Hart, and his wife, Hannah (Williams), born November 8th, 1788, at Farmington. · He first located in Wintonbury, (now Bloomfield,) Conn., and from thence he removed to Natchez, Miss., where he became a distinguished and successful physician. He died there of yellow fever, July 6th, 1823, aged 33 years. He left no family.

<h3 style="text-align:center">1893.   Natchez, Miss.</h3>

DOCTOR JOHN ARIADNA HART, Natchez, Miss., third son of Dr. John Hart, of Farmington, and his wife, Hannah (Williams), born November 17th, 1790, at Farmington; married February 27th, 1815, Joanna Porter, daughter of Samuel, of Berlin, born March 20th, 1792, at Berlin, where he was a practicing physician until he removed to Natchez, where he became associated with his brother, James, and was highly successful until his premature death. He taught penmanship from Gettysburg to Tennessee. He was a botanist, and was familiar with plants—from the lichen on the bleak rock of the north, to the magnolia of the south. He died of yellow fever, October 23d, 1822, aged 32 years.

THEIR CHILDREN, BEING THE SEVENTH GENERATION.

Son, born March 2d, 1816, at Farmington; died March 3d, 1816, aged 28 hours.

2189. James Porter, born July 27th, 1817, at Farmington. He graduated at Yale College in 1840.

John Linne, born at Natchez, March 6th, 1822; died July 30th, 1823, aged 1 year.

<h3 style="text-align:center">1893½.   Farmington, Conn.</h3>

ELIZABETH LAWRENCE HART, only daughter of Dr. John Hart, of Farmington, and his wife, Hannah (Williams), born April 9th, 1793, in Farmington, and died there November 13th, 1807, in her 15th year. A sermon was preached at her funeral by Rev. Noah Porter, D. D., from 1 Peter i. 24, 25—"For all flesh is as grass, and all the glory of man as the flower of grass. The grass withereth, and the flower thereof falleth away; but the word of the Lord endureth for ever."

<h3 style="text-align:center">1894.   Blendon, Ohio.</h3>

GIDEON WILLIAMS HART, Worthington, Ohio, fourth son of Doctor John Hart, of Farmington, and his wife, Hannah (Williams), born July

21st, 1795, in Farmington; married November 26th, 1818, Nancy Langdon. They removed to the town of Blendon, Franklin County, Ohio. His avocation is farming. He died.

THEIR CHILD, BEING THE SEVENTH GENERATION.

2190. Henry Clay, born

1895. *Blendon, Ohio.*

THOMAS JOSEPH YOUNG HART, youngest child of Dr. John Hart, of Farmington, and his wife, Hannah (Williams), born January 11th, 1798, at Farmington; married . They settled at Blendon, Franklin County, Ohio, where, it is reported, he died from eating poisoned pork, when she second married ,
——— Jones, and removed to Columbus, Ohio.

THEIR CHILDREN, BEING THE SEVENTH GENERATION.

2191. Joseph, born
2192. Thomas, born

1896. *New Britain, Conn.*

DEACON ELIJAH HART, 3d, New Britain, Conn., son of Elijah 2d, and his wife, Sarah (Gilbert), and grandson of Elijah 1st, born May 7th, 1759, at New Britain; baptized May 13th, 1759; married December 21st, 1780, Anna, eldest daughter of Hezekiah Andrews, of the same place, and his wife, Anna (Stedman), born September 6th, 1760, at New Britain, Conn. They lived at the south part of the parish, and owned Hart's Mills, which were located there. He was a large farmer, and an extensive manufacturer of corn meal for the West India trade. He was admitted to the church October 3d, 1784, was chosen deacon in 1805, and held the military rank of captain. He enlisted into the army of the revolution, March 18th, 1778, for three years, and was at the taking of Burgoyne. In 1824 he and his wife were dismissed from the church in New Britain, and were admitted to the church at Mount Carmel, in Hamden, Conn., where he had built a house and mill, and where they lived several years. They returned, however, to their old home in New Britain, and he died from the sting of a bee, August 4th, 1827, aged 68 years, 2 months, 27 days. His widow died December 2d, 1835, aged 75 years, 2 months, 26 days.

THEIR CHILDREN, BEING THE SEVENTH GENERATION.

2193. Elijah, born February 11th, 1782; died May 13th, 1802, aged 20 years.
2194. Selah, born November 6th, 1784; married October 5th, 1805, Jemima Webster.
2195. Samuel, born April 7th, 1786; married March 18th, 1812, Orpha North.
2196. Jesse, born April 20th, 1789; married April 5th, 1810, Lucina Cowdry.

2197. Jonathan, born February 20th, 1792; died March 4th, 1863, aged 71.

2198. Norman, born August 5th, 1794; married September 8th, 1818, Minerva Lee.
Anna, born December 5th, 1796; died young.

2199. Ira, born July 22d, 1798; married May 3d, 1820, Orpha Hart.
Anna, born November 17th, 1801; died August 8th, 1807, aged 6 years.

2200. Elijah, born September 11th, 1804; married March 15th, 1826, Louisa Warner.

1897.　　　　　　*New Britain, Conn.*

AARON HART, New Britain, Conn., second son of Deacon Elijah
Hart, of Kensington and New Britain, and his wife, Sarah (Gilbert),
born October 16th, 1761, at New Britain; married March 4th, 1790,
Sarah Francis, daughter of Joseph, of Newington, and his wife, Milly
(Stoddard), born April 6th, 1769. He held the military rank of captain. His avocation is farming, and he inherited the old homestead of
his father, in the south-west corner of the parish, since occupied by his
son, Horace, Levi O. Smith, Kelly, and others. He was a large, portly
man, of stern virtue and integrity, and was admitted to the church,
May 26th, 1793. He made weavers' reeds with tools used by his father,
which were inherited by him from his grandfather, Deacon Thomas
Hart, of the Great Swamp Society. The will or deed conveying the
tools is dated March 14th, 1760, by which he gives them to his grandson, Elijah Hart, Jr. Aaron died July 2d, 1829, aged 67 years, 8
months, and 16 days. His wife died January 1st, 1847, aged 77 years,
8 months, and 25 days. She possessed a social, genial spirit, and was
quick and active even in old age.

THEIR CHILDREN, BEING THE SEVENTH GENERATION.

2201. Francis, born December 18th, 1791; married December 30th, 1812, Dolly
Stanley.

2202. Chester, born February 7th, 1793; married September 19th, 1821, Hannah
Wells; second
Betsey, born　　　　　, 1795; baptized October 18th, 1795; died September
5th, 1798, aged 3 years.

2203. Sarah, born　　　　　, 1798; baptized April 29th, 1798; died June 24th,
1814, aged 16 years.

2204. Anson, born　　　　　; baptized August 24th, 1800; died single
May 13th, 1850, aged 51.

2205. Betsey, born February 26th, 1803; married April 10th, 1822, John Judd.

2206. Aaron, born November 25th, 1805; married November 27th, Abigail Andrews.

2207. Horace, born July 29th, 1808; married December 2d, 1831, Harriet J. Church.

2208. Walter, born　　　　　. He was a silver plater by trade, and died single
September 10th, 1847, aged 40.

CORNWALL.

1898.　　　　　　*New Britain, Conn.*

SARAH HART, New Britain, eldest daughter of Deacon Elijah Hart,
of Kensington and New Britain, and his wife, Sarah (Gilbert), born

February 21st, 1765, at New Britain; married March 3d, 1785, Robert Cornwall, of Berlin, son of Captain Timothy, of Middletown, and his wife, Mary (Warner), born August 30th, 1757. He was a cooper by trade, and lived in Hart Quarter, New Britain. The house was in good condition in 1873, and was owned by Charles L. Baldwin. Mr. Cornwall kept a tavern there after the Middletown Turnpike was built. He and his wife were admitted to the church, April 20th, 1800. He died October 5th, 1819, aged 62 years. She died September 15th, 1846, aged 81 years. They had—1, Sarah Gilbert, born June 2d, 1786, married October 1st, 1812, Erastus Storrs; 2, Robert, born October 7th, 1788, died August 30th, 1798, aged 10 years; 3, George, born November 7th, 1791, married August 24th, 1815, Hannah Hooker, daughter of William; 4, Chauncey, born September 22d, 1791, married July 15th, 1819, Mary Coslett; 5, Mary, born July 12th, 1798, married April 4th, 1816, Moses W. Beckley; 6, Robert, born August 16th, 1801, died single March 21st, 1839; 7, Julia Ann, born February 16th, 1804, married October 3d, 1821, Harvey Dunham, Jr., of Southington.

1899.   *New Britain, Conn.*

OZIAS HART, New Britain, third son of Deacon Elijah Hart, of Kensington and New Britain, and his wife, Sarah (Gilbert), born August 8th, 1768, at New Britain; married   , Sarah, daughter of Deacon John Lee, of Worthington Society, Conn., and his wife, Sarah (Cole), and granddaughter of Deacon Jonathan Lee, the blacksmith of Great Swamp Society, baptized August 16th, 1761. Mr. Hart was a farmer, but he built and ran a saw-mill on the north branch of the Mattabesett River, at the south end of the parish. The house where he lived was owned by Frederic North in 1873. He died February 6th, 1845, aged 77. His wife died October 19th, 1829, at Holland Patent, in New York.

THEIR CHILDREN, BEING THE SEVENTH GENERATION.

2209. Ozias, born December 9th, 1793; married November 15th, 1816, Pamela Baggs.
     John Lee, born   ; died in infancy.
     Emily, born   ; baptized April 1st, 1798; died April 3d, 1813, aged 15 years.
2210. Otis, born, February, 1800; died July 1st, 1819, aged 19 years.
     Sarah Cole, born   ; baptized April 3d, 1803; died January 12th, 1804, aged 1 year and 1 month.
2211. Sarah Cole, born March 27th, 1805. She was living single at New Britain in 1874, and was a dress-maker.
     Eliza Ann, born   , 1808; baptized April 21st, 1808; died May 8th, 1808, aged 3 months.

CHURCHILL.

1900.   *New Britain, Conn.*

SELINA HART, New Britain, second daughter of Deacon Elijah Hart, of Kensington and New Britain, and his wife, Sarah (Gilbert), born August 30th, 1770, at New Britain; married December 30th, 1790, Solomon, son of Nathaniel Churchill, and his second wife, Jane (Bushnell), born April 24th, 1767. He died April 27th, 1841, aged 81 years. She died November 22d, 1845, aged 75 years. They had—1, Solomon, born October 20th, 1791, married December 1st, 1812, Candace Gilbert; 2, Amzi, born December 11th, 1793, married Maria White, of Long Island; 3, Prudentia, born 1795, died September 24th, 1798; 4, Cyrus, born December 15th, 1797, married Clarissa Bradley, of Guilford; 5, Selina Hart, born 1799, died November 17th, 1799; 6, Selina Hart, born March 5th, 1801, married Andrew Rapylee; 7, Prudentia, born July 15th, 1804, married in 1820, Albert Webster; 8, Louisa, born November 20th, 1807, died January 5th, 1808; 9, Louisa, 2d, born February 8th, 1809, married Ebenezer Evans, of Southington, and she died December 18th, 1862; 10, Jane Bushnell, born May 20th, 1810, married Ebenezer Evans, and she died September 11th, 1866; 11, John, born August 10th, 1813, married Emeline Cleaveland.

MERRILLS.

1901.   *New Britain, Conn.*

OLIVE HART, New Britain, youngest child of Deacon Elijah Hart, of Kensington and New Britain, and his wife, Sarah (Gilbert), born 1775; baptized August 27th, 1775, in New Britain; married August 8th, 1803, Seth Merrills, son of Allen, and his wife, Mary (Andrews). They lived in the yellow house on Dublin Hill. in New Britain. Allen Merrills was killed at the raising of Farmington meeting-house, July 11th, 1771, at 1 o'clock P. M., aged 37. They had two daughters, Anna and Maria. They were both single in 1870.

ROBERTS.

1902.   *New Britain, Conn.*

RUTH HART, New Britain, eldest daughter of Thomas Hart, of the same place, and his wife, Mehitabel (Bird), born November 10th, 1758, at New Britain; married February 17th, 1785, Aaron Roberts, son of Dr. Aaron, and his wife, Hepzibah (Shepherd), born April 20th, 1758, at Middletown. He was admitted to the Congregational Church. December 5th, 1784, and his wife was admitted August 7th, 1785. He was a joiner and cabinet maker, and he lived in a house that he bought of Daniel Ames, a fellow-apprentice. His wife died February 18th, 1828, aged 70. She had no children. He married second, May 20th, 1829, Mary, widow of Eliphalet Wadsworth, and daughter of Jehudi Hart, and his wife, Mary (Munson), born August 5th, 1769. He died September 27th, 1831, aged 73 years. His widow died in Farmington, November 11th, 1847, aged 78 years.

SEYMOUR.

1903. *New Britain, Conn.*

ABIGAIL HART, New Britain, Conn., second daughter of Thomas Hart, of the same place, and his wife, Mehitabel (Bird), born October 27th, 1761, at New Britain; baptized there November 1st, 1761; married February 15th, 1781, Jonathan Seymour, of Kensington, son of Eliakim, and his wife, Susanna (Judd), born, October, 1757. He was a blacksmith, built the Saxy Hooker house in Kensington, and had his shop opposite. She was admitted to the church at New Britain, December 5th, 1784, and to the church at Kensington with her husband, May 5th, 1788. They moved west, and she died January 1st, 1833, at Harford, Penn., aged 72 years. He became a deacon at Otsego, where he located, and where he died, July 26th, 1819, aged 62 years. They are the grand-parents of Professor Tyler, of Amherst College. Jonathan Seymour was a great-grandson of Captain Richard Seymour, of the Seymour Fort, in Great Swamp.

1904.
New York City, New Britain, Conn.

ABIJAH HART, New Britain, eldest son of Thomas Hart, of the same place, and his wife, Mehitabel (Bird), born April 7th, 1764, at New Britain; married September 22d, 1794, Anna, daughter of Captain Giles Hall, of Middletown, and his wife, Anna (Lord), born August 24th, 1765, and was a woman of rare accomplishments. Mr. Hart took an honorary degree at Yale College in 1795, and taught school several years at Middletown. He became extensively engaged in merchandise and commerce in New York City, in the firm of Hicks, Vanderbilt & Hart. They failed in business in consequence of the French spoliation, and he returned to the old home of his father about 1808, where he followed farming. His wife died January 15th, 1824, aged 58 years, when he second married October 26th, 1826, Lucy, widow of Samuel Dunham, of Southington, and daughter of John Ariail, and his wife, Hannah (Rich), born August 27th, 1781, at Southington. He died

May 3d, 1829, aged 65 years, when his widow third married, September, 1831, Isaac Stearns, of Lanesboro, Mass.

THEIR CHILDREN, BEING THE SEVENTH GENERATION.

2212. Julia Ann, born September 1st, 1795; married December 16th, 1818, Seth Lewis; second   ; third

2213. Caroline Bird, born April 15th, 1798, in New York City; married December 16th, 1818, Alfred Andrews, of New Britain.

2214. Thomas Giles, born December 2d, 1800; died at Raleigh, N. C. He was never married.

2215. Henry Abijah, born August 9th, 1805; married April 24th, 1827, Eliza Shipman.

2216. Samuel Mansfield, born August 30th, 1807; died single in Texas, in 1838.

1905.   *New Britain, Conn.*

ISMENA HART, New Britain, Conn., third daughter of Thomas Hart, of the same place, and his wife, Mehitabel (Bird), born   , 1768; baptized July 17th, 1768, at New Britain. She was admitted to the Congregational Church there, February 6th, 1785. She was never married, but lived and died on the old premises of her father, where Henry K. Smith owned and occupied in 1873. She was remarkably devoted and conscientious as a Christian, and gave the residue of her estate to the Home Missionary Society, by Will, appraised at $750. She died February 20th, 1854, aged 86 years.

1906.
New Britain, Conn., Candor, N. Y.

REV. WILLIAM HART, New Britain, Conn., youngest son and child of Thomas Hart, of the same place, and his wife, Mehitabel (Bird), born 1772; baptized March 16th, 1772. He graduated at Yale College in 1792, and married in 1798, Hannah Bridge Campe, at Shoreditch Church, Wapping, London, Eng. She was born at London in 1765. He prepared for college with Dr. Smalley, and was licensed to preach by the Hartford South Association at Southington, June 3d, 1800. His wife died April 30th, 1817, at Hartford, Conn., aged 52 years. He was of feeble health and constitution, and only preached occasionally. He was never settled. He second married at Madison, Conn., Widow Joanna Hand, a sister of Return G. Meigs. He died in Candor, N. Y., at the residence of his son, Deacon Jonathan Bird Hart, August 2d, 1836, aged 64 years.

THEIR CHILDREN, BEING THE SEVENTH GENERATION.

2217. Hannah Bridge, born February 11th, 1799; married March 25th, 1818, Henry M. Pratt.

2218. Jonathan Bird, born August 25th, 1800; married, March, 1823, Elvira Humiston.

2219. Mehitabel, born January 11th, 1806; married March 20th, 1844, Peter G. Broom.

WADSWORTH. ROBERTS.

1907. *Farmington, New Britain, Conn.*

MARY HART, New Britain and Farmington, eldest daughter of Jehudah Hart, of New Britain, and his first wife, Mary (Munson), born August 5th, 1759, at New Britain; admitted to the Congregational Church there, March 30th, 1800; married December 24th, 1806, Eliphalet Wadsworth, of Farmington, and was his second wife. He died January 21st, 1823, aged 75 years, when second she married May 20th, 1829, Aaron Roberts, of New Britain, and was his second wife. He died at New Britain, September 27th, 1831, aged 73. She was a discreet, patient, and good woman. She returned again to Farmington, where she died, November 11th, 1847, aged 78 years. Her grave is in the old cemetery at Farmington, on the hill.

1908. *New Britain, Conn.*

ASAHEL HART, New Britain, Conn, eldest son of Jehudah Hart, of the same place, and his first wife, Mary (Munson), born May 24th, 1771, at New Britain; married, January, 1790, Hannah Langdon, daughter of Captain John, and his wife, Mercy (Eno), who were near neighbors, born November 11th, 1771. She died November 12th, 1792, when second he married July 30th, 1793, Sarah, daughter of Judah Hart, Jr., and his wife, Sarah (North), born November 7th, 1770, at New Britain. She died at the house of Horace Butler, in New Britain, December 19th, 1841, aged 71 years. He died at Charleston, S. C., July 22d, 1804, aged 35. He was of slender make, and studied with his uncle, Dr. Josiah Hart, of Wethersfield, and was thus fitted for a school teacher. After some years experience here, and he had built the Francis Hart house, near the corner of Lake and Hart Streets, he went south teaching. The inventory of his estate was taken by Ephraim Doolittle and Robert Cornwall, December 4th, 1804; amount, £66 11s. 11d.; and the court granted the widow, for support, £22 1s. 6d., and £6 16s. for the support of the children.

CHILDREN BY HIS FIRST WIFE, BEING THE SEVENTH GENERATION.

Amon, born November 18th, 1790; died of dysentery, August 17th, 1798, aged 7 years.

2219¼. Hannah, born October 7th, 1792; married　　　　, 1810, Sylvester Clark, son of Abel.

CHILDREN BY HIS SECOND WIFE.

Amzi, born June 13th, 1795; died August 25th, 1798, of dysentery, aged 3 years.

Sarah, born March 20th, 1797; died March 20th, 1797, aged 1 hour.

2220. Eliza, born October 10th, 1799; married April 18th, 1824, Ralph Pearl.
2221. Amzi Woodruff, born November 3d, 1801; died August 10th, 1823, of spotted fever, aged 22 years.
      Amon, born December 19th, 1802; died December 22d, 1803, aged 1 year.

. **1909.**   *New Britain, Conn.*

JAMES HART, New Britain, second son of Jehudah Hart, of the same place, and his wife, Mary (Munson), born May 22d, 1773, at New Britain; married, June, 1793, Sylvia, daughter of Nathaniel Pennfield, of New Britain, and his wife, Lydia (Barnes), born, June, 1774, at New Britain. He was a farmer by occupation, and built opposite his father in Hart Quarter. He died in a fit, March 29th, 1813, aged 40 years. His family became scattered, and his house finally disappeared. His widow second married January 7th, 1818, John Wyard, of Wolcott. She died at St. Mary's, Anglaise County, Ohio, October 20th, 1852, in her 79th year.

ᶜTHEIR CHILDREN, BEING THE SEVENTH GENERATION.

2222. Lydia, born May 13th, 1796; married November 25th, 1818, John C. Root.
2223. Ethan, born, September, 1799; married November 3d, 1819, Martha Wyard.
2224. Clarissa, born February 22d, 1803; married, June, 1822, Enos Beckwith.
2225. Harriet, born October 6th, 1806; married, April, 1821, William McCreary.
2226. Mary, born, January, 1810; married May 18th, 1839, George McLaughlin.
      James, born, March, 1812; died, November, 1819, aged 7 years.

1910.   *New Britain, Conn.*

SYLVIA HART, New Britain, Conn., third daughter of Jehudah Hart, of the same place, and his first wife, Mary (Munson), born April 15th, 1777, at New Britain. She lived at the home of her father during his life, and then in various families—having no certain dwelling place. She was never married. She retained her faculties to old age, especially her memory. She was admitted to the Congregational Church in New Britain, October 1st, 1809, and from thence she went to the South Church in 1842. She was supported in old age in part by the church and in part by the town, but chiefly by her nephew, O. Seymour. She died at the old house of Chester Hart's, New Britain, May 9th, 1864, aged 87 years and 24 days.

1911.   *New Britain, Conn.*

JOEL HART, New Britain, Conn., third son of Jehudah Hart, of the same place, and his first wife, Mary (Munson), born June 14th, 1779, at New Britain; married September 17th, 1800, Lydia North, daughter of Jedediah, of Berlin, and his second wife, Abigail (Andrews), born 1780. Mr. Hart died October 16th, 1811, aged 32 years, when second she married ———— Riley, and after living in Worthington, Ohio, for a time, they removed to Meredith, N. Y., in 1804, where he died, October 17th, 1811. She died March 28th, 1857, aged 77 years.

CHILDREN OF JOEL AND LYDIA, BEING THE SEVENTH GENERATION.

2227. Stephen, born April 12th, 1801; married, July, 1831, Eliza Buck.
2228. Seth, born November 13th, 1804; married Vesta Curtiss; second, Mary Wilson. He was a physician.
2229. Lydia G., born July 9th, 1806; married June 12th, 1828, Carlisle Olmsted.
2230. Mary, born November 9th, 1808; married October 8th, 1827, Salman Baldwin.

1912. *Watertown, Marietta, Ohio.*

DEACON. BENJAMIN HART, New Britain, fourth son of Jehudah Hart, of the same place, and his first wife, Mary (Munson), born November 20th, 1781, at New Britain; married July 28th, 1805, Honor Deming, of Watertown, Ohio, daughter of Colonel Simeon Deming, of Wethersfield, Conn., born September 28th, 1789. She died December 19th, 1825, aged 36 years, when second he married August 26th, 1826, by Rev. Jacob Linsley, Mrs. Esther Miner, whose maiden name was Esther Wilson, born August 25th, 1795. She died at Watertown, August 9th, 1833, when third he married October 15th, 1834, Widow Lawrence, whose name was Rebecca White, born November 11th, 1802. She died September 19th, 1856. Mr. Hart settled in Watertown, Washington County, Ohio, about 1820, and was chosen a deacon of the Presbyterian Church there at its organization. From thence he removed to Marietta in 1852, and died at the house of his youngest son by his second wife, Henry Converse, December 24th, 1867, aged 72 years and 4 months.

CHILDREN BY HIS FIRST WIFE, BEING THE SEVENTH GENERATION.

2231. Austin, born March 4th, 1808; married April 9th, 1842, Clarinda Star.
2232. Columbus, born July 7th, 1810; married September 10th, 1833, Nancy Proctor.
2233. Mary Ann, born May 24th, 1813; married September 25th, 1833, Joseph Hayward.
2234. Lucy Wolcott, born December 2d, 1815; married October 12th, 1836, Samuel · Payne; second
2235. Simeon Deming, born August 13th, 1818; married July 24th, 1846, Minerva Lawrence.
    Sally Emeline, born September 20th, 1820; died September 19th, 1828, aged 8 years.
2236. Benjamin Franklin, born January 5th, 1823; married October 19th, 1848, Sally Maria Alcock, of Marietta, Ohio.
    Joel North, born September 4th, 1825; died October 5th, 1825, aged 1 month.

CHILDREN BY HIS SECOND WIFE.

2237. Esther Minor, born May 8th, 1827; married   , Charles Stratton.

2238.   Honor Deming, born January 4th, 1829; married October 30th, 1852, Thomas
        Ralph Eckley.

        Child, born February 8th, 1831; died February 9th, 1831.

2239.   Henry Converse, born March 4th, 1833; married September 4th, 1860, Han-
        nah Rood.

THIRD WIFE.

        William Morrison, born November 13th, 1836; died April 9th, 1840, in his
        4th year.

2240.   Frances Adelia, born August 10th, 1839; married January 16th, 1868, John
        A. Plumer.

SEYMOUR.

1913.   *New Britain, Conn.*

ABIGAIL HART, New Britain, Conn., youngest daughter and child of
Jehudah Hart, of the same place, and his first wife, Mary (Munson),
born October 28th, 1786, at New Britain. She was admitted to the
Congregational Church there, June 6th, 1819. She married January
29th, 1807, Moses D. Seymour, son of Aaron, of West Hartford, and
his wife, Anna (Phelps), of Litchfield, born June 3d, 1782. He was
a clothier by trade, which he learned of the Talcotts, of West Hartford. He built his house at the south part of New Britain, and it was
owned and occupied by William Wallace in 1873. He had his shop
near the saw-mill of Ozias Hart. He left this place later in life, and
built in the village under Dublin Hill, where he spent his last days.
He was admitted to the Congregational Church, April 4th, 1819. He
died July 7th, 1839, aged 57 years. She died in Hartford, March 16th,
1858, aged 71, but was buried in New Britain, and a neat stone tells
where she lies in the cemetery. She was a discreet and worthy woman.
They had—1, Orson Hart, born September 1st, 1807; 2, 3, twin sons,
died March 17th, 1809; 4, Mary Ann, died   ; 5,
Mary Ann, 2d, born October 4th, 1813; 6, Henry Phelps, born August
2d, 1818; 7, Oliver Dewitt, born December 31st, 1820, lives in Hartford, and has drawn more votes than any man there.

1914.   *Hinkley, Copley, Ohio.*

OLIVER HART, New Britain, eldest son of Jehudah Hart, of the same
place, and his second wife, Mrs. Elizabeth (Mazuzen) Judd, born December 13th, 1788, at New Britain. He was a farmer, and married
January 3d, 1838, Deborah E. Hurlburt, who died, when he second
married Lurana Osborn, and lived on the old homestead of his father
until about 1832, when he removed to Hinkley, Madison County, Ohio,
and afterwards lived at Copley, Summit County, where he died, September 6th, 1864, aged 76 years.

Harriet, born   ; died August 3d, 1840.

2441.   Elizabeth, born February 3d, 1844.

1915.   *Hinkley, Ohio.*

ELIZUR HART, New Britain, second son of Jehudah Hart, of the same place, and his second wife, Mrs. Elizabeth (Mazuzen) Judd, born October 9th, 1794, at New Britain. He was a joiner by trade, which he learned of Captain Porter, of Farmington. He married September 11th, 1832, Sophronia Jerome, of Bristol. He removed to Hinkley, Ohio, 'where he perished in a snow storm, February 16th, 1842, aged 48 years.

THEIR CHILDREN, BEING THE SEVENTH GENERATION.

2442.   Walter, born August 30th, 1833.
2443.   Henry, born August 15th, 1836.
2444.   Elizabeth, born October 10th, 1838.
2445.   Mary, born March 8th, 1841.

WELLS.

1916.   *Wethersfield, Conn., Windsor, Vt.*

ABIGAIL HART, eldest daughter of Dr. Josiah Hart, of New Britain and Wethersfield, Conn., and Marietta, Ohio, and his first wife, Abigail (Sluman), of Stonington, Conn., born February 3d, 1766, at Wethersfield; married   , Thomas Wells, of Hartford. He was a tailor by trade. They lived for a time on what is now called Wethersfield Avenue, when they removed to Windsor, Vt., where they had a family of five children, viz: 1, Abigail, 2, Sarah, 3, Emily, 4, Thomas, 5, Josiah. The sons learned book binding in Hartford, and went to sea. Abigail married a Stone, and Emily a Stimson, a wealthy man of Boston. The parents died at Windsor, Vt.

ROBBINS.

1917.   *Wethersfield, Conn.*

HANNAH HART, Wethersfield, Conn., second daughter of Dr. Josiah Hart, of New Britain and Wethersfield, Conn., and Marietta, Ohio, and his first wife, Abigail (Sluman), born   24th, 1769, at Wethersfield, Conn.; married   , Joshua Robins. She died May 28th, 1862, at Avon, Conn., aged 94 years. They had —1, Hannah Hart, married Romanta Woodruff; 2, Abigail, married Colier Steele; 3, Thomas, married Mary Burkitt; 4, Daniel, died single.

WELLS.

1918. *Wethersfield, Conn.*

EMILY HART, third daughter of Dr. Josiah Hart, of Wethersfield, and his first wife, Abigail (Sluman), born February 5th, 1771, at Wethersfield; married, March, 1789, Gideon Wells, of that town, born July 16th, 1764. He was a farmer, lived on West Main Street, and died there March 19th, 1810, aged 45 years, 8 months, 3 days. She died February 21st, 1860, aged 89 years and 16 days. They lived in the house owned and occupied by their grandson; Dudley Wells, in 1874, about one and a half miles west of the village, where I found a family tablet beautifully wrought and embroidered in colors by their daughter, Mary Wells. Although faded, it shows taste, skill, and utility. They had—1, Sluman, born June 12th, 1790; 2, William Hart, born December 15th, 1792; 3, Emily, born October 13th, 1796; 4, Romanta, born May 4th, 1798; 5, Dudley, born August 13th, 1800; 6, Mary, born December 30th, 1802; 7, Pamela, born May 3d, 1806; 8, Prudence, born April 21st, 1808, died January 25th, 1816.

1919. *Wethersfield, Conn.*

JOSIAH SLUMAN HART, Wethersfield, Conn., second son of Dr. Josiah of New Britain and Wethersfield, Conn., and Marietta, Ohio, and his first wife, Abigail (Sluman), born January 6th, 1773, at Wethersfield; baptized February 7th, 1773, at New Britain, by Dr. Smalley. He learned the trade of cabinet making of Aaron Roberts, at New Britain. He left before his time was out, and died in Wethersfield at his father's house, in his 18th year.

1920. *Wethersfield, Conn., Marietta, O.*

MAJOR WILLIAM HART, Marietta, Ohio, third son of Dr. Josiah Hart, of New Britain and Wethersfield, Conn., and Marietta, Ohio, and his first wife, Abigail (Sluman), of Stonington, Conn., born March 4th, 1775, at Wethersfield, Conn.; married   , Sarah Waters Wolcott, daughter of Gershom, and his wife, Rhoda (Robbins), of Wethersfield, born there November 27th, 1779. They removed to Marietta, Ohio, and were said to be the handsomest couple that settled in the place. He was a farmer, and had his farm opposite the island of Marietta, now a part of the city, and one of the streets is called Hart, in honor of him. Major Hart was on active military duty and watch at the time of Aaron Burr's insurrection in 1806-7, to prevent the boats in the Muskingum River from joining the fleet of Burr. Mrs. Hart died, March, 1824, aged 44 years. He second married

, Mary Cass, cousin to Governor Lewis Cass. He was intelligent, amiable, and brave. He died January 28th, 1836, aged 60 years, 10 months, and 24 days. He has a beautiful monument in Mound Cemetery, Marietta, Ohio.

THEIR CHILDREN, BEING THE SEVENTH GENERATION.

2446. Camillus, born   . He was killed young by the kick of a horse.

2447. Sally, born   . She was scalded to death young, at Marietta, Ohio.

2448. Rhoda Robbins, born •   ; died at Memphis, Tenn., in 1855.

2449. William Wolcott, born   ; married   , Areli Gates.

2450. Royal Robbins, born March 4th, 1808. He was never married. He died of consumption in 1839.

2451. Charlotte, born   , 1810; married   , 1833, James Price, of Kentucky.

2452. Harriet C., born March 10th, 1814; married   , 1843, James N. Foley, of Parkersburg.

2453. Eliza Buck, born   ; married   , 1833, Hon. Solon Borland.

2454. Camillus Sluman, born July 10th, 1823; married September 27th, 1865, Joanna B. Krebs, of Winchester.   .

SECOND WIFE.

2455. Josiah Thomas, born September 13th, 1827; married November 27th, 1849, Elizabeth A. Harris.

2456. Henry W., born   ; married December 15th, 1869, Mary C Skinner, of Lagrange, Mo.

·

1921.   *Lancaster, Ohio.*

THOMAS HART, Lancaster, Ohio, youngest son of Dr. Josiah Hart, of New Britain and Wethersfield, Conn., and subsequently of Marietta, Ohio, and his first wife, Abigail (Sluman), of Stonington, born December 14th, 1776, at Wethersfield, Conn.; married   , 1800, in Kentucky, Elizabeth, daughter of Robert McClelland, and his wife, Margaret (Howe). They lived at Lancaster, Ohio, to which place they removed in   , where he was engaged in the mercantile business, and where he died, March 13th, 1825, aged 48 years and 4 months.

THEIR CHILDREN, BEING THE SEVENTH GENERATION.

2456. Sarah, born   ; married   , Luman Baker, of Lancaster, Ohio.

2457. Cynthia, born   ; married   , Charles Borland, of Virginia.

2458. Jesse Beecher, born December 31st, 1812; married May 11th, 1837, Susan Rebu; second, Sallie C. Coleman.

2459. Samuel McClelland, born February 9th, 1814; married   , Mary E. Pugh.

2460. William McClelland, born   ; married
   Susan Saffin.
2461. Thomas Ewing, born   ; married   ,
   Adaline Woods, of Virginia.
2462. Susan Cecelia, born   , 1824; married   , 1844, Samuel
   C. Stambaugh.

BUCK.

1922.   *Marietta, Ohio.*

BETSEY HART, eldest daughter of Dr. Josiah Hart, of Wethersfield, Conn., and his second wife, Mrs. Abigail Harris, born December 22d, 1778, at Wethersfield; married   , Titus Buck, son of Samuel, of Wethersfield, and his wife, Elizabeth Blinn, and lived in Marietta, Ohio. When the family of Dr. Hart was about to remove to Marietta, she objected to going until she had married Titus Buck, and she did it.

DEVOE.

1923.   *Marietta, Ohio.*

CLARISSA HART, second daughter of Dr. Josiah Hart, of New Britain and Wethersfield, Conn., and subsequently of Marietta, Ohio, and his second wife, who was the Widow Abigail Harris, of Wethersfield, born about 1780, at Wethersfield. After the decease of her mother at Wethersfield, about 1796, she went with her father to Marietta, Ohio. She married   , Wing Devoe, of Marietta, and lived on the Muskingum River, some four miles above Marietta. They had a son, Josiah, who lives on the old homestead, a daughter, Emeline, who married Hon. George Barker, of Ohio, and lived in Missouri in 1874, and a son, William, who married a granddaughter of General Israel Putnam, and they have his military coat, and his wife's bridal dress, which is made of brocade silk. Mrs. Devoe died January 25th, 1871, aged 88. Mr. Devoe died, February, 1868, in his 90th year.

VANCE.

1924.   *Columbus, Ohio.*

CYNTHIA HART, youngest daughter of Dr. Josiah Hart, of New Britain and Wethersfield, Conn., and subsequently of Marietta, Ohio, and his second wife, who was Mrs. Abigail Harris, of Wethersfield, born about 1782, at Wethersfield, and after the decease of her mother at Wethersfield, she removed with her father to Marietta in 1796, and there married   , Vance, and they lived at the state capital, Columbus. She died in 1872, aged 90 years.

1925. *New Britain, Kensington, Conn.*

BENJAMIN HART, New Britain, eldest son of Benjamin Hart, of the same place, and his wife, Mary (Fuller), born February 7th, 1773; married January 30th, 1800, Hannah Kellogg, of Newington, daughter of Martin, and his wife, Hannah (Robbins), born January 17th, 1774, at Newington. She died there of cancer, July 28th, 1824, aged 50 years, when second he married July 15th, 1832, Almira Carter, daughter of Ithiel, of Kensington, and his wife, Lois (Deming), born 1782. She died September 11th, 1847, aged 65 years, and has a tombstone in the cemetery south of the railroad station in Kensington. Mr. Hart was a farmer by occupation. He taught school several seasons in early manhood. He lived in Newington several years, but made it his home in Kensington, half a mile south-west of the church. He bought his farm of Phineas Andrews when he went to Leyden, N. Y. He was occasionally partially insane the last few years of his life. He died July 11th, 1856, aged 83 years, 5 months, and 4 days.

THEIR CHILDREN, BEING THE SEVENTH GENERATION.

2463. Benjamin Kellogg, born January 27th, 1801; married April 22d, 1824, Olivia Cowles.

2464. Thomas Robbins, born August 27th, 1803; married December 18th, 1836, Cecelia Beaumont.

2465. Walter Ward, born November 17th, 1804; married May 28th, 1829, Sarah Bennett.

BELDEN.

1926.

New Britain, Conn., East Windham, N. Y.

ROXANNA HART, New Britain, third daughter of Benjamin Hart, of the same place, and his wife, Mary (Fuller), born June 21st, 1780, at New Britain; married November 9th, 1797, Leonard Belden, Jr., son of Leonard, Sr., and his wife, Hannah (Judd), born July 13th, 1778. He lived at the home of his father and grandfather, Ezra, on East Street, in New Britain, and was a farmer. He died March 8th, 1807, aged 29 years. She was admitted to the Congregational Church in New Britain, April 3d, 1808, and was dismissed by letter to the church at East Windham, N. Y. She lived at Big Hollow, Green County, N. Y., where she died, February 12th, 1864, in her 84th year. Children, viz: 1, Emily Hart, born September 12th, 1798; 2, Hannah Judd, born July 23d, 1800; 3, Rhoda Roxalina, born August 24th, 1802; 4, George Dunham, born February 7th, 1805; 5, Leonard Dix, born January 29th, 1807.

THERON HART, New Britain, second son of Benjamin Hart, of the same place, and his wife, Mary (Fuller), born December 29th, 1782; married   , Abiah Warner, of Hamden. She died December 16th, 1832, aged 50 years, when second he married April 27th, 1834, Lydia, daughter of Ebenezer Hart, of Kensington, born 1780. She died July 18th, 1850, aged 70 years. Her Will was made January 24th, 1846, and was proved in the court of probate for the district of Berlin, on the 25th of July, 1850. She gave her nephew, Jonathan T. Hart, of Kensington, the use, during his natural life, of all her real estate, amounting to $5,935, as appraised by Captain Jabez Langdon and William Kellogg, provided that he paid three legacies, to wit: first, to her niece, Maria, wife of Truman Cole, $50; second, to her niece, Mrs. Elizabeth, wife of Riley Gladden, $50; and to my brother, Ichabod Hart, $300. And I give to the legal male heirs of my nephew, Jonathan T. Hart, at the time of his death, all the above lands, (except what my executor shall sell for a grave-stone, &c.,) and buildings, to be equally divided between them. To my husband, Theron Hart, I give the use of all my buildings for three months after my death.   Signed, Lydia Hart and seal.

She has a grave-stone in the Bridge Cemetery at Berlin. She inherited the estate of her uncle, Thomas Hart, at the corner west of the Second Church in Kensington. She and her husband lived on this place several years, although he owned a place on Arch Street, in New Britain. Mr. Hart was a prominent member of the Methodist Church in New Britain. He died January 16th, 1859, aged 76 years, 2 months, and 17 days.

THEIR CHILDREN, BEING THE SEVENTH GENERATION.

2466. Sabrina Abia, born   , 1817, married January 18th, 1844, Curtiss C. Camp.

2467. Mary, born April 1st, 1822; married January 13th, 1848, Curtiss C. Camp.

ANDREWS.

FANNY HART, fifth daughter of Benjamin Hart, of New Britain, and his wife, Mary (Fuller), born February 17th, 1785, in New Britain; married April 4th, 1804, Dr. Chauncey Andrews, of Southington, son of Benjamin, and his second wife, Mary (Barnes), born May 8th, 1783, at Southington. He was a physician, and took his medical degree at Yale College in 1805. They lived in Hamden, Killingworth, and Durham, Conn., where he died of cancer, October 14th, 1863, aged 80 years. She died February 7th, 1860, aged 75 years. Children, viz: 1, Benjamin Hart, born March 10th, 1805, died June 23d, 1832; 2, Erasmus Darwin, born September 28th, 1806, at Killingworth; 3, Chauncey W., born January 30th, 1809; 4, Theron Hart, born January 26th, 1813; 5, Frances C., born July 26th, 1814.

TULLER.

1929. *Simsbury, New Britain, Conn.*

RHODA HART, New Britain, sixth daughter of Benjamin Hart, of New Britain, and his wife, Mary (Fuller), born February 8th, 1788, at New Britain; baptized there March 30th, 1788, by Rev. John Smalley; married March 28th, 1839, Asa Tuller, of Simsbury. He died November 7th, 1853, at Simsbury, when she returned to New Britain, and owns and occupies a place on Arch Street. They attended the Methodist Church. She was admitted to the First Congregational Church in New Britain, April 3d, 1808, and has never been dismissed. She taught school in early life. She has never had children. She was in comfortable health in 1873, aged 85.

1931. *New Britain, Conn.*

CYRUS HART, New Britain, fourth son of Benjamin Hart, of the same place, and his wife, Mary (Fuller), born July 19th, 1795, at New Britain; married March 31st, 1819, Betsey, daughter of Solomon Clark, and his wife, Elizabeth (Smith), born December 20th, 1794. His avocation is farming. He inherited his father's homestead, and has sold his lands for building lots until he has become rich, and in 1872 built an elegant house on Arch Street, just north of his old one, and his son-in-law, Imlay Bird Veits, also lives in his family. His wife died February 22d, 1862, aged 66 years.

THEIR CHILDREN, BEING THE SEVENTH GENERATION.

2468. Juliaetta Andrews, born May 20th, 1820; married June 27th, 1838, Imlay Bird Veits.
2469. Angeline Clark, born July 11th, 1822; married June 27th, 1843, Imlay Bird Veits.
Elizabeth, born December 19th, 1824; died August 24th, 1827.

GRIDLEY.

1932. *Southington, Conn.*

ESTHER HART, Southington, youngest daughter and child of Benjamin Hart, of New Britain, and his wife, Mary (Fuller), born March 5th, 1798, at New Britain; married March 16th, 1819, Edwin, son of

Noah Gridley, of Southington, and his wife, Luanna (Andrews). She was admitted to the Congregational Church in Southington, by letter from New Britain, December 5th, 1819. He was admitted on profession, December 1st, 1833, but afterwards joined the Unitarians. His avocation was farming. He died October 3d, 1852, aged 55 years. She was living in Southington with her children in 1873.

1933.   *Albion, N. Y.*

JOSEPH HART, New Britain, eldest son of Joseph Hart, of New Britain, Conn., and New Durham, N. Y., and his wife, Huldah (Smith), born November 20th, 1773, at New Britain, Conn.; married May 3d, 1798, Lucy (Kirkland), of Saybrook, born November 11th, 1778, at Saybrook. Soon after marriage he removed to Durham, Green County, N. Y., where they lived a few years. He then went to Seneca, Ontario County, N. Y., bought a quarter section of land of the Holland Land Company, then a dense forest, cut some trees, rolled together a few logs for a cabin, and in 1812 he moved into it with his wife, four sons, and an infant daughter; and thus began a settlement, which was known in 1873 as Albion, Orleans County, N. Y. His house was the missionary's home, his barn the meeting-house, and he was an elder of the Presbyterian Church. He died July 22d, 1853, aged 80 years. His widow died at Adrian, Mich., where she had gone to be with her daughter, Mrs. Berry, January 4th, 1867, aged 88 years.

THEIR CHILDREN, BEING THE SEVENTH GENERATION.

2470. William, born February 23d, 1801; married September 23d, 1834, Pamelia Wells.

2471. Elizur, born May 23d, 1803; married June 11th, 1834, Loraine Field.

2472. John J., born April 8th, 1805; died single, May 24th, 1868, aged 63.

2473. Benjamin Kirkland, born July 2d, 1807; married, November, 1839, Sophia E. Mix.

Christopher, born December 25th, 1809; died January 28th, 1810.

2474. Lovisa Lord, born April 27th, 1811; married September 3d, 1833, Orange Martin Roode.

2475. Lucy Kirkland, born January 22d, 1814; married August 19th, 1839, Ambrose Spencer Berry.

2476. Mary Ann, born June 2d, 1817; married, September, 1846, Langford Green Berry.

2477. Joseph Smith, born February 2d, 1820; married   , 1861, Harriet Cole.

2478. Samuel E., born August 13th, 1823; married October 7th, 1852, Anna D. Criney.

1934.   *Marshall, Mich.*

DR. LUTHER W. HART, M. D., Marshall, Calhoun County, Mich., second son of Joseph Hart, of New Britain, and his wife, Huldah (Smith), born September 2d, 1778, at New Britain. He was a graduate of Williams College, and was a physician in Durham, N. Y., for thirty years. "Then, as a pioneer, he removed to Marshall. He was a scholar, a patron of education, a supporter of the institutions of the gospel, and a man of virtue and worth." He married April 27th, 1806, Sibil Selden, of Windsor, Conn., and removed from New Britain, Conn., to Durham, N. Y., soon after marriage, and from thence to Marshall, Mich., in July, 1833. He and his wife were members of the Presbyterian Church in Durham. He died at Marshall, September 10th, 1842, aged 64 years. When they removed to Marshall they united with the Congregational Church, and he was elected a deacon, which office he held until his decease. The church was a very feeble one, and he was very active and useful in it. He was in the midst of his activity when taken with his last sickness, and at first expressed great regret that he must leave his work; but it was only a momentary feeling. He almost immediately expressed his perfect resignation to God's will, saying, "God knows best whether he has any more work for me to do." He was sick but a few days, and I always look back to them in his sick room as among the most blessed of my life. I remember repeating at the time those beautiful lines—"The chamber where the good man meets his fate is privileged beyond the common walks of virtuous. life, quite in the verge of heaven." His beautiful death was a fit close to such a life.

THEIR CHILDREN, BEING THE SEVENTH GENERATION.

2479. Mary Ann, born February 16th, 1807; married May 17th, 1825, Charles Thayer.

2480. Delia Selden, born January 26th, 1811; married August 26th, 1834, Abner C. Parmelee.

2481. Clarissa Selden, born April 3d, 1814; married August 2d, 1830, Dr. Andrew L. Hayes.

2482. Charlotte Eaton, born September 6th, 1820; married April 10th, 1839, Charles T. Gorham.

2483. Joseph, born August 9th, 1822, at Durham, N. Y.; died there March 9th, 1825, and was buried there.

CLARK. LEE.

1937. *New Britain, Conn.*

SALLY HART, New Britain, Conn., eldest child of Elizur Hart, the school-master, of the same place, and his wife, Sarah (Langdon), born November 9th, 1778, at New Britain; married November 9th, 1797, Manly, son of Abel Clark, of New Britain, and his wife, Abigail (Judd), born April 1st, 1776, at New Britain. They lived with his father in Stanley Quarter. He died May 1st, 1812, aged 30 years, when second she married February 27th, 1824, Martin Lee, of Southington, son of Timothy, and his wife, Lucy (Camp), born October 10th, 1778, at Southington. His avocation was farming. He lived on the old place of his father and grandfather, on the west side, just north of the churches, where he died January 21st, 1841, aged 61 years. She died December 19th, 1860, aged 82 years. Her children by Clark were—1, Abigail Judd, born March 28th, 1799, died July 3d, 1804; 2, Elizur Hart, born August 17th, 1801, died December 6th, 1824, at Southington; 3, Julia Abigail, born July 23d, 1807, died February 1st, 1813, in New Britain. Her child by Lee was—4, Lucretia Sarah, baptized August 7th, 1831, married June 21st, 1842, Dr. Frederick Hart, of Southington.

HITCHCOCK.

1939.   *Southington, Conn.*

SOPHIA HART, New Britain, third daughter of Elizur Hart, the school-master, and his wife, Sarah (Langdon), born September 3d, 1785, at New Britain; married November 30th, 1809, Franklin Hitchcock, of Southington, son of Samuel, and his wife, Tamar   .
He lived in Southington, on West Street. He was a large, well proportioned, and powerful man, and a famous wrestler. He died November 8th, 1827, aged 43 years. They had one child, Sophia Hart, born   ; married September 18th, 1827, John Nelson Hart.

1940.

DOCTOR ERASTUS LANGDON HART, only son of Elizur Hart, the school-master, of New Britain, and his wife, Sarah (Langdon), born May 8th, 1787, at New Britain. He became a physician of celebrity, and married September 12th, 1810, Mary Parmelee, of Goshen, Conn., born March 6th, 1788. He studied for the medical profession with Dr. Everest, of Canton, Conn., and began his practice in Goshen, Conn., in 1809, where he found his first wife, who died at Elmira, N. Y., where he located in 1824, when second he married November 1st, 1843, Harriet Hepburn, born November 23d, 1804. He died October 23d, 1871, at Elmira, N. Y., aged 84 years.

THEIR CHILDREN, BEING THE SEVENTH GENERATION.

2484. Emma Goodrich, born July 12th, 1811; married September 21st, 1842, Hon. Samuel Partridge.

2485. Julia Clark, born July 6th, 1813; married September 8th, 1836, Arials Thurston; died April 17th, 1844.

2486. Sarah Keziah, born July 7th, 1815; married   , William R. Judson.

2487. William Elizur, born September 26th, 1817; married September 3d, 1844, Elizabeth Morse Hull.

2488. Erastus Parmelee, born May 6th, 1822; married January 6th, 1846, Eliza Haight.

2489. Mary Parmelee, born March 12th, 1825; married August 8th, 1843, Henry M. Partridge.

CHILD BY THE SECOND WIFE.

2490. Charles Langdon, born April 10th, 1845. He was living single at Elmira, N. Y., in 1872.

1941. *Hartford, Conn.*

COLONEL RICHARD WILLIAM HART, Hartford, Conn., only son and child of General William Hart, of Saybrook, and his first wife, Esther (Buckingham), born January 15th, 1768, at Hartford; married October 29th, 1795, Elizabeth Bull, of Newport, R. I., born September 17th, 1772. His residence was near the Deaf and Dumb Asylum, some two doors east, with large high pillars in front, and where his daughter, Hetty Buckingham Hart, lived in 1873. He inherited the wealth of his father. He died January 13th, 1837, at Saybrook, aged 68 years, 10 months, and 28 days. His widow died at Hartford, August 31st, 1843, in her 71st year.

THEIR CHILDREN, BEING THE SEVENTH GENERATION.

William Richard, born November 17th, 1796; died January 30th, 1807, aged 10 years.

2491. Elizabeth Miller, born June 26th, 1798; married December 22d, 1825, Rev. William Jarvis.

2492. Hetty Buckingham, born April 19th, 1800. She is living single in the family mansion on Asylum Hill.

1943. *Saybrook, Conn.*

SAMUEL HART, Saybrook, eldest son of Samuel Hart, of the same place, and his wife, Lucy (Bushnell), born February 13th, 1778, at Saybrook; married April 3d, 1813, Mercy Pratt, of Saybrook. He died January 10th, 1833, aged 55 years. She died May 8th, 1847.

THEIR CHILDREN, BEING THE SEVENTH GENERATION.

2493. Henry, born August 16th, 1815; married November 17th, 1836, Mary Ann Welton.

Harriet, born April 16th, 1817; died August 17th, 1834, aged 17 years.

1946. *Saybrook, Conn.*

NATHANIEL LYNDE HART, Saybrook, youngest son and child of Samuel Hart, of the same place, and his wife, Lucy (Bushnell), born

October 25th, 1791; married February 17th, 1822, Emeline E. Ingraham, of Saybrook. He died June 6th, 1833, aged 42 years.

2494. Samuel Lynde, born February 8th, 1823.
2495. Maria, born May 18th, 1830.

1947.   *Lyme, Conn.*

JOHN HART, Lyme, Conn., eldest son of John Hart, of Saybrook, Conn., and his wife, who was Widow Nancy Bull, born March 11th, 1784, at Saybrook, and settled at Lyme as a merchant in 1807; married June 25th, 1811, Nancy Matthews, of Old Lyme, daughter of Sylvester, and his wife, Elizabeth. She died June 22d, 1834, when second he married August 25th, 1835, Margaret, daughter of Thomas Sill, and his wife, Mehitabel, of Old Lyme. He was a merchant in Old Lyme some forty years, and from thence he removed to Clinton, Oneida County, N. Y., in 1853, with his family, where he died, July 7th, 1858, aged 74 years. The widow and her three children were still there in 1871.

CHILDREN BY HIS FIRST WIFE, BEING THE SEVENTH GENERATION.
Sylvester Mather, born May 29th, 1812; died December 7th, 1816, aged 4 years.
2496. Ann Elizabeth, born June 17th, 1814; married October 8th, 1833, Willys Warner, of New Haven.
2497. John Alexander, born July 5, 1816; married May 7, 1839, Louisa Edgarton.
2498. Louisa Ely, born September 10th, 1822; married September 9th, 1845, Rev. William Whittlesey.

CHILDREN BY THE SECOND WIFE.
2499. Philip Augustus, born September 9th, 1839. He was single in 1874, and is a merchant at Clinton, N. Y.
2500. Louis Henry, born June 7, 1846; married March 18, 1874, Mary Williams.
2501. Margaret Sill, born July 13th, 1850.

1952.   *Edinburgh, Ohio.*

RICHARD MORRISON HART, Edinburgh, Portage County, Ohio, third son of John Hart, of Saybrook, Conn., and his wife, who was Widow Nancy Bull, born May 9th, 1795, at Saybrook. He was a farmer at Edinburgh, Ohio, in 1873. He married, May, 1818, Betsey Ingham, daughter of William, who died in 1838, at Edinburgh, Ohio, when second he married   , Sarah R. Averill, daughter of Nathaniel P., of Salisbury, Conn. She had no children.

CHILDREN BY HIS FIRST WIFE, BEING THE SEVENTH GENERATION.

2502. Elizabeth, born, July, 1819; married   , Henry J. Canriff, of
        Detroit.
2503. Emeline, born September 18th, 1820; never married; died   , 1841,
        at Edinburgh, Ohio.
2504. Charles Richard, born February 16th, 1825; married, August, 1836, Lorinda
        R. Davis, of Edinburgh, Ohio.

1954.   *Clinton, N. Y.*

CHARLES EDWARD HART, Clinton, N. Y., fifth son of John Hart, of
Saybrook, and his wife, who was Widow Nancy Bull, born, January,
1797; married   , Phebe Mather Sill, daughter of
Thomas, and his wife, Mehitabel, of Old Lyme, where she was born,
November 27th, 1802, and died August 30th, 1869, at Clinton. He
died April 14th, 1869.

THEIR CHILDREN, BEING THE SEVENTH GENERATION.

2505. Henry Sill, born May 4th, 1827, at East Haddam, Conn.; married
2506. Richard Morrison, born March 16th, 1829; married   , 1860, Ruth
        M. Gleason; second,   Brooks.
2507. Sarah Mehitable, born December 25th, 1832, at Marlboro, Conn.; married
        Nelson Bradley, of New York.
2508. Mary Sill, born Sept. 4th, 1837; married Henry D. Pixley, of Utica, N. Y.

1959.   *New Britain, Middletown, Conn.*

FERDINAND AUSTIN HART, Middletown, fifth son of Joseph Hart, of
Saybrook, and his wife, Eunice (Ellery), born September 10th, 1796,
in Hartford; married June 12th, 1827, Sarah A. Cook, daughter of
George and Phebe, of Hartford. He settled in New Britain, Conn.,
where he became one of the trustees of the Methodist Church. He
also engaged somewhat largely in the manufacture of suspenders, but
removed to Middletown, April, 1832, where he has carried on the same
business. He wrote, September 10th, 1873, and said: "I am 77 to-day,
and I am in good health." But he died December 27th, 1873, aged
77 years, 3 months, 17 days.

THEIR CHILDREN, BEING THE SEVENTH GENERATION.

2509. Joseph Austin, born April 2d, 1824; married   , 1844, Clarissa
        Hubbard.
2510. William Ellery, born October 22d, 1826; died January 24th, 1858.
2511. Ann A., born May 14th, 1829.
2512. Ellen A., born March 5th, 1833; died May 30th, 1867.

59

JARVIS.

1960.   *Middletown, Conn.*

SARAH McCURDY HART, Saybrook, Conn., eldest daughter of Elisha
Hart, of Saybrook, and his wife, Jannette (McCurdy), born   ,
1787, at Saybrook; married   , Rev. Samuel Jarvis,
D.D., LL.D., of Middletown, from whom she had been divorced.

HULL.

1961.   *Philadelphia, Penn.*

NANCY McCURDY HART, Saybrook, second daughter of Elisha Hart,
of the same town, and his wife, Jannette (McCurdy), born   ,
1790; married   , Commodore Isaac Hull, United
States Navy. He died in Philadelphia, February 13th, 1843, aged 68
years. He was appointed lieutenant in the navy in 1798, and first distinguished himself in 1800, during the short war with France, by cut-
ting out the French letter-of-marque Sandwich, then lying in the harbor of Port au Platts, in St. Domingo. He subsequently commanded
the schooner Enterprise, twelve guns, attached to the squadron under
Commodore Morris, off Tripoli. In this vessel he aided Captain Rogers,
of the John Adams, in capturing a large cruiser of twenty-two guns.
During the Tripolitan war he was promoted to the rank of master
commandant, and in 1806 was made captain. In the war of 1812 he
commanded the frigate Constitution, and distinguished himself by
capturing the English frigate Guerriere.

ALLEN.

1963.   *Burlington, Vt.*

ELIZABETH HART, Saybrook, Conn., fifth daughter of Elisha Hart,
of the same town, and his wife, Jannette (McCurdy), born   ,
1796, at Saybrook, Conn.; married   , Hon. Heman
Allen, formerly member of Congress from Vermont, and minister
plenipotentiary to Colombia, S. A. He died at Burlington, Vt., December 11th, 1844. His wife also died at Burlington. They had one
child who died in infancy.

1966.   *Guilford, Conn.*

COLONEL WILLIAM HART, Guilford, eldest son of Thomas Hart, of
the same town, and his wife, Mary (Parmalee), born May 5th, 1788, at
Guilford; married November 29th, 1814, Lydia Griffing, daughter of
Joel. She died April 8th, 1819, when second he married Catharine

Starr, daughter of Deacon William, who died April 8th, 1860. He was a carpenter by trade, and held the military rank of colonel. He removed to Mendon, Ill., and died there, August 18th, 1862, aged 74 years.

CHILDREN BY THE FIRST WIFE, BEING THE SEVENTH GENERATION.

Sally Amelia,   ⎫   married Henry Frisbee; died May 4th, 1855.
             ⎬ born August 20th, 1815;
Clarissa Adelia, ⎭   died September 18th, 1817, aged 2 years.

2512¼. William Henry, born November 28th, 1818; died March 17th, 1852, aged 34 years.

CHILDREN BY HIS SECOND WIFE.

Lydia Clarissa, born December 23d, 1823; died December 22d, 1828.

2513. Catharine Elizabeth, born May 9th, 1826; married January 30th, 1849, David Lyman.

2514. Richard Edwin, born April 24th, 1828; married November 28th, 1854, Jane Loper.

2515. Lydia Griffing, born April 3d, 1832; married September 23d, 1864, G. D Colton, of Galesburg.

2516. Harriet Lavinia, born July 22d, 1837; married September 22d, 1869, Rev. A. C. Denison.

1968.   *Guilford, Conn.*

GEORGE HART, Guilford, Conn., second son of Thomas Hart, of the same town, and his wife, Mary (Parmalee), born February 8th, 1794, at Guilford, Conn.; married March 27th, 1816, Clarissa Parmelee, daughter of David. He died May 25th, 1848, aged 54 years.

THEIR CHILDREN, BEING THE SEVENTH GENERATION.

Parnel, born December 7th, 1816; died May 28th, 1828, aged 12 years.

2517. Clarissa, born December 28th, 1817; married July 21st, 1845, William Nash, of Westport.

2518. Ruth, born July 20th, 1819. She was living single at Guilford in 1847.

George Thomas, born June 7th, 1824; died March 11th, 1826.

2519. Henry Thomas, born February 18th, 1827; married   , 1848, Elizabeth Babcock.

2520. George Benjamin, born April 21st, 1831; married September 14th, 1853, Harriet R. Wildman.

2521. Charles Seth, born February 25th, 1833.

TROWBRIDGE.

1970.   *Guilford, Conn.*

ELIZA HART, Guilford, Conn., youngest child of Thomas Hart, of the same town, and his wife, Mary (Parmelee), born, March, 1800, in Guilford; married August 31st, 1823, Stephen Trowbridge, son of Deacon Thomas, and his wife, Sally (Peck), born February 13th, 1798. Their children were—1, Maria Hall, born October 24th, 1824, married

Frederic Goodwin; 2, Frederic Hart, born July 31st, 1828, died, July, 1854; 3, Sarah Elizabeth, born October 12th, 1834, married Samuel G. Dickinson; 4, Julia Caroline, born July 30th, 1837, died, 1839. Mrs. Trowbridge died May 5th, 1841, aged 41 years, when he second married June 27th, 1848, Grace Ann Umberfield.

1973. *Guilford, Conn.*

SAMUEL S. HART, Guilford, second son of John Hart, of the same town, and his wife, Betsey (Field), born November 7th, 1808, at Guilford, Conn.; married   , Mary Coulter. He committed suicide by drowning himself in West River, Guilford, December 10th, 1862, aged 54 years.

THEIR CHILDREN, BEING THE SEVENTH GENERATION.

2522. Henry Thomas, born August 27th, 1856.
2523. George Burdett, born October 27th, 1857.
2524. Mary Ellen, born March 31st, 1859.
2525. Catharine Jane, born August 23d, 1860.
2526. Clarissa Ann, born February 10th, 1862.
2527. John Loomis, born March 29th, 1863.

1977. *Guilford, Conn.*

THOMAS HART, Guilford, third son of John Hart, of the same town, and his wife, Betsey (Field), born August 8th, 1819, at Guilford; married   , Elizabeth Fuller, of New Haven.

THEIR CHILDREN, BEING THE SEVENTH GENERATION.

2528. John, born
2529. George, born
2530. Mary, born

1978. *Guilford, Conn.*

ELISHA HART, Guilford, Conn., fourth son of John Hart, of the same place, and his wife, Betsey (Field), born November 11th, 1823, at Guilford; married October 14th, 1862, Sarah Beardsley.

THEIR CHILDREN, BEING THE SEVENTH GENERATION.

2531. Sherman Elisha, born July 7th, 1864.
2532. Frederick Zebulon, born February 4th, 1866.
2533. Richard Pratt, born February 23d, 1868.

BROWN. KENT.

1982. *Kensington, Conn.*

ROXANNA HART, only child of David Hart, of Berlin, and his wife, Ann (Benjamin), born   , at Berlin; married October

31st, 1799, Bridgman Brown, of Kensington. They had children, viz:
1, Lydia, married William Lewis, of Southington, and died December
6th, 1861, aged 56 years; 2, David, married Hannah Hart, of Middletown; 3, Horace, born . Mr. Brown died, when
his widow married second, June 29th, 1829, John Kent, of Kensington,
his second wife. He died September 2d, 1842. She died at Southington, in the house of Widow Crissey, on West Street, of pneumonia,
October, 1859.

WILLIAMS. ELTON.

1984. *Berlin, Conn.*

LOIS HART, Berlin, Conn., eldest child of Submit Hart, of the same
place, and his wife, Clarissa (Hopkins), born at Berlin in 1797; married
July 29th, 1818, Norman Williams, of Berlin, who died, when second
she married at Berlin, in 1826, Sylvester Elton, of that place, who died
January 17th, 1859, aged 77 years. His widow died at Hartford, January 24th, 1866.

HOLLISTER.

1985. *Kensington, Conn.*

MARILLA HART, Berlin, second daughter of Submit Hart, of the
same town, and his wife, Clarissa (Hopkins), born there in 1799, and
married , Russel Hollister, of Berlin, where she
died March 31st, 1823, aged 23 years, when second he married
, and third he married . A tomb-
stone in the South Cemetery at Berlin shows where Mrs. Marilla Hollister was interred.

1988. *Morrison, Ill.*

SUBMIT HART, youngest child of Submit Hart, Sr., of the same town,
and his wife, Clarissa (Hopkins), born September 28th, 1810, in Berlin,
posthumous; married , Mary Cone, daughter of
Edward, and his wife, Eunice (Belden), born September 29th, at Middletown, Conn. She lives at Morrison, Whiteside County, Ill., and is
a member of the church, where he died, August 9th, 1870, aged 59
years, 10 months, and 11 days.

THEIR CHILDREN, BEING THE SEVENTH GENERATION.

2534. Stephen Pierce, born January 11th, 1835; married July 3d, 1858, Adelia
Qualters, of Boston.
2535. William Samuel, born ; died
[There were other children, but nothing is definitely known of them.]

1989. *Plymouth, Conn.*

REV. LUTHER HART, Plymouth, Conn., eldest son of David Hart, of Goshen, Conn., and his wife, Hannah (Hudson), of Long Island, born July 27th, 1783, at Goshen, Conn. He learned his father's trade of carpenter, but having a great fondness for books, he was fitted for college by Rev. Alexander Gillett, of Torrington, where his father then lived, and became a member of Mr. Gillett's church. In September, 1803, he entered Yale College, and at once took a high rank; and at his graduation in 1807 he received one of the highest honors of the institution. After a year devoted to teaching at Litchfield South Farms he studied theology with Rev. Ebenezer Porter, at Washington, Conn., graduated at Andover, Mass., and was licensed to preach by the Essex Middle Association of Massachusetts. In September, 1811, he married Minerva, daughter of General Potter, of Plymouth, where he received a call and was ordained the year previous, the sermon on the occasion being preached by his tutor, Rev. Ebenezer Porter. This marriage connection is said to have contributed greatly to his comfort and usefulness. Great accessions were made to the church there in 1812, 1824, 1827, and 1831. Some 500 were added during his ministry. In 1818 he aided in the publication of doctrinal tracts, also in the establishment of the *Christian Spectator*, and contributed largely to both. On the 18th of April, 1834, he was seized with lung fever, which at first was not deemed alarming, but on the 25th terminated fatally. He passed away in the triumphs of faith. Rev. Noah Porter, of Farmington, preached his funeral sermon, and it was published in the *Christian Spectator*. The Rev. Laurens P. Hickok, of Auburn, N. Y., says of Mr. Hart: "One of his marked characteristics was an indescribable expression of cheerfulness and hearty good will, diffusing its sweet savor wherever he was, so that his presence and society were always sought." He had a quick and keen discernment of men and things. His intercourse with his church and people was very frank and familiar. His manner of preaching was serious, pungent, and discriminating. His sermons abounded less in long drawn argument, but were exceedingly rich in condensed, sententious thoughts, and concise declarations. He died at Plymouth, April 25th, 1834, aged 51 years. Their only child, Luther Potter, died August 28th, 1829, aged 5 months.

1990. *Goshen, Conn., Farmington, Ill.*

DEACON HENRY HART, Goshen, second son of David Hart, of the same town, and his wife, Hannah (Hudson), of Long Island, born February 28th, 1785, at Goshen; married   , Ann Street, daughter of Samuel D., of Goshen. He was chosen deacon, and served until he removed, January, 1838, to Farmington, Fulton County, Ill., or near there. He represented Goshen in the state legislature in 1822 and 1823.

THEIR CHILDREN, BEING THE EIGHTH GENERATION.

2536. Elizabeth L., born December 1st, 1809; married   , 1838, Rev. Henry D. Pendleton.
2537. William, born April 1st, 1811; married   , Adaline Candee, of Farmington, Ill.
2538. Mary, born October 3d, 1813; married   , Amos D. Thomas.
2539. Catharine, born April 15th, 1815; married June 7th, 1837, John Wright, of Hanover, N. H.
2540. Minerva, born October 3d, 1813; married, April, 1840, Rev. Samuel Wright.
2541. Margaret F., born February 9th, 1818; married   , James M. Flint, of Toulon.
2542. Luther, born   . He is living single in Canton, Ill.
2543. Henry Hudson, born June 14th, 1821; married December 8th, 1847, Martha J. Warnock.
2544. Calvin, born September 30th, 1822; married December 29th, 1853, Mary Ann Holgate, of Illinois.
2545. Louisa, born March 8th, 1825; married April 10th, 1845, Joel W. Dewey.
2546. Edward, born February 7th, 1827; married May 6th, 1857, Lucy B. Robbins.
2547. David, born about 1828; married   , 1852, Dorcas Heacock, of Canada.

1991. *Goshen, Conn.*

Miles Hart, Goshen, third son of David Hart, of the same town, and his wife, Hannah (Hudson), of Long Island, born December 10th, 1786; married June 1st, 1820, Laura Clark, daughter of Nehemiah, of Cornwall, Conn. They were members of the North Church in Goshen, and lived on the old homestead of his father. He represented that town in the state legislature two years. He died July 25th, 1862, aged 76 years.

THEIR CHILDREN, BEING THE EIGHTH GENERATION.

2548. Victor Clark, born March 26th, 1821; married May 16th, 1850, Weltha E. Hanks.
2549. Frederick Miles, born May 4th, 1823; died single December 7th, 1845.
2550. Laura Ann, born July 26th, 1824.
2551. Charles Conkling, born March 6th, 1826; married   , 1852, Helen Paine.
2552. John Hudson, born January 6th, 1828. He was living in California in 1871.
2553. Luther Potter, born April 23d, 1835. He is an imbecile, and lives with Victor.

1992. *Goshen, Conn.*

Alpha Hart, Goshen, Conn., fourth son of David Hart, of the same town, and his wife, Hannah (Hudson), of Long Island, born September 17th, 1788, at Goshen; married December 15th, 1814, Betsey Dutton, of Plymouth, Conn. He has represented Goshen twice in the state legislature. He is a farmer and mechanic. They reside in the limits of Goshen, but his post-office address is Torrington, Conn.

THEIR CHILDREN, BEING THE EIGHTH GENERATION.

2554. Abraham Parmelee, born April 23d, 1816; married September 5th, 1839, Angeline Badger.
2555. Harriet Newell, born December 14th, 1818; died October 16th, 1838, aged 20 years. She was a teacher.
2556. Jane, born October 11th, 1821; married　　　　　　　　, William Martin.
2557. Matthew Rice, born June 28th, 1824; married October 23d, 1845, Adeline Chase.

1996.　　　　　　　　Brookfield, Ohio.

SEELYE HART, Brookfield, Portage County, Ohio, second son of Reuben Hart, and his wife, Ruth (Ives), born February 1st, 1798, at Goshen. He removed to　　　　, Ohio, in 1821, and there married October 16th, 1823, Jemima Thirza Chapman, daughter of Constant, and his wife, born March 30th, 1806. They have no children.

1998.　　　　　　　　Brimfield, Ohio.

REUBEN HART, Brimfield, Portage County, Ohio, third son of Reuben Hart, of Goshen, Conn., and his wife, Ruth (Ives), born May 2d, 1803, at Goshen, Conn. He removed to Ohio, November 17th, 1826, and married there, July 2d, 1829, Nancy Ann Law, born November 19th, 1810. He was a carpenter by trade.

THEIR CHILDREN, BEING THE EIGHTH GENERATION.

2558. Charles Wallis, born December 5th, 1837; married October 28th, 1863, Eleanor N. Stilwell.
2559. Lois Law, born June 17th, 1840, at Brimfield, Portage County, Ohio.

1999.　　　　　　　　Goshen, Conn.

ELIAS HART, Goshen, youngest son and child of Reuben Hart, of the same town, and his wife, Ruth (Yale), born May 2d, 1807, in Goshen, Conn.; married January 20th, 1830, Julia Ann Page, of Warren. He lives on his father's old place.

THEIR CHILDREN, BEING THE EIGHTH GENERATION.

2560. Seelye, born December 20th, 1831.
2561. Lois Catlin, born May 1st, 1833.
2562. Harriet Potter, born January 23d, 1836.
2563. Mary Elizabeth, born May 19th, 1839.
2564. Martha Blake, born September 13th, 1842.

BARTHOLOMEW.

2000. *Harwinton, Conn.*

LOIS HART, Litchfield, Conn., eldest daughter of Benjamin Hart, of the same town, and his wife, Hannah (Curtiss), born October 4th, 1775; married   , Heman Bartholomew, of Harwinton, Conn. She died at Milton, Saratoga County, N. Y.

WEBSTER.

2003. *Kingsville, Ohio.*

PHEBE HART, Litchfield, Conn., third daughter of Benjamin Hart, of Wallingford and Litchfield, and his wife, Hannah (Curtiss), of Wallingford, born August 28th, 1784, a twin with Lucy; married   , White Webster. She died at Kingsville, Ashtabula County, Ohio.

CURTISS.

2004. *Litchfield, Conn.*

LUCY HART, Litchfield, Conn., fourth daughter of Benjamin Hart, of Wallingford and Litchfield, and his wife, Hannah (Curtiss), born August 28th, 1784, a twin with Phebe; married   , Eliakim Curtiss. They lived in Litchfield, where she died   , 1834.

2005. *Litchfield, Conn.*

JONATHAN HART, Litchfield, Conn., second son of Benjamin Hart, of Wallingford and Litchfield, and his wife, Hannah (Curtiss), of Wallingford, born August 11th, 1786; married   , 1810, in Kingsville, Ohio, Anna Webster, born October 15th, 1792, in Litchfield, Conn. They removed to Kingsville, Ashtabula County, Ohio, where he died May 25th, 1845, aged 59 years. His avocation was farming. She died in Kingsville, March 6th, 1872, aged 80 years.

THEIR CHILDREN, BEING THE EIGHTH GENERATION.

2565. Henry, born February 2d, 1812; married   , 1834, Louisa Stone.
2566. Truman, born October 14th, 1814; married June 22d, 1845, Sarah Eugenia Pease.
2567. Benjamin, born, September, 1816; married   , Mary McAlister.
2568. Julia, born, September, 1818, at Kingsville; died there, March 21st, 1839, aged 21 years.
2569. Anna, born, April, 1820; married   , 1839, Lyman Webster.
2570. Jonathan, born, November, 1824; married   , 1846, Louisa Barnes

60

2006. *Kingsville, Ohio.*

ISAAC HART, Litchfield, Conn., third son of Benjamin Hart, of Wallingford and Litchfield, and his wife, Hannah (Curtiss), of Wallingford, born April 1st, 1788, at Litchfield; married March 19th, 1812, Martha Butler, of Harwinton, daughter of Timothy, of Southington, and his wife, Priscilla (Pelton), born October 21st, 1787. He was a cooper by trade, and a farmer by occupation, and lived in Northfield Society. In 1816 he removed with his family to Kingsville, Ashtabula County, Ohio, and about 1819 to Sheffield, in the same county. In the fall of 1822 he returned to Litchfield, Conn., where he died, March 6th, 1834, aged 47 years. She died April 18th, 1839, aged 52 years. They were buried in the old cemetery on Litchfield Hill.

THEIR CHILDREN, BEING THE EIGHTH GENERATION.

2571. Sophronia L., born July 9th, 1813; married January 22d, 1840, Sylvester Saxton, of Watertown.
2572. Lucy Ann, born June 7th, 1816; married September 17th, 1835, Lewis Morris. Luther, born July 12th, 1818; died August 2d, 1819.
2573. Luther Butler, born March 9th, 1821; married March 31st, 1852, Lydia Skiff, of Elsworth.
2574. Lamira W., born December 31st, 1822; married February 6th, 1843, Thomas F. Hickok.
2575. Timothy, born October 27th, 1825; married June 18th, 1848, Martha E. Benham.
2576. Martha Sophia, born June 30th, 1828; married October 18th, 1847, Roswell Atkins.
2577. Mary Jane, born June 19th, 1831; married July 3d, 1853, Norridson Bennet.
2578. Isaac Phineas, born July 16th, 1834; married March 28th, 1857, Jane Hill.

STONE.

2007. *Vernon, N. Y.*

MERAB HART, Litchfield, Conn., fifth daughter of Benjamin Hart, of Wallingford and Litchfield, and his wife, Hannah (Curtiss), of Wallingford, born   ; married   , Abner Stone. She lived and died at Vernon, Oneida County, N. Y.

HUNTLEY.

2009. *Ashtabula County, Ohio.*

LYDIA HART, Litchfield, Conn., youngest daughter of Benjamin Hart, of Wallingford and Litchfield, and his wife, Hannah (Curtiss), of Wallingford, born September 3d, 1794, at Litchfield; married   , —— Huntley, and lived at   , Ashtabula County, Ohio.

2010. *Colebrook, Conn.*

TRUMAN HART, Colebrook, Conn., eldest son of Titus, of the same town, and his wife, Lucy (Johnson), born November 23d, 1785; married, April, 1812, Polly Spencer, daughter of Amos, of New Hartford, and his wife, Millicent (Sanford), born May 29th, 1786, at Torrington. He died August 16th, 1867, aged 79 years. She was living, in 1873, at Colebrook, with her daughter, Mrs. Augusta Barnard.

THEIR CHILDREN, BEING THE EIGHTH GENERATION.

Child, born October 5th, 1813; died October 11th, 1813.

2579. Eliza Lucy, born November 17th, 1814; married, November, 1836, Abner Wilcox.
2580. Albert S., born May 3d, 1820; married   , 1842, Maria Gaylord.
2581. Louisa Jane, born September 30th, 1817; married March 24th, 1841, Austin A. Spaulding.
2582. Augusta C., born August 18th, 1822; married November 17th, 1850, Nelson Barnard.
2583. Jerusha, born
2584. Phebe, born
2585. Miles S., born October 1st, 1827. He was living in Oregon in 1873.

GILLETT.

2011. *Colebrook, Conn.*

MARY JOHNSON HART, Colebrook, Conn., eldest daughter of Titus Hart, of the same town, and his wife, Lucy (Johnson), born July 17th, 1788, in Litchfield, Conn.; married   , James Gillett, of Hartland, Conn. She was living, in 1872, at Cheshire Corners, Ontario County, N. Y., in her 85th year.

2013. *Kentucky.*

LEWIS HART, Kentucky, second son of Titus Hart, of Colebrook, and his wife, Lucy (Johnson), born September 30th, 1793, at Colebrook; married November 1st, 1815, at Colebrook, Persis Swift, daughter of Deacon William, and his wife, Almira (Butrick), born February 20th, 1796, at Goshen, Conn. He joined the church in Colebrook. He has lived in Ohio, and in Lexington and Green, Ky. He first located at Winchester, Conn., and lived there until June, 1838, when he emigrated to Pennfield, Ohio, with all his family, except the eldest daughter, who was married. His wife died June 23d, 1855, aged 59 years, when second he married October 29th, 1861, Almira B. Swift, sister of his first wife. He died November 29th, 1866, aged 73.

THEIR CHILDREN, BEING THE EIGHTH GENERATION.

2586. Almira, born October 23d, 1816; married March 30th, 1836, Lewis Barnard.
2587. William, born September 12th, 1819; married, April, 1841, Harriet Smith.

2588. Lucy, born September 17th, 1821; married January 12th, 1840, Hawley Hart.

2589. Lewis, born April 11th, 1824; married September 9th, 1846, Melinda Starr.

2590. Erastus Swift, born June 27th, 1826; married   , Harriet Newell Gilbert.

2591. Heman, born August 14th, 1828; married May 11th, 1853, Martha Ingersol.

2592. Persis, born July 20th, 1830.

2593. Henry, born October 16th, 1831; married December 28th, 1854, Jane L. Edwards.

2594. Ralph, born April 11th, 1834; married May 25th, 1859, Diana A. Noble.

2595. Miles, born September 14th, 1839; married   , 1865, Sarah Kemp.

2014. *Colebrook, Conn.*

Titus Hart, Jr., Ohio, third son of Titus Hart, Sr., of Colebrook, Conn., and his wife, Lucy (Johnson), born May 5th, 1795, in Colebrook, Conn.; married at Manchester, July 14th, 1820, Amanda Webster. He removed to Ohio, but in 1871 was a farmer in Colebrook, Conn. His wife died August 10th, 1866, aged 66, when second he married October 5th, 1866, Almira Hawley, who died, July, 1872.

THEIR CHILDREN, BEING THE EIGHTH GENERATION.

2596. Lewis, born August 26th, 1821, at Winchester; married   , Esther Works.

2597. Amanda, born May 31st, 1823, at Norfolk; married January 1st, 1851, Harvey Rood.

2598. Jay, born March 16th, 1826, at Norfolk; married, May, 1862, Jane Sage.

2599. William, born April 18th, 1829, at Norfolk; married, May, 1849, Emeline Snyder.

2600. Grove, born June 5th, 1831, at Norfolk; married, May, 1860, Emeline Hart.

2601. Webster, born November 29th, 1833, at Norfolk; married   , 1863, Ann Maxwell.

2602. Wilbur, born July 16th, 1836; died June 5th, 1864, in the late war, aged 28 years.

NORTH.

2015. *Alexander, N. Y.*

Lucy Hart, Colebrook, third daughter of Titus, of the same town, and his wife, Lucy (Johnson), born January 1st, 1799, at Colebrook, Conn. She married February 22d, 1824, Lester North, of Colebrook, Conn. Their present residence is Alexander, Genesee County, N. Y., and his avocation is farming.

VINING.

2016. *Colebrook, Conn.*

Orpha Hart, Colebrook, fourth daughter of Titus Hart, of the same place, and his first wife, Lucy (Johnson), born April 11th, 1802, at Colebrook; married December 13th, 1831, William Vining, son of Thomas, of Simsbury, and his wife, Weltha (Weston), of Wethersfield.

They had children, viz: 1, Albert, born December 2d, 1832; 2, Weltha Ann, born October 17th, 1834; 3, Robert, born May 30th, 1836; 4, Mary Etta, born April 20th, 1838, married Cornelius Chapin, of Collinsville, and she died July 25th, 1870; 5, William Henry, born March 10th, 1840; 6, Julius Hart, born July 12th, 1842, married May 3d, 1868, Maggie Glenketchen; 7, Elizabeth, born March 2d, 1844, died June 2d, 1863, aged 8 years; 8, Alice Jennette, born June 12th, 1846, died May 6th, 1863.

2017. *Winchester, Conn.*

MILO ROBERTS HART, Winchester, eldest son of Titus Hart, of Colebrook, Conn., and his second wife, Elizabeth, daughter of Elijah Andrews, of Windsor and Colebrook, and his wife, Mary (Roberts), born June 30th, 1806, at Colebrook; married   , Julianna Cowdry. His avocation is farming, and he was living in 1871, either in Winchester or Watertown.

THEIR CHILD, BEING THE EIGHTH GENERATION.

2603. Melissa, born

GILLETT.

2018. *Colebrook, Conn.*

PHEBE FENN HART, Colebrook, Conn., second daughter of Titus Hart, of the same place, and his second wife, Elizabeth (Andrews), of Colebrook, born February 29th, 1808, at Colebrook; married   , Leonard Gillet, of Colebrook, a brother of James Gillet, who married her sister, Mary. She died November 5th, 1850, aged 42 years.

2018½. *Colebrook, Conn.*

TIMOTHY ORSON HART, Colebrook, Conn., second son of Titus Hart, of the same town, and his second wife, Elizabeth (Andrews), born November 30th, 1809, at Colebrook; married March 30th, 1845, Margaret, daughter of Adin Wakefield, of Colebrook, and his wife, Susanna (Barney), born August 9th, 1806. In 1872 he lived on the old homestead of his father, in the south part of Colebrook. His post-office address is Mill Brook, Conn.

THEIR CHILD, BEING THE EIGHTH GENERATION.

2604. Jane Susanna, born August 15th, 1847; married November 26th, 1867, William Henry Vining.

ROGERS.

2020.   *Colebrook, Conn., Pecatonica, Ill.*

JERUSHA HART, Colebrook, third daughter of Titus Hart, of the same town, and his second wife, Elizabeth (Andrews), born August 31st, 1813, at Colebrook, Conn.; married September 15th, 1834, Horatio Nelson Rodgers. He was a blacksmith by trade. He died April 15th, 1867. She lived at Pecatonica, Winnebago County, Ill., in 1872. They had children, viz: 1, Titus Hart, born December 3d, 1835, at Colebrook, married May 18th, 1867; 2, Oliver C., born March 1st, 1838, at Colebrook; 3, Aaron D., born December 23d, 1840, in Green County, N. Y.; 4, Phebe G., born December 31st, 1844, in Green County, N. Y.; 5, Henry A., born April 12th, 1847, in Green County, N. Y., died May 24th, 1864.

WELLS.

2021.   *Norfolk, Conn.*

SYLVIA HART, Colebrook, fourth daughter of Titus Hart, of the same town, and his second wife, Elizabeth (Andrews), born October 10th, 1815, at Colebrook; married   , James Hubbard Wells, of Norfolk, Conn., where they were residing in 1872.

2022.   *Woodbury, Conn.*

CHARLES WILLIAM HART, Woodbury, Conn., youngest son of Titus Hart, of Colebrook, Conn., and his second wife, Elizabeth (Andrews), born January 2d, 1818, at Colebrook; married at Norfolk, Conn., November 20th, 1842, Ann, daughter of Darius Camp, of Norfolk, and his wife, Eliza (Parrot), born in 1820. He was living at Woodbury, Conn., in 1871, and is a farmer by occupation. His wife died at Derby, Conn., October 20th, 1866, aged 46 years, when second he married at Derby, January 15th, 1868, Mrs. Lucy Lane, widow of Abner Lane, of Huntington, and daughter of Samuel Hubbell, and his wife, Lucy (Wilson), born August 26th, 1822, at Newtown, Conn. He has no children by either wife.

ARNOLD.

2023.   *Colebrook, Conn.*

JANE MINERVA HART, Colebrook, youngest daughter of Titus Hart, of the same town, and his second wife, Elizabeth (Andrews), born August 23d, 1820, at Colebrook, Conn.; married, May, 1846, Henry Arnold, of   . She died July 5th, 1847, aged 27 years. She was the seventeenth child of her father, Titus Hart, of Wallingford, Litchfield, and Colebrook.

2042. *Buffalo, N. Y.*

WILLIAM AUSTIN HART, Buffalo, N. Y., eldest son of Aaron, of Wallingford and Barkhamsted, and his wife, Annis (Austin), born January 13th, 1797, at Barkhamsted, Conn.; married January 22d, 1821, Mary Ann Sumorton, of Sempronius, N. Y., born, February, 1801. He was a gunsmith at Buffalo, N. Y., and learned his trade at Hartford, Conn., where he spent several years in gunsmithing and making cutlery. A very lengthy article was published at Buffalo as an eulogy and obituary at his decease, August 9th, 1865, aged 68 years, in the *Daily Courier* of August, 1865, in which his character as a man and Christian is highly extolled. Mr. Hart was a natural mechanic, and took out the first patent for a percussion lock when the old flint lock was given up. This patent is dated February 20th, 1827, and is signed John Quincy Adams, President, Henry Clay, Secretary of State, and William Wirt, Attorney-General. It sets forth that William A. Hart has invented a new and useful improvement in the percussion gun lock for rifles, muskets, fowling-pieces, pistols, &c., called *"Hart's Percussion Gun Lock."* The improvement in those days attracted no little attention, and on the 23d of February the commissioner of patents wrote him a congratulatory letter, in which he said, "I am pleased to find so much *genius* accompanied with so much *morality.*" He became a member of the Episcopal Church at Fredonia, N. Y., where he resided for a time. When he removed to Buffalo he joined Trinity Church, and became a vestry-man, and subsequently assisted in organizing St. John's Church, of which he was a constituent member. His widow died May 3d, 1871, aged 70 years.

THEIR CHILDREN, BEING THE EIGHTH GENERATION.

2605. Austin Sumerton, born January 2d, 1827. He is a tinner.
2606. Ellen Douglass, born April 25th, 1829; died October 24th, 1868.

2045. *Erie, Penn.*

IRA WILDER HART, Erie, Penn., second son of Aaron Hart, of Pomfret, Chautauqua County, N. Y., and his wife, Annis (Austin), born , 1804; married Eliza Metcalf, who died, when second he married her sister, Lucy, who also died, when third he married Martha Mason, of Vermont. He was a stage and ticket agent, in 1871, at Erie, Penn., and was living there, but in 1873 his son, James, took his position as general freight agent there.

CHILD BY HIS FIRST WIFE, BEING THE EIGHTH GENERATION.

2607. James Charles, born December 20th, 1832; married September 11th, 1862, Adelaide Marvin.

CHILD BY HIS SECOND WIFE.

A daughter, born   ; died young.

CHILD BY HIS THIRD WIFE.

A son, born   ; died young.

2044.   *Fredonia, N. Y.*

SALMON HART, Fredonia, Chautauqua County, N. Y., third son·of Aaron, of Wallingford and Barkhamsted, Conn., and his wife, Annis (Austin), born September 19th, 1807; married Mary Ann Starr, who died, January, 1839. He second married Mary A. Redington, of Westfield, N. Y., who died April 25th, 1853. He third married Helen Wilder, born at Canandaigua, N. Y., in 1827. He was a gunsmith, and died March 4th, 1861, aged 53 years, 5 months, and 15 days. Their children were all born at Fredonia, N. Y. His widow was living at Canandaigua in 1873.

CHILDREN BY HIS FIRST WIFE, BEING THE EIGHTH GENERATION.

2608. Henry Starr, born July 18th, 1834; married Mary Jones. He died April 4th, 1868, at Buffalo, N. Y.

SECOND WIFE.

2609. Walter John, born, July, 1841. He entered the Union Army, and was killed on the peninsula.

Martha Redington, born October 18th, 1846; died at Parma, N. Y., April 15th, 1868.

2610. Frederick William, born April 18th, 1853. He is clerk in a drug store in Chicago.

2045½.

AARON H. HART, Fredonia, Chautauqua County, N. Y., youngest son of Aaron Hart, of Wallingford and Barkhamsted, Conn., and Bristol, N. Y., and his wife, Annis (Austin), born September 19th, 1810, at Barkhamsted. He went with his parents to Bristol, N. Y., in 1817. They removed to Fredonia, N. Y., in 1827. He married August 29th, 1833, Hepsibah Hart, of Victor, N. Y. He is a tinner by trade, and resides at Buffalo, N. Y. She died May 12th, 1837. His second wife was Florilla Emmons, born at Litchfield, Conn., February 11th, 1811; married June 7th, 1838, and was living in 1873.

CHILD BY HIS FIRST WIFE, BEING THE EIGHTH GENERATION.

2611. Harriet Emeline, born September 29th, 1834; married May 2d, 1855, Amon L. Barmore, of Fredonia.

SECOND WIFE.

Mary Eliza, born April 23d, 1839; died December 23d, 1847.

Francis Snodon, born January 24th, 1841; died January 18th, 1848.

2612. Flora Adalaide, born May 13th, 1846.

2613. Kate Eliza, born August 8th, 1848.

2046. *Barkhamsted, Conn.*

CHESTER HART, Barkhamsted, Conn., eldest son of Hawkins Hart, of Wallingford and Barkhamsted, Conn., and his wife, Lois (Slade), born July 16th, 1806, at Barkhamsted; married March 13th, 1833, Julia Case, daughter of Alexander, and his wife, A. (Mindwell), born May 21st, 1808, at   . His avocation is farming.

THEIR CHILDREN, BEING THE EIGHTH GENERATION.

Julia, born January 21st, 1837; died January 12th, 1840.

2614. Monroe, born April 31st, 1842; married December 8th, 1869, Annice Case.
2615. Walter, born August 4th, 1846. He is a farmer, and was single in 1873.

2047. *Barkhamsted, Conn.*

WILLIAM HENRY HARRISON HART, Barkhamsted, Conn., second son of Hawkins Hart, of Wallingford and Barkhamsted, Conn., and his wife, Lois (Slade), born August 28th, 1812, at Barkhamsted; married October 26th, 1840, Eliza Scovil, born December 6th, 1822, at Winsted. His avocation was farming. He died at Washington, D. C., June 24th, 1864, aged 51 years, 9 months, 26 days, and was buried there.

THEIR CHILDREN, BEING THE EIGHTH GENERATION.

2616. Mary C., born March 10th, 1842; married October 10th, 1860, Wolcott Little.
2617. William Burton, born October 7th, 1843; married January 1st, 1867, M. G. Kitchen.
2618. Truman H., born September 30th, 1846; married November 20th, 1870, Sarah Saunders.
2619. Frederick, born September 22d, 1848, at Torrington.
2620. Willie H., born November 22d, 1851, at Torrington.
2621. Charles G., born November 11th, 1858, at Torrington.
2622. Eliza, born   ; married March 17th, 1870, A. G. Kitchen.

2049. *Riverton, Conn.*

ABNER S. HART, Riverton, Litchfield County, Conn., third son of Hawkins Hart, of Wallingford and Barkhamsted, and his wife, Lois (Slade), born July 15th, 1823, at Barkhamsted; married April, 1848, Julia Rose, who died June 8th, 1863. His avocation was farming until 1866, when he removed to the village of Riverton, and engaged in the drug business in company with his son, Myron.

THEIR CHILDREN, BEING THE EIGHTH GENERATION.

2623. Myron, born January 17th, 1849.
2624. Leveret C., born September 9th, 1850. He works in the rule shop.

Henry W., born August 8th, 1858, at Riverton.

2053. *Canaan, Conn.*

DIADAMIA HART, Winchester, Conn., second daughter of Selah Hart, of the same town, and his wife, Rachel (Hemsted), born at Winsted in 1793; married at the age of 60 years, Luke Hadsell, of Canaan, as his second wife. She died April 11th, 1866, at Canaan, aged 66 years.

ANDREWS.

2054. *Binghamton, N. Y.*

SALLY HART, Winchester, Conn., third daughter of Selah Hart, of the same town, and his wife, Rachel (Hemsted), born at Winchester, and married there in 1812, David Andrews, who was a blacksmith by trade. They removed to Canaan Mountain, and from thence to Binghamton, Broome County, N. Y., where they died about 1866.

2055. *Vineland, N. J.*

PHŒBUS HART, Vineland, N. J., eldest son of Selah Hart, of Winchester, Conn., and his wife, Rachel (Hemsted), born April 19th, 1798, at Winsted, Conn.; married in 1833, Rhoda Dorman, of Canaan, daughter of Chauncey, and his wife, Obediance (Dickerman), born July 2d, 1814, at Canaan, Conn. He died at Vineland, N. J., October 17th, 1865, aged 67 years. His avocation was farming. His widow was residing at Vineland, N. J., in 1872.

THEIR CHILDREN, BEING THE EIGHTH GENERATION.

2625. Lewis, born April 27th, 1835, at Canaan.
2626. Adaline Louisa, born October 1st, 1838; married September 25th, 1862, Frederic M. Hadsell.
2627. Mary Cornelia, born May 2d, 1849. She was living single at Vineland, N. J., in 1872.
2628. Martin Lee, born January 24th, 1855.

2056. *Winchester, Conn.*

NEWTON HART, Winchester, Conn., youngest son and child of Selah Hart, of the same town, and his wife, Rachel (Hemsted), born January 11th, 1800, at Winchester; married March 1st, 1824, Ruth Hadsell, of Canaan, born September 12th, 1806.

THEIR CHILDREN, BEING THE EIGHTH GENERATION.

2629. Julia, born February 11th, 1828. She was living single with her parents in 1872.
2630. Norman, born April 21st, 1831; married, May, 1862, Jane E. Curtiss.
2631. Matilda, born February 2d, 1835; married December 21st, 1859, Cyrus H. Miller.
2632. Phebe, born September 5th, 1845; married August 27th, 1869, Francis Hatch, of Massachusetts.

2060. *Winsted, Conn.*

WILLARD HART, Winsted, Conn., eldest son of Samuel Hart, of Southington, and his wife, Mariam (Bassett), born, January, 1798, at Winsted; married December 11th, 1822, Rhoda Benedict, daughter of Timothy, and his wife, Lydia (Crocker). She died May 12th, 1824, at Winsted, aged 24 years, when second he married May 29th, 1828, Maria, eldest daughter of Daniel Andrews, Jr., of Winchester, and his wife, Sarah (Platt), of Danbury, Conn., born November 15th, 1808. He died May 5th, 1840. His widow was living in 1873, on Meadow Street, in West Winsted, where she owns a nice and pleasant home.

THEIR CHILDREN, BEING THE EIGHTH GENERATION.

633. Rhoda Matilda, born January 26th, 1824; married   , William Miner.

SECOND WIFE.

634. Sarah, born September 20th, 1829; married September 19th, 1850, George Camp, and was divorced.
635. Henry, born April 20th, 1832; died of consumption, at Winsted, in 1856.
636. Elizabeth, born April 8th, 1835; married July 8th, 1855, James C. Ferris, of Winsted.
637. Lewis Daniel, born April 14th, 1837. He lives with his mother.
638. Henrietta M., born January 8th, 1839; married February 3d, 1862, Nelson Beers, of Roxbury.
639. Willard, born April 11th, 1840; married May 6th,   . He was killed at Cold Harbor.

2061. *Hartland, Conn.*

SYLVESTER HART, Hartland, Conn., second son of Samuel Hart, of Southington, and his wife, Mariam (Bassett), of Winchester, born May 2d, 1800, at Hartland; married June 22d, 1822, Charlotte Walter, of Torrington, daughter of Andrew, and his wife, Abigail, born January th, 1805, at Winchester, Conn. He is a cooper by trade and occupation, and lives in Hartland. He removed with his father's family, when about eight years old, from Hartland to Winchester, and moved back to Hartland in 1862.

THEIR CHILDREN, BEING THE EIGHTH GENERATION.

640. Cynthia Emily, born August 17th, 1823; married   , Silas R. Gridley, of Bristol.
    Lyman, born February 24th, 1825, at Winchester; died December 26th, 1826.
641. George Washington, born June 8th, 1827; married, October, 1851, Laura Ann Hill.
642. Mary Abigail, born June 20th, 1829; married, May, 1852, Jefferson Monroe Tyler.
    Jane, born October 21st, 1830; died May 4th, 1836, at Winchester.

2643. Luther Warren, born April 27th, 1832; married January 31st, 1857, Nancy Elizabeth Burr.

Sarah Ann, born January 18th, 1834; died at Winchester, May 16th, 1836.

2644. Ellen Charlotte, born November 30th, 1836; married in 1855, James Miles, of Colebrook.

BANDELL.

2062. *Winchester, Conn.*

AMELIA HART, Winchester, second daughter of Samuel Hart, of Southington and Winchester, and his wife, Mariam (Bassett), of Winchester, Conn., born in 1802; married   , Samuel Bandell, of Winchester, and a blacksmith by occupation. They had two sons and three daughters. Mrs. Bandell died at the west, aged about 60 years.

TUTTLE.

2063. *Winchester, Conn.*

POLLY HART, Winchester, Conn., third daughter of Samuel Hart, of Southington and Winchester, Conn., and his wife, Mariam (Bassett), of Winchester, born   ; married   , Levi Tuttle, a farmer of Winchester. They had two sons and two daughters. Mrs. Tuttle died.

2064. *Torringford, Conn.*

WELLS HART, Torringford, third son of Samuel Hart, of Southington and Winchester, Conn., and his wife, Mariam (Bassett), of Winchester, born February 4th, 1805, at Barkhamsted; married November 1st, 1826, at New Durham, N. Y., Susan, daughter of Richard Tryon, of that place, but formerly of Saybrook, and his wife, Betsey (Tripp), born June 25th, 1807, at New Durham. He is a mighty fox hunter, and has killed some 500 foxes. The skins are sold for $2 each. He has sold two fox hounds at $50 each. They have lived in various localities, and in 1871 were living on a farm of General Tuttle's, formerly of Torringford. Mr. Hart is much respected.

THEIR CHILDREN, BEING THE EIGHTH GENERATION.

2645. Samyria B., born January 15th, 1828, at Winchester; died single, March 6th, 1847, aged 18 years.

2646. Phidelia E., born June 20th, 1831; married   , Levi Eaton.

2647. Huldah Mariam, born February 20th, 1833; married   , Luther Leach.

2648. Lurinda A., born August 5th, 1836; married   , Samuel Sperry.

2649. Susan M., born January 11th, 1839, at Winchester; died single, July 26th, 1862, aged 23 years.

2650. Caroline A., born January 17th, 1841; married   , Chauncey
      Messenger.
2651. Sarah Jane, born May 17th, 1843, at Torrington; died single, July 26th, 1862,
      aged 19 years.
2652. William Wells, born December 10th, 1845; married October 21st, 1866, Lydia
      Waugh.
2653. Frederic Alvin, born April 18th, 1848; married   , Jennie
      Fancher.
2654. Richard Elias, born June 18th, 1850. He is a mechanic, and works in Water-
      bury, Conn.
      Matilda S., born   ; died October 6th, 1861.

2065.   *Winchester, Conn.*

HAWLEY HART, Winchester, Conn., fourth son of Samuel Hart, of
Southington and Winchester, Conn., and his wife, Mariam (Bassett),
born February 10th, 1807, at Hartland; married   ,
Hannah Tryon, daughter of Richard, of Saybrook, Conn., and New
Durham, N. Y., and his wife, Betsey (Tripp), a sister of his brother
Wells' wife. She died   , when second he married
January 12th, 1840, at Pennfield, Ohio, Lucy, daughter of Lewis Hart,
formerly of Winchester, Conn., where she was born, September 17th,
1821. They were living at Pennfield, Lorain County, Ohio, in 1871.
His avocation is farming, and she is a member of the Methodist Church.

THEIR CHILDREN, BEING THE EIGHTH GENERATION.

2655. Willard, born October 12th, 1840; married January 15th, 1861, Ann E. Soog.
2656. Chester, born April 11th, 1842; died August 10th, 1859, aged 17 years.

ALBRO.

2067.   *Granville, Mass.*

SYLVIA HART, Granville, Mass., sixth daughter of Samuel Hart, of
Southington and Winchester, Conn., and his wife, Mariam (Bassett), of
Winchester, born   ; married   ,
Edward Albro, of Winchester. He is a farmer, and lived in Gran-
ville, Mass., in 1871. They have one son and one daughter.

2072.   *Melrose, Wis.*

BENJAMIN PECK HART, Melrose, Jackson County, Wis., the youngest
child of Webb Hart, of Meriden, Conn., and his wife, Clarissa (Peck),
born June 26th, 1811, at Meriden; married August 5th, 1835, Jane
Brooks, who died December 24th, 1849, when second he married December 30th, 1852, Nancy A. Wentworth. They reside in Melrose,
Wisconsin.

CHILD BY HIS FIRST WIFE, BEING THE EIGHTH GENERATION.

!656½. Harriet Ann, born May 27th, 1836.

CHILDREN BY HIS SECOND WIFE.

Sarah Jane, born January 23d, 1861.
Carrie Bell, born April 23d, 1862.

2073.   *Meriden, Conn.*

DANIEL HALL HART, Meriden, Conn., eldest son of Samuel Ives Hart,
)f the same town, and his wife, Abigail D. (Hall), born June 19th,
815, at Meriden; married May 14th, 1840, Harriet G. Miller, of Mid-
lletown, Conn. He is a farmer, and lives east of the city of Meriden,
·n East Main Street.

THEIR CHILDREN, BEING THE EIGHTH GENERATION.

657. Ives W., born October 4th, 1841; married November 24th, 1870, Elsie Lane,
of Madison.
658. Ellen C., born November 23d, 1843.
659. Edmund B., born December 31st, 1845.

2076.   *Stonington, Conn.*

DOCTOR DAVID SHERMAN HART, Stonington, Conn., eldest son of Rev.
ra Hart, of the same town, and his wife, Maria, daughter of John
herman, and granddaughter of Hon. Roger Sherman, of New Haven,
·ho was a signer of the Declaration of Independence, born September
6th, 1799, at Middlebury, Conn. He graduated at Yale College in
823, as a medical student. He is a druggist and book-seller in Ston-
igton, and occasionally instructs young men fitting for teachers or for
·ollege. He was single in 1873.

2077.   *Stonington, Conn.*

CHARLES THEODORE HART, second son of Rev. Ira Hart, of Middle-
ury and Stonington, and his wife, Maria, daughter of John Sherman,
nd granddaughter of Hon. Roger Sherman, of New Haven, born
une 14th, 1801. He died of quick consumption proceeding from
emorrhage, October 13th, 1819, aged 18 years. He was a member of
ie Sophomore Class in Yale College. He gave abundant evidence of
eing sanctified in early childhood, and not being able to ascertain the
me of his conversion, his fears prevailed over his hopes; but in the
st conflict he was enabled, with humble confidence, to commit his soul
ito the hands of Jesus.

PALMER.

2078. *Mystic, Conn.*

HARRIET ELIZA HART, eldest daughter of Rev. Ira Hart, of Middle bury and Stonington, Conn., and his wife, Maria, daughter of John Sherman, born March 12th, 1803; married December 31st, 1823, Benjamin F. Palmer, of Mystic, Conn. She died, December, 1842, aged 39 years, leaving six children. Her son, Franklin, succeeds his uncle, David S. Hart, M. D., in business. Her youngest child was born five days before her death.

2084. *Canandaigua, N. Y.*

THEODORE EPHRAIM HART, Canandaigua, N. Y., second son of Jonathan Hart, of Kirkland, Ontario County, N. Y., and his wife, Orphia (Chapin), of Springfield, Mass., born December 22d, 1802; married January 11th, 1826, Eliza Collins. He was a merchant in Canandaigua fourteen years, and a banker ten years. He retired from business wealthy in 1873, and says he is waiting to join his children, who are all dead but one.

THEIR CHILDREN, BEING THE EIGHTH GENERATION.

2660. Samuel Collins, born May 20th, 1828; married   , Catharine M. Buell.

Adeline Eliza, born August 22d, 1829; died May 3d, 1851.

2661. Theodore Henry, born January 26th, 1831; married October 11th, 1859, Caroline S. Stone; died April 12th, 1861.

Caroline Maria, born July 29th, 1832; died January 3d, 1860.

Samanthe, born July 23d, 1835; died June 26th, 1854.

2086.

JONATHAN WALTER HART, fourth son of Jonathan Hart, of Kirkland, Oneida County, N. Y., and his wife, Orphia (Chapin), born in 1807. It is related of him that about 1830 he left Harford, Cortland County, in search of a home in some western state. Nothing was heard from him until his return in 1835. He then said he was unmarried, was living in Missouri, had been unfortunate and lost all by the sinking of a boat in the Mississippi River, caused by striking a snag, and he wished for some pecuniary aid. He only staid a few days and left, since which time nothing definite has been heard of him.

2093. *Caroline, N. Y.*

ALONZO ORVILLE HART, Caroline, Tompkins County, N. Y., eldest son of Josiah Hart, of Paris, N. Y., and his wife, Sophronia (Gridley), born February 1st, 1806, at Paris, Oneida County, N. Y.; married at

Caroline, N. Y., February 19th, 1829, Eveline M. Tobey, daughter of Nathaniel, and his wife, Eunice (Pierce), born October 24th, 1806, at Middleborough, Plymouth County, Mass. He is a member of the Congregational Church. His avocation is farming, and he was residing at Caroline, Tompkins County, N. Y., in 1873.

THEIR CHILDREN, BEING THE EIGHTH GENERATION.

2662. Ira Fayette, born November 17th, 1829; married   , Marion E. Cook.

2663. Evelyn Maria, born December 7th, 1835; married   , Christopher Preswick.

2094.   *Janesville, Wis.*

SAMUEL HART, Janesville, Rock County, Wis., second son of Josiah Hart, of Paris, N. Y., and his wife, Sophronia (Gridley), born December 14th, 1807, at Paris; married January 17th, 1832, Sarah S. Potter, daughter of James, of East Haven, Conn., and his wife, Lydia (Smith), born May 3d, 1813. They were residing at Janesville, Wis., in 1872.

THEIR CHILDREN, BEING THE EIGHTH GENERATION.

2664. James Potter, born February 24th, 1833, at Harford, N. Y.; married in 1855, Nancy J. Blodgett.

2665. Edwin, born February 2d, 1835, at Harford, N. Y.; married December 28th, 1865, Ruth E. Woodward.

2666. Henry, born April 3d, 1837, at Harford, N. Y.; married September 30th, 1863, Rachel Schenck.

2667. Mary Elizabeth, born February 10th, 1839, at Harford, N. Y.; married December 7th, 1865, Garry Nettleton.

2668. Esther Cornelia, born June 17th, 1841, at Harford, N. Y.; married November 6th, 1862, Cyrus Miner.

2669. Samuel Willard, born February 9th, 1844, at Harford, N. Y.; married October 18th, 1871, Frankie Yost.

2670. Josiah Fayette, born April 2d, 1848, at Harford, N. Y.; married November 14th, 1871, Harriet M. Campbell.

Frederic Lewis, born September 17th, 1850, at Harford, N. Y.; died September 26th, 1852, aged 2 years.

2671. Sara Louise, born January 5th, 1855, at Turtle, Rock County, Wis.

TOBEY.

2094½.   *Caroline, N. Y.*

ESTHER MARIA HART, Paris, N. Y., eldest daughter of Josiah Hart, of the same town, and subsequently of Cortlandville, N. Y., and his wife, Sophronia (Gridley), born November 27th, 1814. She married, December 24th, 1839, Nathaniel M. Tobey, of Caroline, Tompkins County, N. Y., born April 25th, 1813. He is a farmer and lumber dealer, and a captain of cavalry. She died of apoplexy, September

10th, 1868, aged 64 years, when second he married May 9th, 1870, Mary T. Andrews, daughter of Simon, neice of William Andrews, of Walton, N. Y., and cousin to William Andrews, of New York City. The children of Esther were—1, Nathaniel M., 2, Josiah Gridley—six in all. Two of them died young.

MONTGOMERY.

2095. *Dryden, N. Y.*

SOPHRONIA HART, second daughter of Josiah Hart, of Paris, N. Y., and other localities, and his wife, Sophronia (Gridley), born November 25th, 1817; married   , Dr. J. W. Montgomery, of Dryden, Tompkins County, N. Y., where she died, May 5th, 1862, aged 45 years. She was a member of the Universalist Church. Dr. Montgomery died, August, 1872. He had been a lunatic for several years.

BULLEN. BENNETT.

2100. *Oswego, N. Y., Kenosha, Wis.*

JULIA ANN HART, eldest daughter of Judge Orris Hart, of Oswego, N. Y., and his wife, Elizabeth (Bigelow), born March 2d, 1814, at Clinton, Oneida County, N. Y.; married February 24th, 1830, Hon. William Bullen, who was born at Clinton, February 24th, 1805, and died at Southport, (now Kenosha,) Wis., October 27th, 1846, aged 41 years, 8 months, 3 days, when second she married June 20th, 1849, Deacon George Bennett, of Ottawa, La Salle County, Ill., at her father's house in Oswego, N. Y. He was born at Ridgefield, Fairfield County, Conn., April 15th, 1806. She had four children by her first husband, viz: 1, Orris Hart, born July 1st, 1832, and died much respected, January 5th, 1865; 2, Mary Gertrude, married Peter Emslie, who is a civil engineer of high repute, and lives at Buffalo—no children; 3, William Herbert, married, is a lumber merchant and a first class business man, and lives in Chicago—no children; 4, Julia Frances, born, December, 1844, died October 9th, 1859, aged 15—an estimable girl. A lengthy obituary notice of the death of Judge Bullen was published, at the time of his decease, in the *Southport Telegraph*, setting forth his character for integrity and intelligence in the highest terms. He was a member of the Congregational Church, and contributed largely to its support. The last hours of his life were strongly marked with his abiding confidence in the truths of Christianity, and the goodness of the Great Author of his being. Her second husband is no less honored in both church and state, having been a representative and senator several terms in the Wisconsin Legislature.

GLOVER.

2101.   *Chicago, Ill.*

JEANNETTE HART, second daughter of Judge Orris Hart, of Oswego, N. Y., and his wife, Elizabeth (Bigelow), born June 24th, 1817, at New Haven, Oswego County, N. Y.; married August 3d, 1837, at Oswego, Joseph Otis Glover, who was born April 13th, 1812, at Scipio, Cayuga County, N. Y. He is a lawyer, and in 1872 was United States District Attorney, residing in Chicago, Ill. They have children, viz: 1, Julia Hart; 2, Henry Tifft; 3, Otis Randall, who graduated at Hamilton College in 1869.

HAMILTON.

2102.   *New York City.*

MARY GERTRUDE HART, third daughter of Judge Orris Hart, of Oswego, N. Y., and his wife, Betsey (Bigelow), born March 25th, 1819; married, September, 1840, Dr. Frank H. Hamilton, of Buffalo, N. Y., formerly professor of surgery in the Geneva Medical College, but in 1873 was professor of surgery in New York City.

RANDALL.

2103.   *Norwich, N. Y.*

ELLEN HART, fourth daughter of Judge Orris Hart, of Oswego, N. Y., and his wife, Betsey (Bigelow), born April 23d, 1821, at Oswego; married, September 1841, John S. Randall; a lawyer of Oswego. They had no children. They removed from Oswego to some place in Wisconsin in 1850, where she soon after died. He was residing at Norwich, Chenango County, N. Y., in 1872.

COOK.

2104.   *Chicago, Ill.*

ELIZABETH HART, fifth daughter of Judge Orris Hart, of Oswego, N. Y., and his wife, Elizabeth (Bigelow), born June 24th, 1823, at Oswego; married   , Hon. Burton C. Cook, late member of Congress from Illinois. They were residing in Chicago in 1872, where he was attorney for the North-Western, and Chicago, Burlington and Quincy Railroads, and had one daughter about 20 years of age.

2106.   *Oakland, Wis.*

ORLANDO PALMER HART, Oakland, Jefferson County, Wis., eldest son of Warren Hart, of Volney, N. Y., and his first wife, Harriet (Page),

of Ephraim, Wis., born November 1st, 1818, in Oneida County, N. Y.;
married   , 1840, Florinda Goodrich, of Stockbridge,
N. Y. His avocation was farming. He removed to Oakland, Wis.,
where his wife died, October 6th, 1859, when second he married April
8th, 1860, Mrs. Elizabeth Barger. He was a very worthy member of
the Free Will Baptist Church. He died at his home in Oakland, October 5th, 1873, aged 54 years, 11 months, and 4 days.　•

THEIR CHILDREN, BEING THE EIGHTH GENERATION.

2672. Henry, born, October, 1842.
2673. Frank, born, November, 1844.
2674. Maria Amelia, born, June, 1847; married March 27th, 1865, Charles Eustis.
2675. Edward C., born, Oct., 1849; married November 14th, 1872, Ellen Orndorf.
2676. Charles, born July 1st, 1851.
2677. Ina, born October 6th, 1853; married October 19th, 1873, George Perry.
2678.ʼ Warren, born October 1st, 1859.
2679. Royal, born June 8th, 1866.

2107.　　　　　　　　　　　　Oakland, Wis.

Lucius Leander Hart, Oakland, Jefferson County, Wis., second son
of Warren Hart, of Volney, N. Y., and his first wife, Harriet (Page),
of Ephraim, Wis., born August 30th, 1819, at Virgil, N. Y.; married
March 6th, 1844, Rebecca Goodrich, of Stockbridge, Madison County,
N. Y., born February 22d, 1823, daughter of Josiah, and his wife,
Hepzibah Lovel. He is a farmer at Oakland, where their children
were all born.

THEIR CHILDREN, BEING THE EIGHTH GENERATION.

2680. Mary Louisa, born December 20th, 1846; married October 6th, 1864, James
        Chapman.
2681. Newton Josiah, born June 20th, 1849; married March 8th, 1870, Cynthia
        Baldwin.
2682. Hattie Angeline, born May 28th, 1854; married October 11th, 1873, William
        W. Ives.
2683. Flora Ellen, born August 30th, 1858.
2684. Cora Bell, born November 16th, 1862.　　　　　　　　　•

2109.　　　　　　　　　　　　Oakland, Wis.

Ephraim Alvaro Hart, Oakland, Wis., fourth son of Warren, of
Volney, N. Y., and his first wife, Harriet (Page), of Ephraim, Wis.,
born March 3d, 1825, at Marshall, N. Y.; married February 12th, 1850,
Marinda Goodrich, daughter of Josiah, born April 14th, 1829. He is
a farmer and justice of the peace.

2685. Fayette W., born October 31st, 1852.
2686. Jessie M., born May 6th, 1857.
2687. Florence M., born January 10th, 1860.
2688. Eleanor L., born May 19th, 1865.
2689. Mary M., born May 25th, 1869.

2110. *Deansville, N. Y.*

ORRIS JOSIAH HART, Deansville, Oneida County, N. Y., fifth son of Warren Hart, of Volney, N. Y., and his first wife, Harriet (Page), of Ephraim, born December 11th, 1826, at Marshall, Oneida County, N. Y.; married September 12th, 1855, Laura Betsey Young, daughter of Young, and his wife, Polly (Whiting), born April 29th, 1831, at Kirkland, Oneida County, N. Y. Mr. Hart's avocation is farming.

2690. Florence Augusta, born November 3d, 1856.
2691. Annie Laura, born June 21st, 1860.
2692. Hattie Adelia, born September 9th, 1861.
2693. Charles Roscoe, born October 13th, 1864.

2113. *Scriba, N. Y.*

HIRAM LORENZO HART, Scriba, Oswego County, N. Y., eighth son of Warren, of Volney, N. Y., and his first wife, Harriet (Page), of Ephraim, Wis., born July 30th, 1830, in Marshall, Oneida County, N. Y.; married January 15th, 1857, Catharine Annie Hubbard, daughter of Thomas, and his wife, Charilla, born September 3d, 1831, at Volney, Oneida County, N. Y. He was formerly a merchant, but is now a dealer in lumber and wood, and was residing at Scriba, Oswego County, N. Y., in 1874.

2694. Frederic Augustus, born October 5th, 1860, at Oswego, N. Y.
　　　　William Arthur, born ; died, May, 1861.
2695. Jessie Luella, born December 24th, 1863, at Oswego, N. Y.
2696. Florence May, born September 14th, 1865, at Scriba, N. Y.
2697. Albert Warren, born February 1st, 1868, at Scriba, N. Y.

JENKS.

2114. *Janesville, Wis.*

HARRIET EMELINE HART, third daughter of Warren, of Volney, Oneida County, N. Y., and his first wife, Harriet (Page), of Ephraim, born January 5th, 1832, at Marshall, Oneida County, N. Y.; married

October 23d, 1856, Ira C. Jenks, a lawyer, of Janesville, Wis. She died April 7th, 1863, aged 31 years, 3 months, and 2 days. Their children were—Harriet May, born March 19th, 1859, at Janesville; Edwin Hart, born March 24th, 1862, at Janesville.

LYMAN. JENKS.

2115. *Janesville, Wis.*

SOPHRONIA JANE HART, fourth daughter of Warren Hart, of Volney, Oneida County, N. Y., and his first wife, Harriet (Page), of Ephraim, Wis., born July 2d, 1833, at Marshall, Oneida County, N. Y.; married January 4th, 1856, Edwin O. Lyman, and had children, viz: Orrin A., born September 25th, 1855, and Mary Emeline, born March 2d, 1859. Mrs. Lyman's husband died, when she second married March 29th, 1865, Ira C. Jenks, the former husband of her sister, Harriet.

DUNN.

2119. *Syracuse, N. Y.*

AUREL AUGUSTA HART, fourth daughter of Edwin Clark Hart, of Oswego, N. Y., and his wife, Aurel (Anderson), born October 25th, 1837, at Oswego City, N. Y.; married August 17th, 1859, John Dunn, Jr. They were residing at Syracuse, N. Y., in 1872. They had—1, Kittie Clark, born about 1861; 2, Nettie, born in 1865; 3, Frankie Hart, born about 1869.

2120. *Oswego, N. Y.*

HAYNES LORD HART, youngest son of Edwin Clark Hart, and his first wife, Aurel (Anderson), both of Oswego, N. Y., born March 13th, 1844, at Oswego City, N. Y.; married October 24th, 1866, Rosie Jones, daughter of Solomon Jones, and his wife, Eliza (Parkhurst), of De Witt, Onondaga County, N. Y., born May 16th, 1845. He is a boot and shoe dealer in Oswego, N. Y., where they were residing in 1872.

THEIR CHILD, BEING THE EIGHTH GENERATION.
2698. Effie Jones, born February 12th, 1869.

2120½. *Crystal Lake, Ill.*

EDWIN ROSE FRISBEE HART, Crystal Lake, McHenry County, Ill., second son of Rev. Ichabod Andrews Hart, of Southport, Wis., and his second wife, Damask Rose (Frisbee), born December 31st, 1839, at Sandusky City, Erie County, Ohio; married Margaret Elizabeth Kull, born November 16th, 1842, at Bloomfield, Wis.

THEIR CHILDREN, BEING THE EIGHTH GENERATION.

2699.   Edwin Orris, born March 29th, 1866, at Crystal Lake, Ill.
2700.   Mabel Rose, born February 20th, 1868, at Crystal Lake, Ill.
2701.   Sherman Alexis, born April 20th, 1870, at Crystal Lake, Ill.

2121.   *Muscatah, Kan.*

CHARLES CARLTON HART, Muscatah, Atchison County, Kan., third son of Rev. Ichabod Andrews Hart, of Southport, Wis., and his third wife, Harriet Eliza (Whitcomb), born December 6th, 1842, at Sandusky City, Ohio; married at Bloomfield, Wis., December 12th, 1867, Emma Amelia Olden, daughter of Enos H., and his wife, Julia Ann (Griggs), born August 28th, 1847. His residence in 1872 was on a farm, near Muscatah, Kan., where his children were born.

THEIR CHILDREN, BEING THE EIGHTH GENERATION.

2702.   Arthur Carlton, born January 2d, 1870.
     Mortimer Dwight, born August 16th, 1872; died October 1st, 1872, aged 1 month and 15 days.

2122.   *Oberlin, Ohio.*

WALTER OSGOOD HART, Oberlin, Ohio, fourth son of Rev. Ichabod Andrews Hart, of Southport, Wis., Wheaton, Ill., and other places, and his third wife, Harriet Eliza (Whitcomb), born August 13th, 1844, at Medina, Ohio; married at Wheaton, Ill., August 2d, 1871, Margaret Ferguson, daughter of James, and his wife, Jane (Reddigh), born March 28th, 1846, at Kempfield, C. W. He was a theological student at Oberlin, Ohio.

THEIR CHILD, BEING THE EIGHTH GENERATION.

2703.   Harriet Mabel, born November 11th, 1872, at Oberlin, Ohio.

2145.   *Kirkland, N. Y.*

EUROTAS HART, Clinton, N. Y., eldest son of Abel Hart, of Bristol, Conn., and his wife, Lovina (Gridley), born October 25th, 1799, at Kirkland, N. Y.; married October 28th, 1823, Betsie S. Walker, of Marshall, N. Y., born October 12th, 1804, and died October 25th, 1844, aged 40 years, when second he married April 20th, 1846, Jane H. Snell, of Oswego, N. Y. He is a farmer in Kirkland, and a justice of the peace.

THEIR CHILDREN, BEING THE EIGHTH GENERATION.

2704.   Maria L., born June 26th, 1826; married April 5th, 1855, Joseph Space.
2705.   Charlotte G., born August 26th, 1828.
2706.   Seth H., born December 20th, 1830; married April 29th, 1863, Isabella Mosher.

2707. Susan E., born February 7th, 1833.
2708. Eurotas, Jr., born December 19th, 1836.
2709. Thomas E., born December 31st, 1839; married August 17th, 1863, Maria
     Gumman.
2710. William L., born August 17th, 1841; married August 17th, 1870, Alice Ogden.
     Betsey L., born October 7th, 1844; died June 3d, 1847.

SECOND WIFE.

2711. Adella J., born February 9th, 1848.
2712. Walter L., born November 28th, 1854.

CAMP.

2157. *Durham, Conn.*

ELIZABETH HART, Durham, Conn., eldest daughter of William A.
Hart, of the same town, and his wife, Sally (Jones), born May 17th,
1831, at Durham; married January 15th, 1855, Charles E. Camp, of
Durham. He is an excellent mechanic, and was residing in Middlefield, Conn., in 1874. Their children are—1, Anna, born, October,
1855; 2, Nellie, born, January, 1857; 3, Frank, born, July, 1861; 4,
Charles, born, June, 1863.

2158. *New Haven, Conn.*

FRANKLIN HART, Durham, Conn., eldest son of William A. Hart, of
the same town, and his wife, Sally (Jones), born April 29th, 1834, at
Durham; married December 25th, 1860, Adaline Jackson, of Durham.
He spent two years in Kansas, and was a participant in the attempt to
protect the territory and state from border ruffians. He was living in
New Haven in 1870, and was one of the firm of Strong, Hart & Co.,
City Market.

THEIR CHILD, BEING THE EIGHTH GENERATION.

2713. Horace, born August 30th, 1865.

2160. *Pennfield, Ohio.*

LEWIS HART, Durham, Conn., second son of William A. Hart, of
the same town, and his wife, Sally (Jones), born December 28th, 1838,
at Durham; married March 31st, 1867, Harriet Hart, widow of the late
George Hart, of Pennfield, Lorain County, Ohio. He served nine
months in the late war as a private in the First Connecticut Regiment,
and was honorably discharged on account of ill health. He was residing in Pennfield, Ohio, in 1874.

THEIR CHILD, BEING THE EIGHTH GENERATION.

2714. Alice, born February 17th, 1868.

HALE.

2161.   *Wallingford, Conn.*

ELLEN HART, Durham, Conn., third daughter of William A. Hart, of the same town, and his wife, Sally (Jones), born March 11th, 1841, at Durham; married August 29th, 1861, Isaac Hale, of Wallingford, the youngest son of Peter Hale, and his wife, Delight (Kirtland). He is a farmer, and resides at the house of his father, in Wallingford.

2162.   *New Haven, Conn.*

CHARLES HART, Durham, Conn., third son of William A. Hart, of the same town, and his wife, Sally (Jones), born April 2d, 1843, at Durham; married February 8th, 1870, in New Haven, Isabella Burns, of Scotch descent. He served four years in the late war, first as corporal in the Fifteenth Regiment Connecticut Volunteers, and then as captain in the One Hundred and Ninth Regiment United States Colored Infantry, where he remained in service until the war closed. In 1874 he was one of the firm of Strong, Hart & Co., City Market, New Haven, Conn.

2163.   *New Haven, Conn.*

FREDERIC HART, Durham, Conn., fourth son of William A. Hart, of the same place, and his wife, Sally (Jones), born February 2d, 1845, at Durham; married November 27th, 1867, Fannie J. Frost, of New Haven. He served four years in the late war, first as a private in the First Connecticut Regiment, then as lieutenant in the One Hundred and Ninth United States Colored Infantry. In 1872 he was in the employ of the Hartford and New Haven Railroad Company as freight agent, and resided in New Haven.

2166.   *Pennfield, Ohio.*

GEORGE F. HART, Pennfield, Lorain County, Ohio, eldest son of Edward Hart, of Durham, Conn., and his wife, Emma L. (Merriman), born May 4th, 1836, at Durham. He went with his parents to Pennfield, Ohio, in 1837, and married February 18th, 1857, Harriet L. Hull. He was a member of the Congregational Church. He removed from Pennfield, Ohio, to Athens, Mich., thence to Sherwood, and then back to Pennfield, where he died, September 18th, 1864, aged 28 years, when second she married March 31st, 1867, Lewis Hart.

THEIR CHILDREN, BEING THE EIGHTH GENERATION.

2715.   Emma, born June 19th, 1859, at Pennfield, Ohio.
2716.   Sarah, born September 26th, 1861, at Athens, Mich.
        Minnie, born June 8th, 1863, at Sherwood, Mich.; died January 11th, 1865, at Pennfield, Ohio.

2167. *Pennfield, Ohio.*

HENRY I. HART, Pennfield, Lorain County, Ohio, second son of Edward Hart, of Durham, Conn., and Pennfield, Ohio, and his wife, Emma L. (Merriman), born September 26th, 1838, at Pennfield. He served two years in the late war, first as color-bearer of a regiment of Ohio Volunteers, and served six months as sergeant-major in a pioneer corps. He was finally honorably discharged on account of illness, and died at Pennfield, November 10th, 1863, aged 25 years. He was a Christian hero, being a member of the Congregational Church. The following shows his appointment:

"NEW MARKET, VA., May 14th, 1862.

I hereby certify that I have this day appointed Corporal Henry I. Hart, Company I, Eighth Regiment Ohio Volunteers, sergeant-major of the Pioneer Corps, in accordance with an order from Major-General Banks. E. B. OLMSTED, *Captain and Chief of Pioneers, Shields' Division."*

Here follows the recommendation for his promotion:

"WASHINGTON, D. C., September 24th, 1862.

This is to certify that H. I. Hart has faithfully and ably performed the duties of sergeant-major in the corps under my command, since April 25th, 1862. He posseses a thorough knowledge of the business of a military company, and is withal a brave and well drilled officer. Above all he has ever maintained a character above reproach, and has proved that a man may be a *soldier* and not yield to temptation. He would fill a position of a commissioned officer with credit to himself, satisfaction to the army, and honor to the country. E. B. OLMSTED, *Captain and Chief of Pioneers."*

HALE.

2172. *Wallingford, Conn.*

JANE HART, Durham, Conn., eldest daughter of Samuel Hart, of the same town, and his wife, Lydia R. (Davidson), born March 22d, 1841, at Durham; married January 1st, 1863, William Hale, of Wallingford, where they went to live. They had—1, Edgar, born in 1865; Frances, born in 1867, and died   ; 3, Infant, born August 12th, 1870.

GLADDEN. ESTGATE.

2175. *Iowa.*

ELIZABETH LAWRENCE HART, Kensington, eldest daughter of Era B. Hart, of the same place, and his wife, Lydia (Gilbert), daughter of John, born July 25th, 1811; baptized June 7th, 1818, at Kensington; married   , 1834, Riley W. Gladden, son of Samuel, of New Britain, and his wife, Phebe (Pennfield), baptized May 10th, 1812.

63

They went to Pennsylvania, where they had three children, but settled in Iowa, where he died, when she second married Stephen Estgate. She had by her first husband—1, Maria, who married Byron Wather, a farmer; 2, Mary Jane, who married Samuel Stansburgh, a farmer in Iowa; 3, Wallace J., who is a missionary in India, and married January 1st, 1874, Dora Estgate.

COLE.

2176. *Kensington, Conn.*

ELIZA BENTON HART, Kensington, second daughter of Era Benton Hart, of the same place, and his wife, Lydia (Gilbert), daughter of John, born January 22d, 1818; baptized June 7th, 1818, at Kensington; married October 2d, 1836, Truman Cole, son of Job, and was born March 4th, 1807, at Kensington. They had children, viz: 1, Elizabeth Maria, born October 18th, 1837, married in 1869, George A. Hooker, of New Britain; 2, Truman Hart, born August 2d, 1840, died August 31st, 1869; 3, Alice Lucy, born August 1st, 1843, died June 24th, 1871; 4, Georgie Ella, born February 29th, 1848, died March 10th, 1862; 5, Wilbur Fiske, born September 28th, 1849, died August 6th, 1872; 6, Frank Era, born August 20th, 1851; 7, Charlie Delane, born August 24th, 1853; 8, Arthur Byron, born February 22d, 1857, died October 4th, 1857. The parents and the children that are living all belong to the Methodist Church.

2177. *Kensington, Conn.*

JONATHAN THOMAS HART, Kensington, only son of Era Benton Hart, of the same parish, and his wife, Lydia (Gilbert), daughter of John, and his wife, Anna Steele, born December 2d, 1818, at Kensington; married June 3d, 1842, Maria Woodruff, of New Britain, daughter of Norman, and his wife, Abigail (Booth), born May 5th, 1820. She united with the First Congregational Church of New Britain, August 6th, 1837, but was dismissed, and recommended to the church in Kensington, December, 1854. She died there, June 5th, 1862, aged 42. He was a brass founder, which trade he learned of his wife's father. He united to the church in New Britain, August 6th, 1837, and removed his connection to the Kensington Church in 1854. He second married September 20th, 1864, Alice R. Upson, daughter of Gustavus, and his wife, Rachel (Woodruff), of West Hartford, born August 2d, 1837. His residence is half a mile north of the church in Kensington, on an eminence overlooking the factory pond and the rich valley of Berlin. He is considered the leading and efficient spirit of the Hart Manufacturing Company, of Kensington, located on Mill River, a

branch of the Mattabesett, and the former site of Percival's Mills. His face is very fairly represented in the engraving on the opposite page, and furnished by him at my urgent solicitation, for which he has my thanks.

THEIR CHILDREN, BEING THE EIGHTH GENERATION.

2717. Louisa M., born August 28th, 1845; married October 20th, 1866, Frederic A. Cowles.

Sarah Woodruff, born August 18th, 1847; died May 30th, 1864, aged 16 years and 9 months.

Ella M., born November 11th, 1849; died of consumption, November 20th, 1860, aged 11 years.

2718. Era Thomas, born July 25th, 1852.

2719. Francis Gillette, born March 15th, 1855.

2720. Leuman Pease, born June 11th, 1858.

2189.　　　　　*New Haven, Conn.*

JAMES PORTER HART, New Haven, Conn., second son of Dr. John Ariadna Hart, of Natchez, Miss., and his wife, Joanna (Porter), born July 27th, 1817, at Farmington, Conn. He graduated at Yale College in 1840, and studied theology at New Haven, where he was residing in 1872, and proposes to represent languages by letters.

2194.　　　　　*New Britain, Conn.*

SELAH HART, New Britain, Conn., second son of Deacon Elijah Hart, of the same place, and his wife, Anna, daughter of Hezekiah Andrews, born November 6th, 1784, at New Britain. He was a cooper by trade, but followed farming. He married October 5th, 1805, Jemima, daughter of David Webster, Esq., of Berlin, Conn., and his wife, Anna (Kelsey), born April 5th, 1783. They settled in Hart Quarter, a locality of New Britain, only a few rods from the site of his great-grandfather, the first Deacon Elijah. They became members of the First Church, August 5th, 1821. He had the military rank of major. He kept a hotel some years, and had one in Saratoga, N. Y. He was an effective farmer. He died of dropsy, September 7th, 1851, aged 68. His widow died July 6th, 1872, aged 89 years, 3 months, and 1 day. She was distinguished for her tall, queenly form, and ladylike appearance and manners.

THEIR CHILDREN, BEING THE EIGHTH GENERATION.

2721. Edward, born September 4th, 1806; married March 26th, 1834, Viana Perry, of Egremont.

2722. Selah, born November 25th, 1808; married November 11th, 1829, Sarah North.

2723. Nelson, born November 25th, 1812; married October 8th, 1834, Lucy Jane Dewy.

2724. Lura Ann, born November 15th, 1816; married April 13th, 1837, Anson W. Francis.

2725. Harriet, born December 10th, 1821; married October   , 1835, Cary B. Moon.

2195.   *New Britain, Conn.*

DOCTOR SAMUEL HART, New Britain, third son of Deacon Elijah Hart, of the same place, and his wife, Anna, daughter of Hezekiah Andrews, born April 7th, 1786, at New Britain; married March 18th, 1812, Orpha, daughter of James North, Esq., and his wife, Rhoda (Judd), born August 12th, 1793. She was baptized and united with the Congregational Church, February 2d, 1812. She was an ardent and exemplary Christian, and died January 12th, 1847, aged 53 years. He was the principal physician of the town for many years, and was an active and laborious man. He built his house on the west side of Central Park. He was successful in farming as well as medicine. He was of slender form and constitution, and for many of his last years was unable to walk, on account of rheumatic affection or paralysis, yet retained his mental faculties in full. He was an early subject of divine grace, and joined the Congregational Church, October, 1802, and in 1842 was one of the constituent members of the South Church. He died June 20th, 1863, aged 77 years.

THEIR CHILDREN, BEING THE EIGHTH GENERATION.

Anna, born September 9th, 1813; died July 23d, 1819, aged 6 years.

Samuel B., born September 23d, 1818; died October 10th, 1818, aged 17 days.

2726. Lucinda Andrews, born August 30th, 1820; married April 27th, 1842, William H. Smith.

2727. Samuel Waldo, born May 22d, 1825; married October 22d, 1851, Cordelia M. Smith.

2728. Louisa, born October 5th, 1828; married December 1st, 1846, Rev. Jared B. Flagg.

2196.   *New Britain, Conn.*

JESSE HART, New Britain, Conn., fourth son of Deacon Elijah Hart, of the same parish, of Berlin then, and his wife, Anna, daughter of Hezekiah Andrews, born April 20th, 1789, at New Britain; married April 5th, 1810, Lucina, daughter of Asa Cowdry, of Hartland, Conn., and his wife, Abigail (Ensign), born September 17th, 1788. She united with the Congregational Church, March 17th, 1816, and he united October 3d, 1819. He was a blacksmith by trade, which he learned of Orrin Lee, in Hartland. His shop stood where the Baptist Church now stands, and his house is the one next west of the bank, which was in good condition in 1874. He died in New Britain, February 21st, 1825, aged 36 years.

2729. Artemas Ensign, born February 11th, 1812; married August 24th, 1836, Elizabeth Ann Clark.

2730. Lucina, born December 3d, 1821; married October 29th, 1850, John H. Goodwin, of Hartford.

2197. Troy, N. Y.

JONATHAN HART, New Britain, Conn., fifth son of Deacon Elijah Hart, of the same place, and his wife, Anna, daughter of Hezekiah Andrews, born February 20th, 1792, at New Britain. He became a member of the Congregational Church, August 5th, 1821. He was never married. He traveled through the south and became dissipated, but returned to West Troy, N. Y., where he acted as magistrate and judge of the police court many years. He died there March 4th, 1863. Nature had lavished on him largely in body and mind few more favored.

2198.

NORMAN HART, New Britain, sixth son of Deacon Elijah Hart, of the same place, and his wife, Anna, daughter of Hezekiah Andrews, born August 5th, 1794, at New Britain; married September 8th, 1818, Minerva, daughter of Thomas Lee, Esq., of New Britain, and his wife, Electa (Riley), born April 22d, 1798, at New Britain. He was a cloth dresser by trade, and resided near Hart's Mills, in the south part of the city, where he carried on wool carding and cloth dressing many years. In 1851 he sold his mill and residence, and built at the foot of Dublin Hill, in New Britain, which place he sold, and he was residing on Walnut Street in 1874. She became a member of the Congregational Church, April 4th, 1813, and he became a member, April 2d, 1843, and was chosen deacon, September 21st, 1843.

From a Newspaper.

"The golden wedding of Deacon Norman Hart and Mrs. Minerva Lee Hart was observed at their residence in New Britain, Conn., on the 8th day of August, 1868. There were present nine persons who were at the wedding fifty years ago, two of whom were brides-maids, and one was groomsman. There were also present the children of Rev. Burdett Hart and Norman Lee Hart, of Philadelphia, and their wives, and Mrs. Ellen H. Wells, of New Britain, and all the grandchildren. For fifty years there had been no death in this family of Deacon Hart. He is the sole survivor of his father's family. An appropriate address was made by Rev. Mr. Perrin, pastor of the First Church in New Britain. Also an address, largely historical, was made by Deacon

Alfred Andrews, the historian of New Britain, in which he particularly referred to the good services of prominent ancestors of both families in civil, ecclesiastical, and military affairs. A poem, written by Mrs. Ellen H. Wells for the occasion, was read, as well as a longer one, by Mrs. Almira Hart Lincoln Phelps, of Baltimore. The occasion was one of great interest in New Britain, and one which will be long and pleasantly remembered by all who enjoyed the exercises and festivities of this delightful family re-union. Deacon and Mrs. Hart are in the enjoyment of a ripe and vigorous old age, promising them yet many years of comfort and happiness."

They were in comfortable health, January, 1875.

THEIR CHILDREN, BEING THE EIGHTH GENERATION.

2731. Burdett, born November 16th, 1821; married August 21st, 1849, Rebecca W. Fiske.

2732. Norman Lee, born February 2d, 1826; married December 6th, 1854, Lavinia M. Kellogg.

2733. Ellen, born February 23d, 1828; married June 15th, 1853, Lemuel R. Wells.

2199.   *New Britain, Conn.*

IRA HART, seventh son of Deacon Elijah Hart, of the same place, and his wife, Anna (Andrews), born July 22d, 1798, at New Britain; married May 3d, 1820, Orpha, daughter of Salmon Hart, of New Britain, and his wife, Sarah (Goodrich), born April 2d, 1800. They both united with the Congregational Church, August 5th, 1821. He was a clothier by trade, and lived in the north part of his father's house, but died December 1st, 1824, aged 26 years, leaving no children. His widow married May 2d, 1835, Horace Butler, of New Britain, as his second wife. He died April 17th, 1870, aged 80 years. She was living on Stanley Street, New Britain, in 1874.

2200.   *New Britain, Conn.*

ELIJAH HART, New Britain, Conn., fourth of the name, and tenth child of Deacon Elijah, and his wife, Anna (Andrews), born September 11th, 1804, at New Britain; married March 15th, 1826, Louisa Warner, of Hamden, daughter of Isaac, and his wife, Damaris (Wooding), born February 23d, 1804, at Hamden. He was a farmer, and lived in his father's old house by the Hart Mills, in the south part of New Britain. He died April 5th, 1856, aged 52 years. He was a man of very strong passions and prejudices, and was often employed in public business. His widow died at Middletown, December 21st, 1870, aged 66 years.

THEIR CHILDREN, BEING THE EIGHTH GENERATION.

2734. Henrietta W., born March 25th, 1827; married September 14th, 1846, Darwin Francis.

2735. Eliza Ann, born July 12th, 1828; married May 31st, 1849, Hector F. Humphrey.

2736. Augusta Cornelia, born May 12th, 1830; married September 5th, Henry Humphrey.

Elijah William, born March 13th, 1832; died September 17th, 1822, aged 6 months.

2737. Mary Jane, born September 5th, 1834; married, February, 1862, Julius S. Doolittle.

2738. Isaac Warner, born April 22d, 1838; married February 5th, 1865, Emily N. Warner; second married

2739. Emma Louisa, born July 14th, 1844; married , June, 1861, Elijah R. Ward, of Middletown.

2201. *New Britain, Conn.*

COLONEL FRANCIS HART, New Britain, eldest son of Captain Aaron, of the same place, and his wife, Sarah (Francis), born December 18th, 1791, at Hart Quarter, in New Britain; married December 30th, 1812, Dolly Stanley, daughter of Lot, (son of Thomas third,) and his wife, Rhoda (Wadsworth), of Farmington, born February 15th, 1794, at New Britain. He was a tanner and shoe-maker by trade, which he learned of Treadway, of Torringford. He located in Hart Quarter. His house, near Shuttle Meadow Road, was formerly owned and occupied by Asahel Hart. He was often engaged in public affairs as a civil officer, and also held the military rank of colonel. She united with the Congregational Church, January 6th, 1811. He united, August 4th, 1811. He was a constituent member of the South Church in 1842. He died June 27th, 1845, aged 54 years, and left no children. She second married October 22d, 1860, Solomon D. Gridley, of Southington, and was his second wife. He was son of Joel Gridley, and his wife, Amanda (Woodruff), born July 14th, 1805. She was a most worthy woman, and died April 26th, 1868, aged 74 years, 2 months, and 11 days.

2202. *New Britain, Conn.*

CHESTER HART, second son of Captain Aaron, of New Britain, and his wife, Sarah (Francis), of Newington, born February 7th, 1793; married September 19th, 1821, Hannah, daughter of Levi Wells, of New Britain, and his wife, Hannah (Wells), born, August, 1797, and died September 1st, 1823, aged 26 years, when he second married May 12th, 1824, Elva Wells, sister of his first wife, born September 11th, 1800, at New Britain, and was baptized there by Rev. William Robinson, of Southington. She is a good woman and scholar. She had a

patrimony from her uncle, Lemuel, of Yonkers, N. Y., with which
they built a good and substantial dwelling-house on the corner of Middletown Turnpike and Shuttle Meadow Road. He died there March
20th, 1865, aged 72 years. This place was sold to Mr. Albert A.
Mason, and she removed to her house on Arch Street, next south of
the South Church, in the city of New Britain.

CHILDREN BY HIS SECOND WIFE, BEING THE EIGHTH GENERATION.

2740. Levi Wells, born June 7th, 1825; married December 27th, 1854, Georgiana
       North.
2741. John Henry, born April 13th, 1828; married Jan. 4th, 1853, Jane Griswold.
2742. Hannah Jennette, born March 9th, 1835; died March 16th, 1853, aged 18
       years, and 1 week.

JUDD.

2205.   *New Britain, Conn.*

BETSEY HART, New Britain, second daughter of Captain Aaron, of
the same place, and his wife, Sarah (Francis), of Newington, born
February 26th, 1803, at New Britain; married April 10th, 1822, John,
son of John Judd, and his wife, Ursula (Stanley), born March 25th,
1796, at New Britain. He is a shoe-maker by trade, and lived many
years on the Shuttle Meadow Road; but in 1875 he is in the city, on
Arch Street. She was admitted to the Congregational Church, October
7th, 1827. He was admitted, January 4th, 1829. They were both
admitted to the South Church in 1842. Their children were—1, Luman Stanley, born June 9th, 1824, married, February, 1844, Martha
Hotchkiss, of Boston; 2, Francis Deming, born February 3d, 1827; 3,
Sarah Hart, born July 10th, 1829; 4, John Bernard, born December
18th, 1831, married November 30th, 1854, Eliza H. Keeney, of New
York; 5, Frederick William, born June 31st, 1834; 6, Ellen Nancy,
born September 27th, 1837, married April 10th, 1860, George C. Gridley, son of Solomon D.

2206.   *New Britain, Conn.*

AARON HART, New Britain, fourth son of Captain Aaron, of the
same place, and his wife, Sarah (Francis), of Newington, born November 25th, 1805, at New Britain; married November 27th, 1827, Abigail Bronson Andrews, daughter of Dr. John, and his second wife,
Caroline, daughter of Jesse Bronson, of Kensington, born May 16th,
1806. He was a joiner, which trade he learned of Captain Selah Porter, of Farmington. He built nearly opposite his father's place in Hart
Quarter, but sold, and lived in various localities. They were members
of the Congregational Church. He died by being pricked with the

spur of a fowl, May 20th, 1845, aged 39 years. She second married May 11th, 1848, Comfort Hewlett, son of Comfort, of Groton, Conn.

THEIR CHILDREN, BEING THE EIGHTH GENERATION.

2743. Newton Francis, born January 2d, 1829; married May 4th, 1852, Nancy Phinney.

2744. John Andrews, born May 2d, 1830. He was killed by the kick of a horse, June 11th, 1843.

Aaron Adolphus, born December 22d, 1831; died September 12th, 1832, aged 9 months.

2745. Jane Abigail, born June 2d, 1837; married December 25th, 1860, John G. Lewis, of Hampton.

2207. *New Britain, Conn.*

HORACE HART, New Britain, Conn., fifth son of Captain Aaron, and his wife, Sarah (Francis), of Newington, born July 29th, 1808, at New Britain; married December 2d, 1831, Harriet J. Church, daughter of James, and his wife, Huldah (Barnes), of Haddam, born February 16th, 1813, at Haddam, Conn. They are living in Washington, Mass., in 1875, where he owns a farm. They formerly lived on Arch Street, in New Britain, in the house built by Bennet J. Andrews, deceased, which Hart bought of Andrews. They have no children.

2209. *Buffalo, N. Y., Chicago, Ill.*

OZIAS HART, New Britain, eldest son of Ozias, of the same place, and his wife, Sarah (Lee), born December 9th, 1793, at New Britain; married November 15th, 1816, Pamelia Baggs, of Durham, who died at St. Louis, when second he married, January 25th, 1831, Triphenia Elmer, who died, March, 1845, when third he married January 11th, 1852, Mrs. Mary Conover, who died soon after. He left New Britain in 1819, and in 1861 lived at Buffalo, N. Y. He now lives in Chicago, where he fourth married July 18th, 1869, Mrs. Elizabeth Bushnell. He has been a miller by occupation.

CHILDREN BY HIS FIRST WIFE, BEING THE EIGHTH GENERATION.

2746. Emily Eliza, born January 8th, 1818; married about 1839, Lewis Potter, a lawyer.

George Henry, born, March, 1819. He left home for parts unknown.

William Otis, born   , 1821; died in infancy.

CHILDREN BY HIS SECOND WIFE.

Charles Augustus, born October 30th, 1837; died, April, 1842.

2747. Willard Otis, born February 13th, 1838; married May 21st, 1867, Martha J. Lucas.

2748. Sarah Ann, born March 5th, 1845; married January 1st, 1864, James W. Winbolt.

64

LEWIS. OAKLEY. HULL.

2212.   *Farmington, Conn.*

JULIA ANN HART, New Britain, Conn., eldest daughter of Abijah, and his wife, Anna (Hall), born September 1st, 1795, at Middletown, Conn.; married December 16th, 1818, Seth Lewis, son of Phineas, of Farmington. He died at Farmington, December 19th, 1833, aged 68 years, when second she married September 27th, 1838, Mr. Oakley, of Pennsylvania. He died, when third she married December 27th, 1842, Samuel Hull, of Candor, N. Y. She was admitted to the Congregational Church at Farmington, August 9th, 1821, and from there to New Britain by letter, April 5th, 1835, and from New Britain to Pennsylvania. She was intelligent and attractive, experienced various vicissitudes of life, and died of dropsy, at Candor, N. Y., August 22d, 1859, aged 63 years. Her children, all by her first husband, were— 1, John Sedgwick, born September 27th, 1824, married December 10th, 1851, Harriet Alden, of Mich.; 2, Thomas Norton, born March 27th, 1827, married April 27th, 1853, Mary F. Lake; 3, Henry Hart, born June 13th, 1829, married March 10th, 1852, Mary Chaine; 4, William Hall, born May 22d, 1831, and went to California.

ANDREWS.

2213.   *New Britain, Conn.*

CAROLINE BIRD HART, New Britain, Conn., second daughter of Abijah, of the same place, and his first wife, Anna (Hall), daughter of Captain Giles, of Middletown, born April 15th, 1798, in New York City; married December 16th, 1818, before Rev. Newton Skinner, pastor, Alfred Andrews, eldest son of Ezekiel, and his first wife, Roxana Hinsdale, daughter of Elijah, born October 16th, 1797, at New Britain. He was a teacher, mechanic, and farmer, and is sometimes called the historian of the town. They were admitted to the Congregational Church, August, 1821. She bore two daughters, viz: 1, Julia Ann, born November 15th, 1819, and is single in 1875; 2, Caroline Hart, born December 4th, 1822, married January 21st, 1852, Elisha B. Bridgman, then of Belchertown, Mass., but now of Boston, Mass. Mrs. Andrews died August 22d, 1823, of spotted fever, aged 25 years. She was intelligent and reflective, and taught school before marriage.

2214.   *Hartford, Conn.*

THOMAS GILES HART, New Britain, eldest son of Abijah, of the same place, and his first wife, Anna (Hall), daughter of Captain Giles, of Middletown, born December 2d, 1800. He was never married. He vas educated a druggist in Hartford, went south, and died in Raleigh, N. C., July 26th, 1825, aged 25 years.

2215. *North Haven, Conn.*

DOCTOR HENRY ABIJAH HART, New Britain, Conn., second son of Abijah Hart, of the same town, and his first wife, Anna (Hall), daughter of Captain Giles, of Middletown, born August 9th, 1805, at New Britain. He studied medicine, and took the degree of M. D. at Yale Medical College in 1826. He married April 24th, 1827, Eliza, second daughter of Joseph Shipman, of New Britain, and his wife, Mary Lee), born February 18th, 1807. He located in North Haven, Conn., is a physician, where he gave promise of skill and success, but was soon prostrated with typhus fever, of which he died March 24th, 1828, aged 22 years, and was buried in New Britain Cemetery, where a ombstone has been erected to his memory. His widow second married February 22d, 1837, David Martin, M. D., of Springfield, N. J., who died March 24th, 1838, when third she married March 13th, 1839, Major Sandford Brown, of New Hartford, who died September 16th, 857, aged 65. He was a man of great executive force, having built oads and bridges in the south, and constructed the big dam for the Green Woods Company. Dr. Martin was an eminent physician and counselor in New Jersey. The wife of these three prominent men was talented, pious, and benevolent. In early life she was a teacher in public and private schools, and was the first pioneer of the infant class in the New Britain Sunday School. She died at New Hartford, Conn., of cancer, July 8th, 1866, aged 59, leaving one son by her first husband, and a son and daughter by her third husband, viz: Hubert Sanford, born March 28th, 1840, and Ellen Elvira, born June 10th, 1843.

CHILD OF DR. HART, BEING THE EIGHTH GENERATION.

1749. Henry Abijah, born November 13th, 1828; at New Britain; married Josephine Estella Essex.

2216. *Texas.*

SAMUEL MANSFIELD HART, New Britain, youngest son of Abijah Hart, of the same town, and his wife, Anna, daughter of Captain Giles Hall, of Middletown, Conn., born August 30th, 1807, at New Britain. He was a brass founder by trade, which he learned of Deacon Chauncey Cornwall, but afterwards became a farmer. In 1837 he went to Texas with a colony from New Britain and New York, and while prospecting near Austin, was killed by a poisoned arrow from the bow of an Indian, and died in 1838, aged 30 years. He was single.

PRATT.

2217.   *Marietta, Ohio.*

HANNAH BRIDGE HART, New Britain, Conn., eldest child of Rev.
William Hart, of the same town, and his wife, Hannah Bridge (Campe),
of Shoreditch Church, Wapping, London, Eng., born February 11th,
1799; married March 25th, 1818, Henry Morgan, son of Andrew Pratt,
Esq., of New Britain, and his third wife, Hannah (Andrews), born
February 23d, 1797, at New Britain. He is a farmer by occupation.
They removed to Marietta, Ohio, where she died, August 15th, 1823,
aged 25 years, leaving one son, William Hart Pratt, born August 20th,
1819; married December 26th, 1841, Esther Caldwell, of Hartford,
Conn.; died June 11th, 1849, aged 30. Mr. Pratt returned from Marietta to his old home, and second married June 18th, 1826, Mary S.,
daughter of Elijah Loveland, of Kensington, and his wife, Azuba Scovill), born January 27th, 1802, at Kensington; died May 23d, 1863, of
consumption, aged 61.

2218.   *Candor, N. Y.*

JONATHAN BIRD HART, New Britain, only son of Rev. William Hart,
of the same town, and his wife, Hannah Bridge (Campe), of Shore-
ditch Church, Wapping, London, Eng., born August 25th, 1800, at
New Britain; married March 26th, 1823, at Northfield, Conn., Elvira
Humiston, of Plymouth. He learned cabinet making of his uncle,
Roberts, and in 1825 removed to Candor, N. Y., where he followed his
business to a limited extent. He and his wife were admitted to the
Congregational Church in 1826, and he became an elder and deacon.
They celebrated their golden wedding March 26th, 1873, a large num-
ber of their friends being present. They have no children.

KROM.

2219.   *Candor, N. Y.*

MEHITABEL HART, youngest daughter of Rev. William Hart, of New
Britain, and his wife, Hannah Bridge (Campe), of England, born January 11th, 1806, at Middletown, Conn. She went with her father to
Candor, N. Y., and married there March 20th, 1844, Peter J. Krom,
of that place, and was living there in 1862, near her brother, Jonathan.

CLARK.

2219½.   *Hartford, Conn.*

HANNAH HART, New Britain, eldest daughter of Asahel, of the same
town, and his first wife, Hannah, daughter of Captain John Langdon,

and his wife, Mercy (Eno), born October 7th, 1792, at New Britain; married in New York, 1810, Sylvester, youngest child of Abel Clark, of New Britain, and his wife, Abigail (Judd), born February 18th, 1789. They lived in Hartford, Conn., where he died, and she survived him many years.

PEARL.

2220.   *Southington, Conn.*

ELIZA HART, New Britain, second daughter of Asahel, and his second wife, Sarah Hart, daughter of Judah Hart, Jr., born October 10th, 1799, at New Britain; married there April 18th, 1824, Ralph Pearl, son of Frederic, of Southington. He went to Southington with his brother, Orrin, from the east part of the state, about 1820. In 1825 he had part of his hand shot off by the accidental discharge of a pistol in the hands of a cavalry officer. They lived in the west part of the town, where he died, January 14th, 1855, aged 62 years. The record says he died of intemperance. They had an infant die of fever, April 15th, 1826, aged 3 months.

2221.   *New Britain, Conn.*

AMZI WOODRUFF HART, New Britain, second son of Asahel, and his second wife, Sarah, daughter of Judah Hart, Jr., and his wife, Sarah (North), born November 3d, 1801, in New Britain. He was never married. He was a cooper by trade, which he learned of Major Selah Hart, and died at his house, of spotted fever, August 10th, 1823, aged 22 years. He was a young man of good habits and much promise.

ROOT.

2222.   *Tallmadge, Ohio.*

LYDIA HART, eldest daughter of James, of New Britain, and his wife, Sylvia, daughter of Nathaniel Pennfield, born May 13th, 1796, at New Britain; married November 25th, 1818, John C. Root, son of Ezekiel, of Farmington, and his wife, Cynthia (Cole), of Kensington. He was a shoe-maker by trade and avocation, and removed to Ohio, where he died, December 10th, 1862, aged 67. She was living, not long since, at Tallmadge, Summit County, Ohio.

2223.   *Southington, Conn.*

ETHAN HART, eldest son of James, of New Britain, and his wife, Sylvia, daughter of Nathaniel Pennfield, born, September, 1799, at New Britain; married May 3d, 1819, Martha Wiard, daughter of

Smith, of Southington. She died March 20th, 1834, aged 34. Mr. Hart was a carpenter and joiner, and died at sea, while on his passage south in pursuit of work, May, 1834, aged 35 years. They left one child.

THEIR CHILD, BEING THE EIGHTH GENERATION.

2750. Henry James, born July 24th, 1820; married August 25th, 1842, Sophia Peck.

2224. *Martinsburg, Ohio.*

CLARISSA HART, second daughter of James, of New Britain, and his wife, Sylvia, daughter of Nathaniel Pennfield, born February 22d, 1803, at New Britain; baptized there June 12th, 1803; married, June, 1822, Enos Beckwith. They went to Martinsburg, Knox County, Ohio, where she died, August 26th, 1831, aged 28 years.

McCREARY.

2225. *Ohio.*

HARRIET HART, third daughter of James Hart, of New Britain, and his wife, Sylvia (Pennfield), born October 6th, 1806, at New Britain; married, April, 1821, William McCreary. They lived in Ohio.

McLAUGHLIN.

2226. *Martinsburg, Ohio.*

MARY HART, fourth daughter of James Hart, of New Britain, and his wife, Sylvia (Pennfield), born, January, 1810, at New Britain. She went to Ohio in 1827, and married there, May 18th, 1829, George W. McLaughlin, a merchant of Martinsburg. They removed to St. Mary's, Ohio, in 1837, where their first son was born. They had—1, Almira, born December 1st, 1830; 2, Amanda, born August 31st, 1832, died June 26th, 1834; 3, Eliza, born November 8th, 1834; 4, Sarah, born May 24th, 1837; 5, William, born January 20th, 1841, died December 30th, 1849, of small pox; 6, Mary Ellen, born August 1st, 1843; 7, George Cannon, born April 18th, 1846; 8, Martha Antoinette, born February 26th, 1849, died August 3d, 1850; 9, John Charles, born September 22d, 1851.

2227. *Madison Co., Ill.*

STEPHEN HART, New Lebanon, St. Clair County, Ill., eldest son of Joel, and his wife, Lydia (North), of Berlin, born April 12th, 1801; married, July, 1831, Eliza Buck, of Marietta, Ohio, born January 5th, 1805. He is a farmer in Madison County, Ill., about twenty-five miles from St. Louis. Their children were all born in Illinois, but at different localities.

2751. Elizabeth, born August 28th, 1833.
2752. George, born July 26th, 1835; married, May, 1863, Sarah Parrot.
Alonzo, born August 4th, 1837.
2753. Albert, born March 6th, 1839; married   , 1868, Anna Radcliff.
2754. Ellen, born December 9th, 1840; died April 5th, 1864, aged 23.
Jane, born January 10th, 1844.
Julia, born January 9th, 1849; died September 22d, 1851, aged 2 years.

2228.   *Harmar, Ohio.*

DOCTOR SETH HART, Harmar, Washington County, Ohio, second son of Joel, of New Britain, Conn., and his wife, Lydia (North), of Berlin, Conn., born November 13th, 1804, at Berlin, Conn.; married at Meredith, N. Y., February 19th, 1825, Vesta Curtis, daughter of Bildad, and his wife, Thankful (Orcutt), born September 6th, 1805, at Plainfield, Mass.; died March 22d, 1827, when second he married June 7th, 1828, Mary Wilson, widow of Benjamin Converse, born in Waterford, Washington County, Ohio, to Deacon David Wilson, and his wife, —— Grovesnor, July 8th, 1798; died June 14th, 1863, when third he married October 22d, 1863, Emma Lewis Hiatt, who died February 16th, 1865, when fourth he married November 16th, 1870, Elizabeth Donover Marshall, the widow of Joseph L. Parker, of Marietta. They were living in Harmar, Washington County, Ohio, February, 1874, where he has been in the practice of medicine since 1825, most of the time for nearly fifty years, from which place he sent me, in 1872, a photograph of his eldest daughter holding in her arms his youngest daughter—lacking only twenty-three days of being forty-six years difference in their ages.

2755. Vesta Curtiss, born December 1st, 1826; married May 13th, 1844, Frederick Edwin Kemper, of Walnut Hills.

SECOND WIFE.

2756. Samuel, born June 7th, 1830; married   , Sarah Elizabeth Purple.
2757. Mary Wilson, born November 26th, 1831; married November 20th, 1870, James Hopkins Nixon, of Ironton, Ohio.
2758. Romayn Beck, born November 30th, 1833; married November 11th, 1856, Martha Eliza Metcalf.
2759. Henry Lyman,   } married September 21st, 1858, Lucy Wolcott Deming.
              } born October 10th, 1835;
2760. Samuel Manson, }
2761. David Wilson, born March 26th, 1838; married December 23d, 1865, Marian Adalade Cox.
2762. Lydia North, born August 30th, 1840. She was single, March, 1874, and was a teacher.
2763. Minnehaha Grace, born November 8th, 1872, at Harmar, Ohio.

OLMSTED.

2229.   *Otsego, N. Y.*

LYDIA G. HART, Otsego, N. Y., eldest daughter of Joel Hart, of New Britain, Conn., and his wife, Lydia, daughter of Jedediah North, and his second wife, Abigail (Andrews), born July 9th, 1806, at Berlin, Conn.; married June 12th, 1828, Carlisle Olmsted, of Otsego, Otsego County, N. Y.

BALDWIN.

2230.   *Otsego, N. Y.*

MARY HART, Otsego, Otsego County, N. Y., second daughter of Joel Hart, of New Britain, Conn., and his wife, Lydia, daughter of Jedediah North, of Berlin, Conn., born November 9th, 1808, at   ; married October 8th, 1827, Salmon Baldwin, of Otsego, Otsego County, N. Y.

2231.   *Cambria, Mich.*

AUSTIN HART, Cambria, Hillside County, Mich., eldest son of Deacon Benjamin Hart, of New Britain, Conn., and Watertown, Washington County, Ohio, and his first wife, Honor (Deming), born March 14th, 1808, at Watertown, Ohio; married April 7th, 1842, Clarinda Star, of Greenfield, Ohio, born July 27th, 1812. They were residing as above in 1874, and he was a farmer.

THEIR CHILD, BEING THE EIGHTH GENERATION.

2764.   Frank B., born June 18th, 1847; married October 23d, 1872, Anne E. Fox.

2232.   *Harmar, Ohio.*

COLUMBUS HART, Harmar, Washington County, Ohio, second son of Deacon Benjamin, of New Britain, Conn., and his wife, Honor (Deming), of Watertown, Ohio, born July 7th, 1810, at Watertown, Ohio; married September 10th, 1833, by Rev. Jacob Lindsley, Nancy Proctor, of Watertown, Ohio. They reside at Harmar, Washington County, Ohio, near Lake Erie, and have six children. He is a carpenter and joiner by trade and occupation.

THEIR CHILDREN, BEING THE EIGHTH GENERATION.

2765.   Emily Beckwith, born October 31st, 1834; married October 20th, 1853, John Q. A. Dye, son of Thomas and Hannah.
        Percival Proctor, born April 24th, 1837; died June 12th, 1863.
2766.   Malvina Emeline, born December 21st, 1838; married June 22d, 1869, Rev. Albert Bowers, of Macon, Mo.

767. Augusta Elizabeth, born April 10th, 1842; married December 19th, 1864, D. H. Zeigler.

768. Benjamin Franklin, born March 31st, 1849; married December 30th, 1873, Laura E. Gearhart, and live at Harmar, Ohio.

Delbert Abdella, born February 16th, 1852; died July 18th, 1853, and was buried at Mound Cemetery.

HAYWARD.

2233. *Waterford, Ohio.*

MARY ANN HART, Watertown, Washington County, Ohio, eldest daughter of Deacon Benjamin Hart, of New Britain, Conn., and Watertown, Ohio, and his first wife, Honor (Deming), born May 24th, 1813, at Watertown, Ohio; married September 25th, 1833, Joseph Hayward, of Watertown, Ohio, born January 10th, 1808. They reside at Waterford, Ohio. They had—1, Charles Austin, born February 12th, 1835, married March 24th, 1870, Nettie Hawley; 2, Lucy Minerva, born May 23d, 1837, died September 28th, 1838; 3, Mary Sophia, born December 13th, 1839, married June 16th, 1869, Douglas P. Leonard; 4, Newell Deming, born February 18th, 1842, married May 24th, 1865, Eliza Bartlett, died September 9th, 1865; 5, Josephine Ann, born April 13th, 1844, and was living with his parents at Waterford in 1874; 6, Arthur Winchester, born June 16th, 1846, and is in a china store at South Bend, Ind.; 7, Emma Hart, born August 10th, 1851, and was living with her parents in 1874.

PAYNE. GROUT.

2234. *Burlington, Iowa.*

LUCY WOLCOTT HART, Burlington, Iowa, second daughter of Deacon Benjamin Hart, of New Britain, Conn., and Watertown, Ohio, and his first wife, Honor (Deming), born December 2d, 1815, at Watertown, Ohio; married October 12th, 1836, Rev. Samuel Payne, born July 21st, 1806. They located at Burlington, Iowa, where he died, January 8th, 1845. They had—1, Sarah, born August 6th, 1838, died December 14th, 1839; 2, Dorcas, born December 24th, 1839, died August 16th, 1844; 3, Sarah Clark, born November 16th, 1841, married July 11th, 1861, William Triggs, who died in the army, when second she married Josiah Fisher; 4, Rebecca, born March 21st, 1844, married Samuel Brunt. Mrs. Payne second married April 1st, 1847, Jonathan Grout, born June 13th, 1811, and died at Lancaster, Iowa, December 2d, 1866. They had one child, Catharine Florence, born August 14th, 1858, and died in infancy.

65

2235. *Marietta, Ohio.*

DOCTOR SIMEON DEMING HART, Marietta, Ohio, third son of Deacon Benjamin Hart, of New Britain, Conn., and Watertown, Ohio, and his first wife, Honor (Deming), born August 13th, 1818, at Watertown, Ohio; married July 24th, 1846, Minerva Lawrence, of Watertown, Ohio, before Rev. Lucien Ford. He is superintendent and she is matron of the Children's Home in Marietta, Ohio. He is also a physician. They had no children in 1874.

2236. *Marietta, Ohio.*

DOCTOR BENJAMIN FRANKLIN HART, Marietta, Washington County, Ohio, fourth son of Deacon Benjamin Hart, of New Britain, Conn., and Watertown, Ohio, and his first wife, Honor (Deming), born January 5th, 1823, at Watertown, Washington County, Ohio. He left home when he was eleven years old, and took the responsibility of caring for himself. Being determined to acquire an education, he worked for $4 per month, went to school winters, and paid his board by doing chores night and morning; but when he became older he paid his expenses by sawing wood and shoveling coal, or any work he could find. He united with the Congregational Church at Harmar, Ohio, April 3d, 1840, at the age of seventeen, and began the study of medicine with his cousin, Dr. Seth Hart, of Harmar, Ohio, but taught school in 1841-2. He worked in a saw-mill one winter, took daguerreotypes for a time, and then worked on a farm, but all the time was studying for his profession. In the fall of 1843 he took his worldly goods, consisting of scanty clothing, one sheet, one blanket, two comfortables, and a few cooking utensils, on the deck of a steamer, and went to Cincinnati. He hired a room in the third story of a house on Vine Street, did his own cooking, washing, and ironing, heard six medical lectures per day, and run in debt for half the lectures. He started for home in the spring of 1844 with $1.50, paid $1 for deck passage to Harmar, and for lack of funds went thirty-six hours without eating, when he landed, and found Dr. Seth Hart very sick. He took care of him and his patients the best he could, and in November went four miles up the Ohio River, to the mouth of the Muskingum, where he began business, soon had a large practice, and in two years had paid all his debts for tuition, horse, house, library, and office. Having a large practice over the Ohio, in Virginia, he relinquished his business in Ohio to his brother, Simeon, and removed to Bull Creek, Wood County, Va., where he remained two years. He married October 19th, 1848, Sally M., daughter of Thomas Alcock, of Marietta, Ohio, and his wife, Sally Holliday (Wells), born December 27th, 1830,

B. F. Hart. M. D.

ear Marietta, and united with the Congregational Church at Harmar,)hio, in 1855. Dr. Hart removed from Virginia to Harmar in 1849, where he followed the practice of medicine until 1863, when he re-1oved to Marietta. At the breaking out of the rebellion in 1861 he vas active in furnishing the Union soldiers with such medicines as they vere likely to need; he also saw to the wants of those families whose athers had gone to the war. In 1862 he spent much time and money a visiting the battle-fields—all gratuitously. He went to Pittsburgh Janding and Shiloh, Tenn., collected as many of the sick and wounded s the boat would accommodate, (some 300,) brought them to Cincin-ati, and returned again for more. Thus he spent some months in isiting Gettysburg, Frederick City, Baltimore, and Washington. He vas assistant surgeon in pursuit of the rebel general, Morgan, appointed y Governor Brough, with rank of major. His face is represented on he opposite page. In 1875 he is still following his profession in Ma-ietta. Mrs. Hart is a woman of intelligence, energy, and benevolence, nd an artist as well as a good housewife. She is interested in mission nd Sunday Schools, and every good work.

THEIR CHILDREN, BEING THE EIGHTH GENERATION.

769. Mary Franklin, born January 27th, 1850; married January 27th, 1870, J. C. Bartlet, M. D., of Marietta, Ohio.

70. Nannie Holliday, born May 19th, 1853; died July 26th, 1854, and was buried in Mound Cemetery, Marietta, Ohio.

71. Charles Seymour, born May 13th, 1856. He was in Roanoke College, Vir-ginia, in 1874, and is to be a physician. He was admitted to membership in the Congregational Church at Marietta, Ohio, April, 1869.

ECKLEY.

2238.   *Lancaster, Iowa.*

HONOR DEMING HART, Lancaster, Iowa, fifth daughter of Deacon enjamin Hart, of New Britain, Conn., and Watertown, Washington ounty, Ohio, and his second wife, Mrs. Esther Miner (Wilson), born anuary 4th, 1829, at Watertown, Ohio; married October 30th, 1852, homas Ralph Eckley, born June 5th, 1831, at Sharon, Morgan County, hio. He is a carriage maker, was married at Lancaster, Iowa, and as living there in 1874. They had—1, Jennie, born August 20th, 853, died December 19th, 1854; 2, William Thomas, born September th, 1855; 3, Henry Converse, born March 12th, 1858; died April 7th, 859; 4, Rosa Adel, born March 8th, 1860, died September 26th, 1861; Abe Lincoln, born March 1st, 1862; 6, Clara, born June 26th, 1865, ed August 22d, 1867; 7, Romain, born March 11th, 1868; 8, Anna ary, born January 14th, 1870; 9, Maggie, born November 13th, 1872.

2239.   *Marietta, Ohio.*

HENRY CONVERSE HART, Marietta, Ohio, only son of Deacon Benjamin Hart, and his second wife, Esther (Wilson), born March 4th, 1833, at Watertown, Ohio; married September 4th, 1860, Hannah Rood, born May 30th, 1829. They live near Marietta, Ohio, where he is a farmer.

THEIR CHILD, BEING THE EIGHTH GENERATION.

2772. Seth Wilson, born August 17th, 1861.

PLUMER.

2240.   *Marietta, Ohio.*

FRANCES ADELIA HART, youngest child of Deacon Benjamin Hart, and his third wife, Widow Rebecca (White) Lawrence, born August 10th, 1839, at Marietta, Ohio; married January 16th, 1868, John A. Plumer, born October 26th, 1833. He is a land surveyor, and lives at Marietta, Ohio. They have had—1, George McAllister, born February 5th, 1869; 2, William Simeon, born July 31st, 1870.

PRICE.

2451.   *Lexington, Ky.*

CHARLOTTE HART, Lexington, Ky., third daughter of Major William Hart, of Marietta, Ohio, and his first wife, Sarah Waters (Wolcott), of Wethersfield, Conn., born at Marietta, Ohio, in 1810; married there in 1833, James Price, of Kentucky. He was a farmer, who owned 1,000 acres of the best blue grass land in Clarke County, and some thirty negro servants, some of whom he inherited from his father, and some were bought with money like Abraham of old, "All of whom," she writes me, "the best government in the world liberated without compensation, notwithstanding the constitution provides that no man is to be deprived of his property without due process of law." He died February 14th, 1865, and has a beautiful monument at his grave in Winchester, Ky., where four of his sons were also buried. Mrs. Price is a lady of culture, intelligence, and discrimination, and has aided me in this work, for which she has my thanks. They had—1, John William, 2, Daniel Webster, 3, Austin Hart, 4, James Royal, 5, Samuel Harris, 6, Eliza Hart, 7, Camillus Hart, 8, Oliver Wolcott, 9, Charles Hart, 10, Charlotte Elizabeth.

FOLEY.

2452.   *Parkersburg, Va.*

HARRIET C. HART, fourth daughter of Major William Hart, of Marietta, Ohio, and his first wife, Sarah Waters (Wolcott), of Wethers-

field, Conn., born March 10th, 1814, at Marietta, Ohio; married
, 1843, James N. Foley, a merchant of Parkersburg, Va. They
have had four daughters, three of whom were living in 1874, viz: 1,
Mrs. Stewart, of Covington, Ky.; 2, Camille Hart; 3, Hattie Hart.
They are all accomplished ladies.

<h3 style="text-align:center">2454. Winchester, Va.</h3>

· MAJOR CAMILLUS SLUMAN HART, Winchester, Va., fourth son of
Major William Hart, of Marietta, Ohio, and his first wife, Sarah Waters (Wolcott), born July 10th, 1823, at Marietta, Ohio, and from the
time he was eight years old was raised at Memphis, Tenn.; married
September 27th, 1865, Joanna B. Krebs, of Winchester, Va., where
they live and keep the hotel in that city, which the visitors at the
Springs patronize largely. He served as major in the Confederate
Army from Manassas to Appomattox. He was a heavy loser both in
friends and means.

THEIR CHILDREN, BEING THE EIGHTH GENERATION.

2773. Camille, born , 1869, at Covington, Ky.
2774. Florence Louisa, born , 1873, at Memphis, Tenn.
2775. Alice Virginia, born , 1874, at Winchester, Va.

<h3 style="text-align:center">2455. Harmar, Ohio.</h3>

JOSIAH THOMAS HART, Harmar, Ohio, fifth son of Major William
Hart, of Marietta, Ohio, and his second wife, Mary (Cass), a cousin of
Governor Lewis Cass, born September 13th, 1827, at Marietta, Ohio;
married November 27th, 1849, Elizabeth A. Harris, born September
12th, 1827. He is a merchant, an architect and builder, a member of
the church, and a good temperance man, and is wealthy.

THEIR CHILDREN, BEING THE EIGHTH GENERATION.

2776. Independence E., born June 17th, 1851; married October 1st, 1872, William
Loffland.
2777. Henrietta Minerva, born November 27th, 1854, at Harmar, Ohio.
2778. Olive Urania, born February 2d, 1856, at Harmar; Ohio.
2779. Josephine Matilda, born December 25th, 1858, at Harmar, Ohio.
2780. Royal Camillus, born May 1st, 1861, at Harmar, Ohio.
2781. Mary Harriet, born August 30th, 1863, at Harmar, Ohio.
2782. Charlotte Irene, born May 6th, 1866, at Harmar, Ohio.

<h3 style="text-align:center">2456. Cincinnati, Ohio.</h3>

CAPTAIN HENRY N. HART, Marietta, Ohio, sixth son of Major William Hart, of Marietta, Ohio, and his second wife, Mary (Cass), cousin
of Governor Lewis Cass, born , at Marietta, Ohio;

married December 5th, 1869, Mary Chambers Skinner, of La Grange, Mo., born August 28th, 1840. In 1874 he was in command of the Steamer Thomas Sherlock, on the Ohio and Mississippi Rivers, with head-quarters at Cincinnati, Ohio.

THEIR CHILDREN, BEING THE EIGHTH GENERATION.
2783. Mary, born July 22d, 1871.
2784. William S., born January 29th, 1873.

BAKER.

2456½.

SARAH HART, Lancaster, Ohio, eldest daughter of Thomas Hart, of Wethersfield, Conn., and Marietta, Ohio, and his wife, Elizabeth (McClelland), born   , at   ; married   , Luman Baker, a cabinet maker, of Lancaster, Ohio.

BORLAND.

2457.   *Lancaster, Ohio.*

CYNTHIA HART, Lancaster, Ohio, second daughter of Thomas Hart, of Wethersfield, Conn., and Marietta, Ohio, and his wife, Elizabeth (McClelland), born   ; married   , Charles Borland, Esq., of Virginia. He lives in Lancaster, Ohio, where he practiced law very successfully for several years, but more recently he has been engaged in railroad enterprises in Ohio and Michigan. They have five children.

2458.   *San Francisco, Cal.*

JESSE BEECHER HART, Esq., San Francisco, Cal., eldest son of Thomas Hart, of Wethersfield, Conn., and Marietta, Ohio, and his wife, Elizabeth (McClelland), of Kentucky, born December 31st, 1812, at Lancaster, Ohio; married May 11th, 1837, Susan Rebu, born in 1817, at Lancaster, Ohio. He is a lawyer by profession, and has an office at No. 330 Pine Street, in the city of San Francisco, Cal. He was admitted to the bar at Lancaster, Ohio, in 1836, and practiced there until 1849, and then removed to California. His wife died September 10th, 1859, when second he married August 1st, 1861, Sallie C. Coleman, of San Francisco, where they now reside.

THEIR CHILDREN, BEING THE EIGHTH GENERATION.
2785. Charles Borland, born January 30th, 1838; married about 1869, Mrs. Spencer, of San Jose, Cal.

John Rebu, born April 9th, 1840, at Lancaster, Ohio; died there, September, 1842.

2786. Thomas, born July 9th, 1842, at Lancaster, Ohio; married   ,
      Miss Woodworth.
2787. Mary, born February 15th, 1845, at Lancaster, Ohio. She is living single
      with her brother, Charles, at Oakland.
      George Rebu, born March 15th, 1847, at Lancaster, Ohio; died at Lancaster,
      September 6th, 1853.
2788. Sallie, born August 30th, 1849, at Lancaster, Ohio.
2789. William, born October 29th, 1856, at Lancaster, Ohio.

SECOND WIFE.

2790. Susan Stambaugh, born September 8th, 1863, at Santa Clara, Cal.
2791. Frances Cornelia, born March 6th, 1868, at Santa Clara, Cal.
2792. Louis Eugene Ritter, born June 20th, 1872, at San Francisco, Cal.

2459.   *Cincinnati, Ohio.*

SAMUEL MCCLELLAND HART, Esq., Cincinnati, Ohio, second son of
Thomas Hart, of Wethersfield, Conn., and Marietta, Ohio, and his wife,
Elizabeth (McClelland), born February 9th, 1814, at Lancaster, Ohio;
married   , Mary E., sister of Hon. George E. Pugh,
member of Congress. He was a lawyer and judge in Cincinnati, and
was killed accidentally on the railroad. His family reside at Cincinnati, Ohio.

THEIR CHILDREN, BEING THE EIGHTH GENERATION.

2460.   *Cincinnati, Ohio.*

WILLIAM MCCLELLAND, Cincinnati, Ohio, third son of Thomas Hart,
of Wethersfield, Conn., and his wife, Elizabeth (McClelland), of Kentucky, born   , at Lancaster, Ohio; married
      , Susan, daughter of Judge Saffin, of Cincinnati, Ohio.
Mr. Hart was a printer by trade, and lived in Cincinnati after he was
twenty-one years of age. He died, July, 1868. His family were living
in Cincinnati in 1874.

THEIR CHILDREN, BEING THE EIGHTH GENERATION.

2461.   *Lancaster, Ohio.*

THOMAS EWING HART, Lancaster, Ohio, fourth son of Thomas Hart, of Wethersfield, Conn., and Marietta, Ohio, and his wife, Elizabeth (McClelland), of Kentucky, born   , at Lancaster, Ohio; married   , Adaline Woods, of Virginia. They had three children.   He was a tinner and coppersmith.   He died   , at Lancaster, Ohio.

THEIR CHILDREN, BEING THE EIGHTH GENERATION.

STAMBAUGH.

2462.   *Lansing, Mich.*

SUSAN CECELIA HART, Lansing, Mich., youngest daughter and child of Thomas Hart, of Wethersfield, Conn., and Marietta, Ohio, and his wife, Elizabeth (McClelland), of Kentucky, born   , 1824, at Lancaster, Ohio; married   , 1844, Samuel C. Stambaugh, of Franklin County, Penn. He was a merchant and banker at Lancaster, where he died, July 9th, 1854, aged 39 years, leaving four children, viz: 1, Charles Borland, born February 19th, 1845. He was first lieutenant in the United States Army, and was killed by Indians in the battle at Wyoming Territory, May 6th, 1870. He was a brave officer, and fell at Atlantic Gulch. The *Cincinnati Commercial* of November 27th, 1870, had an interesting obituary notice of him. 2, Elienor Ewing, born January 14th, 1850. 3, Louis Hart, born May 2d, 1852. 4, Samuel Augustus Daugherty, born August 5th, 1854, at Lancaster, Fairfield County, Ohio.

2463.   *New Britain, Conn.*

BENJAMIN KELLOGG HART, Kensington and New Britain, Conn., eldest son of Benjamin Hart, of New Britain and Kensington, and his wife, Hannah, daughter of Martin Kellogg, of Newington, born January 7th, 1801, at Kensington; married at Southington, Conn., before Rev. David L. Ogden, April 22d, 1824, Olivia, daughter of Thomas Cowles, of Southington, and his second wife, Tamar (Hitchcock), born May 15th, 1802, at Southington. He is a farmer by occupation, and built himself a house just south of Moore's Mills, in Kensington, on land belonging to his father's farm. He sold and removed to Hart Quarter in New Britain, and bought on the corner of Camp Street and Park Avenue, in the city, worth some $8,000.

THEIR CHILDREN, BEING THE EIGHTH GENERATION.

Hannah Kellogg, born August 18th, 1825, at New Jersey.

Nancy Cowles, born July 8th, 1827; died Nov. 22d, 1828, aged 16 months.

2793. William Cowles, born July 30th, 1829; married February 18th, 1873, Eleanor Medora Porter.

Olivia, born September 5th, 1831; died November 15th, 1860, at Kensington, and was buried there.

Adaline, born June 25th, 1833; died February 1st, 1853, aged 19 years.

Lucinda A., born February 1st, 1836; died Feb. 5th, 1859, aged 23 years.

2794. Thomas Kellogg, born April 30th, 1838. He was single in 1871.

2464. *Kensington, Conn.*

THOMAS ROBBINS HART, Kensington, Conn., second son of Benjamin Hart, of New Britain and Kensington, Conn., and his wife, Hannah (Robbins), born August 27th, 1802, at Kensington, Conn.; married December 18th, 1836, Cecelia Bemont, daughter of Joseph, and his wife, Lois (Bacon), of Middletown, Conn., born March 20th, 1817, at Middletown, Conn. He is a farmer, and resides just west of Kensington Church, on the west side of the north and south road, on the old farm and place of Captain Norman Winchell, deceased.

THEIR CHILDREN, BEING THE EIGHTH GENERATION.

2795. Harriet S., born September 2d, 1837; married March 14th, 1860, Adna Woodruff.

2796. Walter Scott, born February 4th, 1840; married June 21st, 1863, Helen Thalia Welch.

2797. Benjamin Franklin, born February 27th, 1842; married September 27th, 1866, Elizabeth Parsons.

2798. George Washington, born October 11th, 1844; married November 18th, 1865, Alice Deming.

2799. Samuel James, born March 28th, 1849.

Nellie Celia, born February 14th, 1856.

2465. *Freehold, N. J.*

WALTER WARD HART, Freehold, Monmouth County, N. J., third and youngest son of Benjamin Hart, of New Britain and Kensington, Conn., and his wife, Hannah (Kellogg), daughter of Martin, of Newington, born November 17th, 1804, at Berlin, Conn.; married May 28th, 1829, Sarah, daughter of William Bennett, and his wife, Jane (Jefferson), born October 11th, 1801, at Freehold, N. J. He was a goldsmith by trade, which he learned of Jacob Sargeant, of Hartford, and was a man of much promise. He carried on the business of his trade, and at the same time cultivated a farm. He held the position of judge of the court of common pleas of the county of Monmouth during his residence at Freehold. He subsequently opened, at Philadelphia, a factory for making spoons according to an improved method, which he had patented. After a few years of success he became embarrassed, and failed. He became partially insane, and died at the Retreat for the Insane at Brattleboro, Vt., April 21st, 1868, aged 64 years, and was buried at Freehold, N. J., on the 24th of the same month.

THEIR CHILDREN, BEING THE EIGHTH GENERATION.

2800. Jane Ann, born April 30th, 1830; married September 28th, 1852, David Mills Rue.

William Bennett, born August 24th, 1832; died August 10th, 1833, aged 1 year.

2801. Emily Augusta, born September 29th, 1835; married June 12th, 1856, Solomon Brock.

2802. Charles Edward, born February 28th, 1838. He graduated at Princeton College.

2803. Evelina McLean, born January 28th, 1841; married June 9th, 1869, John Fressales Mount.

CAMP.

2466.   *New Britain, Conn.*

SABRINA ABIA HART, New Britain, Conn., eldest daughter of Theron Hart, of the same place, and his wife, Abiah (Warner), born , 1817, at New Britain; married January 18th, 1844, Curtiss Coe Camp, a wealthy farmer of New Britain. His residence is on Arch Street, and he is a member of the Methodist Church. She had one son, and died September 6th, 1846, aged 29 years, when second he married her sister, Mary, born April 1st, 1823, at New Britain; married January 13th, 1848, who had one son, and died January 4th, 1861, aged 39 years. The child of Sabrina, Theron Hart, was born March 1st, 1845; married December 1st, 1870, Nora Veits. The child of Mary, Waldo, was born April 7th, 1852; married November 2d, 1870, Fannie Webster.

VIETS.

2468.   *New Britain, Conn.*

JULIAETTA ANDREWS HART, New Britain, Conn., eldest daughter of Cyrus Hart, of the same place, and his wife, Betsey (Clark), born May 20th, 1820, at New Britain; married June 27th, 1838, Imlay Bird Viets, son of John, of Granby, and his wife, Abigail (Eno), born December 19th, 1808. He is a farmer, and resides with his father-in-law, who has a beautiful residence on the corner of Arch Street and Hart Avenue. She died in Granby, February 23d, 1842, aged 22, when he second married her sister, Angeline Clark Hart, born July 11th, 1822, and married June 27th, 1843. She was admitted to the Congregational Church, April, 1841. They had—1, Mary Adelia, born March 10th, 1847; married March 10th, 1875, by Rev. J. H. Denison, in the Centre Church, New Britain, Charles A. Blair, of Lebanon, Madison County, N. Y., born October 5th, 1844. He was educated at Genesee College, New York, and trained as a clerk for a merchant. Their residence is at Milford, Kent County, Del. 2, Eleanora Juliaetta, born July 22d, 1849; married December 1st, 1870, Theron Hart Camp, of New Britain, and had—1, Florence Angie, born March 6th, 1872; 2, Mortimer Hart, born August 21st, 1874.

2470. *Albion, N. Y.*

WILLIAM HART, Albion, Orleans County, N. Y., eldest son of Joseph, of New Britain, Conn., and New Durham, N. Y., and his wife, Lucy (Kirtland), of Saybrook, Conn., born February 23d, 1801, at Durham, Green County, N. Y.; married September 23d, 1834, Pamelia Wells, of Wethersfield, Conn., who died January 25th, 1864.. He was living in 1872 with his son, on a portion of the land which his father bought of the Holland Company in 1812.

THEIR CHILD, BEING THE EIGHTH GENERATION.

2804. John Wells, born, September, 1836, at Albion, N. Y.

2471. *Albion, N. Y.*

ELIZUR HART, Albion, Orleans County, N. Y., second son of Joseph, of New Britain, Conn., and New Durham, N. Y., and his wife, Lucy (Kirtland), born May 23d, 1803, at Durham, Green County, N. Y.; married June 11th, 1834, Loraine Field, of Albion, N. Y., who died February 11th, 1843, when he second married ', 1846. Cornelia Ann King, of Jonesville, N. Y. Previous to his second marriage he started the Orleans County National Bank, of which he was president and the principal stockholder. He was a straight forward business man, liberal with his means during life, and at his death, which occurred at Jonesville, August 13th, 1870, he gave to the Presbyterian Church of Albion, of which he was a member, $50,000 to build a stone church, and giving directions how it should be built; $5,000 as a sinking fund, the interest to be used for the benefit of the Sabbath School, and $2,000, the interest of which was to be expended for missionary purposes at the west.

THEIR CHILDREN, BEING THE EIGHTH GENERATION.

2805. Frances Ellen, born , 1835, at Albion, N. Y.
2806. Jane King, born , 1837, at Albion, N. Y.
2807. Elizur Kirtland, born , 1839, at Albion, N. Y.
Henry Martin, born , 1841; died in his second year.

2472. *Louisville, Ky.*

JOHN J. HART, Louisville, Ky., third son of Joseph, of New Britain, Conn., and New Durham, N. Y., and his wife, Lucy (Kirtland), of Saybrook, Conn., born April 8th, 1805, at Durham, N. Y. He printed and published the *Louisville Journal-Courier* in Louisville. He was never married. He died at Jackson, Mich., on his way to Adrian, May 24th, 1868, aged 63 years, saying "He could trust his mother's Saviour."

2473. *Alton, Ill.*

DOCTOR BENJAMIN KIRTLAND HART, Alton, Ill., fourth son of Joseph, of New Britain, Conn., and New Durham, N. Y., and his wife, Lucy (Kirtland), born July 2d, 1807, at Seneca, Ontario County, N. Y. He was educated at Boston, where he received his diploma, and studied medicine at Henrietta and Middlebury, N. Y. He traveled in the west, and after six months prospecting located at Alton, Ill., then a town only thirteen months old, nailed his tin to the wall, and in July, 1832, wrote to his brother: "I am going to try my luck among the active mass of mankind, and I assure you I shall not give up the ship until disease or age incapacitates me from walking with a firm step on its deck." He married, November, 1839, Sophia E. Mix, of New Orleans. He was a skillful physician and surgeon, and accumulated a handsome property. He was very benevolent, having educated many young men and women to fill useful places in society. He was an elder in the Presbyterian Church, and the right hand man of his pastor. After some thirty years practice, his health beginning to fail him, he started for the seaside with his family, and got as far as his sister's, at Adrian, where he died, August 30th, 1864, aged 57 years. A sermon was preached at his funeral entitled "The Beloved Physician," from the text—"For me to live is Christ, to die is gain." His widow was living in 1871, at Alton, Ill.

THEIR CHILDREN, BEING THE EIGHTH GENERATION.

2808. Lucy Maria, born
2809. Charles Kirtland, born   ; died July 24th, 1854, aged 10 years.
2810. Sophia, born

ROODE.

2474. *Rome, Mich.*

LOVISA LORD HART, eldest daughter of Joseph, of New Britain, Conn., and New Durham, N. Y., and his wife, Lucy (Kirtland), of Saybrook, Conn., born April 27th, 1811, at Seneca, Ontario County,

N. Y.; married September 3d, 1833, Orange Martin Roode. They have one child, Bertrand Elizur, born December 21st, 1835, at Rome, Mich., married October 5th, 1871, Eli B. Moffitt. The parents and daughter are members of the Presbyterian Church.

BERRY.
2475. *Adrian, Mich.*

LUCY KIRTLAND HART, Adrian, Mich., second daughter of Joseph, of New Britain, Conn., and New Durham, N. Y., and his wife, Lucy (Kirtland), of Saybrook, Conn., born January 22d, 1814, at Albion, Orleans County, N. Y., being the first child born in the county; married August 19th, 1839, Ambrose Spencer Berry, of Adrian, Lenawee County, Mich. He is a dealer in real estate, and both are members of the Presbyterian Church.

BERRY.
2476. *Adrian, Mich.*

MARY ANN HART, Adrian, Mich., third daughter of Joseph Hart, of New Britain, Conn., and New Durham, N. Y., and his wife, Lucy (Kirtland), of Saybrook, Conn., born June 2d, 1817, at Albion, Orleans County, N. Y.; married, September, 1841, Langford Green Berry, of Adrian, only brother of A. S. Berry, who married her sister, Lucy. She died May 8th, 1849, aged 32 years. Some twenty-four hours before her death she called for her son and daughter, laid her emaciated hands upon their heads and gave them her parting blessing, and also gave them to a covenant-keeping God, and then said, "Take them away." She then sang—

"Jesus can make a dying bed,
Feel soft as downy pillows are"—

and sweetly passed away. Their children are—1, Benjamin Hart, born August 20th, 1842, at Adrian, Mich. He enlisted in the Twentieth Regiment Michigan Volunteers, and was at the seige of Knoxville, in the battle of the Wilderness, at the surrender of Vicksburg, and was taken prisoner, but escaped, and was promoted to captain. His health failed and he was sent to the hospital, but subsequently was honorably discharged. 2, Emily Alice, born March 19th, 1845; married December 25th, 1868, Scyler F. Segar, a lawyer of Lansing, Mich. 3, Mary Hart, born February 6th, 1849; died January 26th, 1863.

2477. *Seneca, N. Y.*

JOSEPH SMITH HART, sixth son of Joseph Hart, and his wife, Lucy (Kirtland), of Saybrook, born February 2d, 1820, at Albion, N. Y.;

married in 1861, Harriet Cole, of Barre, N. Y. He and his brother, William, owned, in 1872, the section of land their father bought of the Holland Company in 1812. Instead of a wilderness as it then was, it was beautiful to look upon for situation in 1874.

THEIR CHILDREN, BEING THE EIGHTH GENERATION.

2811. Lucy Kirtland, born
2812. Alice Josephine, born
2813. Harriet Cole, born
2814. Jennie Snow, born

2478.   *Adrian, Mich.*

SAMUEL ELLIS HART, Adrian, Mich., youngest child of Joseph Hart, of New Britain, Conn., and New Durham, N. Y., and his wife, Lucy (Kirtland), of Saybrook, Conn., born August 13th, 1823, at Albion, Orleans County, N. Y. He went to Adrian, May, 1840, and married October 7th, 1852, Anna D. Crissey, of Astoria, L. I., daughter of Ebenezer A., and his wife, Dolly Ann (Barnes), born April 6th, 1835, at Buffalo, N. Y. In 1872 he was residing at Adrian, Mich., where he carried on a successful business as druggist, and was an elder in the Presbyterian Church. He obtained a divorce from his wife about 1868, when second he married March 11th, 1872, Hattie A. King, of Palmyra, N. Y., widow of Marvin S. King, and daughter of Thomas Galloway, and his wife, Azuba (Gifford), born May 20th, 1841, at Palmyra, N. Y. She first married November 19th, 1863, Marvin S. King, who died March 14th, 1865.

CHILDREN BY HIS FIRST WIFE, BEING THE EIGHTH GENERATION.

2815. Otho Spencer, born January 9th, 1856, at Adrian, Mich.
2816. Kate Elizabeth, born August 21st, 1861, at Adrian, Mich.

THAYER.

2479.   *Ann Arbor, Mich.*

MARY ANN HART, Ann Arbor, Mich., eldest daughter of Doctor Luther W. Hart, of Marshall, Calhoun County, Mich., and his wife, Sibil Selden, born February 16th, 1807, at Durham, Green County, N. Y.; married there May 17th, 1825, Charles Thayer, and removed immediately to Ann Arbor, Washtenaw County, Mich., where they resided in 1872. She united with the Presbyterian Church at Ann Arbor. They had one child, Delia Hart, born in 1826, died   , aged 11 years.

PARMELEE.

2480. *Marshall, Mich.*

DELIA SELDEN HART, Ann Arbor, Mich., second daughter of Doctor Luther W., of Marshall, Mich., and his wife, Sibil (Selden), born January 26th, 1811, at Durham, N. Y.; married at Marshall, Calhoun County, Mich., August 26th, 1834, Abner C. Parmelee. She was a member of the Presbyterian Church at Durham, N. Y. She died at Ann Arbor, April, 1851, aged 40 years. Their children were—1, Emily Brace, born, August, 1835, at Buffalo, N. Y., died, June, 1848, aged 2 years; 2, Delia Thayer, born, April, 1837, at Marshall, Mich., married there, May, 1861, H. E. Phelps.

HAYS.

2481. *Marshall, Mich.*

CLARISSA SELDEN HART, Marshall, Mich., third daughter of Dr. Luther W., and his wife, Sibil (Selden), born April 5th, 1814, at Durham, Green County, N. Y.; married at Ann Arbor, Washtenaw County, Mich., Andrew L. Hayes, and in 1831 removed to Marshall, Mich., where she remained until 1866, when she removed to Clinton, Iowa, where she was residing in 1873, and was a member of the Presbyterian Church. Their children were—1, Luther Hart, born January 7th, 1832, at Marshall, Mich., died there October 16th, 1848, aged 16 years; 2, Sara Thompson, born January 15th, 1835, at Marshall, Mich., married there, May, 1858, P. S. Schuyler; 3, Walter Ingals, born December 9th, 1841, married Francis L. Coon, a lawyer of Clinton, Iowa, where they now reside.

GORHAM.

2482. *Marshall, Mich.*

CHARLOTTE EATON HART, Marshall, Mich., fourth daughter of Dr. Luther W. Hart, of the same town, and his wife, Sibil (Selden), born September 6th, 1820. at Durham, Green County, N. Y.; married at Marshall, April 10th, 1839, Charles T. Gorham, a banker. Her home is still in Marshall, but she is at present in Europe, her husband being United States Minister at the Hague, Netherlands, in 1872. She is a member of the Presbyterian Church. Their children are—1, Selden Hart, born, June, 1840; married Lizzie Dwight, of Jackson, Mich. He served in the late war as major in the Second Michigan Cavalry, and later as lieutenant-colonel. 2, Isabella Wilbur, born October 18th, 1848; married Norris S. Frink. 3, Charles Edward, born September 5th, 1855, in Marshall. He was in Europe in 1872, at school in Brussels.

PARTRIDGE.

2484.   *Elmira, N. Y.*

EMMA GOODRICH HART, eldest daughter of Dr. Erastus Langdon Hart, of Elmira, N. Y., and his first wife, Mary (Parmelee), born July 12th, 1811, at Wolcott, Conn.; married September 21st, 1842, at Elmira, Chemung County, N. Y., Hon. Samuel Partridge, born November 29th, 1795, at Norwich, Windsor County, Vt. He is a merchant, and was a member of Congress in 1840. They have no children.

THURSTON.

2485.   *Elmira, N. Y.*

JULIA CLARK HART, second daughter of Dr. Erastus Langdon Hart, and his first wife, Mary (Parmelee), born July 6th, 1813, at Goshen, Conn.; married September 8th, 1836, at Elmira, Chemung County, N. Y., Ariel Standish Thurston, who was born June 11th, 1810, at Goffstown, N. H. He is a lawyer in Elmira. She died at Elmira, April 17th, 1844, aged 31. Their children are—1, Theodore, born April 9th, 1838, died August 14th, 1839; 2, Mary Parmelee, born July 20th, 1840, married November 19th, 1862, Curtiss C. Gardner, of Elmira; 3, Clara Standish, born November 3d, 1842, married October 9th, 1867, Henry White Strang, of Elmira.

2487.   *Elmira, N. Y.*

WILLIAM ELIZUR HART, Elmira, Chemung County, N. Y., eldest son of Dr. Erastus Langdon Hart, of Goshen, Conn., and subsequently of Elmira, N. Y., and his first wife, Mary (Parmelee), of Goshen, Conn., born September 26th, 1817, at Goshen, Conn.; married September 3d, 1844, at Angelica, Allegany County, N. Y., Elizabeth Morse Hull, born November 1st, 1823. She died July 20th, 1855, aged 32 years, when he second married at Earlville, N. Y., November 25th, 1856, Delia A. Case, born December 28th, 1827, at Smyrna, Chenango County, N. Y. He is a merchant.

THEIR CHILDREN, BEING THE EIGHTH GENERATION.

2817. Alice Elizabeth, born October 17th, 1845; married January 9th, 1868, Seward A. Gould.

Frederic Hull, born December 17th, 1850; died March 18th, 1864.

2818. Frank Parmalee, born June 2d, 1852.

CHILD BY HIS SECOND WIFE.

2819. William Case, born October 24th, 1857, at Elmira, N. Y.

2488. *Elmira, N. Y.*

ERASTUS PARMELEE HART, Esq., Elmira, Chemung County, N. Y., second son of Dr. Erastus Langdon Hart, of the same town, and his first wife, Mary (Parmelee), born May 6th, 1822, at Goshen, Conn.; married January 6th, 1846, at Havana, N. Y., Eliza Haight, born March 5th, 1825, at Canaan, N. Y. He is a lawyer.

THEIR CHILDREN, BEING THE NINTH GENERATION.

2820. Emma, born October 22d, 1846; married January 12th, 1871, D. J. Scott.
2821. Erastus Langdon, born May 24th, 1851.
2822. Hattie, born April 14th, 1854, at Elmira, N. Y.

PARTRIDGE.

2489.

MARY PARMELEE HART, fourth daughter of Dr. Erastus Langdon Hart, of Goshen, Conn., and Elmira, N. Y., and his first wife, Mary (Parmelee), of Goshen, Conn., born March 12th, 1825, at Elmira, Tioga County, N. Y., and later Chemung County; married August 8th, 1843, at Elmira, N. Y., Henry Norton Partridge, born April 20th, 1820, at Norwich, Windsor County, Vt. He is a lumber merchant. Their children are—1, Henry F., born June 15th, 1844, died August 18th, 1848; 2, Julia Hart, born August 23d, 1846, married August 23d, 1869, Eugene Devin; 3, Hetty Few, born May 17th, 1848, died April 7th, 1849; 4, Robert, born August 10th, 1850, died October 12th, 1850; 5, Mary Parmelee, born October 10th, 1852; 6, Sarah Elizabeth, born July 8th, 1854; 7, Edward Langdon, born March 21st, 1856, died September 14th, 1859; 8, Charles Royal, born October 1st, 1859; 9, Samuel, born January 16th, 1861, died April 9th, 1861; 10, Louisa Loveland, born May 19th, 1862; 11, Florence Lee, born September 2d, 1868.

JARVIS.

2491. *Middletown, Conn.*

ELIZABETH MILLER HART, Hartford, eldest daughter of Colonel Richard William Hart, of that city, and his wife, Elizabeth (Bull), of Newport, born June 26th, 1798, at Hartford; married December 22d, 1825, Rev. William Jarvis, son of Hezekiah, of Norwalk, Conn., born February 29th, 1796, and was eight years old before he had a birthday. He is a presbyter of the Protestant Episcopal Church, but having lost the use of his voice from bronchitis in the early years of his ministry, he has not been able to do any professional work for many years. His health in July, 1871, was very infirm. Of their nine children two sons

67

and two daughters died under twelve years of age, and one son died at twenty-nine years of age.

2493. *Saybrook, Conn.*

HENRY HART, Saybrook, Conn., only son of Samuel Hart, of the same town, and his wife, Mercy (Pratt), born August 16th, 1815, at Saybrook, Conn.; married November 17th, 1836, Mary Ann Welton, of Norwich, Conn., where she was born, October 17th, 1816.

THEIR CHILDREN, BEING THE EIGHTH GENERATION.

Harriet, born September 15th, 1842; died September 23d, 1842.
2823. Samuel, born June 4th, 1845.
2824. George, born April 30th, 1848.
2825. Elizabeth, born May 23d, 1854.

WARNER.

2496. *New Haven, Conn.*

ANN ELIZABETH HART, New Haven, Conn., eldest daughter of John Hart, of Lyme, Conn., and his wife, Nancy (Mather), of Old Lyme, where she was born, June 17th, 1814; married October 8th, 1833, Rev. Willys Warner, of New Haven, Conn., for many years the treasurer of Yale College.

2497. *Cleveland, Ohio.*

JOHN ALEXANDER HART, Greenport, L. I., second son of John Hart, of Lyme, Conn., and his wife, Nancy (Mather), born July 5th, 1816, at Lyme, Conn.; married May 7th, 1839, Louisa Edgerton, of New London, Conn., daughter of James, Jr., and his wife, Charlotte (Wilson), born February 27th, 1817, at New London, Conn. They were at No. 249 Perry Street, Cleveland, Ohio, in 1874, and he was in the coal mining business.

THEIR CHILDREN, BEING THE EIGHTH GENERATION.

2826. William Henry, born July 27th, 1840; married December 5th, 1864, Alice Martin.
2827. Mortimer Edgerton, born September 5th, 1844; married November 23d, 1868, Alice J. McCurdy.
2828. Edward Learned, born May 3d, 1848; married November 3d, 1870, Anna Sullivan.
2829. Nannie Louise, born June 11th, 1853. She is a noted songstress, and was single in 1874.

WHITTLESEY.

2498. *New Britain, Conn.*

LOUISA ELY HART, New Haven, Conn., second daughter of John Hart, of Lyme, and his first wife, Nancy (Mather), born September 10th, 1832, at Lyme, Conn.; married September 9th, 1845, Rev. William Whittlesey, eldest son of Deacon David, of New Britain, Conn., and his wife, Rebecca (Smalley), born September 19th, 1805, at New Britain, Conn., where he was admitted to the church, October 7th, 1821. He graduated at Yale College in 1827, and was ordained to the ministry in 1837. He was a Sunday School Missionary at the west, preached in various places, and was a teacher in several localities. He built near his father in New Britain, but sold, and was living at New Haven in 1874. She was admitted to the church in New Britain, October 8th, 1854, by letter from the Chapel Street Church, New Haven. She is an intelligent and well educated woman. They have one child, Louise Hart, born May 23d, 1847, at New Haven. She was admitted to the Congregational Church in New Britain, June 6th, 1858, and is living single with her parents at New Haven in 1875.

2500. *Clinton, N. Y.*

LEWIS HENRY HART, Clinton, N. Y., second son of John Hart, the merchant, of Lyme, Conn., and Clinton, N. Y., and his second wife, Margaret, daughter of Thomas Sill, of Lyme, Conn., born June 7th, 1846, at Lyme, Conn.; married at Utica, N. Y., before Rev. Dr. Correy, Miss Mary Williams, of Utica, N. Y., March 18th, 1874. He is a dry goods merchant in Clinton, N. Y.

2504. *Edinburgh, Ohio.*

CHARLES RICHARD HART, Edinburgh, Ohio, only son of Richard Morison Hart, of the same town, and his first wife, Betsey (Ingham), daughter of William, of Saybrook, Conn., born February 16th, 1825, at Edinburgh, Portage County, Ohio; married, August, 1836, Lorinda R. Davis, of the same place, where he followed farming. He was a soldier in the late war, in Company F, Ohio Volunteer Infantry. He died at his home in Portage County, April 25th, 1862, aged 37. His widow and children were residing there in 1874. He was a member of a masonic lodge, who attended his funeral, and followed him to his grave in Ravenna, Ohio.

THEIR CHILDREN, BEING THE EIGHTH GENERATION.

2830. Mary Louisa, born February 25th, 1856.
2831. Annie Averill, born April 7th, 1859.
2832. Charles Richard, born August 29th, 1861.

2505. *Saybrook, Conn.*

HENRY SILL HART, New York City, eldest son of Charles Edward Hart, of Clinton, N. Y., and his wife, Phebe Mather (Sill), of Lyme, daughter of Captain Thomas, and his wife, Mehitabel (Mather), born May 4th, 1827, at East Haddam, Conn.; married June 18th, 1850, at Auburn, N. Y., Mary Eliza Clark, daughter of Silas, born February 23d, 1828, at Watertown, N. Y. He is a dry goods merchant in New York City, and they live in Saybrook, Conn.

THEIR CHILDREN, BEING THE EIGHTH GENERATION.

2833. Mary Williams, born June 12th, 1851; married April 4th, 1870, Thomas B. Doane.
2834. Annie Sill, born December 25th, 1853, in Brooklyn, N. Y.
2835. Amelia Sheffield, born June 25th, 1855, in New York City.
    Lilie, born July 13th, 1856, in New York City; died August 17th, 1856.
2836. Richard Bushnel, born July 11th, 1860, in Saybrook, Conn.
2837. Cornelia Martin, born January 13th, 1867, in Saybrook, Conn.

2506. *Clinton, N. Y.*

RICHARD MORRISON HART, Clinton, N. Y., second son of Charles Edward Hart, and his wife, Phebe Mather (Sill), born March 6th, 1829, at Newark, N. J.; married in 1860, at Kirtland, N. Y., Ruth Morrison Gleason. She died there in 1867, when second he married at Clinton, N. Y., November 4th, 1869, Jeannette Adelphi Brooks. Mr. Hart was a farmer at Clinton, Oneida County, N. Y., in 1874.

THEIR CHILDREN, BEING THE EIGHTH GENERATION.

2838. Henry Norton, born, November, 1861, in Kirtland, N. Y.
2839. Jennie Gertrude, born, April, 1864, in Kirtland, N. Y.

CHILD BY HIS SECOND WIFE.

Sarah Lillian, born   , 1871; died September 5th, 1872, in Clinton, N. Y.

PERKINS. BRADLEY.

2507.

SARAH MEHITABEL HART, Clinton, N. Y., eldest daughter of Charles Edward Hart, of the same place, and his wife, Phebe Mather (Sill), born December 23d, 1832, in Marlboro, Conn.; married in Clinton, N. Y., June 1st, 1864, Sherlock William Perkins, a merchant of Cazenovia, N. Y., who died there, August 16th, 1865, leaving no issue, when second she married October 22d, 1867, in Clinton, N. Y., Nelson Bradley, a merchant of New York City.

THEIR CHILDREN, BEING THE EIGHTH GENERATION.

Clinton Hart, born February 15th, 1870, in Clinton, N. Y.
Child, born August 9th, 1873, in Clinton, N. Y.

2509.   *Middletown, Hartford, Conn.*

JOSEPH AUSTIN HART, Middletown, Conn., eldest son of Ferdinand Austin Hart, and his wife, Sarah (Cook), born April 2d, 1824, in Hartford, Conn.; married in 1844, Clarissa Hubbard, daughter of Sylvester, and his wife, Clarissa (Smith). He died July 11th, 1860, aged 36 years, 3 months, 9 days, and his widow was residing in Hartford in 1874.

THEIR CHILDREN, BEING THE EIGHTH GENERATION.

2840. William Henry, born November 30th, 1844; married   ,
       Isabella J. Weildon.
2841. Ferdinand Austin, born August 30th, 1846, in Middletown, Conn.; married
       December 10th, 1874, in Christ Church, Hartford, Conn., Miss Emma
       Tomlinson, of that city. He is an insurance agent.

2512½.   *Guilford, Conn.*

WILLIAM HENRY HART, Guilford, Conn., eldest son of Colonel William Hart, of the same town, and his first wife, Lydia (Griffing), born November 28th, 1818, at Guilford, Conn.; married November 13th, 1842, Maria H. Griffing, daughter of William H. He died March 19th, 1851, aged 34 years.

LYMAN.

2513.   *Middlefield, Conn.*

CATHARINE ELIZABETH HART, Middlefield, Conn., fourth daughter of Colonel William Hart, of Guilford, Conn., and his second wife, Catharine (Starr), born May 9th, 1826, at Guilford, Conn.; married there January 30th, 1849, David Lyman, of Middlefield, a great farmer and an extensive manufacturer. He was the moving spirit in putting through the Air Line Railroad, which probably hastened his premature end. He died at his home, January 24th, 1871, aged 50 years. He was a man widely known and highly esteemed, and his death was greatly lamented. Their children were—Mary Elizabeth, born December 2d, 1850; Harriet Augusta, born September 9th, 1852; William, born May 3d, 1854; Henry, born March 3d, 1856; Charles Elihu, born November 3d, 1857; John, born September 1st, 1860; James, born September 1st, 1862; Adaline, born September 24th, 1864; David, born April 6th, 1867.

2514.   *Guilford, Conn.*

RICHARD EDWIN HART, Guilford, second son of Colonel William Hart, of Guilford, and his second wife, Catharine (Starr), born April 24th, 1828, in Guilford; married November 28th, 1854, Jane Soper.

2842. William Henry, born December 13th, 1855.
2843. Edward Soper, born March 31st, 1857.
  Catharine Starr, born November 2d, 1859; died February 17th, 1864, aged 5 years.
  Alice Bernard, born February 18th, 1861; died April 20th, 1862, aged 1 year.
  Wallace Coan, born February 17th, 1863; died May 1st, 1863.
  Thomas, born

COLTON.

2515.   *Galesburg, Ill.*

LYDIA GRIFFING HART, Galesburg, Ill., fifth daughter of Colonel William Hart, of Guilford, Conn., and his second wife, Catharine (Starr), born April 3d, 1832, in Guilford, Conn.; married September 23d, 1864, G. D. Colton, of Galesburg, Ill. She died August 27th, 1868, 36 years, 4 months, and 24 days.

DENISON.

2516.   *Middlefield, Conn.*

HARRIET LAVINIA HART, Middlefield, Conn., sixth daughter of Colonel William Hart, of Guilford, Conn., and his second wife, Catharine (Starr), born July 22d, 1837, at Guilford, Conn.; married September 22d, 1869, at Middlefield, Conn., Rev. Andrew C. Denison, stated pastor of the Congregational Church at that place in 1874. He graduated at Yale College in 1847, and was located for several years at Portland, Conn. She was his third wife. They had a daughter, Catharine Mabel, born December 8th, 1870, died February 15th, 1872, and a son, William, born October 6th, 1873.

2519.   *Chicago, Ill.*

HENRY THOMAS HART, Guilford, Conn., second son of George Hart, of the same town, and his wife, Clarissa (Parmelee), daughter of David, born February 18th, 1827, at Guilford, Conn.; married 1848, Elizabeth Babcock, of New Haven, Conn. Their residence in 1874 was in Chicago, Ill., where their last children on the following list were born:

  Elizabeth, born June 9th, 1849; died
2844. Henry, born November 3d, 1851.
2845. Clara, born November 24th, 1853.
2846. Mary Babcock, born February 7th, 1856.

2520. *Guilford, Conn.*

GEORGE BENJAMIN HART, Guilford, Conn., third son of George Hart, of the same town, and his wife, Clarissa (Parmelee), born April 21st, 1831, at Guilford, Conn.; married September 14th, 1853, Harriet R. Wildman, of Danbury, Conn., who died May 2d, 1857.

THEIR CHILDREN, BEING THE EIGHTH GENERATION.

2847. Fanny Rebecca, born December 25th, 1855.
2848. David Wildman, born January 31st, 1857.

2534. *Milwaukee, Wis.*

STEPHEN PIERCE HART, Berlin, Conn., eldest son of Submit Hart, of the same town, and his wife, Mary (Cone), born, January, 1836, at Berlin, Conn.; married July 3d, 1858, Adelia Qualters, of Boston. He enlisted at Portland, Maine, in the Seventeenth Regiment Maine Volunteers, in the late war, and was wounded at the battle of Gettysburg, July 2d, 1863. He never asked a pension. In 1865 he was in the Invalid Corps at Indianapolis, Ind. In 1874 he was in a britannia and silver ware factory at Milwaukee, Wis., at work at his trade.

THEIR CHILDREN, BEING THE EIGHTH GENERATION.

Nellie Adelaide, born August 11th, 1860, at Dorchester, Mass.; died November 17th, 1861, in Westbrook, Maine.
Charles Elmer, born February 22d, 1863, in Westbrook, Maine. He lives in Aurora, Ill.
Nelly Qualters, born about 1868, an adopted daughter of his wife's brother.

PENDLETON.

2536. *Henry, Ill.*

ELIZABETH LAMONT HART, Goshen, Conn., eldest daughter of Deacon Henry Hart, of Goshen, Conn., and his wife, Annie Elizabeth (Street), born December 1st, 1809, in Goshen, Conn.; married in 1838, Rev. Henry D. Pendleton, of Cornwall, Conn., who was preaching in Illinois in 1874. She died of consumption, in Henry, Ill., February, 1850, in her 41st year. They had children, viz: 1, William Henry, born March 7th, 1840, died January 29th, 1842; 2, Lucretia Ann, born October 1st, 1844, and died the same day; 3, Ann Lucretia, born April 16th, 1848; died, May, 1851.

2537. *Farmington, Ill.*

WILLIAM HART, Goshen, Conn., eldest son of Deacon Henry Hart, of that town, and Farmington, Fulton County, Ill., and his wife, Ann

Elizabeth, daughter of Samuel D. Street, of Goshen, Conn., born
April 1st, 1811, at Goshen; married   , Adaline
Candee, of Farmington, Fulton County, Ill.

THEIR CHILDREN, BEING THE NINTH GENERATION.

THOMAS.

2538.   *Mt. Desert, Maine.*

MARY HART, Mt. Desert, Maine, second daughter of Deacon Henry
Hart, of Goshen, Conn., and subsequently of Farmington, Fulton
County, Ill., and his wife, Ann Elizabeth, daughter of Samuel D.
Street, of Goshen, Conn., where she was born, October 3d, 1813;
married   , Amos D. Thomas, of Mt. Desert, Maine.

WRIGHT.

2539.   *Hanover, N. H.*

CATHARINE HART, Canton, Ill., third daughter of Deacon Henry
Hart, of Goshen, Conn., and his wife, Ann Elizabeth, daughter of
Samuel D. Street, of Goshen, Conn., where she was born, April 15th,
1815; married June 7th, 1837, John Wright, of Hanover, N. H. He
settled at Canton, Ill., where he was a farmer, and deacon of a Congregational Church. Their children were—1, Royal H., born in 1839,
married Violetta Fulton; 2, Chester, born in 1841; 3, James, born in
1842; 4, Julia, born in 1845; 5, Charles, born in 1846; 6, Asher, born
in 1848; 7, Franklin C., born in 1852; 8, Frederic F., born in 1856.
The second and third sons died in infancy, and all the others, except
one, are members of the Congregational Church.

WRIGHT.

2540.   *Burlington, Kan.*

MINERVA HART, Goshen, Conn., fourth daughter of Deacon Henry
Hart, of Goshen, Conn., and subsequently of Farmington, Fulton
County, Ill., and his wife, Ann Elizabeth, daughter of Samuel D.
Street, of Goshen, Conn., where she was born, October 5th, 1816;
married April 30th, 1840, Rev. Samuel Guild Wright, of Hanover,
N. H., born December 26th, 1809. In 1874 he was stated preacher
and acting pastor of the Congregational Church at Burlington, Coffey
County, Kan. Since his marriage he has been in active labor as a Con-
gregational minister in Taulon, Galva, and Neponset, Ill., and other
places, some of the time as a home missionary. Their children were

—1, Eliza Maria, born July 21st, 1841; married August 25th, 1866, Henry F. Knapp, of New York. He graduated at Adrian, Mich., and was a teacher. 2, Minerva, born January 2d, 1843; married January 4th, 1864, Captain Henry H. Bush, of New York. 3, Mary, born September 15th, 1844; died July 19th, 1845. 4, Mary Page, born February 17th, 1848. 5, Samuel Frederick, born April 22d, 1851; married February 17th, 1872, Charlotte Rule. 6, Henry Hart, born March 19th, 1854. 7, Joel, born April 29th, 1856; died June 5th, 1857. 8, Alfred Clarence, born June 15th, 1858.

FLINT.

2541. *Toulon, Ill.*

MARGARET FULLERTON HART, Toulon, Stark County, Ill., fifth daughter of Deacon Henry Hart, of Goshen, Conn., and his wife, Ann Elizabeth, daughter of Samuel D. Street, of Goshen, Conn., where she was born, February 9th, 1818; married   , James M. Flint, son of Caleb P., and his wife, Sarah, born May 25th, 1816, at Methuen, Essex County, Mass. He is a farmer, at Toulon, Stark County, Ill. Their children were—1, Emma A., born November 20th, 1853; 2, Lucretia M., born May 20th, 1855. They were all members of the Congregational Church.

2543. *Luzerne, Iowa.*

HENRY HUDSON HART, Luzerne, Benton County, Iowa, third son of Deacon Henry Hart, and his wife, Ann Elizabeth, daughter of Samuel D. Street, of Goshen, Conn., where he was born, June 14th, 1821; married December 8th, 1847, Martha Jane, daughter of Samuel and Mary Warnock, born January 8th, 1826, in Dearborn County, Ind. She is a member of the Congregational Church. He is a farmer in Luzerne, Benton County, Iowa.

THEIR CHILDREN, BEING THE NINTH GENERATION.

2849. Emeline Frances, born October 11th, 1848; married October 24th, 1872, George Reuben Folsom.

2850. Charles Henry, born July 19th, 1850, at Farmington, Fulton County, Ill.

2851. Mary Ellen, born March 7th, 1853, at Whitefield, Marshall County, Ill.

2852. Chester Warnock, born May 22d, 1855, at Leroy, Benton County, Iowa.

2853. Ann Elizabeth, born February 16th, 1867, at Leroy, Benton County, Iowa. Alice, born March 24th, 1869; died the same day.

2854. Frederic, born January 15th, 1860, at Leroy, Benton County, Iowa.

2855. Laura, born November 10th, 1861, at Leroy, Benton County, Iowa. Samuel, born October 13th, 1863; died the same day.

2856. Ernest, born May 18th, 1865, at Leroy, Benton County, Iowa.

2857. Winfred, born April 1st, 1867, at Leroy, Benton County, Iowa.

68

DEWEY.

2545.   *Canton, Ill.*

LOUISA HART, Canton, Ill., sixth daughter and tenth child of Deacon Henry Hart, of Goshen, Conn., and his wife, Ann Elizabeth, daughter of Samuel D. Street, born March 8th, 1825, at Goshen, Conn.; married April 10th, 1845, Joel W. Dewey, a farmer, of Canton, Ill. He and his wife and the two eldest daughters are members of the Congregational Church. He died of heart disease, August 2d, 1870. Their children were—1, Mary Loranie, born January 15th, 1846; 2, Frederick O., born June 8th, 1848; 3, Edward Hart, born October 3d, 1850; 4, Charles Carol, born September 3d, 1852; 5, Catharine Louise, born July 31st, 1856; 6, Ellen Frances, born July 26th, 1863.

2546.   *Elmwood, Ill.*

EDWARD HART, Elmwood, Ill., fifth son of Deacon Henry Hart, and his wife, Ann Elizabeth, daughter of Samuel D. Street, of Goshen, Conn., where he was born, February 7th, 1827; married May 6th, 1857, Lucy B., daughter of Henry and Elizabeth Robbins, born July 18th, 1835, at Bristol. They were admitted to the Congregational Church at Elmwood in 1863.

THEIR CHILDREN, BEING THE NINTH GENERATION.

2858.   Edith Eliza, born September 16th, 1858.

     Isabel Jane, born October 22d, 1861; died April 7th, 1863.

2859.   Walter Seymour, born December 23d, 1867.

2860.   Edward Amos, born September 8th, 1873.

2547.   *New Kirtland, Ill.*

DAVID HART, New Kirtland, Ill., youngest son of Deacon Henry Hart, of Goshen, Conn., and subsequently of Farmington, Ill., and his wife, Ann Elizabeth, daughter of Samuel D. Street, of Goshen, Conn., where he was born about 1828; married in 1852, Dorcas Heacock, of Canada, who died, October, 1861. He enlisted, September, 1861, in Company I, Forty-Seventh Regiment Illinois Volunteers, as second sergeant, but was soon promoted to orderly, and served three years. He was at the fight of Island No. 1, at the siege of Corinth, subsequently at the siege of Vicksburg, at the fight of Jackson, and other places. He was promoted to be first lieutenant in a colored regiment, and detailed as sub-commissioner of freedmen, and was honorably discharged, March, 1866, when he went to California, and has not been heard from by his friends since.

THEIR CHILDREN, BEING THE NINTH GENERATION.

2861.   Addie, born   ; died in the winter of 1857.

2862.   Annie, born in the spring of 1859; died   , aged 3 years.

2548. *Goshen, Conn.*

VICTOR CLARK HART, Goshen, Conn., eldest son of Miles Hart, of the same town, and his wife, Laura (Clark), born March 26th, 1821; married May 16th, 1850, at North Mansfield, Conn., Weltha Elizabeth Hanks, who died August 8th, 1862, when he second married March 24th, 1864, Mrs. Adaline Hall Peterson. He is a farmer and mechanic, and was living in Goshen, Conn., in 1874. He was not drafted in the late war, but sent a substitute, at an expense of $500.

THEIR CHILDREN, BEING THE NINTH GENERATION.

Child, born ; died in infancy.
Child, born ; died in infancy.
Child, born ; died in infancy.
Elizabeth Hale, born May 26th, 1859.

CHILDREN BY HIS SECOND WIFE.

Hannah Hanks, born March 14th, 1865.
Edward Victory, born January 27th, 1867.
Stedman Hall, born February 19th, 1870.

2549. *Goshen, Conn.*

FREDERIC MILES HART, Goshen, Conn., second son of Miles Hart, of the same town, and his wife, Laura (Clark), born May 4th, 1823. He was a young man of much promise, and was studying for a physician, when he died very suddenly of heart disease, on Long Island, December 7th, 1845, aged 22 years.

WHITING.

2550. *Torrington, Conn.*

LAURA ANN HART, eldest daughter of Miles Hart, of Goshen, Conn., and his wife, Laura (Clark), born July 26th, 1824, at ;
married , John N. Whiting, of Torrington, Conn., where they now reside. Their children were—1, Charles, died, November, 1864; 2, Ella, killed by the accidental shot of a pistol; 3, George, living at the age of 17 years; 4, Louise Helen, living at the age of 14 years. 5, Hubert, died, , aged 2 years; 6, Mary, died , aged 6 months.

2551.

CHARLES CONKLIN HART, Goshen, Conn., third son of Miles Hart, of the same town, and his wife, Laura (Clark), born March 6th, 1826, in Goshen, Conn.; married , 1852, Helen Paine, of New

York. He went to California, accompanied by his wife and brother,
John, where they were residing in 1871, in Tulare County.

THEIR CHILDREN, BEING THE NINTH GENERATION.

2863. Frederick, born
2864. Charles, born
2865. John, born
2866. Caroline, born
      Infant, born

2554.   *Elmira, N. Y.*

ABRAHAM PARMELEE HART, Goshen, Conn., eldest son of Alpha Hart,
of the same town, and his wife, Betsey (Dutton), of Plymouth, Conn.,
born April 23d, 1816, at Goshen, Conn.; married September 5th, 1839,
Angeline Badger, of Elmira, N. Y. He is a professional artist, and
they were residing at Elmira, Chemung County, N. Y., in 1873.

THEIR CHILD, BEING THE NINTH GENERATION.

2867. Harriet, born December 20th, 1840; married   , E. More-
      house, of Medina, N. Y.

MARTIN.

2556.   *Goshen, Conn.*

JANE HART, second daughter of Alpha Hart, of Goshen, Conn., and
his wife, Betsey (Dutton), born October 11th, 1821, at Goshen, Conn;
married   , William Martin, of
They had—1, Clarence, whom they say was 15 years old in 1872; 2,
Harriet, died in infancy.

2557.   *Goshen, Conn.*

MATTHEW RICE HART, Goshen, Conn., youngest child of Alpha Hart,
of the same town, and his wife, Betsey (Dutton), born June 28th, 1824,
at Goshen, Conn.; married October 23d, 1845, Adeline Chase. He
was a farmer by avocation. He died February 26th, 1855, aged 31
years.

THEIR CHILDREN, BEING THE NINTH GENERATION.

2868. Reuben Chase, born January 2d, 1847.
2869. Marion Issadore, born December 9th, 1848.

2558.   *Brimfield, Ohio.*

CHARLES WALLIS HART, Brimfield, Portage County, Ohio, only son
of Reuben Hart, of the same town and county, and his wife, Nancy

Ann (Law), born December 5th, 1837, in Brimfield, Ohio, where he is a farmer; married October 28th, 1863, Eleanor N. Stilwell.

THEIR CHILDREN, BEING THE NINTH GENERATION.

2870. Minnie G., born July 14th, 1865, in Brimfield, Ohio.
2871. Harry S., born March 12th, 1867, in Brimfield, Ohio.
2872. Jennie L., born January 28th, 1869, in Brimfield, Ohio.
2873. Addie, born July 24th, 1873, in Brimfield, Ohio.

2565. *Kingsville, Ohio.*

HENRY HART, eldest son of Jonathan Hart, of Litchfield, Conn., and his wife, Anna (Webster), born February 2d, 1812, in Litchfield, Conn.; married in 1834, Louisa Stone, of Sheffield, Ashtabula County, Ohio. His avocation is farming, and he resides in Kingsville, Ashtabula County, Ohio. No children reported.

2566. *Kingsville, Ohio.*

TRUMAN HART, Litchfield, Conn., second son of Jonathan Hart, of the same place, and his wife, Anna (Webster), born October 14th, 1814, at Litchfield, Conn.; married June 22d, 1845, Sarah Eugenia Pease, of Sempronius, Cayuga County, N. Y., born December 3d, 1819. His avocation is farming, and he resides at Kingsville, Ashtabula County, Ohio.

THEIR CHILDREN, BEING THE NINTH GENERATION.

Albert Alpine, born August 14th, 1846, in Kingsville, Ohio; died August 3d, 1854, in Wayne, Ill.
2874. Emeretta Arminda, born January 10th, 1848, in Kingsville, Ohio, where he was residing single in 1872.
Infant son, born February 4th, 1853, in Kingsville, Ohio; died there March 2d, 1853.
2875. Verona Rowena, born October 24th, 1858, in Kingsville, Ohio.

2567. *San Francisco, Cal.*

BENJAMIN HART, third son of Jonathan Hart, of Litchfield, Conn., and his wife, Anna (Webster), born, September, 1816, at Litchfield, Conn.; married   , in Rockford, Winnebago County, Ill., Mary McAllister. He was a tailor by trade, and died in California, when second she married   Field, and was residing in San Francisco, Cal., in 1872.

WEBSTER.

2569. *Kingsville, Ohio.*

ANNA HART, Kingsville, Ohio, second daughter of Jonathan Hart, of Litchfield, Conn., and his wife, Ann (Webster), born, April, 1820, at Kingsville, Ashtabula County, Ohio; married, 1839, Lyman Webster, of Kingsville, a tanner by trade, but is now a farmer there.

2570.   *Perrysburg, Ohio.*

JONATHAN HART, youngest child of Jonathan Hart, of Litchfield, Conn., and his wife, Anna (Webster), born, November, 1824, at Kingsville, Ashtabula County, Ohio; married in 1846, Louisa Barnes, of New York. He is a carpenter, and was residing at Perrysburg, Wood County, Ohio, in 1872.

SAXTON.

2571.   *Middlebury, Conn.*

SOPHRONIA L. HART, eldest daughter of Isaac Hart, of Litchfield, Conn., and his wife, Martha (Butler), of Harwinton, Conn., born July 9th, 1813, at Litchfield, Conn.; married January 22d, 1840, Sylvester Saxton, of Middlebury, Conn., who died August 22d, 1854. They had—1, Albert D., born February 20th, 1849, married March 22d, 1871, Eliza Roberts, of Burlington, Conn.; 2, Franklin Hart, born March 15th, 1851.

MORRIS.

2572.   *Wolcottville, Conn.*

LUCY ANN HART, Litchfield, Conn., second daughter of Isaac Hart, of the same town, and his wife, Martha (Butler), born June 7th, 1816, at Litchfield, Conn.; married September 17th, 1835, Lewis Morris, of Torrington, Conn. He is a jeweler. They live in Wolcottville, Conn. They have had two sons and three daughters. She was living in 1871.

2573.   *Ellsworth, Bristol, Conn.*

REV. LUTHER BUTLER HART, Ellsworth, Conn., second son of Isaac Hart, of Litchfield, Conn., and his wife, Martha (Butler), born March 9th, 1821, at Sheffield, Ohio. He learned the printer's trade, but became a Baptist minister, and subsequently located in Norfolk and Ellsworth, Conn.; married May 31st, 1852, Lydia Skiff, of Ellsworth, Conn., daughter of Herman, and his wife, Caroline (Whitcomb). They were residing in Bridgeport in 1871. He graduated at Union College, Schenectady, N. Y., July 25th, 1849, and was called to the Baptist Church in Cornwall, Conn., from there to North Norfolk, Conn., thence to Ellsworth, Conn., from thence, in 1861, to Amenia, Dutchess County, N. Y., then in 1866 to Poughkeepsie, N. Y., thence to Bridgeport, Conn., thence to Bristol, Conn., where he was residing in 1872, but his health does not admit of his professional labors.

2876. Seth Skiff, born July 9th, 1853.
2877. Isaac Harmon, born December 18th, 1855.
2878. William Luther, born April 10th, 1867.

HICKOK.

2574. *Jefferson, Ohio.*

LAMIRA W. HART, Litchfield, Conn., third daughter and child of Isaac Hart, of the same town, and his wife, Martha (Butler), born December 31st, 1822, at Litchfield, Conn.; married September 15th, 1843, in Kingsville, Ashtabula County, Ohio, Thomas F. Hickok, of Jefferson, in the same county and state. They have two sons and five daughters married and living in Kingsville. Mrs. Hickok is still living.

2575. *Winfield, Kan.*

TIMOTHY HART, Litchfield, Conn., third son of Isaac Hart, of the same town, and his wife, Martha (Butler), born October 27th, 1825, in Litchfield, Conn.; married June 18th, 1847, Martha E. Benham, of Watertown. He is a joiner by trade, and has lived in various localities. He was living in Winfield, Cowles County, Kan., in 1872.

2879. Nellie, born
2880. Burdett, born
2881. Oscar, born

ATKINS.

2576. *Bristol, Conn.*

MARTHA SOPHIA HART, fourth daughter of Isaac Hart, of the same town, and his wife, Martha (Butler), born June 30th, 1828, in Litchfield, Conn.; married October 18th, 1847, Roswell Atkins, of Bristol, Conn., son of Deacon Lloyd Atkins, deceased. He is a deacon of the Baptist Church. She died of dysentery, in the Insane Retreat, Hartford, Conn., September 24th, 1852, aged 24 years, when second he married Sarah Barnam.

BENNET.

2577. *Bristol, Conn.*

MARY JANE HART, fourth daughter of Isaac Hart, of Litchfield, Conn., and his wife, Martha (Butler), born June 19th, 1831, in Litchfield, Conn.; married July 3d, 1853, Norridson Bennett, a mechanic of Torringford, Conn., who worked at Bristol, Conn. He became a soldier in the late war, and was supposed to have been killed at Antietam.

2578. *Bristol, Conn.*

ISAAC PHINEAS HART, Bristol, Conn., fourth son of Isaac Hart, of Litchfield, Conn., and his wife, Martha (Butler), born July 16th, 1834, in Litchfield, Conn.; married March 28th, 1857, in New Haven, Conn., Jane, daughter of William Hill, of London, Eng., and his wife, Harriet (Mason). Their home is on Pine Hill, west of Bristol, Conn., where he has a farm of some ninety acres, and grows small fruits. He is an active and intelligent man.

THEIR CHILDREN, BEING THE NINTH GENERATION.

2882. Ettie Sophronia, born March 28th, 1858, in Bristol, Conn.
2883. William Timothy, born September 1st, 1859, in Bristol, Conn.
2884. Mary Jane, born July 24th, 1861, in Bristol, Conn.
2885. Charles Henry, born September 26th, 1864, in Bristol, Conn.
2886. Isaac Truman, born October 13th, 1867, in Bristol, Conn.
2887. Benjamin Franklin, born April 9th, 1871, in Bristol, Conn.

WILCOX.

2579. *Sandwich Islands.*

ELIZA LUCY HART, eldest daughter of Truman Hart, of Colebrook, Conn., and his wife, Polly (Spencer), born November 17th, 1814, in Colebrook, Conn.; married   , 1836, Abner Wilcox, of Harwinton, Conn. He is a missionary to the Sandwich Islands. She is a teacher, and has spent thirty-three years at the islands. They have had eight sons.

2580. *Norfolk, Conn.*

ALBERT S. HART, Norfolk, Conn., eldest son of Truman Hart, of Colebrook, Conn., and his wife, Polly, daughter of Amos Spencer, of New Hartford, born May 3d, 1820; married in 1842, Maria Gaylord.

SPAULDING.

2581. *Norfolk, Conn.*

LOUISA JANE HART, Norfolk, Conn., second daughter of Truman Hart, of Colebrook, Conn., and his wife, Polly, daughter of Amos Spencer, of New Hartford, born September 30th, 1817, at Colebrook, Conn.; married March 24th, 1841, Austin A. Spaulding, of Norfolk, Conn. He was a farmer in 1874.

BARNARD.

2582. *Colebrook, Conn.*

AUGUSTA C. HART, third daughter of Truman Hart, of Colebrook, Conn., and his wife, Polly, daughter of Amos Spencer, of New Hartford, Conn., born August 18th, 1822, in Colebrook, Conn.; married November 17th, 1850, Nelson Barnard.

BARNARD.

2586. *Colebrook, Conn.*

ALMIRA HART, Colebrook, Conn., eldest daughter of Lewis Hart, of the same place, and his wife, Persis, daughter of Deacon William Swift, born October 23d, 1816, in Colebrook, Conn.; married there March 30th, 1836, Lewis Barnard, son of Asa, and his wife, Elizabeth Hart. He is a farmer, and they were residing in Colebrook, Conn., in 1872. Their children were—1, Elizabeth, born March 7th, 1838; 2, George Lucian, born May 23d, 1840, married, May, 1871, Mary Hoyt; 3, Harriet Ann, born May 29th, 1843, married December 16th, 1863, Samuel A. Cooper; 4, Julius Hart, born March 19th, 1845, married October 22d, 1872, Clara Mattison; 5, Almira Swift, born July 1st, 1848, married November 16th, 1870, Albert B. Sage, died July 9th, 1871.

2587. *Grafton, Ohio.*

WILLIAM HART, Grafton, Ohio, son of Lewis Hart, of Colebrook, Conn., and his wife, Persis (Swift), of Winchester, Conn., where he was born, September 12th, 1819; married in Pennfield, Lorain County, Ohio, April, 1841, Harriet E. Smith, born July 8th, 1821, in Rome, N. Y. He is a merchant in Grafton, Lorain County, Ohio, and he wrote to me, February, 1874.

THEIR CHILDREN, BEING THE NINTH GENERATION.

2888. Sarah L., born March 26th, 1843; married December 12th, 1861, William McGraw.

2889. Myra P., born May 3d, 1847; married May 6th, 1866, G. W. Lavoo.

2890. William, born January 14th, 1858, in Grafton, Ohio.

HART.

2588. *Pennfield, Ohio.*

LUCY HART, Winchester, Conn., second daughter of Lewis Hart, of Colebrook, Conn., and his wife, Persis (Swift), born September 17th, 1821, in Winchester, Conn.; married in Pennfield, Ohio, January 12th, 1840, Hawley Hart, of Winchester, Conn., son of Samuel, and his wife, Mariam (Bassett), born February 10th, 1807, in Hartland, Conn. She is his second wife, and is a member of the Methodist Church. He is a farmer, and they were residing in Pennfield, Lorain County, Ohio, in 1871.

69

2891.　Willard, born October 12th, 1840; married January 15th, 1861, Ann E. Soog.
　　　　Chester, born April 11th, 1842; died August 10th, 1859, aged 17 years.

2589.　　　　　　　*Pennfield, Ohio.*

LEWIS HART, Pennfield, Ohio, second son of Lewis Hart, of Cole-brook, Conn., and his wife, Persis (Swift), born April 11th, 1824, in Winchester, Conn.; married in Pennfield, Lorain County, Ohio, September 9th, 1846, Melinda, daughter of Orris Starr, and his wife, Abby (Hickox). He was a farmer by occupation, and died April 6th, 1863, aged 39 years. His widow second married in Pennfield, Ohio, May 12th, 1864, James M. Pierce.

CHILDREN OF LEWIS AND MELINDA, BEING THE NINTH GENERATION.

　　　　Lucy M., born March 13th, 1848; died September 13th, 1850, in Pennfield, Ohio.
　　　　Persis S., born February 15th, 1850; died November 12th, 1856, in Pennfield, Ohio.
2892.　Jay, born November 10th, 1851. He was single, February, 1874.
　　　　Horace, born January 12th, 1854; died February 22d, 1854, in Pennfield, Ohio.
2893.　Hattie, born April 8th, 1858.

2590.　　　　　　　*Colebrook, Conn.*

ERASTUS SWIFT HART, Colebrook, Conn., third son of Lewis Hart, of the same town, and his wife, Persis (Swift), born June 27th, 1826, in Winchester, Conn.; married in Winchester, November 30th, 1848, Harriet Newell Gilbert, where she was born, December 19th, 1826. He is an insurance agent, and they were residing in Colebrook, Conn., in 1874.

THEIR CHILDREN, BEING THE NINTH GENERATION.

2894.　Erastus Swift, born October 26th, 1849; married February 22d, 1870, Emma Jane Messenger. He is a farmer.
　　　　Edgar Howard, born March 25th, 1851, in Simsbury, Conn.; died there, March 31st, 1851.
2895.　Gilbert Lyman, born September 23d, 1854.
　　　　Hattie Gilbert, born January 24th, 1858.
　　　　Charles Potter, born December 6th, 1865.

2591.　　　　　　　*Pennfield, Ohio.*

HEMAN HART, Pennfield, Lorain County, Ohio, fourth son of Lewis Hart, and his wife, Persis (Swift), born August 14th, 1828, in Winchester, Conn.; married in Grafton, Lorain County, Ohio, May 11th, 1853, Martha C. Ingersol, daughter of　　　　　　　, and his wife, Mary (Simons), born March 8th, 1831, in Grafton, Ohio, where he engaged in the mercantile business, but died in Pennfield, Ohio, January 5th, 1858, aged 29 years, when second she married in Elyria, Ohio, March 13th, 1871, William H. Tucker, where they were residing in 1872.

CHILD OF HEMAN AND MARTHA, BEING THE NINTH GENERATION.

2896. Frances Marion, born August 27th, 1855, in Grafton, Ohio; died April 17th, 1857, in Oberlin, Ohio.

2593. *Elyria, Ohio.*

HENRY HART, Elyria, Lorain County, Ohio, fifth son of Lewis Hart, of Colebrook, Conn., and his wife, Persis (Swift), born October 16th, 1831, at Winchester, Conn.; married in Elyria, Ohio, December 28th, 1854, Jane L. Edwards, where he was a mechanic in 1872.

THEIR CHILDREN, BEING THE NINTH GENERATION.

2897. Frank, born
2898. Walter, born
2899. Heman, born
     Lucy, born
     Burton, born

2594. *Lagrange, Ohio.*

RALPH HART, Lagrange, Lorain County, Ohio, sixth son of Lewis Hart, of Winchester, Conn., and his wife, Persis (Swift), born April 11th, 1834, in Winchester, Conn.; married in Grafton, Ohio, May 25th, 1859, Diana A. Noble. He is a farmer, and was residing at Lagrange, Ohio, in 1872.

THEIR CHILD, BEING THE NINTH GENERATION.

2900. Chester, born

2595. *Wheeler, Ind.*

MILES HART, Wheeler, Porter County, Ind., seventh son and youngest child of Lewis Hart, of Colebrook, Conn., and his wife, Persis (Swift), born September 14th, 1839, in Pennfield, Lorain County, Ohio; married in Ridgeville, Ohio, June 20th, 1866, Sarah, daughter of Henry Kemp, and his wife, Harriet (Foster), born April 24th, 1844, in Litchfield, Medina County, Ohio. He is a farmer, and was located in Wheeler, Ind., in 1872. He served nearly four years in the late war, mostly guarding prisoners on Johnson's Island, in Lake Erie. She is of English descent, and both are members of the Methodist Church.

THEIR CHILD, BEING THE NINTH GENERATION.

2901. Angie, born March 19th, 1867, in Lagrange, Ohio.

2596. *Marbledale, Conn.*

LEWIS HART, Marbledale, Litchfield County, Conn., eldest son of Titus Hart, of Colebrook, Conn., and his wife, Amanda (Webster), born August 26th, 1821, in Winchester, Conn.; married , Esther, daughter of Weeks, and his wife, Lucy (Tucker), born, May, 1842. He is a cabinet maker, and resides in Marbledale, Conn.

THEIR CHILD, BEING THE NINTH GENERATION.
2902. Edwin, born July 3d, 1860.

ROOD.

2597. *Norfolk, Conn.*

AMANDA HART, Norfolk, Conn., eldest daughter of Titus Hart, of Colebrook, Conn., and his wife, Amanda (Webster), born May 31st, 1823, in Norfolk, Conn.; married January 1st, 1851, Harvey Rood, of Norfolk, Conn. Their children were—1, Eliza, born February 24th, 1852; 2, Maria, born February 16th, 1854; 3, Grove, born July 16th, 1855; 4, William, born August 6th, 1857; 5, Mary, born October 10th, 1859; 6, Maria, married, December, 1870, Martin Kelley, of Canada.

2598. *Pittsford, N. Y.*

JAY HART, Pittsford, Monroe County, N. Y., second son of Titus Hart, of Colebrook, Conn., and his first wife, Amanda (Webster), born March 16th, 1826, in Norfolk, Conn.; married in Pittsford, Monroe County, N. Y., May, 1862, Jane Sage.

THEIR CHILD, BEING THE NINTH GENERATION.
2903. Frederick Gay, born September 4th, 1865, in Pittsford, N. Y.

2599.

WILLIAM HART, Norfolk, Conn., third son of Titus Hart, of Colebrook, Conn., and his first wife, Amanda (Webster), born April 18th, 1829, in Norfolk, Conn.; married, May, 1849, Emeline Snyder. She died , when he second married , 1852, Elizabeth Hines.

THEIR CHILD, BEING THE NINTH GENERATION.
2904. Sarah, born November 22d, 1852; married October 21st, 1821, Hubert Harris.

2600. *Norfolk, Conn.*

GROVE HART, Norfolk, Conn., fourth son of Titus Hart, of Colebrook, Conn., and his first wife, Amanda (Webster), born June 5th, 1831, in

Norfolk, Conn.; married   , 1860, Emeline Hart, daughter
of   . He died June 12th, 1863.

2601.   *Norfolk, Conn.*

WEBSTER HART, Norfolk, Conn., fifth son of Titus Hart, of Colebrook, and his first wife, Amanda (Webster), born November 29th,
1833, in Norfolk, Conn.; married   , 1863, Ann Maxwell.

VINING.

2604.   *Simsbury, Conn.*

JANE SUSANNAH HART, Simsbury, Conn., only daughter of Timothy
Hart, of Colebrook, Conn., and his wife, Margaret (Wakefield), born
August 15th, 1847, at Mill Brook, Conn.; married November 26th,
1867, William Henry Vining, of Simsbury, Conn., son of William.
They had—1, Aden Wakefield, born November 8th, 1868; 2, William
Roscoe, born April 7th, 1872.

2605.   *Buffalo, N. Y.*

AUSTIN SUMMERTON HART, Buffalo, N. Y., only son of William Austin
Hart, of the same place, and his wife, Mary Ann (Summerton), born
January 2d, 1827, in Fredonia, N. Y. He was a tinner by trade. He
went to Buffalo with his father in 1837, and subsequently became a
partner in the firm of Hart, Ball & Hart. He was a good mechanic,
and a thorough business man. He was identified with the interests of
the Episcopal Church, although not a communicant. He was a man of
true culture and of refined taste. By his death, which occurred at St.
Augustine, Fla., January 8th, 1874, he leaves a wife and one child.

THEIR CHILD, BEING THE NINTH GENERATION.
2905. William Austin, born

2607.   *Erie, Penn.*

JAMES CHARLES HART, Erie, Erie County, Penn., eldest son of Ira
Wilder Hart, of the same town, and his first wife, Eliza (Metcalf), born
December 20th, 1832, at Erie, Penn.; married September 11th, 1862,
Adalaide Marvin, daughter of John, and his wife, Mary (Judson), born
December 11th, 1840. He is the general freight agent of the Lake
Shore & Michigan Southern Railroad, at Erie, Penn.

THEIR CHILDREN, BEING THE NINTH GENERATION.
Belle M., born April 5th, 1867, in Erie, Penn.
Annie Louise, born February 19th, 1874, in Erie, Penn.

2608.   *Fredonia, Buffalo, N. Y.*

HENRY STARR HART, Fredonia and Buffalo, N. Y., eldest son of Salmon Hart, of Fredonia, N. Y., and his first wife, Mary Ann (Starr), born July 18th, 1834, in Fredonia, N. Y.; married
Mary E., daughter of Alfred Jones, of Binghamton, N. Y., and his wife, Hannah (Lamont), born March 18th, 1837, in Binghamton, Boone County, N. Y. He was a printer by trade, and died in Buffalo, N. Y., April 4th, 1868, aged 33 years, 8 months, and 12 days, leaving one child, when second his widow married August 11th, 1872, Mr. Ray, of Lodi, Wis., where they were residing in 1874.

CHILD OF H. S. AND MARY HART, BEING THE NINTH GENERATION.

2906. Amia May, born April 5th, 1860, in Buffalo, N. Y. She was living with her mother in 1874.

2609.   *Fredonia, N. Y.*

WALTER JOHN HART, Fredonia, N. Y., second son of Salmon Hart, of the same place, and his second wife, Mary A. (Reddington), of Westfield, N. Y., born July 6th, 1841, in Fredonia, N. Y. He was a printer by trade. He entered the Union Army of the late war, was wounded before Richmond, October 24th, 1864, and died on the 28th.

BARMORE.

2611.   *Fredonia, N. Y.*

HARRIET EMELINE HART, eldest daughter of Aaron H. Hart, of Fredonia, N. Y., and his first wife, Hepsibah Hart, of Victor, N. Y., born September 29th, 1834, in Fredonia, N. Y.; married May 2d, 1855, Amon L. Barmore, of Fredonia, N. Y.

2614.   *Barkhamsted, Conn.*

MONROE HART, Barkhamsted, Conn., eldest son of Chester Hart, of the same town, and his wife, Julia (Case), born April 30th, 1842, in Barkhamsted, Conn.; married December 8th, 1869, Annice Case, daughter of Ormand, and his wife, Ann (Tiffany), born June 23d, 1849, in Hartland, Conn. He is a carpenter and joiner, and was residing in Barkhamsted, Conn., in 1873. He has manifested much interest in this Genealogy, by furnishing much valuable information concerning his grandfather's and father's family, as well as his own, for which he has my hearty thanks.

THEIR CHILD, BEING THE NINTH GENERATION.

2907. Georgie Annie, born August 20th, 1871.

LITTLE.

2616. *Torrington, Conn.*

MARY C. HART, Torrington, Conn., eldest daughter of William Henry Harrison Hart, of Barkhamsted, Conn., and his wife, Eliza (Scovill), born March 10th, 1842, in Barkhamsted, Conn.; married October 10th, 1860, Wolcott Little, of Torrington, Conn. They had—1, Ella C., born June 22d, 1861; 2, Angeline E., born December 31st, 1863; 3, William, born January 20th, 1867, died February 3d, 1869.

2617. *Barkhamsted, Conn.*

WILLIAM BURTON HART, eldest son of William Henry Harrison Hart, of Barkhamsted, Conn., and his wife, Eliza (Scovill), born October 7th, 1843, in Barkhamsted, Conn.; married in Torrington, Conn., January 1st, 1867, M. G. Kitchen. He was a farmer by occupation, and died August 7th, 1871, aged 29 years.

THEIR CHILDREN, BEING THE NINTH GENERATION.

Burton A., born November 1st, 1867; died February 6th, 1868, aged 3 months.
Eddie B., born August 28th, 1870; died May 20th, 1871, aged 8 months.

2618. *Barkhamsted, Conn.*

TRUMAN H. HART, second son of William Henry Harrison Hart, of Barkhamsted, Conn., and his wife, Eliza (Scovill), born September 30th, 1846, in Barkhamsted, Conn.; married November 20th, 1870, Sarah Saunders.

KITCHEN.

2622. *Torrington, Conn.*

ELIZA HART, youngest daughter of William Henry Harrison Hart, of Barkhamsted, Conn., and his wife, Eliza (Scovill), born
, in Torrington, Conn.; married March 17th, 1870, A. G. Kitchen.

2625. *Vineland, N. J.*

LEWIS HART, eldest son of Phœbus Hart, of Vineland, N. J., and his wife, Rhoda (Dorman), born April 27th, 1835, in Canaan, Conn. He went to Wisconsin, where he was when the late war broke out, and he enlisted for three months and served out his time, when he returned to Connecticut in October, 1861, and in November enlisted again for three years, and died July 9th, 1864, in the United States Barracks Hospital at New Orleans, aged 29 years.

HADSELL.

2626. *Canaan, Conn., Vineland, N. J.*

ADALINE LOUISA HART, eldest daughter of Phœbus Hart, of Vineland, N. J., and his wife, Rhoda (Dorman), born October 1st, 1838, in Canaan, Conn.; married September 25th, 1862, Frederick M. Hadsell, of Massachusetts. They had—1, Wallace Frederick, born May 25th, 1863, in Canaan, Conn.; 2, Joseph Lewis, born October 17th, 1866, in Vineland, N. J.; 3, Nellie May, born September 19th, 1869, in Vineland, N. J.

2630.

NORMAN HART, eldest son of Newton Hart, of Winchester, Conn., and his wife, Ruth (Hadsell), of Canaan, Conn., born April 21st, 1831, in   ; married, May, 1852, Jane E. Curtiss. He served three years in the late war in a Wisconsin Regiment. He is now a farmer, and was residing in Wisconsin in 1874.

THEIR CHILDREN, BEING THE NINTH GENERATION.

2908. Arthur Lurin, born
2909. Ira, born

MILLER.

2631. *Springfield, Mass.*

MATILDA HART, second daughter of Newton Hart, of Winchéster, Conn., and his wife, Ruth (Hadsell), born February 2d, 1835; married December 21st, 1859, Cyrus H. Miller, of Springfield, Mass. She died July 6th, 1866, aged 31 years. They had—1, Mary Ellen, born July 14th, 1862; 2, Samuel, born May 5th, 1863; 3, Son, born

HACK.

2632. *Monterey, Mass.*

PHEBE HART, Monterey, Mass., youngest daughter of Newton Hart, of Winchester, and his wife, Ruth (Hadsell), of Canaan, born September 5th, 1845; married August 27th, 1869, Francis Hack, of Monterey, Mass.

MINER.

2633. *Glastonbury, Conn.*

RHODA MATILDA HART, eldest child of Willard Hart, of Winsted, Conn., and his first wife, Rhoda, daughter of Timothy Benedict, and his wife, Lydia (Crocker), born January 26th, 1824, in Winsted, Conn.;

married
she died.
, William Miner, of Glastonbury, where

2637.
West Winsted, Conn.

LEWIS DANIEL HART, Winsted, Conn., second son of Willard Hart, of the same town, and his second wife, Maria, eldest daughter of Daniel Andrews, Jr., of Winchester, and his wife, Sarah (Platt), born April 14th, 1837, in Winsted, Conn.; married June 9th, 1869, Eveline Helen Meriam. They have a residence on Wheeler Street, Winsted, and he is a brick mason by trade. He is a member of the order of Freemasons.

FERRIS.

2636.
Ballston Springs, N. Y.

ELIZABETH HART, Winsted, Conn., third daughter of Willard Hart, of the same town, and his second wife, Maria, eldest daughter of Daniel Andrews, Jr., and his wife, Sarah (Platt), born April 8th, 1835, at Winchester, Conn.; married July 8th, 1855, James G. Ferris, a scythe maker of Winsted. They were living at Ballston Springs, N. Y., in 1871, and have two sons and one daughter.

BEERS.

2638.
Roxbury, Conn.

HENRIETTA MARIA HART, Winsted, Conn., fourth daughter of Willard Hart, of the same place, and his second wife, Maria (Andrews), born January 8th, 1839, in Winsted, Conn.; married February 3d, 1862, Nelson Beers, of Roxbury, Conn. He is a brick mason by trade. They have one daughter. He is a Freemason.

2639.
West Winsted, Conn.

WILLARD HART, Winsted, Conn., youngest son and child of Willard Hart, of the same place, and his second wife, Maria (Andrews), daughter of Daniel, born April 11th, 1840, in Winsted, Conn.; married May 5th, * , Maryette Hill, of Winsted. He was a mechanic. He enlisted in Company E, Second Regiment Connecticut Volunteers, and was killed at Cold Harbor, Va., June 2d, 1864, aged 24 years.

GRIDLEY.

2640.
Bristol, Conn.

CYNTHIA EMILY HART, eldest child of Sylvester Hart, of Hartland and Winchester, Conn., and his wife, Charlotte (Walter), born August

70

17th, 1823, in Winchester, Conn.; married at her father's residence, November 23d, 1846, Silas Riley Gridley, son of Cyrus, of Bristol, Conn., and his wife, Elizabeth (Benton), of Harwinton, Conn., born September 16th, 1820, in Bristol, Conn. He is a clock maker by trade, but was a farmer and cattle dealer in 1874, and was living on his father's old place on West Street, Bristol, Conn. They have three daughters, all living. His place was the old home of his father.

2641.   *Hartland, Conn.*

GEORGE WASHINGTON HART, Hartland, Conn., second son of Sylvester Hart, of the same place and Winchester, and his wife, Charlotte (Walter), born June 8th, 1827, in Winchester; married October 13th, 1850, in Colebrook, Conn., Laura Ann Hill, daughter of Daniel, and his wife, Fanny (Markam,) born December 25th, 1826, in Colebrook, Conn. He is a cooper by trade, and lived in Hartland in 1872. His present avocation is farming, having rented a farm in West Hartland.

THEIR CHILDREN, BEING THE NINTH GENERATION.

2910. Washington Constantine, born July 14th, 1856, in Colebrook, Conn.
2911. Flora Elizabeth, born July 21st, 1862, in Hartland, Conn.

TYLER.

2642.   *Colebrook, Conn.*

MARY ABIGAIL HART, second daughter of Sylvester Hart, of Winchester, Conn., and his wife, Charlotte (Walter), born June 20th, 1829, in Winchester, Conn.; married, May, 1852, Jefferson Monroe Tyler, a wagon maker of Colebrook, Conn. They had two sons and one daughter in 1871.

2643.   *Burrville, Conn.*

LUTHER WARREN HART, Burrville, Conn., third son of Sylvester Hart, of Winchester, Conn., and his wife, Charlotte (Walter), born April 27th, 1832, in Winsted, Conn.; married January 31st, 1857, Nancy Elizabeth Burr, of Winsted, Conn. He is a wood turner, and worked in Waterbury in 1871, but lives in Burrville.

THEIR CHILDREN, BEING THE NINTH GENERATION.

2912. Leon Warren, born June 25th, 1859, in Riverton, Conn.
2913. Jennie Augusta, born September 20th, 1864, in Colebrook, Conn.

MILES.

2644.   *Colebrook, Conn.*

ELLEN CHARLOTTE HART, youngest daughter of Sylvester Hart, of Winchester, Conn., and his wife, Charlotte (Walter), born November

30th, 1836, in Winsted, Conn.; married   , 1855, James
Miles, of Colebrook, Conn., where he is a butcher. They have three
sons and three daughters.

EATON.

2646.   *Torringford, Conn.*

PHIDELIA E. HART, Torringford, Conn., second daughter of Wells
Hart, of the same place, and his wife, Susan, daughter of Richard
Tryon, born June 20th, 1831, in Winchester, Conn.; married
        , Levi Eaton, of New Hartford, Conn. His avocation is
farming, and they were living on Torringford Street in 1871. They
have three sons.

LEACH. LATHAM.

2647.   *Plymouth, Conn.*

HULDAH MARIAM HART, Plymouth, Conn., third daughter of Wells
Hart, of Torringford, Conn., and his wife, Susan, daughter of Richard
Tryon, of Saybrook, Conn., born February 20th, 1833, in Winchester,
Conn.; married Luther Leach, a farmer of Torrington, Conn. They
had two sons, when he died   , and she second married
Lyman Latham, of Tolland, Conn. They were living in Plymouth,
Conn., in 1871, where has a farm. They had one son in 1871.

SPERRY. GOODWIN.

2648.   *Torrington, Conn.*

LURINDA A. HART, Wolcottville, Conn., fourth daughter of Wells
Hart, of Torringford, Conn., and his wife, Susan, daughter of Richard
Tryon, of Saybrook, Conn., born August 5th, 1836, in Winchester,
Conn.; married   , Samuel Sperry, a farmer of
Torrington, Conn., who died   , when second she
married   , Lewis Goodwin, a mechanic of Wolcott-
ville, Conn. She had three daughters by Sperry, but no children by
Goodwin in 1871.

MESSENGER.

2650.   *Torringford, Conn.*

CAROLINE A. HART, sixth daughter of Wells Hart, of Torringford,
Conn., and Susan, daughter of Richard Tryon, of New Durham,
N. Y., born January 17th, 1841, in Winchester, Conn.; married
        , Chauncey Messenger, of New Hartford, Conn. She

died March 6th, 1862, in Torringford, Conn., when he second married
, and lives in Bridgeport, Conn.
She had three sons by Messenger, but they are all dead.

2652.   *Torringford, Conn.*

WILLIAM WELLS HART, Torringford, Conn., eldest son of Wells
Hart, of the same place, and his wife, Susan (Tryon), born December
10th, 1845, in Winchester, Conn.; married October 21st, 1866, Lydia
Waugh, daughter of Frank, born April 21st, 1850. They were living
with his father, in Torringford, Conn., in 1871.

THEIR CHILD, BEING THE NINTH GENERATION.
2914.   Hattie Emily, born August 13th, 1869, in Winchester, Conn.

2653.   ·   *Torringford, Conn.*

FREDERICK ALVIN HART, Torringford, Conn., second son of Wells
Hart, of the same town, and his wife, Susan (Tryon), born April 18th,
1848, in Torrington, Conn.; married   , Jennie
Fancher, of Colebrook, Conn. They had no children in 1871.

2655.   *Pennfield, Ohio.*

WILLARD HART, Pennfield, Lorain County, Ohio, eldest son of Hawley Hart, of Winchester, Conn., and his second wife, Lucy Hart, born
October 12th, 1840, in Pennfield, Ohio; married January 15th, 1861,
at Huntington, Ohio, Ann E. Soog, daughter of   Soog, and his
wife, Margery Hayes, born May 24th, 1837, in Spencer, Ohio. He
was a farmer in 1871, and was living in Pennfield, Ohio.

THEIR CHILD, BEING THE NINTH GENERATION.
2915.   Carrie L., born November 25th, 1861, in Pennfield, Ohio.

2657.   *Meriden, Conn.*

IVES W. HART, Meriden, Conn., eldest son of Daniel H. Hart, of
the same town, and his wife, Harriet G. (Miller), of Middletown, born
October 4th, 1841, in Meriden, Conn.; married November 24th, 1870,
Mrs. Elsie Lane, a widow, of Madison, Conn. He is a farmer, and
resides in Meriden, Conn. They are members of the First Baptist
Church.

THEIR CHILD, BEING THE NINTH GENERATION.
2916.   Arthur M., born May 20th, 1872, in Meriden, Conn.

2660.

SAMUEL COLLINS HART, eldest son of Theodore Ephraim Hart, of Canandaigua, N. Y., and his wife, Eliza (Collins), born May 20th, 1828, at Harford, Cortland County, N. Y.; married   ,
Catharine M. Buell.

THEIR CHILDREN, BEING THE NINTH GENERATION.

2917. Caroline Maria, born March 24th, 1863.
2918. Edna Augusta, born December 22d, 1864.   .
2919. Olive Eliza, born August 26th, 1867.
2920. Miriam Louise, born March 27th, 1871.

2661.   *Canandaigua, N. Y.*

THEODORE HENRY HART, second son of Theodore Ephraim Hart, of Canandaigua, N. Y., and his wife, Eliza (Collins), born January 26th, 1831, at Harford, Cortland County, N. Y.; married October 11th, 1859, Caroline S. Stone, of Philadelphia, Penn. He was a graduate of Hamilton College, Clinton, N. Y., in 1852. He died in Philadelphia, Penn., April 12th, 1861, aged 30 years, 2 months, and 16 days.

Obituary Notice from a Daily Paper.

"Theodore Henry Hart was born in Harford, Cortland County, N. Y., January 26th, 1831; died in Philadelphia, Penn., April 12th, 1861. While a junior in college Mr. Hart made a public profession of religion, and united with the Congregational Church of Canandaigua, N. Y. In the fall of 1853 he entered the Union Theological Seminary, but was compelled, by loss of health, to leave for a warmer climate. This breaking up of his cherished plans he reconciled himself to by helping a number of young men in preparing for the ministry. He engaged in active business in Philadelphia, and was very successful. In 1857 he visited Europe, and sent home sketches of travel, that were published in the *Northern Independent.* They reveal a genial nature, with the nice tastes of the scholar, and such pleasant power of expression, that they deserve to be preserved in a more permanent form. Mr. Hart's life was short, but was filled up with acts of usefulness and charitable beneficence, and was rich with tokens, that it answered life's great end. He leaves a wife and one son, who bears his name."

THEIR CHILD, BEING THE NINTH GENERATION.

2921. Theodore Henry, born August 11th, 1860, in Philadelphia, Penn.

2662.   *Elmira, N. Y.*

DOCTOR IRA FAYETTE HART, Elmira, Chemung County, N. Y., eldest son of Alonzo Orville Hart, of Tompkins County, N. Y., and his wife,

Eveline M., daughter of Nathaniel Tobey, and his wife, Eunice (Pierce), born November 17th, 1829, at Harford, Cortland County, N. Y.; married March 10th, 1852, Marion E., daughter of Chauncey Culver Cook, and his wife, Esther Elmina (Hills), born November 15th, 1827, in Augusta, Oneida County, N. Y. He graduated at Hamilton College, July, 1849, and at Jefferson Medical College, Philadelphia, Penn. He was a physician in 1872, and was residing at Elmira, Chemung County, N. Y. He and his family are all members of the Congregational Church there, Rev. Thomas K. Beecher, pastor.

THEIR CHILDREN, BEING THE NINTH GENERATION.

2922. Fannie Evelyn, born December 15th, 1852, in Elmira, N. Y.

     Orville Kennedy, born February 1st, 1856; died December 31st, 1871, in Elmira, N. Y.

     Martha Lillybridge, born October 13th, 1860; died January 26th, 1861, in Elmira, N. Y.

2923. Esther Hastings, born February 22d, 1862, in Elmira, N. Y.   .

PRESWICK.

2663.   *Elmira, N. Y.*

EVELYN MARIA HART, Elmira, N. Y., only daughter of Alonzo Orville Hart, of Caroline, Tompkins County, N. Y., and his wife, Eveline M. Tobey, born December 7th, 1835, in Harford, Cortland County, N. Y. She was educated for a music teacher, but married June 17th, 1857, Christopher Preswick, a dealer in books and stationery in Elmira, N. Y., who was born August 18th, 1820, in Ithaca, N. Y. They are members of the Congregational Church, Rev. Thomas K. Beecher, pastor. They had no children, February, 1874.

2664.   *Chicago, Ill.*

JAMES POTTER HART, Chicago, Ill., eldest son of Samuel Hart, of Janesville, Rock County, Wis., and his wife, Sarah S., daughter of James Potter, of East Haven, Conn., born February 24th, 1833, in Harford, Cortland County, N. Y.; married in 1855, Nancy J. Blodget, of Dryden, Tompkins County, N. Y. He was a lumber merchant in Chicago, Ill. They had no children in 1874.

2665.   *Dryden, Iowa.*

EDWIN HART, Dryden, Tama County, Iowa, second son of Samuel Hart, of Janesville, Wis., and his wife, Sarah S., daughter of James Potter, of East Haven, Conn., born February 2d, 1835, at Harford, Cortland County, N. Y.; married December 28th, 1865, Ruth Emma

Woodward, of Lyons, Iowa. His avocation is farming, and he resided in Dryden, Iowa, but in 1874 he left Iowa, and removed to Riverside, San Bernardino County, Cal. He was a soldier in Company I, Sixth Regiment Iowa Cavalry.

THEIR CHILDREN, BEING THE NINTH GENERATION.
2924. Effie Elizabeth, born May 23d, 1867.
2925. Mary Louise, born April 15th, 1870.
2926. Samuel Henry, born January 9th, 1873.

2666.   *Greenville, Mich.*

HENRY HART, Greenville, Montcalm County, Mich., third son of Samuel Hart, of Janesville, Wis., and his wife, Sarah S. (Potter), born April 3d, 1837, at Harford, Cortland County, N. Y.; married September 30th, 1863, Rachel Schenck, of La Prairie, Wis. He was engaged in the lumber business in Greenville, Mich., in 1872.

THEIR CHILDREN, BEING THE NINTH GENERATION.
Josiah William, born December 29th, 1864; died August 25th, 1866.
Frank Willard, born December 4th, 1869; died October 8th, 1871.
2927. Harry, born May 13th, 1873.

NETTLETON.

2667.   *Janesville, Wis.*

MARY ELIZABETH HART, eldest daughter of Samuel Hart, of Janesville, Wis., and his wife, Sarah S. (Potter), born February 10th, 1839, at Harford, Cortland County, N. Y.; married December 7th, 1865, Garry Nettleton, of Janesville, Rock County, Wis., formerly of Milford, Conn. She died May 24th, 1871, aged 32 years. They had no children in 1874.

MINER.

2668.   *Janesville, Wis.*

ESTHER CORNELIA HART, Janesville, Wis., second daughter of Samuel Hart, of the same place, and his wife, Sarah S. (Potter), born June 17th, 1841, in Harford, Cortland County, N. Y.; married November 6th, 1862, Cyrus Miner, a merchant of Janesville, Rock County, Wis., where they resided in 1872. They had Mary Hart, died August 7th, 1864, Florence Hart, J. Potter, and Frederick, born February 27th, 1871.

2669.   *Beloit, Wis.*

SAMUEL WILLARD HART, Beloit, Wis., fourth son of Samuel Hart, of Janesville, Wis., and his wife, Sarah S. (Potter), born February 9th,

1844, at Harford, Cortland County, N. Y.; married October 18th, 1871, Franke Yost, of Beloit, Wis. He is a farmer, and resided in Beloit in 1872. They have no children.

2670.   *Janesville, Wis.*

JOSIAH FAYETTE HART, Janesville, Wis., fifth son of Samuel Hart, of the same place, and his wife, Sarah S. (Potter), born April 2d, 1848, in Harford, Cortland County, N. Y.; married November 14th, 1871, Harriet M. Campbell, of Janesville, Wis., where he is a clerk, and where he was residing in 1874.

THEIR CHILD, BEING THE NINTH GENERATION.
Marie, born September 30th, 1872; died August 27th, 1873.

EUSTIS.

2674.   *Oakland, Wis.*

MARIA AMELIA HART, Oakland, Wis., eldest daughter of Orlando Palmer Hart, and his first wife, Florinda (Goodrich), born, June, 1847, in Oakland, Jefferson County, Wis.; married March 27th, 1865, Charles Eustis, of Sangamond County, Ill. They have three children.

2675.

EDWIN CLARK HART, Oakland, Wis., third son of Orlando Palmer Hart, of the same place, and his first wife, Florinda (Goodrich), born, October, 1849, in Oakland, Wis.; married November 14th, 1872, Ellen S. Orndorf, daughter of Philander J. Mr. Hart is a farmer in Oakland, Wis., where his wife was born. They have no issue.

PERRY.

2677.

INA HART, Oakland, Jefferson County, Wis., second daughter of Orlando Palmer Hart, of the same town and county, and his first wife, Florinda (Goodrich), born October 6th, 1853, in Oakland; married October 19th, 1873, George Perry.

CHAPMAN.

2680.   *Koshkonong, Wis.*

MARY LOUISA HART, Oakland, Wis., eldest daughter of Lucius Leander Hart, of the same town and county, and his wife, Rebecca

(Goodrich), born December 20th, 1846, in Oakland; married October 6th, 1864, James Chapman, born March 13th, 1841, in England. He is a farmer. They have two children.

2681. *Oakland, Wis.*

NEWTON JOSIAH HART, Oakland, Wis., eldest son of Lucius Leander Hart, of the same town and county, and his wife, Rebecca (Goodrich), born June 20th, 1849, in Oakland; married March 8th, 1870, Cynthia Baldwin, of Farmington. They had William Arthur, born October 4th, 1871.

IVES.
2682.

HATTIE ANGELINE HART, Oakland, Wis., second daughter of Lucius Leander Hart, of the same town and county, and his wife, Rebecca (Goodrich), born May 28th, 1854, in Oakland; married October 11th, 1873, William W. Ives, born September 11th, 1850. He is a farmer. They had Rosamond Belle, born July 11th, 1874, and died February 4th, 1875.

COWLES.
2717. *Cheshire, Conn.*

LOUISA MARIA HART, Southington, eldest daughter of Jonathan Thomas Hart, the great manufacturer of Kensington, and his first wife, Maria (Woodruff), of New Britain, born August 28th, 1845, in New Britain; married October 20th, 1866, Frederick A. Cowles, of Southington, son of Charles A., and his wife, Widow Delia V. Bradley, whose maiden name was Stedman, born May 15th, 1843, in Southington. They were living in Cheshire, New Haven County, Conn., where he was keeping a drug store in 1874.

2721. *New Britain, Conn.*

EDWARD HART, New Britain, Conn., eldest son of Selah Hart, of the same place, and his wife, Jemima, daughter of David Webster, Esq., born September 4th, 1806, in New Britain; married March 26th, 1834, Vianer Perry, of Egremont, Mass. He was a farmer, and lived in a part of his father's house in Hart Quarter, where he died of consumption, September 1st, 1845, aged 39 years.

THEIR CHILDREN, BEING THE NINTH GENERATION.

John Burnham, born   , 1835; died March 7th, 1853, aged 18 years.
2928. Edward, born October 8th, 1836; married October 8th, 1861, Jane Eliza Webster.
2929. Stephen Perry, born   , 1837.

71

2722.   *New Britain, Conn.*

SELAH HART, New Britain, second son of Selah Hart, Sr., of the same place, and his wife, Jemima, daughter of David Webster, born November 25th, 1808, in New Britain; married November 11th, 1829, before Rev. Dr. Cogswell, in New Britain, Sarah, daughter of Henry North, of New Britain, and his first wife, Sally (Coslett), born December 24th, 1811, in New Britain. He has been a manufacturer and merchant in New York and Philadelphia. The residence of this family has been in Philadelphia, although he spends much of his time on his farm in Hart Quarter, New Britain.

THEIR CHILDREN, BEING THE NINTH GENERATION.

2930. Caroline E., born January 21st, 1832; married July 14th, 1852, S. B. Pratt.
2931. Julia Maria, born May 5th, 1834; died July 1st, 1853, aged 19 years.
2932. Katharine Harriet, born June 3d, 1840; married December 2d, 1864, William R. Buck, of Philadelphia.

2723.   *Fort Abercrombie, Minn.*

NELSON HART, New Britain, third son of Selah Hart, Sr., and his wife, Jemima (Webster), born November 25th, 1812, in New Britain; married October 8th, 1834, Lucy Jane Dewey, daughter of Josiah, Jr., and his wife, Betsey (Recor), born November 8th, 1816, in New Britain. In 1837 he went to Texas with that ill-fated colony from his native town. After some two years he went to Wisconsin, and at length located at Fort Abercrombie, Minn., where he and his son have spent some fifteen or twenty years in the government service, as commissary for the United States Army stationed there.

THEIR CHILD, BEING THE NINTH GENERATION.

2933. Franklin Dewey, born August 8th, 1837, in New Britain.

FRANCIS.

2724.   *New Haven, Conn.*

LURA ANN HART, eldest daughter of Selah Hart, Sr., of New Britain, and his wife, Jemima (Webster), born November 15th, 1816, in New Britain; married April 13th, 1837, in New Britain, Anson W. Francis, a carriage painter of Wethersfield and New Haven. She died February 20th, 1839, aged 22 years, leaving one child, Lura Ann, born July 14th, 1837. She is intelligent and pious, but was unfortunately lame in 1874, and is residing in Berlin.

MOON.

2725.   *Saratoga, N. Y.*

HARRIET HART, Saratoga, N. Y., youngest daughter of Selah Hart, Sr., of New Britain, and his wife, Jemima (Webster), born December

10th, 1821, in New Britain, Conn.; married, October, 1835, Cary B. Moon, of Saratoga, N. Y., where they kept a popular hotel, and where she died October 2d, 1869, aged 47 years, 11 months, and 22 days. Their children were Henry S. and Charles H.

SMITH.

2726. *New Britain, Conn.*

LUCINDA ANDREWS HART, New Britain, Conn., second daughter of Dr. Samuel Hart, of the same place, and his wife, Orpha, daughter of James North, Esq., born August 30th, 1820; united with the Congregational Church, December, 1835; married April 27th, 1842, William H. Smith, son of William, born October 22d, 1800, in New Britain. She was his second wife. He was a manufacturer, and was an active business man. He united with the Congregational Church in 1829, and was a deacon of the South Church. He was a man of integrity, very kindly disposed, and was much in public employment. He had just finished a beautiful residence on Main Street, in the south part of the city, when he was suddenly taken ill, and died August 20th, 1873, aged 72 years, 9 months, 27 days. They had—1, Willie Hart, born June 11th, 1846, died September 16th, 1847; 2, Annie Louisa, born October 19th, 1849, married November 5th, 1874, before Rev. Henry L. Griffin, and Rev. John H. Denison assisting, at the residence of the bride's mother, Frederick H. Churchill, Esq., a young lawyer of much promise, born March 27th, 1847, in New Britain, and graduated at Cambridge, Mass., in 1873.

2727. *New Britain, Conn.*

DOCTOR SAMUEL WALDO HART, New Britain, Conn., second son of Dr. Samuel Hart, of the same town, and his wife, Orpha, daughter of James North, Esq., and his first wife, Rhoda (Judd), born May 22d, 1825; married October 22d, 1851, Cordelia M. Smith, daughter of William H. Smith, and his first wife, Marsha (North), born June 7th, 1828, in New Britain. He is a successful practicing physician in New Britain. He has traveled in Europe, and has been to California. He resided in the old house of his father, on Main Street, opposite the Central Park. He was mayor of the city in 1873, 1874, and 1875. His wife died June 16th, 1857, aged 29 years, when he second married November 10th, 1864, in St. Mark's Church, Margaret C. Smyth, daughter of William B., and his wife, Annie (Goldsborough), born October 18th, 1846, in Easton, Md.

CHILDREN BY HIS FIRST WIFE, BEING THE NINTH GENERATION.

2934. Mary Louise, born October 8th, 1852.
2935. Gerald Waldo, born July 23d, 1856.

William Goldsborough, born April 6th, 1870; died July 20th, 1870.

2936. Anna Smyth, born September 13th, 1872.

FLAGG.

2728.   *New Haven, Conn.*

LOUISA HART, youngest daughter of Dr. Samuel Hart, of New Britain, and his wife, Orpha, daughter of James North, Esq., and his first wife, Rhoda (Judd), born October 5th, 1828, at New Britain; married December 1st, 1846, Rev. Jared B. Flagg, son of Henry C., of South Carolina, and his wife, Martha (Whiting), born June 16th, 1820. They lived in Brooklyn, N. Y. She died January 18th, 1867, in New Haven, aged 38. They had—1, Charles Noel, born December 25th, 1848, in Brooklyn; 2, Jared, born February 26th, 1853, in New Haven; 3, Earnest, born February 6th, 1857, in Brooklyn; 4, Washington Allston, born June 2d, 1860, in Brooklyn; 5, Louisa, born February 15th, 1862, in Brooklyn; 6, Rosalie, born November 9th, 1866, in New Haven.

2729.   *Hartford, Conn.*

ARTEMAS ENSIGN HART, New Britain, Conn., only son of Jesse Hart, the blacksmith, of the same place, and his wife, Lucina (Cowdrey), born February 11th, 1812, in New Britain; married August 24th, 1836, Elizabeth Ann, daughter of Abel Clark, of Litchfield, Conn., now Morris, and his wife, Catharine (Eckerst), born December 7th, 1816, in Litchfield, now Morris. He is a jeweler by trade. He built the house on Washington Street, which was used as a parsonage for the Episcopal Church in 1874. He lived for a time in Newington, but was living in Hartford in 1874.

THEIR CHILDREN, BEING THE NINTH GENERATION.

2937. Virginia Veeder, born August 1st, 1838; married November 4th, 1857, Henry Pember.

2938. Charles Richmond, born June 17th, 1840; married   , Ellen M. Woodruff.

2939. Artemas Elijah, born June 20th, 1842; married October 13th, 1865, Kate Litchfield.

Lucina, born September 27th, 1844; died   , aged 1 year.

2940. Elizabeth Ann, born November 10th, 1846; married October 9th, 1866, Charles Makin.

Henry Lockwood, born November 19th, 1848; died August 27th, 1849, aged 9 months.

2941. Joseph Clark, born June 4th, 1850. He was living with his parents in Hartford in 1871.

GOODWIN.

2730.   *Hartford, Conn.*

LUCINA HART, only daughter of Jesse Hart, the blacksmith of New Britain, and his wife, Lucina (Cowdrey), born December 3d, 1821, in New Britain; united with the Congregational Church there, April 4th, 1841; married October 29th, 1850, John H. Goodwin, of Hartford, son of John, and his wife, Anna (Belden), born March 2d, 1809. She was his second wife, his first wife being Nancy, daughter of Dr. Adna Stanley, of New Britain, and his wife, Nancy (Deming). He died January 20th, 1873, aged 64 years.

2731.   *Fair Haven, Conn.*

REV. BURDETT HART, New Britain, eldest son of Deacon Norman Hart, of the same town, and his wife, Minerva, daughter of Thomas Lee, Esq., and his wife, Electa (Riley), born November 16th, 1821, in New Britain, Conn.; graduated at Yale College in 1842, and settled in the ministry at Fair Haven, Conn.; married August 21st, 1849, Rebecca W., daughter of David Fiske, and his wife, Laura (Severance), of Shelburne, Mass., born February 22d, 1823.* His voice having partially failed, he traveled in Europe, and visited St. Paul, Minn., for a season, where he gathered a Congregational Church, and preached to them some twelve months, but not gaining much relief he was dismissed from Fair Haven, and removed to Philadelphia, where he engaged in mercantile pursuits. He was a good scholar, an easy writer, and a popular preacher. He returned to Fair Haven in 1874.

Since the above brief sketch was prepared the following communication has been received from a better informed source:

"His work in Fair Haven lasted some fifteen years. During the time he had invitations from Syracuse, N. Y., Manchester, N. H., Detroit, Mich., Middletown, Conn., St. Paul, Minn., and other places, to become their pastor. The church at Fair Haven was increased by 390 additions, 271 of them being heads of families. Through his influence the cause of education and social life was greatly promoted. During his ministry the church sent out over 100 members to form the second church. In St. Paul his congregation was one of the most intelligent in the city. Twelve lawyers were regular attendants. On thanksgiving day he preached a sermon on "Northern and Southern Civiliza-

---

* Mrs. Hart was president of the New Haven branch of the Women's Board of Missions in 1874, and often addresses public assemblies on the subject of missions, with great acceptance, which fact, perhaps, sufficiently indicates the quality of her talents and address.

tion," the first anti-slavery sermon ever preached in that city. It created a great excitement, and led to much discussion in the press. Thirty lawyers were present. The church, during his short pastorate, increased nearly threefold. On leaving he received a unanimous call to become their pastor. Perhaps the most important work of his life has been done in Philadelphia. It was owing to his influence that the Congregational Churches have been planted there. Dr. J. P. Thompson once said to him—'I could not understand why you were removed from Fair Haven; but in the planting of Congregationalism in Philadelphia I see the reason.' And many have said to him—'the work you have done here is vastly more important than you could have done in Fair Haven.' By personal effort he enlisted a sufficient number of New Englanders to organize a church. Soon after he movéd for a second church in another section of the city. Now they have two vigorous churches of that order there. The Central Church has just finished its ecclesiastical buildings, which, with the land, cost $120,000, and has a membership of over 200. The Plymouth Church has a commodious chapel, and a membership of about 100. The future of both seems to be assured. This work has not been confined to Philadelphia. Churches have followed at Baltimore, Washington, Vineland, and other places holding Congregational principles. It is said the establishing of the Congregational Church in Washington was owing to his influence. It would be impossible to measure the extent of this work. The Church of the Pilgrims, which he organized in Vineland, N. J., a flourishing and interesting community of 10,000 inhabitants, thirty-four miles south of Philadelphia, has prospered. Its membership has gone up from twenty-four to seventy-three. He was urged to become the permanent pastor. Quite a number of his sermons, as well as articles, have been published in the *New Englander*."

THEIR CHILDREN, BEING THE NINTH GENERATION.

Frederick Burdett, born August 2d, 1850; died August 6th, 1851.
2942. Arthur Burdett, born September 5th, 1852.
2943. Mary Arabella, born May 30th, 1855.
2944. Minerva Lee, born November 9th, 1859.

2732. *Philadelphia, Penn.*

NORMAN LEE HART, second son of Deacon Norman Hart, of New Britain, and his wife, Minerva (Lee), born February 2d, 1826, in New Britain; married December 6th, 1854, Lavinia M. Kellogg, of Philadelphia, daughter of M. A. Kellogg, of Avon, Conn., and his wife, Marilla (Cooley), of Hartford, Conn., born June 24th, 1834, in Hartford. He has been engaged in the mercantile business in Philadelphia for a number of years. He is very benevolent, having contributed some $10,000 to build up the Central and Plymouth Churches of that city, besides the aid he bestowed some years since to the First Church in his native town, showing his New England principles and attachments.

THEIR CHILDREN, BEING THE NINTH GENERATION.

2945. Marilla Mellen, born January 31st, 1858, in Philadelphia.
2946. Norman Elwood, born January 21st, 1861, in Philadelphia.

WELLS.

2733. *New Britain, Conn.*

ELLEN HART, New Britain, only daughter of Deacon Norman Hart, of the same place, and his wife, Minerva, daughter of Thomas Lee, Esq., born February 23d, in New Britain, where she joined the church, December 3d, 1848; married June 15th, 1853, Lemuel Russell Wells, son of Horace, and his wife, Pamela (Sedgwick), born January 2d, 1827, in New Britain. He was a farmer, and a deacon in the First Church. His residence was opposite his father's, on East Street, New Britain. He died February 25th, 1867, aged 40 years, and was greatly lamented. They had no children. Mrs. Wells was educated at Holyoke Seminary, Holyoke, Mass.

FRANCIS. RATCLIFF.

2734. *New Britain, Conn.*

HENRIETTA WOODING HART, New Britain, eldest daughter of Elijah Hart, 4th, of the same town, and his wife, Louisa (Warner), of Hamden, born March 25th, 1827, in New Britain; married September 14th, 1846, Darwin, son of Dr. Miles C. Francis, of Kensington, and his wife, Lydia (Bishop), of Stockbridge, Mass., born, August, 1823; died July 5th, 1854, aged 31 years, when second she married May 9th, 1860, Thomas Smith Ratcliff, son of Ezekiel, of Middletown, and his wife, Eunice (Winship), of Middletown, born January 6th, 1826, in Middletown. They live on Kensington Street, in the south part of the city of New Britain. He is a wagon maker by trade, which he learned in Middletown. She had one son and one daughter by Francis, and three sons and one daughter by Ratcliff.

HUMPHREY.

2735. *Bolton, Conn.*

ELIZA ANN HART, New Britain, Conn., second daughter of the fourth Elijah Hart, of the same town, and his wife, Louisa (Warner), born

July 12th, 1828, in New Britain; married　　　　　　, Hector
Humphrey, of Bloomfield, Conn. He is a farmer, and was living in
Bolton, Conn., in 1871. They have had two sons and two daughters.

HUMPHREY.

2736.　　　*Bloomfield, New Britain, Conn.*

AUGUSTA CORNELIA HART, New Britain, third daughter of the fourth
Elijah Hart, of the same town, and his wife, Louisa (Warner), of
Hamden, Conn., born May 12th, 1830, at New Britain; married September 5th, 1850, Henry Humphrey, a sash and blind maker of Bloomfield. In 1873 he built a house and shop on Kensington Street, in the
city of New Britain. They had one son in 1874.

DOOLITTLE.

2737.　　　　　　　　*Bethany, Conn.* ·

MARY JANE HART, Bethany, Conn., fourth daughter of the fourth
Elijah Hart, of New Britain, and his wife, Louisa (Warner), born September 5th, 1834, in New Britain; married, February, 1862, Julius S.
Doolittle, a farmer of Bethany, Conn. They had one son in 1874.

2738.　　　　　　　　*New Britain, Conn.*

ISAAC WARNER HART, New Britain, second son of the fourth Elijah
Hart, of the same town, and his wife, Louisa (Warner), born April
22d, 1838, in New Britain; married February 5th, 1865, Emily N.
Warner, daughter of Lewis, of Hamden, and his wife, Harriet (Scranton), of Madison, Conn., born December 15th, 1842, in Hamden; died
April 7th, 1868, in New Britain, aged 25 years, leaving no children,
when second he married, in Middletown, January 1st, 1874, before
Rev. J. P. Taylor, Lucina S. Lane, of Killingworth, Conn., daughter
of Bela, and his wife, Lucinda (Burr), born September 7th, 1852, in
Killingworth. He is a sash and blind maker. In 1873 he built a fine
house on Kensington Street, in the south part of the city of New
Britain.

WARD.

2739.　　　　　　　　*Middletown, Conn.*

EMMA LOUISA HART, youngest child of the fourth Elijah Hart, of
New Britain, and his wife, Louisa (Warner), of Hamden, born July
14th, 1844, in New Britain; married, June, 1861, Elijah R. Ward, a
joiner of Middletown. They lived in Newfield, a locality of Middletown, and had one daughter, Jennie, born April 3d, 1865. He was

killed May 6th, 1874, by being thrown from a wagon while the horses were running, in Fair Haven, Conn.

2740. *Brooklyn, N. Y.*

REV. LEVI WELLS HART, New Britain, Conn., and Brooklyn, N. Y., eldest son of Chester Hart, of New Britain, and his second wife, Elvey (Wells), daughter of Levi, born June 7th, 1825, in New Britain. He graduated at Yale College in 1846, and studied theology at Union Seminary, New York. He taught at the academy in Wallingford, Conn., in 1846-9. In 1852 he was licensed to preach by the South Presbytery of New York. He was one year a missionary to the Germans of the city, having a good knowledge of their language, as well as several others, when he became rector of the College Grammar School in Brooklyn, N. Y., established in 1849, where he remained until September, 1874, except four months spent with the State Normal School, located in New Britain, Conn., in the winter of 1855-6. His pupils at Brooklyn have numbered about 1,000, and were from four or five nationalities. He had an interesting Bible class in Mr. Beecher's church some sixteen years. He has preached as a supply and given lectures, and written on various subjects, both literary and religious, for periodicals, especially on education. He married December 27th, 1854, Georgiana, daughter of William B. North, of New Britain, and his wife, Sarah (Burger), born June 4th, 1825, in New Britain.

THEIR CHILDREN, BEING THE NINTH GENERATION.

2947. Louisa Wells, born September 8th, 1856. She is a member of Mr. Beecher's church.

Herbert Winthrop, born September 23d, 1865; died September 2d, 1867, aged 2 years.

2948. William North, born August 11th, 1869. He is a member of Dr. Talmage's church.

2949. Alice Bertha, born November 5th, 1870, in Brooklyn, N. Y.

2741. *New Britain, Conn.*

JOHN HENRY HART, New Britain, second son of Chester Hart, of the same town, and his second wife, Elvey, daughter of Levi Wells, of New Britain, and his wife, Hannah, born April 13th, 1828, in New Britain; baptized there, June, 1828; married January 4th, 1853, Jane, daughter of Deacon Josiah Griswold, of West Hartford. He was a farmer, and lived with his father on the Shuttle Meadow road, in Hart Quarter, in a good house and on a fine farm. This was sold, and they bought on Arch Street, in the center of the city. His wife died previous to this removal, April 7th, 1864, which induced in him a melan-

72

choly state of mind, and, in spite of all his efforts, was led to suicide by drowning in the factory pond, August 20th, 1869, aged 41 years, 4 months, and 7 days. He had a fine cultivated mind, was eminently pious, and gentlemanly in his deportment.

THEIR CHILDREN, BEING THE NINTH GENERATION.

2950. Anna Jane, born January 21st, 1855.
2951. Ellen Wells, born January 12th, 1857.

2743. *Galesburg, Ill.*

NEWTON FRANCIS HART, New Britain, Conn., eldest son of Aaron Hart, of the same place, and his wife, Abigail (Andrews), daughter of Dr. John, born January 2d, 1829, in New Britain; married May 4th, 1852, Nancy Phinney, of Plainville, Conn., daughter of Isaac, and his wife, Dolly (Phelps), widow of Sherman Carter, born November 13th, 1828, in Plainville, Conn. He was bred a merchant, and served his clerkship with Adna Whiting, of Plainville, Conn. In 1863 he was a druggist in Meriden, Conn., but in 1874 was a traveling agent for a hardware firm in Philadelphia, and resided at Galesburg, Ill.

THEIR CHILD, BEING THE NINTH GENERATION.

Ella, born December 9th, 1856; died January 29th, 1857, aged 1 year and 1 month.

LEWIS.

2745. *New Haven, Conn.*

JANE ABIGAIL HART, New Britain, Conn., youngest child of Aaron Hart, of the same town, and his wife, Abigail (Andrews), daughter of Dr. John, born June 2d, 1837, in New Britain, where she graduated at the State Normal School, and became a model teacher; married December 25th, 1860, John G. Lewis, of Hampton, Conn., and a teacher in New Haven, Conn., where they reside. He is at the head of the Webster School there. They had—1, Caell Andrews, born January 2d, 1862; 2, Robert Hart, born December 1st, 1864; 3, Mary Mumford, born December 4th, 1866; 4, John Newton, born January 11th, 1869, died July 12th, 1870; 5, Sarah Knowles, born July 5th, 1870, died June 10th, 1871; 6, Harry Blakeman, born August 17th, 1872.

POTTER.

2746.

EMILY ELIZA HART, eldest daughter of Ozias Hart, Jr., of Chicago, Ill., and his first wife, Pamelia (Baggs), born January 8th, 1818, in

New Britain, Conn. When she was about one year old she went to the west with her parents, and married about 1839, Lewis Potter, a lawyer from Vermont. He was a student of Dartmouth College until his health failed, when he went south teaching, where he found his wife, who was also a teacher.

2747. *Lombard, Ill.*

WILLARD OTIS HART, Lombard, Ill., second son of Ozias Hart, Jr., of New Britain, Conn., but in 1874 of Chicago, Ill., and his second wife, Triphena (Elmer), born February 13th, 1838, in Henderson, Jefferson County, N. Y.; married in Chicago, May 21st, 1867, Martha Jane Lucas, born in Trumansburg, N. Y., February 2d, 1844. He is a house painter by occupation, and lives in Lombard, Ill.

THEIR CHILDREN, BEING THE NINTH GENERATION.

2952. John Ozias, born March 7th, 1868, in Chicago, Ill.
2953. Willard Lucas, born January 11th, 1870, in Chicago, Ill.
2954. Myrtle Edna, born October 19th, 1871, in Chicago, Ill.
2955. Edith Louise, born January 10th, 1874, in Lombard, Ill.

WINBOLT.

2748. *West Brooklyn, Ill.*

SARAH ANN HART, West Brooklyn Station, Lee County, Ill., only daughter of Ozias Hart, of New Britain, Conn., but now of Chicago, and his second wife, Triphena (Elmer), born March 5th, 1845; married January 1st, 1864, James W. Winbolt, born March 23d, 1835, in Port Rowin, Canada. His avocation is farming, and they were living at West Brooklyn Station, Lee County, Ill., in 1874. They have had— 1, Charles Walter, born November 10th, 1864; 2, George Edward, born November 18th, 1866, and died February 10th, 1867.

2749. *Millerton, N. Y.*

DR. HENRY ABIJAH HART, JR., New Hartford, Conn., and Millerton, N. Y., only son of Dr. Henry Abijah Hart, Sr., of New Britain and North Haven, Conn., and his wife, Eliza (Shipman), daughter of Joseph, of New Britain, born November 30th, 1828, in New Britain. He graduated at the Medical College, New Haven, as a physician, and practiced for a time in Forestville and Watertown, Conn., but removed to New Hartford, Conn., and at his mother's death came into possession of the homestead and farm left at the decease of Major Brown, subject to legacies. He married January 26th, 1868, Josephine Estella Essex, of New Hartford, Conn., daughter of William F., of Colchester, Conn., and his wife, Eliza Ann (Clark), of Brooklyn, Conn., born February 11th, 1846, in Mansfield, Conn. He was a farmer in New Hartford, Conn., in 1873, but was a physician in Millerton, N. Y., in 1874.

THEIR CHILD, BEING THE NINTH GENERATION.

2956. Josephine Louisa, born February 20th, 1871, in New Hartford, Conn.

2750. *Southington, Conn.*

HENRY JAMES HART, Southington, Conn., only son of Ethan Hart, of New Britain, Conn., and his wife, Martha (Wiard), born July 24th, 1820, in Southington, Conn.; married August 25th, 1842, Sophia, daughter of Caleb Peck, and his wife, Lucy (Dutton), born April 11th, 1822, in Southington, Conn. She died April 1st, 1865, aged 43 years. He is a farmer by occupation, and owns and occupies the house built by Selah W. Thorp, on the west side of the West Mountain Road.

THEIR CHILDREN, BEING THE NINTH GENERATION.

Lucy Ann, born April 1st, 1843; died young. .
2957. Henry Ethan, born May 20th, 1844; married, December, 1864, Gelina Lewis, Amelia Sophia, born June 16th, 1846; died young.
2958. Charles Emerson, born July 16th, 1847; married   , Henrietta Stedman.
2959. Lucy Ann, born November 23d, 1851.
2960. Amelia Sophia, born August 23d, 1854.
2961. Inez A., born February 22d, 1856.
Gilbert, born April 14th, 1861; died February 28th, 1862, aged 11 months.

2752. *Palatka, Ill.*

GEORGE HART, Palatka, Ill., eldest son of Stephen Hart, of Palatka, Ill., and his wife, Eliza (Buck), born July 26th, 1835, in Palatka, Ill.; married, May, 1863, Sarah Parrot.

THEIR CHILDREN, BEING THE NINTH GENERATION.

2753. *Palatka, Ill.*

ALBERT HART, Palatka, Ill., third son of Stephen Hart, of Palatka, Ill., and his wife, Eliza (Buck), born March 6th, 1839, in   ;
married   , 1868, Anna Radcliff.

KEMPER.

2755. *Bantam, Ohio.*

VESTA CURTISS HART, Bantam, Claremont County, Ohio, eldest daughter of Doctor Seth Hart, of Harmar, Ohio, and his first wife,

Vesta (Curtiss), born December 1st, 1826, in Watertown, Washington County, Ohio; married in Harmar, Ohio, May 13th, 1844, Frederick Edwin Kemper, of Virginia, by birth. He is a farmer in Bantam, Ohio, about twenty-five miles from Cincinnati. They had—1, Olive Orcott, born August 2d, 1848, married Albert Martin Palmer, a hardware merchant in Cleveland, Ohio, October, 1868; 2, Fayette M., born March 3d, 1851; 3, Lydia North, and 4, Mary Hart, twins; 5, Edwin Wilson, born October 19th, 1857; 6, Vesta Curtiss, born January 10th, 1862.

2756. *Marietta, Ohio.*

DOCTOR SAMUEL HART, Marietta, Ohio, eldest son of Dr. Seth Hart, of Harmar, Ohio, and his second wife, Mary (Wilson), born June 7th, 1830, in Watertown, Washington County, Ohio. He removed with his father's family to Marietta in 1837. He finished his course in the Academy in 1848, studied medicine with his father, and graduated at the Medical College of Cincinnati in 1852. He practiced medicine in Marietta until October, 1861, when he became surgeon of the Seventy-Fifth Regiment Ohio Volunteers, and served in it until February, 1863, when he was breveted lieutenant-colonel and surgeon of United States Volunteers. After the war closed he resumed medicine at Bellevue Hospital Medical College, taking the *ad eundem* degree in 1867. He has had a large professional business since in Marietta, Ohio. He married June 11th, 1856, Sarah Elizabeth, daughter of Ezra Purple, of Gill, Mass., and his wife, Clara   , born March 14th, 1827, in Gill, Franklin County, Mass.

THEIR CHILD, BEING THE NINTH GENERATION.

2962. Donald Purple, born October 12th, 1868, in Marietta, Ohio.

NIXON.

2757. *Ironton, Ohio.*

MARY WILSON HART, eldest daughter of Dr. Seth Hart, of Harmar, Ohio, and his second wife, Mary (Wilson), born November 26th, 1831, in Watertown, Ohio; married November 20th, 1870, James Hopkins Nixon, of Ironton, Ohio, born September 8th, 1834, in Lawrence County, Ohio. They were living in Ironton in 1874.

2758. *Harmar, Ohio.*

ROMAYN BECK HART, Harmar, Ohio, second son of Dr. Seth Hart, of the same town and county, and his second wife, Mary (Wilson), born November 30th, 1833, in Watertown, Ohio; married November 11th, 1856, Martha Eliza Metcalf, born in Cincinnati, September 22d, 1834·

married in Walnut Hills, Ohio, near Cincinnati. He is a book-keeper, and was residing in Harmar, March, 1874.

THEIR CHILDREN, BEING THE NINTH GENERATION.

2963. Romayn Beck, born June 19th, 1858.
     Infant daughter, born January 6th, 1860; died in a few hours.
2964. Willie Metcalf, born February 27th, 1862.
2965. Helen Wilson, born March 29th, 1871.
2966. Harry Munson, born April 29th, 1873.

2759.   *Constitution, Ohio.*

HENRY LYMAN HART, Constitution, Washington County, Ohio, third son of Dr. Seth Hart, of Harmar, Ohio, and his second wife, Mary (Wilson), a twin with Samuel Mansun, born October 11th, 1835, in Watertown, Ohio; married September 21st, 1858, Lucy Wolcott Deming, born May 8th, 1838. His avocation is farming, but is interested in the gold and silver mines of Colorado, and was residing in Watertown, March, 1874.

THEIR CHILDREN, BEING THE NINTH GENERATION.

2967. Charles Grosvenor, born June 19th, 1859.
2968. Mary Deming, born September 11th, 1861.
2969. Lucy Wolcott, born January 20th, 1864.
2970. Eleanor, born September 26th, 1866.

2761.   *Denver, Col.*

DAVID WILSON HART, Denver, Col., fifth son of Dr. Seth Hart, of Harmar, Washington County, Ohio, and his second wife, Mary (Wilson), born March 26th, 1838, in Watertown, Ohio; married December 23d, 1865, Marian Adelaide Cox, daughter of Samuel N., and his wife, Charlotte (Rowland), born April 29th, 1845. He was a book-keeper in Denver, Col., March, 1874.

THEIR CHILD, BEING THE NINTH GENERATION.

2971. Frederick Wilson, born November 8th, 1868.

2762.   *Harmar, Ohio.*

LYDIA NORTH HART, youngest daughter of Dr. Seth Hart, of Harmar, Ohio, by his second wife, Mary (Wilson), born August 30th, 1840, in Watertown, Ohio. She has been employed as a teacher in Harmar and Marietta, Ohio, for some twelve years.

2764.   *Cambria, Mich.*

* FRANK B. HART, only son of Austin Hart, of Cambria, Hillsdale County, Mich., and his wife, Clarinda (Star), born June 19th, 1847, in

Cambria, Mich.; married October 23d, 1872, Annie E. Fox, born May 2d, 1850. He is a farmer, and they live in Cambria, Mich.

DYE.

2765. *Harmar, Ohio.*

EMILY BECKWITH HART, eldest daughter of Columbus Hart, of Huron County, Ohio, and his wife, Nancy (Proctor), born October 31st, 1834, in Harmar, Ohio; married October 20th, 1853, John Quincy Adams Dye, son of Thomas, and his wife, Hannah, born, October, 1831. They had—1, Nettie Zenette, born April 1st, 1854; 2, Lizzie Nan, born September 8th, 1856; 3, John Judson, born July 3d, 1858; 4, Delbert Hart, born March 13th, 1861.

BOWERS.

2766. *Huntington, W. Va.*

MALVINA EMELINE HART, second daughter of Columbus Hart, of Huron County, and his wife, Nancy (Proctor), born December 21st, 1838, in Harmar, Ohio; married June 22d, 1869, Rev. Albert Bowers, in Macon, Mo., born April 11th, 1837, in Hancock, N. H. He graduated at Dartmouth College in 1863, and at Andover Theological Seminary in 1868. He was ordained February 28th, 1869, and has charge of the Congregational Church in Huntington, W. Va. They had—1, Roy Edwin, born January 7th, 1872, in Macon, Mo.

ZEIGLER.

2767. *Columbus, Ohio.*

AUGUSTA ELIZABETH HART, third daughter of Columbus Hart, of Huron County, Ohio, and his wife, Nancy (Proctor), born April 10th, 1842; married December 19th, 1864, D. H. Zeigler, before Rev. I. W. Andrews, president of Marietta College. He was a son of Nicholas Zeigler, and his wife, Elizabeth (Bugh), born in Somerset, Ohio, March 3d, 1838. He graduated at Marietta College in 1863, and was a teacher, but died April 22d, 1871, in Columbus, Ohio. They had one child, Jessie, born February 22d, 1866, in Columbus, Ohio.

2768. *Harmar, Ohio.*

BENJAMIN FRANKLIN HART, Harmar, Ohio, second son of Columbus Hart, of Huron County, Ohio, and his wife, Nancy (Proctor), born March 31st, 1849; married December 30th, 1873, Laura E. Gearhart. He is a machinist, and they live in Harmar, Washington County, Ohio.

BARTLETT.

2760.   *Marietta, Ohio.*

MARY FRANKLIN HART, eldest daughter of Dr. Benjamin Franklin Hart, of Marietta, Ohio, and his wife, Sally Maria (Alcock), born January 27th, 1850, in Marietta; married January 27th, 1870, J. C. Bartlett, M. D., of Marietta, son of Hon. Levi, and his wife, Maria (Dickey), born September 23d, 1838. He graduated at the Medical College in Cincinnati, March, 1865, and at the University of Michigan in 1868. He has a drug store in Marietta. They became members of the Con gregational Church in Marietta, April, 1869.

LOFFLAND.

2766.   *Harmar, Ohio.*

INDEPENDENCE E. HART, Harmar, Washington County, Ohio, eldest daughter of Josiah Thomas Hart, of the same town and county, and his wife, Elizabeth A. (Harris), born June 17th, 1851, in Harmar; married October 1st, 1872, William Loffland, of Scotch origin, born June 17th, 1846. He is a business contractor, and lives on the banks of the Muskingum River. They have had one child, William Arthur, born August 2d, 1873, in Harmar, Ohio.

2783.   *New Britain, Conn.*

WILLIAM COWLES HART, New Britain, second son of Benjamin Kellogg Hart, of Kensington and New Britain, Conn., and his wife, Olivia (Cowles), born July 30th, 1829, in Kensington; married February 18th, 1873, in New York City, by Rev. Mr. Quackenbush, Eleanor Medora, daughter of Joseph Porter, of Waterbury, Conn., and his wife, Charlotte Ann (Tompkins), of Camden, N. Y., born March 24th, 1845, in Waterbury, Conn. She was educated at the high school there, and has been a teacher several years. He is a house builder, and a speculator in houses and lands, in and near Hart Avenue, in the south part of the city of New Britain.

THEIR CHILD, BEING THE NINTH GENERATION.
2972. Agnes Porter, born December 9th, 1873, in New Britain, Conn.

WOODRUFF.

2785.   *Southington, Conn.*

HARRIET SELENAH HART, eldest daughter of Thomas Robbins Hart, of Kensington, Conn., and his wife, Cecelia (Bement), born September

2d, 1837, in Kensington; married March 14th, 1860, Adna Woodruff, son of Samuel, and his wife, Emeline (Neal), of Southington, where he was born. He is a master carpenter and joiner, which he learned of his father. He built himself a house one and a half miles east of the village of Southington, on the corner of the road leading to East Street. They had no children in 1871.

2786. *Berlin, Conn.*

WALTER SCOTT HART, Berlin, Conn., eldest son of Thomas Robbins Hart, of Kensington, and his wife, Cecelia (Bement), born February 4th, 1840, in Kensington; married June 21st, 1863, Helen Thalia Welch, daughter of Hiram G., of Bristol, and his wife, Sophronia (Atwater), of Berlin, born March 22d, 1847, in Bristol. He is a carpenter and joiner, and owns a small place, well located near the old place of Henry Sage, in the south part of the village of Berlin.

THEIR CHILDREN, BEING THE NINTH GENERATION.
Walter Barton, born March 18th, 1867, in Berlin, Conn.
Lucius Robbins, born August 7th, 1869, in Berlin, Conn.

2787. *New Britain, Conn.*

BENJAMIN FRANKLIN HART, New Britain, Conn., second son of Thomas Robbins Hart, of Kensington, Conn., and his wife, Cecelia (Bement), born February 27th, 1842, in Kensington; married September 27th, 1866, Elizabeth, daughter of Hosmer Parsons, of New Britain, and his wife, Mahala (Tuller), of Simsbury, Conn., born June 21st, 1837, in New Britain. He is a mechanic, and works and lives in New Britain.

THEIR CHILD, BEING THE NINTH GENERATION.
Frank Hosmer, born January 14th, 1869, in New Britain, Conn.

2788. *Kensington, Conn.*

GEORGE WASHINGTON HART, Kensington, Conn., third son of Thomas Robbins Hart, of Kensington, and his wife, Cecelia (Bement), born October 11th, 1844, in Kensington; married November 18th, 1865, Alice Deming, daughter of Stillman, of Durham, Conn., and his wife, Roxy (Potter), of Rhode Island, born August 23d, 1846, in Middletown. He is a farmer and mechanic, and they were living with his father in Kensington in 1871.

THEIR CHILDREN, BEING THE NINTH GENERATION.
Ida Stillman, born October 3d, 1866, in Durham, Conn.
George Edwin, born August 10th, 1868, in Berlin, Conn.

73

RUE.

2790. Freehold, N. J.

JANE ANN HART, Freehold, N. J., eldest child of Walter Ward Hart, of Freehold, Monmouth County, N. J., and his wife, Sarah (Bennett), born April 30th, 1830, in Freehold; married September 28th, 1852, David Mills Rue, of Freehold, where they reside.

BROCK.

2791. Brooklyn, N. Y.

EMILY AUGUSTA HART, Brooklyn, N. Y., second daughter of Walter Ward Hart, of Freehold, N. J., and his wife, Sarah (Bennett), born September 29th, 1835; married June 12th, 1856, Solomon Brock. He is a wholesale dealer in patent articles in New York City, and they reside in Brooklyn, N. Y. They have one child, Edward Rue, born August 16th, 1860.

2792. Newark, N. J.

REV. CHARLES EDWARD HART, Newark, N. J., second son of Walter Ward Hart, of Freehold, N. J., and his wife, Sarah (Bennett), born February 28th, 1838, in Freehold. He graduated at Princeton College, N. J., in 1858, and at the Theological Seminary there in 1860. He was installed pastor of Murray Hill Presbyterian Church, New York City, December 6th, 1863, and of the North Reformed Church, Newark, N. J., June 3d, 1866. His residence was at No. 56 Park Place, Newark, N. J., in 1871. He was not married.

MOUNT.

2793. Brooklyn, N. Y.

EVELINA McLEAN HART, youngest daughter of Walter Ward Hart, of Freehold, N. J., and his wife, Sarah (Bennett), born January 28th, 1841, in Freehold; married June 9th, 1869, John Fressaler Mount, importer of furs and confidential clerk in New York City. They reside in Brooklyn, N. Y., and have had one child, Jennie Rue, born September 1st, 1870.

SCOTT.

2810. Patterson, N. J.

EMMA HART, eldest daughter of Erastus Parmelee Hart, Esq., of Elmira, Chemung County, N. Y., and his wife, Eliza (Wright), born October 22d, 1846, in Elmira, N. Y., and married there January 12th,

1871, D. J. Scott, of Patterson, N. J. They have had one child, Isabella Langdon, born November 25th, 1871.

2816. *Tennessee.*

WILLIAM HENRY HART, eldest son of John Alexander Hart, of Greenport, L. I., and his wife, Louisa (Edgerton), born July 27th, 1840; married in Marshville, Tenn., December 5th, 1864, Alice Martin. He was a railroad superintendent in Tennessee in 1871. They have no children.

2817. *Santa Barbara, Cal.*

MORTIMER EDGERTON HART, Cleveland, Ohio, second son of John Alexander Hart, formerly of Greenport, L. I., but now of Cleveland, and his wife, Louisa (Edgerton), of New London, Conn., born September 5th, 1844, in Greenport; married in Cleveland, November 25th, 1868, Alice Josephine McCurdy, of Lyme, Conn. He served his country as a soldier in the late war. In 1872 he went to California for his health, and has much improved by the change. He is now (1875) located at Santa Barbara, Cal., where he is a banker.

THEIR CHILD, BEING THE NINTH GENERATION.

2973. Alice Louise, born August 20th, 1869, in Cleveland, Ohio.

2818. *Montana.*

EDWARD LEARNED HART, Montana, third son of John Alexander Hart, of Greenport, L. I., and subsequently of Cleveland, Ohio, and his wife, Louisa (Edgerton), of New London, Conn., born May 3d, 1848, in Greenport, L. I.; married November 3d, 1870, Anna Sullivan. He is a miner in Montana in 1875.

DOANE.

2823. *Saybrook, Conn.*

MARY WILLIAMS HART, New York, eldest daughter of Henry Sill Hart, of Saybrook, Conn., and subsequently of New York City, and his wife, Mary E. (Clark), born June 12th, 1851, in Utica, N. Y.; married April 4th, 1870, in Saybrook, Conn., Thomas Benjamin Doane, son of Hon. John J. Doane, of that place.

2830. *Hartford, Conn.*

WILLIAM HENRY HART, Hartford, Conn., eldest son of Joseph Austin Hart, of the same city, and his wife, Clarissa (Hubbard), born November 30th, 1845, in Middletown, Conn.; married   ,

Isabella J. Weildon, of Hartford. He is a general agent of the Charter Oak Life Insurance Company, of Hartford.

THEIR CHILDREN, BEING THE NINTH GENERATION.

2974. Annie Clarissa, born May 17th, 1871, in Hartford, Conn.
2975. Mary Francis, born February 10th, 1873, in Hartford, Conn.

FOLSOM.

2839. *Luzerne, Iowa.*

EMELINE FRANCES HART, eldest daughter of Henry Hudson Hart, of Luzerne, Benton County, Iowa, and his wife, Martha Jane (Warnock), born October 11th, 1848, in Farmington, Fulton County, Ill.; married October 24th, 1872, near Luzerne, Iowa, George Reuben Folsom, son of Samuel, and his wife, Achsah, born May 23d, 1846, in Sandwich, Carrol County, N. H. He is a member of the society of Friends.

MOREHOUSE.

2857. *Medina, N. Y.*

HARRIET HART, Medina, N. Y., only child of Abraham Parmelee Hart, of Goshen, Conn., and subsequently of Elmira, Tioga County, N. Y., and his wife, Angeline (Badger), of Elmira, N. Y., born December 20th, 1840; married   , E. Morehouse, of Medina, N. Y.

HARRIS.

2904. *Richmond, Mass.*

SARAH HART, only daughter of William Hart, of Norfolk, Conn., and his first wife, Elizabeth (Snyder), born November 22d, 1852, in Norfolk, Conn.; married October 21st, 1871, Hubert Harris, of Richmond, Mass. They had one child, Nellie Eliza, born May 18th, 1872.

2928. *Plainville, Conn.*

EDWARD HART, Plainville, Conn., second son of Edward Hart, of New Britain, Conn., and his wife, Viana (Perry), born October 8th, 1836, in New Britain; married October 8th, 1861, Jane Eliza, daughter of Ebenezer Webster, of Plainville, Conn., and his wife, Sarah Jane (Grimes), born November 11th, 1838, in Plainville. He was a carriage trimmer by trade and avocation. He was a most devoted Christian, and early joined the Congregational Church, but died prematurely of consumption, in Plainville, December 26th, 1865, aged 29 years, leaving a devoted wife and two children.

2976. Edward Perry, born June 24th, 1864, in Plainville, Conn.
2977. Frederick Wells, born July 12th, 1866, in Plainville, Conn.

PRATT.

2930.   *Charlestown, Mass.*

CAROLINE ELIZABETH HART, eldest daughter of Selah Hart, of New
Britain, Conn., and subsequently of Philadelphia, Penn., and his wife,
Sarah (North), born January 21st, 1832, in New Britain; married in
Philadelphia, July 14th, 1852, S. B. Pratt, of Boston, Mass., by his
father, Rev. Parsons Pratt, of New York. Their child, Willys Herbert, born, February, 1854, died March 3d, 1860. Mrs. Pratt died
March 4th, 1859, in Charlestown, Mass., aged 27 years. They were
both buried in Mount Auburn. The following obituary notice is from
a newspaper:

"Mrs. Carrie E. Pratt, daughter of Selah Hart, Esq., formerly of
New Britain, Conn., died in Charlestown, Mass., on Thursday, March
3d, 1860. In her decease not only her husband and parents and immediate relatives have sustained a great loss, but a far wider circle, to
whom she was greatly endeared by her Christian graces, refinement,
and labors of love. She had charge of the infant department in the
Sunday School of which her husband was superintendent, and we learn
that the services of the Sabbath preceding her death were virtually a
united prayer meeting for her recovery. The afflicted parents will have
the sincerest sympathy of all who knew them here in this second be-
reavement."

An obituary notice of her child, Willys Herbert, a very extraordinary lovely child, mentioned above, was published in the *Sunday School
World* of the period, occupying one and a half columns of the paper
too lengthy for our space.   ✦

BUCK.

2932.   *Philadelphia, Penn.*

KATHARINE HARRIET HART, Philadelphia, Penn., youngest daughter
of Selah Hart, of New Britain, Conn., and subsequently of Philadelphia, Penn., and his wife, Sarah (North), born June 3d, 1840, in New
Britain; married December 2d, 1864, William R. Buck, of Philadelphia, Penn.

PEMBER. SMITH.

2937.   *Morrisania, N. Y.*

VIRGINIA VEEDER HART, eldest daughter of Artemas Ensign Hart,
of New Britain and Hartford, Conn., and his wife, Elizabeth Ann

(Clark), born August 1st, 1838, in New Britain; married November 4th, 1857, Henry Pember, son of Elisha, and his wife, Persis (King), born August 2d, 1833, in Vernon, Conn. He died November 30th, 1866, in Hartford, aged 33 years, when second she married January 5th, 1869, J. Charles Smith, son of Nathaniel C., and his wife, Charlotte (Strong), born May 14th, 1832, in East Hampton, Conn. Her children by Pember were—1, Elisha Hart, born November 22d, 1858, in Rockville, Conn.; 2, Persis King, born May 10th, 1862, in Willimantic, Conn. She was residing with her second husband in Morrisania, N. Y., in 1874.

2938. Hartford, Conn.

CHARLES RICHMOND HART, Hartford, Conn., second son of Artemas Ensign Hart, of New Britain, but now of Hartford, and his wife, Elizabeth Ann (Clark), born June 17th, 1840, in Milford, Conn.; married in Christ Church, Hartford, April 4th, 1866, Ellen Maria Woodruff, daughter of Orrin D., and his wife, Mary Jane (Crosby), born February 9th, 1843, in Hartford. He is in the firm of Hart, Merriam & Co., dry goods merchants, No. 325 Main Street, Hartford, and is doing a good business. His residence is No. 171 Sigourney Street.

THEIR CHILDREN, BEING THE TENTH GENERATION.

Son, born December 6th, 1868; died December 8th, 1868.

2978. Edith Woodruff, born September 21st, 1869, in Hartford.

2939. Hartford, Conn.

ARTEMAS ELIJAH HART, Hartford, Conn., second son of Artemas Ensign Hart, of Hartford, and his wife, Elizabeth Ann (Clark), born June 20th, 1842, in New Britain; married October 13th, 1865, Katharine A. O. Litchfield, of Hartford, where she was born, September 29th, 1845. He is cashier of the Pratt Street Savings Bank. Hartford.

THEIR CHILDREN, BEING THE TENTH GENERATION.

2979. Elizabeth Katharine, born January 19th, 1867.
Alida May, born May 9th, 1870; died March 8th, 1873.
2980. Sara Litchfield, born February 16th, 1872.

MACKIN.

2940. Hartford, Conn.

ELIZABETH ANN HART, third daughter of Artemas Ensign Hart, of Hartford, and his wife, Elizabeth Ann (Clark), born November 10th, 1846, in New Britain; married October 9th, 1866, Charles Mackin, of New York. He was a contractor for clothing the army during the late war, and was a man of wealth. He died February 24th, 1868, in New York. They had no children.

2957. *Southington, Conn.*

HENRY ETHAN HART, Southington, eldest son of Henry James Hart, of the same town, and his wife, Sophia (Peck), born May 20th, 1844, in Southington; married, December, 1864, Gelina, daughter of Lloyd Lewis, of Southington, and his wife, Diadama (Phinney), daughter of Martin, born   . They live in the west part of Southington, on the West Mountain Road, and his avocation is farm-ing. They have no children at this writing.

2958. *Southington, Conn.*

CHARLES EMMERSON HART, Southington, Conn., second son of Henry James Hart, of the same town, and his wife, Sophia (Peck), born July 16th, 1847, in Southington; married December 9th, 1869, Henrietta Stedman, daughter of William and Priscilla Stedman, of Southington, born August 20th, 1849. Mr. Hart works in a saw-mill, and they live on High Street.

THEIR CHILD, BEING THE TENTH GENERATION.

2981. Ada Louise, born September 2d, 1870, in Southington, Conn.

ADDENDA.

The following items were received after the pages to which they belong were printed:

The following is in addition to the Introduction to this work:

MISCELLANEOUS HARTS NOT OF DEACON STEPHEN HART.

"*Isaac Hart* came over in 1637, as a servant of Richard Carver, and stopped first at Watertown. He was at Lynn in 1640, and removed to Reading in 1647. His wife's name was Elizabeth. Their children were—Elizabeth, born in 1651, and married in 1667, in Malden, John Winborn; Samuel, born in 1656; Adam, born in 1666; Reuben, died in 1670. He first settled in the south part of that town, near and west of the present site of the Congregational meeting-house, and removed to North Reading." (From a Deed, July 6th, 1703.)

"*Adam Hart* married Elizabeth Colston, daughter of Adam Colston, and Adam Hart was made guardian to Mary Colston." (Genealogical History of the town of Reading, Mass., by Hon. Lilley Eaton, page 85.)

MRS. RUTH (COLE) HART, widow of General Selah Hart, No. 41, page 57, gave to the ecclesiastical society of Kensington, Conn., in March, 1837, the sum of $500, to re-model and modernize their meeting-house, provided the society would add to it an equal sum. At a legal meeting held on the above date the society appointed Benjamin Allen, Esq., as moderator, when, on motion, the society voted to accept the gift with the conditions annexed, and appointed Colonel Isaac Botsford, Linas Cowles, and Roswell Moore, Jr., a committee to thank her for the gift, and laid a tax of ten cents on a dollar of each man's list to raise the money to fulfill the condition.

Otho, Iowa.

Deacon Norman Hart, Otho, Webster County, Iowa, No. 229, Branch of John, page 107, youngest son of Deacon Seth Hart, of Kensington, Glastonbury, and Rocky Hill, Conn., and his second wife, Lydia (Williams), who was the widow of Dr. Bull, born October 10th, 1805, in Rocky Hill, and baptized there by Rev. Calvin Chapin, D. D., December 22d, 1805. He was left an orphan at the age of seven years, and went to live with Deacon Oliver Hale, of Glastonbury. In March, 1825, he married his daughter, Marcia, who was born November 21st, 1801, and died in Otho, Iowa, February 11th, 1875. Her mother was Betsey Hale, daughter of Colonel John Hale, of Glastonbury. Mr. Hart was a farmer, and they lived in Glastonbury until 1834, when they removed to Illinois, where they resided twenty years, but in 1854 they removed to Iowa. He was chosen deacon of the church in Mechanicsville, Ill. Mr. and Mrs. Hart and three of their children were organized into a Congregational Church in Otho, in March, 1855, which church now (1875) has eighty members.

THEIR CHILDREN, BEING THE EIGHTH GENERATION.

Norman Hale, born July 10th, 1826, in Glastonbury, Conn.; married Jane Fuller, of Ohio.

Lucius Williams, born October 26th, 1827, in Glastonbury, Conn.; married Katharine Livingstone, of Illinois.

Caroline E., born May 14th, 1833, in Glastonbury, Conn.; married Francis B. Drake, of New York.

George Dwight, born July 26th, 1835, in Illinois; married Orlinda Moore, of Ohio.

Note.—These children have all settled within sight of their father's house, are all members of the church there, and are a great comfort to their father in his old age, and more especially in the loss of their mother as above stated.

William Strickland Hart, New Britain, Conn., No. 265, page 122, Branch of John, and son of Roger Hart, No. 116, page 85, was a shoemaker by trade, and died in New Britain, March 15th, 1875, aged 69 years, 5 months, and 1 day. He was an active member of the Methodist Church, having united with that church in early life. His last sickness was fever, which lasted but one week. He made himself useful for several years as a night watchman in one of our largest manufacturing establishments. After his decease his widow removed to Hartford, where she formerly belonged.

Edward Gardner Hart, No. 519, page 124, fourth son of Salmon North Hart, No. 270, page 124, Branch of John, born October 9th,

1852; married December 7th, 1874, before Rev. Mr. Gage, Mary Scoville Calhoun, daughter of David Samuel Calhoun, Esq., and his wife, Harriet Antoinette (Gilbert), born July 23d, 1854, in Hartford, Conn. His avocation is carriage making, and he is supposed to be in company with his father, in his extensive establishment on Albany Avenue.

The following narrative and pedigree was kindly furnished by Rev. C. H. Hart, now of Logan, Ohio:

JOSEPH HART AND HIS DESCENDANTS.

JOSEPH HART was born in Botetourt County, Va., June 22d, 1760. The Christian names of his father and mother I am not able to give. The maiden name of his mother was Stout. She, with a brother older than herself, came from Wales, G. B., about the year 1750, and settled in South Carolina, where a Mr. Hart was married to Miss Stout, probably in the year 1758. One child, Joseph, was born to them, and during his infancy the mother died. The father married a second time. Of his children by the second wife I can not speak. When Joseph was eighteen or twenty years of age the family moved to the colony of Tennessee, on to the French Broad River.

During the last year of the revolutionary war Joseph became a soldier in the continental army, and in the third month of his soldier life he was engaged in a battle with the British and tories, in which he was wounded in the right hip, and from which he did not recover until after peace was declared. In the year 1785 Joseph Hart was married to Miss Nancy Shanklin, of East Tennessee, and settled in Blount County, near Maryville. To them there were born six children, viz: Edward, Thomas, Elizabeth, Joseph, Gideon Blackburn, and Silas. In 1810 the mother died, and the father married his second wife—Miss Mary Means, of Blount County, in the year 1812. To them were born five sons, viz: William, Samuel, James Harvey, Isaac Anderson, and Charles Coffin. These eleven children were all born in Blount County, Tennessee.

In October, 1821, Mr. Hart, with his wife and four younger sons, emigrated to Indiana, and settled on Clifty Creek, in Bartholomew County. Here Gideon B. soon joined the family, he having gone to Vincennes, on the Wabash, the year before. Before leaving Tennessee Isaac Anderson, the ninth son, was choked to death with a grain of coffee before he was two years old. William, the sixth son, was drowned in Clifty Creek while bathing, June 6th, 1826, aged 14 years. Mr. Hart buried his second wife September 11th, 1827.

The most remarkable feature of Joseph Hart's character was his deep, fervent, practical piety. He was converted in early life, and for more than half a century he literally walked with God, "and was not, for God took him," June 25th, 1840, aged 80 years and 3 days.

Edward Hart married in Blount County, Tennessee, was the father of nine children, and died in his 76th year.

Thomas married in Blount County, and was the father of one son and nine daughters. The son died in infancy. The daughters are all still living, and bringing up children. Thomas, with all his family, emigrated to Indiana, and settled on Clifty Creek in 1846, where he died in July, 1866, aged 74 years.

Elizabeth Hart was married to Mr. William Trotter, of Blount County, Tennessee, in September, 1821. She became the mother of eight children. The family emigrated to Indiana, and settled on Clifty Creek in 1834, and in 1839 settled in Clarke County, Indiana, nine miles east of Charleston, where he died in 1869, aged 74 years.

Gideon Blackburn was married to Miss Hetty Ann Taylor, of Bartholomew County, in 1825, and was the father of nine children. He was at one time sheriff of his county, and for many years held the office of school commissioner. He represented his county in the state legislature one term. He died in 1854, aged 56.

Joseph Hart, Jr., married, and settled in Columbia, Maury County, Tenn., where he died without children.

Silas Hart married Miss Susan Strain, of East Tennessee. They had but one child, Silas Hart, Jr., now living in California. Silas died in East Tennessee about the year 1824.

In 1832 Samuel, the seventh son, went to Mississippi, and settled at Carrollton as a merchant, where he still continues in business. In 1840 he married Miss Amanda Ayres, of Elkton, Ky. They have had ten children. Samuel Hart served his county for many years as probate clerk.

James Harvey, the eighth son, served an apprenticeship to the tailoring business, in Columbus, Ind., and in September, 1836, when the Ohio River was very low, he, with two shop-mates, purchased a skiff at New Albany, Ind., in which, with fishing tackle and guns, they made a journey of 600 miles, to the mouth of the Wabash River, thence to Shawneetown, where he still resides as a merchant tailor. He was married to Miss Achsa Gold, of Shawneetown, in 1857. They have had four children.

Charles Coffin Hart was born in Blount County, Tennessee, March 29th, 1820, and accompanied the family to Indiana in 1821. He served an apprenticeship to the cabinet making business in Salem, Washington County, Ind., from February, 1836, to February, 1840, and worked as a journeyman for two years. He graduated at Marietta College in 1848, and at Lane Theological Seminary in 1852, and was ordained as a minister of the gospel at Carrollton, Miss., by the presbytery of Lexington South, January 1st, 1853. He supplied the churches of Carrollton, Middleton, and Greenwood, all in Carroll County, Miss., from early in the year 1852 to January, 1856. April 1st, 1856, he was settled over the Presbyterian Church of Logan, Hocking County, Ohio, in which capacity he continued until October, 1868, when he removed to Shawneetown, Ill., and was settled as pastor over the Presbyterian Church of that place, and continued his labors there for three years, when the church of Logan, Ohio, re-called him, and on the 1st of November, 1871, he was re-installed as pastor in Logan, where he still continues his labors, December, 1874. He was married in St. Louis, Mo., September 6th, 1853, to Miss Olivia Page Studley, of Boston, Mass., a granddaughter of Major Isaac Andrews, of Hillsboro, N. H. They have six children, three sons and three daughters, viz: 1, Edward Studley, born March 9th, 1855, in Carrollton, Miss.; 2, Horace Pierce, born March 12th, 1858, in Logan, Ohio; 3, Alice Whipple, born July 17th, 1859, in Logan, Ohio; 4, Mary Pamelia, born April 19th, 1862, in Logan, Ohio; 5, Olivia Rochester, born July 10th, 1865, in Logan, Ohio; 6, Joseph Charles, born November 20th, 1866, in Logan, Ohio.

NOTE.—For one hundred years religion has had a home in this family. The descendants of Joseph Hart to the fifth generation are known. There are to-day more than a hundred who are consistent Christians, adorning the gospel of our Lord Jesus Christ.

Quotation from the will of William Shakespeare, A. D. 1616:

" *Item.* I give and bequeath unto her (i. e., his sister Joan), three sons William Hart, —— Hart,* and Michael Hart, five pounds apiece, to be paid one year after my decease."

I quote the above from an edition of Shakespeare published in 1656.

It seems that he bequeathed to this sister (Joan) 20 pounds, his wearing apparel, "and the house in Stratford wherein she dwelleth, for her natural life, under the yearly rent of twelve pence."

---

*Malone says: "It is singular that neither Shakspeare nor any of his family should have recollected the name of his nephew, who was born at Stratford but eleven years before the making of his will. His christian name was Thomas; and he was baptized in that town July 24, 1605."

ALPHABETICAL INDEX

OF

HARTS.

A.

Page.	Person.	Father.	Grandfather.	Page.	Person.	Father.	Grandfather.
440	Aaron,	Elijah,	Elijah,	540	Albert S.,	Truman,	Titus,
476	Aaron H.,	Aaron,	Hawkins,	568	Albert,	Stephen,	Joel,
500	Aaron,	Elijah,	Elijah,	437	Alces E.,	Jonathan,	Ebenezer,
417	Aaron,	Hawkins,	Nathaniel,	96	Alfred,	Solomon,	Solomon,
97	Abel,	Abel,	Ebenezer,	128	Alfred,	Eliphaz,	Judah,
68	Abel,	Ebenezer,	Isaac,	156	Alfred D.,	Salmon N.,	Salmon,
146	Abel,	Abel,	Abel,	208	Alice G.,	Rev. Levi,	Dea.Thomas,
390	Abel,	Thomas,	Hawkins,	215	Alice,	Gideon,	Joseph.
430	Abel,	Amasa,	Thomas,	79	Almira,	Samuel,	Samuel,
353	Abbie M.,	Dennis,	Linas,	95	Almon,	Solomon,	Solomon,
331	Abia,	Joseph,	Asahel,	142	Alonzo G.,	Almon,	Solomon,
56	Abigail,	Nathaniel,	Capt. John,	142	Alvira S.,	Almon,	Solomon,
106	Abigail,	Gideon,	Nathaniel,	214	Almira,	Gideon,	Joseph,
106	Abigail,	Deacon Seth,	Nathaniel,	226	Almira,	Lent,	Samuel,
110	Abigail,	Cyprian,	Nathaniel,	239	Almon,	Chauncey,	Amos,
127	Abigail,	Judah,	Judah,	249	Alvin,	Timothy,	Reuben,
132	Abigail E.,	Dea. Nathan,	Titus,	267	Alonzo,	Abner,	Gideon,
137	Abigail B.,	Oliver B.,	Titus,	272	Almira L.,	Joseph,	Gideon,
167	Abigail,	Stephen 3d,	Stephen,	273	Alva,	Gad,	Ambrose,
171	Abigail,	Timothy,	Stephen,	305	Alphonzo,	Chauncey,	Ard,
187	Abigail,	Eldad,	Daniel,	309	Almira E.,	Edward,	Chauncey,
192	Abigail,	Samuel,	Serj.Thomas,	313	Almon J.,	Joel,	Calvin,
194	Abigail,	Stephen,	Stephen,	317	Alvin C.,	Asahel W.,	Timothy W.,
315	Abigail B.,	Julius,	Roswell,	425	Alvaro,	Jonathan,	Thomas,
409	Abigail,	Hezekiah,	Hezekiah,	467	Alpha,	David,	Nathaniel,
410	Abigail,	Zachariah,	Hezekiah,	483	Alonzo O.,	Josiah,	Jonathan,
443	Abigail,	Thomas,	Elijah,	541	Almira,	Lewis,	Titus,
448	Abigail,	Jebudah,	Elijah,	93	Alvin N.,	Elias,	Salmon,
449	Abigail,	Dr. Josiah,	Elijah,	94	Amanda,	Solomon,	Solomon,
443	Abijah,	Thomas,	Elijah,	141	Amanda,	Reuben,	Solomon,
214	Abner,	Gideon,	Joseph,	174	Amos,	Thomas,	Thomas,
335	Abner N.,	Noadiah,	Noadiah,	196	Amos,	Amos,	Thomas,
477	Abner,	Hawkins,	Hawkins,	205	Ambrose,	Simeon,	Thomas,
536	Abraham P.,	Alpha,	David,	234	Amos,	Lemuel,	Amos,
286	Adaline,	Edward,	Stephen,	252	Ambrose,	Ambrose,	Simeon,
330	Adaline F.,	J. Chester,	Simeon,	255	Amanda,	Bliss,	Simeon,
343	Adelbert M.,	Joseph C.,	Gideon B.,	273	Ambrose,	Gad,	Ambrose,
548	Adaline L.,	Phœbus,	Selah,	291	Amanda,	Erastus,	Lent,
580	Adam, see Addenda.			293	Amos E.,	Araunah,	Lent,
253	Adna,	Ambrose,	Simeon,	299	Amelia,	Edward,	Josiah,
261	Adna T.,	Asahel,	Joseph,	302	Amos B.,	Ard,	Lemuel,
264	Adna,	Bethel,	Joseph,	907	Amos,	Jude,	Jude,
278	Adna,	Linas,	Elnathan,	340	Amos G.,	Luther W.,	Gideon B.,
158	Albert J.,	John C.,	Dea. Nathan,	390	Amasa,	Thomas,	Hawkins,
321	Albert J.,	John,	Ambrose,	406	Amelin,	Rev.William,	Rev. John,
346	Albert G.,	Ambrose,	Gad,	415	Amos,	Timothy,	Nathaniel,
356	Albert W.,	Sidney,	Sidney,	415	Amasa,	Timothy,	Nathaniel,
357	Albert J.,	Chauncey,	Zenas,	480	Amelia,	Samuel,	Luke,
362	Albert B.,	Albert G.,	Ambrose,	505	Amzi W.,	Asahel,	Jehudah,

F.

Page.	Person.	Father.	Grandfather.	Page.	Person.	Father.	Grandfather.
259	Fanny,	Simeon,	Simeon,	359	Frank,	Richard,	Zenas,
272	Fannie,	Joseph,	Gideon,	362	Frances A.,	Hiram,	Obed,
275	Fanny W.,	Gad,	Ambrose,	491	Franklin,	William A.,	Samuel,
330	Fanny,	J. Chester,	Simeon,	499	Francis,	Aaron,	Elijah,
454	Fanny,	Benjamin,	Elijab,	512	Frances A.,	Benjamin,	Jehudah,
285	Fidelia,	Stephen,	Stephen,	570	Frank B.,	Austin,	Benjamin,
299	Fidelia,	Edward,	Josiah,	103	Freedom,	Asahel,	Samuel,
461	Ferdinand A.,	Joseph,	Rev. William,	98	Frederick,	Jabish,	Job,
361	Florence E.,	Robert S.,	Orenus,	125	Frederick,	Salmon,	Judah,
152	Frances L.,	Rev. Wm. H.,	Rev. Seth,	320	Frederic A.,	John A.,	Levi,
288	Francis,	William,	Stephen,	323	Frederic M.,	Ambrose,	Ambrose,
326	Frances M.,	Levi,	Bliss,	492	Frederic,	William A.,	Samuel,
343	Frances K.,	Joseph C.,	Gideon B.,	535	Frederic M.,	Miles,	David,
348	Franklin,	Gad,	Gad,	552	Frederic A.,	Wells,	Samuel.
356	Frances,	Sidney,	Sidney,				

G.

Page.	Person.	Father.	Grandfather.	Page.	Person.	Father.	Grandfather.
194	Gad,	Stephen,	Stephen,	334	George A.,	Adna,	Bethel,
216	Gad,	Ambrose,	Joseph,	339	George,	Luther W.,	Gideon B.,
274	Gad,	Gad,	Ambrose,	356	George L.,	Chauncey,	Zenas,
293	Gad H.,	Stephen W.,	Gad,	437	George W.,	Ebenezer,	Ebenezer,
101	George,	Matthew,	Matthew,	463	George,	Thomas,	Thomas,
104	George.	Jesse,	Samuel,	492	George F.,	Edward,	Samuel,
119	George,	Hiram,	Selah,	531	George B.,	George,	Thomas,
129	George,	Eliphaz,	Judab,	550	George W.,	Sylvester,	Samuel,
139	George S.,	Julius,	Elias,	568	George,	Stephen,	Joel,
153	George L.,	Truman,	Cyprian,	573	George W.,	Thomas R.,	Benjamin,
154	George,	Bera,	Cyprian,	81	Gideon,	Nathaniel,	Nathaniel,
157	Georgiana,	Alfred,	Eliphaz,	181	Gideon,	Joseph,	Thomas,
159	George A.,	Joseph B.,	Oliver B.,	215	Gideon B.,	Gideon,	Joseph,
223	George,	Stephen,	Stephen,	270	Gideon W.,	Gideon B.,	Gideon,
247	George,	Timothy,	Reuben,	438	Gideon W.,	Dr. John,	Ebenezer,
282	George,	Obed,	Elnathan,	142	Gilbert D.,	Almon,	Solomon,
202	George L.,	Newton,	Lemuel,	200	Gilbert,	Thomas,	Thomas,
321	George,	Orrin,	Ambrose,	544	Grove,	Titus,	Titus.

H.

Page.	Person.	Father.	Grandfather.	Page.	Person.	Father.	Grandfather.
57	Hannah,	Nathaniel,	John,	530	Harriet L.,	Col. William,	Thomas,
184	Hannah,	James,	Thomas,	317	Harriet G.,	Levi,	Timothy,
213	Hannah,	Noah,	Joseph,	322	Harriet I.,	Orrin,	Ambrose,
262	Hannah D.,	Asahel,	Joseph,	328	Harriet E.,	Oliver E.,	Bliss,
289	Hannah J.,	William,	Stephen,	346	Harriet R.,	Joseph N.,	Joseph,
375	Hannah,	Thomas,	Thomas,	546	Harriet E.,	Aaron H.,	Aaron,
389	Hannah,	Thomas,	Hawkins,	558	Harriet,	Selah,	Elijah,
397	Hannah,	Ebenezer,	Thomas,	572	Harriet S.,	Thomas R.,	Benjamin,
409	Hannah,	Hezekiah,	Hezekiah,	576	Harriet,	Abraham P.,	Alpha,
417	Hannah,	Hawkins,	Nathaniel,	362	Hastings H.,	Albert G.,	Ambrose,
449	Hannah,	Dr. Josiah,	Elijah,	366	Hawkins,	Thomas,	Stephen,
504	Hannah B.,	Rev. William,	Thomas,	371	Hawkins,	Hawkins,	Thomas,
504	Hannah,	Asahel,	Jehudah,	384	Hawkins,	Nathaniel,	Hawkins,
98	Harriet,	Abel,	Ebenezer,	385	Hawkins,	Hawkins,	Hawkins,
98	Harvey,	Jabish,	Job,	417	Hawkins,	Hawkins,	Nathaniel,
104	Harriet,	Jesse,	Samuel,	481	Hawley,	Samuel,	Luke,
127	Harriet E.,	Judah,	Judah,	489	Haynes L.,	Edwin C.,	Jonathan,
130	Harriet,	Eliphaz,	Judah,	557	Hattie A.,	Lucius L.,	Warren,
148	Harriet N.,	Isaac,	Job,	110	Henry C.,	Cyprian,	Nathaniel,
153	Harriet,	George,	Jesse,	126	Henry,	Judah,	Judah,
162	Harriet L.,	Walter S.,	Truman,	129	Henry H.,	Eliphaz,	Judah,
276	Halsey P.,	Gad,	Ambrose,	151	Henrietta V.,	Velina,	Stephen H.,
283	Harvey,	Obed,	Elnathan,	154	Henry,	Bera,	Cyprian,
295	Harriet P.,	Julius,	Gad,	161	Henry G.,	Daniel,	Abel,
435	Harriet,	John,	Samuel.	233	Henry,	Amanda,	Seth,
483	Harriet E.,	Rev. Ira,	Jonathan,	240	Henry,	Chauncey,	Amos,
488	Harriet E.,	Warren,	Jonathan,	277	Helena,	Hosea,	Medad,
506	Harriet,	James,	Jehudab,	322	Henry C.,	Orrin,	Ambrose,
512	Harriet C.,	William,	Dr. Josiah,	325	Henry C.,	Oremus,	Bliss,

75

M.

O.

P.

R.

S.

INTERMARRIAGES WITH THE HARTS.

A.

9707

CPSIA information can be obtained
at www.ICGtesting.com
Printed in the USA
BVHW04*2148080918
526295BV00012B/36/P